Electric Railway Dictionary

DEFINITIONS AND ILLUSTRATIONS OF
THE PARTS AND EQUIPMENT OF
ELECTRIC RAILWAY CARS AND TRUCKS

COMPILED UNDER THE DIRECTION OF A COMMITTEE APPOINTED BY
THE AMERICAN ELECTRIC RAILWAY ASSOCIATION

BY RODNEY HITT
Associate Editor, Electric Railway Journal

SUPERVISING COMMITTEE

H. H. ADAMS, *Superintendent of Rolling Stock and Shops, Metropolitan Street Railway Company, New York, Chairman.*

PAUL WINSOR, *Chief Engineer of Motive Power and Rolling Stock, Boston Elevated Railway Company.*

RICHARD MCCULLOCH, *Vice-President and Assistant General Manager, United Railways of St. Louis.*

FIRST EDITION

NEW YORK
McGRAW PUBLISHING COMPANY
PUBLISHERS OF
ELECTRIC RAILWAY JOURNAL
1911

©2008-2010 PERISCOPE FILM LLC
ALL RIGHTS RESERVED
ISBN #978-1-935700-25-8
WWW.PERISCOPEFILM.COM

Resolution Adopted at the Atlantic City Convention of the American Electric Railway Association, October 14, 1908, approving the publication of the Electric Railway Dictionary:

"Whereas, the McGraw Publishing Company has proposed to publish an illustrated dictionary describing the apparatus and defining the terms used in electric railway work, under the direction of a supervising committee to be appointed by the president of the association;"

"Resolved, that this association approves of this proposal without expense to this association, and the president is hereby directed to appoint such a supervising committee to consist of three members of this association, with instructions to assist in the preparation of such a book in every way possible, and to report at the convention next year."

Editor's Note

Every industry has a technical language of its own and the terms and names of apparatus used cannot be found in any of the standard dictionaries. In the electric railway field, the evolution of motive power from horse to cable, and from cable to electricity, has resulted in many changes in the character of the rolling stock and its equipment. The terminology of the art has undergone a similar change. New names have been created and others have been borrowed from steam railway practice. Owing to the widely scattered growth of electric railways standardization of terms has been as slow as the standardization of parts. This has resulted in much confusion in ordering parts from manufacturers and in interpreting communications between railway companies. As a step toward standardizing the nomenclature of electric railway car construction the compilation of the Electric Railway Dictionary was undertaken.

The plan adopted in this work of defining the location and purpose of a part and referring to an illustration of that part in another section of the book simplifies the finding of a term and makes possible a logical arrangement of the illustrations. The definitions are arranged alphabetically, with numerous cross references. Where more than one name is commonly applied to a part the preferred name is defined and the other names are also given in their proper places with a cross reference to the preferred name. The nomenclature of the manufacturers has been retained in most instances, so that but little trouble will be experienced in consulting this book in connection with catalogues and other manufacturers' literature. As an aid in ordering parts from the illustrations the manufacturer's name has been added below the title to each engraving.

The editor and the supervising committee wish to acknowledge, with thanks, the assistance which has been rendered by manufacturers in furnishing most of the material for the illustrations.

New York, March, 1911.

ELECTRIC RAILWAY DICTIONARY

A

A. C. A common abbreviation for **Alternating Current**, which see.

Acceleration. The rate of change of velocity of a moving body. Under normal conditions an average acceleration of 1½ miles per hour, per second on level track is about the maximum which has been obtained in practice with well-designed railway motors and control apparatus. Higher accelerations are, of course, possible, and are sometimes attained. Acceleration is sometimes expressed as positive when the velocity is increasing and negative when the velocity is decreasing. Negative acceleration is often termed retardation.

Ackley Adjustable Brake. Figs. 583-587. A type of **Geared Brake**, which see.

Acme Cable Curtain Fixture. Figs. 645-646.

Acorn Butt Hinge. Fig. 756. A butt hinge with a pin ornamented with an acorn on the top and bottom.

Adjustable Brake Rod. See **Bottom Truck Connection**.

Adjustable Motorman's Seat. Figs. 1266-1267, 1302.

Adlake Lamps. Figs. 1078-1093.

Advertising Frame or Panel. A frame or glass panel in the end of a car, in or behind which advertising cards can be placed. The upper and lower deck end panels are frequently used for displaying advertisements.

Advertising Rack Rail. 51, Fig. 306. A narrow, grooved molding placed along the bottom edge of the lower deck just above the side windows, in which are inserted the bottom edges of advertising cards. A similar molding is used to confine the top edges of the cards, which are curved to conform to the contour of the lower deck.

Agard Vestibule Door Fixture. Figs. 681-688.

Agasote. A fireproof and waterproof composition material made up in the form of sheets, and used in place of wood veneers for the headlining and other interior finish of cars.

Air Brake. Figs. 451-567. A brake operated by admitting air behind a piston moving in a brake cylinder mounted under the car body. The pressure against the piston is transmitted through a system of rods and levers to the brake shoes on the trucks, bearing against the treads of the wheels. Air brakes are in universal use on all heavy, high-speed elevated, subway and interurban electric cars, and have been applied to many of the larger surface cars now operated by city street railways. The supply of compressed air for operating air brakes is furnished either by a motor-driven air pump mounted on the car, or storage tanks may be used in which the supply is renewed from time to time from a compressing station. See **Storage Air Brake**.

There are two general types of air brake apparatus in use on electric cars, **Straight-Air Brakes** and **Automatic Air Brakes**, which see. Straight-air brakes are used only on cars operated singly and occasionally for two-car trains. For cars to be operated in trains of more than two units, automatic air brakes are usually used. Some types of brake apparatus combine the principal features of both the straight-air and the automatic brake. See also **Electro-Pneumatic Brake**.

Air Brake Hose. See **Brake Hose**.

Air Brake Lubricator. Fig. 560. A holder containing a stick of soft graphite lubricant, which is inserted in the brake pipe between the main reservoir and the brake cylinder. The passage of the air through the pipe erodes the graphite, which is carried along with the air and serves to lubricate the triple valve and the brake cylinder walls.

Air Compressor. Figs. 474-476, 530, 534-535, 544-545. A motor-driven air pump, usually mounted in a cradle hung from the underframe of the car body, which supplies compressed air at a pressure of from 90 to 120 lb. per sq. in. for operating the air brakes. The compressed air is stored in a main reservoir, from which the supply is drawn to feed the brake cylinders. Compressors for air-brake service are usually of the gear-driven, single-stage, two-cylinder type without cooling jackets on the cylinders. They range in capacity from 5 to 40 cu. ft. of free air per minute. The pressure in the main reservoir is maintained at any desired point by means of a **Pump Governor**, which see, which automatically starts the compressor motor when the pressure drops and stops it when the pressure rises above the desired point.

Air Compressor Cage. See **Air Compressor Cradle**.

Air Compressor Cradle. Figs. 453, 546. A detachable steel or wooden frame or closed box in which an air compressor is mounted. It is often secured to the underframe of a car body by bolts or lag screws, with rubber washers interposed between the bearing surfaces, to prevent objectionable vibration and noise being transmitted to the car body.

Air Compressor Governor. See **Pump Governor**.

Air Compressor Switch. Fig. 460. A small snap switch used to turn on or off current in an air-compressor motor circuit. It is inserted between the trolley and the governor, and should not be confused with the governor which automatically starts and stops the motor when the air pressure in the main reservoir rises or falls beyond the desired limits. In the Westinghouse governor synchronizing system for trains containing more than one motor car the local compressor switch on each car is an electro-pneumatic switch or governor, which controls the compressor either through the fall of pressure in the main reservoir on that car or through the flow of current in a synchronizing wire running through the train. This wire is energized through any one of the master governors on the train. See **Governor Synchronizing System**.

Air Compressor Suction Pipe. See **Suction Pipe**.

Air Gage. Figs. 472-473. A device for indicating the pressure of air in the main reservoir of an air brake system. It is similar in form and operation to an ordinary steam pressure gage, and is usually mounted in the motorman's vestibule alongside of the brake valve or on one of the vestibule posts in plain sight. For automatic air brake systems, a duplex gage with a red hand and a black hand revolving on a single index dial is used. The red hand indicates main reservoir pressure and the black hand indicates brake pipe pressure.

Air Gap. The space between a magnet pole piece and its armature through which the magnetic lines of force pass. The strength of a magnet decreases very rapidly as the air gap is increased, and this principle is utilized in some types of tripping switches for multiple-unit control apparatus. The calibration of these devices is accomplished by adjusting the magnetic air gap instead of attempting to adjust a strong spring.

Air Hose. See **Brake Hose**.

Air Pipe. A common name for the **Brake Pipe**, which see.

Air Pump. More properly **Air Compressor**, which see.

Air Purifier. Fig. 561. A device for purifying the intake air before it reaches the air compressor. It consists of a small settling tank, partially filled with oil or other liquid, into which the heavy particles of dirt fall as the air passes over the surface of the liquid. The liquid holding the dirt in suspension can be drawn off and replenished with clean liquid as frequently as may be necessary.

Air Signal. Figs. 514-520. Apparatus for giving communicating signals from one car to another in a train by means of compressed air taken from the air brake system. A separate train line pipe is required, and in each car a conductor's signal valve is connected to this pipe. On the head car of the train is a signal valve connected to a small whistle. When any conductor's valve is opened the air pressure in the continuous signal pipe is reduced, and this causes the signal valve to open a port connecting the whistle to the reservoir pipe. Seldom used on electric cars but in use on all steam railroad passenger cars and electric locomotives which are intended to haul such cars. An **Electro-Pneumatic Train Signal**, which see, is intended to serve the same purpose.

Air Signal Valve. Fig. 514. A valve used for admitting air to the whistle on a locomotive or head car of a train equipped with air signal apparatus.

Air Strainer. Figs. 466-468. A fine metal screen, or bundle of curled hair, placed in the brake pipe or over the end of the air compressor suction pipe to prevent dust and dirt being drawn in with the air and clogging the compressor valves or triple valves. See **Brake Pipe Air Strainer** and **Suction Strainer**.

Air Whistle. Fig. 546. An alarm whistle blown by compressed air drawn from the brake system. Used on all interurban and other high-speed motor cars. It is usually mounted on top of the front vestibule hood.

Air Whistle Valve. Figs. 562-563. A self-closing valve inserted in the pipe connecting the air whistle with the brake system. It is opened by pulling down the handle with a cord or pressing it down with the thumb.

Aisle. The longitudinal space in the center of a car floor between the seats.

Aisle Matting. A long strip of fiber matting laid in the aisle of a car to deaden the noise, absorb the dirt and provide a safer foothold to standing passengers. Seldom used in modern cars.

Aisle Seat Back Arm. A **Seat Back Arm**, which see, next to the aisle as distinguished from a wall seat back arm. See Fig. 1294.

Aisle Seat End. The support and arm rest of a cross-seat frame next to the aisle. See **Wall Seat End** and **Seat End**.

Aisle Strip. 87, Fig. 259. One of a number of narrow pieces of hardwood fastened to the floor of a car in the aisle and occasionally between the cross seats to take the wear and prevent slipping. Sometimes made in sectional squares, which can be lifted from the floor to give access to the motor trap doors.

Alarm Gong. See **Gong**.

Alcove. Any recess in a wall or partition such as a **Water Alcove**, which see, containing a tank of drinking water.

Allis-Chalmers Air Brakes. Figs. 529-531.

Allis-Chalmers Motors. Figs. 1706-1709.

Alternating Current. "A current of electricity which, when plotted, consists of half-waves of equal area in successively opposite directions from the zero line."—A. I. E. E.

Alternating current is used in railway work for the transmission of electrical energy at high tension from a central generating station to converter sub-stations, in which it is converted to direct current and fed to the trolley wire at a potential of from 550 to 700 volts. It is also used on a number of interurban and electrified steam roads for direct propulsion with trolley wire potentials of from 3000 to 11,000 volts. See **Single-Phase System, Three-Phase System**.

American Car & Foundry Trucks. Figs. 1441-1453.

American Electric Railway Engineering Association Standards. See **Engineering Association Standards**.

American Mason Safety Step Tread. Fig. 927.

American Wire Gage. Another name for the Brown & Sharpe wire gage which is in general use in the United States. See **Wire Gage**.

Ammeter. An instrument for measuring the flow of electric current in a circuit in terms of amperes.

Ampere. The unit of measurement of the rate of flow of electricity through a conductor. It may be defined as the amount of current which will pass with an electromotive force of one volt through a circuit having a resistance of one ohm.

Ampere Hour. A unit of measurement of electricity, being the amount represented by the flow of one ampere for one hour.

Ampere Hour Meter. Figs. 1831-1832. An instrument for measuring the consumption of electricity of a motor or other piece of electrical apparatus in terms of ampere hours. Ampere hour meters mounted on cars have been extensively used in Europe for keeping a check on the skill of the motormen in operating their cars. There are two main classes of these meters—the commutator and the mercury-motor types. The latter is practically the only one used for traction work, as the mercury acts as a buffer against the jarring of the car, while the former is too delicate in its construction to withstand this. In the mercury-motor type the armature consists of a copper disc floating in mercury in the field of a permanent magnet. For convenience of reading such meters are fitted with dials of the springing figure type.

Ampere Turn. A single turn or winding in a coil of wire through which a current of one ampere passes. The number of amperes flowing through a coil multiplied by the number of turns of the conductor gives the total number of ampere turns in the coil. The number of ampere turns is a measure of the magnetizing force of the coil.

Angle or **Angle Iron.** Rolled iron or steel sections consisting of two narrow plates uniting to form an angle of 90 deg., more or less. Special forms of angles include square root angles, in which the interior angle is finished sharp without a fillet and bulb angles, in which the outer edge of one leg is thickened and finished with a semi-circular contour. Angles are extensively used in steel and composite wood and steel car construction.

Angle Cock. Fig. 479. A two-way cock inserted in the brake pipe under the end of a car equipped with train air brakes, for the purpose of closing the pipe to prevent the escape of the air. It is usually bent downward at an angle of about 60 deg., and the brake hose nipple is screwed into the downwardly projecting arm. When two or more cars are coupled together the angle cocks between the cars must be opened, while the angle cocks at each end of the train must be closed.

Angle Iron Bumper. Fig. 598. A bumper made of a heavy angle curved to the contour of the end of the car and bolted to the platform sills.

Anti-Climber. Figs. 590-597. A corrugated channel section used in place of a bumper to prevent cars in collision from overriding. The anti-climber is either rolled of structural steel and cut in lengths to suit and bent to fit the curved contour of the platform end sill, or it may be made of cast steel of any width and depth. When cars equipped with anti-climbers collide the corrugations interlock and tend to prevent one car from rising and riding over the other.

Anti-Friction Bearings. Ball or roller bearings which have a low coefficient of friction as compared with the ordinary sleeve bearing. Anti-friction bearings have been tried experimentally for car journals and motor armatures, but they have not yet come into general use for these purposes. See **Ball Bearing** and **Roller Bearing**.

Anti-Friction Metal. A soft alloy, such as Babbitt Metal, which see, having a low coefficient of friction and used for lining bearings. Many alloys differing only slightly in their composition are used for this purpose.

Application Valve. (Electro-Pneumatic Brake.) Fig. 454. The magnet valve under each car which, when energized, admits air from the auxiliary reservoir to the brake cylinder to apply the brakes. See **Electro-Pneumatic Brake** and **Release Valve**.

Apron. An overhanging edge of a car roof. See **Deck Apron, Platform Hood Apron**.

Arc. The flame produced momentarily when two electrodes which are in contact and in which an electric current is flowing are separated. The arc is formed by the intense heat generated by the air gap resistance which is inserted in the path of the current at the instant of breaking contact.

Arc Chute. (Of Circuit Breaker.) An open extension on an automatic circuit breaker box to conceal the arc which is formed on breaking the circuit.

Arc Deflector. See **Controller Arc Deflector**.

Arc Headlight. Figs. 1028-1030, 1042-1045, 1051-1054. An electric headlight in which the light is emitted by the arcing of an electric current across the gap between two carbon or metallic electrodes. The electrodes are kept separated automatically by a solenoid in circuit with the arc. When the electrodes burn away the resistance of the air gap is increased, and the current flowing through the solenoid is cut down, thereby weakening the lifting power of the solenoid which holds the two electrodes apart. See **Headlight, Luminous Arc Headlight**.

Arc Light. See **Arc Headlight**.

Arch Bar. The top member of a diamond-shaped trussed side frame of a truck. It passes over the columns or bolster guide bars and rests on top of the journal boxes. An inverted arch bar passes under the columns, and is bent up to lie on top of the journal boxes under the arch bar. The tie bar is straight, and is below the inverted arch bar, running out under the journal boxes. These three members, together with the columns, when bolted up on both sides of the journal boxes, form a stiff side frame.

Arch Bar Truck. Figs. 1382-1383, 1399. A truck having diamond-shaped arch bar side frames. Used by electric railways only for work cars and occasionally for trailer express and freight cars. It is the common type of truck in use under steam railroad freight cars. A modified form of arch bar truss is used in a number of types of equalized trucks. See Figs. 1388-1390, 1405.

Arched Roof. Fig. 78. A roof having a continuous symmetrical curve from one side of the car to the other and not broken up by a monitor. Arched roofs are often used for freight and express cars and for some recent types of passenger cars. Also called turtle-back roof.

Arm. See **Seat Arm.**

Arm Rest. A narrow wooden or metal shelf attached to the inside lining or posts of a car at a suitable height above the cross-seat cushions to form a convenient resting place for the arm. A similar support is sometimes provided by a cap or rail on top of the aisle seat end. See Fig. 1288.

Armalac. An insulating compound for armatures, fields and commutators.

Armature. Figs. 1661, 1688-1704. The revolving element of an electric railway motor or direct-current generator. It is composed of a spider surrounded by a cylindrical core of iron, usually built up of thin sheets to reduce hysteresis loss, on the surface of which are wound conductor coils of insulated copper wire or ribbon. These coils are imbedded in slots in the surface of the core parallel to the axis of the shaft on which the core is mounted. The ends of the coils are connected symmetrically to segments of a commutator mounted on one end of the shaft. Pairs of carbon brushes bear on the commutator, and are so mounted around the commutator that a complete circuit is formed in successive series of coils on the armature as the commutator segments pass under the brushes, which are electrically connected to the external circuit of the motor. The passage of current through a conductor placed in a field of magnetic lines of force created between the energized poles of a motor tends to cause the conductor to move through the field, and it is this principle which causes the armature to revolve. Each coil, while current flows through it, tends to move through the magnetic field between the poles, and as one coil moves out of the field another coil, also carrying current, moves into the field.

Railway motor armatures are universally of the drum wave-wound type, in which the coils are disposed on or near the outer surface of the iron core, so as to give the maximum torque to the motor. The spider is usually made with air passages through it connecting with openings through the walls of the core, so as to provide means for ventilating and cooling the coils on the outer surface. See **Wave Winding.**

Armature Band. 17, Fig. 1661. A steel wire wrapped around the core of an armature after the coils are in place, to prevent the coils from working out of the slots under the effect of centrifugal force. Several bands are usually wound on the armature, spaced close together from end to end of the core.

Armature Band Clip. 18, Fig. 1661. A small piece of tin plate inserted under a number of continuous turns of banding wire and bent over and soldered down. Its purpose is to keep the band wires from spreading or unwinding in case one turn should break.

Armature Bearing. A contraction of **Armature Shaft Bearing,** which see.

Armature Bearing Cover. A removable lid on top of an armature shaft bearing which can be lifted to inspect the bearing or renew the lubricating materials.

Armature Bearing Housing. Figs. 1672, 1678. A removable casting inserted in some types of motor frames in which the armature bearing sleeves are mounted. The housing is hollow and forms an oil well for the bearing.

Armature Bearing Lid. See **Armature Bearing Cover.**

Armature Bearing Lining. Figs. 1674-1675. A brass, bronze or cast-iron sleeve filled with babbitt or other anti-friction metal, inserted in an armature shaft bearing to provide a smooth surface on which the shaft can turn. The babbitt filling is usually made very thin to prevent the armature dropping on the field pole pieces in case the soft metal melts and runs out.

Armature Bearing Sleeve. See **Armature Bearing Lining.**

Armature Coil. One or more turns of insulated copper wire or ribbon formed in the shape of a rectangular coil and inserted in slots on the surface of the armature core. The ends of the coil are bent around the end of the armature core and soldered to the proper commutator segments. Armature coils are usually wrapped with tape and dipped in or impregnated with an insulating compound before being put in place.

Armature Core. Fig. 1693. A cylindrical shell built up of laminated soft iron punchings, assembled and bolted together on the armature spider. Slots to hold the armature coils are formed on the surface of the core.

Armature End Plate. Figs. 1688-1692; 20, Fig. 1661. A malleable iron disc keyed, or otherwise fastened, on the armature shaft to confine the core laminations horizontally and also to form a support for the overhanging ends of the armature coils.

Armature Shaft. 8, Figs. 1659-1661. A steel arbor revolving in bearings formed in the motor frame. On it is mounted the armature spider, the commutator and a toothed pinion engaging with a gear on the truck axle.

Armature Shaft Bearing. Figs. 1674-1675. A bearing formed in the motor frame, or in a removable housing, in which one end of the armature shaft turns. The two bearings are distinguished as commutator end bearing and pinion end bearing.

Armature Spider. Figs. 1688-1692. A cast or malleable iron skeleton center pressed and keyed on an armature shaft and surrounded by the laminated iron core in which the armature coils are imbedded.

Armature Thrust Collar. S, Fig. 1657. A collar on an armature shaft which bears against the frame head or bearing lug, and takes the side thrust of the armature, due to irregularities in the gear and pinion teeth or their alignment.

Armature Wire. See **Magnet Wire.**

Armbrust Brake Shoe. Fig. 1509.

Armstrong Journal Oiler. Fig. 1568.

Arrester. See **Lightning Arrester.**

Art Glass. Colored glass with a rough, pebbled surface, sometimes used for the semi-elliptic top sashes of twin windows.

Asbestos. A non-combustible mineral, fibrous in texture, which is used for electrical insulation. Asbestos-covered wire is used in some types of motor field coils on account of its heat-resisting qualities.

Ash Car. Figs. 230-232. A car built especially for hauling ashes or other refuse. Usually a gondola car with a hopper bottom or drop sides.

Ash Pan. A sheet metal pan sliding into the ash pit under the grate of a hot-water heater or car stove, to receive the ashes as they fall through the grate.

Ash Pit. A space under the grate of a hot-water heater or car stove, into which a removable ash pan is fitted to receive the ashes as they fall through the grate.

Ash Pit Door. A hinged door containing a damper, used to close the opening in the front of the ash pit of a hot-water heater or car stove.

Association Standards. See **Engineering Association Standards.**

Atlanta Car Wheels. Figs. 1606-1608.

Automatic Air Brake. Fig. 456. A type of **Air Brake,** which see, universally used on steam railroad passenger and freight cars and on high-speed interurban, subway and elevated cars operated in trains. It differs from the **Straight-Air Brake,** which see, in that the brakes are applied by reducing the pressure in the brake pipe instead of admitting air under pressure. In the simplest form compressed air is supplied by an air pump or compressor mounted on one or more cars in the train. From the main reservoir the compressed air is supplied through a feed valve to the motorman's brake valve, and thence to the brake pipe. To apply the brakes the supply from the main reservoir is cut off, and the pressure reduced in the brake pipe through an open port in the motorman's brake valve. Under each car is mounted a small auxiliary reservoir, connected to the brake pipe and to the brake cylinder through a **Triple Valve,** which see. The pressure in the auxiliary reservoir is normally the same as in the brake pipe, but when the brake pipe pressure is reduced the triple valve moves to a position in which the auxiliary reservoir feed port is closed and another port is opened, admitting the auxiliary reservoir pressure to the brake cylinder and thus applying the brakes. To release the brakes, the normal brake pipe pressure is restored by moving the brake valve to the release position. This restoration of pressure in the brake pipe moves the triple valves to the exhaust and recharge position, in which the brake cylinders on all cars in the train are open to the atmosphere, and the auxiliary reservoirs are recharged from the brake pipe. The automatic feature consists in the instantaneous application of the brakes on all the cars in the train, in case the train breaks in two or any of the flexible couplings between cars should part or rupture.

To suit the many and widely varying conditions of number of cars, kind of cars, number of stops, etc., which are encountered in electric railway service, a number of modifications of the elementary forms of the straight-air brake and the automatic air brake have been brought out, but the essential principles of one or both are maintained in the modified apparatus. The modifications in general consist of (1) means for making straight-air applications on a trailer car with an emergency feature similar to the automatic air brake; (2) means for more quickly applying the brakes with full power on long trains and recharging the auxiliary reservoirs after an application, and (3) means for graduating the release of the brakes.

Automatic Circuit Breaker. See **Circuit Breaker.**

Automatic Control. A type of **Multiple-Unit Control,** which see, in which a current-limit relay automatically limits the flow of current in the motor circuit to a predetermined maximum. The controller handle is moved to the full "on" position, and the contactors automatically cut out the resistance as the speed increases. Any desired rate of acceleration can be obtained by adjusting the current-limit relay.

Automatic Coupler. Figs. 600-601, 605-608, 611-625. A car coupler, which will couple automatically by impact with a similar coupler when two cars thus equipped are brought together. See **Coupler.**

Automatic Fender. Fig. 714. A **Fender**, which see, designed to pick up or catch a person struck by a car without being dropped by the motorman.

Automatic Slack Adjuster. See **Brake Slack Adjuster.**

Automatic Ventilator. Figs. 1340-1366. A device for automatically exhausting or forcing air into a car while the car is running in either direction. See **Ventilator.**

Automatic Wheel Guard. Figs 707, 712-713, 718. A **Wheel Guard,** which see, which is automatically dropped down on the pavement when the tripping apron under the front end of the platform strikes a prostrate person on the track.

Automotoneer. Figs. 1725-1728. A device attached to the top of a controller case and designed to limit the speed with which the controller handle may be revolved in moving from the "off" to the "on" position. It does not affect the quick movement of the handle back to the "off" position. The purpose of the device is to prevent fast feeding of current to the motors.

Auto-Transformer. Fig. 1803. A special transformer used as part of the control equipment of cars operating on single-phase alternating current. A part of the primary winding is used also as the secondary winding. The transformer serves to reduce the trolley voltage to that required at the motor terminals, and, as the speed of single-phase motors is controlled by varying the e. m. f. at the motor terminals, this can be accomplished readily by connecting the motors successively to different voltage taps on the secondary coil of the transformer. The normal maximum e. m. f. used at the motors is usually from 250 to 300 volts. See **Single-Phase Control Apparatus.**

Auxiliary Compression Beam Brace. 125, Figs. 356-358. A short brace in a trussed side frame of a long interurban car, slanting upward and toward the center of the car body, between the side sill and the compression beam. A similar beam, when slanted toward the end of the car, is called a counterbrace.

Auxiliary Contactor. Figs. 1721, 1764, 1783-1784. A **Contactor,** which see, applied to a type K control system to open and close the main motor circuits at a point remote from the platform controller. By this means heavy arcing is eliminated in the controller. The contactors are mounted under the car body and the magnets are connected in series with the contacts of a tripping switch supplied as part of the equipment. The contactor magnets are energized through auxiliary contacts mounted on the controller drum in such a way that the contacts are broken just before the controller segments leave the fingers in returning to the "off" position, and also during the period when the controller cylinder is passing from series to parallel connections, or vice versa. When the controller is in any of the "on" positions the auxiliary contacts in the controller are closed and the main power circuit is, therefore, closed through the contactors. If the tripping switch opens, due to the passage of excessive current, or the controller is moved to the "off" position, or passes from series to parallel connections, the contactor magnets are de-energized and the power circuit is broken.

Auxiliary Reservoir. Fig. 500. (Automatic Air Brake.) A small reservoir mounted near the brake cylinder and connected to it, as well as to the brake pipe, by the triple valve. Normally the air in the auxiliary reservoir is maintained at brake-pipe pressure. When the brake-pipe pressure is reduced to apply the brakes, a port in the triple valve opens, at the same time closing the brake-pipe feed connection and opening a connection to the brake cylinder from the auxiliary reservoir. When the brakes are released by restoring the brake-pipe pressure, the feed connection in the triple valve between the brake pipe and the auxiliary reservoir is again opened and the auxiliary reservoir is recharged.

Axle. Figs. 1594-1601; 2, Figs. 1388-1390. A shaft or cross-bar supporting a vehicle, on or with which the wheels turn. Car axles have the wheels pressed on firmly and have journals formed on their ends which project beyond the wheel hubs and turn in suitable bearings carried in journal boxes mounted in the truck side frames. The American Electric Railway Engineering Association has adopted four standard designs of axles for motor trucks, which are shown in Figs. 1948-1951. The M. C. B. standard axles for trailer trucks are shown in Figs. 1594-1597. Axles are made of cold-rolled shafting, hot forgings of plain carbon steel and of special heat-treated steel.

Axle Bearing. 25, Fig. 1660. (Motor.) One of a pair of bearings usually formed integrally with the motor frame, by which the motor is supported at one side on the axle. The opposite side of the motor is supported from the truck frame. See **Motor Suspension.**

Axle Bearing Bracket. A projection cast on a motor frame to receive a bearing shell in which the axle turns.

Axle Bearing Cap. 12, Figs. 1659-1660. A separate casting bolted to an axle-bearing bracket which holds the bearing shell or lining securely in place. In some designs of split frame motors the bearing cap is attached on the under side of the axle.

Axle Bearing Oil Well Lid. 11, Fig. 1660. A removable lid on top of an axle bearing which can be lifted to inspect or renew the packing and lubrication.

Axle Bearing Dowel Pin. Cb, Fig. 1657. A small steel pin let into the axle bearing cap and fitting into a hole in the bearing lining. Its purpose is to prevent the bearing lining from turning with the axle.

Axle Bearing Lining. L, Fig. 1657. A brass, bronze or cast-iron split sleeve inserted in the axle bearing of a motor and lined with anti-friction metal, to provide a smooth surface in which the axle turns.

Axle Box. More properly **Journal Box,** which see.

Axle Cap. See **Axle Bearing Cap.**

Axle Collar. The shoulder or ring formed on the end of the journal of an axle to take the end thrust of the journal bearing. In some types of journal bearings and boxes the end thrust is taken by the box itself against the end of the axle and the collar is omitted. In some older types of journals the axle collar is replaced by a groove, in which is fitted a check plate. The thrust of the journal bearing is taken by this check plate.

Axle Fit. The surface of the bore in the hub of a car wheel or motor gear. The corresponding surface of the axle is called the wheel fit or gear fit.

B

Babbitt. A contraction of **Babbitt Metal**, which see.

Babbitt Metal. A soft, anti-friction metal containing copper, tin and antimony, so called from the original inventor, Isaac Babbitt. Tin predominates, giving the metal a white appearance and distinguishing it from other bearing metals in which copper is the principal element. Extensively used for lining bearings.

Back. See **Seat Back**.

Back Lash. (Of Motor Gears.) The lost motion between the teeth of two engaging gears caused by wear of the teeth or change in the distance between gear centers.

Back Platform. The rear platform of a car on which the conductor stands, as distinguished from the front, or motorman's, platform.

Back Seat Bottom Rail. See **Seat Bottom**.

Baggage Car. Figs. 195, 199. A car having wide side doors intended particularly for the transportation of trunks and personal baggage of passengers. Baggage is usually transported by interurban railways either in a compartment in a passenger car or in freight and express cars which also carry package freight.

Baggage Compartment. A compartment in a passenger car separated by a partition from the main passenger compartment and used for storing trunks and light freight and express matter while in transit. The baggage compartment of most interurban cars is equipped with folding seats, and is used as a smoking compartment when not occupied by baggage. The baggage compartment is often lined with wooden slats to protect the windows and sheathing. See Figs. 132-160.

Baggage Door. A wide sliding door in the side of the baggage compartment of a car through which large pieces of baggage can be handled.

Baggage Door Handle. Fig. 847. A U-shaped handle fastened near the edge of a sliding baggage door to pull it open or shut.

Baggage Door Latch. Figs. 823-824.

Baggage Door Plate. A metal plate sometimes screwed to the floor of a car in front of the baggage door to prevent the wood flooring from being damaged by the dropping of heavy trunks.

Bail. See **Motor Frame Bail**.

Baldwin Trucks. Figs. 1385-1399.

Ball Bearing. A bearing for moving parts, consisting of one or more hardened steel balls rolling between hardened steel plates. The theoretical contact surfaces in a ball bearing are two points on each ball, and the friction is correspondingly low. Ball bearings are used for truck center plates and side bearings and trolley base bearings, and have been tried experimentally for journal bearings and armature bearings. See **Roller Bearing**.

Ballast Car. A car used for hauling ballast. Usually arranged for either side or center dumping.

Baltimore Ball-Bearing Center Plate. Figs. 1516-1517.

Band Wire. See **Armature Band Wire**.

Bar Wound Coil. An armature or field coil wound with bar or strap copper instead of round wire.

Barber Car. Figs. 11-13. A type of single-truck car for city service having square ends and a curved roof without monitor. It has a very light weight per seated passenger.

Barber Truck. Fig. 1420.

Barney & Smith Trucks. Figs. 1464-1466.

Base Board. A finishing board sometimes applied on the inside of the truss plank just above the floor.

Basin. A semi-spherical receptacle made of porcelain or white metal, used to hold water in which passengers may wash. It is usually mounted in a flat slab in a small closet or toilet room at one end of a passenger car, and water is supplied either by a hand pump or by a compressed air system. Only a few of the most elaborate interurban limited cars are supplied with such facilities.

Basin Pump. A small hand pump used for lifting water into a wash basin from a tank underneath.

Basket Rack. Figs. 720-727. A shelf made of rods and wire netting or cast in metal in the form of an open grill, supported from the side of the car just below the plate and above the seats. It provides a place where passengers may stow their small parcels and hand baggage. Basket racks are made in short, separate sections and also to extend continuously from end to end of the car on each side.

Basket Rack Bracket. A support for an end or an intermediate section of a basket rack.

Batten. A strip of wood or metal secured to parallel strips of wood to fasten them together as in a door or hatch cover.

Battery. A group of two or more primary or storage cells delivering electric current. See **Storage Battery, Primary Battery**.

Battery Relay and Charging Switch. Figs. 891-892. A device for automatically cutting in and out an auxiliary lighting circuit supplied from a storage battery whenever the trolley current fails. A similar device, Fig. 1789, is used to control the charging of the control circuit storage battery used with a Westinghouse unit-switch control equipment.

Bay State Cord Connector. Figs. 753-754.

Bayonet Trolley Base. Fig. 1872.

Bead. A small semi-circular molding. In window frame construction the sash parting strips are also called beads.

Beam. A timber of considerable cross-section subjected to compression or transverse stresses. The term is also applied to rolled iron and steel sections such as I-beams. See **Brake Beam, Bumper Beam, Compression Beam**.

Bearing. "That which supports or rests on something. A block on or in which a journal rotates."—Standard Dictionary. See **Armature Shaft Bearing, Axle Bearing, Brake Shaft Bearing, Center Bearing, Journal Bearing, Side Bearing**.

Bearing Lining. See **Bearing Shell, Axle Bearing Lining, Armature Bearing Lining**.

Bearing Metal. Any soft anti-friction metal used for lining bearing shells.

Bearing Shell. Figs. 1674-1675. A cylindrical or split sleeve made of cast or malleable iron or bronze, lined with bearing metal and surrounding the journal of a shaft. Also called bearing lining.

Bell. A hollow piece of metal, which when struck emits a sharp, clear sound. See **Signal Bell and Gong**.

Bell Clapper. A pivoted counterweighted hammer with which a signal bell is struck. The bell cord is attached to one end of the clapper, and the counterweight serves to pull the clapper quickly away from the gong after it strikes.

Bell Cord. Figs. 750-752. A small leather or woven cotton rope, carried in hangers under the car roof and extending from end to end of the car. It is attached to the signal bell on the platform, and is used by the conductor to give signals to the motorman according to a code of bell taps. In closed cars, the bell cord is usually carried under the deck sill and on open cars under the side plate, where it can be conveniently reached by the conductor standing on the running board.

Bell Cord Bushing. Figs. 741-742. A tube with rounded ends inserted in the end bulkheads, through which the bell cord is passed.

Bell Cord Connector. See **Bell Cord Splice**.

Bell Cord End Hook. Figs. 743-744, 748-749. A hook fastened to the end of a bell cord and fitted with an eye attached to the platform hood, to prevent the bell cord from being pulled through the guides when signals are given.

Bell Cord Guide. An eye or ring through which the bell cord is passed. It is often formed as part of the hand strap rod brackets or register rod brackets.

Bell Cord Handle. A small wooden knob fastened to the bottom of a bell cord which hangs down from the platform hood within easy reach of the conductor.

Bell Cord Hanger. Figs. 735-740. A rod or strap with an eye or pulley at the lower end, hung from the center of the upper deck, where the bell cord is carried over the center of the aisle.

Bell Cord Holder. Fig. 745. See **Bell Cord End Hook**.

Bell Cord Splice. Figs. 746-747, 753-754. A split metal sleeve with interior corrugations, which is slipped over the ends of two pieces of bell cord and pinched together, so as to grip both ends firmly and fasten them together.

Bell Cord Pulley. Fig. 742. A substitute for a bell cord guide in which a small grooved sheave is used to carry the cord and prevent excessive wear.

Bell Crank. An angular lever, pivoted at the apex and used to change the direction of motion by 90 deg., more or less, of the rods connected to it at each end.

Bell Mouth. A metal nipple used in connection with a soft rubber gasket, to make a water-tight joint surrounding a wire passing through the wall of a contactor box, motor frame or similar enclosure.

Bell Rope. See **Bell Cord**.

Belt Rail. 15, Figs. 271-273. A narrow strip of wood framed horizontally into the side posts of a car body just below the windows on the outside to form a support for the outside window sills. The end belt rail is a similar piece framed across the end posts of a car body.

Bench. A wooden seat. The cross seats of open cars are usually referred to as benches, and the size of such cars is designated by the number of benches with which they are fitted, as a 10-bench car. The usual spacing between benches is 2 ft. 8 in.

Berg Fenders. Figs. 708-710.

Berth. (Sleeping Cars.) A narrow bed, which can be made up by pulling out the seat cushions of two adjoining seats. An upper berth is sometimes formed by a shelf, which, when not in use, folds up against the lower deck. See Fig. 366.

Binding Post. A threaded metal post with nut, used to make a readily removable wire connection. The wire is bent around the post and the nut is screwed down tight on it. One or more wires may be attached to a post in this manner and another wire may be fastened with solder or a nut on the base of the post where it projects through the board on which it is mounted. See **Controller Connection Board**.

Birmingham Wire Gage. The British standard **Wire Gage**, which see.

Blind. See **Window Blind**.

Bliss Gears. Figs. 1520-1522.

Block. A short, thick piece of timber or metal used as a filling piece or as a support for some other part resting on it.

Blow-Out Coil. (Of Circuit Breaker.) A magnet coil inserted in an automatic circuit breaker to produce a magnetic field surrounding the arc which is ruptured when the circuit is broken. The presence of this magnetic field extinguishes the arc as it is formed. A similar device is used to extinguish the arcs formed in platform controllers, contactors and other apparatus in which heavy currents are broken.

Blower. A motor-driven pressure fan used with some single-phase car equipments of large capacity to provide forced ventilation for the auto-transformer and the motors. See Fig. 1705.

Board. A thin, narrow piece of wood. See **Floor Board, Running Board, Letter Board, Trolley Board, Tread Board, Roof Board**.

Body. (Of a Car.) The box or platform resting on the truck, or trucks. It includes the underframing, floor, sides and roof, but not the platforms, which are usually framed separately.

Body Bolster. 3, Figs. 271-370. A cross member of the body underframing of a double-truck car which transmits the load carried by the longitudinal sills to the body center plate. It is made of a single heavy timber or built up of timbers reinforced with flitch plates of steel. The body bolsters of long, heavy interurban and city cars are usually made entirely of metal, either in the form of a built-up truss with top and bottom plates or a single steel casting. In a trussed bolster, the top member, which is a steel plate 6 in. to 10 in. wide and ½ to ¾ in. thick, is called the top plate. The bottom member, which is a similar plate, is called the bottom plate, or compression bar. The two are riveted together at the ends, and are separated by filler blocks, increasing in depth toward the centre plate.

Body Bolster Bottom Plate. 102, Figs. 349-351. See above.

Body Bolster Fillers. Distance blocks bolted in between the top and bottom plates of a trussed body bolster. Also called body bolster thimbles.

Body Bolster Flitch Plates. Reinforcing plates of iron or steel sandwiched in on edge between two or more pieces of wood, giving to the bolster greater stiffness and strength. Also called sandwich plates.

Body Bolster Thimble. See **Body Bolster Fillers**.

Body Bolster Top Plate. 101, Figs. 271-370. See **Body Bolster**.

Body Center Plate. 26, Figs. 1388-1390; Figs. 1516-1517. The **Center Plate**, which see, attached to the under side of the body bolster and resting on the truck center plate.

Body Corner Post. 25, Figs. 259-370. An upright post in the body framing at the intersections of the sides and ends. Together with the vestibule corner post it forms the door opening over the vestibule steps. A grab handle is usually fastened to the body corner post to facilitate ascending or descending the steps.

Body End Door. See **End Door**.

Body End Plate. See **End Plate**.

Body End Sill. See **End Sill**.

Body End Spring. 19, Fig. 1378. An elliptic or semi-elliptic spring resting on the end of the side frame of a single truck, and designed to prevent galloping of the car.

Body Framing. The skeleton framework of a car body above the underframe and not including the roof framing or vestibule framing.

Body Grab Handle. Figs. 899-900. A vertical or curved rod or stick fastened to the end of the car body above the platform steps, to be grasped in boarding or alighting.

Body Hand Rail. Fig. 899. A curved or horizontal **Body Grab Handle**, which see.

Body Rib. Figs. 277-278; 35, Fig. 367. A light, vertical post extending from the side sill to the belt rail between the window posts. The ribs are shaped to conform to the curved or straight contour of the side panels, which are fastened to them and to the posts on the outside. Where vertical sheathing is used for the sides, light horizontal sticks are framed in the posts between the belt rail and the sill. These are also called body ribs.

Body Side Bearing. 98, Figs. 271-370. The **Side Bearing**, which see, attached to the under side of the body bolster immediately above a corresponding part carried on top of the truck bolster.

Body Spring. 21, Fig. 1376. (1) Single-Motor Truck. A spiral spring supporting one of the body spring posts.

(2) Single Truck. 12, Fig. 1378. One of the springs resting on top of the truck side frame and supporting the car body directly. Spiral and elliptic or semi-elliptic springs are used for the purpose.

Body Spring Post. 14, Fig. 1376. (Single-Motor Truck.) Spring-supported posts on the side frames of a single-motor truck having no bolster. They carry the side bearings on which the weight of the car body rests. A similar part is used in the coil springs of single trucks on which the body side sills rest.

Body Spring Post Stay. 5, Fig. 1378. A rod connecting the bottom ends of the spring posts on one side of a single truck.

Body Truss Rod. 4, Figs. 356-370. A round iron or steel rod from 1 in. to 1½ in. in diameter extending from end to end of the car under the longitudinal sills. It is anchored near the ends of the longitudinal sills or to the end sills, and passes over the bolsters and under queen posts dropped from the needle beams. It thus forms a shallow truss with the longitudinal sill above it, and materially stiffens the underframe against sagging in the center. From two to four truss rods are used under long interurban cars and many double-truck city cars of only moderate length. See **Overhang Truss Rod**.

Body Truss Rod Anchor. 127, Figs. 356-370. A casting bolted to the under side of the side sills at or outside of the bolsters to which the ends of a body truss rod are secured. The truss rod is sometimes carried on a saddle on top of the bolster and extends through the end sill, where it is fastened with a large nut and washer on the outside face

Body Truss Rod Queen Post. 5, Figs. 356-370. A strut dropped from the needlebeam against which the body truss rod bears.

Body Truss Rod Saddle. A bearing for a continuous body truss rod on top of the body bolsters.

Body Truss Rod Turnbuckle. A turnbuckle used to tighten up the body truss rods. Inserted at or near the center of the car.

Body Truss Rod Washer. See **Body Truss Rod Anchor.**

Bogie Truck. The British term for a four-wheel swiveling truck.

Bolster. The **Body Bolster**, which see, is a cross member of the body underframing which transmits the weight carried by the longitudinal sills to the body center plate, through which it is transmitted to the truck. Single-truck cars have no body bolsters. The **Truck Bolster**, which see, is a corresponding part of the truck which distributes the weight on the truck center plate equally between the two side frames and thence to the journals.

Bolster Chafing Plate. 12, Fig. 1368. A removable hardened steel plate attached to the side of a truck bolster to take the wear caused by the vertical and transverse movement of the bolster between the transoms. Similar plates, called **Transom Chafing Plates**, are usually provided on the transoms. In some designs of cast-steel bolsters bosses are cast on the sides in place of the chafing plates.

Bolster Guide Bar. More commonly called **Column**, which see.

Bolster Hanger. A **Swing Hanger**, which see.

Bolster Spring. 22, Fig. 1368; 20, Figs. 1388-1390. A coil or elliptic spring carried on the spring plank or directly on the bottom member of the truck side frame and supporting one end of the truck bolster.

Bolster Spring Cap. A metal plate on top of a bolster spring on which the truck bolster bears.

Bolster Spring Link. 21, Fig. 1374. In a Brill No. 39-E. truck, a part which performs the same function as an **Equalizer Spring Link**, which see.

Bolster Spring Scroll. 23, Fig. 1368. See **Scroll.**

Bolster Spring Seat. 24, Fig. 1368. A metal plate on top of the spring plank on which a bolster spring rests.

Bolster Spring Seat Rocker. 25, Fig. 1368. A curved rocker casting secured to the spring plank on which the bolster spring seat rests. Its purpose is to permit free radial swing of the spring plank without distortion of the bolster spring, due to side displacement.

Bolster Wear Plate. Another name for a **Bolster Chafing Plate,** which see.

Bolt. (1) A short, round bar of metal having a head formed on one end and screw threads to take a nut on the other end.

(2) The short bar or rod of a lock, which can be forced out or withdrawn into the lock by turning the knob or key.

Bolted Commutator. Figs. 1694-1695. A motor commutator in which the segments and mica insulation are assembled and held in place between two retaining rings by bolts.

Bolted Fastening. Figs. 1615-1616. A type of fastening for the tires of steel-tired wheels.

Bottom. See **Seat Bottom.**

Bottom Arch Bar. See **Arch Bar** and **Inverted Arch Bar.**

Bottom Door Track. A tongued or flat bar on which the bottom edge of a sliding door runs. See **Door Track.**

Bottom End Panel. A panel on the outside of the end of a car body below the continuation of the fender rail.

Bottom Framing. More properly **Underframe**, which see.

Bottom Plate. (Body Bolster.) 102, Figs. 271-370. The lower of two wide plates fastened together at the ends and spread apart at the center to form a trussed body bolster.

Bottom Sash. 46, Fig. 334. The lowest sash in a car window. The top sash, when used, is usually stationary, while the bottom sash is arranged to raise or lower.

Bottom Side Panel. 129, Fig. 334. A panel on the outside of a car below the fender rail. It is frequently curved in to clear wheel hubs and then becomes a **Concave Panel**, which see.

Bottom Truck Connection. 46, Fig. 1370. The rod, or turnbuckle, connecting the lower ends of the live and dead levers on a truck. With inside-hung brakes, it is in compression, and with outside-hung brakes it is in tension. Also called brake-lever coupling bar, brake turnbuckle and adjustable brake rod. See **Slack Adjuster.**

Bow. See **Platform Hood Bow.**

Bow Collector. A flexible horizontal bar or light roller 2 ft. or 3 ft. long which slides on the under side of an overhead trolley wire and is used instead of a trolley wheel for collecting current. Bow collectors are in general use in Europe, but have not found favor in the United States.

Box. A receptacle containing a bearing, as a **Journal Box**, which see.

Box Bolt. See **Journal Box Bolt.**

Box Car. A term commonly applied to any type of closed passenger or freight car. More properly a car completely enclosed with sides, ends and roof and having no windows, such as is used for the transportation of freight on steam railroads.

Box Frame Motor. Figs. 1645-1647, 1663, 1666-1667. A motor in which the frame or shell is made in one piece in the form of a rectangular box with the corners rounded off. The G. E.-66 and Westinghouse-300 motors are typical of this type. The armature can only be removed by taking the motor off of the truck, removing the frame heads and sliding or lifting the armature out through the circular hole in the end of the shell. A special machine, having a long arbor on which the armature can be carried and a sliding carriage for moving the frame lengthwise of the armature, has been designed to facilitate the removal of armatures in motors of this type. See **Split Frame Motor.**

Brace. 11, Figs. 356-370. In a framed structure, an inclined compression or tension member connecting two or more points where the vertical and horizotal members are joined. In the trussed side frames of cars such a member, when subjected only to compression, is usually termed simply a brace, and, when subjected only to tension, is termed a brace rod.

Brace Pocket. A cast or malleable-iron shoe screwed or bolted to the sills or plates of the body framing and forming a receptacle for the end of a brace. They are also made to receive the end of a brace and also the end of the adjoining vertical post. Seldom used in passenger-car framing.

Brace Rod. See **Brace.**

Bracket. (1) A support for any piece or part projecting from a wall or other surface.

(2) A curved stiffening rib formed on the plate of a cast-iron car wheel.

Bracket Lamp. A lamp fixture projecting from a wall, as distinguished from a ceiling lamp.

Bradshaw Skid. Fig. 1474.

Brake. A device for absorbing, through friction, and dissipating in the form of heat, the kinetic energy of a moving mass. Electric car brakes in common use are divided into those in which the pressure of the shoes on the wheels or rails is applied by hand through a system of levers, those in which the pressure is applied by compressed air admitted behind a piston working in a cylinder mounted under the car body, and those in which the motor connections are reversed to cause the motors to run as generators, the current generated being used to energize magnets which are attracted to the rails and at the same time apply pressure on the shoes bearing on the wheels. See **Air Brake, Hand Brake, Magnetic Brake, Slipper Brake, Momentum Brake, Electro-Pneumatic Brake.**

Brake Beam. Figs. 1510-1515; 50, Fig. 1370. A rod or trussed beam hung from the truck frame and carrying on each end a brake head and shoe which bears against the wheel tread. Pressure is applied longitudinally at the center of the beam, and is distributed equally against the wheels on each side. Only a few designs of motor trucks employ brake beams, owing to the difficulty of forming a connection between them around the motors; but in most trailer trucks the brake rigging is designed for the use of beams. Brake beams may be either inside-hung, when supported from the transoms, or outside-hung, when supported from the truck end frame.

Brake Beam Adjusting Spring. 41, Fig. 1372. A coil or flat spring designed to keep the brake shoes attached to a brake beam clear of the wheels when the brakes are released. See **Brake Shoe Spring.**

Brake Beam Hanger. More commonly called **Brake Hanger,** which see.

Brake Beam Release Spring. See **Brake Release Spring.**

Brake Beam Safety Hanger. 17, Fig. 1370. A strap attached to a truck transom and passing underneath a brake beam. Its purpose is to prevent the beam from dropping on the track in case one or both of the brake hangers breaks or works loose.

Brake Beam Slide. 43, Fig. 1374. A guide for the end of a brake beam.

Brake Beam Strut. In a trussed brake beam, Figs. 1510-1515, the post in the center, which also serves as the **Brake Lever Fulcrum,** which see.

Brake Beam Truss Rod. A truss rod applied to a brake beam to stiffen it. The king post or strut in the center is used as the brake lever fulcrum. See Figs. 1510-1515.

Brake Block. A combined brake head and shoe formed in one piece.

Brake Chain. A chain wound around the barrel or spiral drum on the lower end of the brake shaft, and connected to a brake chain connecting rod, which in turn is fastened to one of the brake levers under the car body. By turning the brake shaft the chain is wound up and a pull applied to the brake leverage. Either flat or twisted link chain is used. See Figs. 577-584.

Brake Chain Connecting Rod. An iron rod, usually ½ in. to ⅝ in. in diameter, connecting the brake chain to one of the levers of the foundation brake gear. Where hand brakes are used in connection with air brakes, the rods from the two ends of the car are attached usually to the extremities of a centrally-pivoted lever, which in turn is connected through another lever to a short piece of chain fastened to the cross-head of one of the cylinder levers. The movement of the air-brake piston does not affect the hand-brake connection, and when the hand brake is applied its power is multiplied from two to three times up to the point of attachment to the cylinder lever. See Fig. 458.

Brake Chain Sheave. A pulley around which the brake chain passes to change its direction of pull. Sometimes required to avoid interference of the chain with other apparatus mounted under the car body.

Brake Chain Worm. A spirally grooved drum attached to the bottom of a brake shaft and on which the brake chain is wound. The spiral groove is intended to cause the chain to wind evenly. In some types of geared brakes the worm is conical in shape, to increase the speed at the beginning of the brake application and to increase the power near the end when the chain is winding on the groove of smallest diameter. See Figs. 577-584.

Brake Connection. A general term for any of the rods connecting two brake levers of the foundation brake gear. The rods usually are designated according to the levers to which they are attached farthest from the brake cylinder.

Brake Cylinder. (Air Brake.) Figs. 498-500. An iron cylinder bolted to the underframe of a car and containing a piston which is forced outward by the admission of compressed air behind it. The pressure exerted on the piston is transmitted to the end of a cylinder lever and through a system of connecting rods and levers to the brake shoes bearing on the wheels. When the pressure is released the piston is returned to its normal position by a helical spring coiled around the piston rod.

Brake Cylinder Bracket. A forging bolted to the underframe of a car body to which a brake cylinder is attached.

Brake Cylinder Head. A circular metal disc bolted to the end of an air brake cylinder. They are distinguished as pressure heads and non-pressure heads.

Brake Dead Lever. More commonly, simply **Dead Lever,** which see.

Brake Dog. See **Brake Pawl.**

Brake Drum. See **Brake Shaft Drum** and **Brake Chain Worm.**

Brake Gear. The entire group of parts which operate to retard the motion of a car. See **Foundation Brake Gear.**

Brake Handle. Figs. 568-572. The S-shaped handle or crank attached to the top of a brake shaft, by means of which the shaft is revolved and the chain wound up to apply the brakes. The handle is made of polished brass or bronze, and usually includes a ratchet attachment, whereby it may be revolved in one direction without turning the brake shaft.

Brake Hanger. 53, Fig. 1370; 55, Figs. 1388-1390. A bar, link, or eye bolt, attached to the truck frame or equalizer bars by which the brake heads or brake beams are suspended. A variety of forms of brake hangers and attachments are in use, many of which are designed to prevent chattering of the brake shoes on the wheels at the end of a stop.

Brake Hanger Carrier. 22, Figs. 1480-1481. A bracket or bearing casting attached to or forming part of the truck frame from which a brake hanger is suspended. For inside-hung brakes on double trucks the carriers are attached to or formed integrally with the transoms, side frames or equalizers, and for outside-hung brakes they are attached to the truck end frames.

Brake Hanger Pin. 56 and 57, Figs. 1388-1390. A pin securing a brake hanger to a brake hanger carrier.

Brake Head. 2, Figs. 1480-1481. A casting attached to the lower end of a brake hanger or on the end of a brake beam, to which is keyed a separable brake shoe. The American Electric Railway Engineering Association has adopted standard designs of brake head and shoe, shown in Figs. 1952-1965, which are being widely adopted.

Brake Head Pin. 59, Figs. 1388-1390.

Brake Hose. Fig. 480. Laminated rubber and cotton tubing attached to a nipple screwed in the angle cock of the brake pipe and carrying at the other end a simple form of coupling. It forms a flexible connection between the brake pipes of two adjoining cars through which compressed air for operating the train brakes is conducted.

Brake Hose Band. See **Hose Band.**

Brake Hose Coupling. Fig. 480. A casting fastened into the lower end of a brake hose and engaging with a coupling of similar shape on the hose of the adjoining car. The two couplings can only be connected together by bending up the ends of the hose, and when the hose falls to its normal position the couplings are securely locked together and are air-tight. If the cars break apart the couplings disengage when the hose pulls out straight without tearing the hose loose from the nipples. Where a separate control pipe must be coupled between cars, as in some types of automatic air brakes, the control pipe hose couplings are of slightly different form from the brake hose couplings, so that the brake hose on one car cannot be coupled with the control pipe hose of the adjoining car.

Brake Hose Dummy Coupling. Fig. 482. A blank coupling similar in shape to a standard hose coupling, which is hung by a chain from the bumper beam. When the hose coupling is not connected to that of another car it is hooked into the dummy coupling to prevent its being damaged and to keep dirt out of the hose.

Brake Hose Nipple. A short piece of pipe fitted into the end of a piece of brake hose and securely held by a hose band. The nipple is threaded and is screwed into the angle cock on the end of the brake pipe. See Fig. 480.

Brake Lever. Any lever forming part of the foundation brake gear of a car. See **Dead Lever, Live Lever, Cylinder Lever, Floating Lever.**

Brake Lever Bracket. A fulcrum for a body brake lever attached to the underframe of a car body.

Brake Lever Carrier. A slide or support for one end of a body brake lever.

Brake Lever Carrier Beam. A short beam sometimes framed between two transverse floor timbers in the center of the underframe to support a body brake lever carrier.

Brake Lever Coupling Bar. The compression rod connecting the two brake beams, or brake heads, of an inside-hung truck brake gear. Also called bottom truck connection, brake turnbuckle and adjustable brake rod. The preferable name is bottom truck connection.

Brake Lever Fulcrum. 41 and 44, Fig. 1370. Any bearing about which a brake lever turns. Specifically, the bearing on a brake beam to which one of the truck brake levers is attached. In trussed metal brake beams the brake beam strut serves as the brake lever fulcrum.

Brake Lever Guide. See **Dead Lever Guide**.

Brake Lever Stop. See **Dead Lever Guide**.

Brake Live Lever. More commonly, simply **Live Lever**, which see.

Brake Pawl. A pointed dog pivoted at the center and engaging in the teeth of a brake ratchet wheel, to prevent the brake shaft from turning backward while the chain is being wound up. It is arranged to be moved in or out of engagement by pressing with the foot against the outer end. See Figs. 576 and 583.

Brake Pin. A term applied to any of the numerous pins used to connect the brake rods to the brake levers.

Brake Pipe. Also called train pipe and train line. An iron pipe carried under a car body equipped with automatic or straight-air train brakes and connected through brake hose and couplings with the brake pipes under adjoining cars in the train, thus forming a continuous connection from the front car to the rear car. It serves to convey compressed air from the main reservoirs of cars carrying motor compressors to recharge the auxiliary reservoirs, or, in the case of straight-air brakes, to fill the brake cylinders direct. See **Automatic Air Brake, Control Pipe, Emergency Pipe, Reservoir Pipe.**

Brake Pipe Air Strainer. Figs. 467-468. A fine mesh wire screen inserted in the brake pipe under each car to prevent the entrance of dirt or foreign matter into the triple valve or brake cylinder. Also called **Air Strainer**, which see.

Brake Pipe Vent Valve. Fig. 454. An electro-pneumatic valve used to vent the brake pipe pressure in an emergency application of an **Electro-Pneumatic Brake**, which see.

Brake Ratchet Wheel. 74, Fig. 260. A toothed disc keyed to the brake shaft just above the floor of the platform with which a brake pawl engages to prevent the shaft from turning backward when pressure on the brake handle is removed while the brake chain is wound up and under tension.

Brake Release Spring. 48, Fig. 1370. A flat bar of steel bent to a suitable shape and attached to the truck frame and to the brake beams or brake hangers. It serves the double purpose of a **Brake Beam Safety Hanger**, which see, and also to pull the brake shoes off of the wheels when the brakes are released. In some types of truck brake gear the release spring (5, Figs. 1480-1481) is a coil spring which is placed under tension or compression when the brakes are applied, and when the pull on the truck connection rod is released the spring returns the truck brake levers to their normal position, in which the brake shoes are clear of the wheels. A brake release spring should not be confused with the spring surrounding a brake cylinder piston rod.

Brake Rod. Any of the rods connecting levers of the foundation brake gear.

Brake Rod Roller. 69, Figs. 1388-1390. A sheave attached to the end of a truck brake rod and moving on the edge of a **Radius Bar**, which see.

Brake Safety Strap. 17, Fig. 1370. A flat bar of iron fastened to the truck frame and bent under the brake beam, or, in some types of trucks, under the bottom truck connection connecting the two brake levers on each side of the truck. Its purpose is to prevent the brake beam or bottom truck connection from falling to the track in case the hangers or the rod should break. Also called **Brake Beam Safety Hanger**, which see. See **Brake Release Spring**.

Brake Shaft. Figs. 574-576; 72, Fig. 260. An iron rod supported vertically on the platform and extending below the floor. It carries a brake handle or wheel at its upper end, by which it is turned. The brake chain is wound around the lower end, which projects through the floor. The brake ratchet wheel is usually keyed to the shaft just above the floor and forms a step bearing for the shaft.

Brake Shaft Bearing. A bearing for the upper end of a brake shaft, carried by an A-frame brace bolted to the dasher of an enclosed vestibule. In open vestibule cars the bearing is usually attached to the dasher rail.

Brake Shaft Brace. A bent iron bar bolted to the dasher and forming a support at the upper end to hold a brake shaft in a vertical position.

Brake Shaft Chain. See **Brake Chain**.

Brake Shaft Drum. An enlargement on the lower end of a brake shaft on which the brake chain is wound. It is sometimes formed with a conical spiral groove to obtain speed in taking up slack in the brakes at the beginning of the application, and greater power but less speed as the chain winds up on the grooves of smaller diameter. See Figs. 577-584.

Brake Shaft Step. A U-shaped support and bearing for the lower end of a brake shaft, hung from the under side of the platform floor.

Brake Shoe. Figs. 1484-1509. A curved block of metal 8 in. to 12 in. long which is pressed against the tread of a car wheel when the brakes are applied to arrest the motion of the car. The kinetic energy of the moving car is thus transformed into heat by the friction between the brake shoes and the wheels, and the heat is dissipated by radiation.

Many of the older types of electric trucks employed a combined brake shoe and head, which was often called a brake shoe. Properly speaking, a brake shoe is a separable block of metal attached by a key to a **Brake Head**, which see, riveted or bolted to one end of a brake beam or to one of the brake levers. The American Electric Railway Engineering Association has adopted standard designs of brake shoes, brake shoe heads and keys, which are patterned after the M. C. B. or Christie type in universal use on steam roads. These are shown in Figs. 1952-1965. Brake shoes are commonly made of cast iron, with or without hardened inserts in the face or with chilled ends.

Brake Shoe Adjusting Spring. 62, Figs. 1388-1390. See **Brake Shoe Spring**.

Brake Shoe Key. 23, Figs. 1480-1481. A tapered piece of steel with an upset end which is inserted in slots in the brake head and the projecting lug on the back of a brake shoe to fasten the shoe to the head.

Brake Shoe Spring. 4, Figs. 1480-1481. A flat spring used to keep the face of a brake shoe parallel with the face of the wheel when the brakes are released, so as to prevent the top of the shoe from dragging on the wheel. It should not be confused with a **Brake Release Spring**, which see.

Brake Slack Adjuster. Figs. 523-528, 1482. A turnbuckle or automatic device to take up the slack in the foundation brake gear caused by the wear of the shoes and the pin connections. The most common form is a turnbuckle inserted in the bottom truck connection, as in Figs. 1480-1481. Several types of automatic slack adjusters are also in use.

Brake Spool. See **Brake Chain Worm**.

Brake Staff. See **Brake Shaft**.

Brake Strut. See **Bottom Truck Connection**.

Brake Turnbuckle. 43, Fig. 1368; 45, Figs. 1388-1390. An elongated nut with a right-hand thread in one end and a left-hand thread in the other, which is inserted between two turnbuckle ends of a **Bottom Truck Connection**, which see. By turning the turnbuckle to the right or left the length of the bottom truck connection can be increased or decreased and the slack in the truck brake rigging adjusted. See **Brake Slack Adjuster**.

Brake Turnbuckle End. 42, Fig. 1368. See **Brake Turnbuckle**.

Brake Turnbuckle Lock. 44, Fig. 1368. A cotter pin or other fastening used to prevent a brake turnbuckle from turning and becoming loose.

Brake Valve. Figs. 483-499, 542-543, 549-559. A valve operated by the motorman to apply and release the air brakes. It is mounted alongside the motor controller in the vestibule. Also called motorman's valve, motorman's brake valve and operating valve.

Brake Valve Handle. Figs. 564-565. A removable handle used to turn the spindle of a motorman's brake valve. It can be removed only when the valve spindle is in the lap position, in which all ports in the valve are blanked.

Brake Wheel. Figs. 573-575. A spoke wheel 12 in. to 15 in. in diameter and made of iron or brass, sometimes used instead of a brake handle to turn a brake shaft. The hub of the brake wheel may be fitted on a square end formed on top of the brake shaft and thus revolve in a horizontal plane, or it may be mounted to turn in a vertical plane and be connected to the brake shaft through bevel gears.

Brass. An alloy composed of copper and zinc in proportions varying from 98 per cent copper to 34 per cent copper. The harder alloys are used as bearing metals, and hence the name is a common abbreviation for a journal bearing.

Breaker. A contraction of **Circuit Breaker**, which see

Bridge. See **Trolley Bridge.**

Bridge Connections. Connections made inside of K-34 and K-35 controllers and so arranged that full current is maintained through the motors when passing from the series to the parallel grouping. In other K-type controllers one of the motors is shunted or short circuited when changing from series to parallel grouping.

Bridging. 115, Figs. 259-370. Short, transverse timbers framed between the longitudinal sills of a car-body underframe to prevent buckling of the sills and to serve as floor joists. The sills are prevented from bulging outward by sill tie rods, which are usually placed alongside of the bridging. Bridging should not be confused with transverse floor timbers, which are framed across from side sill to side sill.

Bridging Relay. Fig. 1797. In an automatic multiple-unit equipment a device for accomplishing the same function as the bridge connections on the cylinder of a platform controller.

Brill Fare Boxes. Figs. 1198-1202.

Brill Journal Box. Figs. 1553-1554.

Brill Radial Drawbar. Fig. 631.

Brill Trucks. Figs. 1367-1384.

Brinkerhoff Pressed Steel Side Construction. Figs. 697-704.

Broad Gage. Any gage of track wider than the standard of 4 ft. 8½ in. Broad gage is used in Philadelphia, Baltimore, and a few other cities. Also termed wide gage. See **Narrow Gage.**

Bronze. An alloy of copper, tin and zinc, with or without lead. Used for journal bearings and car fittings.

Broom. (Sweeper.) A revolving shaft on which are mounted radially pieces of rattan of even length. The broom is mounted in hangers diagonally across the under side of the sweeper, so as to throw the snow out to one side of the track. It is driven through chains and sprockets by an independent motor mounted in the car body. See **Sweeper.**

Brown & Sharpe Wire Gage. The **Wire Gage**, which see, commonly employed in the United States.

Brush. (1) A collection of bristles or straws secured in a back or handle, as a paint brush.
(2) 13, Fig. 1659. A stick of carbon carried in a **Brush Holder**, which see, and bearing on the commutator of a motor armature with a pressure of from 4 lb. to 7 lb. It transmits current from the leads attached to the brush holder to the commutator segment, on which it bears. The current then passes through the armature coils connected in series with the positive commutator segment and out through the negative commutator segment and brush. See **Armature.**

The American Electric Railway Engineering Association in 1908 approved as good practice the following specifications for motor brushes:

Each brush should be plainly stamped with the name of the manufacturer and grade of the brush. The stamping should be placed on the brush so that the marking will not be destroyed when the brush is worn.

The thickness of the brush should not be greater than exact size or less than 0.01 in. under exact size. The width and length of the brush should not be greater than exact size or less than 1/32 in. under exact size. The standard method of box gage should be used.

All copper plating should be omitted.

Brushes, when broken, should show a fracture of uniform appearance and fine grain.

Stratification and shrinkage cracks are objectionable, and should be avoided as far as possible. When the brush is broken crosswise and lengthwise, the appearance of the two fractures should be similar in texture.

Brushes should be classified into:

Class 1. Coke brushes, which are suitable for motors of 50 hp. or less with ungrooved commutators operating in slow-speed service;

Class 2. Composite coke and graphite brushes, which are suitable for motors of from 50 hp. to 100 hp. operated in suburban or interurban service, normally with grooved commutators;

Class 3. Graphite brushes, which are suitable for general use on grooved commutators on motors of 100 hp. and over.

When tested on a vibrator wheel having a diameter of 8¼ in. and eight ratchet teeth 1/16 in. deep running at 250 r.p.m., a class 1 brush under a pressure of 7 lb. per sq. in. of contact area should stand 20,000 revolutions. Class 2 brushes should stand 30,000 revolutions, and class 3 brushes should stand 50,000 revolutions.

When tested for current-carrying capacity on a hard copper slip ring 8 in. in diameter running at 500 r.p.m. under a spring pressure of 7 lb. per sq. in. of contact area, a class 1 brush should transmit a current of 100 amperes per sq. in. at 25 volts without glowing. Class 2 brushes should transmit 150 amperes per sq. in., and class 3 brushes 200 amperes per sq. in. without glowing.

Brush Board. In a short-broom snow sweeper, a plank with a rattan brush attached to the bottom edge. It is mounted diagonally under the sweeper to one side of the revolving broom, and its purpose is to push the snow off of the rail and out to one side.

Brush Holder. Figs. 1650, 1676-1677, 1710. A metal casting, usually of brass, attached to but insulated from the inside of the motor frame and carrying from one to four narrow carbon brushes which bear on the commutator of the armature. The brushes are inserted in rectangular tubes in the holder, which are radial to the commutator. A finger is pressed down on top of the brush by a spring mounted on the holder, and this holds the bottom end of the brush firmly on the surface of the commutator. Suitable terminals are provided on the brush holder for connecting the brushes to the external circuits of the motor.

Brush Holder Shunt. A flexible conductor attached to the finger which presses the brush down and to the terminal of the motor lead connected to the brush holder. It provides a path of low resistance for the current flowing through the brush and prevents overheating of the brush holder spring, through which the current would otherwise have to pass.

Brush Holder Spring. A flat or coil spring mounted in a brush holder and pressing down the brush against the commutator with a force of from 4 lb. to 7 lb. The springs are designed to maintain an almost constant pressure on the brush, regardless of the amount of brush wear.

Bucking. (Of a Motor.) A peculiar phenomenon of railway motors, which is the result of the motor acting momentarily as a generator and exerting a reverse torque which tends to check the motion of the car with great force and suddenness. It is usually due to the existence of a ground in the armature or commutator. When a second ground occurs in any part of the motor between the armature and the trolley, a heavy current flows and produces an intense magnetic field, as the counter electromotive force in the armature drops to zero value, owing to the short circuit within it, and does not oppose the flow of current from trolley to ground. The short-circuited armature, revolving in the strong magnetic field, exercises a powerful reverse torque, which checks the motion of the car. The same effect can be produced by reversing the motors when the car is moving in a forward direction, opening the circuit breaker and turning the controller on one or two notches. The residual magnetism of the motors tends to cause them to act as generators, but one motor will usually be stronger than the other and will generate enough current to cause the other motor to run as a motor in the reverse direction.

Buffer. A device attached to the bumper beam for absorbing the compressive shocks between two cars coupled together. Seldom used on street or interurban railway cars.

Buffet Car. Figs. 174-175. An interurban car having facilities for serving light meals to passengers. Also called café car. Such cars are operated on one or two of the longer interurban roads in the Middle West.

Bulb Angle. See **Angle**.

Bulkhead. A cross partition in a car body. See **End Bulkhead**.

Bulkhead Sash. 78, Fig. 260. A fixed or drop window sash in the end bulkhead of an open car. Three sashes are usually used. When arranged to drop, they are lowered into a pocket between the backs of the two bulkhead seats.

Bulkhead Seat. A cross seat in an open car built with the back against the end bulkhead. Such a seat may or may not be built on the platform side of the bulkhead.

Bulkhead Top Light. 80, Fig. 260. A fixed sash in an end bulkhead above the drop sashes and below the end plate. Also called bulkhead upper sash.

Bull's-Eye Lens. A plano-convex glass lens used in signal lamps and incandescent headlights to project the light rays in a straight beam. See **Fresnel Lens**.

Bull Rope. See **Switching Rope**.

Bumper. See **Bumper Beam** and **Seat Back Bumper**.

Bumper Beam. 26, Figs. 259-370; Figs. 590-598. The curved block of wood or piece of metal fastened to the ends of the platform sills or on the outside of the crown piece to resist compressive shocks.

Bumper Beam Cover Plate. An iron or steel plate attached to the top surface of a projecting bumper beam. On many city cars the plate is inclined upward at an angle of about 45 deg. and riveted to the dasher, so that no foothold is afforded on the bumper beam.

Bumper Beam Face Plate. An iron plate fastened with screws to the outside face of a wooden bumper beam to protect it from abrasion.

Bundle Rack. More properly **Basket Rack**, which see.

Burlap. Coarse hemp cloth used in upholstering car seats.

Bus. A common conductor to which several other conductors are joined. The term is sometimes applied to a power cable connecting all the motor cars in a train and connected, in turn, to each trolley or third-rail shoe.

Bushing. A hollow metal cylinder inserted in a hole to make it of smaller size or to form a bearing in which a shaft can turn. See **Trolley Wheel Bushing**.

Butt Hinge. Figs. 755-756. A hinge for a swinging door, so called because the two leaves are fastened to the abutting edges of a door and jamb.

Button. See **Push Button**.

Buzzer. Figs. 1236, 1246. An electrical device which, when supplied with current, emits a buzzing sound. It consists of a spring-pivoted armature and a magnet coil, together with an interrupter. When the circuit is made and broken in the interrupter the magnet is intermittently energized and attracts the armature. The rapid movement of the armature produces the buzzing sound.

Buzzer Signal System. Fig. 1237. A system of push buttons and signal buzzers by means of which passengers inside of a car may signal to the conductor and motorman that they wish to alight at the next stopping place. A buzzer is mounted on each platform and both are connected in circuit with a number of push buttons mounted in the side posts of the car. Current is supplied from primary batteries or from the trolley through suitable resistance. When any one of the buttons is pushed the circuit through the battery or trolley feed is established and both buzzers sound.

C

Cab. See **Motorman's Cab**.

Cab Heater. Fig. 1157. A portable electric heater used to warm a motorman's cab.

Cable. An insulated electrical conductor of large size, containing one or more wires. The wires leading from the controller to the trolley and to the motors are usually called car cables. See **Jumper**.

Cable Car. A car propelled by a grip attached to a cable running on sheaves in an underground conduit. Cable cars have been supplanted by overhead trolley or underground conduit electric cars in nearly every city in the United States in which they were at one time used.

Cable Clamp. A band partly or wholly encircling one or more car cables and used to fasten them in place on the car framing.

Cable Fixture. Figs. 644-646. A type of curtain fixture for open cars in which the two ends of the bottom rod of the curtain run on small wire cables let into grooves cut in the posts.

Cafe Parlor Car. Figs. 174-176. A luxuriously appointed car equipped with facilities for serving light meals. Such cars are operated by a few long-distance interurban railways in the Middle and Far West.

California Type Car. Figs. 29, 83. A car designed for all-year service, in which the body is built with a closed compartment in the center and with cross-bench open seats occupying the remaining space between the platforms. So-called because cars of this type were first used in the warm, equable climate of California.

Cam Curtain Fixture. Fig. 652.

Camber. The rise or upward deflection given the center of a car body when built to compensate for any sagging which may take place after the car has been run for some time.

Candle. A round stick of tallow or paraffin wax, in the center of which is placed a loosely woven cotton thread or wick. When lighted the wick draws up the melted wax, which burns slowly and evenly.

Candle Lamp. An emergency lamp burning a candle, sometimes carried in interurban cars to supply light in case of failure of the trolley current for any length of time.

Candle Power. A measure of the comparative illumination of a source of light. A 16-candle power lamp is a lamp which gives an illumination equivalent to that produced by 16 standard candles. A standard candle was originally a sperm oil candle burning a given number of grains of wax per hour, but comparisons of illuminants are now made with standardized incandescent electric lamps.

Canopy. (1) A term sometimes applied to a **Platform Hood**, which see.

(2) A canvas roof over an open car, as shown in Fig. 163. See **Moonlight Car**.

Canvas. A closely-woven heavy cotton cloth, used for the backing of rattan seating and for the outside covering of car roofs. See **Roofing Canvas**.

Cap. The upper part or covering of anything. See **Seat Arm Cap**, **Spring Cap**, **Pedestal Cap**.

Car. Figs. 1-450. A vehicle mounted on wheels and running on rails. Electric railway cars may be divided into motor or self-propelling cars and trail cars. They include a great variety of types for city and interurban service.

Cars for city passenger service include:

California Type Car	Open Car
Closed Car	Parlor Car
Convertible Car	Pay-as-You-Enter Car
Double-Deck Car	Pay-Within Car
Double-End Car	Semi-Convertible Car
Double-Truck Car	Single-End Car
Funeral Car	Single-Truck Car

Cars for interurban passenger service include:

Cafe Car	Office Car
Combination Passenger and Baggage Car	Parlor Car
Excursion Car	Passenger Car or Coach
Observation Car	Smoking Car

Cars for company's service and freight service include:

Ash Car	Line Car
Baggage and Express Car	Salt Car
Box Car	Snow Plow
Coal Car	Snow Sweeper
Flat Car	Sprinkler Car
Gondola Car	Work Car

Car Body. The main structure of a car which is mounted either on one or two trucks. It includes the underframe, sides, ends and roof, but not the platforms at the ends, which are usually framed separately.

Car Cleaner. Any compound used with or without water for cleaning the exterior varnished surface of cars. A great variety of such cleaners are sold.

Car Coupler. Figs. 600-635. A device for connecting two cars together for train operation. See **Coupler**.

Car Discharge Valve. Figs. 518-519. Another name for a **Conductor's Signal Valve**, which see.

Car Door. See **Door**.

Car Fittings. Figs. 636-658, 720-1027, 1094-1207, 1235-1318. The miscellaneous hardware attached to a car body. The term is general, and includes seats, fare registers, heaters, lamps, bells and other equipment in addition to the door and window fixtures, hand-pole rods and similar small parts.

Car Floor. 42, Figs. 259-370. The platform of boards laid over the underframing and forming the bottom of the car body.

Car Heater. Figs. 1094-1157. A stove or hot-water heater or an electric resistance coil, used for warming the air in the interior of a car body. See **Electric Heater**, **Hot-Water Heater** and **Stove**.

Car Roof. 48 and 49, Figs. 259-370. The covering over the body of a car. The roofs of electric railway cars usually consist of a frame composed of the side and deck plates, deck sills and deck posts on which are framed the upper and lower deck carlines. The roof boards are laid longitudinally on the carlines and covered with heavy roofing canvas. See **Roof**.

Car Seat. See **Seat**.

Car Truck. See **Truck**.

Car Wheel. See **Wheel**.

Car Wiring. Figs. 1838-1854. The wires mounted in or under a car body to serve as conductors for the various electrical circuits required for the motors, control apparatus and lights.

The National Board of Fire Underwriters has approved the following requirements for car wiring:

32. CAR WIRING AND EQUIPMENT OF CARS

A. Protection of Car Body, Etc.

1. Under side of car bodies to be protected by approved fire-resisting, insulating material, not less than $\frac{1}{8}$ in. in thickness, or by sheet iron or steel, not less than 0.04 in. in thickness, as specified in Section A, 2, 3 and 4. This protection to be provided over all electrical apparatus, such as motors with a capacity of over 75 hp. each, resistances, contactors, lightning arresters, air-brake motors, etc., and also where wires are run, except that protection may be omitted over wires designed to carry 25 amp. or less if they are encased in metal conduit.

2. At motors of over 75 hp. each, fire-resisting material or sheet iron or steel to extend not less than 8 in. beyond all edges of openings in motors, and not less than 6 in. beyond motor leads on all sides.

3. Over resistances, contactors and lightning arresters and other electrical apparatus, excepting when amply protected by their casing, fire-resisting material or sheet iron or steel to extend not less than 8 in. beyond all edges of the devices.

4. Over conductors, not encased in conduit, and conductors in conduit when designed to carry over 25 amp., unless the conduit is so supported as to give not less than $\frac{1}{2}$ in. clear air space between the conduit and the car, fire-resisting material or sheet iron or steel to extend at least 6 in. beyond conductors on either side.

The fire-resisting insulating material or sheet iron or steel may be omitted over cables made up of flame-proof braided outer covering when surrounded by $\frac{1}{8}$-in. flame-proof covering, as called for by Section I, 4.

5. In all cases fireproof material or sheet iron or steel to have joints well fitted, to be securely fastened to the sills, floor timbers and cross braces, and to have the whole surface treated with a waterproof paint.

6. Cut-out and switch cabinets to be substantially made of hardwood. The entire inside of cabinet to be lined with not less than $\frac{1}{8}$-in. fire-resisting insulating material, which shall be securely fastened to the woodwork, and after the fire-resisting material is in place the inside of the cabinet shall be treated with a waterproof paint.

B. Wires, Cables, Etc.

1. All conductors to be stranded, the allowable carrying capacity being determined by the following table, except that motor, trolley and resistance leads shall not be less than No. 7 B. & S. gage, heater circuits not less than No. 12 B. & S. gage, and lighting and other auxiliary circuits not less than No. 14 B. & S. gage.

CARRYING CAPACITY OF RUBBER-COVERED WIRE

B. & S. G.	Amperes.	Circ. Mils.	B. & S. G.	Amperes.	Circ. Mils.
18	3	1,624	4	65	41,740
16	6	2,583	3	76	52,630
14	12	4,107	2	90	66,370
12	17	6,530	1	107	83,690
10	24	10,380	0	127	105,500
8	33	16,510	00	150	133,100
6	46	26,250	000	177	167,800
5	54	33,100	0000	210	211,600

Circular Mils.	Amperes.	Circular Mils.	Amperes.
200,000	200	1,200,000	730
300,000	270	1,300,000	770
400,000	320	1,400,000	810
500,000	390	1,500,000	850
600,000	450	1,600,000	890
700,000	500	1,700,000	930
800,000	550	1,800,000	970
900,000	600	1,900,000	1,010
1,000,000	650	2,000,000	1,050
1,100,000	690		

The current used in determining the size of motor, trolley and resistance leads shall be the per cent of the full-load current, based on one hour's run of the motor, as given by the following table:

Size Each Motor.	Motor Leads.	Trolley Leads.	Resistance Leads.
75 h. p. or less	50%	40%	15%
Over 75 h. p.	45%	35%	15%

Approved fixture wire will be permitted for wiring approved clusters.

2. To have an insulation and braid approved for wires carrying currents of the same potential.

3. When run in metal conduit to be protected by an additional braid.

Where conductors are laid in conduit, not being drawn through, the additional braid will not be required.

4. When not in conduit, in approved moulding, or in cables surrounded by $\frac{1}{8}$-in. flame-proof covering, must be approved rubber covered (except that tape may be substituted for braid) and be protected by an additional flame-proof braid, at least 1/32 in. in thickness, the outside being saturated with a preservative flame-proof compound. Except that when motors are so enclosed that flame cannot extend outside of the casing, the flame-proof covering will not be required on the motor leads.

5. Must be so spliced or joined as to be both mechanically and electrically secure without solder. The joints must then be soldered and covered with an insulation equal to that on the conductors.

Joints made with approved splicing devices and those connecting the leads at motors, plows or third-rail shoes need not be soldered.

6. All connections of cables to cut-outs, switches and fittings, except those to controller connection boards, when designed to carry over 25 amp., must be provided with lugs or terminals soldered to the cable, and securely fastened to the device by bolts, screws or by clamping; or the end of the cable, after the insulation is removed, shall be dipped in solder and be fastened into the device by at least two set screws having check nuts.

All connections for conductors to fittings, etc., designed to carry less than 25 amp., must be provided with up-turned lugs that will grip the conductor between the screw and the lug, the screws being provided with flat washers, or by block terminals having two set screws, and the end of the conductors must be dipped in solder. Soldering, in addition to the connection of the binding screws, is strongly recommended, and will be insisted on when above requirements are not complied with.

This rule only to apply to circuits where the maximum potential is over 25 volts and current exceeds 5 amp.

C. Cut-Outs, Circuit Breakers and Switches

1. All cut-outs and switches having exposed live metal parts to be located in cabinets. Cut-outs and switches, not in iron boxes or in cabinets, shall be mounted on not less than ¼-in. fire-resisting insulating material, which shall project at least ½ in. beyond all sides of the cut-out or switch.

2. Cut-outs to be of the approved cartridge or approved blow-out type.

3. All switches controlling circuits of over 5-amp. capacity shall be of approved single-pole, quick-break or approved magnetic blow-out type.

Switches controlling circuits of 5 amp. or less capacity may be of the approved single-pole, double-break, snap type.

4. Circuit breakers to be of approved type.

5. Circuits must not be fused above their safe carrying capacity.

6. A cut-out must be placed as near as possible to the current collector, so that the opening of the fuse in this cut-out will cut off all current from the car.

When cars are operated by metallic return circuits, with circuit breakers connected to both sides of the circuit, no fuses in addition to the circuit breakers will be required.

D. Conduit

When from the nature of the case, or on account of the size of the conductors, the ordinary pipe and junction box construction is not permissible, a special form of conduit system may be used, provided the general requirements as given below are complied with.

1. Metal conduits, outlet and junction boxes to be constructed in accordance with standard requirements except that conduit for lighting circuits need not be over 5/16 in. internal diameter and ½ in. external diameter, and for heating and air motor circuits need not be over ⅜ in. internal diameter and 9/16 in. external diameter, and all conduits where exposed to dampness must be watertight.

2. Must be continuous between and be firmly secured into all outlet or junction boxes and fittings, making a thorough mechanical and electrical connection between same.

3. Metal conduits, where they enter all outlet or junction boxes and fittings, must be provided with approved bushings fitted so as to protect cables from abrasion.

4. Except as noted in Section **I**, 2, must have the metal of the conduit permanently and effectively grounded.

5. Junction and outlet boxes must be installed in such a manner as to be accessible.

6. All conduits, outlets or junction boxes and fittings to be firmly and substantially fastened to the framework of the car.

E. Moulding

1. To consist of a backing and a capping, and to be constructed of fire-resisting insulating material, except that it may be made of hardwood where the circuits which it is designed to support are nominally not exposed to moisture.

2. When constructed of fire-resisting insulating material the backing shall be not less than ¼ in. in thickness, and be of a width sufficient to extend not less than 1 in. beyond conductors at sides.

The capping, to be not less than ⅛ in. in thickness, shall cover and extend at least ¾ in. beyond conductors on either side.

The joints in the moulding shall be mitered to fit close, the whole material being firmly secured in place by screws or nails, and treated on the inside and outside with a waterproof paint.

When fire-resisting moulding is used over surfaces already protected by ⅛-in. fire-resisting insulating material no backing will be required.

3. Wooden mouldings must be so constructed as to thoroughly encase the wire and provide a thickness of not less than ⅜ in. at the sides and back of the conductors, the capping being not less than 3/16 in. in thickness. Must have both outside and inside two coats of waterproof paint.

The backing and the capping shall be secured in place by screws.

F. Lighting and Lighting Circuits

1. Each outlet to be provided with an approved receptacle, or an approved cluster. No lamp consuming more than 128 watts to be used.

2. Circuits to be run in approved metal conduit or approved moulding.

3. When metal conduit is used, except for sign lights, all outlets to be provided with approved outlet boxes.

4. At outlet boxes, except where approved clusters are used, receptacles to be fastened to the inside of the box, and the metal cover to have an insulating bushing around opening for the lamp.

When approved clusters are used, the cluster shall be thoroughly insulated from the metal conduit, being mounted on a block of hardwood or fire-resisting insulating material.

5. Where conductors are run in moulding the receptacles or cluster to be mounted on blocks of hardwood or of fireproof insulating material.

G. Heaters and Heating Circuits

1. Heaters to be of approved type.

2. Panel heaters to be so constructed and located that when heaters are in place all current-carrying parts will be at least 4 in. from all woodwork.

Heaters for cross seats to be so located that current-carrying parts will be at least 6 in. below under side of seat, unless under side of seat is protected by not less than ¼-in. fire-resisting insulating material, or 0.04-in. sheet metal with 1-in. air space over same, when the distance may be reduced to 3 in.

Truss plank heaters to be mounted on not less than ¼-in. fire-resisting insulating material, the legs or supports for the heater providing an air space of not less than ½ in. between the back of the heater and the insulating material.

3. Circuits to be run in approved metal conduit, or in approved moulding, or if the location of conductors is such as will permit an air space of not less than 2 in. on all sides except from the surface wired over, they may be supported on porcelain knobs or cleats, provided the knobs or cleats are mounted on not less than ¼-in. fire-resisting insulating material extending at least 3 in. beyond conductors at either side, the supports raising the conductors not less than ½ in. from the surface wired over, and being not over 12 in. apart.

H. Air Pump Motor and Circuits

1. Circuits to be run in approved metal conduit or in approved moulding, except that when run below the floor of the car they may be supported on porcelain knobs or cleats, provided the supports raise the conductor at least ½ in. from the surface wired over and are not over 12 in. apart.

2. Automatic control to be enclosed in approved metal box. Air pump and motor, when enclosed, to be in approved metal box or a wooden box lined with metal of not less than 1/32 in. in thickness.

When conductors are run in metal conduit the boxes surrounding automatic control and air pump and motor may serve as outlet boxes.

I. Main Motor Circuits and Devices

1. Conductors connecting between trolley base and main cut-out or circuit breakers in hood to be protected where wires enter car to prevent ingress of moisture.

2. Conductors connecting between third-rail shoes on same truck to be supported in an approved fire-resisting insulating moulding, or in approved iron conduit supported by soft rubber or other approved insulating cleats.

3. Conductors on the under side of the car, except as noted in Section **I**, 4, to be supported in accordance with one of the following methods:

a. To be run in approved metal conduit, junction boxes being provided where branches in conduit are made, and outlet boxes where conductors leave conduit.

b. To be run in approved fire-resisting insulating moulding.

c. To be supported by insulating cleats, the supports being not over 12 in. apart.

4. Conductors with flameproof braided outer covering, connecting between controllers at either end of car, or controllers and contractors, may be run as a cable provided the cable where exposed to the weather is encased in a canvas hose or canvas tape, thoroughly taped or sewed at ends and where taps from the cable are made, and the hose or tape enters the controllers.

Conductors with or without flameproof braided outer covering connecting between controllers at either end of the car, or controllers and contactors, may be run as a cable, provided the cable throughout its entire length is surrounded by ⅛-in. flameproof covering, thoroughly taped or sewed at ends, or where taps from cable are made, and the flameproof covering enters the controllers.

Cables where run below floor of car may be supported by approved insulating straps or cleats. Where run above floor of car to be in a metal conduit or wooden box, painted on the inside with not less than two coats of flameproof paint, and where this box is so placed that it is exposed to water, as by washing of the car floor, attention should be given to making the box reasonably waterproof.

Canvas hose or tape, or flameproof material surrounding cables after conductors are in same, to have not less than two coats of waterproof insulating material.

5. Motors to be so drilled that, on double-truck cars, connecting cables can leave motor on side nearest to king bolt.

6. Resistances to be so located that there will be at least 6 in. air space between resistances proper and fire-resisting material of the car. To be mounted on iron supports, being insulated by non-combustible bushings or washers, or the iron supports shall have at least 2 in. of insulating surface between them and metal work of car, or the resistances may be mounted on hardwood bars, supported by iron stirrups, which shall have not less than 2 in. of insulating surface between foot of resistance and metal stirrup, the entire surface of the bar being covered with at least ⅛-in. fire-resisting insulating material.

The insulation of the conductor, for about 6 in. from terminal of the resistance, should be replaced, if any insulation is necessary, by a porcelain bushing or asbestos sleeve.

7. Controllers to be raised above platform of car by a not less than 1-in. hardwood block, the block being fitted and painted to prevent moisture working in between it and the platform.

J. Lightning Arresters

1. To be preferably located to protect all auxiliary circuits in addition to main motor circuits.

2. The ground conductor shall be not less than No. 6 B. & S. gage, run with as few kinks and bends as possible, and be securely grounded.

K. General Rules

1. When passing through floors, conductors or cables must be protected by approved insulating bushings, which shall fit the conductor or cable as closely as possible.

2. Moulding should never be concealed except where readily accessible. Conductors should never be tacked into moulding.

3. Short bends in conductors should be avoided where possible.

4. Sharp edges in conduit or in moulding must be smoothed to prevent injury to conductors.

Carbon. A non-metallic element found in all organic matter. It is a good conductor of electricity and is universally used for motor brushes. Also used for contact pieces in switches and for arc headlight electrodes. See **Brush**.

Carborundum. An extremely hard form of crystalline carbon produced in an electric furnace. It is used as an abrasive and in finely powdered form as the wearing surface of some types of safety step treads.

Carline. 19, 20 and 21, Figs. 259-370. One of the transverse members of the roof framing of a car on which the roof boards or sheets are laid. In monitor deck roofs the transverse members, which are continued across the car from side plate to side plate, are termed main carlines. The cross members in the upper deck are termed deck carlines and those in the lower deck are called lower deck carlines or rafters. Main carlines rest on the side posts, and are sometimes framed with a piece of steel plate between two pieces of wood to add strength. See **Platform Hood Carline, End Carline, Compound Carline**.

Carpet. A woven floor covering. The only carpet ordinarily used in electric railway cars is the **Aisle Matting**, which see. A heavy plush material resembling ordinary carpet is sometimes used to cover wooden seats in closed cars instead of upholstering the seat back and bottom.

Carry Iron. See **Drawbar Carry Iron**.

Casing. (1) (Of a Motor.) The shell or frame surrounding the field magnets, armature and commutator. See **Motor Frame**.
(2) (Hot-Water Heaters). The outside shell separated from the fire pot by an air space to prevent overheating.

Cast Iron. Iron containing from 3 to 5 per cent. of carbon, melted in a furnace or cupola and poured into a suitable mold. Cast iron is low in tensile strength and comparatively brittle. See **Malleable Iron**.

Cast Iron Wheel. See **Chilled Cast Iron Wheel**.

Cast Steel. Steel which is melted in an open-hearth furnace, crucible or converter and poured into suitable moulds. It has high tensile strength and ductility when properly annealed.

Cast Steel Wheel. Figs. 1611-1614.

Castle Nut. A nut with grooves cut across the top to receive a cotter pin put through the end of the bolt to which the nut is applied. The cotter pin prevents the nut from turning off.

Catch. A device used to prevent a door, window or gate from opening or closing. See **Door Catch**.

Catcher. See **Trolley Catcher**.

Ceiling. 53 and 54, Figs. 259-370. The inside sheathing under the car roof. Also called **Headlining**. Painted canvas, wood veneer and sheets of composition board are used for car ceilings.

Ceiling Cluster. Fig. 872. A **Cluster**, which see, of electric incandescent lamps mounted in the center of the upper deck ceiling.

Ceiling Furring. Light strips of wood attached to the roof carlines and used for nailing or gluing on the ceiling sheets.

Cell. (1) A small, enclosed space.
(2) An electro-chemical device for producing electrical energy, consisting of two metal or metaloid elements immersed in a liquid electrolyte. When the two plates are connected by an exterior conductor a current of electricity is caused to flow from one element to the other through the liquid electrolyte and the exterior circuit. Such a device is called a voltaic or primary cell. A group of such cells connected together is called a battery, and a single cell is also commonly referred to as a battery. See **Primary Battery, Storage Battery**.

Center (Steel-Tired Wheel). The hub, spokes or web and blank rim on which the tire is shrunk and otherwise fastened.

Center Bearing. The point about which a swiveling truck rotates. A body center plate attached to the middle of the body bolster rests on a corresponding truck center plate attached to the middle of the truck bolster. The weight of one end of the car body is transmitted through this bearing to the truck. See **Side Bearing** and **Center Plate**.

Center Dump Car. A dump car with doors arranged to drop the load entirely between the rails.

Center Pin. A round steel bolt passing through the body and truck center plates. The annular grooves and flanges on the center plates which fit into each other relieve the center pin of any severe shearing stresses. Also called king pin and king bolt.

Center Pin Floor Plate. A small, round casting let into the floor flush with the surface to cover the hole through which the center pin is dropped down through the center plates.

Center Pin Key. A flat key inserted through a slot near the bottom of the center pin so as to prevent the pin from pulling out through the truck bolster center plate in case of derailment.

Center Plate. 16, Fig. 1368; 26 and 27, Figs. 1388-1390; Figs. 1516-1517. One of two metal plates attached at the center of the body and truck bolsters and forming a bearing about which the truck can swivel in rounding a curve. See **Body Center Plate, Truck Center Plate**.

Center Side Door. A door in the side of a car body at or near the center of its length, as distinguished from platform side doors at the end of the car. Many subway cars, and some cars for city service, are now being built with center side doors. See Figs. 11-13, 84-85, 87-89, 209-212.

Center Side Entrance Car. Figs. 11-13, 84-85, 87-89, 209-212. A car with an entrance door in the center of the side of the car body.

Center Sills. 2, Figs. 259-370. The central pair of longitudinal members of the underframe of a car body, as distinguished from the **Intermediate Sills** and **Side Sills**, which see. They are often formed of steel I-beams, or channels, or built-up fish-belly girder sections.

Center Sill Filler. 104, Figs. 259-370. A stick of wood used to square out the cross-section of a structural steel center sill. It serves no structural purpose in the underframe of a car except as a nailing strip for the floor boards.

Centering Gage. A special gage used in mounting wheels to insure that they are pressed on equidistant from the center of the axle.

Centrifugal Sprinkler. Figs. 223-224. A sprinkler in which the water is forced through the nozzles by a motor-driven centrifugal pump. See **Sprinkler.**

Chafing Plate. A removable metal plate fastened to a truck bolster, transom, or other part subjected to wear to resist the abrasion. Also called **Wear Plate**, which see.

Chain. A succession of metal rings interlinked together. See **Brake Chain, Check Chain.**

Chair. An individual car seat, as distinguished from a double cross seat or a continuous longitudinal seat. Chairs are used only in parlor cars and in the smoking compartments of some limited interurban cars.

Channel. A U-shaped section of rolled iron or steel used for sills in car-body underframes and for transoms and spring planks of trucks. Light-weight channels are used for many purposes in steel car construction, including door and window posts and carlines.

Chattering. (Of Brakes.) The noise emitted by the vibration of loose brake hangers and other parts of the truck brake gear at the end of a stop when the coefficient of friction of the brake shoes rises rapidly and the shoes tend to stick on the wheels.

Check Chain. 13, Fig. 1376. A chain attached to the car body side sills and to one corner of a swiveling truck with a check chain hook and check chain eye. Its purpose is to prevent the truck from slewing across the track in case of derailment. Seldom used for electric car trucks.

Check Chain Eye. See **Check Chain.**

Check Chain Hook. See **Check Chain.**

Check Plate. (Brill Journal Bearing.) A semi-circular block fitting into the top of a groove cut around the outer end of the axle journal. It is held in place by a wooden wedge under the top of the journal box and takes the end thrust of the journal bearing. See **Axle Collar.**

Check Valve. (Quick Action Triple Valve.) A small valve included in the triple valve which prevents the flow of air back from the brake cylinder into the brake pipe following an emergency application. See **Triple Valve.**

Chilled Cast Iron Wheel. Figs. 1602-1610. A car wheel made of iron which is cast in a sand mold containing a heavy iron ring or chill mold forming the circumference of the tread and throat of the flange. The molten iron, coming in contact with the cold iron chill mold, is cooled suddenly and crystallizes to a depth of from ½ in. to ¾ in., forming an extremely hard surface skin on the tread where the wear takes place.

Chimney. See **Smoke Pipe.**

Choke Coil. A number of concentric turns of wire in a conductor which offers low ohmic resistance to the flow of direct current but which impedes the flow of alternating current or sudden discharges such as lightning due to the impedance of self-induction. Also called **Kicking Coil**, which see.

Chord. (Of a Truss.) The top or bottom member of a truss. In car-body framing, the side sills form the bottom chords of the side frames and the side plates form the top chords. See **Top Chord.**

Christensen Air Brake. Figs. 520-531.

Christie Brake Head and Shoe. Figs. 1952-1965. A type of brake head and removable shoe which was adopted as standard by the American Electric Railway Engineering Association in 1907. The shoe is held in the head by a long, tapered key. The Christie brake head and shoe has been long the standard of the Master Car Builders' Association. See **Brake Head.**

Cincinnati Tool-Steel Gear. Fig. 1518.

Circuit. A path for the flow of a current of electricity.

Circuit Breaker. Figs. 1751-1757. A device for automatically opening the circuit of an electric current when the flow of current exceeds a predetermined rate. It consists essentially of a fixed and a movable contact, a spring to force the movable contact out of engagement, and a latch on the movable contact, which may be released by the pull on the armature of a solenoid magnet in shunt with the main circuit. When the flow of current through the solenoid produces sufficient magnetic flux to pull down the armature and release the latch, the contact pieces are separated by the action of the spring. To restore the circuit, the movable contact is replaced by hand and again latched. Electric cars are usually provided with one or more circuit breakers inserted in the main circuit between the trolley or third-rail shoe and the controller. They are provided with a magnetic blow-out for extinguishing the arc, and are mounted either under the car body or under the vestibule hood, over the controller. From this latter common location they are sometimes called hood switches. A **Tripping Switch**, which see, is a small circuit breaker used with auxiliary contactor-control apparatus to break the holding current of the contactors when the motor current exceeds a safe value.

Circuit Breaker Box. The wooden or metal box enclosing the coil, contacts and tripping mechanism of an automatic circuit breaker.

Circuit Breaker Handle. An insulated handle on a circuit breaker latch projecting through the end of the box enclosing the contacts and solenoid, by means of which the contact can be opened or closed by hand. A circuit breaker can thus be made to serve as a manually-operated main switch.

Circular Loom Conduit. A form of flexible conduit for electric wiring, approved by the National Board of Fire Underwriters. It is composed of a spirally wound paper tube surrounded by cotton sleeving impregnated with a stiff compound and dusted with flake mica.

Circular Mil. See **Mil** and **Wire Gage.**

Circulating Drum. Another name for an **Expansion Drum**, which see, used with hot-water heaters.

Circulating Pipe. See **Heater Pipe.**

Clamp. A clip used to fasten one part to another, as a **Cable Clamp** or **Pipe Clamp**, which see.

Clapper. See **Bell Clapper** and **Gong Clapper.**

Clark Fender and Wheelguard. Figs. 715-716.

Clark Track Scraper. Fig. 1322.

Classification Lamp. Figs. 1078, 1083-1084. A **Marker Lamp**, which see, used on the front end of a car.

Clear Story. Also spelled clerestory. An obsolete name for the deck of a monitor car roof. Properly applied to the entire space enclosed by the upper deck.

Cleat. A small wooden, porcelain or vulcanized rubber block used to fasten a wire on a wall or partition.

Clevis. A U-shaped shackle fastened with a pin to a bar or rod and used to attach a chain or another rod. Clevises are sometimes used to connect the rods and levers of the foundation brake gear.

Climax Cable Curtain Fixture. Figs. 644-645.

Clip. A U-shaped clamp used for attaching a pipe or cable to a flat surface.

Closed Car. Figs. 1-14, 35-67. A car which is completely enclosed on the sides and ends by panels and windows, as distinguished from an open car which can be closed at the sides only with curtains. The term box car is sometimes applied to closed cars. **Convertible Cars**, which see, may be changed quickly from open cars to closed cars by inserting the removable side panels and window sashes, which in the Brill type of car are carried in pockets under the roof.

Closet. In general, any small compartment in a car, such as a **Heater Closet**, which see; but the term is usually restricted to the lavatory or saloon.

Cluster. Fig. 872. A group of two or more lamps having a common reflector. From two to five incandescent lamps are used in deck clusters for illuminating electric cars.

Coach. A term borrowed from steam railroad practice to designate an interurban passenger car having, in general, no baggage or smoking compartment.

Coal Car. Figs. 230-233. A car used for carrying coal. A large variety of dump cars have been built especially for carrying coal and ashes to and from street railway power houses. Interurban railways which haul coal as freight ordinarily use standard steam railroad gondola cars for the purpose.

Coasting Register. Figs. 1827-1830. A device for integrating and recording the total time during the run of a car or train in which the car is coasting without taking power and without brakes applied. The record so made is an indication of the efficiency of operation of the train, since with a given scheduled running time the longer the coasting time the less will be the time during which power is being taken from the trolley.

Coat Hook. Fig. 870. A small brass or bronze hook attached to the inside window panels of interurban cars above the windows and used to hang up overcoats. A hook for this purpose is often formed on the bottom of the basket rack brackets.

Coat and Hat Hook. Fig. 871. A coat hook combined with a longer vertical post on which a hat can be hung. Seldom used in interurban cars.

Cock. A small valve and spout used to draw off the contents of a tank. See **Drain Cock**.

Coil. (1) A number of concentric turns of wire forming a path for the flow of a current of electricity. See **Armature Coil, Field Coil**.

(2) A spiral nest of piping inserted in the fire pot of a hot-water car heater, through which the water circulates as it is heated.

Coleman Fare Box. Figs. 1205-1206.

Collar. See **Axle Collar**.

Color and Varnish Process. See **Paint**.

Color Coat. In car painting, the coat, or coats, applied after the surface of the wood has been filled and scraped and before the lettering and varnish coats are applied.

Columbia Ratchet Brake Handle. Fig. 572.

Columbia Sheet Steel Gear Case. Fig. 1540.

Columbian Single Truck. Figs. 1400-1401.

Column. 16, Figs. 1388-1390. (Arch Bar Truck Side Frame.) One of a pair of spreaders inserted between the top and bottom arch bars and serving as a vertical guide for the bolster. Both columns are sometimes formed in one piece with the bolster spring seat. Also called truck frame center.

Column Bolt. A long bolt passing through the arch bars and holes in the projecting feet of a column casting to hold the column in place.

Combination Car. Figs. 132-160. Any car having one or more compartments for passengers and a separate compartment for baggage, mail or express.

Commonwealth Trucks. Figs. 1454-1463.

Commutating Pole. See below.

Commutating Pole Motor. Figs. 1645-1656. A type of railway motor in which four auxiliary coils and pole pieces called commutating poles are mounted between the four main field poles. The windings of the commutating poles are connected in series with each other and with the armature. The magnetic strength of the commutating poles varies, therefore, with the current passing through the armature, and an intermediate magnetic field is produced of such intensity as to properly reverse the current in the armature coils short circuited during commutation. The commutating poles are so proportioned and wound as to compensate for the armature reactions, and a marked improvement in commutation under the severest overloads is secured. As the magnetizing current around the commutating poles is reversed with the armature, the poles perform their functions equally well in whichever direction the motor is run.

Commutating pole motors are also termed **Interpole Motors**, which see.

Commutating Switch. A hand or pneumatically-operated switch forming part of the car equipment of a 1200-volt, direct-current system in which equally high speeds on 600-volt and 1200-volt sections are required. Its purpose is to effect the connection of the four motors into two groups of two motors in series when passing from a 600-volt section to a 1200-volt section. It also changes the connections of the rheostats so that the proper values of resistance are obtained for the various steps in the control. A similar switch is used on a. c.-d. c. car equipments to change the necessary trolley and auxiliary connections when passing from an a. c. section to a d. c. section, or vice versa.

Commutation. The transfer of a current of electricity between the brushes and the commutator segments of a motor.

Commutator. O, Fig. 1675; Figs. 1694-1695. The complete assemblage of copper segments, insulation, supporting shell and retaining rings on one end of a railway motor armature by which current is passed from the positive brush bearing on one segment through the armature coils connected in series with that segment and out again through the segment under the negative brush. See **Armature**.

Commutator Bar. A **Commutator Segment**, which see.

Commutator Cap. An iron ring with a V-shaped groove cut in one face which fits over the dovetails formed on the bottom of the commutator segments. The shell has an undercut shoulder formed in the back, into which the dovetails also fit, and when the cap is pressed in tight by the clamping ring the segments are held firmly in place. The segments are insulated from the cap and shell by a flat mica collar on the bottom and by inner and outer conical mica collars surrounding the dovetails.

Commutator Clamping Ring. A ring screwed on the outer end of a commutator shell to hold the cap firmly in place against the segments. From four to six flush-head screws are used to fasten the clamping ring to the cap.

Commutator Groove. See **Commutator Slot**.

Commutator Insulation. The moulded or sheet mica used to insulate the segments from each other and from the shell and clamping ring with which they are assembled and held in place.

Commutator Key. A key used to secure a commutator shell securely on the armature shaft.

Commutator Segment. A flat bar of copper with a wide dovetail cut on one edge which is assembled radially on the commutator shell with other similar segments and securely clamped to form the cylindrical surface on which the brushes bear. The segments are insulated from each other and from the shell and clamping cap by sheet or moulded mica. The terminals of the armature coils are soldered to the segments, and when two segments, spaced the proper distance apart around the commutator, pass simultaneously under positive and negative brushes, a complete circuit is formed through the armature coils, which are connected in series with those segments.

Commutator Shell. A cast-iron cylinder or bushing pressed and keyed on the armature shaft, on the circumference of which the commutator segments are assembled and clamped.

Commutator Slot. The space between adjoining commutator segments which is filled with sheet mica insulation. The practice of cutting out this mica to a depth of from 1/32 in. to 3/32 in. is termed grooving or slotting the commutator. It is done to reduce brush wear and prevent jumping of the brushes over ridges of high mica, which produces sparking.

Compartment. A section of a car body separated from the main room by an interior bulkhead. Some large interurban cars have three compartments, one for ordinary passengers, one for smokers, and one for baggage or express.

Composite Board. Thin sheets of prepared fiber, pulp and other ingredients made up by a special process to render them hard, yet pliable, and to make them more or less waterproof.

Composite Sills. Main longitudinal members of a car-body underframe built up of timbers enclosing a steel plate or rolled steel I-beam or channel.

Compound Bolster. A body or truck bolster built up of two or more pieces of wood stiffened with vertical plates of steel, all firmly bolted together. Built-up or one-piece metal bolsters have almost entirely superseded wooden and compound bolsters.

Compound Carline. 20, Figs. 259-370. A main carline extending across the car roof from side plate to side plate and built up of two pieces of wood bolted on the outside of a flat bar of iron placed on edge and bent to the contour of the upper and lower deck. They sometimes project through the headlining, breaking it up into panels, and they are then called contour carlines, or outline carlines.

Compressed Air. Atmospheric air which is confined in a closed receptacle under a pressure of more than 14.7 lb. absolute. Air under a pressure of between 90 lb. and 120 lb. per sq. in. above atmosphere is used on electric cars for operating **Air Brakes, Pneumatic Doors** and **Sanders,** which see.

Compression Beam. 122, Figs. 356-360. In the trussed side frame of long interurban cars the horizontal compression member in the center of the truss just below the belt rail. Compression beam braces inclined upward and toward the center of the car from the bolsters abut against the compression beam at each end, and shorter auxiliary braces and counterbraces are sometimes used between the main end braces.

Compression Beam Brace. 123, Figs. 356-360. See **Compression Beam.**

Compression Block. 30, Fig. 1376. See **Single-Motor Truck.**

Compression Device. 27-31, Fig. 1376. A device for transferring weight to the pony wheels of a **Single-Motor Truck,** which see, when rounding curves. Experience has shown that a compression device is not necessary for safe operation of a single-motor truck, and many trucks of this type are now built without it.

Compression Spring. 27, Fig. 1376. See **Single-Motor Truck.**

Compression Spring Bracket. 29, Fig. 1376. See **Single-Motor Truck.**

Compressor. See **Air Compressor.**

Concave Panel. A bottom outside panel curved inward from the fender rail to clear the hubs of wheels on vehicles standing close to the track. The upper side panel is made straight, or sometimes slightly convex. See Fig. 258.

Conductivity. The reciprocal of electrical **Resistance,** which see.

Conductor. (1) The member of a car crew who collects the fares from passengers and gives signals to the motorman to start and stop the car. He usually stands on the rear platform when not required to go inside the car to collect fares.

(2) A metal wire or rod serving as a path for the flow of a current of electricity.

Conductor's Control Stand. Figs. 667-668. An iron pipe stand separating the opening from the rear platform to the car body of a pay-within car into entrance and exit passages. The spindles for operating the pneumatic door valves are mounted in the top of this stand so that they can be turned with a removable handle by the conductor.

Conductor's Signal Valve. Fig. 517. A valve connected to the signal pipe of a train air-signal equipment, which, when opened, causes the air in the signal pipe to escape. This causes the signal whistle to blow in the locomotive or head car of the train. The handle of the conductor's signal valve is usually connected to a cord, similar to a bell cord, running through the car. By pulling on this cord a signal can be given to the motorman on the head car.

Conductor's Valve. (Air Brake.) In an automatic train brake equipment, an emergency valve mounted in some convenient place inside of the car body, which, when opened, will release the pressure in the brake pipe and cause the brakes to be applied. See Fig. 454.

Conductor's Valve Pipe. A branch pipe connecting the conductor's valve with the brake pipe.

Conduit. (1) Iron pipe or other fireproof tubing mounted in and under a car body and through which the wires for the electrical circuits on the car are drawn. See Figs. 1845-1854.

(2) See **Conduit System.**

Conduit Plow. Fig. 1863. A narrow steel plate supported on a car truck so that it is free to move transversely and projecting downwardly through a slot in the pavement into the conduit between the rails. The plow carries on its lower end two sliding contact pieces, which are pressed against the positive and negative conductor rails in the conduit by flat springs. Connectors are brought up along the edges of the plow to the car cables leading to the controller on the platform.

Conduit System. A system of current distribution for street railways in which the positive and negative conductors carrying the propulsion current are mounted in a conduit below the level of the street. The current is collected by a plow mounted on the car truck and projecting down into the conduit through a continuous slot in the pavement between the rails. The conduit system is used in the United States only in Washington, D. C., and New York City.

Condulets. Figs. 1845-1849. A trade name applied to a complete line of junction boxes, outlets, and other fittings for rigid conduit used in electric wiring.

Cone Mica. The mica insulation in a commutator placed between the dovetails on the segments and the central shell and cap. See **Commutator Cap.**

Congdon Brake Shoe. Fig. 1485.

Connection Board. See **Controller Connection Board.**

Connection Box. Fig. 1791. A sheet-iron box containing a connection board on which are mounted a number of binding post terminals. The wires in two or more cables entering the box are interconnected, as desired, by short connectors between proper binding posts. In a multiple-unit control system such boxes are used for connecting the main control cables to the short cables leading into the master controllers and to the contactors. Also called junction box.

Connector. Any loose cable or wire connecting one piece of electrical apparatus on a car with another, as a motor connector or control-line connector in a multiple-unit control system.

Consolidated Buzzer Signal System. Figs. 1237-1247.

Consolidated Electric Heaters. Figs. 1132-1157.

Construction Car. A **Work Car,** which see.

Contact. The coming together of two bodies in space; the condition of being in touch. Hence the term is applied to any movable conductor which touches another conductor and completes an electric circuit.

Contactor. Fig. 1764. A magnetic switch used to make or break a circuit in a motor control system. It consists of a magnet coil and a pivoted armature carrying a contact piece, which is forced against another fixed contact piece when the magnet coil is energized by the control current. A magnetic blow-out is provided for disrupting the arc formed when the contactor armature drops by gravity and opens the circuit. See **Auxiliary Contactor, Unit Switch** and **Multiple-Unit Control.**

Contactor Box. A waterproof sheet iron box in which one or more contactors are mounted under a car body. See Figs. 1758-1759.

Continuous Basket Rack. A **Basket Rack,** which see, made in sections, but extending continuously from one end of the car to the other above the seats.

Continuous Brake. A general term for any brake system which may be applied or released simultaneously on all cars in a train from one point. All automatic air brake systems are continuous brakes.

Continuous Deck Sash Opener. Figs. 1019, 1025. A device for opening or closing simultaneously several deck sashes on one side of a car.

Control Pipe. A secondary line of pipe, sometimes called a supply pipe, required for some modified types of automatic air brakes. (See Fig. 454.) The main reservoir is connected to the control pipe through a feed valve, and the brake pipe is charged through a supply pipe connecting the control pipe with the operative motorman's brake valve. The pressures in the brake pipe and control pipes are therefore normally the same. The control pipe as well as the brake pipe is connected to the triple valve under each car, and in recharging the auxiliary reservoirs air flows from the control pipe and from the brake pipe. This decreases materially the time required for recharging between applications. The control pipe makes possible a **Graduated Release**, which see.

Control Resistor. Figs. 1780-1781. A resistance unit for lowering the voltage of the current used for energizing the control circuits of a Westinghouse unit-switch control equipment.

Control Stand. See **Conductor's Control Stand**.

Control Switch. See Figs. 1773-1774. A device used in connection with Westinghouse unit-switch control apparatus to serve the purpose of a control circuit fuse box and resetting switch. When the overload trip operates the operating circuit of the control switch must be opened, and the reset circuit momentarily closed before the current can again be supplied to the motors.

Control System. Figs. 1715-1803. The electric switching mechanism on a car by means of which the speed and direction of rotation of the motor are regulated. Nearly all direct-current railway motors are operated in pairs in the so-called series-parallel or series-multiple relation, in which the two motors of each pair are first connected in series with each other across the power mains and then in parallel. Suitable external resistances are inserted in the motor circuits at the beginning of each period of acceleration with the series and parallel combinations, and these resistances are cut out in steps as the speed increases. The control of these steps is accomplished in one of two ways. For equipments of moderate horsepower requiring comparatively small amounts of current, all the switching is done through contacts inside of a hand-operated controller mounted on the car platform. This is the method used on ordinary street cars operated singly. The main power circuit is brought from the trolley through a suitable fuse box or automatic circuit breaker to the connection board in the controller. The leads from the motors and resistance rheostats under the car body are also brought into the controller, and all connections are made by segments mounted on a revolving drum or cylinder, which come in contact with fixed wipers or fingers mounted on springs inside of the controller case.

Where the motor equipment requires the switching of such large amounts of current as would cause excessive arcing when the contacts are broken in the confined space of a platform controller, or when several motor cars are to be operated simultaneously in trains, the so-called system of **Multiple-Unit Control**, which see, is generally used.

Controlator. Fig. 1731. A type of **Controller Regulator**, which see.

Controller. Figs. 1715-1719. The complete assemblage of parts whereby the switching necessary to regulate the speed and direction of rotation of the motors is accomplished. Street railway controllers in which the switching is done by hand by revolving a cylinder inside of the controller case, mounted on the platform, are of four general types, namely, Type B, which includes necessary contacts for electric braking; Type K, which is the type commonly used for two or four-motor equipments up to a total capacity of 160 hp., giving series and parallel combinations; Type L, which is also of the series-parallel design, but is used for motor equipments aggregating up to 600 hp., and Type R, which is designed to control the motor speeds by means of external resistance only. The table accompanying Figs. 1715-1718 shows the classifications of the hand controllers in general use. Type K controllers are most frequently used for city cars. For interurban service Types K and L controllers are used except where multiple-unit control is employed.

Controller Arc Deflector. A framework of fireproof insulation consisting of two side strips enclosing a number of partitions and mounted on the hinged pole piece of the magnet blow-out coil. When closed the division pieces isolate each segment on the main cylinder and prevent any arc formed from spreading.

Controller Blow-Out Magnet. A powerful magnet coil mounted in a controller case, usually below the reversing cylinder and having a hinged pole piece which is swung around in front of the main cylinder. The other pole is formed by the iron back of the controller case. The magnet is in series with the trolley connection in the controller, and a powerful magnetic field is set up between its poles when current is on. The field encloses the contact segments and fingers, and effectually extinguishes any arcs formed when the contacts are broken.

Controller Bracket. A knee-iron support for securing a platform controller case to the dasher.

Controller Case. The iron case which encloses the cylinder contacts, connection boards and other essential parts of a controller. The back and base are usually made of cast iron and the front, which is made of sheet iron, is hinged so as to swing open from one side, or it may be completely removed by unlocking the special hinges on each side. Some of the larger sizes of controllers have the front of the case sheathed with strips of hardwood.

Controller Connection Board. A board in the bottom of a controller case on which are mounted the cut-out switches and binding posts for all of the cables leading to the trolley, motors and resistances.

Controller Contact Board. A wooden board in a controller case on which are mounted the main contact fingers. A similar board of smaller size is used for mounting the reverser contact fingers.

Controller Cut-Out Switch. A double-pole knife switch mounted on the controller contact board. When opened it cuts out one motor or pair of motors. Two such switches are used.

Controller Cylinder. A spindle mounted in bearings in a vertical position inside of a controller case. It is composed of a plurality of cylindrical sections or iron spiders, insulated from each other and from the supporting shaft. On these sections are mounted copper segments of different lengths, which, as the cylinder is revolved, make contact with fixed fingers attached with springs to the controller contact board. The segments on each insulated section are not insulated from each other, so that when any two segments on one section are in contact with their corresponding fingers a dead short circuit is made through the section of the cylinder on which they are mounted. A K-10A controller, for example, carries six segments on the top section of the cylinder, three on the middle section and two on the bottom section. The six top segment fingers are connected, respectively, to the trolley and the five groups of resistance. The bottom segment finger is connected to ground, and the four intermediate segments to connections on the reversing cylinder, through which the proper grouping of the motors is effected.

The controller cylinder turns in bearings mounted on the controller frame, and carries at the top and bottom insulation discs of large diameter to prevent any leakage of current from the sections to the frame. Above the top insulation disc is a star wheel and check pawl, for momentarily checking the rotation of the cylinder as each step of the switching connections is accomplished. This star wheel also effects an interlock with a similar wheel on the reversing cylinder, to prevent the movement of either cylinder unless the other is in the proper position. See **Multiple-Unit Control** and **Master Controller**.

Controller Drum. More properly **Controller Cylinder**, which see.

Controller Finger. Fig. 1731. One of the fixed spring-supported contacts mounted on the contact board of a controller. Each finger is connected to one of the motor or resistance leads and bears on a segment on the controller cylinder.

Controller Frame. The cast iron back and base of a platform controller on which the main cylinder, contact board, connection board, blow-out magnet coil and reversing cylinder are mounted. The back of the frame forms one pole of the magnetic blow-out, and the hinged pole piece on which the arc deflector is mounted forms the other.

Controller Handle. Figs. 1732-1743. A brass or malleable iron crank with a wooden grip and a square hole socket fitting over the projecting shaft of the main controller cylinder, by means of which the cylinder is revolved. The boss, or water cap, which fits over the cylinder shaft on which the handle rests, is cast with a small teat or pointer, which slides over raised numbers cast on the top plate of the controller to indicate the number of the step for each position of the handle. In some types of multiple-unit master controllers the handle is fitted with a "dead-man," consisting of a button on the top of the grip, which must be pressed down in order to move the handle from the "off" position. If pressure on the button is released while the handle is in any of the "on" positions, the handle is returned to the "off" position by a spring and the power is automatically cut off.

Controller Regulator. Figs. 1725-1731. A general term sometimes applied to any one of several patented devices for controlling the speed of revolution of a controller handle to prevent fast feeding of the motors. See **Automotoneer and Controlator.**

Controller Reversing Cylinder. A small wooden cylinder in a platform controller on which are mounted segments engaging with fixed fingers. Its purpose is to effect the proper connections through the armatures and fields of the motors in order to control their direction of rotation. It has three positions—forward, neutral and reverse. By reason of the interlock it can only be revolved when the main cylinder is in the "off" position. As it cannot be moved unless all current is off no arc deflector is required for it.

Controller Reversing Handle. A metal handle fitting over the projecting shaft of the reversing cylinder by means of which the cylinder is revolved. The top plate of the controller has a boss surrounding the reversing cylinder shaft, which is designed to engage with a projection on the handle in such a way that the handle can only be removed or applied when the cylinder is in the neutral position. The removal of the reversing handle insures that the reversing cylinder is in the neutral position which locks the main cylinder in the "off" position.

Controller Segment. A short strip of copper bent to the radius of a circle and mounted on an iron spider on the main cylinder of a platform controller. The segment engages with a spring-supported finger to make the desired contact. The lengths of the several segments on a cylinder vary according to the contacts desired for each step of rotation.

Controller Star Wheel. A disc mounted on top of the main cylinder shaft, which engages with a similar wheel on the reversing cylinder shaft in such a way that the main cylinder cannot be revolved when the reversing cylinder is in the neutral position and the reversing cylinder cannot be revolved unless the main cylinder is in the "off" position. See **Controller Cylinder.**

Controller Top Plate. The brass casting forming the top of the controller case through which project the spindles of the main and reversing cylinders. A stop lug is cast on the plate against which the controller handle strikes when in the full "on" or "off" positions. The shoulder through which the reverse cylinder spindle projects is formed so that the reverse handle is locked on the spindle and cannot be lifted off except when the reverse cylinder is in the neutral position with all contacts open.

Contour Carline. See **Compound Carline.**

Convertible Car. Figs. 26-27, 80-82. A type of car which can be operated with the sides entirely enclosed with panels and window sashes, or with both the sashes and the panels removed, leaving the space between posts entirely open from floor to plate. In the Brill patent convertible car, the bottom side panels and the upper and lower window sashes may be raised in suitable grooves in the side posts and stored in pockets between the roof and the headlining. A folding running board is sometimes used when convertible cars are operated as cross-bench cars without side screens. See **Half-Convertible Car** and **Semi-Convertible Car.**

Convex Panel. A top outside panel between the windows and the fender rail, which has a slight outward curvature above the fender rail. See **Concave Panel.**

Cooke Ventilating System. Figs. 1352-1359.

Cooler. See **Water Tank.**

Cooling Coil. See **Radiating Pipe.**

Cooper Heater. Figs. 1098-1099.

Copper. A metallic element, redish brown in color, ductile and of high electrical conductivity. Copper in the form of round wire and flat straps or ribbons is universally used for the conductors of motor armatures and field coils and for making connections between all the electrical apparatus mounted on a car.

Cord. See **Bell Cord, Register Cord, Trolley Cord.**

Cord Connector. See **Bell Cord Splice.**

Core. See **Armature Core.**

Corner Brace. 111, Figs. 259-370. In the underframe of a single-truck car, one of the diagonal floor timbers framed between the end of the transverse floor timber and the center of the end sill. In open car underframes in which no drop platforms are used the corner braces sometimes cross each other and extend out to the platform end sill. Similar diagonal cross braces are often inserted in the center of the underframe between the transverse floor timbers.

Corner Post. See **Body Corner Post, Platform Corner Post** and **Vestibule Corner Post.**

Corner Seat. A short, longitudinal seat in the corner of a car equipped with cross seats. Corner seats accommodating from two to four passengers are commonly used. They are sometimes made to fold up against the car side when the space occupied by them is required as an aisle to reach an exit door.

Cornice. A molding on the outside of a car just below the eaves is called an outside cornice. A molding on the inside at the junction of the inside lining above the windows and the lower deck headlining is called an inside cornice.

Corridor. A narrow passageway on one side of an inclosed compartment of a car.

Cotton Covered Wire. Figs. 1712-1714. Copper wire wound with one or more layers of cotton thread for insulation. Extensively used for winding field and armature coils. See **Magnet Wire.**

Cotton Sleeving. Woven cotton tubing, used for surrounding and insulating short pieces of wire or cable, such as motor leads. It is usually impregnated with some liquid insulating compound.

Counterbrace. 124, Figs. 259-370. In express car side frames, the inclined brace extending from the end of the body bolster to the top of the corner post. In long passenger car side frames the timber framed into the side sill near the needlebeam and supporting the compression beam brace approximately in the center of its length.

Counter Electromotive Force. Electromotive force set up in the revolving armature of a motor which tends to resist the impressed electromotive force. The counter electromotive force is directly proportional to the speed of rotation, and as the speed rises the effect of the impressed electromotive force is gradually diminished until a balance is reached, at which the motor will run at constant speed as long as the impressed current and the load remain constant. See **Electromotive Force.**

Coupler. Figs. 600-635. In general, any device which fastens two similar parts together. Specifically in car construction the iron bar and head by means of which two cars are connected for train operation. The term is also applied to electric cable jumpers used to connect the control circuits on adjoining cars of a multiple-unit train and to the connections on the ends of air-brake hose. The American Electric Railway Engineering Association has adopted as recommended practice for interurban cars a vertical plane type of automatic coupler with a movable knuckle, which will couple with M. C. B. type steam railroad couplers. See **Drawbar.**

Coupler Attachments. The complete assemblage of springs, yokes and other parts by which a coupler is attached to the car body.

Coupler Guard Arm. See **Guard Arm.**

Coupler Head. 27, Figs. 259-370. The outer end of an automatic coupler which, together with the movable knuckle, engages and interlocks with the head and kunckle of the coupler on an adjoining car.

Coupler Jumper. See **Jumper.**

Coupler Knuckle. A steel casting pivoted in the head of an automatic M. C. B. type coupler and arranged to interlock with the knuckle of an adjoining coupler when brought in contact with it. The knuckle is locked by a lock casting in the coupler head, which engages with the knuckle automatically by gravity when dislodged by the impact of two cars coming together. See **Knuckle.**

COU   CYL

Coupler Plug. A round, insulated plug containing a number of brass studs on its face which are connected to the ends of the several wires in the coupler jumper cable. The plug fits into a socket mounted on the end of an adjoining car and the studs are inserted in brass tubes in the socket. These tubes are connected to the wires in the car control cable. The studs and tubes are arranged so that the plug cannot be inserted so as to make wrong connections. See Figs. 1765-1766.

Coupler Socket. Fig. 1766. See **Coupler Plug.** The socket is usually located under the bumper beam to one side of the drawbar, or on the dasher above the bumper beam.

Coupling. A term nearly synonymous with **Coupler,** which see, commonly applied to such connections as brake-hose couplings, link and pin drawbar couplings, pipe couplings, etc.

Coupling Chain. See **Safety Coupling Chain.**

Coupling Link. An open link or flat bar used to connect two drawbar heads together. The link is inserted in the jaw of the drawbar head and secured with a coupling pin.

Coupling Pin. A metal pin fitting in a hole in a drawbar head or drawbar pocket and securing a coupling link inserted in the head.

Coupling Pin Chain. A short chain attached to the end of a coupling pin and to the drawbar head or pocket to prevent the pin from getting lost.

Cradle Suspension. See **Motor Suspension.**

Craighead Destination Sign. Fig. 654.

Crane Car. Figs. 234-239. A flat car on which is mounted a pillar crane to handle rails and heavy construction material.

Cripple Post. An end window post or stud between the end door post and body corner post, used where the end window does not occupy the entire width above the end panel.

Cross Bar. 3, Fig. 1376. (Single-Motor Truck.) A cross piece bolted to the truck frame inside of the pony axle, and carrying at its center the compression device which transfers part of the load to the pony wheels when rounding curves.

Cross Bar Brace. 6, Fig. 1376. (Single-Motor Truck.) An iron knee attached to the truck side frame to stiffen the cross bar longitudinally.

Cross Bar Carrier. 4, Fig. 1376. (Single-Motor Truck.) A bracket bolted to the truck side frame to support the ends of the cross bar.

Cross Beam. A **Transverse Floor Timber,** which see.

Cross Bearer. See **Needlebeam.**

Cross Frame Tie. Another name for a **Needlebeam,** which see.

Cross Seat. Figs. 1259-1301. A car seat placed crosswise in a car as distinguished from a longitudinal seat. Cross seats are almost universally used for interurban and suburban cars, and are coming more and more into use for city cars. For cars operated always in one direction the cross seats are sometimes made with fixed backs, but most cross seats have reversible backs.

Cross Seat Heater. Figs. 1112-1116, 1145-1148. A pattern of electric car heaters designed for attachment under the frames of cross seats. They consist of one or more coils enclosed in a cylindrical, perforated sheet-iron case.

Cross Sill. A **Transverse Floor Timber,** which see.

Cross Tie Rod. A **Sill Tie Rod,** which see.

Cross Tie Timber. One of the numerous names applied to a **Needlebeam,** which see. The name is also abbreviated to cross tie, especially where a light I-beam is used instead of a piece of wood.

Crosshead. A clevis on the end of a brake cylinder piston rod by means of which one of the cylinder levers is attached with a pin.

Crown Molding. 61, Fig. 306. A light molding in the corner formed by the junction of the upper deck sides and roof. Also called deck plate molding.

Crown Piece. 116, Figs. 259-370. A broad, thick timber of crescent shape, framed across the top of the ends of the platform sills to form a backing for the buffer beam which is framed into the ends of the sills. A separate crown piece is not always used.

Current. The flow of electricity from a point of high potential to a point of lower potential. The measure of the rate of flow is the **Ampere,** which see. The measure of the actual quantity is the coulomb. An ampere is the flow of one coulomb per second.

Current Clock. A device designed to integrate and record the length of time during which the motors under a car are taking current. These records afford a comparison of the power consumption of a number of cars on similar runs, and serve much the same purpose as a recording wattmeter. See **Coasting Register.**

Current Limit Relay. Fig. 1796. An adjustable circuit breaker in series with the main motor circuit of an automatic multiple-unit control equipment. It makes and breaks the contactor energizing circuit, and when open prevents the automatic progression of the contactors. No contactor will open until the motor current flowing is less than the amount necessary to lift the relay armature.

Current Meter. A recording **Ampere-Hour Meter,** which see.

Curtain. A piece of cloth or other material hung in front of a window to keep out the light. It is usually mounted on a spring roller fixed across the top of the window, and may be pulled down or rolled up at will. Curtains have almost entirely superseded slatted blinds in car construction. On open cars the curtains are made of heavy canvas, and are arranged to pull down to the floor to keep out wind and rain.

Curtain Fixtures. Figs. 636-653. The handle, side grips and roller which are fitted to a car curtain. Many types of curtain fixtures are in use, some of which are illustrated.

Curtain Groove. A vertical groove cut in the window posts inside of the sash grooves in which the curtain runs.

Curtain Handle. A handle on the bottom of a car curtain which is used to raise or lower the curtain. It is usually made with pinch arms, which when pressed together release the grips on the side of the curtain which run in the curtain grooves cut in the window posts. See Fig. 652.

Curtain Roller. Figs. 641-643, 647. A cylinder of small diameter on which a curtain is wound. A spring roller contains a coiled spring which is restrained by a centrifugal pawl. When the curtain is pulled down suddenly the pawl is disengaged, and if the curtain is then released the spring will revolve the roller and wind up the curtain.

Curtain Roller Brackets. Figs. 648-651. Small brackets attached to the window casing to support the ends of a curtain roller. One of a pair of brackets has a rectangular notch cut in it to hold the flattened end of the curtain roller spring shaft and prevent it from turning when the curtain is run up or down.

Curtain Wire. A wire within the curtain grooves of open cars which acts as a guide for the curtain and prevents it from leaving the groove. See **Cable Fixture.**

Curtis Trucks. Figs. 1472-1473.

Cushion. See **Seat Cushion** and **Field Coil Cushion.**

Cuspidor. A bell-mouthed pan used as a receptacle for spit. Placed on the floor of the smoking compartment of some interurban cars.

Cut-Out Switch. One of a pair of double-pole knife switches mounted inside of a controller for cutting out of circuit one motor of a two-motor equipment or a pair of motors with a four-motor equipment without affecting the operation of the remaining motor or motors.

Cycle. In an alternating current a complete reversal of direction of the flow as from maximum positive through maximum negative and back to maximum positive. The number of cycles or alternations per unit of time is called the frequency. Frequencies of 15 and 25 cycles per second are used in railway work.

Cylinder. See **Brake Cylinder.**

Cylinder Levers. The levers in the foundation brake gear which are attached to the brake cylinder head and to the piston cross-head. They are connected together near the center of their length by a tie-rod, and their free ends are connected to the truck brakes at each end of the car. The hand brake is usually connected through an auxiliary lever to the cross-head cylinder lever in such a way that the power is multiplied from two to four times. See Fig. 458.

Cylinder Lever Support. A carry iron bolted to the underside of one of the longitudinal sills to support the outer ends of the cylinder levers.

D

D. & W. Fuses. Figs. 1807-1812.

Dash or Dash Board. See **Dasher**, below.

Dasher. 62, Figs. 259-370. The curved metal plate or wooden panels enclosing the end of an electric car platform or vestibule above the floor and below the windows.

Dasher Post. 66, Figs. 259-370. An upright post, pipe or rod resting on the crown piece and supporting the center of the dasher rail. The dasher is fastened to the post on the outside, usually with small clips.

Dasher Rail. 64, Figs. 259-370. An iron bar connecting the platform corner posts just above the top of the dasher. It is surmounted by a rounded wooden or brass dasher rail cap.

Dasher Rail Brackets. 67, Figs. 259-370; Figs. 932-933. A casting riveted on the platform corner post to support the end of the dasher rail.

Dasher Rail Cap. 65, Figs. 259-370. See **Dasher Rail**.

Dayton Multi-Stroke Gong. Fig. 949.

Dead Cylinder Lever. One of the two **Cylinder Levers**, which see, which is pivoted to the pressure head of the brake cylinder. The live cylinder lever is attached to the piston crosshead. See Fig. 458.

Dead Lever. (Truck Brake Gear.) 19, Figs. 1480-1481. The truck lever or levers whose upper end is attached to a dead lever guide on the truck frame and does not move, as distinguished from the live levers whose upper ends are connected to the system of body brake levers.

Dead Lever Guide. 38, Fig. 1372. A yoke or stirrup enclosing the upper end of a dead lever. In some types of brake gear the dead lever is held in the guide by a pin, and a number of holes are provided in the guide to adjust the position of the end of the dead lever and thus take up slack.

Dead Lever Pin. 54, Figs. 1388-1390.

Dead Lever Stop. 53, Figs. 1388-1390.

Deadman's Handle. See **Controller Handle**.

Deafening Floor. A false floor built below the main floor of a car to deaden the noises under the car. Sometimes the intermediate space between the two floors is filled with sawdust, mineral wool or other non-conductor of heat and sound. Seldom used in electric railway cars.

Deck. A term originally applied to the entire roof of a passenger car, but in recent years when used alone almost entirely restricted to the clear story or upper part of a monitor roof. The lower part of the roof near the sides of the car is termed the lower deck. When used in connection with other names to distinguish a part as a deck carline the upper deck is invariably referred to.

Deck Apron. 52, Figs. 259-370. The overhanging part of the upper deck roof outside of the deck posts. The end overhang is sometimes called the deck hood or ventilator hood.

Deck Bottom Rail. A term sometimes applied to the **Deck Sill**, which see.

Deck Carline. 19, Figs. 259-370. A **Carline**, which see, in the upper deck roof.

Deck Cluster. Fig. 872. A group of two or more incandescent lamps with a common reflector mounted under the ceiling of the upper deck.

Deck Collar. A flanged lining for the opening in the roof of a car through which the heater smoke pipe projects.

Deck Corner Post. A short, upright post resting on the end of the deck sill and supporting one end of the deck plate.

Deck Eaves Molding. A light molding on the edge of the deck roof to conceal the turnover of the roofing canvas.

Deck End Panel. The space in the end of the monitor deck. Frequently utilized for displaying destination signs. Colored glass sashes are sometimes used to indicate the destination or route of the car. The panels in the end bulkheads below the lower deck roof are usually distinguished as lower deck end panels.

Deck End Plate. The top cross members of the main framing of the upper deck above the deck end sash.

Deck End Post. A post between the deck end sill and deck end plate dividing the end of the deck into two panels.

Deck End Sash. 82, Figs. 259-370. A fixed or movable sash in the end of the upper deck. See **Deck End Panel**.

Deck End Sill. A cross piece supporting the deck end and corresponding to the **Deck Sill**, which see.

Deck End Ventilator. See **Deck End Sash**.

Deck Inside Cornice. A small molding in the joint between the deck roof and the deck side.

Deck Lamp. A lamp dropped from the ceiling of the upper deck, as distinguished from a lamp dropped from the lower deck. See **Deck Cluster**.

Deck Plate. 18, Figs. 259-370. The longitudinal piece of wood on the top of the deck side. The upper deck carlines rest on it.

Deck Plate Molding. 61, Figs. 259-370. See **Crown Molding**.

Deck Post. One of the uprights supporting the deck plate above the deck sill and separating the side deck sashes.

Deck Sash. 50, Figs. 259-370. A narrow glazed panel in the side of a monitor roof. Deck sashes frequently are made to partially open by revolving about either a horizontal or vertical axis so that they may act as ventilators. For this reason they are sometimes called ventilator sashes.

Deck Sash Catch. Figs. 1016-1018. A spring bolt used to hold a deck sash closed. The end of the bolt, which is not beveled, is usually provided with an eye or hook so that the bolt can be withdrawn from the keeper to open the sash.

Deck Sash Opener. Figs. 1019-1025. A device for conveniently opening or closing a deck sash. In some types two or more sashes on one side are operated simultaneously by one opener. Several types are illustrated.

Deck Sash Pivot. Figs. 1012-1015. A bearing pin on which a deck sash turns. See **Deck Sash Ratchet**.

Deck Sash Pivot Plate. A small metal plate with a hole in it to receive a deck sash pivot attached to the sides of the deck posts.

Deck Sash Pull. Figs. 1010-1011. An eye screwed into one of the rails of a deck sash, by means of which the sash can be revolved on its pivot to open or close.

Deck Sash Ratchet. Figs. 1026-1027. A ratchet stop combined with a deck sash pivot and plate. Designed to hold the sash in any partially open position.

Deck Sash Ventilator. See **Deck Ventilator**.

Deck Side. The entire vertical side of a monitor deck, including the sashes, sill, plate and posts.

Deck Sill. 17, Figs. 259-370. A longitudinal timber in the frame of a monitor deck supporting the upper ends of the lower deck carlines and the deck posts.

Deck Sill Molding. 57, Figs. 259-370. Wide molding strips attached to the inside faces of the deck sill.

Deck Top Rail. A **Deck Plate**, which see.

Deck Ventilator. Figs. 1341-1342, 1350, 1360. An automatic ventilator inserted in the side of a monitor roof in place of one or more deck sash. The term is sometimes used to distinguish the movable deck sashes which act as ventilators when open from the fixed deck sashes.

Deck Window. See **Deck Sash**.

Dedenda Gong. Fig. 939.

Deltabeston Wire. A trade name for magnet wire insulated with treated asbestos and made waterproof by being impregnated with a special compound.

Derrick Car. See **Crane Car**.

Destination Marker Lamp. Fig. 1069. A **Route Signal Lamp**, which see.

Destination Sign. Figs. 654-658. A printed sign or marker prominently displayed on a car to indicate its route or direction. The deck end sash and upper sash of the middle side window are frequently used for displaying destination signs which are mounted inside of the car. Revolving signs are also used on some cars. They are mounted above the platform hood in front or above the lower deck on the sides. Destination signs are frequently illuminated at night by incandescent lamps placed behind them and showing through them, or by mounting lamps in a hood above the sign so that the lamps are hidden but the light is reflected on the sign.

De Witt Sand Box. Figs. 1231-1233.

Diagonal Floor Timber. 118, Figs. 259-370. One of a pair of diagonal timber braces in the center of a car body underframe, between the needlebeams or central transverse floor timbers. See **Corner Brace**.

Diamond Arch Bar Truck. Figs. 1382-1383, 1399. A type of car truck, so called from the shape of the side frames, which are built up of flat iron bars called **Arch Bars**, which see. This type of truck is in wide use under steam railway freight cars and is occasionally used for motor and trailer cars, especially freight and express cars. It is not an easy riding truck and has not been used in passenger service to any extent.

"Diamond S" Brake Shoe. Figs. 1489-1490, 1499.

Dielectric. A substance which permits the phenomena of induction to take place through its mass, but which has high resistivity to the flow of direct current. The term dielectric strength as applied to an insulating material commonly means the insulating property of the material, although dielectric strength is not exactly proportional to non-conducting power.

Dipped Coil. A coil which has been impregnated with an insulating compound by dipping in an open tank filled with the compound.

Direct Current. As commonly employed, a term used to designate a current of electricity flowing always in one direction, due to a uniform difference of potential. A primary battery generates a direct current, and such a current may be generated in a suitable dynamo-electric machine. Direct current at a potential of from 550 to 700 volts is in universal use for the propulsion of electric cars in cities, and with the exception of a few installations of 1200-volt, direct-current and high-tension, single-phase alternating-current systems is also universally used for electric subway, elevated and interurban railways. See **High-Tension Direct-Current System, Single-Phase System**.

Discharge Pipe. A pipe connecting an air compressor to the main reservoir of an air brake. A coil of radiating pipe is usually inserted between the compressor and the reservoir.

Disconnecting Switch. A **Cut-Out Switch**, which see.

Distance Piece. A short timber or block placed between two other timbers, such as sills, to hold them the proper distance apart.

Division Board. See **Seat Bottom**.

Door. Fig. 691. A hinged or sliding framework, usually rectangular in shape, which closes an opening in a wall or partition. The doors used in electric cars are classified as swinging, sliding, double sliding and folding doors. See **Trap Door, Exit Door, Entrance Door, End Door, Side Door**, etc.

Door Bottom Rail. 136, Figs. 259-370. The lowest horizontal member of a door frame.

Door Case. The complete frame into which a door is fitted. It includes the **Door Jambs** or **Door Posts**, the **Door Sill** and **Door Lintel**, which see.

Door Catch. Figs. 790-793. A hook or spring latch used to hold a door open or shut. See **Door Stop**.

Door Chafing Strip. A flat, brass strip fastened on both sides of a sliding door about the center of its height to take the wear of a middle door guide.

Door Check. Fig. 767. A pneumatic or hydraulic dash pot and spring attached with suitable levers to the top of a swinging door and to the door lintel. The spring tends to close the door, and the dash pot arrests its movement sufficiently to prevent the door from slamming shut.

Door Controller. Fig. 689. A device for guiding the movement of a double folding door, such as is used above platform steps. It consists of two top door tracks and pivoted sheaves on each half of the door. The door tracks are bent so that the two halves of the door fold up on each other and swing back against the vestibule corner post out of the way.

Door Corner Plate. A wide, brass plate screwed on the corner of a door frame to keep it square. On sliding doors the top corner plate is usually combined with the door hanger, and the bottom corner plate serves as a chafing plate for the bottom door guides.

Door Frame. The frame surrounding the panels of a door. It consists of the stiles or side uprights, the mullions or center uprights and the top, middle and bottom rails.

Door Guards. (1) Strips of wood attached to a frame on the inside lining and forming a door pocket for a sliding side door in a baggage or freight car.
(2) Brass rods fastened across the glass panel of a swinging door to prevent pushing on the glass to open the door. See **Window Guard**.

Door Guide. Figs. 833-835. A small brass or rubber roller mounted on the sides of the opening of a sliding door pocket to keep the door in line. One is usually mounted on both sides of the opening about the center of the door, and sometimes guides are also used at the bottom of the opening. They rub on horizontal brass chafing strips screwed on the door.

Door Handle. Figs. 845-852. See **Sliding Door Handle**.

Door Hanger. Figs. 839-844. A casting enclosing a grooved sheave and attached to the top of a sliding door. The sheave runs on a cross bar or rod fastened above the door opening. In some forms of double-door hangers the sheave is replaced by a toothed wheel, which runs on a rack rail. See **Double-Door Operating Device**.

Door Hasp. A metal bar with a slot cut in it fastened to a door frame and fitting over a staple in the door jamb. A pin or the shackle of a padlock is put through the staple to hold the hasp in place. Only occasionally used for sliding doors of baggage and freight cars.

Door Hinge. Figs. 755-764. A pivoted support for one edge of a swinging door. They are made to permit a door to swing open in one direction only or in both directions. In the latter case they are usually made with springs to return the door to the central or closed position. From two to four hinges are used to a door.

Door Holder. Figs. 790-793. A device for holding a swinging door open. A door stop and a door holder are usually combined. See **Door Stop**.

Door Hook. Figs. 825-831. A pivoted hook used with a pin or button to fasten a sliding door.

Door Jamb. One of the two finishing boards which, together with the door lintel and door sill, form the casing in which a door is mounted. The jambs are usually applied on the outside of the door posts, which are rough timbers forming part of the body framing.

Door Knob. The round or elliptical knob, usually made of brass, which is fastened on the projecting end of the spindle of a door lock, by means of which the spindle is turned and the catch bolt withdrawn from the keeper. It also serves as a handle to pull or push the door open. See Figs. 768-773.

Door Latch. Figs. 781-782. A spring bolt engaging with a keeper on the door case to hold a swinging door shut. It is often combined with a dead-bolt lock.

Door Latch Keeper. See **Door Lock Keeper**.

Door Lintel. The cross piece forming the top of a door opening above the door. Also called **Head Piece**, which see.

Door Lock. Figs. 768-822. A bolt turned with a key or knob, and engaging with a slotted plate or keeper on the door case to hold a swinging door shut. Door locks usually combine a spring latch bolt withdrawn by turning the knob and a dead bolt moved by turning a removable key inserted in the lock.

Door Lock Keeper. Figs. 768-773. A slotted plate set in flush in a door case in which the bolt of a door lock engages. The edge of the keeper is sometimes slightly beveled to form a strike plate for a beveled spring bolt of a lock or latch.

Door Mullion. The vertical post in the center of a door frame.

Door Panel. 137, Fig. 334. Thin pieces of board or sheet metal fitted into the spaces between the rails, stiles and mullions of a door frame.

Door Pocket. The space between two partitions into which a sliding door moves when opened. Sliding end doors enter a pocket formed by the body end panel on the outside and the seat end panel on the inside.

Door Pocket Sash. 78 and 80, Fig. 334. A fixed or swinging window sash forming the inside wall of a sliding end door pocket above the inside bottom end panel or seat panel.

Door Pocket Transom. A hinged panel above a door pocket sash which can be opened to expose the sprockets of a double sliding door mechanism. A similar half-elliptic panel is often inserted over the doors to give access to the door hangers and track.

Door Post. An upright which forms the side of a door opening. They are designated according to the location of the doors as end door post, side door post, vestibule door post, etc.

Door Rail. 133, 134 and 136, Figs. 259-370. One of the horizontal pieces of a door frame. Door rails are designated as top rail, middle rail and bottom rail.

Door Roller. Figs. 833-836. See **Door Guide.**

Door Sash. A pane of glass used in place of an opaque panel in a car door. The sashes of electric railway car doors are commonly fixed in the door frame and cannot be raised or lowered.

Door Sheave. See **Door Hanger.**

Door Sheave Transom. 132, Fig. 334. A half-elliptic or rectangular panel above a double sliding door. It is hinged to lift up or drop down so as to expose the door sheaves and operating mechanism.

Door Sill. A piece of wood or metal placed across the bottom of a door opening. The metal door sill of sliding end door openings is often cast with small projections on the top surface to act as guides for the bottom rail of the door.

Door Spring. A spiral or rod spring attached to a swinging door to cause it to close when released after opening.

Door Stile. 135, Figs. 259-370. One of the upright sticks forming the side of a door frame.

Door Stop. Figs. 790-793. A wood, metal or rubber block attached to the floor or a partition to prevent a swinging door from opening too far. Sometimes combined with a catch or door holder to hold the door open.

Door Track. The flat bar, rack or rod on which the sheave of a sliding door hanger runs.

Doorway. The opening which is closed by a door.

Dossert Connectors. Figs. 1841-1844.

Double-Acting Hinge. Figs. 757, 765-766. A door hinge designed to permit a swinging door to open in either direction. They are usually made with a spring, which causes the door to return to the central position when released.

Double-Coil Heater. Figs. 1150-1154. An electric car heater having two resistance coils, each connected to a different circuit. The coils are usually made of different capacity, so that when used singly or in combination three degrees of heat may be obtained.

Double-Deck Car. A car with seats on the roof as well as within the body. The roof is reached by a winding staircase from the rear platform. Many double-deck cars are used in Europe but they are not used in the United States.

Double Door. A door made in two halves. Double, triple and quadruple folding doors are used to close the vestibules of enclosed platform cars. Double sliding doors working separately or together are used for body end doors.

Double-Door Operating Device. Figs. 674-680. A mechanism for causing the two halves of a double sliding door to move in or out simultaneously. Several such devices are illustrated.

Double-End Car. Figs. 1-6, 35-49, etc. A car with similar platforms and equipment on each end which may be operated equally well in either direction.

Double Lip Retaining Ring. Figs. 1627-1632. A type of fastening for the tires of steel-tired wheels which employs one or two U-shaped retaining rings. One lip of the retaining ring fits in a groove cut in the side of the tire and the other fits in a similar groove cut in the rim of the wheel center.

Double Plate Wheel. Figs. 1604-1605. A cast-iron wheel in which two plates or webs spring from the hub and join into a single web under the rim.

Double Register. Figs. 1159-1163. See **Fare Register.**

Double Sliding Door. A body end door made in two halves which slide into pockets in the end bulkhead on each side of the door opening. The two halves are usually connected together by suitable mechanism, so that they close or open simultaneously. Several forms of double sliding door operating mechanisms are shown in Figs. 674-680.

Double Trolley Base. A Trolley Base, which see, supporting two trolley poles side by side for use only with a double trolley system.

Double Trolley System. In Cincinnati and the outskirts of the District of Columbia city ordinances prohibit the use of the track rails for the return circuit. Positive and negative overhead conductors are used and two trolleys are required on each car.

Double-Truck Car. Figs. 35-212. A car mounted on two swiveling four-wheel trucks. See **Single-Truck Car.**

Dowel. See **Axle Bearing Dowel Pin.**

Draft Gear. Figs. 599-635. A general term embracing all of the appliances and attachments by which one car is made to pull another. It includes the couplers or drawbars and the springs or pocket castings by which they are attached to the car body.

Draft Pin. A pivot pin in a pocket casting under the platform by means of which a radial drawbar or coupler is attached to the car underframing.

Draft Spring. 31, Figs. 259-370. A coil spring inserted between the drawbar or coupler and the draft pin to relieve the shock on the draft gear.

Drain Cock. Fig. 481. A small cock inserted in the bottom of the auxiliary reservoir to drain off the water of condensation.

Drawbar. 28, Figs. 259-370; Figs. 600-635. An iron bar or casting with a socket head for receiving a coupling link by means of which two cars may be coupled together. The drawbar is usually attached with a draft spring to a pivot casting secured to the underside of the body center sills and projects out under the bumper beam. Drawbars are sometimes made with automatic coupler heads. See **Coupler.**

The term drawbar is also applied to a long coupling link used to connect together two cars which are not equipped with radially pivoted drawbars or automatic couplers.

Drawbar Anchorage. Figs. 629-630. A heavy pivot casting securely bolted to the car body underframe by means of which a radial drawbar is attached under the end of the car.

Drawbar Attachments. Figs. 599-635. The spring, yoke, pivot pin and anchor casting by means of which a drawbar is secured to the car underframing.

Drawbar Carry Iron. 29, Figs. 259-370; Fig. 628. A strap hung from the under side of the bumper beam and supporting the outer end of a pivoted drawbar.

Drawbar Centering Device. A device for maintaining a radial drawbar normally in the center line of draft, but permitting it to deflect to either side when the car is rounding a curve and is coupled to another car.

Drawbar Follower Plate. One of two plates enclosing the ends of a draft spring. The rear plate is fastened to the shank of the drawbar, which passes through the spring and the front plate is connected to a sleeve attached to the draft pin and surrounding the shank of the drawbar. By this means, the pull on the drawbar is transmitted to the draft pin through the draft spring, which is compressed between the follower plates.

Drawbar Head. The recessed enlargement at the outer end of a drawbar which receives a coupling link.

Drawbar Pocket. Fig. 609. A recessed casting bolted below or on the face of the bumper beam and used to attach a coupling link or bar with a coupling pin.

Drawbar Sector. A curved carry iron for a radial drawbar.

Drawbar Stirrup. See **Drawbar Carry Iron.**

Drawbar Yoke. A U-shaped forging attached to the rear end of a drawbar and enclosing the draft spring and follower plates. Used instead of a tail bolt passing through the center of the spring.

Draw Head. See **Drawbar Head.**

Draw Spring. See **Draft Spring.**

Drawing Room Car. See **Parlor Car.**

Dressel Headlights. Figs. 1048-1050.

Drip Rail. A narrow molding above the side windows on the outside intended to prevent water from running down on the windows. Also called water table.

Driving Axle. A car axle geared to a motor. Also called **Motor Axle**, which see.

Driving Wheel. A wheel mounted on an axle which is geared to a motor, as distinguished from an idle wheel which exerts no tractive effort on the track.

Drop Bottom Car. A freight car with doors in the bottom arranged to drop and discharge the load by gravity. Used for hauling ballast, coal and cinders.

Drop Door. A door in the bottom of drop bottom car.

Drop Platform. A platform on the end of a car body, the floor of which is several inches below the level of the car body floor. Drop platforms are used to avoid two platform steps. They are employed generally on closed and semi-convertible city cars, but not on open cars and interurban cars.

Drop Sash. A window sash arranged to open by dropping it into a pocket in the side of the car below the window sill.

Drop Sill. A term sometimes applied to the platform sills of cars having drop platforms.

Drum. See **Expansion Drum** and **Controller Drum.**

Drum Controller. A term applied to any type of controller in which the main motor current is carried through contacts on a revolving cylinder or drum inside the controller case. See **Hand Control** and **Controller.**

Drum Switch. (Train Starting Signal.) Figs. 1257-1258. A switch in the signal train line circuit which is mechanically connected to the lid of the control line jumper socket. The switch is closed when the socket lid is raised to insert a control jumper plug, and is opened when the plug is removed and the lid is shut.

Drum Winding. (Of an Armature.) A form of winding in which all of the wires are laid in slots on the outside of the armature core, as distinguished from a ring winding, in which the core is hollow and the wires are wound over the outside surface and back again through the hole in the center of the core. Drum windings are used exclusively in modern railway motors.

Dry Battery. See **Primary Battery.**

Dry Closet. Fig. 897. A closet for toilet rooms which is not flushed with water.

Duck. A stout, closely woven, cotton cloth used for curtains of open cars, car seat upholstery and car roofs. Duck is the trade name for canvas.

Dummy Hose Coupling. Fig. 482. A casting of the same shape as a brake hose coupling which is hung from the car body by a chain. When the hose is not connected to another on an adjoining car, the hose coupling is hooked into the dummy coupling, and the hose is thus hung up out of the way. The dummy coupling also serves to close the opening in the hose coupling and keep out dirt.

Dump Car. Figs. 231-233. A car arranged to discharge its contents by gravity, either through drop doors, swinging side doors or by tipping the entire body to one side.

Dumpit Sand Box. Fig. 1223.

Duner Water Closet. Fig. 898.

Duo Controller Finger. Fig. 1731.

Duplex Air Gage. (Air Brake.) Figs. 472-473. A pressure gage registering on the same dial with separate pointers the pressure in the main reservoir and in the brake pipe. The red hand registers reservoir pressure and the black hand registers the brake pipe pressure.

Dust Guard. Figs. 1561-1562. A piece of wood, metal, cloth or fibre surrounding an axle in the back of a journal box to exclude the dust and prevent the oil from working out on the axle.

Dynamotor. Fig. 1767. A small motor-generator mounted under the body of a car equipped to operate with 1200-volt direct current. It is designed to deliver 600-volt current for the lighting, compressor motor and control circuits and consists of a single frame and set of field coils, with an armature provided with two commutators and separate sets of windings connected in series across the line. A shunt field is connected across one-half of the armature. The first half of the armature acts as a motor and takes current from the trolley; the second half acts as a generator, producing a current of equal amperage and voltage to that taken from the trolley. The exterior circuit of the dynamotor is connected to a point midway between the two armature windings, and therefore draws equal amounts of current from the trolley through the first half of the armature and from the generator half of the armature. The dynamotor is started automatically when leaving a 600-volt section and entering a 1200-volt section by means of a selector relay, the two coils of which will throw the relay armature at about 250 volts and 750 volts, respectively.

E

Earll Trolley Retriever. Figs. 1325-1328.

Earth. See **Ground.**

Eaves. The lowest edge of a car roof.

Eaves Fascia Board. 55, Figs. 259-370. A narrow board applied on the outside of the letter board just below the eaves of the lower deck.

Eaves Molding. A narrow molding applied on the outside of the letter board or eaves fascia board, when the latter is used, to cover the overlapping edge of the roofing canvas.

Eckert Water Closet. Fig. 896.

Eclipse Destination Sign. Fig. 655.

Eclipse Life Guard. Fig. 714.

Economy Oil Cup. Fig. 1711.

Edwards Sash Fixtures. Figs. 961-965.

Edwards Vestibule Trap Door. Figs. 921-922.

Eickmeyer Coil. One of the early types of formed coils for drum wound armatures, used in the G. E.-800 motors. The coil has a reverse twist in each end, and one-half forms part of the top layer of conductors in one armature slot, while the other half forms part of the bottom layer in another slot, approximately 90 deg. around the armature. See **Straight-Out Winding.**

Electric Arc. See **Arc.**

Electric Bell. A bell which is sounded by a clapper mounted on a spring armature placed in front of a small electro-magnet. When the circuit through the magnet coil is alternately interrupted and restored, the armature is intermittently attracted and released, thus causing the clapper to strike successive blows on the bell.

Electric Buzzer. See **Buzzer.**

Electric Car. Any car propelled by electric motors as distinguished from cable cars, horse cars, steam railroad cars, etc.

Electric Circuit. See **Circuit.**

Electric Current. A flow of electricity.

Electric Headlight. See **Arc Headlight** and **Incandescent Headlight.**

Electric Heater. Figs. 1112-1157. A coil or coils of resistance wire enclosed in a suitable frame and mounted under the seats of a car or along the seat riser. Current is taken through a special heater switch from the trolley circuit, and three degrees of heat are usually provided by proportioning the two coils of each heater so that one will give off twice as much heat as the other. The large coils are placed on one circuit and the small coils on another, and they may be turned on separately or together by the four-point heater switch. In cars equipped with electro-magnetic brakes the current generated by the motors acting as dynamos is turned into the heaters during cold weather.

Electric Heater Switch. Figs. 1108-1111, 1132-1143. A switch used to turn the current on or off in electric heaters. Usually a three-point snap switch. Commonly abbreviated to **Heater Switch**, which see.

Electric Insulation. See **Insulation.**

Electric Lamp. See **Arc Headlight** and **Incandescent Lamp.**

Electric Light. Light emitted from a source which is heated to incandescence by a current of electricity. See **Arc Headlight** and **Incandescent Lamp.**

Electric Locomotive. A Locomotive, which see, propelled by electric motors.

Electric Motor. Figs. 1645-1709. A machine for transforming electrical energy into mechanical energy of rotation. See **Motor.**

Electric Pump Governor. See **Pump Governor.**

Electric Varnish. See **Insulating Varnish.**

Electricity. An intangible medium which carries energy. A current of electricity may be likened to the flow of water in a pipe. The rate of flow, of which the unit is the ampere, may be compared with the number of gallons or cubic feet of water flowing in a given time. The force or pressure, measured in volts, is equivalent to the pressure on the water in the pipe, which is measured in pounds per square inch. The number of amperes multiplied by the number of volts is a measure of the power transmitted and is expressed in terms of watts. See **Ampere, Volt, Watt.**

Electrobestos. A form of fireproof insulating material of which the base is asbestos.

Electrode. A terminal of an electric conductor farthest from the source of supply of the current. See **Arc Headlight.**

Electro-Magnet. An iron core surrounded by a closed coil of wire through which a current of electricity is flowing. Lines of magnetic force in the core are induced by the flow of electricity in the surrounding coil. The quantity of the magnetism so induced is directly proportional to the number of turns of wire in the coil and the rate of flow of current through the coil. See **Ampere-Turn.** Electro-magnets are used to produce the magnetic field of motors, for operating circuit breakers, contactors, track brakes and for many other devices.

Electro-Magnetic Brake. See **Magnetic Brake.**

Electromotive Force. That which moves or tends to move electricity. A difference in electrical potential between two points on a circuit produces a flow of electricity between those points, just as water will flow from one level to another lower level under the force of gravitation. The unit of measurement of electromotive force is the volt.

Electro-Pneumatic Brake. Fig. 454. An improved type of air-brake apparatus for long high-speed trains, such as are used in elevated and subway service. All of the functions of the ordinary quick-action automatic air brake are retained, but in addition means are provided for applying and releasing the brakes on each car through the action of electro-pneumatic valves energized by current taken through contacts on the motorman's brake valve and continuous train wires. Four control wires are required to perform the three functions of service application, emergency application and release. Service applications are made by energizing an electro-pneumatic valve which opens a direct passage from the auxiliary resrvoir to the brake cylinder. Successive applications can be made with all the accuracy of the straight-air brake by admitting more and more air to the brake cylinder. The release is accomplished in the same way by energizing a magnet valve, which bleeds off the brake cylinder pressure with any degree of rapidity and with perfect control. An emergency application opens a magnet valve, which forms part of the triple valve, and admits full auxiliary reservoir pressure to the brake cylinder. Another magnet valve, called a brake pipe vent valve, is also opened, admitting air from the brake pipe direct to the brake cylinder. The necessary contacts on the motorman's brake valve are arranged so that the electric application precedes the automatic air application. At the extreme left-hand position of the valve handle the brakes will release either through the action of the electro-pneumatic valves or the restoration of pressure in the brake pipe. The next position is electric lap, which is the normal running position, and the next is electric application. Then follows automatic lap, first and second automatic service application positions, and at the extreme right emergency application, in which both the air and electric features are operative. If for any reason a movement of the handle from electric lap to electric application fails to apply the brakes, further movement to the right will give an automatic air service application. The application of the brakes on all cars in a long train can be accomplished instantaneously and simultaneously with the electro-pneumatic devices, and this eliminates any tendency to surging, due to the quicker application of the brakes on the head cars than on the rear cars.

Electro-Pneumatic Control. Figs. 1768-1803. A type of **Multiple-Unit Control,** which see, made by the Westinghouse Electric & Manufacturing Company, in which the unit switches or contactors are operated by pneumatic cylinders. The air supply, which is drawn from the air brake system, is admitted to the cylinders through small needle valves, which are raised from their seats by electro-magnets energized by low-voltage control currents. See **Unit-Switch Control.**

Electro-Pneumatic Switch. Figs. 1783-1787. An electric switching device in which the contacts are held open normally by a strong spring, but are closed by a piston actuated by compressed air. The admission and release of the air in the piston cylinder are controlled by an electro-pneumatic valve. See **Unit Switch.**

Electro-Pneumatic Train Signal. A system of communicating signals from one car to another in a train in which the closing of a signal switch on any car sends current through a wire in the control train line to the motorman's cab, where an electro-pneumatic valve is energized to admit air to a small signal whistle. See **Air Signal.**

Electro-Pneumatic Valve. An air valve which is opened by the pull exerted on the armature of an electro-magnet when current is sent through the magnet coil. See **Unit-Switch** and **Electro-Pneumatic Brake.**

Elevated Car. Figs. 202-206. A car designed for use in trains on elevated railways such as are in operation in New York, Boston, Philadelphia, Chicago and other cities. Elevated cars are usually entered from station platforms which are the same height above the rails as the car floor, so that platform steps are not required. The entrances to the platforms or vestibules are closed with gates or sliding doors.

Elevating Wing. (Snow Plow.) A curved surface built above the plow share to throw the snow up and to one side so as to clear the sides of deep cuts.

Elliptic Spring. Figs. 1572-1573. A spring made up of two sets of curved steel strips fastened together at the ends and forming an approximate ellipse. The plates of each half of the spring are secured at the center by a spring band. This form of spring is used for truck bolster springs and also for body supporting springs on single trucks. They are designated as single, double, triple, quadruple, etc., according to the number of complete springs which are placed side by side. A single set of strips is termed a semi-elliptic or half-elliptic spring.

E. M. F. A common abbreviation of **Electromotive Force,** which see.

Emergency Application. An application of air brakes with the maximum power, made in emergencies to stop a car in the shortest possible distance.

Emergency Brake. Fig. 1483. An auxiliary brake for use in emergencies. See **Slipper Brake.**

Emergency Cord. A cord sometimes carried through the car and connected to the handle of the conductor's valve of the air brake system. By pulling on the cord the valve can be opened and the brakes applied.

Emergency Pipe. In a straight-air brake equipment with emergency feature, a separate line of pipe containing air at main reservoir pressure, which is connected to the emergency valves under each car. When the pressure in the emergency pipe is released, either by the movement of the motorman's brake valve to the emergency position or by rupture of the emergency pipe hose couplings, the emergency valves come into action and admit air from the auxiliary reservoirs to the brake cylinders. See Fig. 546.

Emergency Position. (Brake Valve.) The position of the valve handle in which a large port from the brake pipe to the atmosphere is open. The sudden reduction in the brake pipe pressure which results when this port is opened causes the triple valves under the cars to also move to the position in which the full auxiliary reservoir pressure is admitted to the brake cylinders through a large emergency port.

Emergency Straight-Air Brake. Figs. 532-533, 546. A straight-air brake equipment for motor car and trailer, with which is combined an emergency feature designed to apply the brakes automatically in case the cars should part or a brake hose should burst.

Emergency Tools. An axe, saw, sledge hammer and crow-bar, sometimes carried in a box under the lower deck of interurban cars. They are intended for use only in case of emergency, as in a wreck. Jacks are sometimes carried on cars to assist in replacing the trucks on the track after a derailment or in case of accident in which a person gets under the trucks.

Emergency Valve. Figs. 509-510, 539-541. (1) A special valve used in connection with a combined straight-air and automatic brake system to perform the same functions as a quick-acting triple valve in emergencies. During an ordinary application the emergency valve does not come into action. (2) A small slide valve contained within the body of a triple valve. When the pressure in the brake pipe is suddenly released the emergency valve moves to its extreme position in which a large port is opened between the auxiliary reservoir and the brake cylinder and air is also admitted through a check valve from the brake pipe to the brake cylinder.

Emery Pneumatic Lubricator. Fig. 560.

Empire Deck. A type of roof construction for interurban cars. The upper deck ceiling is vaulted and the deck sashes are made half-elliptic in pairs. See **Semi-Empire Deck.**

Enclosed Fuse. Figs. 1807-1815. A fuse enclosed in a fireproof tube with suitable terminals for conveniently inserting in a fuse box or mounting on a fuse block.

End Belt Rail. A horizontal timber framed between the end posts of a car body at the height of the side belt rail. See **Belt Rail.**

End Bulkhead. In open street cars a cross partition in each end of the car dividing the platform from the main body of the car. A non-reversible seat is built against the bulkhead on one or both sides and the upper part contains two or more drop sashes. The term is also applied to the end of a closed car body which separates the body from platform or vestibule.

End Bulkhead Post. 70, Figs. 259-370. A post in an end bulkhead separating two sashes.

End Bulkhead Sash. 78, Figs. 259-370. A fixed or drop sash in an end bulkhead of an open car.

End Carline. A **Carline,** which see, fastened to the inside or on top of the end plate.

End Cover Plates. T and U, Fig. 1657. (Box Frame Motor.) Circular iron disks containing the armature, bearings and bolted over the openings in the end of the motor frame through which the armature is inserted or withdrawn. Also called **Motor Frame Heads,** which see.

End Door. A door in the end of a car body opening onto the platform or vestibule.

End Door Post. One of the posts in the body end framing forming the side of an end door opening.

End Hook. See Bell Cord End Hook.

End Panel. 131, Figs. 259-370. A panel in the end of a car body between the end door posts and the body corner posts. When a sliding end door is used, the end panel or the end seat panel on the inside forms the door pocket. The end panels usually extend up to the height of the end belt rail and an end window is placed above.

End Piece. See Truck End Frame.

End Plate. A horizontal timber connecting the two side plates above the end door. It is frequently cut to the contour of the lower deck and made to serve as an end carline in the lower deck. Also called head piece and end top rail.

End Post. A post in the end framing of a car body or vestibule. The posts in the end of a car body are the two door posts, the body corner posts and occasionally one or two **Cripple Posts,** which see.

End Rib. A short stud connecting the end sill with the end belt rail between the end door post and the body corner post.

End Rib Rail. A narrow strip of wood framed in flush with the outside surface of the end posts and ribs back of the continuation of the fender rail around the end of the body.

End Roof Panel. 132, Fig. 334. A wide low panel on the inside of a car between the top of the end door opening and the lower deck. It is often made with hinged door sheave transoms to give access to the double sliding door mechanism.

End Seat. More properly, **Corner Seat,** which see.

End Seat Panel. A panel on the inside of a car at the end of a longitudinal seat below the end window.

End Sill. 117, Figs. 259-370. The cross member of the body underframing connecting the ends of the longitudinal sills which are mortised into it.

End Sill Knee Iron. A bent steel plate inserted in the interior angle of the joint between the end sill and one of the longitudinal sills to stiffen the joint and keep it square.

End Sill Diagonal Brace. See Corner Brace.

End Top Rail. See End Plate.

End Ventilator. See Deck End Ventilator.

End Window. 78 and 80, Fig. 334. A window in the end of a car body above the end panel. The sash is usually stationary. In cars having sliding end doors the end window forms part of the outside wall of the door pocket. A sash of similar size, usually hinged, is inserted on the inside of the car above the end seat panel.

Engineering Association Standards. Figs. 1948-1987. The American Electric Railway Engineering Association has adopted a number of standards and recommended practices affecting car construction as follows:

Standards:
    Motor Axles.
    Brake Heads and Shoes.
    Wheel Tread and Flange Contours.
    3¾-in. x 7-in. Journal Box.
    4½-in. x 8-in. Journal Box.
    5-in. x 9-in. Journal Box.
    5½-in. x 10-in. Journal Box.

Recommended practice:
    Height of Car Steps.
    Height of Couplers.
    Height of Bumpers.

Entrance Door. A door in the end of a car body or in the side of a platform which is used only for the entrance of passengers. See **Exit Door.**

Entrance Step. A step below an entrance door opening. See **Exit Door Step.**

Equalizer. 21, Fig. 1368. A bent steel bar whose ends rest on top of the journal boxes of a four-wheel truck. The truck frame rests on helical equalizer springs which are carried on the equalizer bars near their ends. The purpose of the equalizer is to distribute the load equally on both axles and to support the load as near to the axles as possible, in order to prevent tilting of the truck frame in starting and stopping. In the Brill type 27-E, 27-F and 27-G trucks the equalizer supports the spring plank and is hung below the top bar of the side frame with spring stirrups located near the journal boxes.

Equalizer Nut. 27, Fig. 1370. A castle nut used to fasten one end of an equalizer of a Brill No. 27-F truck into an equalizer spring eye-bolt.

Equalizer Separator. 12, Figs. 1388-1390. A thimble surrounding a bolt, fastening the two plates of a double equalizer bar together.

Equalizer Spring. 18, Fig. 1368. A coil spring resting on an equalizer and supporting the truck frame.

Equalizer Spring Cap. 19, Fig. 1368. A cast iron seat on top of an equalizer spring on which the truck frame rests.

Equalizer Spring Eye Bolt. 24, Fig. 1370. An eye bolt passing up through the center of one of the equalizer springs of a Brill No. 27-F truck and supporting one end of the equalizer.

Equalizer Spring Link. 22, Fig. 1370. A hanger suspended from the side frame of a Brill No. 27-F truck and supporting the seat of one of the equalizer springs.

Equalizer Spring Seat. 20, Fig. 1368. A casting bolted on top of the equalizer bar on which the equalizer spring is seated.

Equalizing Bar. See **Equalizer**.

Equalizing Brake Gear. Figs. 588-589. A system of body brake levers and connecting rods designed to equalize the braking pressure on the two trucks of a double-truck car when the hand brakes are applied from either end of the car. One or two floating levers are employed.

Equalizing Lever. A floating lever in an **Equalizing Brake Gear**, which see.

Escutcheon. A small brass guard plate surrounding a key hole in a door.

Eureka Trolley Wheels. Figs. 1914-1917.

Excursion Car. Figs. 161-163. A light trail car having large seating capacity used by some city and interurban railways for transporting special excursion parties. They are usually open cars and have inexpensive wooden slat seats and fixtures. See **Moonlight Car**.

Exhaust Muffler. (Air Brake.) Fig. 469. A device attached to the exhaust pipe from the brake valve of a straight-air equipment to silence the noise of escaping air when the brakes are released.

Exhaust Pipe. A pipe connecting the exhaust port of a motorman's brake valve and extending down through the car floor to carry off the exhaust air when the brakes are released. See Fig. 455.

Exit Door. A door in a car body or platform side, used only for the exit of passengers. In prepayment type cars the front platform door on the right-hand side is generally used as an exit door.

Exit Step. A platform step under an exit door. On the rear platforms of pay-as-you-enter cars the right-hand step is usually divided into an exit step next to the car body and an entrance step next to the platform corner post. A vertical iron pipe separates the opening above the step into exit and entrance passageways. On several types of pay-as-you-enter cars the front exit step and the sliding door above it are connected by suitable mechanism, so that when the door is closed the step is folded up against the platform side sill. See Figs. 659-664.

Expansion Drum. A closed metal cylinder partly filled with water and connected to the piping of a hot-water heating system. It contains a reserve supply of water to make up for slight leakage and the air space above the water level permits the expansion of the water in the heating system as its temperature rises.

Express Car. Figs. 191-200. A box car with side doors used for the transportation of small parcels, baggage and light freight. Interurban express cars are usually well finished on the outside, as they are frequently operated through city streets during the day.

F

Falk Gear. Fig. 1519.

Fare Box. Figs. 1198-1207. A box mounted on the rear platform of prepayment type cars into which passengers drop cash fares or tickets on entering the car. A variety of types of fare boxes have been placed on the market, some of which are illustrated. Most of the successful designs embody a glass chute through which the coins drop on to an inspection plate. By moving a handle on the outside of the box the inspection plate can be tilted and the coin caused to drop into a cash box below. Some types of fare boxes combine also a registering device, change making mechanism and coin separating mechanism.

Fare Register. Figs. 1158-1165. A mechanical counting device for registering the number of fares collected by the conductor. It is usually mounted on one of the end bulkheads inside the car over the door, where it can be seen plainly. The registering mechanism is contained in a case, through the glass-covered face of which the figure wheels and indicators show. The case is preferably dust proof, with a separate compartment for the bell, having perforations to let out the sound. The operating levers are mounted on a metal register back screwed to the bulkhead and arranged with suitable fasteners to facilitate the removal or replacement of the register. The levers on the back are connected to operating rods or cords running down the car within easy reach of the conductor.

A single register for recording one class of fares only contains the mechanism of a trip register showing in large figures the number of registrations in any half trip and so connected with a direction indicator and resetting key that on turning the latter the trip register is reset to zero and the direction indicator is reversed. A totalizer, which is usually read once a day by the auditor's representative for checking the conductors' trip sheets, and a bell, ringing once for each registration, are also included.

A double register for recording two classes of fares has the mechanism of a single register duplicated, except that one direction indicator serves for both mechanisms. There is also a fare indicator showing the kind of fare last registered.

A multi-fare register has one trip register, direction indicator and bell, and several totalizers and fare indicators, with means for registering and indicating separately several classes of fares.

A recording register may be any of the above types, with the addition of a printing mechanism for printing on a strip of paper contained within the register a record of the totalizer readings whenever desired. They sometimes print other information, such as the date, car number, conductor's number, trip number, etc.

For names of fare register fittings, see **Register**.

Fascia Board. See **Eaves Fascia Board**.

Feed Valve. (Air Brake.) Figs. 501-503. In an automatic air brake equipment, a valve inserted between the main reservoir and the brake valve for automatically maintaining a fixed brake pipe pressure, while the brake valve handle is in the release or running position.

Felt. A thick fabric made of animal hair, which is pressed and not woven together. Felt is extensively used as a backing for the upholstery of car seats.

Fender. Figs. 705, 708-710, 717. A projecting basket made of wire netting, rope or metal slats and attached to the front of a street car to catch persons when struck. A **Wheel-guard**, which see, is an apron mounted under the car body in front of the truck and arranged to drop on the track and pick up or push to one side prostrate bodies which have been thrown under the car. Many forms of fenders and wheel-guards are in use, some of which are illustrated. Some fenders are fixed in position; others are arranged to be dropped down on the track by hand or automatically when a person is struck. On interurban cars a fixed V-shaped pilot fender made of heavy wooden slats or iron bars is commonly used.

Fender Bracket. A casting fastened to the dasher or bumper and used to attach a fender.

Fender Chain. A chain with a ring fitting over an eye on the dasher, used with some types of fenders to support them above the rails. By unhooking the chain the fender can be dropped onto the track.

Fender Rail. 128, Fig. 334. A projecting wooden strip sometimes sheathed with iron, separating the lower or concave side panel from the upper or straight panel. Its purpose is to prevent the thin panels from coming in contact with wheels or wagon bodies when the car rubs another vehicle.

Fender Rail Guard. A narrow strip of iron screwed to the outside surface of a fender rail.

Fiber Insulation. Vegetable fibers which are treated and compressed into sheets or blocks for use in insulating electrical conductors.

Fiber Matting. See **Aisle Matting**.

Field. (Of Motor.) The space between opposite pole pieces through which pass the magnetic lines of force set up by the passage of current through the field coils. The armature rotates in this magnetic field.

Field Coil. Figs. 1682-1687; 14, Figs. 1659-1661. A large number of concentric turns of wire surrounding an iron pole piece. When current flows through the coil a magnetic field is created in front of the pole piece and the tendency of the conductors in the armature carrying current to move out of this magnetic field causes the armature to revolve. Field coils are made up of heavy insulated wire or copper ribbon compactly formed, taped to prevent mechanical injury and thoroughly impregnated with an insulating compound. Usually they are held tightly in the motor shell by the pole pieces, which are bolted on. A compression pad is sometimes placed under the coils to prevent their working loose and chafing. In other types of motors the field coils are held between upper and lower face plates, which form a spool, inside of which is the pole piece.

Field Coil Clamp. A flat plate bolted to the motor frame and used to clamp down one corner of a field coil. Not used in modern types of motors.

Field Coil Compression Pad. Da, Fig. 1657. A flat spring or compressible canvas pad placed between a field coil and the field frame to prevent the field coil from working loose or chafing.

Field Coil Cushion. Another name for a **Field Coil Compression Pad**, which see.

Field Coil Leads. Ub, Fig. 1657. Flexible leads of heavily insulated wire connecting the terminals of the field coils with each other or passed through bushings in the motor frame and connected to the car cables leading to the controller. The outside leads are usually made with a brass connector, which can be readily connected or disconnected with the car cables when necessary to remove the trucks and motors from under the car.

Field Coil Spool. An iron or brass form about which a field coil is wound. The spool fits over and is bolted down with the pole piece. Not used in modern types of motors having mummified coils.

Field Pole. 1, Figs. 1659-1661. A laminated iron core which is surrounded by a field coil. Magnetic lines of force are induced in the pole piece by the flow of current through the coil.

Field Pole Bolts. 22, Figs. 1659-1661. Bolts passing through a field pole and the motor frame to hold the pole securely in place.

Filament. A thin metallic or carbonized thread used as the conductor in an **Incandescent Lamp**, which see. The resistance of the filament is great enough to cause it to heat to incandescence when a current of electricity of sufficient voltage is passed through it.

Filler. See **Filling Piece**.

Filling Piece. A casting or block of wood which serves no purpose other than to close an opening or provide backing for another piece laid over it.

Filtering Lubrication. Fig. 1678. A method of lubricating the armature and axle bearings of Westinghouse motors with oil supplied from a well in the bearing housing or axle cap. The housing is divided by an interior wall into a waste pocket and an oil reservoir, which are connected by an opening in the bottom. Wool waste is packed in the waste pocket against the shaft or axle, through an opening in the bearing lining. The oil is poured into the reservoir and through the communicating opening in the bottom it is filtered and fed to the bearing by capillary attraction in the fibers of the wool waste. All dirt and impurities in the oil are kept away from the bearing. The oil in the reservoir may be gaged by a measuring rod to insure a sufficient supply at all times.

Finger. See **Controller Finger**.

Finishing Varnish. A varnish applied as the last coat in painting a car body. It is compounded to give a hard, but elastic surface with good lustre.

Fire Extinguisher. A closed receptacle containing a dry or liquid chemical compound which, when thrown on a fire, extinguishes it more effectively than water. Fire extinguishers usually form part of the emergency equipment of interurban cars.

Fire Pot. The cylinder in the center of a hot-water heater containing the fire of coals, which is supported on a grate in the bottom. The heater coil is placed inside of the fire pot, where it is exposed to the heat of the fire.

Fittings. See **Car Fittings** and **Register Fittings**.

Flag. A square piece of red, white or green cloth attached to a short staff and displayed on the front or rear of interurban cars as a marker signal.

Flag Holder. A socket casting attached to the vestibule corner posts of interurban cars for holding a marker signal flag. They are commonly made to also take a marker lamp which is displayed at night in place of a flag.

Flange. The projecting rim on the periphery of a car wheel, which prevents the wheel from running off the rail. The standard wheel flanges of the American Electric Railway Engineering Association are ¾ in. and ⅞ in. high and 1 3/16 in. thick. See Figs. 1966-1967.

Flange Brake Shoe. Figs. 1496-1499. A brake shoe formed with a groove which fits over and bears on the flange of the wheel, as well as the tread.

Flanger. See **Snow Flanger**.

Flap Curtain. A car curtain which is not confined at the bottom by grooves or wires in the window posts.

Flashing. Arcing in a controller or on the surface of a motor commutator. Flashing on the commutator may be caused by rough surface, weak brush holder springs or short-circuited armature coils or commutator segments.

Flat Car. Figs. 227-229. A car with a floor, but no sides or ends, used for hauling ballast, ties, rails, etc.

Flat Wheel. A car wheel which has one or more flat spots of considerable size worn on the tread by skidding on the rails.

Flitch Plates. Iron or steel plates placed on edge between pieces of wood to form a built-up beam, such as a bolster. Also called sandwich plates.

Floating Lever. A body brake lever which has no fixed fulcrum. Such a lever is sometimes used to equalize the braking pressures on the two trucks of a double-truck car when the brakes are applied by hand. See **Equalizing Brake Gear**.

Floor. 42, Figs. 259-370. The layer of boards or metal plates on top of the underframe of a car body, forming a platform to support the seats and standing passengers.

Floor Beam. 109 and 118, Figs. 259-370. A transverse or diagonal beam in a car underframe, on which the flooring is placed. Short beams used for filling blocks between sills or transverse floor beams are commonly called bridging.

Floor Board. 42, Figs. 259-370. One of the narrow wooden boards which form the floor of a car.

Floor Joist. See **Floor Beam**.

Floor Mat. See **Aisle Mat**.

Floor Stop. Figs. 790-793. A **Door Stop**, which see, fastened to the floor of a car.

Floor Strips. 87, Figs. 259-370. Narrow pieces of hard wood screwed on top of the floor boards in the aisle and occasionally between the seats to protect the floor from wear. In some cars the strips are made up into rectangular frames, which are laid on top of the floor, but are not fastened down.

Floor Timber. 109 and 118, Figs. 259-370. A **Floor Beam**, which see. The term floor timber is commonly used when wooden beams are referred to.

Flooring. Narrow tongued and grooved or matched boards used for car floors.

Flush Door Lock. A door lock, the handle of which is in a recessed plate and does not project beyond the surface of the door.

Flush Sash Lift. Figs. 983-984. A recessed casting let in flush with the surface of the bottom rail of a movable sash so as to provide a hold for the fingers in raising the sash.

Flushing Tank. A small tank mounted under the roof in a lavatory compartment to hold a supply of water for flushing a water closet.

Flux. (1) A substance such as borax, which promotes the fusion of metals. Some form of flux is usually used when applying solder to make a joint.
(2) The amount of flow of magnetic lines of force through a magnetic circuit.

Folding Door. Fig. 689. A door made in two or more sections, hinged together so as to fold up into the width of one section. Folding doors are used in car construction for vestibule entrances.

Folding Gate. Fig. 690. A gate made of latticed metal strips which can be folded back into a small space. Frequently used for platform gates.

Folding Seat. A seat which can be folded up against a partition or the side of the car out of the way when not wanted. Such seats are often used in the baggage compartments of interurban cars and in the corners of city cars having entrance or exit doors which are in use only when running in one direction.

Follower Plate. See Drawbar Follower Plate.

Foot Board. See Running Board.

Foot Gong. Figs. 939, 941, etc. An alarm gong sounded by depressing a foot pedal in the platform floor, as distinguished from a roof gong (Fig. 943) mounted on top of the platform hood and struck by pulling on a cord which hangs down in front of the motorman.

Foot Rail. See Foot Rest.

Foot Rest. 97, Fig. 341. A wooden slat or rod under a cross seat serving as a support for the feet of passengers occupying the seat behind. Also called foot rail.

Force. That which tends to change the condition of rest or motion of a mass. See **Electromotive Force.**

Form Wound Coil. An armature coil which is wound on a form to the proper shape for insertion in the core slots, as distinguished from a coil which is wound in place in the slots turn by turn. All railway armature coils are now form wound for convenience of making repairs.

Forsyth Steel Doors and Sashes. Figs. 691-692.

Foundation Brake Gear. The complete assemblage of parts by means of which the force exerted by turning the brake handle or admitting compressed air to the air brake cylinder is transmitted to the brake shoes on the trucks. It includes the body and truck levers and all connecting rods.

Four-Wheel Truck. A **Truck**, which see, having two axles and four wheels. Four-wheel trucks are used exclusively in electric railway service.

Fowler Brush Holder. Fig. 1710.

Frame. (Car Body.) Figs. 250-450. The skeleton structure on which the side panels, floor and roof are placed. The framing of a car body may be divided into the underframe, body frame and roof frame. See **Door Frame, Motor Frame** and **Window Frame.**

Frame Head. See Motor Frame Head.

Freight Car. Figs. 191-201. A general term including all cars used for the transportation of commodities. In electric railway practice a distinction is often made between a freight car which is used for rough bulk freight and an express car which is used for package freight.

Frequency. The number of cycles or complete reversals of the direction of flow of an alternating current per unit of time. Frequencies of 15 and 25 cycles per second are used in railway work.

Fresnel Lens. Fig. 1034. A glass lens for signal lamps and headlights having a plano-convex center surrounded by ring-shaped prisms that project the light rays in parallel beams.

Friction Plate. See Wear Plate.

Friction Tape. A common name for **Insulating Tape,** which see.

Frieze. The upper part of the side of a car between the lower deck eaves and the top of the windows. This space is commonly occupied by the letter board.

Front Door. A door in the end of a car body opening onto the front platform.

Front End. The forward end of a car as referred to its direction of motion. The front end of a single-end car usually differs in construction from the rear end.

Front Platform. The platform at the front end of a car. On double-end cars the front and rear platforms are usually identical in size, arrangement and equipment.

Fulcrum. The point of support of a lever about which it moves. See **Brake Lever Fulcrum.**

Funeral Car. Figs. 97-99. A car built especially for the transportation of funeral parties to cemeteries on the outskirts of a city. They are usually divided into a compartment for the casket and a compartment for the mourners. Used only in a few large cities.

Furring. Small pieces of wood nailed or glued to the frame of a car to support panels or moldings placed outside of them.

Fuse. Figs. 1807-1815. A piece of wire having a low melting point, which is inserted in an electric circuit as a protective device. When an excessive current flows through the circuit the fuse is heated to the melting point and opens the circuit. Fuses are distinguished by the names of the circuits which they protect as lighting fuse, control fuse and main fuse. The latter is placed in the trolley circuit between the trolley and the controller. See **Enclosed Fuse.**

Fuse Block. Fig. 1807. A block of wood, slate or other material on which a fuse and terminals are mounted without covering, as distinguished from a **Fuse Box,** which see.

Fuse Box. Figs. 1804-1815. An enclosed box containing binding posts or terminals to support a fuse wire, with means for readily inserting new fuses when required. Sometimes provided with an **Arc Chute,** which see.

G

Gage. (Of Track.) The distance between the inside of the heads of the two track rails. The standard steam and electric railway track gage is 4 ft. 8½ in., but 3 ft. 6 in. and 5 ft. 2½ in. gages are also used by street railway companies in a few cities.

Gain. A groove cut out of one timber to receive the end of another timber which is to be framed into it.

Gap. See Air Gap.

Garland Ventilator. Figs. 1360-1366.

Garton-Daniels Lightning Arrester. Figs. 1820-1822.

Gas-Electric Car. Figs. 34 and 188. A self-propelled car carrying a gasoline-engine driven dynamo which supplies current to motors mounted on the trucks, as in an ordinary trolley car. A storage battery is sometimes used in connection with the self-contained power plant to supply current during periods of acceleration and it is recharged, when the car is standing and the dynamo is running light. Gas-electric cars are equipped with standard control apparatus for varying the speed of the motors. They have been used by only a few companies in an experimental way.

Gasket. A thin sheet of compressible material such as rubber or soft metal placed between the two surfaces of a metallic joint to prevent leakage. A bell-mouth gasket is used to surround a wire leading out of a weather-proof box or case, as for example a contactor box.

Gasoline Motor Car. Figs. 186-187. A self-propelled car which is driven by a gasoline engine mounted in the car body or on the truck, and connected with gears or chains and sprockets to the driving wheels.

Gate. Fig. 690. A slatted door used to close an opening. A **Platform Gate,** which see, is used instead of a paneled or glazed door to close the opening between the body and vestibule corner posts above the steps.

Gear. Figs. 1518-1530. A toothed wheel or disc pressed or keyed on the axle of a motor truck and engaging with the teeth on a smaller wheel or pinion mounted on the end of the motor armature shaft. The wheel of larger diameter is commonly called the gear, while the smaller wheel with which it engages is called a pinion. Railway motor gears are made of tough steel and are either split in half and bolted together and keyed on the axle or made solid and pressed and keyed on. See **Pinion.**

Gear Case. Figs. 1535-1540. A malleable iron, sheet metal or wooden case completely enclosing the gear and pinion of a railway motor to exclude dirt and water. It is supported by a gear case bracket formed on the motor frame.

Gear Case Bolt. C, Fig. 1657. A bolt used to fasten together the two halves of a gear case.

Gear Case Bracket. 15, Figs. 1659-1661. A projection on a railway motor frame to which a gear case is bolted.

Gear Case Safety Strap. A steel strap fitted around the two halves of a gear case and its supporting bracket in such a way that if the bolts holding the lower half of the case should break or the nuts should come off the case could not fall on the track.

Gear Fit. The length on the surface of a motor axle which is turned to fit into the hub of the gear.

Gear Grease. A thick, pasty lubricant for the teeth of motor gears and pinions.

Gear Ratio. The ratio between the number of teeth on the armature pinion and the number of teeth on the axle gear. It expresses the relative speed of rotation of the armature and the axle.

Geared Brake. Figs. 577-587. A form of hand brake in which the brake shaft is connected to the winding drum with reduction gearing so as to decrease the speed of winding up the brake chain but at the same time increase the pull on the chain with a given force applied on the brake handle. Another type of geared brake (Figs. 573-575) uses a vertical hand wheel geared to the top of the brake shaft with bevel gears.

General Electric Air Brakes. Figs. 544-559.

General Electric Motors. Figs. 1645-1657.

Giant Geared Brake. Fig. 577.

Gibson Retaining Ring. Figs. 1638-1640. A type of fastening for the tires of steel-tired wheels in which a light, steel ring is riveted over in suitable grooves in the wheel center and the tire. No bolts or rivets passing through the center and the tire are used.

Girth. Another name for a **Belt Rail**, which see.

Glass. See **Window Glass**.

Globe Ventilator. Fig. 1351. An automatic exhaust ventilator of semi-spherical shape, which is sometimes used as a roof ventilator on cars.

Glue. An adhesive substance prepared from the hoofs, bones and hides of animals. It is melted in hot water before use, and is extensively employed in car building for fastening together small wooden parts of the car body, such as moldings, furring, panels, etc.

Gold Electric Car Heaters. Figs. 1107-1131.

Gondola Car. Figs. 230-232. A car with sides and ends, but no roof. Used for hauling coal, ballast and other rough bulk freight.

Gong. Figs. 939-949. A loud-sounding bell mounted under the platform floor and used to warn pedestrians and drivers of vehicles of the approach of a car. It is struck by a clapper actuated by a foot pedal projecting through the floor of the platform near the base of the controller. On some cars the gong is mounted on the platform hood, and is sounded by pulling a cord which hangs in front of the motorman. Multiple-stroke foot gongs and pneumatic gong ringers are sometimes used to give a number of strokes in quick succession.

Gong Clapper. A pivoted and counterweighted hammer, with which a gong is struck to cause it to emit sound.

Gong Pedal. A short stem projecting through the platform floor, which, when depressed by the foot, raises the gong clapper against the gong.

Gong Ringer. See **Pneumatic Gong Ringer**.

Gothic Sash. A half-elliptic sash of plain or art glass, sometimes used above a pair of twin side windows.

Gould Storage Battery. Figs. 1833-1834.

Governor. See **Pump Governor**.

Governor Synchronizing System. See **Pump Governor Synchronizing System**.

Grab Handle. 69, Figs. 259-370; Figs. 899-916. A vertical handle secured to the body or platform corner post above the platform steps to provide a hand hold for passengers when boarding or alighting. Made of hard wood or brass tubing. On cross-bench open cars grab handles are usually applied to the outside of each side post.

Grab Handle Socket. 70, Figs. 259-370; Figs. 903-910. A casting attached to a body post in which is inserted one end of a wooden grab handle.

Graduated Release. In the plain automatic air brake the pressure in the brake cylinder is entirely exhausted when the brakes start to release, and another application must be made to bring the pressure up to a lower point than was reached during the first application. With improved apparatus the cylinder pressure can be released as gradually as it is applied, and held at any desired point. This is accomplished by using an auxiliary train line called a control pipe, which feeds air to the auxiliary reservoirs during release. To release the brakes partially, the brake pipe pressure is increased slightly. This causes the feed port from the control pipe to open and recharge the auxiliary reservoir, at the same time opening the brake cylinder to atmosphere. As soon as the auxiliary reservoir pressure has again equalized with the brake pipe pressure the recharge ceases and the exhaust of the brake cylinder to atmosphere is cut off. This may be repeated until the brake cylinder pressure is entirely exhautsed.

Graduating Valve. A small valve inside of a triple valve, which serves to open the feed connection between the auxiliary reservoir and the brake cylinder in a service application. It closes the connection when the brake pipe and auxiliary reservoir pressures have equalized. A gradual application of the brakes is thereby secured by making successive small reductions in the brake pipe pressure.

Graphite. A form of crystalline carbon extensively used for motor brushes on account of its lubricating qualities.

Gravity Brake Handle. Figs. 569-570. A ratchet brake handle in which the ratchet pawls engage by gravity and not by spring pressure.

Gray Iron Brake Shoe. Fig. 1484. A brake shoe made of soft cast iron.

Grid. Fig. 1747. A resistance unit in the form of an iron plate, providing a long, continuous path for the flow of current. Usually a casting composed of a continuous strip bent back on itself a number of times. See **Rheostat**.

Griffin Wheels. Figs. 1602-1605.

Grooving. (Of Commutators.) See **Slotting**.

Ground. An electrical connection to the earth or track rails to complete the path for the flow of electricity from the trolley wire back to the power house. The usual method of grounding motors is to connect the fields on one side to the truck bolster or side frame.

Ground Cable. The cable connecting one side of a motor to the truck frame and ground.

Guard. Any piece designed to protect another piece from abrasion or breakage.

See **Door Guard,**   **Fender Rail Guard.**
    Dust Guard,   **Window Guard.**

Guard Arm. The projecting arm of an automatic coupler head which guides the knuckles into engagement with each other and prevents their lateral displacement when coupled.

Guard Rail. 68, Figs. 259-260. A railing or wire or rod screen on the outside of the posts of an open car to prevent passengers on the inside seats from falling out. The guard rail on double-end open cars is usually made of a board about 3 in. wide which can be raised or lowered between the side posts and the grab handles. When down it rests on the grab handle brackets, and when raised it is held under the eaves by spring catches in the body corner posts.

Guard Rail Catch. 86, Fig. 260. A spring catch inserted in the body corner posts of an open car to hold the guard rail up under the eaves.

Guide. See **Bell Cord Guide, Dead Lever Guide**.

Guiding Wheel. More properly **Pony Wheel**, which see.

Gusset Plate. 4, Fig. 1368. A small flat metal plate used to reinforce a joint between intersecting members of a framework, as, for example, an end sill and a side sill. Bent knee irons serve the same purpose and are more commonly employed in electric car construction.

Gutta Percha. A hard resinous gum exuded from a tropical tree. It has a high electrical resistance and is extensively used for insulation and in the compounding of special insulating materials. Unlike rubber, it has little or no elasticity.

H

Half-Ball Brake Hanger. Figs. 1476-1478.

Half-Convertible Car. Figs. 81-82. A car with cross seats, in which the left-hand side is built the same as a closed car and the right-hand side is built like a convertible car, with removable panels and sashes. Such a car is suitable only for single-end operation.

Half-Elliptic Spring. Fig. 1571. A spring made up of one set of curved flat bars, supported in the center and carrying the load at the ends. See **Elliptic Spring.**

Half Open and Closed Car. Figs. 28, 84-88. A car having a closed section or compartment at one end and an open side section at the other end. Used only in mild climates. See **California Type Car.**

Half-Vestibule Platform. A platform enclosed on the end and one side, but having no door to close the opening over the step. See Fig. 39.

Ham Sander. Fig. 1230.

Hand Brake. The assemblage of parts by means of which pressure can be applied to the brake shoes on the wheels by turning a brake wheel or handle on the platform. Practically every car is equipped with hand brakes, even if also equipped with some type of power brake. The hand brakes are connected to the same truck brake rigging as the power brakes, but may be applied independently.

Hand Control. Figs. 1715-1757. A term sometimes used to distinguish control apparatus in which the rate of acceleration is regulated by successive movements of the controller handle from automatic multiple-unit control apparatus, in which only one movement of the controller handle is required, the various control switches opening and closing automatically in regular sequence thereafter. The terms **Drum Controller** and **Platform Controller** are used to distinguish controllers in which the main motor circuits are made and broken inside of the controller case mounted on the platform as distinguished from mastercontrollers used with multiple-unit equipments, in which only the small control currents are broken by the contacts inside of the controller, and the main motor circuits are made and broken by switches or contactors mounted under the car body.

Hand Hold. Figs. 899-916. A handle applied to the side or roof of a car to be grasped by the hand. A **Grab Handle,** which see. See also **Roof Hand Hold.**

Hand Pole. See **Hand Strap Pole.**

Hand Rail. A horizontal grab handle. See **Body Hand Rail.**

Hand Strap Pole. A round wooden rod mounted in brackets just below the deck sill. Straps are suspended from this rod to be grasped by passengers who are required to stand in the aisle.

Hand Strap Pole Brackets. Figs. 853-866. Stout metal brackets attached under the deck sill to support a hand strap pole. They frequently combine, also, the functions of bell cord and register rod guides.

Hand Straps. Figs. 868-869. Leather slings suspended from a hand strap pole to be grasped by passengers standing in the aisle.

Hand Wheel. A **Brake Wheel,** which see.

Handle. That which is grasped by the hand to move the piece to which it is attached. See **Brake Handle, Controller Handle.**

Hanger. A rod, bar or strap by which one part is suspended from another. See **Brake Hanger, Door Hanger, Swing Hanger.**

Hanging Door. A **Sliding Door,** which see.

Hartshorn Shade Roller. Fig. 647. A spring roller, on which a window curtain is wound. The spiral spring inside of the roller is coiled around a shaft mounted in brackets in the window frame and when the curtain is pulled down the spring is in torsion. Centrifugal pawls on the end of the roller prevent the spring from turning the roller to wind up the curtain. When the curtain is given a quick pull downward, and then released, the pawls fly out of engagement and allow the spring to turn the roller and wind up the curtain. As soon as the roller ceases to revolve the pawls fall back into engagement and prevent further movement.

Hasp. See **Door Hasp.**

Hat Hook. See **Coat and Hat Hook.**

H-B Universal Life Guard. Figs. 712-713.

Headlight. Figs. 1028-1058. A lamp with a reflector behind it, mounted on the front dasher or on top of the front platform hood, so as to cast a beam of light on the track ahead of the car. Electric incandescent and arc lamps are usually used on electric railway cars, but oil lamps are also used by some companies. See **Arc Headlight.**

Headlight Bracket. A bracket on the outside of the dasher used for attaching a removable oil or arc headlight. In many types of headlights brackets which fit over the top of the dasher are attached to the back of the headlight case.

Headlight Dimmer. Fig. 1040. A wire gauze screen sometimes placed over the glass in the front of an arc headlight to reduce its brilliancy when the car is running through city streets. An opaque curtain with a small hole in the center is also used. See **Luminous Arc Headlight.**

Headlight Resistance. Fig. 1041. Resistance inserted in the circuit of an arc headlight to cut down the trolley voltage. It is usually mounted under the car, and the headlight connection plugs at each end of the car are connected through it so that one set of resistance is made to serve when the headlight is used on either end of the car.

Headlight Screen. See **Headlight Dimmer.**

Headlight Switch. A switch in the motorman's cab, by which the electric headlight can be turned on or off. Where combined arc and incandescent headlights are used a single switch is used to turn either lamp on and extinguish the other or to turn both off.

Headlining. 53 and 54. Figs. 259-370. The thin layer of veneer, composite board or painted canvas which forms the inside ceiling of a car roof.

Head Piece. More properly an **End Plate,** which see.

Head Roll. (Car Seat.) The padded roll across the top of a high seat back. See Figs. 1259-1260.

Heat Treated Axle. An **Axle,** which see, in which the steel has been given special heat treatment to thoroughly and uniformly anneal it and render it strong and tough against fatigue. Such axles cost more than plain hammered or cold rolled stock, but are specially adapted for heavy motor trucks.

Heater. Figs. 1094-1157. Any apparatus for warming the interior of a car. See **Electric Heater** and **Hot Water Heater.**

Heater Closet. A small closet at one end of an interurban car in which is mounted a hot water heater. The sides and floor on the inside are usually sheathed with sheet iron to prevent scorching of the woodwork.

Heater Coil. (1) A number of concentric turns of iron or steel tubing placed in the fire pot of a hot water heater. The heater pipes are connected to the ends of the coil and the water is heated as it circulates through the coil.
(2) Figs. 1113-1119. A spiral coil of resistance wire in an electric car heater, which becomes hot and radiates the heat when a current of electricity is passed through it.

Heater Deflector. Figs. 1129-1131. A curved steel sheet attached under the overhang of a longitudinal seat bottom to deflect the hot air which rises from the panel heaters set in the seat riser.

Heater Pipe. A pipe through which hot water is circulated to warm a car by radiation. It is usually located along the truss plank on each side of the car, but occasionally is looped under each cross seat.

Heater Pipe Casing. A shelf along the side of the car over the heater pipes to prevent passengers from scorching their feet on the hot pipes. It may be a continuous board or a short metal shelf between each pair of seats.

Heater Switch. See **Electric Heater Switch**.

Heater Train Wire. A power cable connected by jumpers from a motor car having a trolley or third-rail collector to a trail car and carrying current to supply the heaters in the trail car.

Heater Train Line Jumper. Figs. 1134-1135. A **Jumper**, which see, connecting the heater train line cables on two adjoining cars.

Hedley Anti-Climber. Figs. 590-597.

Height of Steps. See **Platform Step**.

Hensley Trolley Harps. Figs. 1929-1939.

Herring-Bone Gear. A form of toothed gear wheel commonly used for the reduction gears of motor-driven air compressors. The teeth, instead of being cut square across the periphery of the gear, are in the shape of a right angle, the pitch lines being at an angle of 45 deg. with the center line of the shaft. There is less lost motion and noise with a gear of this type than with an ordinary spur gear. See Fig. 545.

High Back Seat. Figs. 1259-1260, 1283, 1295. A car seat with an extra high back, and head roll.

High-Tension Direct-Current System. An electric railway equipment designed to use direct current for propulsion at a trolley or third-rail potential of 1200 volts or higher, thereby reducing transmission losses and substations. The car motors may be wound to carry the full trolley voltage when connected in parallel, in which case they will operate at only half speed on sections in cities and towns when the trolley potential is reduced to 600 volts. The more common arrangement is to connect a four-motor car equipment in the ordinary series-parallel combination when using 600-volt current in cities and towns, and by means of a commutating switch connect the four motors in two groups of two motors each when passing to the 1200-volt sections. The four motors thus operate substantially as a two-motor equipment, two motors being always in series with each other. This permits the motors to be insulated for only 600 volts and reduces any tendency to spark at the brushes. The commutating switch may be operated by hand or pneumatically by a motorman's valve, and is provided with an interlock which prevents operation of the contactors if the connections for 1200-volt operation are not properly made. Commutating pole motors of ordinary construction are used with 1200-volt equipment, and the control apparatus, trolley, etc., are similar in design and construction to standard 600-volt equipment. To furnish 600-volt current for the control circuits, lights and air compressor motor when running on 1200-volt sections, a small motor-generator or **Dynamotor**, which see, is installed under the car body. When operating on 600-volt current the dynamotor does not run.

Hinge. See **Door Hinge**.

Holland Trolley Base. Fig. 1874.

Holophane Globe. A glass lamp globe formed with a large number of angular reflecting surfaces to concentrate and thoroughly diffuse the light thrown in one direction. Such globes are coming into use for interurban cars on account of the superior quality of illumination which they afford.

Hood. See **Platform Hood**. **Deck Hood**.

Hood Headlight. Figs. 1035, 1037, 1049. An incandescent lamp headlight mounted on top of a platform hood.

Hood Switch. Figs. 1752, 1755, 1757. A term applied to an automatic **Circuit Breaker**, which see, mounted under the platform hood above the controller.

Hopper. A **Dry Closet**, which see.

Hopper Bottom Car. A car with a floor sloping toward a central hopper closed with drop doors. The load can be discharged by gravity by opening the drop doors. Used for hauling coal and ashes and ballast.

Hopper Car. A **Hopper Bottom Car**, which see.

Hopper Door. See **Drop Door**.

Horse Car. A street car drawn by horses or mules.

Horse Power. The commercial unit of power or rate of doing work. One horse power represents work done at the rate of 33,000 ft. lb. per minute. One horse power is equal to 745.941 watts.

Hose. See **Brake Hose**.

Hose Clamp. A split ring with tightening nut used to clamp a brake hose on a nipple.

Hose Coupling. See **Brake Hose Coupling**.

Hot-Air Heater. Figs. 1094, 1106. A device for heating cars by forcing hot air through ducts having openings under the seats. Cold air is drawn up between the inner and outer shells of a coal stove and after being warmed is forced into the distributing ducts by a small motor-driven fan mounted above the heater. The warm air rises from under the seats and is exhausted through the deck sash ventilators.

Hot-Water Heater. Figs. 1095-1099. A coal stove in the fire pot of which is a coil of pipe through which water is circulated. The hot water passes through heater pipes down one side of the car and back again on the other side to the heater. An expansion drum above the heater contains a supply of water to make up for slight leaks and also serves the purpose of an expansion chamber to relieve the closed system of circulating pipes from excessive pressure.

Hot Water Pipe. See **Heater Pipe**.

Hub. The central boss on a wheel or gear, into which is fitted the shaft or axle on which it is mounted.

Hudson & Bowring Life Guard. Figs. 712-713.

Hydraulic Brake. A type of power brake apparatus for single cars, in which the pressure on the brake shoes is applied by a hydraulic cylinder and pistons. Water is forced into the cylinder between two oppositely moving pistons, by means of a force pump mounted in the motorman's cab. When the pressure is released by moving the pump handle forward beyond the working stroke the water in the cylinder flows back to a supply tank and the pistons are returned to their normal position by coil springs.

Hydraulic Jack. A lifting jack consisting of a hydraulic plunger working in a cylinder, and a small hand pump for forcing the liquid into the cylinder below the plunger.

Hysteresis. Friction between molecules of iron accompanying changes in magnetic stress. An appreciable amount of energy is expended in magnetizing and then demagnetizing a mass of iron, such as an armature core, and this loss takes place many times a minute as the parts of the surface of the armature successively pass in front of and leave the field poles. The energy is dissipated in the form of heat. By building the core up of soft iron laminations the hysteresis loss is greatly reduced.

I

I-Beam. A rolled steel beam having a web and two projecting flanges giving it a section approximating the letter I. Such beams are extensively used in the underframes of long cars for center and side sills and needlebeams.

Ice Box. (Refrigerator Car.) A box on the inside of a refrigerator car in which ice is stored to cool the contents of the car. The ice is usually inserted through doors in the side or roof near the end.

Ice Leveler. Fig. 1324. A device for removing the accumulation of snow and ice between the rails so as to clear the motor frames. It consists of heavy iron bar attached under the front end of a snow plow or sweeper, on which are bolted a number of tool-steel flanged knives, or teeth. Each tooth is held in place by two special tenthead bolts and can be removed for sharpening or replacement, independently of the other teeth on the bar.

Ideal Trolley Catcher. Fig. 1338.

Illuminated Air Gage. An **Air Gage**, which see, the dial of which is illuminated at night by a small incandescent lamp.

Illuminated Destination Sign. Figs. 656-658. See **Destination Sign**.

Impedance. In an alternating-current circuit, that property which opposes the flow of the current. In applying Ohm's law to alternating-current circuits, the quantity of electricity is equal to the electromotive force divided by the impedance.

Imperial Headlights. Figs. 1051-1058.

Impregnation. A method of thoroughly insulating armature and field coils by filling all of the interstices with a plastic insulating varnish, which is solidified by baking in an oven. The vacuum process uses a vacuum tank for dipping the coils to insure that the compound penetrates to every part of the coil.

Incandescent Electric Lamp. A closed glass globe from which the air has been exhausted, containing a carbon or metallic filament. The passage of an electric current through this filament heats it to incandescence. Street railway car lamps are usually of 16 candle power on 110 volts. They are connected in series, five lamps to the circuit, so that on 550-volt trolley current each lamp is subjected to only 110 volts.

Incandescent Headlight. Figs. 1031-1037, 1048-1050, 1055-1058. A **Headlight,** which see, in which one or more incandescent electric lamps are mounted.

India Rubber. See **Rubber.**

Indicating Register. Figs. 1159-1160. A **Fare Register,** which see, which indicates the kind or amount of fare paid.

Inductance. "That property in virtue of which a finite electromotive force, acting on a circuit, does not immediately generate the full current due to its resistance, and when the electromotive force is withdrawn, time is required for the current strength to fall to zero."—Fleming. Inductance is the common term for the property of self-induction.

Induction. An influence exerted by a magnetic field on a neighboring body or conductor. Current is generated in the armature coils of a generator by induction as the coils pass through the magnetic lines of force opposite the poles. The current flowing in the secondary of a transformer is likewise an induced current.

Induction Regulator. See **Single-Phase Control Apparatus.**

Inside Cornice. See **Cornice.**

Inside Hung Brakes. Figs. 1480-1481. Truck brakes in which the brake shoes bearing on both wheels are mounted between the wheels. See **Outside Hung Brakes.**

Inside Hung Motor. A motor which is supported between the truck bolster and the axle to which it is geared. See **Motor Suspension.**

Inside Lining. 44, Figs. 259-370. The layer of boards applied on the side of a car inside of the posts below the windows.

Inside Roof. The **Headlining,** which see.

Inside Sheathing. More properly **Inside Lining,** which see.

Inside Window Panel. A panel on the interior of a car between the windows.

Inside Window Sill. A projecting strip of wood at the bottom of the window frame on the inside of the car. Where the sash is arranged to drop the inside window sill is hinged and can be lifted up to expose the sash pocket in the side of the car.

Inside Window Stop. A narrow strip of wood nailed to the face of the window casing to form, with the outside stop or sash parting strip, a groove in which the window sash slides.

Inspection Plate. 24, Figs. 1659-1661. A removable plate covering a hole in a motor frame through which the brushes and commutator may be inspected without removing the motor from the truck.

Instruction Car. A car equipped for use in instructing motormen in the proper handling of motors and brakes. Such cars are used by only a few of the largest railways.

Insulated Paper. Plain or varnished paper having high dielectric strength, used for insulation in forming motor coils and other similar purposes.

Insulated Wire. A metal wire coated with one or more layers of cotton, silk or rubber compound. Insulated wire is used for connecting all of the electrical apparatus in a car, from the trolley base to the motors.

Insulating Tape. A narrow woven fabric impregnated with an adhesive insulating compound, used for wrapping exposed joints in insulated wires and many other similar purposes. It is put up in rolls for convenient handling.

Insulating Varnish. A liquid compound of high dielectric strength used for insulating electric coils and similar purposes where a thin, continuous and moisture-proof insulated coating is required. Many formulæ for insulating varnishes have been devised, using different bases and vehicles. Some are composed principally of linseed oil, and others of asphaltum. They may be compounded for quick drying at ordinary temperatures or for baking at temperatures up to 200 deg. The varnish may be applied to coils by painting with a brush, by dipping in an open tank, or by impregnation with the vacuum process. See **Impregnation.**

Insulation. Any material having high resistivity to the flow of an electric current which is used to electrically insulate one conductor from another. Cotton, silk, rubber, linseed oil varnishes, asbestos, mica, porcelain, glass and many special vegetable and mineral compounds are extensively employed as insulation in the manufacture of electrical apparatus and machinery.

Insulator. An insulated mounting for an electric conductor.

Interlock. (1) A mechanical device in a controller arranged to prevent the movement of the reverse handle unless the main controller cylinder is in the "off" position, and to prevent the movement of the main cylinder unless the reversing cylinder is in the full forward or reverse position. See **Controller Star Wheel.**

(2) In a multiple-unit control switch group, the contacts through which the control circuits are carried on each contactor or unit switch. These contacts are so arranged that the contactors must open and close in proper sequence; that is, the control circuit of one contactor is carried through the interlock of the preceding contactor, and the second contactor cannot be operated until the first has performed its proper function.

Intermediate Cross Tie. A timber or steel section framed across the bottom of the longitudinal sills between the bolster and the needlebeam. It should not be confused with a floor joist or **Bridging,** which see, which is framed in between the sills. An intermediate cross tie is seldom used, except on very long cars.

Intermediate Sills. 103. Figs. 259-370. Longitudinal main members of an underframe sometimes placed between the side sills and the center sills.

Intermediate Window Post. 13, Figs. 259-370. A light window post separating a pair of twin windows.

International Fare Register. Figs. 1158-1159.

Interpole. Figs. 1679-1681. One of the auxiliary magnetic poles of an **Interpole Motor,** which see. The name commutating pole more nearly describes the purpose of this part.

Interpole Motor. Figs. 1662-1667. A term applied by the Westinghouse Electric & Manufacturing Company to motors built with auxiliary poles between the main field poles to create a magnetic field of sufficient strength to properly reverse the current in the armature coils short circuited during commutation. Motors of the same type are termed by the General Electric Company, **Commutating Pole Motors,** which see.

Interurban Car. Any electric car used in long distance high-speed service, as distinguished from city and suburban cars. Interurban passenger cars are built in lengths up to 65 ft. of very heavy and substantial construction, closely resembling steam railroad coaches. Various types are illustrated in Figs. 100-201.

Inverted Arch Bar. One of the members of a diamond arch bar truck side frame next below the arch bar. It rests on top of the journal boxes and passes under the columns.

Inverted Body Truss Rod. An **Overhang Truss Rod,** which see.

J

Jack. A mechanical contrivance for lifting weights. Jacks are sometimes carried on cars as part of the emergency equipment. See **Ratchet Jack, Hydraulic Jack, Screw Jack.**

Jamb. (Of a Door.) One of the vertical posts or boards forming the sides of a door opening.

Janney Radial Coupler. Figs. 618-620.

Jaw. See **Pedestal Jaw.**

Jewell Car Stove. Figs. 1105-1106.

Jewett Truck. Fig. 1421.

Johnson Fare Box. Fig. 1203.

Journal. That part of a shaft or axle which rotates in a bearing. Specifically in car construction, the end of an axle which projects beyond the wheel hub, and on which a journal bearing rests. Axles are usually designated by the dimensions of the journals as a 5-in. x 9-in. axle.

Journal Bearing. Fig. 1556. A bearing for the journal of a car axle. The American Electric Railway Engineering Association has adopted standard designs for journal boxes for journals 3¾ in x 7 in., 4¼ in. x 8 in., 5 in. x 9 in. and 5½ in. x 10 in. These designs correspond closely with the standards of the Master Car Builders' Association. The journal bearing is semi-cylindrical and rests on top of the axle journal. It is held in place in the box by a wide, flat key or wedge which is inserted on top of it.

Journal Bearing Key. See **Journal Bearing Wedge.**

Journal Bearing Wedge. Figs. 1559-1560. A broad, flat key which fits on top of a journal bearing and supports the top of the journal box.

Journal Box. 4, Figs. 1388-1390; Figs. 1553-1567, 1968-1982. A cast iron, cast steel, or malleable iron box enclosing a journal bearing and wedge, and containing a suitable lubricant in the cellar formed in the bottom. The truck frame or the ends of the equalizer bars rest on the top of the journal boxes. See **Journal Bearing.**

Journal Box Bolts. The bolts inserted on each side of the journal boxes of an arch bar truck to secure the arch bars and the tie bar.

Journal Box Guides. See **Pedestal.**

Journal Box Lid. Fig. 1566. A hinged, bolted or pivoted cover on the outside of a journal box which can be opened to inspect and oil the journal or to remove the bearing and wedge.

Journal Box Lid Bolt. (1) A bolt used to fasten a journal box lid to the box.
(2) The hinge pin of a hinged lid.

Journal Box Lid Spring. A flat or coil spring used to hold a journal box lid securely in place when closed.

Journal Box Spring. A spring supporting the truck frame and resting directly on the journal box. More properly, **Pedestal Spring,** which see.

Journal Packing. Wool or cotton waste inserted in the oil cellar of a journal box and pressing up against the under side of the journal. It forms a wick to carry the oil from the bottom of the box to the surface of the journal by capillary attraction.

Jumper. Figs. 1765, 1793. A short conductor cable used to connect the electrical circuits on two cars which are coupled together. Also called a coupler. The jumper is fitted on each end with a contact plug. One of these plugs is inserted in a fixed socket in the end of the car, which forms a terminal for the car wiring. Jumpers are named from the circuits which they connect as control jumper, power jumper, light jumper.

Junction Box. Fig. 1791. See **Connection Box.**

K

K-Controller. Figs. 1715-1718. The letter K is used to designate a general type of hand-operated platform controllers of moderate capacity for two or four-motor equipments, giving series and parallel combinations with external resistance in the circuit. See **Controller.**

K. W. The common abbreviation for **Kilowatt,** which see.

Kalamazoo Trolley Wheels. Figs. 1940-1943.

Karbolith. A hard composition cement sometimes used for the surface covering of car floors.

Keeper. A metal catch plate on a door jamb with which a door lock bolt engages.

Kerite. A durable and efficient insulating compound composed of crude kerite and pure Para rubber, used for insulating electric wires and cables.

Kewanee Unions. Figs. 566-567.

Key. (1) A removable metal handle used to move the bolt of a door lock.
(2) A **Journal Bearing Wedge,** which see.

Key Hole Escutcheon. A metal plate surrounding a key hole in a door.

Keyless Lamp Socket. Figs. 873-877. See **Lamp Socket.**

Keystone Cord Connector. Figs. 746-747.

Keystone Pneumatic Gong Ringer. Fig. 940.

Keystone Pneumatic Sander. Figs. 1213-1218.

Kicking Coil. Figs. 1825-1826. A protective device inserted in the main power circuit between the circuit breaker and the controller to provide inductive resistance to a lighting discharge. It consists of a few turns of heavy wire about a wooden core.

Kilowatt. One thousand watts. A kilowatt is equivalent to 1.34 horse power. See **Watt.**

King Bolt. A **Center Pin,** which see.

King Post. A single post or spreader placed in the center of a trussed beam and separating the truss rod from the beam. If two such posts are used so that the truss rod lies parallel to the beam between them, they are termed queen posts. Body truss rods are usually braced with queen posts dropped from the two needlebeams.

Kirby-Neal Incandescent Headlight. Figs. 1031-1034.

Kling's Ratchet Brake Handle. Fig. 571.

Knee. An L-shaped timber, casting or forging used to strengthen a joint between two members of a framework. See **Platform Knee, Sill Knee Iron, Gusset Plate.**

Knee Iron. See **Knee.**

Knife Switch. Figs. 1137-1139. A device for making or breaking an electric circuit. It consists of a hinged flat blade which is inserted between two spring leaves. Knife switches are designated as single-pole or double-pole, according to the number of blades which are attached to one handle and are moved simultaneously.

Knob. See **Door Knob.**

Knuckle. (M. C. B. Type Automatic Coupler.) A pivoted casting mounted in the coupler head which hooks around the knuckle of the engaging coupler and is locked in position to effect a coupling.

Knuckle Lock. A casting within the head of an automatic coupler which drops in front of the tail of the knuckle by gravity when dislodged by impact and locks the knuckle in place to prevent uncoupling.

Knuckle Opener. A device used in some types of M. C. B. automatic couplers to open the knuckle by lifting the locking pin. Its use makes it unnecessary to go between the cars to open the knuckles by hand so that they will engage when brought together.

Knuckle Pin. A vertical shaft mounted in the head of an automatic coupler and passing through a hole in the body of the knuckle, thus forming a hinge for the knuckle.

Knutson Trolley Retriever. Fig. 1339.

L

Lag Screw. A bolt with a square head and a shank formed with a wood screw thread and a sharpened point. They are used to screw into wood by turning with a wrench fitted on the square head.

Laminated Pole Piece. A **Field Pole,** which see, made up of thin sheet iron stampings bolted together. The object in using laminated pole pieces is to reduce the hysteresis loss in the magnet core.

Lamp. A source of light. **Incandescent Electric Lamps,** which see, are universally used for illuminating the interior of electric railway cars. See **Tail Lamp, Marker Lamp.**

Lamp Base. Figs. 875-877. A porcelain or metal collar surrounding an incandescent lamp socket by means of which the socket is secured to the wall or ceiling.

Lamp Burner. In an oil lamp, the wick holder and means for turning the wick up or down.

Lamp Cluster. Fig. 872. A group of two or more incandescent lamps mounted on a single bracket. Ceiling clusters of three or five lamps are commonly used for the illumination of the upper decks of electric cars. They are usually mounted under a circular white porcelain reflector.

Lamp Globe. A cup-shaped piece of glass surrounding a lamp to soften the glare or concentrate the light rays in one direction. See **Holophane Globe.**

Lamp Holder. See **Flag Holder.**

Lamp Socket. Figs. 873-874. A threaded porcelain outlet into which an incandescent lamp bulb is screwed to connect it in the circuit. Sockets for use in electric railway cars are usually of the keyless type, the individual lamps on a circuit being turned off by unscrewing them part of a turn and thus breaking the contacts in the bottom of the sockets.

Lancaster Brake Shoes. Figs. 1505-1508.

Lantern. Figs. 1092-1093. A portable oil lamp, the chimney of which is surrounded with a metal guard. Carried on interurban cars and used for giving signals at night.

Latch. Figs. 871-872. A catch for a door having a beveled spring bolt which engages automatically with the keeper when the door is closed. A **Lock,** which see, has a dead bolt moved by turning a key.

Lateral Motion. See **Swing Motion.**

Lavatory. A small compartment on some interurban passenger cars which contains a soil hopper and occasionally a wash basin.

Lead. See **White Lead.**

Lead. A wire connecting one piece of electrical apparatus with another, as a **Motor Lead,** which see.

Lead and Oil Process. See **Paint.**

Lead Battery. See **Storage Battery.**

Leather. Tanned animal hide. Leather and imitations of leather are occasionally used for upholstering car seats, especially in smoking compartments.

Leather Sash Lift. Figs. 992-993. A small leather flap attached to a sash frame by a flat brass plate and used to lift the sash up or down.

Leather Sash Lift Plate. Figs. 990-991. A small rectangular brass plate with beveled edges, screwed to a sash frame and used to fasten a leather sash lift.

Lens. A piece of glass or crystal ground to a semi-spherical surface on one or both sides and placed in front of a source of light to concentrate the light rays into a solid beam. Lenses are used in all signal lamps and often in incandescent electric headlights.

Letter Board. 56, Figs. 259-370. A wide board on the outside of a passenger car body just below the eaves. The name or initials of the railway owning the car is often painted on this board; hence the name.

Lettering Panel. Any outside panel on which is painted the car number or the monogram of the railway company owning the car.

Lever. A beam or bar turning about a fixed point called a fulcrum.

See **Brake Lever,** **Dead Lever,**
Cylinder Lever, **Live Lever.**

Lifeguard. Figs. 712-714. Another name for a **Wheelguard,** or **Fender,** which see.

Lift. See **Sash Lift.**

Lift Sash. A sash arranged to raise into a pocket above the window. See **Drop Sash.**

Lighting Switch. Figs. 880-890, 894. A small snap switch or knife switch, usually combined with a fuse, for controlling the car lights.

Lightning Arrester. Figs. 816-824. A device for protecting the electrical apparatus on a car from the effects of a lightning discharge. It is placed in shunt with the main power circuit between the trolley and the controller, and in most types consists of an air gap in series with a non-inductive resistance connected to ground. The air gap is adjusted to provide a path of less impedance for the discharge to ground than through the electrical apparatus.

Limit Switch. See **Current Limit Relay.**

Limited Car. An interurban car making only a few stops as distinguished from a local car. The term, limited car, has no reference to the type of car used for this service, although the most luxuriously appointed cars are generally assigned to limited runs.

Lindstrom Ratchet Brake Handle. Fig. 576.

Line Car. Figs. 240-244. A work car designed for use in repairing overhead lines. A common type consists of a flat car, in the center of which is a tower surmounted by a working platform. The platform may be raised by a winch to any convenient height for reaching the trolley wire.

Line Switch. Figs. 1783-1784. A group of one or two unit-switches, assembled in a suitable case, for handling main power currents. In a Westinghouse unit-switch control equipment a double line switch is used between the trolley and the switch group which makes the operating connections.

Lining. A layer of boards placed over the framework of a car body to give a smooth surface on the inside. The outside layer of boards is commonly called sheathing. See **Inside Lining, Headlining.**

Link. See **Coupling Link** and **Swing Link.**

Link and Pin Coupler. Figs. 609, 631. A **Coupling Link** and **Coupling Pin,** which see, used to couple two cars together.

Link Hanger. See **Swing Hanger.**

Linseed Oil. Oil extracted by pressing flax seed. It is commonly used as the vehicle for most paints, as it dries in a thin, elastic and impervious film.

Lintel. The top horizontal member of a door or window frame.

Live Cylinder Lever. One of the two **Cylinder Levers,** which see, which is attached to the piston crosshead. The other cylinder lever, which is attached to the pressure head of the brake cylinder, is called the dead cylinder lever. See Fig. 458.

Live Lever. 17 and 18, Figs. 1480-1481. One of the truck brake levers to which the brake connecting rod is attached. With inside hung brakes, the lever nearest the center of the car. See **Dead Lever.**

Live Lever Brake Rod. 51, Figs. 1388-1390.

Live Lever Pin. 49 and 50, Figs. 1388-1390.

Lobdell Cast Steel Wheel. Figs. 1611-1614.

Lock. A fastening for a door, window or other movable part. See **Door Lock, Sash Lock, Knuckle Lock, Interlock.**

Lock Lifter. A device for lifting the lock of an automatic coupler to release the knuckle and permit uncoupling. The handle usually extends out to one or both sides of the car, so that it is unnecessary to go between the cars to uncouple.

Lock Nut. A second nut screwed on a bolt to hold the first nut applied securely in place. See **Nut Lock.**

Lock-on Controller Handle. Figs. 1729-1730.

Locker. A small closet used for the storage of tools and other loose equipment of a car, such as brooms, lanterns and camp stools.

Locomotive. Figs. 443-450. A tractor having no provision for carrying freight or passengers. Electric locomotives are used by a few interurban roads for hauling trains of freight cars. The electric locomotives used for hauling through trains within the electrified zones of steam railroads are equipped with two or more motors aggregating from 1000 hp. to 4000 hp.

Long Broom Sweeper. Figs. 213-214. A type of snow sweeper in which the brooms extend out some distance beyond the trucks on each side. No brush board or wing is used. See **Sweeper**.

Longitudinal Seat. A seat built along the side of a car as distinguished from a cross seat placed at right angles to the car side.

Lower Brake Rod. A rod which connects the lower ends of the truck brake levers on trucks fitted with outside hung brakes. The term bottom truck connection is the common name for this part and is applied also to the compression bar connecting the lower ends of the brake levers of inside hung brakes.

Lower Deck. That part of a car roof between the sides of a car and the monitor or upper deck.

Lower Deck Carline. 21, Figs. 259-370. A **Carline**, which see, forming part of the framing for the lower deck; also called rafter.

Lumen Bronze. A special composition bearing metal used for journal bearings, trolley wheel bushings, etc.

Lumen Trolley Wheel. Fig. 1913.

Luminous Arc Headlight. Figs. 1043-1047, 1051-1052. An electric arc headlight in which the upper electrode is a copper rod and the lower electrode is an iron tube filled with a special composition. A brilliant light is given off by the arc formed when current at about 80 volts passes from the copper or positive electrode to the composition or negative electrode. By reversing the direction of the flow of current and introducing slightly more external resistance, the brilliancy of the arc is greatly dimmed.

Lyon Reinforced Steel Gear Case. Figs. 1537-1538.

M

Magazine. (Hot Water Heater.) A space above the fire pot of some types of heaters to hold a supply of coal which is fed down on the fire by gravity.

Magnet. A body possessing the property of attracting to it another body which has the same property. A body possessing a magnetic field. Magnetic phenomena are closely related to electric phenomena. Thus an iron core on which is wound a number of turns of continuous wire possesses the property of creating a magnetic field when an electric current is sent through the surrounding conductor. A permanent magnet is a bar of iron or steel which contains sufficient residual magnetism to create a magnetic field around itself without excitation.

Magnet Coil. An **Electro-Magnet**, which see.

Magnet Valve. See **Electro-Pneumatic Valve**.

Magnet Wire. Figs. 1712-1714. A copper conductor covered with one or more layers of cotton or other insulating material, wound in opposite directions if more than one layer is used. Magnet wire is used for forming motor field and armature coils and for many similar purposes. The larger sizes of magnet wire, used for railway motors, are usually saturated in some liquid insulating material and the coils are further protected by wrappings of tape or canvas. The smaller sizes of magnet wire are sometimes used without other insulation than the cotton covering. The purest copper, high in conductivity and extremely ductile, must be used in order to permit the wire to be easily wound into any desired shape of coil. The cotton insulation must be firm and adhere to the wire and must be clean and free from injurious oils, knots and breaks. It must be uniform throughout and must not exceed certain well-defined limits of thickness.

Magnetic Blow-Out. A means employed in controllers and other switches to extinguish the arc formed when the contact is broken. A strong magnetic field is maintained around the contact points by an electro-magnet in shunt with the main circuit. The presence of this field effectually repels the arc and thus breaks and extinguishes it.

Magnetic Brake. Fig. 1479. A type of electric car brake in which the retardation is caused by (1) the drag of track magnets on each rail when energized by current from the car motors acting as generators, (2) the pressure of the brake shoes on the wheels resulting from the attraction of the track magnets on the rails which is transmitted and multiplied by a system of levers and (3) the resistance to rotation of the motor armatures when the motors act as generators. The track magnets consist of two steel plates connected by a yoke carrying the magnet coil. The lower edges of the plates are planed and fitted with a wearing shoe shaped to fit the rail head. The magnet shoe is supported between the wheels over the rail head by suitable springs and by toggle arms, which are in turn connected to the wheel brake shoes in such a way that when the magnet shoe is pulled down and drags on the rail the force is transmitted and multiplied as pressure on the wheel brake shoes. A special form of motor controller, known as Type B., is required for magnetic brake equipments. To apply the brakes, the controller handle is moved beyond the "off" position from one to six notches without moving the reverse handle. This cuts out the trolley circuit and reverses the motors so that they run as generators producing a voltage varying with the speed of rotation. The current thus generated is fed through resistance to the track magnets. The resistance used, which is usually divided into six steps, is necessary to regulate the braking power. In cold weather the coils of the electric heaters within the car body are utilized as resistance.

Magnetic Disk Brake. An obsolete form of magnetic brake in which a stationary disk fixed in the motor frame and a revolving disk on the axle are attracted by the action of a magnet coil fixed in the stationary disk. The coil is connected, in series with resistance, to the motor and is energized when the motor runs as a generator. The retardation obtained with this type of brake is due to the negative torque of the motor acting as a generator, the drag due to eddy currents set up in the revolving disk and the sliding friction between the contact surfaces of the two disks.

Magnetic Field. The space surrounding a magnet through which pass the magnetic currents or lines of force.

Magnetism. The property of magnetic bodies which causes them to attract other bodies. According to Ampere's theory, magnetism is caused by the presence of electric currents in the ultimate particles of all magnetizable bodies.

Mail Car. A car for carrying United States mail. See **Postal Car**.

Main Carline. 20, Figs. 259-370. A **Carline**, which see, extending continuously across the lower and upper decks from side plate to side plate. They are usually built up of two sticks of wood and a flat steel plate or bent angle, and therefore are commonly called compound carlines.

Main Fuse. Figs. 1804-1815. A fuse of large current carrying capacity, placed in the main circuit between the trolley and the controller.

Main Reservoir. (Automatic Air Brake.) A large storage tank for compressed air carried on each car equipped with a compressor. The compressor discharges into the main reservoir through a coil of radiating pipes and from the main reservoir air is supplied through the brake valve to the brake pipe. A feed valve inserted between the main reservoir and the brake valve regulates the pressure in the brake pipe. See **Auxiliary Reservoir**.

Main Switch. In a multiple-unit control equipment, a switch placed in the motor circuit of each motor car to cut out all of the electrical apparatus on that car.

Malleable Iron. Cast iron of a special composition which is annealed by packing in pots containing forge scale or other oxide of iron and subjecting it to a bright red heat for from four to six days. Malleable iron castings are not easily broken and may be hammered and bent within moderate limits. They are largely used in car and truck building.

Marker Lamp. Figs. 1059-1091. A **Signal Lamp**, which see, carried on a car to indicate its class and direction of movement. Marker lamps usually are mounted on the vestibule corner posts and have three lenses to display lights to the front side and rear. A **Tail Lamp**, which see, is a powerful lamp with a red lens used to indicate the rear end of a car.

Master Controller. Figs. 1760-1761, 1778-1779. A small platform controller used with multiple-unit control systems Only the current necessary to operate the motor control switches is broken through the contacts in the master controller. The control wires extend throughout a multiple-unit train and the motor control switches under all cars are operated simultaneously by the movement of any master controller. See **Multiple-Unit Control.**

Master Car Builder's Standards. See **M. C. B. Standards.**

Master Governor. Fig. 461. See **Pump Governor Synchronizing System.**

Match Strike. A small metal plate with a roughened surface frequently fastened to the inside window panels of the smoking compartments of interurban cars to be used for striking matches.

Maximum Traction Truck. Figs. 1373-1376, 1406-1408, 1465. A common name for a **Single-Motor Truck,** which see, in which more weight is carried by the driving axle than by the pony axle.

M-B Sand Box. Fig. 1225.

M. C. B. Standards. Standard designs for parts of steam railroad cars adopted by the Master Car Builders' Association, including couplers, wheels, axles and journal boxes, brake shoes and brake heads. They are largely followed in the construction of many interurban cars and trucks.

M. C. B. Type Truck. Figs. 1367-1368, 1385-1394, etc. A four-wheel truck in which the journal boxes are confined in pedestals dropped from the side frames. The bolster rests on elliptic springs supported on a swinging spring plank hung from the truck transoms. The truck frame in turn is supported on four spiral springs carried by the equalizer bars on each side. These equalizer bars rest on top of the journal boxes and distribute the load on each side equally between both axles. This type of truck, which is a modification of the standard steam railroad four-wheel passenger truck, has been widely used under high-speed interurban cars.

McCord Journal Box. Figs. 1555-1558.

McGuire-Cummings Trucks. Figs. 1400-1405.

Metallic Arc Headlight. See **Luminous Arc Headlight.**

Mica. A mineral insulating material extensively employed in the construction of commutators and other parts of electrical machinery. Mica is taken from the earth in large masses, which are readily separated by cleavage into thin sheets. It comes in various grades of hardness and transparency. Moulded mica is made of finely pulverized mica mixed into a paste with some fused or liquid insulating material and moulded into any desired shape.

Micanite. A composition insulating material prepared by mixing small flakes of mica with an insulating compound and pressing into sheets and other forms.

Middle Door Rail. 134, Figs. 259-370. See **Door Frame.**

Mighty Midget Car Heater. Fig. 1096.

Mil. A unit of length equal to 0.001 in. A circular mil is a unit of area used in computing the size of wire. It is the cross-sectional area of a wire one mil in diameter. One circular mil equals 0.000,000,785 sq. in.

Mineral Wool. A fibrous material made by blowing a steam jet into molten blast furnace slag. Mineral wool resembles asbestos somewhat and is occasionally used for filling in the space between sills under car floors to deaden the sound.

Mirror. A piece of plate glass coated on one side with a bright amalgam of mercury. Occasionally used for small interior panels.

Molding. A narrow strip of wood used to conceal a joint or fill a corner between two other pieces of wood. Moldings of many irregular cross-sections are used in electric car building.

Momentum Brake. A type of mechanical brake working on the principle of a friction clutch. The clutch is mounted on the axle and tends to wind up the brake chain on a drum, thereby applying the brakes on the wheels through a suitable system of levers. Not in general use in the United States.

Monitor. The raised central portion of a car roof. The clearstory.

Monitor Deck. The upper deck or roof over the clearstory.

Moonlight Car. Fig. 163. A term sometimes applied to a trail car with low sides and no roof, used for moonlight excursion parties. Iron pipe stanchions are used to support a canvas canopy roof, which can be rolled up in good weather.

Mortise. A recess cut in the surface of one timber to receive a projecting tenon on the end of another timber.

Mosher Arc Headlight. Figs. 1028-1029.

Motor. Figs. 1645-1709. A machine for converting electrical energy into mechanical energy of rotation. Railway motors are of two general types designed to operate on direct current and alternating current. The standard direct current voltage used in electric railway work is 550 to 650 volts, but a few interurban lines have been built to use current at 1200 volts. Direct current motors for operation on 550 to 650-volt current consist of an armature rotating in bearings in the motor frame and carrying on one end a commutator and on the other end a pinion; a cast steel frame enclosing two or more field poles and magnets; and a pair of brushes bearing on the commutator. The armature and fields are connected in series with each other through the brushes. The passage of current through the motor creates a magnetic field between opposite field poles and the armature coils carrying current tend to move in and out of the field, thus rotating the armature. As each coil moves out of the field it is open-circuited at the commutator and the next successive coil is energized. See **Armature.** For description of alternating current motors, see **Single-Phase Motor.**

Details of the types of railway motors in general use are given in the table accompanying Figs. 1710-1714.

See also **Commutating Pole Motor, Box Frame Motor, Split Frame Motor.**

Motor Armature. See **Armature.**

Motor Axle. Figs. 1598-1601. An axle to which a motor is geared. Half of the weight of the motor is carried on the axle, and hence the axle is made of large diameter in the center. In addition to the journals, motor bearings and wheel fits, a gear fit is turned on one end inside of the wheel fit on which is pressed or bolted and keyed a toothed gear engaging with the motor armature pinion. See **Axle** and **Motor Suspension.**

Motor Brush. See **Brush.**

Motor Car. A self-propelled car as distinguished from a trail car.

Motor Compressor. See **Air Compressor.**

Motor Controller. See **Controller.**

Motor Cut-Out. A switch in the bottom of a Type K controller which, when opened, cuts out one motor of a two-motor equipment or two motors of a four-motor equipment.

Motor Frame. 3, Figs. 1659-1661. A cast steel box enclosing the armature, brushes and field coils. The motor frame forms part of the magnetic circuit of the fields and protects all of the enclosed parts from mechanical injury, dirt and water. Two types of motor frames are in use, **Box Frame** and **Split Frame,** which see.

Motor Frame Bail. 9. Figs. 1659-1661. An eye formed in the top of a motor frame for lifting the motor with a crane or hoist. Usually two or four such bails are provided.

Motor Frame Bolts. The bolts which hold together the two halves of a split motor frame.

Motor Frame Head. T and U, Fig. 1657. In a box-frame motor, the two circular discs closing the end of the motor frame and carrying the armature bearings.

Motor Gear. See **Gear** and **Pinion.**

Motor Generator. See **Dynamotor.**

Motor Leads. 6, Figs. 1659-1661. The flexible insulated cables used to connect the motor fields and brushes with the car cables. They are usually provided with brass connectors on their ends for readily connecting or disconnecting them when the motors or trucks are removed from under the car.

Motor Nose. A projecting lug cast on a motor frame on the side opposite to the axle bearings. It rests on the truck transom and supports the motor on one side. See **Motor Suspension**.

Motor Nose Strap. A strap bolted to the truck transom and surrounding the motor nose to prevent it from lifting off of its seat.

Motor Suspension. The method of supporting a railway motor on the truck. The motor frame is formed with two bearings on one side, which surround the axle to which the motor is geared. The other side of the motor is carried in one of four ways. A cradle suspension consists of a U-shaped bar surrounding the motor frame on each side. The ends of the bar rests on coil springs on the axle bearings of the motor frame. Lugs are cast on the motor frame above the armature bearings and these rest on top of the cradle. The cradle bar is bolted at its center to a cross bar supported on coil springs to the truck side frames. A parallel bar suspension is similar to the cradle suspension except that two parallel side bars are used and the outer ends of these bars rest on springs mounted on a rigid cross member of the truck frame. A yoke suspension consists of a spring supported cross bar, which is bolted to or under lugs cast on the outside face of the motor frame. A nose suspension is usually built without springs, and is used only for inside hung motors. A lug cast on the motor frame rests on a bracket, attached to or formed on the truck transom, and a yoke passes over the motor frame lug to hold it down on the transom. The cradle and parallel bar suspensions are obsolete, only the yoke and nose suspensions being used for modern motors.

Motor Suspension Bar. 9, Figs. 1368-1370; 41, Figs. 1388-1390. The cross bar, or yoke, which supports one side of a motor in a yoke suspension.

Motor Suspension Bar Bolt. 10, Figs. 1368-1370; 42, Figs. 1388-1390. A bolt securing a motor suspension bar to the truck frame. Where the suspension bar is spring supported, the bolt passes through the springs and spring caps.

Motor Suspension Bracket. 12, Fig. 1374.

Motor Suspension Spring. 32 and 33, Fig. 1368. A spring mounted on the truck side frame and supporting one end of a motor suspension bar.

Motor Suspension Spring Cap. 34, Fig. 1368.

Motor Suspension Spring Seat. 35, Fig. 1368.

Motor Yoke Bar. See **Motor Suspension Bar**.

Motorman. The member of a car crew who manipulates the controller and brakes to start and stop the car. He usually occupies the front platform, where he has a clear view ahead.

Motorman's Brake Valve. See **Brake Valve**.

Motorman's Cab. A small compartment in the front end of a car and having a clear view forward, which is occupied by the motorman. In most street cars the motorman occupies the front platform and is not shut off in a separate compartment.

Motorman's Cab Door Lock. Figs. 774-780.

Motorman's Stool. Figs. 1266-1267, 1302-1304. A portable seat for a motorman. An ordinary wooden stool is generally used, but in some types of cars a revolving seat supported by a pipe stand set in a socket in the platform floor is substituted.

Motorman's Valve. See **Brake Valve**.

Mud Guard. See **Splash Plate**.

Muffler. See **Exhaust Muffler**.

Mullion. An upright partition post in a door or window frame separating two panels or panes of glass.

Multiple. Another name for the method of connecting two or more pieces of electrical apparatus in **Parallel**, which see.

Multiple Stroke Gong. Figs. 946-947. An alarm gong for street cars in which a number of rapid strokes are given for each depression of the pedal.

Multiple-Unit Control. Figs. 1758-1803. A general term applied to control systems designed for the operation of two or more motor cars in a train. Two different types have been developed, the Sprague, or type M, all-electric system, by the General Electric Company, and the electro-pneumatic system, by the Westinghouse Electric and Manufacturing Company. In the type M control, the switching operations are accomplished by electro-magnetic contactors and reversing switches operated by control circuits carried through each car in the train from the operative master controller, which may be located on any car. In the Westinghouse apparatus, the control switches, which are known as unit-switches, are operated by compressed air taken from the brake system through electro-pneumatic valves actuated by low-voltage control circuits drawing current from storage batteries or from the trolley through suitable resistances.

The type M control apparatus in its simplest form consists of a master controller, master controller switch, a plurality of contactors or electrically-operated switches, a reverser, motor resistance rheostats, control rheostats, control wires, control cable couplers and connection boxes, control cut-out switch, main switch and suitable fuses for protecting the motor and control circuits. The master controller resembles a small type K cylinder controller in all of its essential elements, the principal difference being that it is designed to switch only the small amounts of current necessary to energize the magnets of the contactors and reverser. The contacts in the master controller are connected to the several control wires in the control cable, which extends from end to end of each car and continuously throughout a multiple-unit train with jumpers or couplers between cars. All master controllers have identical connections with the control cable and the contactors and reverser under each car likewise are uniformly connected to the control wires. It will be seen, therefore, that when current is switched through any master controller in a train, it is transmitted through the control cable and actuates the sets of contactors under each motor car simultaneously. The motor circuit is local to each car, and on the first point the main motor current from the trolley or third-rail shoe passes through the following pieces of apparatus in the order named: Main switch and fuse, contactors, resistances, reverser, motors, and to ground. In the control circuit, the course of the current from the trolley is through a shunt connection to the master controller switch and fuse, master controller, connection box, cut-out switch, control cables, operating coils of the reverser and contactors through fuses to ground.

With the simplest form of type M control apparatus the rate of feeding current to the motors is regulated by the movement of the master controller from point to point. Automatic control of the amount of current fed to the motors may be accomplished by the use of interlocking contactors and a current-limit relay in circuit with the master controller. The master controller handle is thrown to the full "on" position, and as each resistance contactor closes, it transfers its operating coil from a lifting to a holding circuit and also connects in the operating coil of the contactor for the next succeeding step. At the same time, the armature of the current-limit relay, which is provided with a lifting coil in the contactor circuit, rises and interrupts the lifting circuit to prevent the further progression of the contactors until it again drops. If the main motor current flowing in series through a holding coil in the current-limit relay exceeds a predetermined value the relay armature will not immediately drop. In this manner the limiting feature is secured. When it is desired to notch up slower than the normal rate, the master controller handle is brought to the first point and the car slowly started. To secure a slight increase in speed the handle is turned to the second point and returned quickly to the first point. This operation lifts the current-limit relay and the contactor for the second step, but as it cuts off the lifting circuit, no more contactors will be closed until the movement is repeated. This method of operation can be repeated until all resistance contactors are closed and full series is reached. After the full series is reached, the resistances in the parallel positions can be cut out step by step in a similar manner by alternately moving the controller handle to the fourth point and back to the third. The current limit relay may be adjusted to hold open with any desired amount of current flowing through the series coil, and thus any predetermined rate of acceleration can be obtained.

The Westinghouse unit-switch system of automatic multiple-unit control operates on much the same principle as the automatic type M control. The unit-switches, which perform the same functions as contactors, are operated by compressed air at 70 lb. per sq. in., taken from the air-brake system, the pistons being controlled by electro-magnetic needle valves. These switches are interlocked and automatically make the proper combinations of motor connections with the resistances. A limit relay is used for arresting the sequence of switch movements when the main motor current value rises above a safe amount. The master controller consists of a small box containing a horizontal drum or roller and suitable contact fingers. The operating handle revolves in a vertical plane, and when moved to the right the motors accelerate forward to full speed; when moved to the left the motors accelerate to full speed reverse.

There are three points or positions in each direction. The first is the switching point and throws all motors in series with full resistance in circuit. The second point is the series position and the motors can be operated continuously in series at half speed with the handle in this position. The third point is the parallel position and the motors are connected in multiple with full power. To cut off the current, the pressure on the controller handle is released and a spring returns it to the "off" position. Current for the control circuits is obtained from a small storage battery of 7 cells, giving 14 volts. See **Unit Switch Control.**

Multiple-unit control apparatus for single-phase equipments differs but slightly from that used for direct-current motors. The contactors control circuits of varying voltage taken from taps on the auto-transformer. The speed of the motors is thus regulated by varying the voltage impressed on them. See **Single-Phase Control System.**

Multiple-Unit Train. A train of cars equipped with multiple-unit control apparatus.

Mummified Coil. A coil of wire which is wrapped with cloth or tape and impregnated with a heavy, viscous compound, which binds the whole coil and its protective wrapping firmly together.

Muntin. Another name for **Mullion,** which see.

N

Nail. A pointed piece of metal with a head formed on one end for driving with a hammer. Used to fasten one piece of wood to another.

Nailing Strip. 43, Fig. 306. A piece of wood fastened by clamps or bolts to a steel sill or other metallic member of a car frame to receive nails driven through an overlying board, such as a floor board.

Narragansett Car. Figs. 93, 341-347. A term applied to open cars embodying a patented construction of the underframe. Z-bars are used for side sills and the horizontal web of the sills forms a middle step between the running board and the car floor. This permits the car floor to be raised high enough to use double trucks and four-motor equipment without sacrificing the width of the body to get in the second step.

Narrow Gage. A track gage less than the standard of 4 ft. 8½ in. See **Broad Gage.**

National Air Brakes. Figs. 532-543.

National Equalizing Wedge. Figs. 1559-1560.

National Metal Molding. Figs. 1838-1840.

National Trolley Base. Fig. 1871.

National Vestibule Trap Door. Figs. 923-926.

Needlebeam. 6, Figs. 259-370. A cross member of the underframe between the bolsters. Two such beams are usually used and the body truss rod queen posts are dropped from them. The terms cross frame tie, cross bearer, cross tie, cross tie timber and body transom are all applied to this piece, but the term needlebeam, which is borrowed from bridge engineering, while not truly descriptive, is accurate and distinctive.

Negative. An arbitrary term used in electrical engineering to distinguish the pole or connection toward which current is considered to flow, from the positive pole or connection away from which the current flows. Thus direct current always flows from the positive pole or brush of a battery or dynamo through the external circuit and back to the negative pole or brush. Positive poles are indicated on drawings by a plus (+) sign and negative poles by a minus (—) sign. In a ground return system the ground connection is always negative.

New Columbia Car Stove. Figs. 1103-1104.

Nichols-Lintern Sander. Figs. 1208-1212.

Nipple. See **Brake Hose Nipple.**

Noark Fuse. Figs. 1813-1815.

Non-Parallel Axle Truck. Figs. 1422-1425. A long wheelbase single-truck, designed so that the two axles are not rigidly confined in a parallel position in the truck frame when rounding a sharp curve, but are free to assume a true radial position on the curve and thereby greatly reduce the track resistance and flange wear. See **Radial Truck.**

Nose Suspension. See **Motor Suspension.**

Nosing. (Of a Step.) The edge of a step tread board which projects beyond the riser board.

Notice Plate. A metal plate having raised letters cast on it forming a notice of some kind to passengers. Notices are commonly painted or gilded on the woodwork in electric railway cars.

Nut. A square or hexagonal block of metal with a threaded hole in the center which screws on the threaded end of a bolt. Nuts usually take their names from the bolts to which they are applied. See **Lock Nut. Castle Nut.**

Nut Lock. A device for securely locking a nut on a bolt. Various types of spring washers and other forms of nut locks are in use. A **Lock Nut,** which see, is a separate nut screwed down on top of a plain nut to hold it tightly in place.

O

Observation Car. Figs. 164-175. A car equipped with an observation platform at one end, or a cross-seat car, used for sight-seeing excursions.

Observation Platform. A platform on the rear end of some interurban cars which is enclosed with glass instead of panels, or is entirely open, so as to afford an unobstructed view to the rear.

O-B Pneumatic Sander. Figs. 1219-1222.

Office Car. A special car used as an office by the manager of a large interurban railway system. It may contain sleeping and dining accommodations.

Ohm. The unit of measurement of electrical resistance. It may be defined as the resistance of a circuit in which a current of one ampere flows with an electromotive force of one volt.

Ohmer Fare Register. Fig. 1160.

Oil. A liquid lubricant refined from crude petroleum. Oil is universally used for lubricating journal bearings and is rapidly superseding grease for lubricating motor bearings.

Oil Box. A **Journal Box,** which see.

Oil Cup. A receptacle for holding a supply of oil to be fed to a bearing or other surface requiring lubrication. Oil cups are used on some types of railway motors for supplying the armature bearings with oil.

Oil Headlight. Figs. 1038-1039. A Headlight, which see, in which the source of light is an oil lamp.

Oil Lamp. A lamp for burning oil. See **Signal Lamp.**

Oil Switch. A switch for breaking high-tension currents in which the contacts are completely immersed in oil in an hermetically-sealed case. The presence of the oil effectually extinguishes any arc which forms.

Oil-Vacuum Heating System. Figs. 1100-1102. A closed circulation system of heating using oil instead of water as the medium. The oil is heated by a small stove under the car body.

Okonite. A rubber compound insulation for wires and cables.

Open Car. Figs. 30-33, 90-96. A type of electric railway car in general use during the summer months for city and suburban service. Open cars have a floor, roof and end bulkheads, but no sides. The seats extend across the car and a continuous step or running board is carried along the side below the sill. Canvas curtains which pull down to the floor between each pair of side posts protect the passengers from wind and rain. Open cars are usually designated by the number of seats or benches which they contain, as 10-bench car.

Operating Valve. See **Brake Valve**.

Osmer Door-Operating Device. Figs. 672-673.

Outline Carline. See **Compound Carline**.

Outside Cornice. See **Cornice**.

Outside Hung Brakes. Figs. 1377, 1384, 1451-1453, 1469-1471. Truck brakes in which the shoes are hung outside of the wheels. See **Inside Hung Brakes**.

Outside Hung Motor. Figs. 1370, 1395, 1406, 1411. A motor which is mounted between the truck end piece and the axle. Outside hung motors require some form of suspension bar resting on springs on the truck side frames. See **Inside Hung Motor** and **Motor Suspension**.

Outside Panel. 129, Figs. 259-370. A wide, thin board or sheet of metal applied on the outside of the body framing. Sheathing made of narrow matched boards is usually used for interurban car sides. City cars are made with straight side panels or with a concave panel along the bottom so as to provide extra clearance for the hubs of vehicles.

Outside Window. A **Storm Sash**, which see.

Outside Window Sill. 60, Fig. 306. A sloping board below a window on the outside. See **Inside Window Sill**.

Overhang. (1) Of a Roof. That part which projects beyond the sides or ends of the upper deck. More commonly called **Apron**, which see. (2) Of a Car Body. The end of the car which projects out beyond the bolster. It does not include the vestibules or platforms, which have separate underframes.

Overhang Brace Rod. See **Overhang Truss Rod**.

Overhang Truss Rod. 8, Figs. 259-370. An inverted body truss rod occasionally used on long cars to support the overhanging ends of the car body. It consists of an iron strap framed into the side posts just below or alongside of the belt rail and extending parallel to the side sill between the bolsters. It is supported by struts or queen posts over the bolsters and is bent downward beyond them to attach to anchors on the side or end sills. Also called overhang brace rod.

Overhang Truss Rod Anchor. 9, Figs. 259-370. A strap or cast washer used to secure an overhang truss rod to the side or end sill.

Overhang Truss Rod Strut. 7, Figs. 259-370. A strut supporting an overhang truss rod on top of the body bolster. In some types of construction it is formed in the shape of a bent knee.

Overhead Switch. A name applied to an automatic **Circuit Breaker**, which see, mounted under the platform hood above the controller.

Overload Relay. Fig. 1796. In an automatic multiple-unit control system, a relay having its magnet coil in series with the motor circuit and its back armature contacts in the lifting circuit of the control apparatus. When the current flowing through the motors exceeds a predetermined value the magnet coil has sufficient force to lift the armature and break the lifting circuit of the control apparatus. When this circuit is broken further progression of the contactors in cutting out resistance is stopped. Also called **Limit Switch** and **Current Limit Relay**, which see. The latter name is preferred as being more accurately descriptive.

Overload Trip. See **Tripping Switch**.

Overrunning Third Rail. A third-rail working conductor arranged so that the third-rail shoes on the cars bear on the top surface either by gravity or spring pressure. See **Underrunning Third Rail**.

P

Package Rack. More properly **Basket Rack**, which see.

Packing. Cotton or wool waste saturated with oil and packed in the oil cellar of a journal box so as to rub against the under side of the journal and lubricate it.

Packing Leather. A leather ring surrounding the piston of a brake cylinder and fitting closely to the walls of the cylinder so as to form an air-tight joint.

Packing Leather Expander. A wire spring surrounding the piston of a brake cylinder and used to keep the packing leather pressed out tight against the cylinder walls.

Padlock. A removable lock, consisting of a body and a hinged shackle, one end of which fits into the body and is secured by a bolt. Padlocks are used on cars for securing locker doors, and occsiaonally for other purposes.

Paint. A liquid, usually boiled linseed oil, containing in suspension a colored pigment. Paints used for finishing the exterior of cars are usually applied in several coats and are followed by one or more coats of varnish. Four processes of car painting are in use, the "lead and oil" process, "surface" process, "color and varnish" process and "sanding" process. The "lead and oil" process consists of priming and filling the wood with white lead and linseed oil paint, building up on this a hard, smooth surface with "rough stuff," applying the body color on this foundation, and finally coating the body color with finishing varnish. This process requires from four to five weeks to complete owing to the slow drying of the lead and oil priming. The "surface" process differs from the "lead and oil" process chiefly in the use of specially prepared quick drying paints for the priming and "rough stuff" upon which are placed the color and varnish coats. This process requires from two to three weeks to complete. The "color and varnish" process uses quick drying priming and surfacing paints, a body color ground in varnish and only one coat of finishing varnish. It can be applied in as short a time as eight days. It is the cheapest method in use, but does not have as good an appearance when completed. The "sanding" process is a modification of the "lead and oil" process, which substitutes a plaster coat of thick white lead in place of "rough stuff." This coat is brought to a smooth surface with sand paper before applying the body color.

Pane. A piece of glass glazed into a window sash.

Panel. A thin board or sheet of metal used to fill the space between the parts of a framework, as a door panel or outside panel.

Panel Furring. Small pieces of wood inserted between the main members of a framework to form a backing for a panel applied over them.

Panel Strip. A narrow strip of wood or metal used to cover the joint between two adjoining outside panels.

Panel Type Electric Heater. Figs. 1125-1131, 1150-1151. A form of electric heater intended to be let in flush with a seat riser panel.

Pantasote. A fabric coated with a secret compound to give it the appearance of leather, used for upholstering car seats and also for curtain material.

Pantograph Trolley. Figs. 1875-1876. A form of current collecting device for an overhead conductor consisting of a jointed frame carrying a transverse bar, shallow pan or roller, which is pressed upward against the wire. The jointed frame is diamond-shaped and may be extended upward or compressed down flat on the car roof. It is operated by a group of springs or by a pneumatic cylinder supplied with compressed air from the brake system.

Parallel. A method of connecting two or more pieces of electrical apparatus on a common circuit so that the positive poles of each are connected to a common positive conductor and the negative poles are connected to a common negative conductor. The drop in voltage through each piece of apparatus is equal to the difference in potential between the positive and negative conductor, while the amount of current which flows through each piece of apparatus is inversely proportional to its resistance. See **Series**.

Parallel Bar Suspension. See **Motor Suspension**.

Parlor Car. Figs. 169-175. A type of luxurious interurban car or special chartered car for city service fitted with individual seats or chairs. An excess fare is usually charged on such cars when used in regular service. Parlor cars are operated by only a few companies.

Parmenter Fender and Wheelguard. Figs. 717-718.

Parting Bead. See **Sash Parting Strip**.

Parting Strip. See **Sash Parting Strip**.

Partition. An interior wall dividing a car body into two or more compartments. The end walls are usually termed end bulkheads or simply ends.

Passenger Car. Figs. 1-189. Any car used for the transportation of passengers. Many interurban passenger cars have a separate compartment for carrying baggage, mail or package freight.

Passenger Compartment. A term sometimes used to distinguish the non-smoking compartment of a car which also contains a smoking compartment.

Pawl. A pivoted detent engaging in the teeth of a ratchet wheel to restrain its movement in one direction. See **Brake Pawl.**

Pay-as-You-Enter Car. Figs. 23-25, 44-50, etc. The original type of prepayment platform car. The conductor stands on the rear platform within a railing which divides the platform and steps into an exit passageway next to the outside corner of the car body and an entrance passageway occupying substantially the entire remaining area of the platform to the inside and rear. Entering passengers pay their fare to the conductor before entering the car body through the door on the inside corner. An exit with a narrower door and step is provided at the side of the front platform, the opening and closing of the door being under the control of the motorman. The entrance and exit passageways on the rear platform may or may not be closed with doors or gates controlled by the conductor or motorman.

Pay-Within Car. Figs. 63-66. A type of prepayment platform car in which the front and rear vestibules are entirely closed while running. The end bulkheads are omitted and the conductor stands within the car facing the rear. Entrance is from the rear platform only, the entering passengers paying their fare as they pass to the right of the conductor. Exit is normally from the front platform, but, if desired, passengers may be allowed to leave by the rear, passing to the conductor's left. No partition railings are used to divide the steps or platforms into entrance and exit passageways, but an iron pipe stand, containing the door operating valve mechanism in the top, is erected in the center of the body end sill to guide the entering passengers around to the right of the conductor, who is behind the stand facing to the rear. The platform steps fold up when the doors above them are closed, and the body grab handles are attached inside of the doors. A pneumatic engine mounted under the corner seat or in a pocket over the door is used for raising and lowering the step and opening and closing the door. The rear platform door is operated by the conductor by moving the operating valve handle in the top of the iron stand which he faces. The front platform door is operated by the motorman in a similar manner, the operating handle being mounted alongside of the brake valve. The operating handles are mechanically connected to the air valves which form part of the pneumatic engines. A supply of compressed air is drawn from the air brake system. Hand operated doors and steps may be used on cars not equipped with air brakes.

Peacock Brake. Figs. 580-581. A type of geared hand brake having a spiral drum on the bottom of the brake shaft to increase the power of the brake as the chain winds up.

Pedal. A foot lever. See **Gong Pedal.**

Pedestal. 31, Figs. 1388-1390. A jaw forming part of a truck side frame and enclosing a journal box between its vertical sides. The journal box is free to move vertically in the pedestal, but is restrained from lateral or longitudinal movement. A **Seat Pedestal**, which see, is a pressed steel column or wooden frame supporting a cross seat frame.

Pedestal Bolt. A contraction of **Pedestal Jaw Bolt**, which see.

Pedestal Brace. A diagonal brace extending from the extension of the side frame to the bottom of the outside leg of the pedestal to stiffen the pedestal longitudinally. The pedestal tie bar braces the inside leg of the pedestal. See Fig. 1405.

Pedestal Cap. 32, Figs. 1388-1390. The casting which closes the space between the bottom ends of the pedestal legs. It is held in place by an extension of the pedestal tie bar or by a pedestal jaw bolt.

Pedestal Filler. 32, Figs. 1388-1390. A piece of metal tubing or a hollow casting surrounding a pedestal jaw bolt or the end of a pedestal tie bar and used as a spacer to spread apart the bottom ends of the pedestal legs. More commonly called **Pedestal Cap**, which see.

Pedestal Gib. See **Pedestal Wear Plate.**

Pedestal Jaw. A **Pedestal**, which see.

Pedestal Jaw Bit. A **Pedestal Cap**, which see.

Pedestal Jaw Bolt. 33, Figs. 1388-1390. A bolt passing through the ends of the pedestal legs under the journal box to hold the legs of the pedestal together and prevent the truck frame from lifting off the journal box. It holds a **Pedestal Cap**, which see, in place. When a pedestal tie bar is used the ends are threaded and pass through the pedestal legs taking the place of the jaw bolt.

Pedestal Leg. One of the two vertical guides for a journal box which together form a pedestal.

Pedestal Spring. A coil spring resting on top of a journal box and supporting one end of the side frame. Also called journal box spring.

Pedestal Tie Bar. 6, Fig. 1370. An iron bar connecting the bottom ends of the four pedestal legs on one side of a truck frame.

Pedestal Truck. A general term properly applied to any type of truck in which the journal boxes are enclosed in pedestals and are free to move vertical in them. It is sometimes used to designate especially trucks having pedestal springs, as distinguished from the M. C. B. equalized type.

Pedestal Wear Plate. 8, Fig. 1368. A removable hardened steel plate inserted on the inside faces of truck pedestals to take the wear caused by the vertical movement of the journal boxes in the pedestals. Also called pedestal gib.

Perry Ventilator. Figs. 1340-1342.

Philadelphia Brake Shoe. Figs. 1502-1503.

Philadelphia Fender. Fig. 719.

Pier Post. 14, Figs. 259-370. A wide window post separating two pairs of twin windows. It is finished with a panel on the inside.

Pilaster. 59, Fig. 306. An ornamental inside panel on a window post.

Pilot. 30, Figs. 356-370. A V-shaped slanting fender mounted under the end of a car body in front of the trucks. Pilots are commonly used on interurban cars in place of projecting fenders or wheelguards. They are framed of heavy wooden slats or steel bars and extend down to about 6 in. or 8 in. above the rail.

Pilot Bar. One of the slanting slats or rods forming the surface of a pilot.

Pilot Bottom Frame. The horizontal timber connecting the bottom ends of the pilot bars.

Pilot Brace. 40, Fig. 367. A rod fastened to the pilot bottom frame and extending upward and back to the car body framing to brace the pilot longitudinally.

Pilot Knee. 10, Fig. 367. A timber or forging bolted to the body or vestibule underframe and supporting the pilot.

Pin. A short rod or bolt used to fasten one piece to another. See **Brake Pin, Center Pin, Coupling Pin**, etc.

Pinion. K, Fig. 1657; Fig. 1528. The smaller of two toothed gear wheels in engagement with each other. The gear wheel on the end of a motor armature shaft is always referred to as a pinion, and the toothed wheel on the axle with which it engages is called a gear.

Pinion Key. A rectangular key driven into a keyway cut in a pinion and an armature shaft to prevent the pinion from turning on the shaft.

Pinion Nut. A thin nut screwed on the end of an armature shaft to keep the pinion wedged up tight on the taper on the end of the shaft.

Pipe. A tube made of iron or other metal used for conveying liquids or gases. Pipes are used on electric railway cars for connecting the various parts of the air brake apparatus, and also are frequently used as conduit for protecting the car wiring. Hot water heaters employ coils of pipe for circulating the hot water within the car body. See **Brake Pipe, Control Pipe, Heater Pipe.**

Pipe Clamp. A strap surrounding a pipe and screwed or bolted to some part of the car framing to hold the pipe in place.

Pipe Conduit. Conduit, which see, formed of iron pipe.

Piston. (Air Brake.) A movable disk fitting closely within the brake cylinder against which the pressure of the compressed air is exerted. This forces the piston outward and its movement is communicated by a piston rod to one end of the cylinder lever, which in turn moves the entire foundation brake gear and applies the brake shoes on the wheels. See Figs. 498-499.

Piston Packing Leather. See **Packing Leather.**

Piston Rod. A rod attached to the piston of a brake cylinder to communicate the movement of the piston to the levers of the foundation brake gear. It is surrounded by a coil spring, which is compressed when the piston moves outward and forces the piston inward when the pressure back of the piston is released. See Figs. 498-499. In some types of brake cylinders the piston rod is a hollow tube enclosing a push rod which is connected to the cylinder lever. See **Push Rod.**

Piston Travel. The distance which the piston in a brake cylinder moves when the brakes are applied. It is an index of the amount of slack in the foundation brake gear and should not be allowed to become excessive, as loss of braking power results. **Brake Slack Adjusters,** which see, have been designed to regulate the piston travel by automatically taking up slack in the brake gear when the travel exceeds a predetermined distance. The piston travel when a car is standing is always considerably less than when the car is running.

Pivot Pin. A term applied to the **Knuckle Pin,** which see, of an automatic coupler.

Plain Triple Valve. A **Triple Valve,** which see, in which the emergency feature of the quick-action triple valves is omitted. Plain triple valves are commonly used for electric car air-brake equipments, the quick-action triple valves being designed especially for use on cars run in long trains.

Plank. A piece of timber wider than it is thick. See **Truss Plank, Spring Plank.**

Plate. (1) 16, Figs. 259-370. A piece of timber framed across the top of the side posts of a car body framing. A **Deck Plate,** which see, is a similar piece across the top of the deck posts and an end plate is framed across the top of the body end posts. The end plate is sometimes called a head piece.

(2) The disk connecting the hub and rim of a car wheel. See **Double Plate Wheel.**

Platform. An extension floor at the end of a car body to facilitate entrance and exit. When completely enclosed with sheathing, windows and doors a platform is termed a **Vestibule,** which see, and the names of parts common to both types of construction are prefixed with the distinguishing term "vestibule" instead of "platform." Platforms of street cars vary in length from 3 ft. to 9 ft. and extend almost the full width of the car body. Except on open cars the platform floor of city cars is universally built from 8 in. to 10 in. lower than the body floor, so as to form a step within the car and thus reduce the height of the steps from the pavement to the platform. The platform floor is usually carried on separate sills attached under the body framing, and the roof is also framed separately. Platforms are distinguished as front and rear, according to the direction of movement of the car. The front platform is occupied by the motorman, and the rear platform, which is used principally for entrance, is occupied by the conductor. Various platform arrangements for prepayment operation are shown in Figs. 44-59.

Platform Bell. See **Signal Bell.**

Platform Brake. A **Hand Brake,** which see, mounted on the platform of a car.

Platform Controller. Figs. 1715-1720. A **Controller,** which see, mounted on a car platform or vestibule. The term is sometimes used to distinguish a type K hand controller from the master controller used with multiple-unit control apparatus.

Platform Corner Post. 32, Figs. 259-370. A post at one of the outer corners of a platform, supporting the platform hood bow and one end of the dasher. It is usually made of iron pipe about 1½ in. in diameter.

Platform Corner Post Bracket. 67, Figs. 259-260. A bracket attached to the underside of a platform hood to secure the top end of a platform corner post.

Platform Corner Post Socket. A cast iron socket washer secured on top of the bumper beam or crown piece to receive the lower end of the platform corner post. A similar casting or bracket is sometimes used to fasten the post to the platform hood bow.

Platform Crown Piece. See **Crown Piece.**

Platform End. The structure enclosing the end of a platform corresponding to the end of the car body. In open platforms the dasher and dasher rail form the platform end.

Platform End Sill. More properly, **Bumper Beam,** which see.

Platform Floor. The layer of boards nailed on top of the platform sills.

Platform Gate. Fig. 690. A swinging or folding gate used to close the opening in the side of the platform over the steps. In enclosed platforms or vestibules, the gate is replaced by a folding or sliding door. Platform gates are usually hinged to the car body, and are fastened with a hook or catch on the platform corner post.

Platform Gong. See **Gong.**

Platform Guard Chain. 93, Figs. 259-260. A chain sometimes used to connect the inside end of the dasher rail and the body corner post of an open car to prevent passengers standing or sitting on the platform from falling out. It serves the purpose of a **Platform Gate,** which see.

Platform Hood. 81, Figs. 259-370. The roof over a platform. It is usually framed separately from the body roof, to which, however, it is joined without a break. The framing consists of a curved bow joined to the body side plates at each end and curved carlines to which the roof boards are nailed.

Platform Hood Apron. The overhanging edge of the roof of a platform. See **Deck Apron.**

Platform Hood Bow. 38, Figs. 259-370. A curved stick forming the lower edge of a platform hood. The ends are fastened to the body side plates and it is also supported by the platform corner posts. The ends of the hood carlines rest on the bow.

Platform Hood Carlines. 24, Figs. 259-370. Curved transverse carlines in the platform hood on which the roof boards are laid.

Platform Hood Plate. 23, Figs. 259-370. A continuation of the deck plate which is carried down to the hood bow in a roof construction in which the monitor deck is carried out over the platform.

Platform Hood Shoulder Carline. A carline in the hood framing placed against the body end plate to support the inner ends of the roof boards.

Platform Hood Side Piece. 22, Figs. 259-370. A plank set on edge as a continuation of the deck sill and rounded off on top to the shape of the curve of the platform hood. Used only where the upper deck is continued out in front to the platform hood bow.

Platform Knee. 71, Figs. 259-370. A common name for a **Platform Sill,** which is the proper term.

Platform Post. 32 and 33, Figs. 259-370. A post in the end of a platform. The posts of an open platform are usually designated as platform corner posts and **Dasher Posts,** which see.

Platform Railing. Pipe partitions erected on a platform to form passageways for entrance and exit. The term is also applied to the **Dasher Rail,** which see.

Platform Roof. See **Platform Hood.**

Platform Safety Chain. See **Safety Coupling Chain.**

Platform Sills. 71, Figs. 259-370. Short timbers or steel beams attached to the underside of the body framing back of the end sill and projecting out under the sill to support the platform floor. Four sills are commonly used, designated as platform outer sills or side sills and platform center sills. The two outside sills are commonly bent inward to taper the width of the platform slightly. The platform sills are bolted to the body framing and are also clamped with stirrups. The outer ends of the sills are framed into the bumper beam or crown piece.

Platform Sill Clamp. A form of fastening for the platform sills under the body end sill. A bolt is put through the end sill on each side of the platform sill and a strap washer is put on these two bolts under the platform sill. By tightening up the nuts on this washer the platform sill is clamped up firmly against the end sill.

Platform Steps. A flight of one or more hanging or built-in steps on the side of a platform to make it easy to board a car or alight to the street pavement. See **Step**. On city cars a single step is commonly used. The American Electric Railway Engineering Association has approved the following dimensions of car steps as recommended practice:

	Interurban Cars	City Cars
Height from top of rail to top of tread of first step	17 in.	17 in.
Height from top of rail to top of tread of second step	29 in.	......
Height from top of rail to top of tread of third step	40 in.	......
Height from top of rail to platform floor	51 in.	31 in.
Height of riser from platform floor to car floor	......	10 in.

Platform Sub-Sill. A timber attached under the body end sill as a spacer to increase the height from the platform floor to the body floor.

Platform Tail Lamp. Fig. 1090. An extra large lamp with a square case and having one large red lens. It is intended to be placed on the rear platform floor or hung from the rear dasher to distinctly mark the rear of the car or train.

Plow. See **Conduit Plow** and **Snow Plow**.

Plush. A heavy woolen cloth with a velvety nap on one side extensively used for upholstering car seats.

Pneumatic Brake. See **Air Brake**.

Pneumatic Door. A sliding or folding vestibule door which is opened and closed by compressed air admitted in a small cylinder behind a piston. Pneumatic doors are used in many elevated and subway cars and in **Pay-Within Cars**, which see.

Pneumatic Engine. Figs. 665-671. A cylinder and piston with suitable valves and cranks used to operate a sliding or folding door.

Pneumatic Gong Ringer. Fig. 940. A device for ringing an alarm gong by means of compressed air. It consists of a partially enclosed circular raceway inside of a gong in which a steel ball runs. The ball is forced around the raceway and in contact with the gong by a blast of compressed air.

Pneumatic Governor. See **Pump Governor**.

Pneumatic Pantograph. A pantograph trolley which is raised and lowered by compressed air. See **Pantograph Trolley**.

Pneumatic Sander. Figs. 1208-1222. A device for applying sand to the rails by means of compressed air drawn from the brake system. A nozzle in the sand box blows the sand into the sand spout.

Pneumatic Sander Valve. Figs. 1208-1210, 1213-1215. A compression valve used to admit air from the brake system to the nozzle of a pneumatic sander. It is usually mounted beside or above the motorman's brake valve, where it can be reached conveniently.

Pneumatic Train Signal System. See **Air Signal**.

Pneumatic Sprinkler. Fig. 226. A **Sprinkler**, which see, in which the water is forced from the tank through the sprinkling nozzles by compressed air introduced in the tank by a geared or motor-driven compressor. In some types of pneumatic sprinklers the water is forced into the tank against the pressure of the air confined in the tank and no independent air compressor is required.

Pneumatic Switch. See **Electro-Pneumatic Switch**.

Pocket. A recess or cavity into which another part is fitted or stored. See **Post Pocket, Sash Pocket, Drawbar Pocket, Door Pocket**.

Pole. See **Field Pole, Hand Pole, Trolley Pole**.

Pole Piece. See **Field Pole**.

Pony Axle. The axle of a single-motor truck which does not carry the motor. The wheels which are mounted on this axle are smaller in diameter than the driving wheels.

Pony Wheel. A wheel of small diameter mounted on the pony axle of a **Single-Motor Truck**, which see.

Portable Fare Register. Figs. 1164-1165. A fare register carried by the conductor. See **Rooke Register**.

Portable Headlight. A **Headlight**, which see, which can be carried from one end of a car to the other.

Portable Vestibule. Figs. 936-938. A frame and sashes used to enclose the end of an open platform above the dasher rail, and which can be readily removed and transferred to another car.

Positive. An arbitrary term used in electrical engineering to denote a pole or connection away from which current flows toward a negative pole or conductor. See **Negative**.

Post. An upright member of a framework which is normally in compression rather than tension. See **Door Post, End Post, Deck Post, Queen Post, Window Post, Corner Post**, etc.

Post Panel. See **Pilaster**.

Post Pocket. A socket casting placed on top of a side sill to receive the bottom end of one of the side posts. Seldom used in passenger car construction.

Postal Car. A closed car used exclusively for the transportation of mail matter. Postal cars are operated in a number of large cities running between the general post office and various sub-stations where the mail is collected and delivered by carriers. Some cars carry only mail in closed pouches, but others are fitted with racks and tables for assorting mail en route.

Potential. Literally, pressure, as applied to an electric current. A difference of potential between two points on a circuit carrying current causes the current to flow from the point of high potential to the point of low potential. The unit of measurement of difference of potential is the **Volt**, which see.

Power. The rate of doing work. The practical unit of mechanical power is the horsepower, which is equal to work done at the rate of 33,000 ft. lb. per minute. The unit of electric power is the watt. One horsepower equals 746 watts. The terms, power, current and energy, are frequently confused in electrical engineering. Electrical energy is the capacity for doing work, and is measured in watt-hours. It may be transmitted through a conductor and converted into mechanical energy by a motor or similar electrical machine. Current is the flow of electricity through a conductor, and power is the rate of doing work when the electrical energy of a current of electricity is transformed into mechanical energy and expended as work.

Power Brake. A car brake actuated by compressed air or electro-magnets, as distinguished from a hand brake.

Prentiss Pneumatic Trolley Retriever. Fig. 1333.

Prepayment Car. Any car which has but a single entrance and in which the conductor collects the fares of passengers on the entrance platform before they enter the car body. See **Pay-Within Car, Pay-as-You-Enter Car**.

Pressure Head. (Air Brake Cylinder.) The circular disc bolted to the end of the brake cylinder opposite to that through which the piston rod passes. The expansive force of the compressed air within the cylinder is exerted equally against the pressure head and the piston. The **Dead Cylinder Lever**, which see, is usually attached to the pressure head. See Figs. 498-499.

Primary Battery. One or more cells consisting of a positive and a negative electro-chemical element immersed in an electrolyte composed of a dilute acid. An electro-chemical action takes place between the two elements when they are connected through an external circuit and a current of electricity of low potential is produced. A dry battery consists of an inert solid conductor saturated with the acid electrolyte which surrounds the two elements and is hermetically sealed to prevent evaporation. Primary batteries are occasionally used to supply current for buzzer signals, instead of taking current from the trolley through a resistance.

Primary Coil. (Of a Transformer.) The coil which is connected to the source of current supply. The secondary coil is connected to the distribution circuit. See **Transformer**.

Priming. (Car Painting.) The first coat of paint applied to the bare wood to fill the pores. See **Painting**.

Printing Register. A recording **Fare Register**, which see.

Private Car. Figs. 166-168, 176-179. A luxuriously appointed car for the exclusive use of an officer of an electric railway. See **Office Car**.

Profile Carline. Another name for an outline carline. See **Compound Carline**.

Protected Groove Curtain Fixture. Fig. 653.

Providence Fenders and Wheelguards. Figs. 705-707.

Pullman Green. A dark olive green color adopted as standard by the Pullman Company for its sleeping and other cars. It is a very satisfactory color for general use on cars and has been adopted by many steam and electric railway companies.

Pullman Window. A form of window construction commonly used on parlor and sleeping cars built by the Pullman Company and occasionally employed in interurban car construction. The windows are arranged in pairs and are surmounted by a narrow fixed sash, usually of art glass or ground glass and either rectangular or semi-elliptical in shape. The posts separating each pair of windows are wider than the division posts between the two windows which comprise the pair.

Pump. An **Air Compressor**, which see.

Pump Governor. Figs. 462-465, 536-538, 547-548. A pneumatically-operated switch designed to start the air compressor motor when the pressure in the main reservoir falls below a predetermined point, and to stop the compressor motor when the pressure is raised to a fixed maximum. For automatic brake equipments the range of pressure is usually 80 to 95 lb., and for straight-air equipments, 50 to 60 lb. Pump governors consist essentially of a piston or diaphragm working against a spring, or a spring and a solenoid magnet, combined with a quick-break switch. The reservoir pressure acts on the piston which moves outward against the spring. When the pressure on the piston exceeds the resistance of the spring the switch opens and cuts out the compressor motor. When the pressure falls the spring moves the piston inward and closes the motor switch. Various auxiliary attachments have been provided on some types of governors to make them sensitive and quick-acting.

Pump Governor Synchronizing System. Fig. 459. A method of simultaneously controlling the operation of the air compressors on all the cars of a train so as to maintain a uniform main reservoir pressure on every car. On each motor car is mounted a master governor and an electro-pneumatic compressor switch. The master governors are all set to cut in and out within close limits, but instead of closing directly the circuit from the trolley to the air compressor, each master governor closes the circuit between the trolley and a common synchronizing wire, which is carried in a cable through the train, when the air pressure in the main reservoir on that car falls below the minimum limit. The magnet coils of the electro-pneumatic switches on each of the cars in the train are connected on one side to the synchronizing wire and on the other to ground. When any master governor closes, due to fall of main reservoir pressure, the synchronizing wire is energized and all of the magnets of the several compressor switches likewise are energized. These switches all close simultaneously and start all of the compressors at one time. They continue to run until the pressure in the supply pipe and in all the main reservoirs is equalized at the cutting out pressure, when all the master governors open and the synchronizing wire becomes dead.

Purlin. Longitudinal members of the roof framing applied over the carlines and to which the roof boards are nailed. Purlins are seldom used in electric car roofs, the roof boards being laid longitudinally on the carlines.

Push Button. Figs. 1234, 1238-1244. A small pearl or ebony disk or brass plunger mounted on a spring contact in the side posts of a car equipped with a buzzer signal system. When any button is pushed in by a passenger the buzzer circuit is closed at that point and the buzzers on the front and rear platforms sound as a warning to the motorman and conductor that the passenger wishes to alight at the next stopping place. See **Buzzer Signal System**.

Push Rod. (Air Brake.) A round iron rod fitting loosely inside of the hollow piston rod of a brake cylinder. It has a cross-head at its outer end attached to the cylinder lever of the foundation brake gear. When the piston moves outward the push rod moves with it, but when the brakes are applied by hand the push rod only moves outward and the piston remains stationary in the brake cylinder. See Figs. 498-499.

Putty. A thick paste made of linseed oil and whiting, used for filling cracks and holes in wood work before painting and for glazing panes of glass in window sashes. It hardens when dry and adheres to the wood.

Q

Quadruple Elliptic Spring. A group of four elliptic springs of the same size placed side by side. Quadruple springs are occasionally used under the bolsters of trucks carrying very heavy car bodies.

Queen Post. 5, Figs. 259-370. One of two struts dropped from a trussed beam and supporting a truss rod. Where only one strut is used it is called a king post. See **Body Truss Rod Queen Post**.

Quick-Action Air Brake. An automatic air brake system equipped with quick-action triple valves. These valves differ from the plain triple valve in that they are much more sensitive to sudden reductions in the brake pipe pressure, and on long trains the brakes are applied on the rear cars almost as quickly as on the forward cars when an emergency reduction is made. In service applications the quick-acting triple valves operate in exactly the same manner as a plain triple valve. See **Triple Valve**.

Quick-Action Triple Valve. See above.

Quick-Break Switch. Figs. 1137-1139. A switch designed to open quickly so as to prevent the formation of destructive arcs.

Quill Drive. Figs. 1531-1534. A form of flexible connection between motors and driving wheels, providing spring suspension for the motors and spring transmission of the motor torque. When gears are used with a quill drive they are mounted on the quills surrounding the axle with ample clearance instead of directly on the axle. The two principal types of quill drive are:

(1) The type in which the quill ends terminate in discs provided with drive pins projecting into corresponding pockets in the wheels. The pin in each pocket is surrounded and supported by a heavy helical spring, wound with progressively eccentric turns of rectangular stock. The spring is assembled with an inner and outer sleeve or bushing. Under load the spring is always under stress and absorbs the greater part of the vibration. A smaller spring inside of the driving pin presses against the cover plate in the outer end of the wheel pocket and takes the end play of the quill. The quill forms journals for the motor axle bearings, and the weight of the motor is divided between the spring-suspended quill and the spring-suspended nose of the motor.

(2) The latest type of quill drive in which direct axial compression of helical springs is employed. Arms on the quill disc project into spaces in the driving wheel hub, and have in their cylindrical faces sockets perpendicular to the plane of the wheel and opposite similar sockets cut in the wheel disc. Stiff helical springs are secured with an end in each socket, and with their

axes in the direction of drive perpendicular to the radius of the wheel. The springs are sufficiently strong to take up lateral vibration while providing smooth transmission of the motor torque.

Quride. A material made from rawhide and used for upholstering seats. It is very tough, and may be moulded into any desired shape.

R

Rabbet or Rebate. A groove cut in the edge of one piece to receive a rib on the edge of an adjoining piece. This method is commonly used in framing doors and applying panels.

Rack. See **Basket Rack**.

Radial Block. 34, Fig. 1376. See below.

Radial Casting. 32, Fig. 1376. (Single-Motor Truck.) A casting attached to the truck end frame. It has a radial slot in which a radial block attached to the car end sill moves. The draft of the truck is transmitted through the radial block and this casting to the body framing. Used only in trucks of this type which have no bolster.

Radial Draft Gear. Figs. 600-603, 610-621. A form of drawbar or coupler attachment designed to permit the outer end of the drawbar to move laterally with respect to the center line of the car body when two cars coupled together move around a sharp curve. In some types of radial gears the drawbar is returned to a central position by side springs.

Radial Truck. Figs. 1422-1425. A long wheelbase, single truck in which the axles are not confined to an exactly parallel position, but are allowed a slight end movement to permit them to assume a radial position when passing around sharp curves. Radial trucks have never found great favor in the United States, but are in limited use in Great Britain and on the Continent. See **Non-Parallel Axle Truck**.

Radiating Pipe. (Air Brake.) A nest of continuous pipe connecting the discharge pipe of an air compressor with the main reservoir. The purpose is to radiate the heat generated by the compression of the air in the pump.

Radiator. A **Heater Pipe**, which see.

Radius Bar. 37, Fig. 1368. (Truck Brake Gear.) A curved, flat bar on top of the truck end piece and attached at its ends to the live levers on each side of the truck. The truck connection brake rod is formed with a jaw enclosing the radius bar and carrying a roller or sheave which pulls against the edge of the bar. This method of connecting the body brake rigging to the truck brake rigging is made necessary by the lack of clearance for a brake rod to pass over the inside motor and connect with a single live lever near the center of the truck. It permits the truck to radiate on curves without affecting the tension on the body brake connections, since the roller moves radially about the truck center pin along the curved radius bar. The terms brake lever equalizer, horizontal lever and brake beam have all been applied to this piece, but none are so distinctive as radius bar.

Radius Bar Clevis. 40, Fig. 1368.

Radius Bar Guide. 39, Fig. 1368. A strap or casting attached to the top of a truck side frame and serving to prevent lateral movement of a radius bar.

Radius Bar Roller. 69, Figs. 1388-1390. A roller or sheave working in a jaw on the end of the truck connection brake rod and running on the inside edge of a radius bar. Also called brake rod roller.

Radius Bar Wear Plate. 38, Fig. 1368. A plate attached to the bottom of a radius bar or on top of the truck side frame to take the wear caused by the movement of the radius bar when the brakes are applied or released.

Rafter. 21, Figs. 259-370. A name sometimes applied to the carlines in the lower deck of a car roof. The proper term is lower deck carline.

Rail. A horizontal member of a framework, as a door rail. See **Belt Rail, Dasher Rail, Door Rail**.

Railway. A pair of continuous parallel track rails on which a car mounted on flanged wheels can run.

Railway Motor. A general name applied to any type of motor used for traction purposes. See **Motor**.

Ratchet Brake Handle. Figs. 568-572. A curved brake handle containing a ratchet connection to the top of the brake shaft. When the handle is turned to wind up the brakes the ratchet teeth engage and the brake shaft is turned. When the handle is moved in the opposite direction the ratchet teeth slip over one another, while the brake shaft is held stationary by the ratchet wheel and pawl mounted on the floor of the platform. The purpose of a ratchet brake handle is to permit the brakes to be applied by moving the handle back and forth a number of times through the short arc in which the maximum force can be exerted by the motorman as he stands in his regular position. See **Brake Ratchet Wheel**.

Ratchet Jack. A jack in which the lifting post is made in the form of a ratchet bar with which a pivoted dog engages. The movement of the handle of the jack moves this dog through a short distance and raises the lifting bar the height of one tooth, or far enough so that another pawl will drop into engagement with the ratchet bar and hold it. The lifting dog can then be lowered over one tooth and again raised by the handle. By reversing the holding pawl the jack can be used to lower a weight as well as to raise it.

Ratchet Sash Lock. Figs. 957, 959. See **Sash Lock**.

Ratchet Wheel. See **Brake Ratchet Wheel**.

Rattan. A tropical reed the stems of which, when dried and split, are woven into a fabric extensively used for upholstering car seats. Rattan seating is made by glueing heavy canvas on the back of the woven rattan and varnishing the surface of the rattan to give a hard, glossy finish.

Raymond Sash Lock. Fig. 956.

Rear Platform. The platform on the back end of a car as referred to its normal direction of motion. The rear platform is occupied by the conductor, and on single-end cars is usually made much longer than the front platform.

Rebate. See **Rabbet**.

Receiver. (Of a Telephone.) The diaphragm and case which is held to the ear and reproduces the sound impressed on the transmitter at the other end of the circuit. The receiver of car telephones is usually a small, hard rubber disc with a metal hook, by which it is hung on the protruding arm of the connection switch inside of the telephone.

Recommended Practice. The American Electric Railway Engineering Association has adopted the following recommended practices affecting car construction:

HEIGHTS OF COUPLERS, PLATFORMS, CAR STEPS AND BUMPERS

	Interurban In.	City In.
Height from top of rail to center of coupler	35	20
Height from top of rail to bottom of bumper	43	25
Height from top of rail to top of bumper	51	31
Width of bumper	8	6
Length of radial coupler from center of pocket-pin to pulling face of coupler	54	54
Height from top of rail to top of tread of first step	17	17
Height from top of rail to top of tread of second step	29	..
Height from top of rail to top of third step	40	..
Height from top of rail to vestibule floor	51	31
Height of riser from vestibule platform to floor of car	..	10

"Your committee also recommends that on city cars where the bumper arrangement will permit, a pocket casting should be placed on the top of the bumper, the center of the pocket to be 35 in. above the top of the rail, and the casting to be of ample strength and properly braced, so that by means of a suitable bar city cars can be coupled on a level with the automatic couplers of interurban cars.

"For this purpose it would appear that for the present at least it would be advisable to maintain a link slot and coupling pin hole in the knuckle of the automatic couplers."

Recording Fare Register. Fig. 1160. A **Fare Register**, which see, in which is included a printing mechanism for recording on a strip of paper whenever desired the totalizer readings and other information, such as the date, car number, trip number, etc.

Reducing Valve. See **Feed Valve**.

Reflector. (Of a Headlight.) A polished metallic mirror, usually of parabolic shape, mounted behind the source of illumination and designed to throw the light rays ahead in a solid beam.

Refrigerator Car. Fig. 201. A freight car built especially for carrying perishable commodities, such as meat, vegetables and beer, at a temperature close to the freezing point. Interior ice boxes are provided, and the sides, floor and roof are insulated against heat. Refrigerator cars have been built for a few interurban railways.

Register. A **Fare Register**, which see.

Register Back. Figs. 1168-1170. A frame permanently mounted in the car body on one of the end bulkheads over the door. The case containing the recording mechanism of a fare register is attached to it and locked on. The back carries a system of levers, crank arms and springs through which the motion of the operating rod or cords is transmitted to the register mechanism inside of the sealed case. Different forms of backs are required for single and duplex registers of different makes and for rod and cord connections.

Register Cord. A leather thong or woven cotton rope strung in guides from end to end of the car and attached to the levers on a register back. It is a substitute for a register rod.

Register Cord Coupling. An interlocking hook on one end of a register cord engaging with a similar hook on another piece of cord to connect them together.

Register Cord Guide. Figs. 1193-1196. A fixed or swinging pulley over which a register cord runs. Various types are used for special locations. From end to end of closed cars the register cord is usually strung through eyes formed in the hand pole brackets.

Register Cord Pull. Fig. 1197. A pivoted bell crank, by means of which the longitudinal movement of a register cord is changed to a lateral movement and is transmitted to the levers on the register back. A cord pull takes the place of a corner pulley, and does away with the excessive wear on the register cord.

Register Rod. A round or square rod running the length of the car and carrying, at frequent intervals, short handles, by which it can be turned through an angle of about 60 deg. to operate the mechanism within the fare register, mounted at one end of the car. The connection from the rod to the register back is made by a rigid crank arm on the register rod and a connecting rod of suitable length attached to the system of levers on the register back. In closed cars the register rod is mounted in brackets, either over the center aisle or under the deck plate. In open cars the rod is mounted inside the car above the openings between posts so that it can be operated from the running board.

Register Rod Bracket. Figs. 1182-1192. A fixed or adjustable bracket mounted on the deck sill or side plate to support a register rod. The hand-strap pole brackets frequently are used to support the register rod also.

Register Rod Bushing. Figs. 1184-1189. A cylindrical sleeve mounted on a square register rod to form a journal turning in a bearing in a register rod bracket.

Register Rod Coupling. Fig. 1101. A metal sleeve fitting over the abutting ends of two sections of a register rod and secured to each by set screws.

Register Rod Crank. Figs. 1179-1180. A short arm fastened to the end of a register rod, and to which is attached one end of a pull bar by means of which the rotation of the register rod is transmitted to the register back mechanism.

Register Rod Handle. Figs. 1171-1178. A metal arm fastened on a register rod to turn it. They are sometimes fitted with hanging straps to enable the conductor to reach them more easily.

Register Rod Pull Bar. Short bars connecting the crank arms on the end of a register rod to the system of levers on the register back.

Registering Fare Box. Fig. 1207.

Regulating Switch. A term occasionally applied to a **Heater Switch**, which see.

Regulator. See **Controller Regulator**.

Relay. An electro-magnetic device for making or breaking small currents by energizing a magnet. A pivoted armature is used which carries on it one or more contacts. See **Current Limit Relay**.

Release Position. The position of the handle of a motorman's brake valve in which the pressure in the brake cylinders is allowed to escape to the atmosphere and hence release the brakes on the trucks. In automatic brake equipments the release position of the brake valve admits air to the brake pipe which causes the triple valves to assume the release and recharge position, in which the brake cylinder is open to the atmosphere and the auxiliary reservoir is connected to the brake pipe for recharging. See **Graduated Release**.

Release Spring. 64, Figs. 1388-1390. A flat or coil spring attached to the truck brake rigging to pull the brake shoes away from the wheels when the brakes are released. The term is also applied to the coil spring surrounding the piston rod in a brake cylinder, which forces the piston back when the air pressure in the cylinder is released.

Release Valve. (Electro-Pneumatic Brake.) See Fig. 454. The magnet valve which, when energized, opens the brake cylinder to atmosphere and causes the brakes to release. See **Application Valve**.

Removable Sash. A window sash which can be entirely removed from the frame so as to convert a closed car into a car with half-open sides. See **Semi-Convertible Car**.

Repulsion Motor. A type of single-phase motor used to some extent in Europe in which the armature currents are produced by electro-magnetic induction. The armature conductors form the secondary of a transformer, the primary of which is wound on the stator.

Reservoir. (Air Brake.) A steel tank for holding a supply of compressed air to operate the brakes. A main reservoir and an auxiliary reservoir are used in an automatic brake system. The compressor discharges into the main reservoir, from which air is supplied to the brake pipe through a feed valve and the motorman's brake valve. The auxiliary reservoir is mounted under the car near the brake cylinder and is connected to the brake pipe and the brake cylinder by a triple valve. In the normal running position the auxiliary reservoir is fed from the brake pipe and the connection to the brake cylinder is closed. To apply the brakes the pressure in the brake pipe is reduced, closing the feed port in the triple valve and opening a port which admits air from the auxiliary reservoir to the brake cylinder.

Reservoir Bracket. A strap or other fastening used to secure a brake reservoir to the car body underframe.

Reservoir Drain Cock. Fig. 481. A small valve in the bottom of an air brake reservoir to drain off any water of condensation which may collect.

Reservoir Pipe. (Air Brake.) The pipe connecting the main reservoir with the motorman's brake valve.

Resistance. That property of a conductor which opposes the flow of a current of electricity through it. Resistance may be expressed as the quotient of the electromotive force divided by the current strength. The unit of resistance is the **Ohm**, which see. The term, resistance, is commonly applied to the coils or grids of metal which are inserted in the motor circuit during acceleration to cut down the current value. See **Rheostat**.

Resistor. Fig. 1748. A term used by the Westinghouse Electric & Manufacturing Company to designate a body having high electrical resistance which is introduced in a circuit to reduce the rate of flow of current in the circuit. It is analogous with the term rheostat, as commonly used.

Rest. A support for anything. See **Arm Rest, Foot Rest**.

Retaining Ring. A device for securing a steel tire to a wheel center. See Figs. 1627-1632.

Retardation. The rate of change of decreasing velocity of a moving body. Negative acceleration.

Retriever Signal Bell. Fig. 732.

Return Circuit. The path of an electric current back to the source of supply. In electric railway work the earth is used for the return circuit, most of the current being carried back to the power house through the track rails, which are bonded at the joints. See **Ground** and **Double Trolley System**.

Reverse Handle. See **Controller Reversing Handle**.

Reverser. Figs. 1762, 1782, 1800-1801. In a multiple-unit control system, a device for changing the motor armature and field connections so as to reverse the direction of rotation of the armatures. In the General Electric Type M. control system, the reverser is a switch, the movable part of which is a rocker arm operated by two electromagnets, one being energized for each direction of motion. The motor field and armature leads are connected to fingers bearing on the ends of the reverser rocker arm. Copper plates on the rocker arm establish the proper connections between the fingers for obtaining forward or backward motion of the car. A similar device operated by an electro-pneumatic cylinder is used in the Westinghouse unit-switch system of multiple control.

Reversible Seat. A cross seat in which the back may be swung or turned on its supports from one side of the seat to the other so that passengers may face forward in either direction the car may be moving. Reversible seats are used on nearly all double-end city cars and on interurban cars.

Revolving Car Seat. Fig. 1265.

Rex Arc Headlight. Fig. 1030.

Rex Basket Rack. Fig. 720.

Rex Curtain Roller. Figs. 641-643.

Rheostat. Figs. 1744-1749. A grid of iron resistance strips mounted on insulation in a frame under the car body and used to limit the flow of current to the motors during the acceleration period. The resistance is divided into a number of steps and taps run from the terminals of each step to the controller. When the controller handle is moved to the first point all of the resistance is in series with the motors. As the handle is moved forward point by point the groups of resistance are successively cut out of circuit until the series running point is reached. When passing from series to parallel conections all of the resistance is again cut in and then cut out, group by group, until the parallel running position is reached.

Rheostatic Brake. A method of retarding the motion of an electric car by reversing the motors and operating them as generators. The energy represented by the current thus generated is dissipated as heat by rheostats. The retardation is increased by adding more resistance while in a **Magnetic Track Brake,** which see, the retardation is increased by cutting out resistance. Now little used.

Rib. See **Body Rib, End Rib.**

Ribbon Wound Coil. A field or armature coil composed of concentric turns of strap or ribbon copper, instead of round wire.

Ridlon Trolley Catcher. Fig. 1332.

Rigid Bolster. A truck bolster having no side play, as distinguished from a bolster supported on a swinging spring plank. Nearly all passenger car trucks have swinging bolsters.

Rim. (Car Wheel.) The outside ring of metal to which the plate or spokes join. It includes the tread and the flange. In steel-tired wheels the tread and flange are formed on the tire, which is shrunk, or otherwise fastened on the rim of the wheel center.

Ring Curtain Fixture. Figs. 636-640.

Ring Nut. Figs. 1688-1690. A type of fastening for an armature end plate and core on an armature spider.

Riser. See **Step Riser.**

Rivet. A piece of metal with a head formed on one end, which is inserted in a hole punched through a plate or other metallic part and hammered out on the other end to form a clinch. Rivets are extensively used for fastening together the parts of a metal underframe.

Rod. A long iron or steel bar of small diameter used as a tension member in a truss or other framework. See **Brake Rod, Sill and Plate Rod, Truss Rod.**

Rod Basket Rack. Figs. 720-721. A Basket Rack, which see, having a bottom composed of metal rods.

Roller. See **Shade Roller, Radius Bar Roller.**

Roller Bearing. A type of shaft bearing in which the journal is surrounded by a cage containing a number of parallel rollers, which are free to revolve in the cage and roll over the surface of the journal. Such bearings have nearly, if not quite, as low a coefficient of friction as ball bearings. See **Anti-Friction Bearing.**

Roller Side Bearing. An anti-friction device for a body and truck side bearing, consisting of two or more conical rollers confined in a cage and bearing on a hardened steel plate.

Roof. 48 and 49, Figs. 259-370. The covering over a car body. Car roofs are commonly of the monitor deck type, consisting of a raised central portion or upper deck and a lower deck along the side. The roof boards are supported on cross pieces called carlines, and are usually covered with heavy painted canvas or tin plate to shed water. See **Arch Roof.**

Roof Apron. See **Deck Apron.**

Roof Boards. Narrow matched boards laid on top of the roof carlines to form the roof covering.

Roof Gong. Fig. 943. An alarm gong mounted on top of the platform hood and struck by pulling a cord hanging down in front of the motorman.

Roof Grab Handle. Figs. 914-916. A hand rod bolted to the corner of the roof above the roof steps to assist in climbing onto the roof.

Roof Ladder. See **Roof Steps.**

Roof Landing. A small platform or group of board strips built on the corner of the roof above the roof steps to stand on while inspecting or repairing the trolley pole.

Roof Running Board. 85, Figs. 259-370. A name sometimes applied to a **Trolley Board,** which see.

Roof Step. Figs. 917-920. One of several cast-iron steps fastened to the outside body corner posts of a car to provide footholds for climbing onto the roof to inspect or repair the trolley. Commonly called **Trolley Steps,** which see.

Roof Ventilator. Figs. 1362-1363. A ventilator rising from the upper or lower deck roofs, as distinguished from a deck sash ventilator.

Roofing Canvas. A heavy grade of closely woven cotton cloth used to cover the outside of car roofs. It is usually painted on the outside, and is bedded in thick white lead paint applied on the roof boards.

Rooke Register. Figs. 1164-1165. A type of portable fare register in which the passenger inserts the proper coin in a slot of the register held in the conductor's hand. When a coin is once inserted in the slot it is gripped and cannot be removed. By pressing a registering grip on the handle of the register the coin passes through the register, is recorded and falls into the palm of the conductor's hand, so that it can be used again for making change.

Root Spring Scraper. Figs. 1319-1320.

Rope. A twisted or woven strand cotton or hemp cord of large diameter. See **Switching Rope, Trolley Rope.**

Rotary Snow Plow. A snow plow having a large revolving screw cutter mounted in front, which bores through the snow drifts and discharges the snow to one side through a chute. Used only in very severe climates.

Rough Stuff. (Car Painting.) The coats applied after the priming to form a surface on which the body color is applied.

Route Signal Lamp. Fig. 1060. A signal lamp used to indicate by colors at night the route or line on which a car is running.

Rub Plate. A Wear Plate, which see.

Rubber. A vegetable gum which is treated under heat with sulphur and other minerals to form a tough and highly elastic substance extensively employed in the arts. Rubber has high resistivity to the flow of an electric current and is widely used for insulating electric conductors which are not subject to excessive heating.

Running Board. 77, Figs. 259-260. A folding step extending along the side of an open car from bumper to bumper and hung below the side sill by hangers attached to the side sill. The running board is also called the side step and folding step, but neither term is distinctive.

Running Board Hanger. 75, Figs. 259-260. A hinged bracket attached to the side of an open car to support the running board.

Running Board Bracket. 75, Figs. 259-260. See **Running Board Hanger.**

Running Board Riser. 76, Figs. 259-260. A vertical plank attached to the running board brackets just above the running board. Its purpose is to prevent the foot from slipping in under the car. It is called side step fender and toe guard, but it is properly termed a riser.

S

Safety Chain. See **Check Chain.**

Safety Coupling Chain. A heavy chain attached to the bumper beam and carrying a hook which engages with an eyebolt attached to the bumper beam of an adjoining car. Its purpose is to prevent the cars from parting in case the couplers should break. Two such chains are used in pairs, the hooks on one car engaging with the eye of the adjoining car. Coupling chains are only occasionally used on electric cars operated in trains.

Safety Gate. See **Platform Gate.**

Safety Hanger. 15, Fig. 1368. A strap secured to one of the main members of a truck frame and passing under a brake beam, brake turnbuckle or spring plank to prevent the part enclosed from falling on the track in case it should break or become loose.

Safety Step Tread. Figs. 927-930. A rubber or roughened metallic plate covering a step tread to prevent persons from slipping on the step.

Safety Valve. Figs. 470-471. A pop valve which opens under excessive pressure and permits the escape of the gas or liquid contained in the reservoir to which it is attached. Safety valves are usually supplied with hot water heating systems and are also inserted in the compressor discharge pipe of all air brake systems to prevent the accumulation of excessive pressure in the main reservoir.

Saloon. A small compartment in an interurban car containing toilet facilities.

Saloon Hopper. Fig. 897. A soil closet in a saloon. Dry hoppers are commonly used on electric interurban cars.

Salt Car. A car used to scatter salt on the track rails during freezing weather so as to keep them free from ice. The salt is shoveled from a bin into a hopper from which it falls through a spout onto the rails.

Samson Bell Cord. Figs. 750-752.

Sand Box. 112, Figs. 259-370; Figs. 1223-1232. A box mounted in a car body and containing dry salt which is dropped through a pipe onto the rails in front of the wheels. A valve in the bottom of the box is used for regulating the flow of sand and this valve is usually operated by a hand or foot lever on the front platform. Pneumatically operated sanding devices are also used. The sand box is ordinarily built in under one of the corner seats in the car and is filled by lifting the seat cushion.

Sand Car. A car used for the distribution of dry sand from a central drying plant to the different car houses and depots. In a few large cities such cars are also used to sand the rails continuously during bad weather. They are run slowly and sand is shoveled from the bin into a hopper and falls through a spout on one rail in a continuous stream. See **Salt Car.**

Sand Plank. A name sometimes applied to a **Spring Plank**, which see.

Sand Spout. 114, Figs. 259-370. An iron pipe or piece of rubber hose dropped from the mouth of the sand valve and reaching nearly to the rail in front of the forward wheel of the truck. The sand is discharged through it onto the rail.

Sand Trap. Figs. 1211, 1216-1218, 1221-1222. The box and nozzle of a pneumatic sander placed below the sand bin and connected to the top of the sand spout.

Sand Valve. 113, Figs. 259-370; Figs. 1226-1227. A valve in the bottom of a sand box to control the flow of sand on the rail.

Sand Valve Lever. A lever on the motorman's platform, operated either by hand or by a foot pedal, which is connected to the sand valve by a rod and serves to open the valve so as to allow the sand to drop on the rail.

Sander. Figs. 1208-1233. A sand box and valve. See **Pneumatic Sander.**

Sanding Process. See **Paint.**

Sandwich Plates. See **Flitch Plates.**

Sash. 46 and 47, Figs. 259-370; Fig. 692. The framework of a window enclosing the glass. In car building the term sash is commonly used to include both the glass and the frame. See **Deck Sash, Drop Sash.**

Sash Balance. Fig. 974. A spring roller similar to a curtain roller to which the sash is attached by light chains. The torsion of the spring in the roller counterbalances the weight of the sash and makes it easy to raise or lower the sash.

Sash Catch. (Semi-Convertible Car.) Fig. 974. A spring catch for holding the sash in place after it has been raised into the deck pocket.

Sash Corner Plate. Figs. 997-1000. An L-shaped plate screwed on the corner of a sash frame to hold it square.

Sash Lift. Figs. 982-993. A handle, knob or recessed casting attached to the bottom rail of a window sash, by which the sash can be raised. A variety of forms of sash lifts are used, some of which are illustrated. A common form is a small leather tab screwed to the bottom sash rail. The handles of a **Sash Lock**, which see, are also used as sash lifts.

Sash Lock. Figs. 952-971. A spring latch attached to the side of a window sash. The bolt, which is withdrawn by pressing together the fixed and movable handles of the sash lock, engages with a sash lock stop on the window post. Several improved types of ratchet sash locks which permit the sash to be raised to any desired height are illustrated.

Sash Lock Stop. A small brass casting screwed to the window post and engaging with the bolt of a sash lock. Sash lock stops are made in two patterns, to hold the window closed and to hold it open. Various forms of ratchet and toothed racks have been devised to take the place of ordinary sash lock stops.

Sash Opener. See **Deck Sash Opener.**

Sash Parting Strip. A narrow strip of wood fastened on the window post and forming a guide to separate the upper and lower sashes. Also called a parting bead.

Sash Pivot. See **Deck Sash Pivot.**

Sash Pocket. A cavity under the lower deck or in the side of the car below the belt rail into which the window sashes of a semi-convertible car can be stored when not in place in the window opening. See **Convertible Car** and **Semi-Convertible Car.**

Sash Spring. Figs. 994-995. A flat spring screwed on the edge of a window sash and bearing against the sash parting strip. Its purpose is to prevent the sash from rattling in the window groove.

Sauvage Slack Adjuster. Fig. 1482.

Schoen Solid Steel Wheel. Figs. 1617-1620.

Screw. See **Wood Screw.**

Screw Jack. A lifting jack consisting of a base, a screw column and threaded nut which rests on the base and can be turned with a bar inserted in holes in the nut. By turning the nut the screw column can be raised or lowered.

Screw Thread. A spiral ridge cut on the surface of a cylinder with a uniform pitch. Screw threads are either square in cross section or V-shaped, the grooves between adjoining threads being of the same cross-section as the thread.

Screw Brake. A mechanical slipper brake which is forced down on the track rails by turning a screw working in a nut fastened to a pair of toggle arms. Not in common use in the United States but employed on many cars in Europe as an emergency brake.

Scroll. (Elliptic Spring.) The casting which confines the ends of the spring leaves.

Seat. (1) Figs. 1259-1304. A place to sit. Electric railway car seats are classified as longitudinal and cross seats according to their location within the car body. Longitudinal seats extending from end to end of the car on each side of the central aisle are commonly used in closed city cars owing to the wide aisle and large amount of standing room afforded. For long distance, city, suburban and interurban service, cars are now commonly built with cross seats holding two persons each. Short longitudinal seats in the rear corners or all four corners are also used in connection with cross seats in city and suburban cars. The cross seats in open cars are commonly called benches since they are made of wooden slats not upholstered. Long longitudinal seats in city cars are frequently covered with a strip of plush or heavy carpet and are not otherwise upholstered. Upholstered car seats are covered with rattan, plush or imitation leather. In double-end city cars and usually in interurban cars the cross seats have reversible backs so that passengers may face in either direction.

(2) A bearing for one piece on another as a spring seat.

Seat Arm. The upper part of a seat end which supports the arm of a person sitting in the seat. The seat arm is often dispensed with on the narrow cross seats used in city cars. The term is also applied to the arms or levers which support the seat back, and the proper name for this part is **Seat Back Arm,** which see.

Seat Arm Cap. A metal cap on a seat end to take the wear. Seldom used in electric car seats.

Seat Arm Pivot. Figs. 1315-1316. A trunnion fastened on the edge of a reversible seat back on which the seat back arm is mounted. The base of the trunnion is often enlarged to secure a firm fastening and the piece thus becomes a seat arm pivot plate. Seat arm pivot plates are attached to the side posts of cross seat open cars to form a pivot for the curved seat back arms which are rigidly attached to the seat backs.

Seat Arm Stop. A metal bracket attached to a seat end or the wall of the car to form a stop for the seat back arm.

Seat Back. 88, Figs. 259-370. The vertical cushion or support for the back of a person sitting on the seat. The seat back may be fixed in position or mounted on seat back arms so that it may be swung or turned over and made to face in the opposite direction.

Seat Back Arm. 89, Figs. 259-370. A metal arm supporting a seat back on one side. With some types of reversible car seats the seat back arms are connected to mechanism under the seat cushion whereby the seat back is made to turn completely over when it is reversed.

Seat Back Bottom Rail. 95, Figs. 259-370. The lowest horizontal member of the frame of a seat back.

Seat Back Bumper. Figs. 1312-1314. A small piece of rubber set in the edge of an open car seat back rail to prevent the seat back rails from striking the seat bottom when the seat back is turned over.

Seat Back Bumper Plate. Figs. 1317-1318. A small brass plate screwed to the edge of a seat back rail and securing a rubber seat back bumper in place.

Seat Back Corner Handle. Figs. 1305-1310. See **Seat Back Handle.**

Seat Back Cushion. An upholstered seat back. For interurban cars they are sometimes made extra high with a projecting roll across the top called a head roll. See Figs. 1259-1260.

Seat Back Frame. The framework of a seat back on which the upholstering is applied or in the case of open car seats the frame in which the slat panels or spindles are inserted.

Seat Back Handle. Figs. 1305-1310. A metal handle formed on the upper outside corner of a seat back to provide a support to be grasped by a person standing in the aisle.

Seat Back Molding. A strip of wood, metal or upholstering fastened along the edge of a seat back to conceal the edges of the upholstering material and to protect the upholstering from wear.

Seat Back Mullion. 96, Figs. 259-370. A vertical post in a wooden seat back frame. See **Mullion.**

Seat Back Rail. 94 and 95, Figs. 259-370. One of the horizontal bars of a slatted seat back frame. They are designated as top and bottom rails.

Seat Back Slat. (1) Thin strips of wood forming the panels of a wooden seat back.

(2) In a seat back cushion, the slats across the back of the box frame which support the seat back upholstery springs.

Seat Back Spindle. One of the small turned wooden rods inserted between the top and bottom rails of an open car seat back. Slat panels are also used for this purpose.

Seat Back Spring. One of a number of coil springs used in upholstering a seat back. Woven wire springs in one piece are also used for this purpose.

Seat Back Top Rail. 94, Figs. 259-370. See **Seat Back Rail.**

Seat Bottom. 91, Figs. 259-370. The boards forming a seat when no upholstered cushion is used. They are fastened on front and back seat bottom rails. In the case of longitudinal seats, the back seat bottom rail is attached to the inside of the body posts and the front rail is supported between the end bulkheads by a continuous riser board or by short posts resting on the floor. Electric heaters are frequently inserted in the panels of the seat riser. In open car cross seats the seat bottom is supported at the ends by the seat end panels, framed to the side posts, and by a wide board placed on edge between the side posts under the center of the seat. This board is known as a division board or post cross rail. The foot rest rod is supported on it by a bracket in the center.

Seat Bottom Cross Bar. A cross piece between the seat bottom rails cut to the desired curve of the seat bottom and supporting the slats or boards forming the seat.

Seat Bottom Rail. See **Seat Bottom.**

Seat Cover. A strip of plush or carpet with which a hard wooden seat is covered.

Seat Cushion. An upholstered box cushion fitted in a seat frame. They are usually made by mounting coil springs on slats placed across the bottom of the box frame. On these springs is placed a layer of heavy webbing and curled hair or thick felt, and an outside cover of plush or rattan seating material. The edges of the cushions are usually padded heavily over the box frame to prevent cutting by the corners of the frame.

Seat Division Arm. A seat arm dividing a longitudinal seat into two or more sections.

Seat End. A wooden frame or metal stand supporting one end of a car seat and projecting above the seat cushion to form an arm rest. In electric railway car seats the arm rest is frequently dispensed with to facilitate entering or leaving the seat. Seat ends are distinguished as aisle and wall seat ends. The curved seat back arms of open car cross seats form seat ends for the benches in the center of the car, but fixed metal seat end brackets are attached to the ends of the bulkhead seats.

Seat End Bracket. 92, Figs. 259-260. A curved arm rest on the end of fixed cross seats of an open car. The seat back arms of the reversible seats serve as arm rests.

Seat End Panel. (Open Car.) 90, Figs. 259-260; Figs. 1291-1293. A vertical panel, the width of the cross seats, attached to the side posts below the seats.

Seat Front. A **Seat Riser,** which see.

Seat Leg. A post supporting the front seat bottom rail of a longitudinal seat.

Seat Lock. A spring latch inserted in the outside seat back arm, seat back stop or seat end to lock the seat back in position. The lock is turned by a special key in the possession of the conductor.

Seat Pedestal. A pressed steel column supporting one end of a cross-seat frame. See Fig. 1294.

Seat Rail. A cross bar connecting the two seat ends of a cross seat and supporting the seat cushion. In longitudinal seats the corresponding parts are designated as front and back seat bottom rails.

Seat Riser. A vertical board or row of narrow panels closing the opening between the floor and the front seat bottom rail of a longitudinal seat. Electric heaters are frequently inserted in the panels of the seat riser.

Seat Slat. A narrow strip of wood used to form part of a wooden seat back or seat bottom.

Seat Spring. A spiral or woven wire spring used in upholstering a seat back or cushion.

Seat Stand. 130, Fig. 334. A support for the outer end of a car seat. It is usually made of iron in the form of a tapered elliptical pillar or a frame having two legs resting on the floor and connected by a cross bar. More commonly called **Seat Pedestal**, which see.

Seat Webbing. Strips of heavy, coarse burlap or canvas, used in upholstering car seats. They are interwoven over the springs and the curled hair or felt is applied over them.

Seating. The outer covering of an upholstered car seat. Plush, rattan and imitation leather are commonly used for this purpose.

Secondary Coil. In a transformer the coil which is not connected to the source of supply of current. See **Transformer**.

Selector Relay. A device for automatically throwing in or out of circuit a dynamotor forming part of a 1200-volt car equipment. See **Dynamotor**.

Semi-Convertible Car. Figs. 16-25, 68-79. A cross-seat, closed car with entrance and exit platforms at the ends which is constructed so that both the upper and lower sashes of the side windows may be removed in warm weather, making the car sides entirely open between the window sills and the side plates. Three types of semi-convertible cars are in use. In the first type the sashes are entirely removed from the car at the beginning of warm weather, and are stored in a car house or shop until replaced in the fall. In the second type the sashes are dropped into wall pockets between the inner and outer sheathing of the body. In the third type the sashes are raised in grooves and stored in pockets formed between the lower deck roof and the headlining.

The Brill patent semi-convertible window system, Fig. 265, consists of an upper and lower sash guided into the roof pocket by trunnions moving in metal runways. The bolts of the window locks form the bottom trunnions of the lower sash while the top trunnions are cast on corner plates screwed to the sash frame. The upper sash has a single pair of trunnions at the top. These trunnions are formed on plates which have an inwardly projecting hook at the top which engages with the top trunnion of the lower sash when it is raised. The trunnion runways in the deck pocket are curved and as the sashes are raised their upper ends are moved inward under the roof. The bottom trunnions of the lower sash drop into notches and hold both sashes securely in the pocket.

Semi-Elliptic Spring. Fig. 1571. A Half-Elliptic Spring, which see.

Semi-Empire Deck. A type of upper deck ceiling construction for interurban cars. The deck headlining is curved down to the deck sill molding except at the deck sashes, where it breaks into flat arches above the semi-elliptic sash frames. In an Empire deck the ceiling is vaulted above each pair of deck sashes. Cars with semi-Empire decks are shown in Figs. 147, 166, etc.

Semi-Steel Car. A car body built largely of steel plates and pressed or rolled sections, and having wooden side and roof framing and interior trim.

Series. A method of connecting two or more pieces of electrical apparatus to a common circuit. The connections are made so that the negative side of one piece of apparatus is connected to the positive of the next and the full current passes successively through each piece of apparatus in the circuit. The drop in voltage on the circuit due to the resistance of the parts in the circuit is the sum of the drops in each part. Railway motors are usually connected through the controller so that on starting two motors and an exterior resistance are in series between the trolley and ground. The exterior resistance is then gradually cut out of the circuit until none remains. The next step changes the connections so that the motors are connected in pairs in parallel between the trolley and ground with all the exterior resistance again in series with the trolley. The resistance is then gradually cut out until each motor is receiving full trolley voltage. See **Parallel**.

Series Motor. A motor in which the armature and field windings are connected in series with each other and both carry the full current supplied to the motor. A shunt motor has a field winding which is connected around the armature and carries only part of the current supplied to the motor. Series motors only are now used for railway work.

Series-Parallel Control. Fig. 1715. The common method of controlling the speed of direct-current railway motors by connecting them first in series in pairs with external resistance in the circuit. To increase the speed the resistance is cut out by steps, and when entirely cut out the motors are then connected in parallel between the trolley and ground with the external resistance again in circuit. The maximum speed is attained when the resistance is entirely cut out and all the motors are receiving full trolley voltage.

Service Application. An application of the air brakes with moderate power such as is made for ordinary stops. The pressure in the brake cylinder is applied in one or more graduated steps and released just before the end of the stop, so as to prevent jerking due to the sudden rise in the coefficient of brake shoe friction at the instant of coming to rest.

Set Screw Fastening. A type of fastening for securing steel tires on wheel centers in which pointed set screws are inserted through the rim of the wheel center into the inside periphery of the tire. Seldom used.

Shade. A window Curtain, which see.

Shade Roller. See Curtain Roller.

Shaft. A rod turning in bearings. See **Armature Shaft, Brake Shaft**.

Shank. The part of a bolt under the head; hence the extended body of a coupler or drawbar between the head and the draft spring.

Share Plow. See Shear Plow.

Shaw Lightning Arrester. Fig. 1824.

Shear Board. Another name for a **Wing Board**, which see.

Shear Guard. Fig. 711. A type of wheelguard in which a single diagonal board or pointed nose is attached to the truck end piece just above the rails. Its purpose is to push and shear a prostrate body to one side of the track.

Shear Plow. Figs. 215, 217, 219, 220. A snow plow having one inclined deflecting plane to push the snow off to one side of the track only. A nose plow has two inclined planes with a central ridge and pushes the snow to both sides of the track.

Sheathing. 107, Figs. 259-370. The narrow vertical matched boards forming the outside surface of a car body below the windows. Wide panels are frequently used for city cars, but sheathing is universally used for wooden interurban car bodies. The covering of the framing on the inside of the body is termed inside lining.

Sheathing Furring. Narrow strips of wood framed horizontally between the side posts to serve as nailing strips for the sheathing. When these strips extend vertically and are used to form a backing for the side panels between the posts they are called side ribs.

Sheathing Lining. 36, Figs. 259-370. A layer of rough boards applied to the outside of the body framing as a backing for the sheathing.

Shelby Seamless Gong. Figs. 944-945.

Shelby Trolley Poles. Figs. 1879-1882.

Shellac. A resinous gum which when dissolved in alcohol forms a clear liquid varnish. Extensively used for insulating purposes.

Shim. A filling piece. See **Side Bearing Shim.**

Shim Slack Adjuster. Fig. 1482.

Shoe. See **Brake Shoe.**

Short Broom Sweeper. See **Sweeper.**

Short Circuit. A direct path for the flow of an electric current. A coil is said to be short circuited when the insulation between two or more adjacent wires breaks down and the current flowing takes the path of least resistance to ground without passing through all the turns of wire.

Short Sill. A term occasionally applied to a short floor timber in the underframe which extends longitudinally between two transverse timbers.

Short Wheelbase Truck. Figs. 1369-1372, 1409-1411, etc. A motor truck in which the axles are placed close to the bolster and the motors are outside hung. The usual wheelbase of such trucks is about 4 ft.

Shunt. A conductor forming a by-path for the flow of part of the current of electricity in a main circuit.

Shunt Motor. See **Series Motor.**

Side Bearings. 98, Figs. 259-370; 28, Figs. 1388-1390. Bearing plates mounted on the body and truck bolsters near their ends to prevent the car body from rocking on the center plates. The upper plate or block of metal is known as the body side bearing and the lower plate on which it rests when the car tilts is known as the truck side bearings. The side bearings are not ordinarily in contact on straight level track when the car body is centrally loaded, but a small amount of vertical play is permitted and the load is normally transmitted from the body bolster to the truck bolster through the center plates. With some types of single-motor trucks the entire load is carried by the side bearings on the truck frames and no center plate or truck bolster is employed. Various forms of anti-friction side bearings are in limited use.

Side Bearing Shims. 30, Figs. 1388-1390. Thin plates of steel placed under a truck side bearing wear plate to compensate for the wear and maintain a uniform clearance between the body and truck bearings.

Side Bearing Wear Plate. 29, Figs. 1388-1390. A removable hardened steel plate secured to either the body or truck side bearing to take the wear. It is bolted down on side-bearing shims which are used to raise or lower the height of the side bearing so as to compensate for wear and maintain a uniform clearance.

Side Deck. See **Deck Side.**

Side Deck Sash. 50, Figs. 259-370. A sash in the side of the upper deck. Commonly termed deck sash.

Side Door. A door in the side of a car body as distinguished from a door in the side of one of the end vestibules. The baggage compartment of combination baggage and passenger interurban cars is usually fitted with a wide sliding side door on one or both sides of the car. See **Center Side Door.**

Side-Dump Car. Figs. 231-233. A car used for hauling coal, ashes or other bulk freight arranged with hinged sides and a sloping floor so that when the doors are unlocked the load discharges to the side by gravity.

Side Frame. (1) The posts, braces and rods forming the framework of the side of a car body.

(2) 1, Figs. 1368-1378. The built-up or forged truss of a truck frame over the journal boxes including the pedestals and columns.

Side Piece. See **Platform Hood Side Piece.**

Side Plate. 16, Figs. 259-370. A continuous timber framed along the top of the body side posts from end to end of the car. The term is usually contracted to **Plate,** which see.

Side Rib. 35, Figs. 259-370. See **Body Rib.**

Side Rib Rail. A narrow piece of wood sometimes framed in flush with the outside surface of the side posts and ribs back of the fender rail.

Side-Rod Truck. Figs. 1379-1380. A single-motor swiveling truck in which the driving axle is connected to the trailing axle with cranks and side rods as in a locomotive driving gear. A few cars in Pittsburgh, Pa., have been equipped with trucks of this type.

Side Seat. A longitudinal seat built along the side of a car.

Side Sill. 1, Figs. 259-370. One of the two outside longitudinal members of a car body underframe. The side sills support the weight of the sides and roof and in double-truck cars transmit this load with part of the floor load to the transverse bolsters. In single-truck cars the side sills usually rest on the top chord of the truck frame, although for wide car bodies an intermediate or sub-sill is sometimes built inside of the side sills to rest on the top chord of the truck.

Side Sill Filling Pieces. 105, Figs. 259-370. Wooden sticks bolted against the web of a structural steel side sill to fill the sill out to a rectangular cross-section.

Side Sill Plate. 108, Figs. 259-370. A thick plate from 10 in. to 20 in. wide placed on edge and forming a stiffening member for a side sill. This form of construction has been extensively used in recent cars owing to its strength and stiffness combined with light weight. A wooden **Truss Plank,** which see, serves a similar purpose.

Side Sill Step. 100, Fig. 341. In a Narragansett type open car a step tread plate attached to the horizontal web of the Z-bar side sill at each opening between posts.

Side Sill Washer. A washer on the outside of a side sill to form a bearing for the nut on the end of a sill tie rod.

Side Step. See **Running Board.**

Side Step Fender. See **Running Board Riser.**

Side Top Rail. See **Side Plate.**

Siding. Another name for **Sheathing,** which see.

Sight-Seeing Car. A car used for conveying parties of tourists on sight-seeing trips to points of interest along a railway company's lines. Many special types of cars have been built for this service. The principal object in the design of such cars is to arrange the seats and windows so that all passengers will have a good view on all sides of the car.

Signal Bell. Figs. 728-734. A small single-stroke clapper gong mounted under the platform hood at each end of a car. A bell cord passes through the car from end to end on guides or hangers and is attached to the counterweighted bell clapper. When the cord is pulled the clapper is raised and strikes the gong a quick sharp blow. The signal bell is used to give signals between the conductor and motorman in accordance with a prearranged code. The standard codes of city and interurban rules of the American Electric Railway Transportation and Traffic Association as of 1910, prescribe the following meanings for bell signals:

Conductor to Motorman.

Sound	Indication.
1 bell	When car is running, stop at next regular stop
2 bells	When car is standing, start forward.
3 bells	Stop immediately.
4 bells	When car is standing, back slowly.

Motorman to Conductor.

1 bell	Come forward.
2 bells	Danger signal to conductor.
3 bells	Set rear brake.
4 bells	Motorman wishes to back car.

For names of signal bell attachments see **Bell.**

Signal Buzzer System. Figs. 1234-1258. A system for enabling passengers within the car to signal to the conductor or motorman that they wish to alight. An electric buzzer is mounted on the bulkhead at each end of the car and is connected in circuit with push buttons mounted on each window post. Current is supplied either by dry batteries or from the trolley through suitable resistance. When any button is pushed in, the circuit through the buzzer is closed and the buzzer sounds, warning the motorman and conductor.

Signal Gong. See **Gong.**

Signal Lamp. Figs. 1059-1093. A three or four-lens lamp used on interurban cars at night to indicate the rear of the train and also whether it is being followed by another section or is running as an extra. The two lamps, one on each side on the rear end, are called marker lamps and should display, when occupying a main track, green lights to the front and sides and red to the rear. When clear of the main track they should show green to the front, side and rear. Similar lamps are used on the front of interurban cars to indicate by two green lights that another section is following and by two white lights that the car is running as an extra train. The lamps are mounted on a bracket which fits into a socket casting set into the vestibule corner posts just below the roof. See **Marker Lamp** and **Tail Lamp**.

Signal Lamp Bracket. See above.

Signal Lamp Socket. See **Signal Lamp**.

Signal Whistle. An air whistle mounted on top of the vestibule hood of interurban cars and operated by pulling a cord suspended in front of the motorman or by a thumb valve near the brake valve. It is used for giving alarm signals instead of a platform gong, which cannot be heard for a long distance. The whistle is only used in the open country. See **Whistle**.

Sill. 1, 2, and 103, Figs. 259-370. One of the main longitudinal members of a car body underframe. They are designated as side, intermediate and center sills. The end cross-pieces of the underframe are called end sills and by analogy the platform floor timbers are called platform sills. A deck sill is a corresponding member in the upper deck roof framing which supports the deck posts. See **Window Sill. Door Sill.**

Sill and Plate Rod. 12, Figs. 259-370. A vertical rod in the side framing of a car body holding together the side sill and the plate. They are usually let into the window posts and are entirely concealed.

Sill Knee Iron. An L-shaped casting or bent plate placed in the angle between the end sill and one of the longitudinal sills to stiffen the joint and keep it square.

Sill Step. See **Side Sill Step**.

Sill Tie Rod. 106, Figs. 259-370. A rod extending across the underframe and used to tie the outside sills together. Transverse floor timbers or bridging pieces serve to keep the sills the proper distance apart.

Single-End Car. Figs. 7, 23, 52, etc. A car designed to be operated always in one direction. The necessary apparatus for operating the car such as the controller, brake wheel or brake valve, etc., is mounted only in the front end.

Single-Motor Truck. Figs. 1373-1376. A four-wheel truck designed for use under city cars. Also called maximum traction truck from the fact that a large proportion of the load on the truck is carried by the driving wheels. The pony wheels are of small diameter compared to the driving wheels so that they will clear the underframe when the truck radiates in rounding sharp curves. Owing to the location of the center of rotation of the truck near the driving axle, the driving wheels are displaced laterally only a small distance so that they can project up between the car sills and thus permit the car body to be mounted low down. In the truck shown in Figs. 1375-1376 the load on the truck is carried by two spring-supported radial side bearings and no bolster is used. The draft of the truck is transmitted through a king bolt carried by the body end sill. This pin works in a radially slotted casting attached to the truck end frame. The theoretical center of rotation of the truck is 6 in. inside the center of the driving axle. The driving wheels carry 75 per cent of the load on straight track, but when rounding curves the pony wheels are additionally loaded by an ingenious device to hold them on the track. A spring-supported post is carried on a cross-member of the truck frame just inside the pony axle. An inverted V-shaped plate is fastened under the car body above this spring post and as the truck radiates the end of the post slides over the inclined surface of the body plate. This compresses the spring post and applies a heavy downward pressure on the pony wheels. As soon as the truck resumes its normal position the extra load on the pony wheels is removed. This type of single-motor truck is designed to operate with the pony wheels nearest the center of the car.

The single-motor truck shown in Figs. 1373-1374 is intended to operate with the pony wheels next to the end of the car. The motor is carried outside of the driving axle and the king bolt on the end piece of the truck frame is replaced by a center plate carried on a bolster disposed nearer the driving axle than the pony axle to give a distribution of load of 75 per cent and 25 per cent respectively on the two axles.

Experience has shown that a compression device is not necessary for the safe operation of a single-motor truck and most trucks of this type are now being built without it.

The truck levers of the brake gear for a single-motor truck are proportioned to exert a braking pressure on the driving and pony wheels proportional to the loads on them.

Single-Phase Alternating Current. An **Alternating Current**, which see, composed of a single set of waves or impulses and requiring for its transmission a single pair of conductors. See **Three-Phase Alternating Current**.

Single-Phase Control Apparatus. Figs. 1722-1724, 1802-1803. The speed of single-phase motors is controlled by varying the voltage of the impressed circuit and not by inserting external resistance in the circuit as in direct-current control apparatus. Two methods are in use, one employing an induction regulator with a fixed secondary transformer voltage and the other a group of switches which connect the motors to different voltage taps in the transformer secondary coil. The induction regulator control is automatic, while the switch group control may be either automatic or non-automatic. The induction regulator is an auxiliary transformer in the form of an induction motor. The primary winding is on the stator and the secondary on the rotor. If the rotor is moved through an angle corresponding to one pole the e.m.f. induced in the secondary is reversed. Thus if the main transformer is wound to give 250 volts and the induction regulator to give 100 volts, the regulator voltage is first subtracted from the main transformer voltage and then by gradually revolving the rotor the regulator voltage is added to the transformer voltage, giving a range at the motors of 150 volts to 350 volts. The induction regulator rotor is revolved through worm gearing by an air motor, the valves of which are electrically operated by the control circuits. The speed of rotation is controlled by the limit switch which can be set to give any desired rate of acceleration of the motors. Whenever the main switch opens, due to excessive current flowing or turning the controller handle to the "off" position, the regulator is revolved back to the starting position of minimum voltage.

This method of control has been generally superseded by the switch group control system in which the control switches or contactors successively connect the motors through taps of increasing voltage on the main transformer. A preventive coil is used to avoid breaking heavy currents when passing from one switch to the next. Alternate voltage taps are connected to the two ends of a single choke coil and the motor lead is connected in the middle of the coil. To increase the voltage the switches of taps 1 and 2 are closed, then 1 is opened and 3 is closed. Each switch carries but half of the main current. The method may be modified by using three preventive coils so that four switches are closed when moving from one tap to another. With this modification 16 switches are required for 13 working voltages. The switches are interlocked so that the proper combinations only can be made. The control apparatus for a single-phase car equipment includes, besides the auto-transformer and tap switches, a reverser, a tap from the auto-transformer for supplying current to the air compressor motor and car lights, motor cut-out switches and an overload relay.

Single-Phase Motor. Figs. 1668-1671. A railway motor designed to operate on single-phase alternating current. Two types have been developed, the single-phase series motor and the compensated repulsion motor. Both employ an armature constructed like a direct current armature and revolving in an alternating magnetic field, but in the series motor the armature conductors form part of the main circuit while in the compensated repulsion motor the armature currents are produced by electro-magnetic induction, the armature conductors forming the secondary of a transformer, the primary of which is wound on the field. The series motor has met with most favor and has been used in most of the notable single-phase installations in the United States and Europe.

The series motor employs an armature with a commutator and brushes exactly like a direct current armature. The field, however, consists of a laminated sheet steel cylindrical shell, on the inside of which are formed four or more curved pole pieces. These pole pieces are wound with heavy copper wire or strap, and auxiliary compensating windings are also threaded through slots in the pole faces and the field frame. The laminated shell is surrounded by an outer cast-steel casing which does not, however, form part of the magnetic field circuit. The armature and field windings are connected in series with each other, hence the name series motor. The characteristics of a series motor are lamination of the entire magnetic circuit, the use of a weak field to prevent self-induction effects, compensating windings in the pole faces to prevent distortion of the field by the armature and the use of preventive leads of high resistance between the commutator segments and the armature windings to reduce the inductive effect of the alternating field on the armature coils temporarily short circuited by the brushes which would otherwise produce large circulating currents in the closed coils and result in excessive sparking when the commutator segments to which they are connected pass from under the brushes.

Single-phase series motors are perfectly adapted for operation on direct current without any changes in their internal connections. The usual practice where cars are operated on both a.c. and d.c. sections is to provide suitable change-over connections for the different types of control employed and to include in the control apparatus means for connecting the motors in pairs in series for d.c. operation and in parallel for a.c. operation.

Single-Phase System. A system of electric traction using single-phase, alternating current of high potential for propulsion as distinguished from a direct current system using 600 or 1200-volt direct current. The single-phase system has been applied to a few interurban roads and a number of electrified steam roads, but in only one or two cities in Europe has it been used for street railway service. Current of 15 or 25 cycles with a potential of from 2000 to 11,000 volts is fed to the overhead trolley wire. Each car carries a transformer which steps down the voltage of the current fed to the motors to a maximum of from 200 to 350 volts. **Single-Phase Motors**, which see, do not differ materially in principle from direct-current motors, and in fact may be and frequently are operated with single-phase current on one section and direct current on an adjoining section. See **Single-Phase Control Apparatus.**

Single Plate Wheel. Figs. 1631-1632. A car wheel in which a single plate of metal is used for the web to unite the hub with the rim. See **Double Plate Wheel.**

Single Register. See **Fare Register.**

Single Truck. Figs. 1377-1378, 1400-1401, etc. A long wheel-base, four-wheel truck, on which a short car body is mounted. The car body underframe rests directly on the truck springs or on the spring-supported top bar of the truck side frame and no pivotal center plate or bolster is used.

Single-Truck Car. Figs. 1-34. A car mounted on a single truck, as distinguished from a car mounted on two swiveling, four-wheel trucks.

Slack Adjuster. Figs. 523-528, 1482. A device inserted in the foundation brake gear for automatically taking up slack caused by wear of the brake shoes and rod connections. The slack also may be taken up by hand by moving the stop pins in the truck dead lever guides or adjusting the turnbuckles in the bottom truck connections.

Slat Seat. A car seat in which the bottom and back are formed of narrow strips of wood set into a wooden frame. Slat seats are universally used for the cross seats of open cars.

Sleeping Car. Figs. 365-366. A closed car fitted with folding berths or beds in which passengers may sleep while traveling at night. Sleeping cars are in operation on only one or two of the longer interurban systems in the Middle West.

Sleet Cutter. Figs. 1911-1912, 1935, 1946-1947. A forked scraper attached to a trolley harp in place of a wheel to cut the ice off of the trolley wire during a sleet storm.

Sleet Wheel. Figs. 1897-1898, 1927-1928. A special form of trolley wheel designed to cut through the ice formed on the trolley wire during a sleet storm.

Sleeving. Woven cotton tubing used for insulating wires. It is usually treated with some insulating compound.

Sliding Door. A door mounted on rollers and moved to one side to open the doorway. Sliding doors are commonly used for body end doors, baggage compartment side doors and sometimes for vestibule doors. They are designated as double sliding doors when they are divided into two halves, each half sliding in an opposite direction. Occasionally the two halves are further divided into half sections which overlap when the door is opened, thus requiring a pocket with a depth equal to only one-quarter of the width of the door opening. Various forms of mechanism for making the two halves of a double sliding door move simultaneously in opposite directions are shown in Figs. 674-680. See **Door.**

Sliding Door Bumper. Fig. 832. A rubber cushion attached to the inside edge of a sliding door which strikes against the end of the door pocket when the door is opened.

Sliding Door Handle. Figs. 845-852. A curved handle attached to a sliding door to pull it open or shut. Some types of sliding door locks have pivoted handles which serve to lift the latch of the lock when pulled to one side.

Sliding Door Hook. Figs. 825-831. A hook catch for locking together the two halves of a double sliding door.

Sliding Door Lock. A type of lock for sliding doors consisting of a hook latch raised by moving the door handle. Several patterns are illustrated in Figs. 797-824.

Sliding Door Roller. (1) Figs. 837-844. A roller or sheave by means of which a sliding door is hung on a door track.

(2) Figs. 833-836. A sliding roller bearing on a strip of brass attached to the face of a sliding door. See **Door Guide.**

Sliding Door Sheave. See **Door Hanger.**

Sliding Door Track. See **Door Track.**

Slipper Brake. Fig. 1483. A mechanical emergency brake for electric railway cars specially suitable for descending long grades. It consists of two or more wooden or metal blocks forced down on the rails by hand power through a system of screws and levers or by pneumatic cylinders and pistons. Seldom used in the United States, but in general use in Europe.

Slot. A groove cut in the surface of an armature core in which an armature coil is embedded.

Slotting. (Of Commutators.) The process of cutting out mica insulation between the bars of a commutator to a depth of from 1-32 in. to 3-32 in. so as to prevent the brushes from jumping over a piece of high mica which has not worn down evenly with the copper bars. It is claimed that it also prevents flashing from one bar to another. The slotting of commutators is now a general practice on many large roads.

Smith Heater. Figs. 1094-1095.

Smoke Pipe. A sheet iron flue rising through the roof from the top of a hot water car heater to carry off the smoke and gases from the fire pot.

Smoking Car. A car in which smoking is permitted.

Smoking Compartment. A compartment in a passenger car, usually separated by a bulkhead from the main compartment, in which smoking is permitted.

Snap Switch. Figs. 883-886. An electric switching mechanism for making and breaking moderate currents. It consists of a rotating handle to which are attached two contacts. When the handle is turned the contacts touch fixed contacts in the switch case and are held in place by light spring pressure. The movement of the handle is checked by this spring pressure with an audible snap whenever the circuit is made or broken; hence the name snap switch. Switches of this type are commonly used for the lighting and heating circuits on cars.

Snow Flanger. See **Snow Scraper.**

Snow Plow. Figs. 215-221. A stoutly built closed car body to which is attached at one or both ends an inclined plane to push the snow outward from the track to one or both sides. A nose plow has inclined planes extending in both directions from a central ridge and pushes the snow to both sides of the track. A shear plow has a single plane extending diagonally across the front of the body which pushes all of the snow to one side of the track.

Snow Scraper. Figs. 1319-1322. A narrow, spring-supported shear board mounted under a car body in front of the trucks which can be lowered on the track to scrape off a light accumulation of snow. It is held down on the pavement by a spring and is raised to clear obstructions by turning a shaft on the platform to wind up a chain passing over a sheave suitably mounted under the platform floor. Scrapers are sometimes made to clean out the groove of the rail and are then called flangers.

Snow Sweeper. See **Sweeper.**

Socket. See **Lamp Socket.**

Soffit. In architecture the under side of an arch or lintel, hence in car building the term is sometimes applied to a finish board nailed to the under side of deck apron.

Soil Hopper. See **Dry Closet.**

Solder. An alloy of soft metals such as lead, tin and antimony having a low melting point. Extensively used for making metallic connections between electric conductors.

Solenoid. A coil of wire surrounding an iron core. When a current of electricity is passed through the coil magnetic lines of force are produced in and around the iron core.

Solid Steel Wheel. Figs. 1617-1620, 1635-1636. A car wheel forged or rolled in one piece from a steel billet as distinguished from a wheel built up with a steel tire shrunk or otherwise fastened on a wheel center.

Spencer Air Purifier. Fig. 561.

Spider. See **Armature Spider.**

Spiral Spring. Figs. 1569-1570. A spring made of a piece of wire or round or square rod, coiled in the shape of a cylindrical helix. See **Elliptic Spring.**

Spittoon. See **Cuspidor.**

Splash Plate. A board or plate of metal dropped from the underframe of a car body to protect the rheostats, compressor or other pieces of auxiliary apparatus mounted under the car from the splash of mud and water thrown up by the trucks. Also called mud guard. See Figs. 1850-1854.

Split Frame Motor. Figs. 1649, 1652, 1658-1662. A motor having the frame divided into two separable halves either in a horizontal plane or at an angle of about 45 deg. with the horizontal. Two field poles are mounted in each half. The two halves are held together by heavy bolt hinges at the corners. By removing the bolts on one side the lower half may be dropped down to inspect or remove the armature without removing the motor fram the truck. Most railway motors of moderate size are of the split frame type. See **Box Frame Motor.**

Split Gear. Figs. 1520-1523. A motor gear which is made in two halves, which are bolted together and keyed on the axle.

Spoke. (Car Wheel.) One of the radial arms which connect the hub with the rim.

Spoke Center. (Steel Tired Wheel.) Figs. 1621-1622. A wheel center having a hub and rim joined by several spokes instead of a circular disk or plate.

Spring. Figs. 1569-1593. A piece of metal or other material of such shape and physical properties that it is capable of being displaced, compressed or elongated under the application of force and will return to its normal shape or position when the force is removed. Springs of various shapes and sizes are used for many purposes in electric railway car construction, taking their names usually from the parts which rest on them or to which they are attached.

Spring Band. A narrow metal band surrounding the plates of an elliptic spring at the center and holding them firmly together.

Spring Cap. 11, Figs. 1388-1390. A plate of metal laid on top of a spring on which the load rests.

Spring Plank. 40, Figs. 1388-1390. A horizontal plank or rolled steel beam below the bolster of a truck on which the bolster springs rest. In most swing motion trucks the spring plank is supported from the transoms by pivoted hangers which permit a slight side motion to the spring plank and bolsters. See **Swing Hanger.**

Spring Plank Carrier. 32, Fig. 1370. A bracket forging riveted on the inside face of one of the equalizers of a Brill No. 27-F truck and supporting one end of the spring plank.

Spring Plank Safety Hanger. 15, Fig. 1368. An iron bar attached to the transoms and passing under the spring plank to hold it up in case one of the swing hanger links or their supports should break.

Spring Plate. A general term applied to either a spring seat or a spring cap.

Spring Post. 14, Fig. 1376. A bolt passing through the center of a spiral spring and screwed into the spring cap to restrain the recoil of the spring. See **Body Spring Post.**

Spring Scraper. See **Snow Scraper.**

Spring Seat. 10, Figs. 1388-1390. A metal plate on which a spring rests as distinguished from a spring cap which rests on top of the spring.

Sprinkler. Figs. 222-226. A car used for sprinkling street pavement adjacent to railway tracks. A large cylindrical tank is mounted on the underframe and is filled with water by a hose attached to a fire hydrant or other source of supply. The water may be sprayed over the pavement from suitable nozzles by one of three methods, gravity, compressed air or a centrifugal pressure pump driven by a motor. Where the distance to one side of the track which the water must be thrown does not exceed 12 ft. or 15 ft. the gravity method is commonly used. When the water must be sprayed out to the curb line the pneumatic or centrifugal pump system is used. In pneumatic sprinklers the air pressure in the tank is supplied by a small compressor driven by a motor or geared to one of the axles with chain and sprockets. Tanks up to 6000 gallons' capacity are employed. Small tanks are mounted on single trucks and the larger sizes on double trucks.

Sprinkler Head. See **Sprinkling Nozzle.**

Sprinkling Car. See **Sprinkler.**

Sprinkling Nozzle. A spray nozzle through which water is discharged in a thin film or spray from the storage tank of a sprinkler. Also called sprinkler head.

St. Louis Car Seats. Figs. 1268-1274.

St. Louis Trucks. Figs. 1422-1447.

Standards. The American Electric Railway Engineering Association, at its convention in 1907, adopted the following standards which are illustrated in Figs. 1948-1967.

(a) Standard Axles and Journal Boxes.
(b) Standard Brake Shoes, Brake Shoe Heads and Keys.
(c) Standard Section of Wheel Tread and Flange.

See **Recommended Practice.**

Standard Gage. The distance of 4 ft. 8½ in. between the inside of the heads of the track rails, which is almost universally used by steam and electric railways. Narrow and wide gages are used in a few localities.

Standard Steel Tired Wheels. Figs. 1621-1634.

Standard Trucks. Figs. 1406-1419.

Stanwood Safety Step Tread. Fig. 929.

Star Wheel. See **Controller Star Wheel.**

Stationary Seat. Figs. 1263, 1275, 1285. A car seat with a fixed back which cannot be reversed when the direction of motion of the car is reversed. Stationary seats are commonly used in single-end cars. See **Reversible Seat.**

Steel. An alloy of iron and carbon with small amounts of other impurities such as phosphorus, sulphur, silicon, etc. Steel contains from 0.20 per cent to 1 per cent of carbon, the higher carbon steels being very hard and brittle and capable of being tempered.

Steel Back Brake Shoe. Figs. 1491-1495. A cast-iron brake shoe with a thin steel plate cast in the back to hold the shoe together in case it should break when worn down thin.

Steel Car. Figs. 207-212. A car built entirely of steel plates and pressed or rolled steel sections.

Steel-Clad Tail Lamp. Fig. 1077.

Steel-Tired Gear. Fig. 1527. A motor gear formed of a solid center and a toothed rim which is shrunk on the center.

Steel-Tired Wheel. Figs. 1621-1644. A car wheel having a hub, spokes or connecting plate and a blank rim on which is shrunk and otherwise fastened a steel tire having a tread and flange formed on it. See **Tire Fastening**.

Steel Wheel. Figs. 1617-1620, 1635-1636. A car wheel forged and rolled from a single billet or slab of steel as distinguished from a steel-tired wheel or a cast-steel wheel.

Step. 120, Figs. 239-370. A shelf or ledge on which to place the foot in ascending or descending from one level to another. Access to closed cars is usually had by one or more steps on the side of the platform or vestibule. In open cars a continuous running board below the side sill serves as a step between the pavement and the car floor. See **Platform Step, Trolley Step**.

Step Facing. A metallic molding sometimes applied to the outer edge of a wooden step hanger.

Step Hanger. A vertical board or metal plate attached to the platform side sill and supporting the step tread boards.

Step Riser. A vertical board connecting the back of one step tread with the front of the next tread board above.

Step Tread. A horizontal board in a flight of steps on which the feet are placed in ascending or descending. See **Safety Step Tread**.

Sterling Destination Sign. Figs. 656-658.

Sterling Fare Register. Figs. 1161-1163.

Sterling Safety Brake. Figs. 578-579.

Sterling Trolley Base. Fig. 1877.

Stile. 135, Figs. 259-370. One of the uprights forming the outside of a wooden sash or door frame.

Stock Car. A car built especially for the transportation of live stock. Usually built with slatted sides and ends and a tight board roof.

Stop Bead. See **Sash Parting Strip**.

Stop Key Journal Bearing. A journal bearing which is held in place in the box by a wedge or stop key inserted between the front of the box and the bearing. This construction, which is now little used, dispenses with a collar on the axle journal.

Storage Air Brake. Figs. 451-452. An air-brake system which is supplied with compressed air for operating the brake piston from large storage tanks mounted under the car. No compressor is carried on the car, but the storage tanks are refilled from time to time as required from stationary compressing stations at terminal car houses or other convenient points.

Storage Battery. Figs. 1833-1834. An electric battery formed of one or more cells, each of which consists of two metallic plates immersed in an acid electrolyte. When one plate is connected to the positive side of a direct current generator and the other plate to the negative side an electro-chemical action takes place and the composition of the two plates is altered. When the two plates are connected to an external circuit a reverse electro-chemical action takes place and current is given off. One cell of a lead storage battery gives a potential of about 2.25 volts.

Storage Battery Car. Figs. 256-258. An electric car propelled by motors which are supplied with current from a storage battery carried on the car. Storage battery cars have been tried experimentally by a number of railways, one of the most recent installations being cars built for the Third Avenue Railroad, in New York City.

Storm Sash. An outside window sash sometimes used on cars operated in very cold climates to keep out the cold and wind.

Stove. Figs. 1103-1105. A closed iron receptacle in which coal or coke is burned to heat a car by direct radiation. Car stoves are usually small cylinders containing a grate and an ash box, placed either at the end of the car or in the center on one of the longitudinal seats. They are usually surrounded on three sides by a non-conducting fender, or guard, to prevent passengers from being burned. The smoke flue passes up through the roof of the lower deck. A stove should not be confused with a **Hot Water Heater**, which see.

Straight-Air Brake. Fig. 453. The common form of air brake used on cars which are operated singly. Air is stored in a main reservoir and is fed directly to the brake cylinder through the motorman's brake valve. To release the brakes the brake valve handle is turned to the release position and the air in the brake cylinder is allowed to escape through a port in the brake valve to the atmosphere. See **Automatic Air Brake**.

Straight-Out Winding. A type of drum armature winding in which the coils are formed in a polygonal shape without intricate curves and the ends project straight out from the ends of the armature slots in a plane parallel to the shaft. The straight-out winding in more or less modified form has been generally adopted for railway motors because it permits the coils to be easily removed.

Strainer. See **Brake Pipe Strainer**.

Strap. See **Hand Strap**.

Strap Copper. Copper rolled in the form of a narrow, thin, rectangular section, used in winding some types of motor armatures and fields.

Strap Hinge. Figs. 759-764. A door hinge with long, narrow leaves fastened to the face of a door and the adjoining door casing.

Street Car. Figs. 1-99. A term used to designate surface cars used only in city passenger service as distinguished from cars used in suburban or interurban service.

Streeter Brake Shoe. Figs. 1487-1498.

Striker Arm. See **Seat Back Arm**.

Stud. A short wooden post in the side or end frame of a car, extending from the sill to the belt rail between the window posts. Commonly called a rib.

Substation Car. Fig. 245. A box car with a specially strong underframe in which are mounted a rotary converter, transformers and all the necessary switching apparatus to permit high-tension alternating current to be converted into direct current for feeding to the trolley wire. Such a car can be moved from place to place, wherever extra substation capacity is required. Also called portable substation.

Suburban Car. Figs. 100-103. A car used for short runs into suburban and country districts. Usually fitted with cross seats and more powerful motors than city cars, but not designed for the high speed of interurban cars. No sharp lines of distinction are drawn between city and suburban cars or between suburban and interurban cars.

Subway Car. Figs. 209-212. A car designed for city subway service. Very similar to an **Elevated Car**, which see.

Suction Pipe. A pipe open to the atmosphere near the side or roof of a car and connected to the inlet valves of the air brake compressor. Its purpose is to draw the air which is to be compressed from a point some distance above the rails where less dust and foreign matter is in suspension.

Suction Strainer. Fig. 466. A fine wire screen placed in the suction opening of an air compressor or in the suction pipe when used, to prevent dirt and foreign matter from being drawn into the compressor and carried into the brake system.

Summer Car. An **Open Car**, which see.

Supply Pipe. (Air Brake.) The pipe connecting the main

reservoir with the brake valve, through which air is supplied to the brake pipe.

Surface Car. A car operated on tracks laid on the surface of the streets as distinguished from a car operated in a subway or on an elevated structure. The terms surface car, street car and city car as commonly used are in general synonymous.

Surface Process. See Paint.

Suspension. See Motor Suspension.

Suspension Cradle. See Air Compressor Cradle.

Sweeper. Figs. 213-214. A machine for sweeping snow off of a street railway track. It consists of a closed car body mounted well above the track on a single truck and carrying below the floor at each end a rotating broom set at an angle of about 45 deg. to the center line so as to throw the snow to one side of the track. The brooms consist of flexible rattan sticks set into a cylindrical center which revolves on a shaft in suitable bearings at each end. The brooms are driven through sprocket wheels and chains by a motor mounted on the floor of the sweeper body. They may be raised or lowered by levers or winches above the cab floor. Two types are in common use—the long broom sweeper shown in Figs. 213-214, which has brooms extending out over the rails on both sides, and the short broom sweeper, which has a shorter broom and in addition a brush board and wing on the left hand side. Sweepers are frequently provided with long wing boards on the sides to push the banks of snow several feet beyond the track on each side.

Swing Bolster. A truck bolster which is supported on a spring plank with a small amount of side play as distinguished from a rigid bolster which has no side play in the truck frames.

Swing Hanger. 27, Fig. 1368. A ling hanging from a pivot bearing on the truck transom and supporting one end of a spring plank by a similar pivot bearing. The links are usually splayed outward at the bottom so as to cause the spring plank to lift as it moves to one side, thus arresting its motion. Also called bolster hanger, swing link and spring plank link.

Swing Link. 27, Fig. 1368. The common name for a swing hanger for a truck spring plank.

Swing Link Pin. 28 and 31, Fig. 1368. A trunnion or shaft turning in bearings and to which the swing links are attached. The pin turns in a bearing casting or pivot resting on top of the transoms and a similar bearing secured to the under side of the spring plank.

Swing Link Pin Bearing. 30, Fig. 1368. A bearing in which a swing link pin turns.

Swing Motion Truck. Figs. 1368, 1385-1394, etc. A truck with a swinging spring plank which permits a side swing to the bolster to relieve the shock when the car body lurches on entering or leaving a curve. Nearly all high-speed electric trucks have swing motion.

Swinging Door. A single door hung on hinges on one side and arranged to swing outward or inward. By using double acting spring hinges such a door may be arranged to swing either in or out and return to the central or closed position when released.

Switch. In electrical parlance a device for opening or closing an electric circuit. See

Cut-Out Switch.   Snap Switch.
Knife Switch.   Unit Switch.

Switchboard. Figs. 1132-1133. A board or slab of stone or other non-combustible material on which are mounted one or more electric switches.

Switch Cabinet. A small locker or closet lined with fireproof material in which small switches and fuses are mounted. Such cabinets are frequently built in the end bulkhead under the end windows with the doors opening onto the platform so that the switches are readily accessible to the motorman.

Switch Group. Figs. 1798-1799. An assembly of two or more unit-switches or contactors mounted in a suitable frame and protected by a removable cover.

Switch Iron Holder. A clip or hook for holding a switch iron used to move the tongues of track switches.

Switching Rope. A strong rope with a hook or link in each end, used for pulling cars around sharp curves where it is impossible to connect the couplers or drawbars owing to the wide lateral displacement. Sometimes carried as part of the emergency equipment of interurban cars. Also called bull rope.

Symington Journal Box. Figs. 1563-1567.

Synchronizing System. See Pump Governor Synchronizing System.

Synchronizing Wire. A wire carried through a train equipped with a pump governor synchronizing system by means of which current from the trolley is transmitted through a contact on the master governor of any car to the electro-pneumatic compressor switches on all cars.

T

Tail Gate. A folding gate or chain used to close the opening between the vestibule center posts in cars provided with a passageway in the end of the vestibule and which are operated in trains.

Tail Lamp. Figs. 1059-1090. A lamp on the rear end of a car, usually displaying a red light at night to the rear as a warning signal to following cars. One or two such lamps are ordinarily mounted on brackets on the rear vestibule corner posts. They may project beyond the sides of the car body and display green lights to the front and side. See Signal Lamp.

Tank. See Water Tank and Sprinkler.

Tank Band. An iron strap used to hold a sprinkler tank down firmly on the tank saddles.

Tank Head. The flanged circular sheet forming one end of a sprinkler tank.

Tank Head Block. A block of wood bolted to the underframe of a sprinkler and bearing against the bottom edge of the tank head to prevent the tank from shifting longitudinally.

Tank Saddle. A curved timber bolted on top of the underframe of a sprinkler to support the tank.

Tap. A lead brought out from the secondary coil of a transformer for the purpose of obtaining a lower voltage than that which can be obtained from the entire secondary coil winding. See Single-Phase Control Apparatus and Transformer.

Tape. See Insulating Tape.

Taylor Steel-Tired Wheel. Fig. 1637.

Taylor Trucks. Figs. 1467-1471.

T. E. C. Fare Box. Fig. 1204.

Telephone. Figs. 1835-1837. A device for receiving, transmitting and reproducing sounds by electric currents. Telephones are in general use on interurban railways for train dispatching and on many roads each car is equipped with a portable telephone set for receiving train orders without leaving the car. The telephone is connected to the line wires either by means of a collapsible bamboo pole, which can be hooked over the wires, or a long cord with a plug is provided and jack boxes are mounted on the telephone poles at intervals of from 1000 ft. to 1 mile. The car is stopped opposite a jack box and the plug inserted to make a connection with the dispatcher's office telephone.

Tenon. A projection on the end of a timber which fits into a mortise in the timber against which it abuts.

Terminal Board. See Controller Connection Board.

Third Rail. An iron conductor rail mounted on insulated brackets outside of and slightly above one of the track rails. A third-rail shoe carried on the truck bears on the head of the third rail either by gravity or spring pressure and collects the propulsion current in the same way as a trolley wheel collects current from an overhead wire. The location of the third rail with respect to the track rail on a number of representative roads using this system is given in the accompanying table:

	Distance from third-rail to top of track rail—in.	Distance from track gage line to center of 3d rail—in.
New York Central & Hudson River Railroad	2¾	28¼
Long Island Railroad	3½	27½
West Jersey & Seashore	3½	27½
Baltimore & Ohio	3½	30
Interborough Rapid Transit Co. (Subway)	4	26
Interborough Rapid Transit Co. (Elevated)	7½	20¾
Boston Elevated Railway	6	20⅜
South Side Elevated, Chicago.	6¾	20⅛
Albany & Southern	6	27
Aurora, Elgin & Chicago	6 5-16	20⅝
Scioto Valley Traction Co	6	28

Third-Rail Shoe. Figs. 1855-1862. A flat iron plate hinged so that it can move vertically and attached to the outside of a car truck so as to bear on a third rail located outside of the track rail. It is held on the third rail either by gravity or spring pressure.

Third-Rail Shoe Beam. A wooden beam attached to the outside of a truck frame or to the journal boxes and carrying at the center a hinge supporting a third-rail shoe.

Three-Phase Alternating Current. Three single-phase alternating currents whose waves bear a definite phase relation to each other, the crests being approximately 120 electrical space degrees apart. Three-phase current requires three conductors for its transmission, the relation of the waves to each other being such that at any instant the positive electromotive force in one conductor is numerically equal to the sum of the negative electromotive forces in the other two conductors. See **Alternating Current** and **Single-Phase Alternating Current.**

Three-Phase System. A system of electric traction employing three-phase alternating current at high potential with two overhead trolley wires. The third conductor required is furnished by the track rails. Two synchronous induction motors are required to be operated together on each car or locomotive. The trolley voltage is stepped down with two transformers to about 400 volts before the current is fed to the motors. The three-phase system is used in the Simplon tunnel and elsewhere in Europe but has been installed in only one place in the United States, the Cascade tunnel of the Great Northern Railroad.

Threshold Plate. An iron plate, usually roughened or corrugated, which forms an end door sill. Threshold plates used with sliding doors frequently have short projections formed on their top surface to act as bottom door guides.

Throat. (Car Wheel.) The rounded angle between the tread and the base of the flange.

Tie. A rod or beam which connects two or more parts of a framework and holds them together. The terms tie, tie bar and tie rod are used in referring to such parts as a cross-frame tie, pedestal tie bar, sill tie rod, etc.

Tie Bar. See **Pedestal Tie Bar.**

Tiger Geared Brake. Fig. 582.

Tire. (Car Wheel.) A steel band or ring with a tread and flange formed on its outer periphery. The tire is shrunk on and otherwise fastened to the blank rim of a wheel center and can be replaced on the center by another tire when worn out. See Figs. 1615-1644.

Tire Fastening. A means for securing a tire on a wheel center in addition to the shrinkage. Various types of fastenings in common use are shown in Figs. 1615-1644.

Toe Guard. See **Running Board Riser.**

Toilet. A **Saloon,** which see.

Tomlinson Radial Coupler. Figs. 621-627.

Tool Box. A box hung under the car body and used for storing emergency tools such as jacks, car replacers, large wrenches, etc. Seldom used except on long interurban cars. See **Emergency Tools.**

Top Chord. (Single Truck.) 4, Fig. 1378. A flat iron bar bolted to the car body side sills and resting on top of the body springs.

Top Door Rail. 133, Figs. 259-370. The horizontal bar across the top of a door frame.

Top Door Track. See **Door Track.**

Top Plate. 101, Figs. 259-370. See **Body Bolster.**

Top Rail. More properly, **Plate,** which see.

Top Sash. 47, Figs. 259-370. The upper sash in a car window. The top sash, when used, is usually stationary and the bottom sash is arranged to lower or raise. See **Gothic Sash.**

Torque. The rotative force exerted by a motor armature when the motor is supplied with electrical energy. The torque is transmitted through gears to the axles and wheels.

Tower Car. Figs. 241-244. A **Line Car,** which see, equipped with a tower or elevating platform on which linemen can stand when repairing or erecting trolley wire.

Track. See **Door Track.**

Track Brake. Figs. 1479 and 1483. See **Magnetic Brake** and **Slipper Brake.**

Track Brush. Fig. 1323. A wire or rattan brush, spring supported on the truck end piece or wheelguard, which is used to clean the top of the rail.

Track Sander. See **Sander.**

Track Scraper. See **Snow Scraper.**

Traction Brake. A type of air brake apparatus designed especially for self-propelled cars as distinguished from brake equipment for steam railway cars. The term is sometimes used to designate straight-air brakes only.

Traction Wheel. A wheel mounted on an axle which is geared to a motor; more properly, driving wheel.

Tractive Effort. The tangential force on the periphery of a car wheel exerted by the torque of the motor which is multiplied and transmitted to the axle through reduction gearing.

Trail Car. Figs. 115, 124, 125, etc. A car mounted on trucks without motors and designed to be hauled by a motor car.

Trailer. A trail car.

Trailer Truck. Figs. 1383, 1399, etc. A truck without motors. Trailer trucks are sometimes used under one end of a motor car which has the other end mounted on a motor truck.

Train. Two or more cars coupled together and operated as a single unit.

Train Control. See **Multiple-Unit Control.**

Train Line. A term loosely applied to the brake pipe, control cable or any other pipe or circuit which is continuous throughout all the cars of a train.

Train Pipe. See **Brake Pipe.**

Train Starting Signal System. Figs. 1248-1258. A system of signals employing a buzzer or lamp in the motorman's cab and contacts on each of the car doors in the train. Current is taken from the last car on the train and the signal lamp or buzzer is not energized unless the circuit is completed through the contacts on all the doors, which are closed only when the doors are closed.

Transformer. Fig. 1803. An induction device for converting an alternating current of high potential and small amperage into a synchronous alternating current of lower potential and relatively larger amperage or vice versa. It consists of an iron core about which is wound one coil consisting of a large number of turns of fine wire and a second coil insulated from the first and consisting of a small number of turns of heavy wire. The ratio of the number of turns in each coil is approximately equal to the ratio of the voltages of the impressed and induced currents. Transformers are used on cars operating on single-phase alternating current to step down the trolley potential to a maximum of about 300 volts before feeding to the motors. See **Auto-Transformer** and **Single-Phase Control Apparatus.**

Transom. (1) A panel or framework over a door or window.

(2) 2, Fig. 1368. A cross member of a truck frame on each side of the bolster.

(3) The term transom is sometimes applied to the needle-beams under a car body.

Transom Chafing Plate. 13, Fig. 1368. A removable hardened steel plate fastened to the inside of a truck transom to take the wear caused by the vertical and lateral movement of the bolster.

Transom Corner Bracket. 3, Figs. 1368-1374. A bent knee bolted in the corner at the junction of the transom and the truck side frame to stiffen the joint.

Transom Gusset Plate. 4, Fig. 1368. A flat plate bolted or riveted on top of the junction between the transom and the truck side frame to hold the two pieces square with each other.

Transom Tie Bar. 14, Fig. 1368. A strap passing over the bolster on each side of the center plate and secured to the two transoms to prevent them from spreading apart.

Transverse Floor Timber. 109, Figs. 259-370. A cross member of the underframe of a car having no center sills. The floor timbers are framed into the side sills between the end sills or body bolsters and the floor boards are nailed to them. The needlebeams which are used to support the queen posts of the body truss rods should not be confused with the floor timbers, as the needlebeams are framed under the longitudinal sills and not between them.

Trap Door. A flush door in the floor of a car over the motors which can be raised to permit inspection of the motors through the inspection lids without removing the truck from under the car. See **Vestibule Trap Door.**

Trap Door Batten. See **Batten.**

Trap Door Beam. 110, Figs. 259-370. A short floor beam running longitudinally between two transverse members of the underframe and forming a ledge on which the trap door over a motor rests. A central trap door beam between two trap doors is sometimes made to be lifted up after the doors are raised so that unobstructed access can be had to the motors.

Trap Door Lift. A flush handle in the top of a trap door by which it is raised.

Tread. (1) The horizontal board of a step on which the foot is placed.

(2) The cylindrical surface on the periphery of a car wheel which rolls on the head of the rail. The American Electric Railway Engineering Association has adopted two standard contours for the flanges and treads of wide and narrow tread wheels which are shown in Figs. 1966-1967.

Tread Board. The board forming the tread of a step.

Triple Valve. (Automatic Air Brake.) Figs. 507-508, 511-512. A valve under each car in a train connecting the brake pipe to the auxiliary reservoir, the auxiliary reservoir to the brake cylinder and the brake cylinder to the atmosphere. In the normal running position the brake pipe is connected to the auxiliary reservoir through a small feed port and air at brake pipe pressure is admitted to the reservoir. When the brake pipe pressure is reduced by a small amount the feed port is closed by the movement of a piston in the valve and another small port is opened admitting air from the auxiliary reservoir to the brake cylinder. As soon as the air in the auxiliary reservoir has expanded down to the reduced brake pipe pressure a graduating valve within the triple valve closes the brake cylinder port and prevents further flow of air from the auxiliary reservoir to the brake cylinder. To apply the brakes harder another reduction is made in the brake pipe pressure. The graduating valve again opens and again closes when the brake pipe and auxiliary reservoir pressures have equalized. This process can be continued until the pressures in the auxiliary reservoir and the brake cylinder have equalized, after which further reductions of the brake pipe pressure have no effect. To make an emergency application of the brakes the brake pipe pressure is suddenly reduced by a considerable amount. This causes the triple valve piston to move suddenly to the emergency position in which a large port is opened between the auxiliary reservoir and the brake cylinder, admitting the air into the cylinder with great rapidity. No more pressure in the brake cylinder is obtained, however, than in the full service application. To release the brakes the brake pipe pressure is raised by admitting air from the main reservoir. The triple valve piston moves to the release position owing to the greater pressure on the brake pipe side of the piston and the feed port to the auxiliary reservoir is opened. At the same time the brake cylinder is connected to the atmosphere and the pressure in it allowed to leak off, thus releasing the brakes. The auxiliary reservoir is recharged to full brake pipe pressure and remains charged until another application of the brakes is made.

The quick-action triple valve is an improvement over the plain triple valve, and is used under cars operated in long trains. It differs from the plain triple valve by the addition of: (1) a brake pipe check valve, the purpose of which is to prevent leakage of the pressure in the auxiliary reservoir and brake cylinder in case the brake pipe pressure is reduced to atmospheric pressure by the bursting of a hose or rupture of a coupling; and (2) of an emergency valve which admits air from the brake pipe direct to the brake cylinder following a quick reduction of brake pipe pressure. This admission of air to the brake cylinder from the brake pipe causes a still further reduction of brake pipe pressure and greatly increases the rapidity of action of all the triple valves in the train. Plain and quick-action triple valves will work perfectly together.

Tripping Switch. A small automatic circuit breaker forming part of a type K control system with auxiliary contactors. The tripping device is actuated by the flow of the main power current through the tripping coil but only the current required to energize the contactor magnets is broken when the contacts are separated. See Fig. 1721.

Trolley. Figs. 1864-1947. The complete device including the spring base, pole, harp and wheel which is mounted on the roof of a car and by means of which current is collected from an overhead trolley wire.

Trolley Base. Figs. 1864-1877. An iron base attached to the roof of the car and having a swiveling socket for the bottom end of the trolley pole. The socket and pole are normally held in an upright position by one or more stiff coil springs which are compressed when the pole is pulled down on an angle. The wheel therefore is always pressed upward on the trolley wire. The base is insulated from the roof of the car by the wooden strips on which it is mounted and an insulated cable conducts the current collected by the trolley wheel from the trolley base down to the platform controller and thence to the motors.

Trolley Base Blocks. 83, Figs. 259-370. Short pieces of wood fastened on top of the trolley board or carried on a bridge above the car roof to which the trolley base is bolted.

Trolley Base Buffer. An attachment to a trolley base to arrest the motion of the pole when it has reached a vertical position after the wheel has left the wire. It may consist of an auxiliary spring or a block of metal bearing against one end of the main compression springs.

Trolley Base Spring. A coil spring attached to a trolley base and a trolley pole socket in such a way that when the socket is deflected from a vertical position the spring is placed under either tension or compression. The force exerted by the spring holds the trolley wheel firmly against the under side of the trolley wire.

Trolley Board. 85, Figs. 259-370. One or more long boards nailed to cleats on top of a car roof to form a platform on which to stand while inspecting or repairing the trolley.

Trolley Board Cleats. 84, Figs. 259-370. Blocks of wood cut to the contour of the upper deck roof and supporting the trolley boards.

Trolley Bridge. One or more cross pieces supported on blocking clear of the upper deck roof and carrying the trolley base blocks. The purpose is to reduce the noise and vibration caused by the revolution of the trolley wheel which is emphasized by the roof acting as a sounding board.

Trolley Car. A common name for an electric car which is propelled by electricity collected from an overhead conductor through a trolley mounted on the car roof.

Trolley Catcher. Figs. 1330-1332, 1334-1336, 1338. A device very similar to a **Trolley Retriever**, which see, which is designed to arrest the upward motion of a trolley pole when the wheel leaves the wire, but contains no spring to pull the pole down to the roof.

Trolley Catcher Socket. Fig. 1329. A casting fastened on the outside of the dasher by means of which a trolley catcher is attached.

Trolley Cord. A stout woven cotton rope about ⅜ in. in diameter fastened to the trolley pole near its upper end and dropped down to the rear platform dasher. It serves to pull the trolley down from the wire. Also called trolley rope.

Trolley Harp. Figs. 1883-1886, 1920-1922. A metal fork or clevis on the upper end of a trolley pole in which the trolley wheel is mounted on a suitable axle and bearing.

Trolley Harp Contact Spring. Figs. 1936-1938. A flat spring riveted on the inside of the arm of a trolley harp and forcing a washer on the axle against the hub of the trolley wheel. The current passes from the wheel through the washer and spring to the harp.

Trolley Harp Contact Washer. See above.

Trolley Hook. An iron hook on the roof of a car under which the trolley pole can be swung so as to hold it down when not in use.

Trolley Pole. Figs. 1879-1882. A piece of iron tubing from 1½ in. to 2 in. in diameter at the lower end and tapered to a smaller diameter at the uper end. The pole is clamped or pinned into the socket of the trolley base and carries a trolley harp on its upper end. Trolley poles are made in lengths from 11 ft. to 18 ft. to suit the height of the car roof and overhead construction.

Trolley Retriever. Figs. 1325-1328, 1333, 1337. A device for automatically pulling down the trolley pole close to the roof when the wheel leaves the wire. It consists essentially of a drum around which the trolley cord is wound, a centrifugal clutch and a strong spring which turns the drum when thrown into engagement by the centrifugal clutch. The trolley cord may be unwound slowly from the drum as the trolley pole rises with an increase in the height of the overhead wire but when the wheel leaves the wire and the pole is thrown upward suddenly by the force of the trolley base springs the cord unwinds from the drum of the retriever fast enough to release the clutch and throw in the retrieving spring, which has strength sufficient to wind up the cord against the trolley base spring tension. The retriever mechanism is enclosed in an iron case which is attached to a bracket on the outside of the rear dasher.

Trolley Rope. See **Trolley Cord.**

Trolley Stand. A framework built in the center of a motor flat car to support a trolley base. See Figs. 227-228.

Trolley Step. Figs. 917-920. A shelf casting attached to a body corner post to afford a foothold in climbing to the roof of a car to inspect or repair the trolley. Also called roof step.

Trolley Wheel. Figs. 1887-1928. A small brass or bronze grooved wheel mounted on an axle in a trolley harp and running on the under side of the trolley wire. They are made in different sizes from 4 in. to 6 in. outside diameter. The hub is often bushed with a thimble made of some antifriction metal.

Trolley Wheel Axle. Fig. 1939. A small pin fitting in holes in the two arms of a trolley harp, on which the wheel turns.

Trolley Wheel Bushing. Fig. 1919. A removable antifriction metal thimble inserted in the hub of a trolley wheel to form a bearing on the axle.

Trolley Wire. The overhead conductor wire under which the trolley wheel runs.

Truck. Figs. 1367-1473. A frame or carriage supported on one or more axles and pairs of wheels. Four-wheel trucks only are used under electric railway cars. When only one truck is used under a car body, supporting it centrally without means for rotating, it is called a single truck. When two four-wheel trucks are pivotally mounted under the two ends of a car body they are called double trucks or bogie trucks. Electric railway trucks are also distinguished as motor trucks and trailer trucks, according to whether they carry motors or run idle. Motor trucks are further designated as single-motor and double-motor trucks.

Truck Bolster. 11, Fig. 1368. The central cross member of a double truck which transmits the load from the body bolster to the truck frame through a pair of center plates revolving around a center pin. In swing motion trucks the bolster rests at each end on bolster springs which are in turn carried on a spring plank. The spring plank is hung from the truck transoms or other parts of the truck frame by links or hangers and thus transmits the load to the journals.

Truck Bolster Chafing Plate. 12, Fig. 1368. See **Bolster Chafing Plate.**

Truck Bolster Spring. 22, Fig. 1368. See **Bolster Spring.**

Truck Check Chain. 13, Fig. 1376. A chain attached to the corner of a double truck and to the side sill of the car body with sufficient slack to permit the truck to rotate only enough to pass around the sharpest curves. Its purpose is to prevent the truck from slewing across the track in the event of derailment. Now seldom used.

Truck Center Plate. 16, Fig. 1368. The **Center Plate** which see, resting on top of the truck bolster.

Truck Connection. See **Bottom Truck Connection.**

Truck End Frame. 5, Fig. 1368. One of the cross members of a truck frame connecting the ends of the side frames. Also called truck end piece, truck end sill and truck end crossing.

Truck End Piece. See **Truck End Frame.**

Truck Frame. 1, 2, and 5. Fig. 1368. The metal framework forming the rigid skeleton of the truck. It includes the side frames, end pieces and transoms.

Truck Frame Center. See **Column.**

Truck Frame Diagonal Brace. 3, Fig. 1378. One of a pair of brace rods crossing diagonally from side to side in the center of a Brill No. 21-E single truck.

Truck Pedestal. See **Pedestal.**

Truck Side Bearing. 28, Figs. 1388-1390. A **Side Bearing**, which see, on top of the truck bolster.

Truck Side Frame. 1, Fig. 1368. The rigid truss, girder or forging forming the side of a truck frame, to which are attached the transoms and end pieces.

Truck Spring. Any spring used to support part of the load on a truck. They are usually designated as bolster springs, equalizer springs or pedestal springs.

Truck Sub-Sill. A timber which is sometimes attached under the side sill of a single-truck car and rests on top of the truck side frame to which it is bolted.

Truss Plank. 126, Figs. 259-370. A wide thick board framed on edge on the inside of the side posts of a car body just above the floor to stiffen the side framing. A steel plate is frequently used for the same purpose.

Truss Plank Electric Heater. Figs. 1122, 1149. A type of electric car heater designed for attachment to the truss plank just above the floor line.

Truss Rod. See **Body Truss Rod.**

Turnbuckle. 20, Figs. 1480-1481. An elongated nut with right and left-hand screw threads cut in opposite ends which is used to vary the length of a rod in which it is inserted. Turnbuckles are used in the center of body truss rods and also in the bottom truck connections of some forms of truck brake gear.

Turtle Back Roof. Fig. 264. A curved roof without a monitor deck. More properly called **Arch Roof**, which see.

Twelve-Hundred-Volt Direct Current System. See **High-Tension Direct Current System.**

Twin Windows. Two side windows enclosed between a pair of wide pier posts and separated by a narrow post which does not carry any of the roof weight. They are usually surmounted by a **Gothic Sash**, which see. Also called **Pullman Windows**, which see.

Two-Motor Equipment. Electrical equipment for a single car consisting of two motors, one or two controllers for single- or double-end operation and the necessary auxiliary equipment such as resistance, fuses, circuit breakers, etc. The two motors may be mounted on a single truck or one motor may be mounted on each of two single-motor double trucks.

U

U-Bolt. An iron rod threaded at both ends and bent over on itself in the shape of the letter U. See **Platform Sill Clamp**.

"U" Brake Shoe. Fig. 1488.

Ulin Sash Lock. Fig. 959.

Uncoupling Rod. (Automatic Coupler.) A rod extending from the coupler head out to the side of the car by means of which the knuckle lock may be raised to uncouple without going between the cars.

Underframe. The framework in the bottom of a car body on which the floor is laid. It is made up of longitudinal sills and end sills, and intermediate cross members, which according to their location and purpose are termed bolsters, needlebeams or transverse floor timbers. The body underframe does not include the platform sills and bumper beams which are usually framed separately and attached to the body underframe.

Underrunning Third Rail. A third-rail working conductor arranged so that the third-rail shoes on the cars bear on the under side of the conductor and are held in contact with it by upward spring pressure. See **Overrunning Third Rail**.

Union. Figs. 566-567. A device for connecting two pipes together.

Union Standard Trolleys. Figs. 1864-1870, 1883-1913.

Unit-Switch. Figs. 1785-1787. An electro-pneumatic switching device for handling main power currents. Several such switches may be assembled together and used for making all the necessary connections for controlling the speed of railway motors. Each unit-switch consists of a pneumatic cylinder and piston connected to the movable contact of the switch, a magnet valve for controlling the admission of compressed air to the cylinder and a magnetic blow-out for extinguishing the arc formed when the circuit is broken by the opening of the switch. The magnet valve is energized by low-voltage control current supplied either from a storage battery or from the trolley through suitable resistance. See **Contactor**.

Unit-Switch Control. Figs. 1768-1803. Control apparatus made by the Westinghouse Electric & Manufacturing Company for single cars and cars operated in multiple-unit trains. All of the essential pieces of apparatus are built on the unit plan, permitting any damaged part to be easily removed and replaced. All of the main power circuit connections are made by pneumatically operated switches assembled in a switch group underneath the car. See **Unit-Switch**. The various magnet valves are operated by low-voltage current through connections in a master controller placed on the platform. The low-voltage control current is obtained either from a storage battery or from the trolley through suitable resistance. The reversing connections are made in a pneumatically-operated reverser mounted in a separate case under the car body. For multiple-unit operation the control circuits are carried throughout the train as explained under **Multiple-Unit Control**, which see.

Four types of unit-switch control apparatus are made. They are: Type AB, automatic operation with control circuits supplied from storage battery. Type AL, automatic operation with control circuits supplied from trolley. Type HB, hand operation, with control circuits supplied from storage battery. Type HL, hand operation, with control circuits supplied from trolley.

Unit-switch control may be applied to either direct current or single-phase alternating current car equipments.

Universal Car Seats. Figs. 1260-1261, 1263-1264.

Universal Deck Sash Ratchet. Fig. 1027.

Universal Safety Step Tread. Fig. 928.

Universal Sash Fixtures. Figs. 950-955.

Upper Deck. The raised central portion of a car roof. Usually contracted to deck except when applied to distinguish a part which is also used in the lower deck.

Upper Deck Apron. See **Upper Deck Roof**.

Upper Deck Carline. 19, Figs. 259-370. A **Carline**, which see, supporting the upper deck roof.

Upper Deck Roof. 49, Figs. 259-370. The covering of the upper deck. It frequently extends out beyond the deck posts, forming an upper deck apron at the ends and sides.

V

Valve. A device for opening or closing an aperture so as to regulate the flow of a liquid or gas. See **Triple Valve**. **Sand Valve**.

Vanderbilt Brake Beams. Figs. 1510-1515.

Van Dorn & Dutton Gears. Figs. 1523-1526.

Van Dorn Couplers. Figs. 610-617.

Varnish. A compound of linseed oil and resinous gums or other substances which, when applied to the surface of wood or metal and allowed to dry, forms a hard, lustrous finish. See **Painting** and **Insulating Varnish**.

Veneer. A thin layer or sheet of hard wood glued to the surface of another piece of inferior wood to give the appearance of solid hard wood. Veneers are used for the interior finish of cars and for headlining.

Ventilator. Figs. 1340-1366. An opening through which fresh air is admitted or foul air is exhausted from a car. Owing to the fact that the only ventilation openings in a closed car were the deck sashes, the name ventilator was at one time applied very generally to the small deck windows and many of their related parts. Recently a number of types of automatic exhaust ventilators have been designed for use on cars. Some of these are intended to be inserted between the deck posts in place of deck sashes.

Ventilator Hood. See **Deck Hood**.

Ventilator Register. Fig. 1366. A perforated plate with a rotating or sliding plate back of it which is used to regulate the flow of air through some types of automatic ventilators.

Vertical Brake Wheel. Figs. 573-575. A hand brake wheel which revolves in a vertical plane and is geared to the brake shaft with bevel gears. The object in using a vertical wheel is to save space in the motorman's vestibule.

Vesta Tail Lamp. Fig. 1076.

Vestibule. An enclosed **Platform**, which see, on the end of a car. The construction of vestibules and open platforms is in many respects the same and most of the parts have either the name vestibule or platform prefixed to them, according to the type of construction, whether open or enclosed.

Vestibule Belt Rail. 34, Figs. 259-370. A horizontal stick framed across the end of a vestibule below the windows. See **Belt Rail**.

Vestibule Center Post. 33, Figs. 259-370. A post in the center of a vestibule end supporting the vestibule belt rail. It corresponds to a **Dasher Post**, which see.

Vestibule Corner Post. 32, Figs. 259-370. An upright post resting on the end of the crown piece and supporting one side of the vestibule hood bow. Together with the body corner post it forms the door opening over the vestibule steps.

Vestibule Door. Fig. 689. A door in the side of a vestibule above the steps. Double folding or single sliding doors are commonly used.

Vestibule Door Controller. Fig. 689.

Vestibule Door Latch. Figs. 783-789.

Vestibule Door Lintel. 39, Figs. 239-370. See **Door Lintel.**

Vestibule Door Rod. A rod fitted across the inside of a double folding vestibule door when closed to prevent its being pushed inward.

Vestibule Hood Bow. 38, Figs. 259-370. See **Platform Hood Bow.**

Vestibule Rib. 37, Figs. 259-370. A light post in the vestibule end or side framing to which the panels are attached. See **Side Rib.**

Vestibule Sash Adjuster. Fig. 935. A fixture for the center sash of vestibules designed to permit the sash to be raised or lowered to any height.

Vestibule Trap Door. Figs. 921-926. A hinged door in the floor of a vestibule closing the opening above the steps.

Vestibule Window. A fixed or drop sash in the end or side of a vestibule.

Vestibule Window Post. A post rising from the vestibule belt rail to the hood bow and separating two vestibule windows.

Voight Door Operating Device. Figs. 659-661.

Volt. The unit of measurement of electromotive force or difference of potential. It may be defined as the difference of potential required to produce the flow of current of one ampere through a circuit having a resistance of one ohm.

Voltage. The value of the electromotive force causing a current to flow in a circuit expressed in terms of volts.

Voltmeter. An instrument for indicating or recording the intensity of electromotive force in terms of volts.

Vulcanizing. A process of treating india rubber or other gums so as to make them hard and durable and capable of being moulded into any desired form.

W

Wainscot. A panel under the windows on the inside of a car. It is finished at the top and bottom by upper and lower wainscot rails. In most electric cars the wainscot is replaced by plain inside lining.

Walkover Seats. Figs. 1278-1286.

Wall Plate. (Seat Mechanism.) A guide plate for the wall seat back arm. See Fig. 1294.

Wall Seat Back Arm. A **Seat Back Arm**, which see, next to the side of a car as distinguished from the aisle seat back arm.

Wall Seat End. A **Seat End**, which see, next to the side of the car. Wall seat ends seldom have arm rests.

Warner Non-Parallel Axle Single Truck. Figs. 1422-1425.

Wash Basin. A receptacle for holding water for washing the hands. Wash basins are installed on only a few of the more luxurious interurban cars used for long distance travel.

Wash Room. A small compartment containing a wash basin. A saloon.

Washburn Couplers. Figs. 605-609.

Washer. A bearing plate under a nut or bolt head to distribute the pressure over a large surface or to take the wear caused by turning the nut on or off.

Waste. Loose fibers of woolen or cotton thread used for packing journal boxes and other bearings lubricated with oil.

Water Alcove. A recess in a partition or bulkhead in which a tank of drinking water is placed.

Water Cap. A small brass collar surrounding the projecting top end of a controller cylinder shaft. See **Controller Handle.**

Water Closet. Figs. 896, 898. A saloon hopper which is flushed with water. Seldom used on electric railway cars. See **Dry Closet.**

Water Cooler. See **Water Tank.**

Water Table. See **Drip Rail.**

Water Tank. Fig. 895. A sheet iron or tin reservoir mounted in a water alcove or in a corner of a car and holding a supply of drinking water.

Watt. The unit of measurement of electrical power. A current of one ampere flowing with an electromotive force of one volt will transmit power of one watt. One horsepower is equal to 746 watts.

Watt-Hour. A unit of measurement of electrical energy. Power of one watt developed for one hour represents energy equal to one watt-hour.

Wattmeter. A device for measuring the power represented by the flow of electricity in a circuit in terms of watts. A recording wattmeter registers watt-hours.

Wave Winding. The common method of winding a railway motor armature, using formed coils. So-called because successive coils advance around the armature continuously instead of returning and lapping over their mates as in a lap winding. Only two brushes are required for a four-pole motor. The commutator is made with an odd number of segments and one terminal of each of two coils is connected to each segment. The other terminals of the pair of coils are connected to adjoining segments diametrically opposite on the commutator. Current entering at the positive brush divides and takes two paths through successive coils connected in series. Each series of coils therefore carries one-half of the total armature current. See **Armature.**

Wear Plate. See **Bolster Wear Plate, Transom Wear Plate.**

Weather Strip. A narrow piece of wood, with a rubber edging, which is nailed to a door or window casing so that the rubber presses against the door or sash and prevents the entrance of air, dust and water through the cracks.

Webbing. Strips of stout, coarse cloth interwoven over the springs of a car seat to form a backing for the curled hair or felt padding which is placed on top.

Wedge. A **Journal Bearing Key**, which see.

Weed Burner Car. Fig. 246. A car equipped with an oil or gasoline tank and suitable burners, used for burning the weeds off of the right-of-way.

Welded Gear Case. Figs. 1535-1536. A sheet steel gear case welded up by the oxy-acetylene process instead of being riveted.

Westinghouse Air Brakes. Figs. 451-522.

Westinghouse Motors. Figs. 1658-1705.

Wheel. Figs. 1602-1644. A circular disk mounted on an axle and rolling on the track rails. Wheels for electric railway cars are made of cast iron, cast steel, solid rolled or forged steel, or built up with a steel tire shrunk and otherwise fastened on a wheel center. All car wheels are rigidly attached to their axles by pressing on and the axles turn in journal bearings with the wheels. See **Cast Iron Wheel, Steel Wheel, Steel-Tired Wheel.**

Wheel Box or Cover. An iron or wooden box placed on the floor of a single-truck car to cover the top of the wheels which project through the floor.

Wheel Center. The hub, plate or spokes and blank rim of a steel-tired wheel on which the annular tire is fastened. See Figs. 1615-1644.

Wheel Fit. (Axle.) That part of the surface of an axle which fits into the wheel hub. See **Gear Fit.**

Wheel Flange. The raised inner edge of the periphery of a wheel which projects below the top of the rail and holds the wheel on the rail. The standard contours of wheel flanges adopted by the American Electric Railway Engineering Association are shown in Figs. 1966-1967.

Wheel Piece. A term sometimes applied to the main member of a truck side frame to which the pedestals are attached.

Wheel Tread. The surface of the periphery of a car wheel which rolls on top of the rail. The standard contours of wheel treads and flanges adopted by the American Electric Railway Engineering Association are shown in Figs. 1966-1967.

Wheel Truing Brake Shoe. Fig. 1504.

Wheeler Car Seats. Figs. 1259-1261.

Wheelguard. Figs. 707, 711-713, 716-718; 10, Fig. 1378. A transverse beam, pointed fender or horizontal tray mounted on the truck or under the car body in front of the wheels and from 3 in. to 6 in. above the rails. Its purpose is to pick up or roll out from under the car prostrate persons on the track so as to prevent them from getting under the wheels. The terms wheelguard and lifeguard are synonymous, but the former is preferred as being more nearly descriptive of the function of the device. A wheelguard should not be confused with a projecting fender or pilot on the front of the car. Several types of automatic wheelguards are in use in which the pick-up tray or fender is normally held far enough above the rails to clear obstructions on the pavement, but is dropped down on the pavement by gravity or spring pressure when the vertical apron which is suspended under the bumper beam strikes an object on the track and is deflected backward. In some types of automatic wheelguards the tray also may be dropped by the motorman depressing a pedal or by making an emergency application of the air brakes and may be restored to the normal position by the motorman from the platform.

Wheelguard Bracket. 11, Fig. 1378. A casting bolted to the end frame of a truck or to an extension of the side frames to which is attached one end of a plank wheelguard.

Whistle. A device for emitting a loud, sharp sound when compressed air is admitted to it. Whistles are used on interurban cars for signaling when running in open country. The whistle is usually mounted on top of the front vestibule hood and is connected to the air brake main reservoir by a branch whistle pipe which has a whistle valve inserted in it.

Whistle Cord. A short cord attached to the handle of a whistle valve which when pulled opens the valve and causes the whistle to sound.

Whistle Pipe. A branch pipe from the main reservoir through which compressed air is carried to the whistle.

Whistle Valve. Figs. 562-563. A spring valve inserted in the whistle pipe below the whistle which when opened admits compressed air to the whistle.

White Lead. An oxide of lead which is pure white in color and is used as a pigment in mixing paint.

Wide Gage. Any track gage more than the standard of 4 ft. 8½ in. Wide gage of 5 ft. 2½ in. is used in a few cities in the United States, notably Philadelphia and Pittsburgh, Pa.

Wilson Trolley Catcher. Figs. 1334-1336.

Winding Drum. (Geared Hand Brake.) Fig. 584. A cylindrical or conical spiral drum on which the brake chain is wound. It is geared to the brake shaft and is carried in a cradle or yoke attached under the platform floor.

Window. An opening in the side or end of a car which is closed by a framework containing one or more panes of glass. The framework is called a window sash, and many of the parts and fittings of windows are prefixed with the name Sash, which see.

Window Blind. A slatted screen mounted on the inside of a car window to exclude light. It will admit air through the openings between slats when the window behind it is opened. Window blinds have been almost entirely superseded by window curtains.

COPPER WIRE TABLE—Matthiessen's Standard of Conductivity

B&S Gage	Size Diam. In.	Area Circular Mils	Weight Lbs. per Ft.	Lbs. per Ohm. @20°C.	@50°C.	@80°C.	Length Ft. per Lb.	Ft. per Ohm. @20°C.	@50°C.	@80°C.	Resistance Ohms per Lb. @20°C.	@50°C.	@80°C.	Ohms per Ft. @20°C.	@50°C.
0000	0.460	211600	0.6405	13039	11679	10579	1.561	20358	18234	16518	0.00007669	0.00008562	0.00009452	0.00004912	0.00005484
000	0.410	168100	0.5088	8230	7369	6676	1.965	16173	14486	13123	0.0001215	0.0001357	0.0001498	0.00006183	0.00006905
00	0.365	133225	0.4032	5168	4630	4193	2.480	12812	11481	10400	0.0001935	0.0002160	0.0002363	0.00007802	0.00008710
0	0.325	105625	0.3192	3249	2909	2636	3.128	10162	9099	8244	0.0003078	0.0003438	0.0003796	0.00009840	0.0001099
1	0.289	83521	0.2528	2032	1820	1648	3.956	8039	7199	6519	0.0004921	0.0005494	0.0006058	0.0001244	0.0001389
2	0.258	66564	0.2015	1291	1156	1047	4.963	6406	5737	5198	0.0007767	0.0008672	0.0009548	0.0001561	0.0001743
3	0.229	52441	0.1597	800.5	717.4	649.8	6.261	5045	4519	4093	0.001249	0.001394	0.001539	0.0001982	0.0002213
4	0.204	41616	0.1260	504.3	451.9	409.3	7.937	4003	3587	3249	0.001983	0.002213	0.002443	0.0002498	0.0002788
5	0.182	33124	0.1003	319.6	286.3	259.3	9.970	3187	2855	2586	0.003129	0.003493	0.003856	0.0003138	0.0003503
6	0.162	26244	0.07944	200.6	179.7	162.8	12.59	2525	2261	2049	0.004985	0.005566	0.006148	0.0003960	0.0004422
7	0.144	20736	0.06277	125.2	112.2	101.6	15.93	1995	1787	1619	0.007983	0.008914	0.009842	0.0005012	0.0005598
8	0.128	16384	0.04959	78.19	70.03	63.41	20.17	1576	1412	1279	0.01279	0.01428	0.01577	0.0006344	0.0007083
9	0.114	12996	0.03934	44.19	44.00	39.90	25.42	1250	1120	1015	0.02035	0.02270	0.02506	0.0007998	0.0008957
10	0.102	10404	0.03149	31.53	28.24	25.58	31.76	1001	898.9	812.3	0.03172	0.03541	0.03909	0.0009990	0.001115
11	0.091	8281	0.02507	19.98	17.90	16.20	39.89	796.8	713.8	646.4	0.05006	0.05588	0.06171	0.001255	0.001401
12	0.081	6561	0.01985	12.54	11.23	10.17	50.35	631.3	565.3	512.3	0.07976	0.08907	0.09829	0.001584	0.001769
13	0.072	5184	0.01569	7.825	7.013	6.349	63.74	498.8	446.8	404.7	0.1278	0.1426	0.1575	0.002005	0.002238
14	0.064	4096	0.01240	4.885	4.376	3.965	80.65	394.0	353.0	319.5	0.2047	0.2285	0.2522	0.002538	0.002833
15	0.057	3249	0.009834	3.074	2.754	2.494	101.7	312.5	278.0	253.6	0.3253	0.3633	0.4010	0.003199	0.003572
16	0.051	2601	0.007873	1.970	1.765	1.598	127.0	250.3	224.2	203.0	0.5076	0.5656	0.6256	0.003996	0.004465
17	0.045	2025	0.006129	1.194	1.070	0.9690	163.2	194.8	174.5	158.1	0.8373	0.9349	1.032	0.005133	0.005730
18	0.040	1600	0.004843	0.7457	0.6676	0.6064	206.5	153.9	137.9	124.9	1.341	1.498	1.653	0.006496	0.007253
19	0.036	1296	0.003923	0.4892	0.4382	0.3968	254.9	124.7	111.7	101.2	2.044	2.282	2.520	0.008025	0.008954
20	0.032	1024	0.003100	0.3054	0.2736	0.2478	322.6	98.52	88.26	79.94	3.274	3.655	4.035	0.01015	0.01133
21	0.0285	812.3	0.002459	0.1921	0.1721	0.1559	406.7	78.13	70.00	63.41	5.205	5.811	6.413	0.01280	0.01429
22	0.0253	640.1	0.001937	0.1193	0.1068	0.09681	516.3	61.58	55.13	49.98	8.384	9.365	10.33	0.01624	0.01814
23	0.0226	510.8	0.001546	0.07599	0.06803	0.06165	646.8	49.14	44.01	39.87	13.16	14.70	16.22	0.02035	0.02272
24	0.0201	404.0	0.001223	0.04753	0.04259	0.03857	817.7	38.87	34.82	31.54	21.01	23.48	25.93	0.02573	0.02872
25	0.0179	320.4	0.0009698	0.02990	0.02677	0.02425	1031	30.85	27.65	25.01	33.45	37.35	41.23	0.03022	0.03622
26	0.0159	252.8	0.0007652	0.01861	0.01667	0.01510	1307	24.52	21.79	19.74	53.75	60.00	66.22	0.04111	0.04590
27	0.0142	201.6	0.0006102	0.01183	0.01060	0.009605	1639	19.39	17.37	15.74	84.50	94.33	104.1	0.05156	0.05756
28	0.0126	158.8	0.0004807	0.007342	0.006579	0.005959	2080	15.28	13.69	12.40	136.2	152.0	167.8	0.06545	0.07307
29	0.0113	127.7	0.0003865	0.004749	0.004254	0.003854	2587	12.39	11.00	9.970	210.6	235.1	259.5	0.08150	0.09088
30	0.010	100.0	0.0003027	0.002914	0.002610	0.002363	3304	9.625	8.621	7.806	343.2	383.2	423.2	0.1039	0.1160
31	0.0089	79.2	0.0002397	0.001827	0.001636	0.001482	4172	7.622	6.826	6.184	547.4	611.2	674.6	0.1312	0.1465
32	0.008	64.0	0.0001935	0.001193	0.001068	0.0009671	5163	6.156	5.516	4.995	838.4	936.0	1034	0.1624	0.1813
33	0.0071	50.4	0.0001525	0.0007396	0.0006625	0.0005988	6557	4.850	4.344	3.936	1353	1510	1667	0.2062	0.2302
34	0.0063	39.7	0.0001202	0.0004591	0.0004112	0.0003724	8319	3.830	3.421	3.099	2178	2432	2685	0.2618	0.2925
35	0.0056	31.4	0.00009505	0.0002872	0.0002572	0.0002326	10522	3.021	2.706	2.454	3482	3888	4292	0.3310	0.3696
36	0.005	25.0	0.00007562	0.0001820	0.0001629	0.0001477	13225	2.405	2.154	1.952	5495	6135	6772	0.4158	0.4642

Values Given Under Weight, Length and Resistance are Accurate to the Third Significant Digit

Window Blind Lift. A handle fastened to a window blind by which it can be raised and lowered. A leather strap attached to the top or bottom rail of the blind is commonly used.

Window Casing. The grooved lining of a window opening in which the sash is fitted.

Window Cove Molding. See **Window Lintel.**

Window Curtain. A piece of thick cloth mounted on a roller above a car window and designed to be pulled down to exclude the light. See **Curtain.**

Window Frame. The posts, sill and lintel which form a window opening. The wooden frame enclosing the glass is called a sash frame or sash.

Window Glass. Thin sheets of transparent glass set into a window sash. Window glass used in electric railway cars is either plate glass from 3/16-in. to 1/4-in. thick, or cylinder glass of single or double thickness (1/16-in. or 1/8-in.). For Gothic and other top sashes, colored art glass or ground glass is often used.

Window Guards. Figs. 1001-1009. Small brass rods or wire grating on the outside of a closed car above the window sills, used to prevent passengers from sticking their heads and arms out of the car when the windows are open.

Window Lintel. The top of a window casing on the outside of a car body. The corresponding piece on the inside is sometimes called a window cove molding.

Window Panel. A panel on the inside or outside of a car between the windows.

Window Pocket. See **Sash Pocket.**

Window Post. 13 and 14, Figs. 259-370. An upright member of the body side framing extending from the side sills to the plate. They are designated as pier posts or wide posts and intermediate posts.

Window Sash. See **Sash.**

Window Shade. See **Curtain.**

Window Sill. 45 and 60, Figs. 259-370. A narrow board at the bottom of a window casing forming a shelf on which the window sash rests. Usually an inside and outside window sill are used, and in drop sash windows the inside window sill forms a hinged cover or flap for the sash pocket.

Window Stop. See **Sash Parting Strip.**

Wing Board. A wide shear board attached to the side of a snow plow or sweeper to push the snow well out beyond the rails. It can be raised or lowered and pulled in or out from the side by chains.

Winner Car Seats. Figs. 1204-1301.

Wire. A metal rod of small diameter. Copper wire insulated with rubber and cotton webbing is commonly used for connecting the electrical apparatus on cars. See **Cable.**

Wire Basket Rack. Figs. 722-723. A **Basket Rack,** which see, having a bottom made up of woven wire screen.

Wire Gage. An arbitrary number used to distinguish a wire of given diameter. Certain standard sizes of wire have long been manufactured and are known by their gage numbers. Several different gages are in use, but the tendency is to abandon the use of gage numbers and use the actual cross-sectional area expressed in circular mils or the diameter expressed in thousandths of an inch. The table on the opposite page gives the sizes, weights and resistance of wire, according to the Brown & Sharpe standard wire gage, which is commonly used in the United States.

Wiring. See **Car Wiring.**

Wood. The vegetable matter forming the trunks of trees. The common woods used in car building include oak, yellow pine, ash, white wood, cherry, maple and mahogany.

Wood Screw. A tapered metal pin having a flat or rounded head with a notch cut across it and a spiral screw thread formed on the shank under the head. Used in place of nails for fastening thin pieces of wood together.

Work Car. Figs. 227-244. Any car used for track construction or repair work. Usually a motor flat car.

Wrecking Car. A car equipped with tools and appliances for clearing up wrecks.

Y

Yoke Suspension. See **Motor Suspension.**

Z

Z-Bar. A rolled structural steel section in the shape of the letter Z. In the Narragansett type of open car, Z-bars are used for side sills.

CITY CARS, Single-Truck, Closed

Fig. 1—Single-Truck, Double-End, Closed Car with Open Platforms and Portable Vestibules
The J. G. Brill Company, Builder

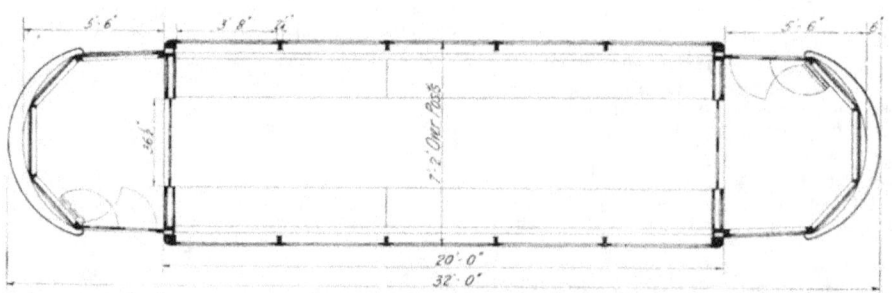

Fig. 2—Floor Plan of Single-Truck, Double-End, Closed Car with Enclosed Platforms and
Longitudinal Seats
Cincinnati Car Company, Builder

Fig. 3—Single-Truck, Double-End, Closed Car; Platforms Enclosed on Both Sides with
Folding Doors and Collapsible Gates
McGuire-Cummings Manufacturing Company, Builder

CITY CARS, Single-Truck, Closed

Fig. 5—Floor Plan of Single-Truck, Double-End, Pay-as-You-Enter, Closed Car with Enclosed Platforms; Aurora, Elgin & Chicago Railroad
Niles Car & Manufacturing Company, Builder

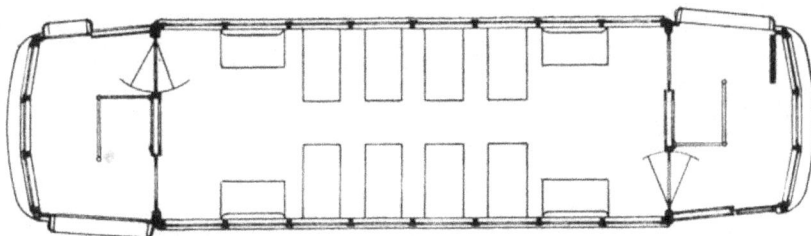

Fig. 5—Floor Plan of Single-Truck, Double-End, Pay-as-You-Enter, Closed Car with Enclosed Platforms; Aurora, Elgin & Chicago Railroad
Niles Car & Manufacturing Company, Builder

Fig. 6—Single-Truck, Double-End, Closed Car with Doors on Right-Hand Side of Platforms Only
The J. G. Brill Company, Builder

CITY CARS, Single-Truck, Closed

Fig. 7—Single-Truck, Single-End, Closed Car with Open Rear Platform and Enclosed Motorman's Vestibule
Barney & Smith Car Company, Builder

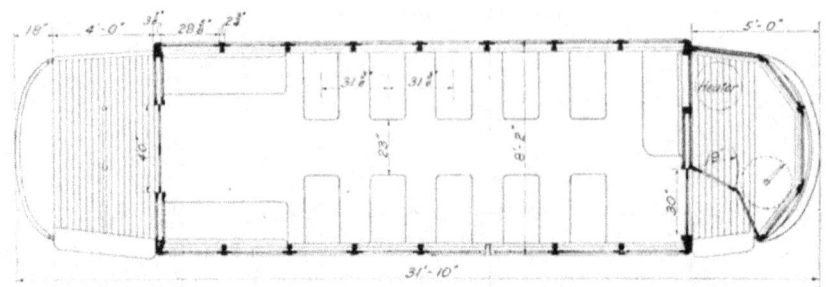

Fig. 8—Floor Plan of Single-Truck, Single-End Car Shown in Fig. 7
Barney & Smith Car Company, Builder

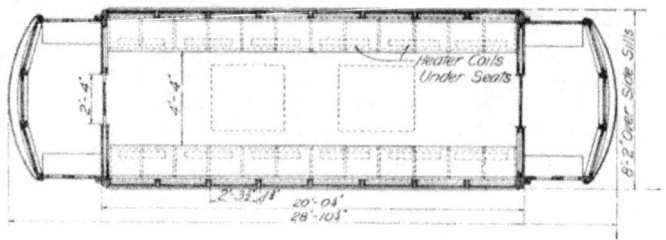

Fig. 9—Floor Plan of Single-Truck, Double-End, Closed Car with Enclosed Platforms and Longitudinal Seats
American Car & Foundry Company, Builder

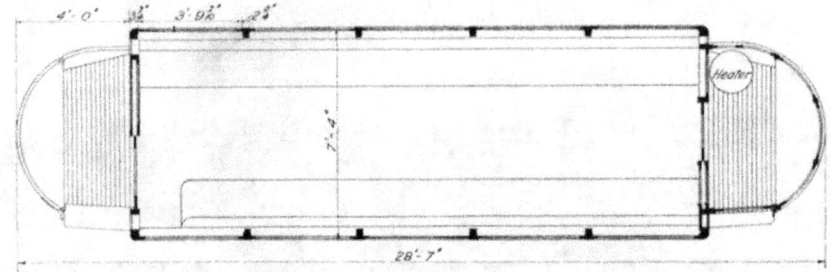

Fig. 10—Floor Plan of Single-Truck, Single-End, Closed Car with Open Rear Platform and Enclosed Motorman's Vestibule
Barney & Smith Car Company, Builder

CITY CARS, Single-Truck, Closed

Fig. 11—Single-Truck, Double-End, Center Side Entrance, Closed Car
Barber Car Company, Builder

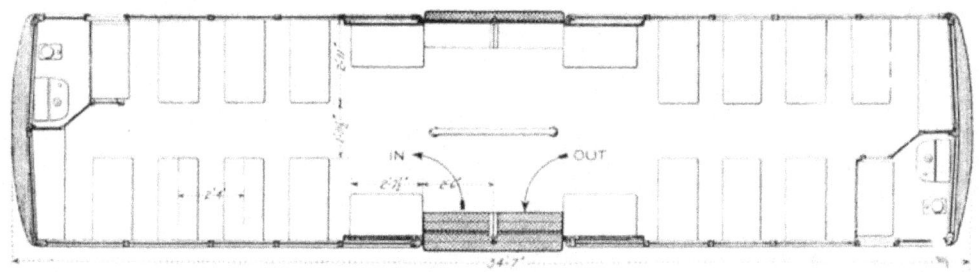

Fig. 12—Floor Plan of Single-Truck, Center Side Entrance, Closed Car
Barber Car Company, Builder

Fig. 13—Interior of Center Side Entrance Car Shown
in Figs. 11 and 12
Barber Car Company, Builder

Fig. 14—Interior of Single-Truck, Closed Car with
Longitudinal Wooden Slat Seats
The J. G. Brill Company, Builder

CITY CARS, Single-Truck, Semi-Convertible — Figs. 15-17

Fig. 15—Single-Truck, Double-End, Closed Car with Enclosed Platforms and Straight Sides
The J. G. Brill Company, Builder

Fig. 16—Standard Single-Truck, Double-End, Semi-Convertible Car with Enclosed Platforms
The J. G. Brill Company, Builder

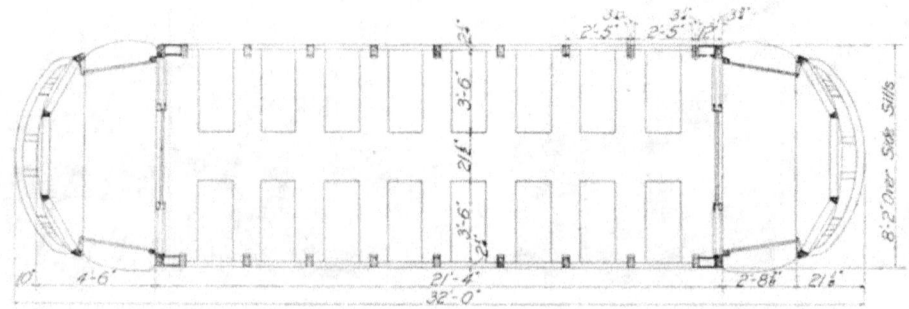

Fig. 17—Floor Plan of Single-Truck, Double-End, Semi-Convertible Car Shown in Fig. 16
The J. G. Brill Company, Builder

CITY CARS, Single-Truck, Semi-Convertible

Fig. 18—Single-Truck, Double-End, Semi-Convertible Car with Sheet Steel Sides
The J. G. Brill Company, Builder

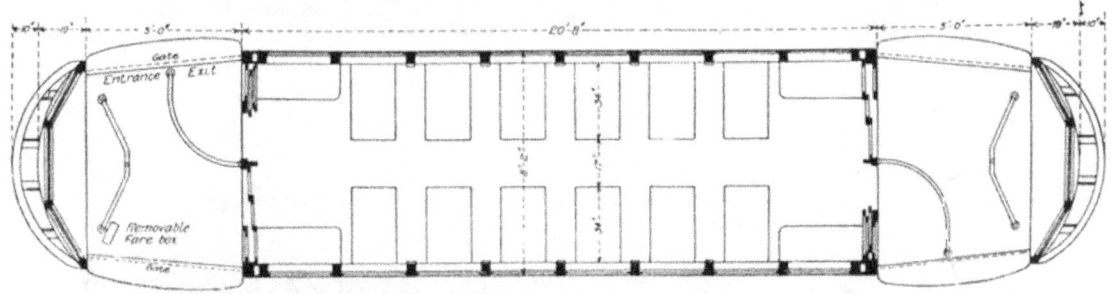

Fig. 19—Floor Plan of Single-Truck, Double-End, Semi-Convertible Car Arranged for One-Man, Pay-as-You-Enter Operation; Brunswick (Ga.) City & Suburban Railway
The J. G. Brill Company, Builder

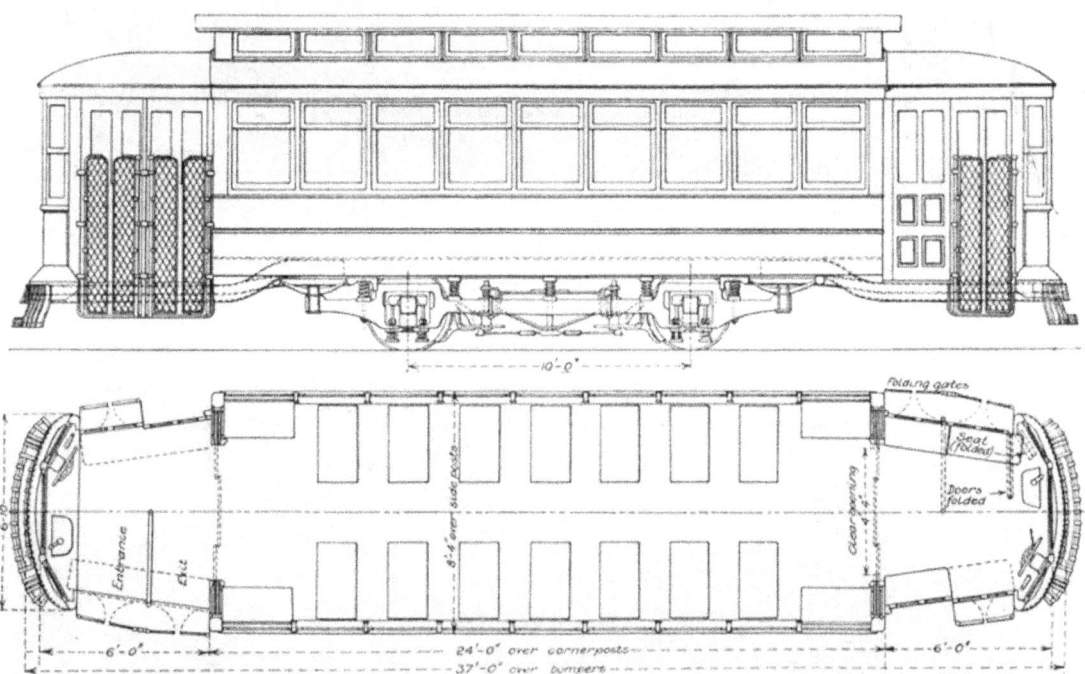

Figs. 20-21—Side Elevation and Floor Plan of Single-Truck, Double-End, Semi-Convertible Car with Long Platforms Enclosed with Folding Doors and Gates; Birmingham Railway, Light & Power Company
St. Louis Car Company, Builder

(6)

CITY CARS, Single-Truck, Semi-Convertible — Figs. 22-24

Fig. 22—Single-Truck, Double-End, Semi-Convertible Car
American Car & Foundry Company, Builder

Fig. 23—Single-Truck, Single-End, Semi-Convertible Car with Open Rear Platform Arranged for Pay-as-You-Enter Operation; Houston Electric Company
Cincinnati Car Company, Builder

(Framing of this car is shown in Figs. 253-255.)

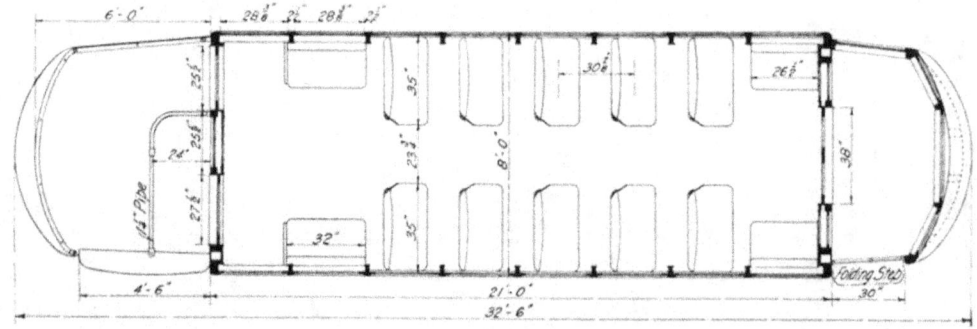

Fig. 24—Floor Plan of Single-Truck, Single-End, Semi-Convertible Car Shown in Fig. 23
Cincinnati Car Company, Builder

Fig. 25—Single-Truck, Double-End, Semi-Convertible Car Arranged for Pay-as-You-Enter Operation
The J. G. Brill Company, Builder

Fig. 26—Standard Single-Truck, Double-End, Convertible Car with Enclosed Platforms
The J. G. Brill Company, Builder

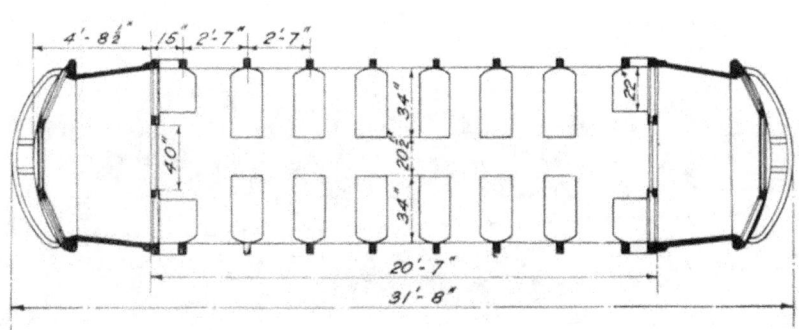

Fig. 27—Floor Plan of Single-Truck, Double-End, Convertible Car Shown in Fig. 26
The J. G. Brill Company, Builder

CITY CARS, Single-Truck, Open

Fig. 28—Half-Open and Closed, Single-Truck, Double-End Car
The J. G. Brill Company, Builder

Fig. 29—Floor Plan of Single-Truck, Double-End, California Type Car with Pair of
Bulkhead Seats at Each End
The J. G. Brill Company, Builder

Fig. 30—Single-Truck, Double-End, Ten-Bench Open Car
American Car & Foundry Company, Builder

Fig. 31—Single-Truck, Double-End, Ten-Bench Open Car
The J. G. Brill Company, Builder

(Side and end elevations and framing of this car are shown in Figs. 259-262.)

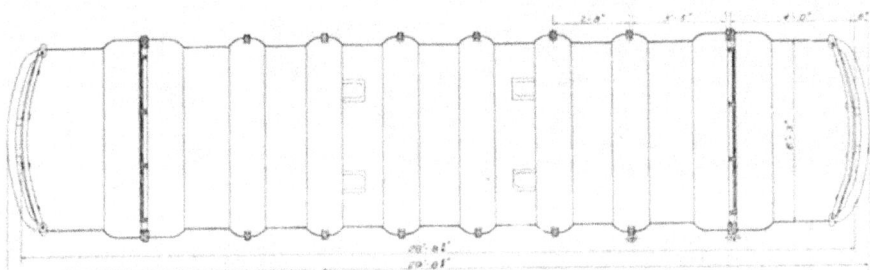

Fig. 32—Floor Plan of Single-Truck, Double-End, Ten-Bench Open Car Shown in Fig. 31
The J. G. Brill Company, Builder

Fig. 33—Single-Truck, Double-End, Ten-Bench Open Car with Center Aisle and Vestibuled
Ends on Platforms
The J. G. Brill Company, Builder

CITY CARS, Double-Truck, Closed

Fig. 34—Single-Truck, Double-End, Gas-Electric Car
General Electric Company, Builder

Fig. 35—Double-Truck, Double-End, Closed Car with Portable Vestibules and Platform Gates
The J. G. Brill Company, Builder

Fig. 36—Double-Truck, Double-End, Closed Car
American Car & Foundry Company, Builder

CITY CARS, Double-Truck, Closed

Fig. 37—Double-Truck, Double-End, Closed Car; Platforms Enclosed with Folding Doors
American Car & Foundry Company, Builder

(Framing of this car is shown in Figs. 288-289.)

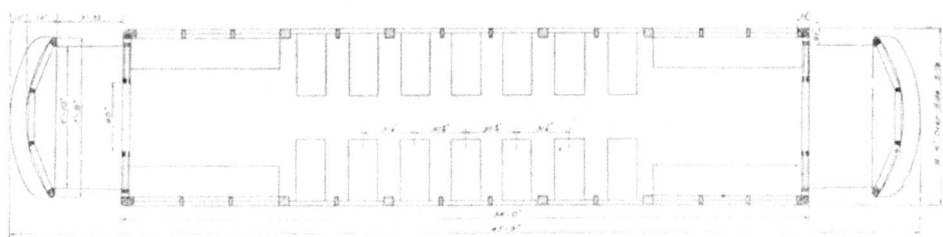

Fig. 38—Floor Plan of Double-Truck, Double-End Closed Car; Washington Railway & Electric Company
The J. G. Brill Company, Builder

Fig. 39—Double-Truck, Double-End, Closed Car; Platforms Open on Right-Hand Side Only
St. Louis Car Company, Builder

CITY CARS, Double-Truck, Closed

Fig. 40—Double-Truck, Double-End, Closed Car with Platforms Arranged for Prepayment Operation; Metropolitan Street Railway, New York
The J. G. Brill Company, Builder

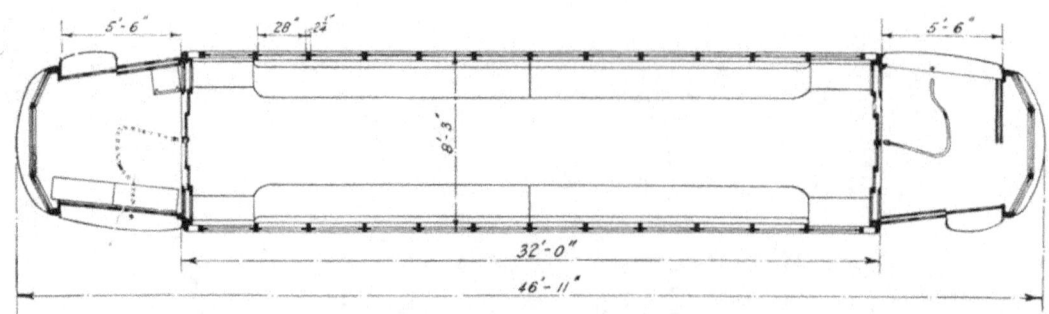

Fig. 41—Floor Plan of Prepayment Type Car Shown in Fig. 40
The J. G. Brill Company, Builder

Fig. 42—Interior of Prepayment Type Car Shown in Fig. 40
The J. G. Brill Company, Builder

Fig. 43—Interior of Double-Truck, Longitudinal Seat Closed Car
The J. G. Brill Company, Builder

CITY CARS, Double-Truck, Closed

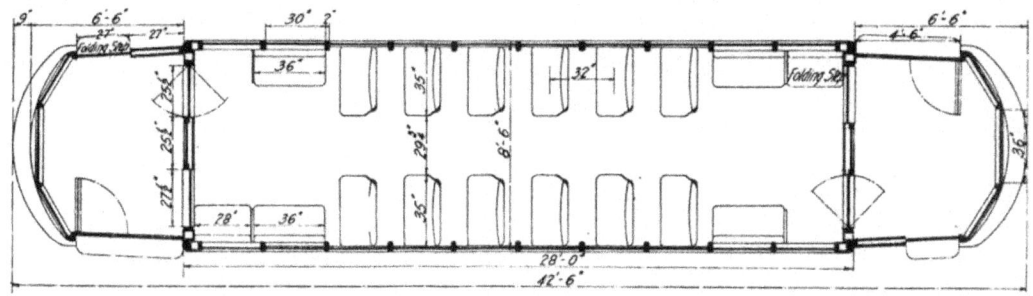

Fig. 44—Floor Plan of Double-Truck, Double-End, Closed Pay-as-You-Enter Car; Northern Texas Traction Company
Cincinnati Car Company, Builder

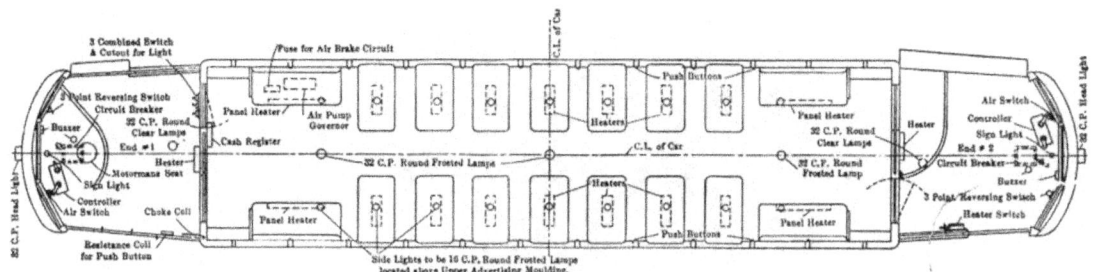

Fig. 45—Floor Plan of All-Steel, Double-Truck, Double-End, Closed Pay-as-You-Enter Car; Chicago Railways Company
Pressed Steel Car Company, Builder

(Framing and cross-section of this car are shown in Figs. 301-306.)

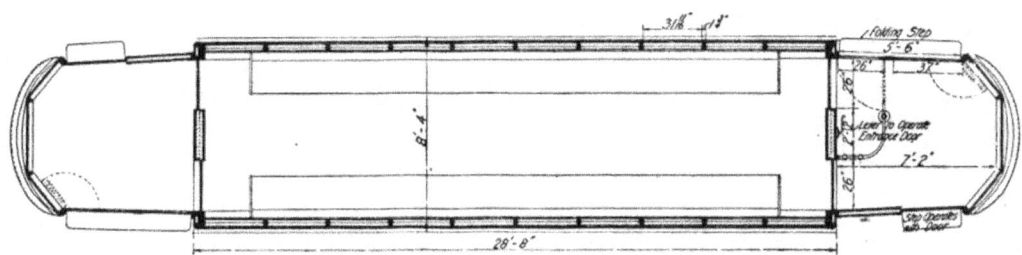

Fig. 46—Floor Plan of Double-Truck, Double-End, Closed Pay-as-You-Enter Car; St. Joseph Railway, Light, Heat & Power Company
St. Louis Car Company, Builder

(Framing of this car is shown in Figs. 332-333.)

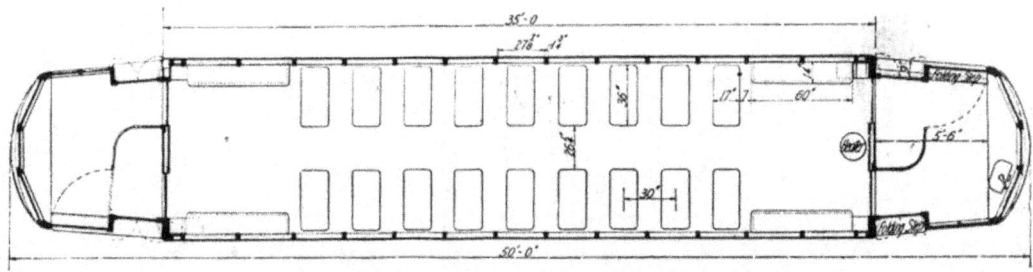

Fig. 47—Floor Plan of Semi-Steel, Double-Truck, Double-End Closed Pay-as-You-Enter Car; Milwaukee Electric Railway & Light Company
St. Louis Car Company, Builder

(Framing of this car is shown in Figs. 274-276.)

CITY CARS, Double-Truck, Closed

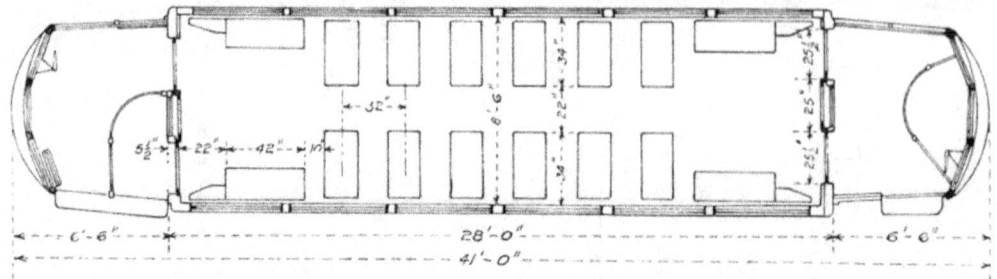

Fig. 48—Floor Plan of Double-Truck, Double-End, Closed, Pay-as-You-Enter Car; Chicago Railways Company
St. Louis Car Company, Builder

Fig. 49—Interior of Double-Truck, Single-End,
Closed, Pay-as-You-Enter Car; Illinois
Traction System
The J. G. Brill Company, Builder

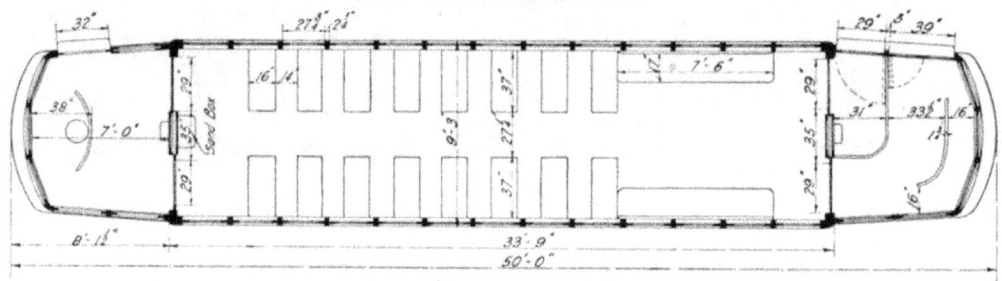

Fig. 50—Floor Plan of Double-Truck, Single-End, Closed, Pay-as-You-Enter Car Shown in Fig. 49
The J. G. Brill Company, Builder
(Cross-section of this car is shown in Fig. 324.)

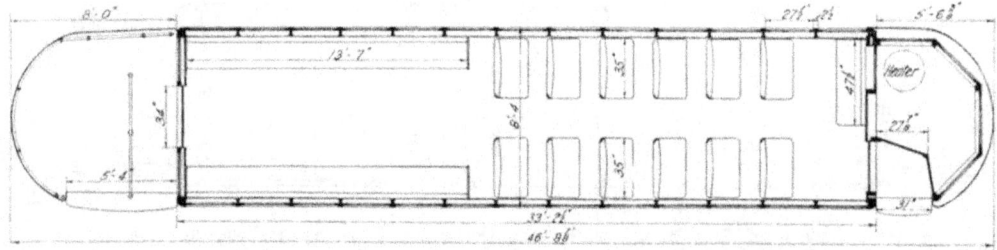

Fig. 51—Floor Plan of Double-Truck, Single-End, Closed Car; Indianapolis Traction & Terminal Company
Cincinnati Car Company, Builder

CITY CARS, Double-Truck, Closed

Fig. 52—Double-Truck, Single-End, All-Steel, Closed, Pay-as-You-Enter Car; Montreal Street Railway
Pressed Steel Car Company, Builder

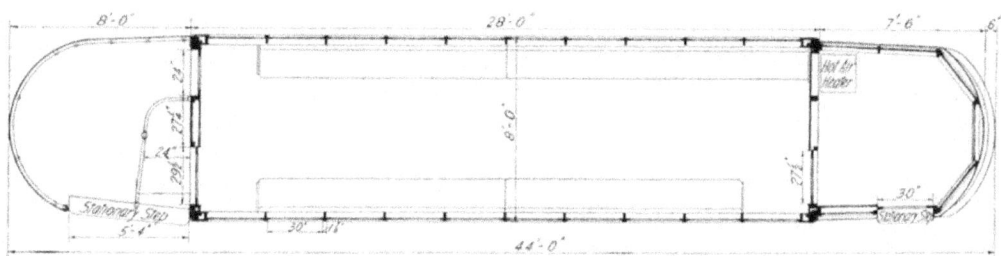

Fig. 53—Floor Plan of Double-Truck, Single-End, Closed, Pay-as-You-Enter Car, Cincinnati Traction Company
Cincinnati Car Company, Builder

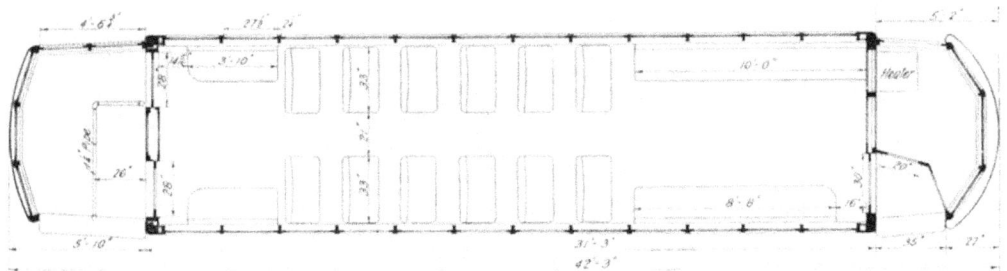

Fig. 54—Floor Plan of Double-Truck, Single-End, Closed, Pay-as-You-Enter Car; Detroit United Railway
Cincinnati Car Company, Builder

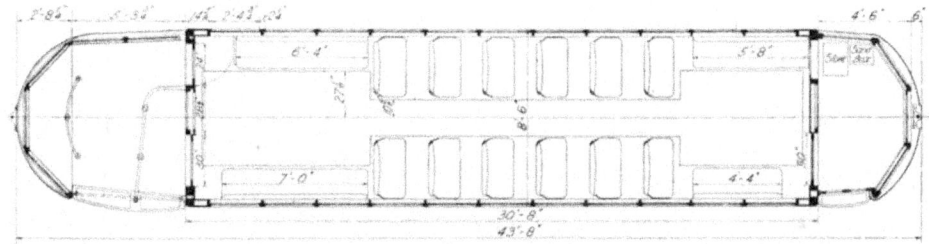

Fig. 55—Floor Plan of Double-Truck, Single-End, Closed, Pay-as-You-Enter Car with Rear
Platform Gates; Public Service Railway
Cincinnati Car Company, Builder

(Cross-sections and framing details of this car are shown in Figs. 279-282.)

Fig. 56—Double-Truck, Single-End, Semi-Steel, Closed, Pay-as-You-Enter Car; United Railways of St. Louis
Built in Company's Shops

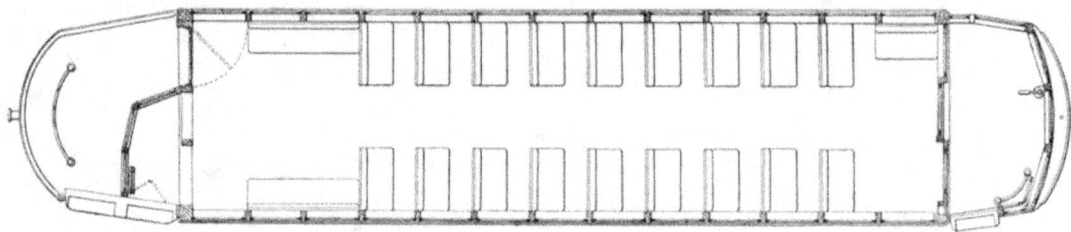

Fig. 57—Floor Plan of Double-Truck, Single-End, Closed, Pay-as-You-Enter Car Shown in Fig. 56

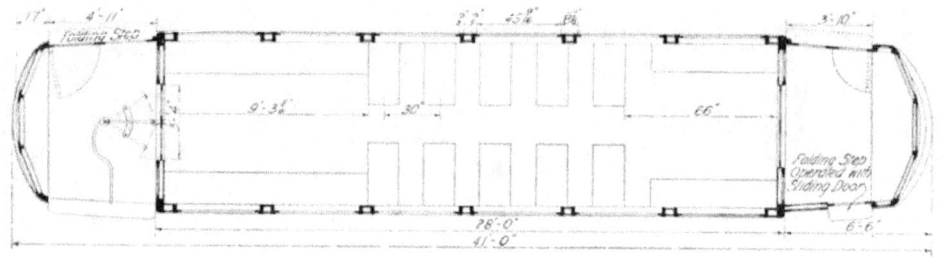

Fig. 58.—Floor Plan of Double-Truck, Single-End, Closed, Pay-as-You-Enter Car; Beloit Traction Company
St. Louis Car Company, Builder

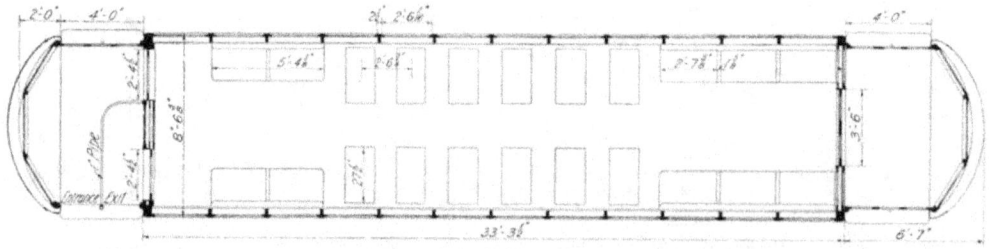

Fig. 59—Floor Plan of Double-Truck, Single-End, Closed, Pay-as-You-Enter Car; Metropolitan Street Railway, Kansas City
St. Louis Car Company, Builder

Figs. 60-63 CITY CARS, Double-Truck, Closed

Fig. 60—Double-Truck, Single-End, Closed Car with Open Rear Platform and Enclosed Motorman's Vestibule
The J. G. Brill Company, Builder

Fig. 61—Double-Truck, Single-End, Closed, Pay-as-You-Enter Car
The J. G. Brill Company, Builder

Fig. 62—Interior of Closed, Pay-as-You-Enter Car Shown in Fig. 61
The J. G. Brill Company, Builder

Fig. 63—Interior of Pay-Within Car, 1909 Type; Capital Traction Company
Cincinnati Car Company, Builder

Fig. 64—Double-Truck, Double-End, Closed, Pay-Within Car, 1909 Type; Capital Traction Company
Cincinnati Car Company, Builder

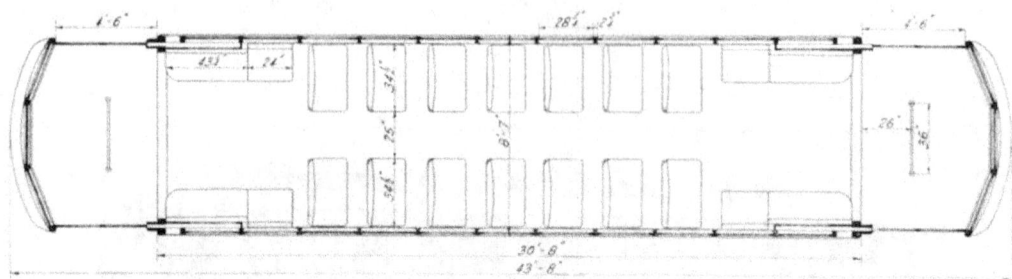

Fig. 65—Floor Plan of Double-Truck, Double-End, Pay-Within Car, 1909 Type; Capital Traction Company
Cincinnati Car Company, Builder

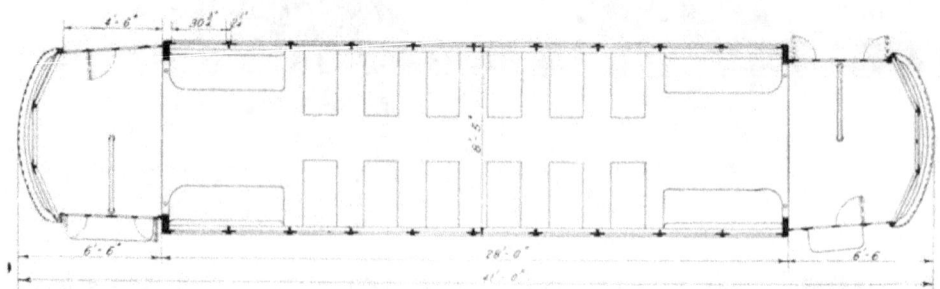

Fig. 66—Floor Plan of Double-Truck, Double-End, Pay-Within Car, 1910 Type; Capital Traction Company
Jewett Car Company, Builder

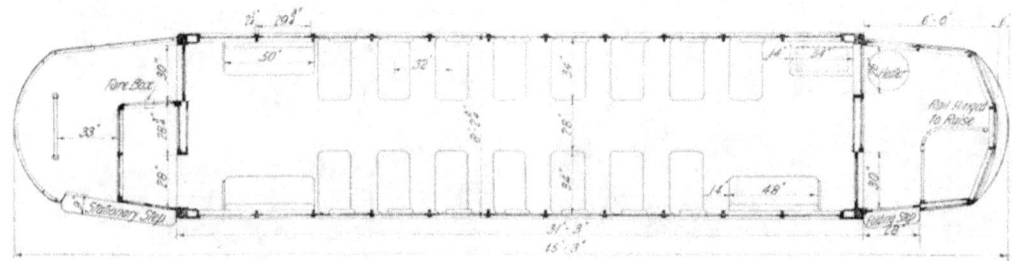

Fig. 67—Floor Plan of Double-Truck, Single-End, Prepayment Car; Louisville Railway
Cincinnati Car Company, Builder

CITY CARS, Double-Truck, Semi-Convertible

Fig. 68—Standard 28-ft. Double-Truck, Double-End, Semi-Convertible Car
The J. G. Brill Company, Builder

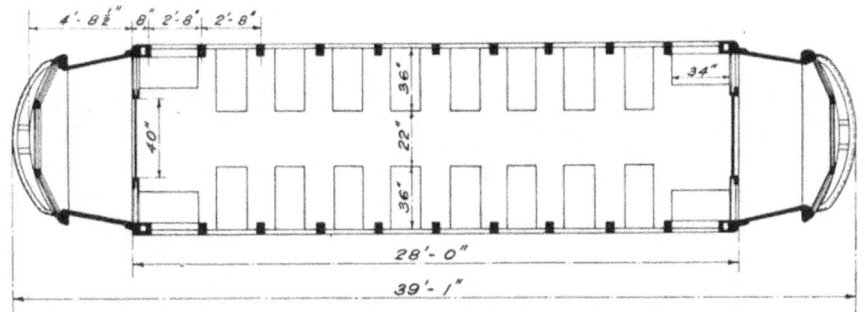

Fig. 69—Floor Plan of Standard 28-ft. Double-Truck, Double-End, Semi-Convertible Car
The J. G. Brill Company, Builder

Fig. 70—Double-Truck, Double-End, Semi-Convertible Car
American Car & Foundry Company, Builder

CITY CARS, Double-Truck, Semi-Convertible — Figs. 71-74

Fig. 71—Double-Truck, Double-End Semi-Convertible Car; Boston & Northern Street Railway
Laconia Car Company Works, Builder

(Framing of this car is shown in Figs. 284-287.)

Fig. 72—Interior View of Semi-Convertible Car
Shown in Fig. 71
Laconia Car Company Works, Builder

Fig. 73—Interior of Semi-Convertible Car Shown
in Fig. 74
The J. G. Brill Company, Builder

Fig. 74—Double-Truck, Double-End, Semi-Convertible, Pay-as-You-Enter Car
The J. G. Brill Company, Builder

Figs. 75-77 CITY CARS, Double-Truck, Semi-Convertible

Fig. 75—Double-Truck, Double-End, Semi-Convertible, Pay-as-You-Enter Car; Capital Traction Company
Cincinnati Car Company, Builder

Fig. 76—Double-Truck, Double-End, Semi-Convertible Car with Portable Vestibules
The J. G. Brill Company, Builder

Fig. 77—Interior of Arch-Roof, Semi-Convertible Car Shown
in Fig. 78
The J. G. Brill Company, Builder

Fig. 78—Double-Truck, Double-End, Semi-Convertible Car with Arch Roof
The J. G. Brill Company, Builder

(Cross-Section of this car is shown in Fig. 264.)

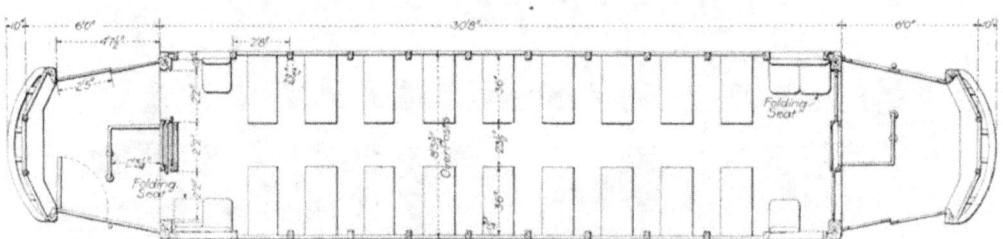

Fig 79—Floor Plan of Double-Truck, Double-End Semi-Convertible Car Shown in Fig. 77
The J. G. Brill Company, Builder

Fig. 80—Standard Double-Truck, Double-End, Narragansett Type, Convertible Car
The J. G. Brill Company, Builder

CITY CARS, Double-Truck, Convertible

Fig. 81—Double-Truck, Single-End, Half-Convertible Car; Toledo Railways & Light Company
The J. G. Brill Company, Builder

Fig. 82—Interior of Half-Convertible Car Shown in Fig. 81
The J. G. Brill Company, Builder

Fig. 83—Double-Truck, Double-End, California Type Car
The J. G. Brill Company, Builder

CITY CARS, Double-Truck, Combination Open and Closed

Fig. 84—Double-Truck, Single-End, Combination Open and Closed Motor Car with Center Side Entrance; Seattle Electric Company
St. Louis Car Company, Builder

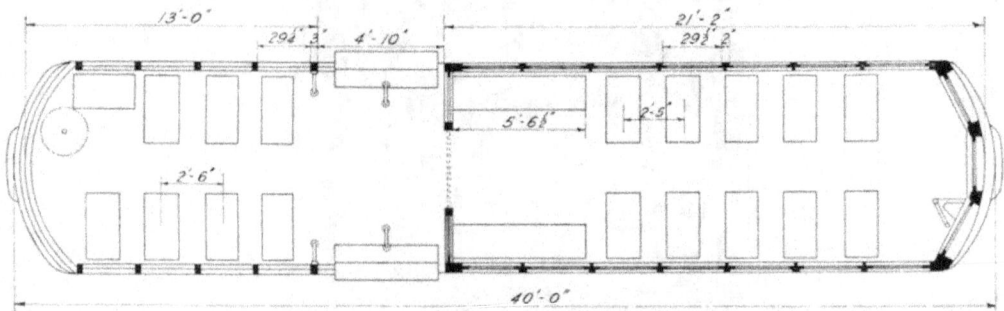

Fig. 85—Floor Plan of Center Side Entrance Car Shown in Fig. 84
St. Louis Car Company, Builder

(Framing of this car is shown in Figs. 335-337.)

Fig. 86—Double-Truck, Double-End, California Type Car
Built by Los Angeles Railway

CITY CARS, Double-Truck, Combination Open and Closed

Fig. 87—Standard Double-Truck, Single-End, Combination Open and Closed Motor Car with Center Side Entrance; Denver City Tramway Company
Woeber Carriage Company, Builder

Fig. 88—Interior of Standard Motor Car; Denver City Tramway Company
Woeber Carriage Company, Builder

Fig. 89—Standard Double-Truck, Center Side Entrance Trailer; Denver City Tramway Company
Woeber Carriage Company, Builder

CITY CARS, Double-Truck, Open

Fig. 90—Double-Truck, Single-End, Open Car with Platforms and Center Aisle; Columbus Railway & Light Company
Barney & Smith Car Company, Builder

Fig. 91—12-Bench, Double-Truck, Double-End Open Car
The J. G. Brill Company, Builder

Fig. 92—14-Bench, Double-Truck, Double-End Open Car with Vestibuled Ends
The J. G. Brill Company, Builder

CITY CARS, Double-Truck, Open

Fig. 93—14-Bench, Double-Truck, Double-End, Narragansett Type Open Car
The J. G. Brill Company, Builder

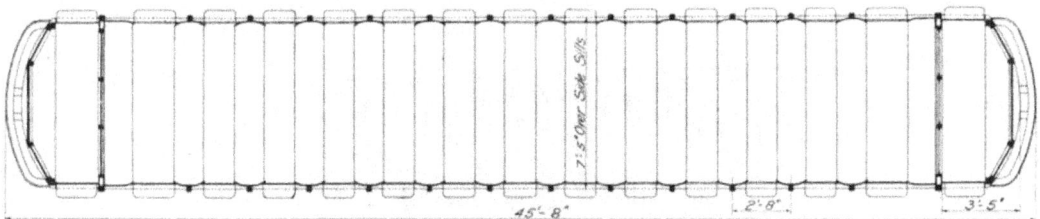

Fig. 94—Floor Plan of 14-Bench, Narragansett Type Open Car Shown in Fig. 93
The J. G. Brill Company, Builder

Fig. 95—Interior of 12-Bench Open Car
The J. G. Brill Company, Builder

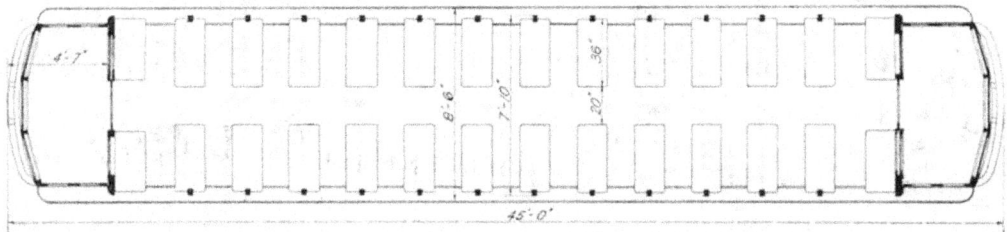

Fig. 96—Floor Plan of Double-Truck, Double-End, Center-Aisle Open Car
St. Louis Car Company, Builder

Fig. 97—Double-Truck, Double-End, Funeral Car; Chicago Railways
The J. G. Brill Company, Builder

Fig. 98—Interior View of Funeral Car Shown in
Fig. 97
The J. G. Brill Company, Builder

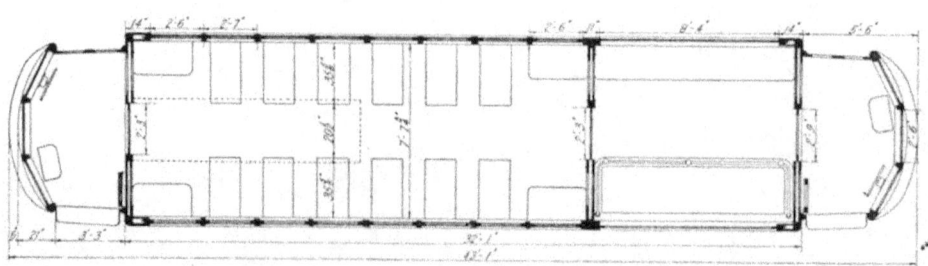

Fig. 99—Floor Plan of Funeral Car; Chicago Railways
The J. G. Brill Company, Builder

INTERURBAN CARS, Passenger

Fig. 100—Single-End, Light Interurban Car with Smoking Compartment; Detroit United Railway
Niles Car & Manufacturing Company, Builder

(Framing of this car is shown in Figs. 290-292.)

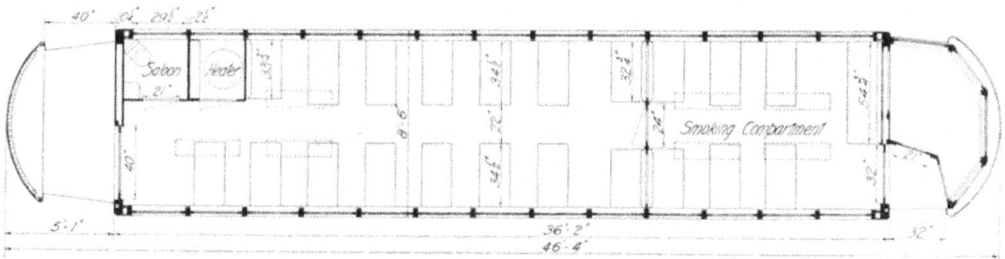

Fig. 101—Floor Plan of Light Interurban Car; Detroit United Railway
Niles Car & Manufacturing Company, Builder

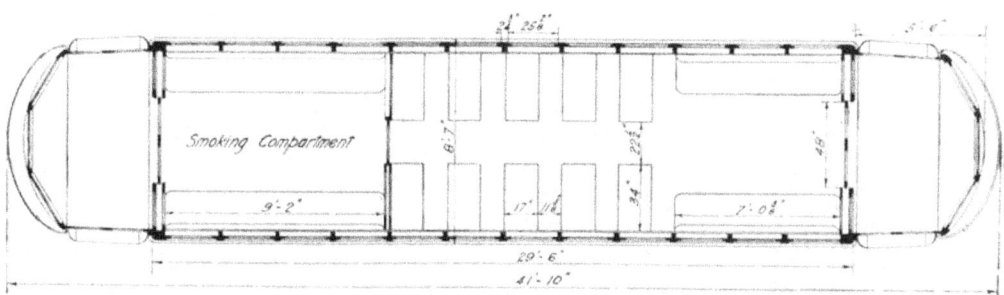

Fig. 102—Floor Plan of Double-End, Light Interurban Car with Smoking Compartment; Schenectady Railway
St. Louis Car Company, Builder

(Underframing of this car is shown in Fig. 293.)

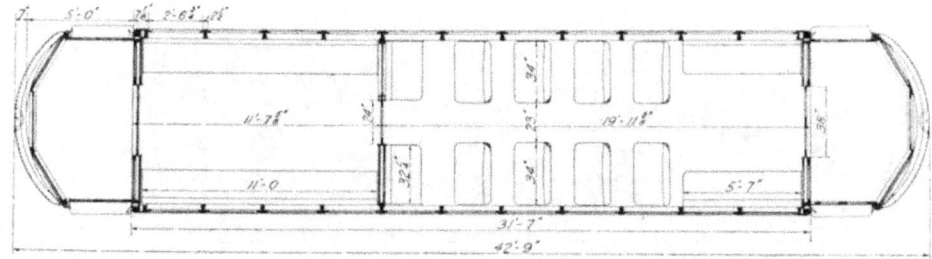

Fig. 103—Floor Plan of Double-End, Light Interurban Car with Smoking Compartment;
Ohio Valley Electric Railway
Cincinnati Car Company, Builder

Fig. 104—Double-End, Single-Compartment, Light Interurban Car
Niles Car & Manufacturing Company, Builder

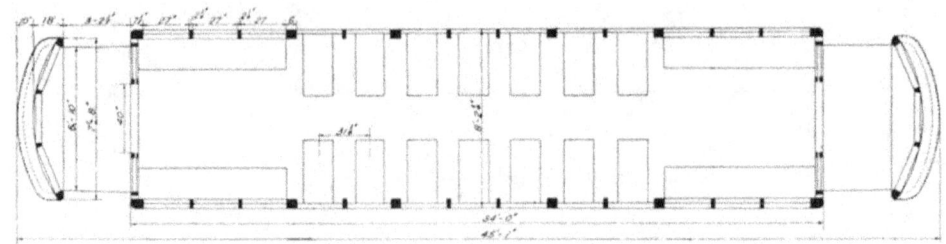

Fig. 105—Floor Plan of Double-End, Light Interurban Car Shown in Fig. 106
The J. G. Brill Company, Builder

Fig. 106—Double-End, Light Interurban Car; Emigration Canyon Railroad
The J. G. Brill Company, Builder

(Framing of this car is shown in Figs. 349-351.)

Fig. 107—Double-End Interurban Car with Smoking Compartment
Barney & Smith Car Company, Builder

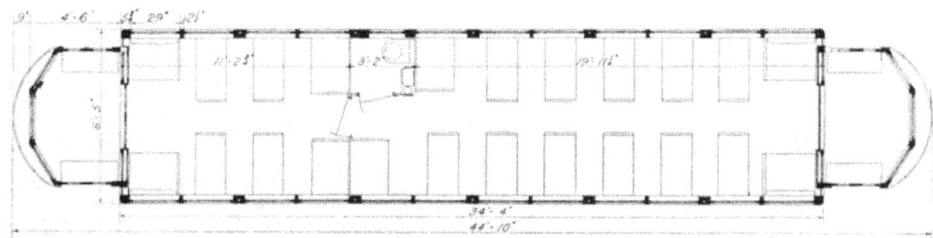

Fig. 108—Floor Plan of Double-End Interurban Car Shown in Fig. 107
Barney & Smith Car Company, Builder

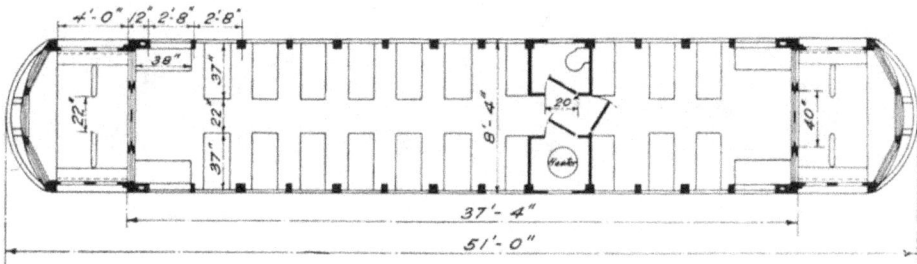

Fig. 109—Floor Plan of Double-End Interurban Car with Smoking Compartment
The J. G. Brill Company, Builder

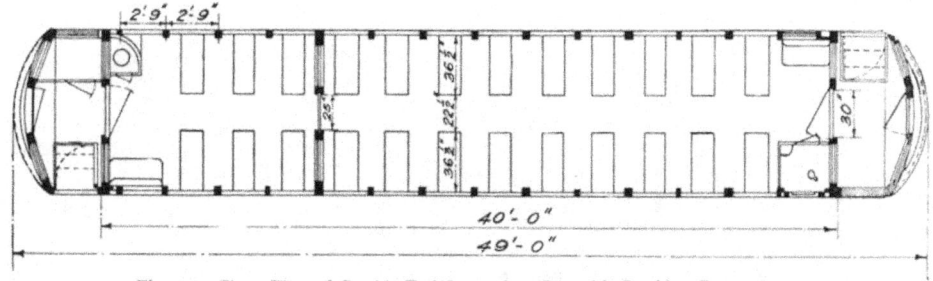

Fig. 110—Floor Plan of Double-End Interurban Car with Smoking Compartment
The J. G. Brill Company, Builder

(32)

INTERURBAN CARS, Passenger — Figs. 111-114

Fig. 111—Double-End Interurban Car with Smoking Compartment
The J. G. Brill Company, Builder

Fig. 112—Interior of Interurban Car with Smoking
Compartment
The J. G. Brill Company, Builder

Fig. 113—Interior of Longitudinal-Seat Interurban
Car Shown in Fig. 114
McGuire-Cummings Manufacturing Company, Builder

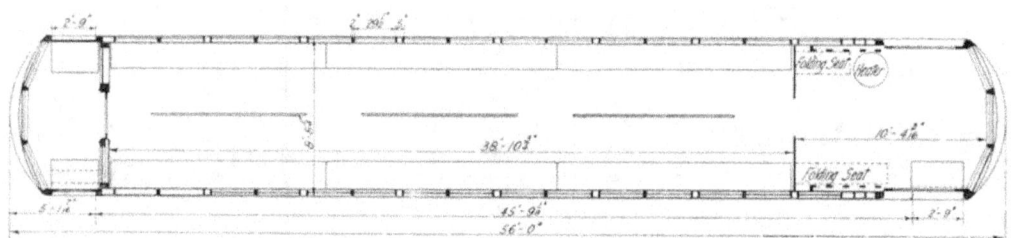

Fig. 114—Floor Plan of Single-End Interurban Car with Longtudinal Seats; Peoria Railway
Terminal Company
McGuire-Cummings Manufacturing Company, Builder

INTERURBAN CARS, Passenger

Fig. 115—Single-Compartment, Double-End Interurban Trail Car
Niles Car & Manufacturing Company, Builder

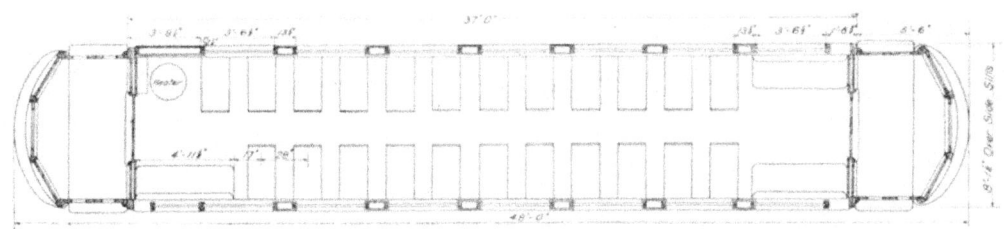

Fig. 116—Floor Plan of Double-End, Single-Compartment Interurban Car; Louisville & Northern Railway & Lighting Company
American Car & Foundry Company, Builder

Fig. 117—Double-End Interurban Car Shown in Fig. 116
American Car & Foundry Company, Builder

(Cross section of this car is shown in Fig. 306.)

Fig. 118—Double-End Interurban Car with Steel Underframe
St. Louis Car Company, Builder

(Framing of this car is shown in Figs. 309-310.)

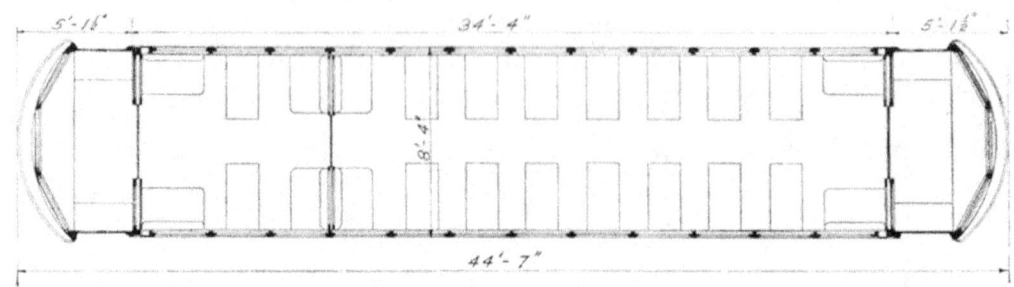

Fig. 119—Floor Plan of Double-End Interurban Car with Smoking Compartment
American Car & Foundry Company, Builder

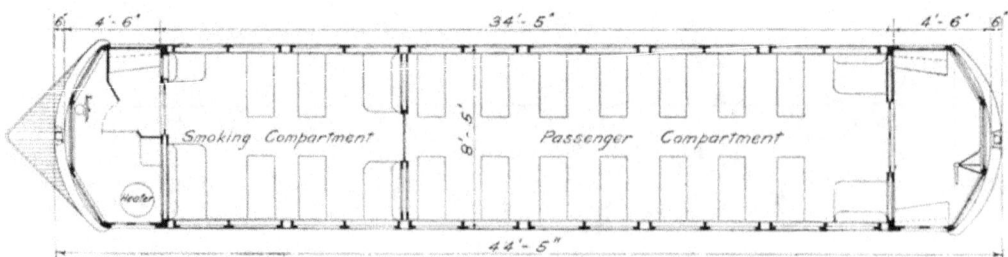

Fig. 120—Floor Plan of Single-End Interurban Car with Smoking Compartment
American Car & Foundry Company, Builder

End Interurban Car with Vestibule End Doors for Train Operation
The J. G. Brill Company, Builder

INTERURBAN CARS, Passenger

Fig. 122—Double-End, Single Compartment, Interurban Car
The J. G. Brill Company, Builder

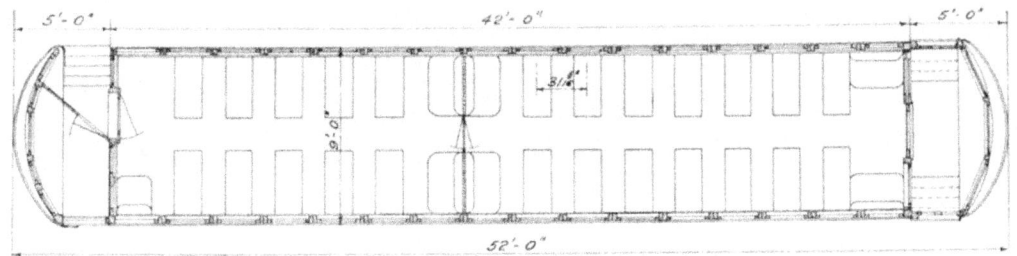

Fig. 123—Floor Plan of Single-End Interurban Car with Smoking Compartment
American Car & Foundry Company, Builder

Fig. 124—Double-End, Single Compartment, Interurban Tra'
Niles Car & Manufacturing Company, Builder

(Framing of this car is shown in Figs. 359-360.)

INTERURBAN CARS, Passenger

Fig. 125—Double-End, Single-Compartment, Interurban Trail Car
The J. G. Brill Company, Builder

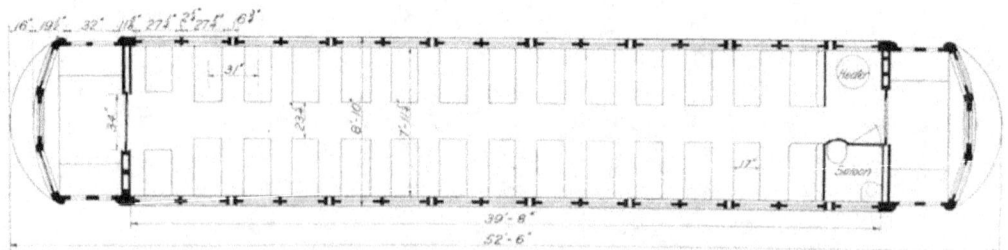

Fig. 126—Floor Plan of Interurban Trail Car Shown in Fig. 127
The J. G. Brill Company, Builder

Fig. 127—Double-End, Single-Compartment, Interurban Trail Car
The J. G. Brill Company, Builder

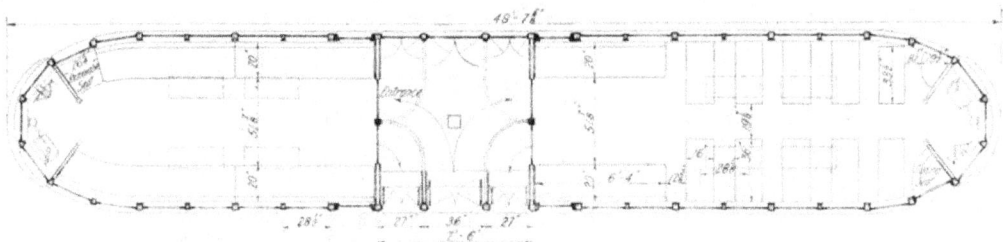

Fig. 128—Floor Plan of Center-Side Entrance, All-Steel, Interurban Car; Oklahoma Railway
Niles Car & Manufacturing Company, Builder

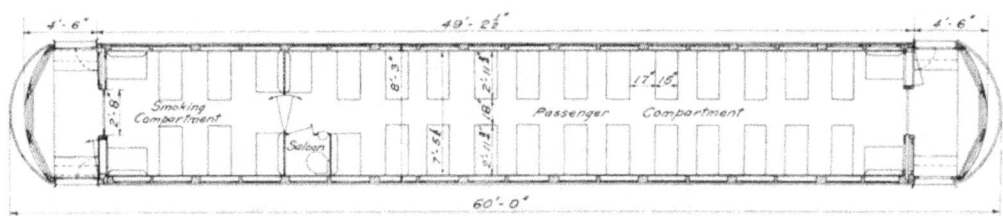

Fig. 129—Floor Plan of Double-End Interurban Trail Car with Smoking Compartment
American Car & Foundry Company, Builder

Fig. 130—Half-Open and Closed, Double-End, Interurban Car
St. Louis Car Company, Builder

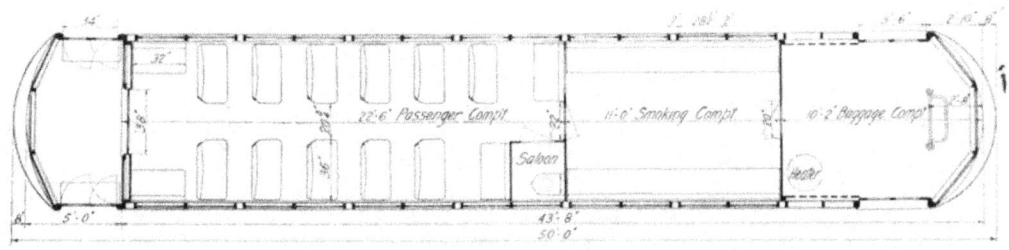

Fig. 131—Floor Plan of Single-End, Combination Passenger, Smoking and Baggage Interurban Car;
Milwaukee & Fox River Valley Railway
Cincinnati Car Company, Builder

Fig. 132—Double-End Combination Passenger and Baggage Interurban Car
McGuire-Cummings Manufacturing Company, Builder

Fig. 133—Interior of Passenger Compartment of
Car Shown in Fig. 132
McGuire-Cummings Manufacturing Company, Builder

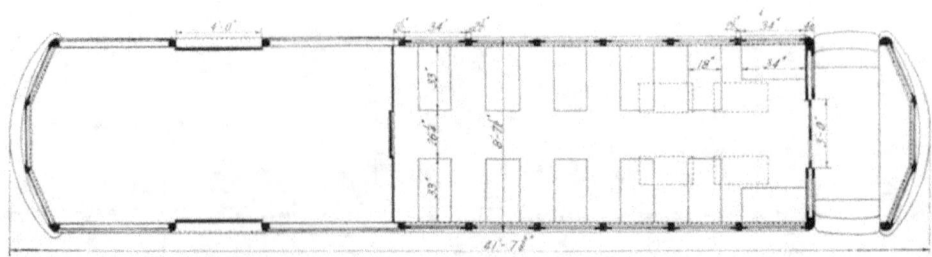

Fig 134—Floor Plan of Double-End Combination Passenger and Baggage Interurban
Car Shown in Figs. 132-133
McGuire-Cummings Manufacturing Company, Builder

Fig. 135—Double-End Combination Passenger and Baggage Interurban Car; Hagerstown Railway
Cincinnati Car Company, Builder

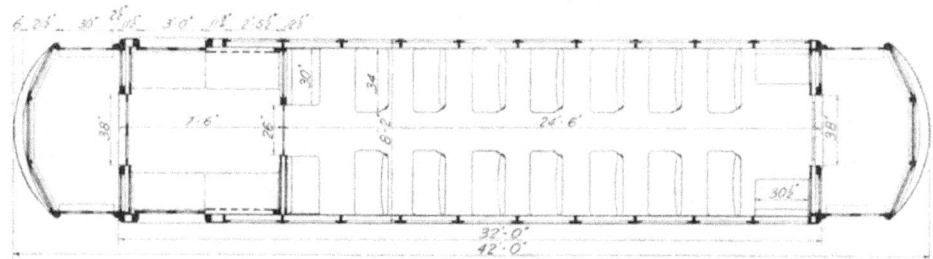

Fig. 136—Floor Plan of Double-End Combination Car Shown in Fig. 135
Cincinnati Car Company, Builder

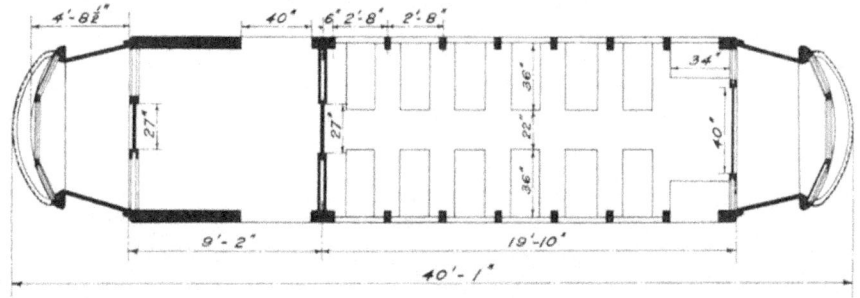

Fig. 137—Floor Plan of Double-End, Semi-Convertible, Combination Passenger and Baggage Interurban Car
The J. G. Brill Company, Builder

Fig. 138—Double-End, Combination, Passenger and Baggage Interurban Car
St. Louis Car Company, Builder

Fig. 139—Double-End Interurban Car with Baggage Compartments at Each End;
Cairo Railway & Light System
The J. G. Brill Company, Builder

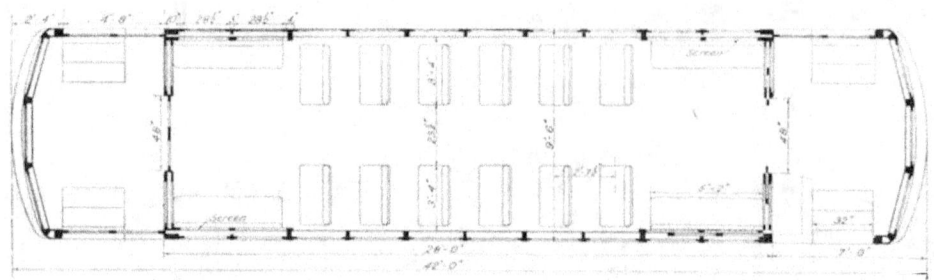

Fig. 140—Floor Plan of Double-End Interurban Car, with Baggage Compartments at Each End,
Shown in Fig. 139
The J. G. Brill Company, Builder

Fig. 141—Single-End Combination Passenger and Baggage Interurban Car
American Car & Foundry Company, Builder

Fig. 142—Double-End Combination Passenger and Baggage Interurban Car
Niles Car & Manufacturing Company, Builder

Fig. 143—Interior of Passenger Compartment of Car
Shown in Fig. 142
Niles Car & Manufacturing Company, Builder

Fig. 144—Single-End Combination Passenger and Baggage Interurban Car with Steel Sides
American Car & Foundry Company, Builder

(Framing of this car is shown in Fig. 367.)

Fig. 145—Double-End Combination Passenger, Smoking and Baggage Interurban Car
Niles Car & Manufacturing Company, Builder

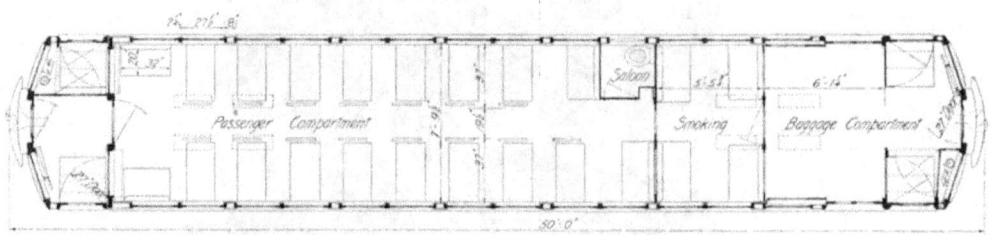

Fig. 146—Floor Plan of Combination Interurban Car Shown in Fig. 145
Niles Car & Manufacturing Company, Builder

Fig. 147—Interior of Passenger Compartment of Combination Interurban Car Shown in Fig. 145
Niles Car & Manufacturing Company, Builder

Fig. 148—Interior of Combination Interurban Car Shown in Fig. 149
The J. G. Brill Company, Builder

INTERURBAN CARS, Combination Passenger and Baggage

Fig. 149—Double-End, Combination Passenger, Smoking and Baggage Interurban Car; Wisconsin Traction, Light, Heat & Power Company
The J. G. Brill Company, Builder

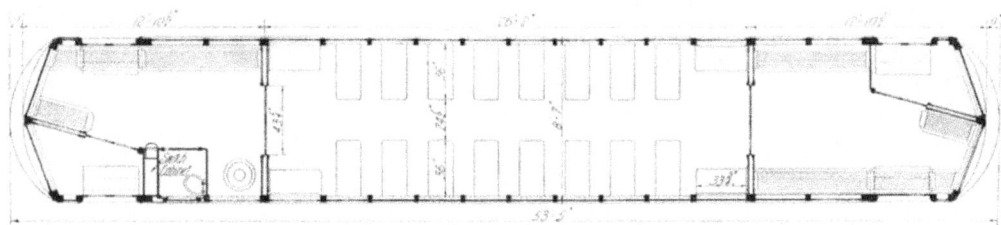

Fig. 150—Floor Plan of Combination Interurban Car Shown in Fig. 149
The J. G. Brill Company, Builder

Fig. 151—Single-End, Combination Passenger, Smoking and Baggage Interurban Car
Barney & Smith Car Company, Builder

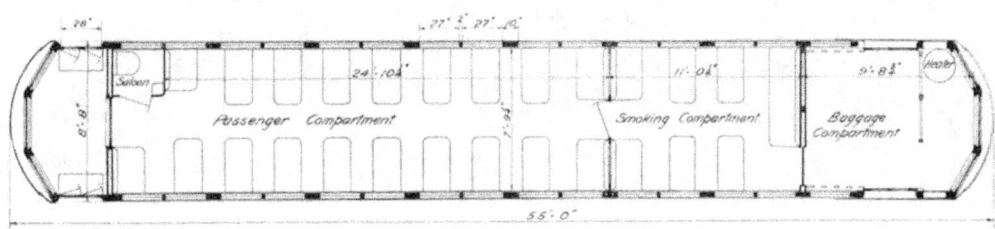

Fig. 152—Floor Plan of Single-End Combination Car Shown in Fig. 151
Barney & Smith Car Company, Builder

(44)

Fig. 153—Single-End, Combination Passenger, Smoking and Baggage Interurban Car
American Car & Foundry Company, Builder

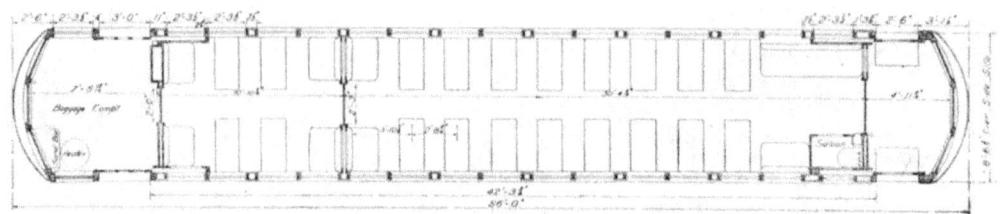

Fig. 154—Floor Plan of Single-End, Combination Interurban Car Shown in Fig. 153
American Car & Foundry Company, Builder

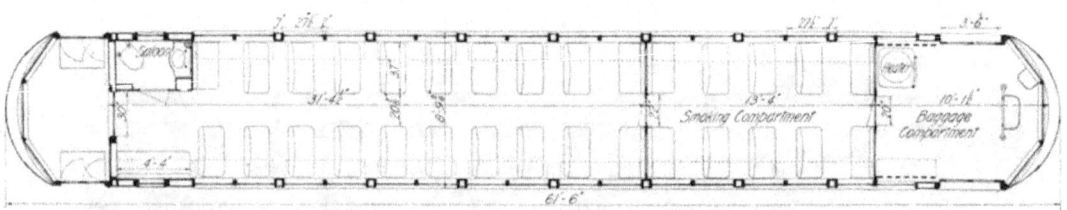

Fig. 155—Floor Plan of Single-End, Combination Passenger, Smoking and Baggage Interurban Car;
Chicago, South Bend & Northern Indiana Railway
Cincinnati Car Company, Builder

Fig. 156—Single-End, Combination Passenger, Smoking and Baggage Interurban Car
The J. G. Brill Company, Builder

INTERURBAN CARS, Combination Passenger and Baggage

Fig. 157—Single-End, Combination Passenger, Smoking and Baggage Interurban Car
Jewett Car Company, Builder

Fig. 158—Single-End, Combination Passenger, Smoking and Baggage Interurban Car;
Indianapolis, Newcastle & Toledo Electric Railway
Jewett Car Company, Builder

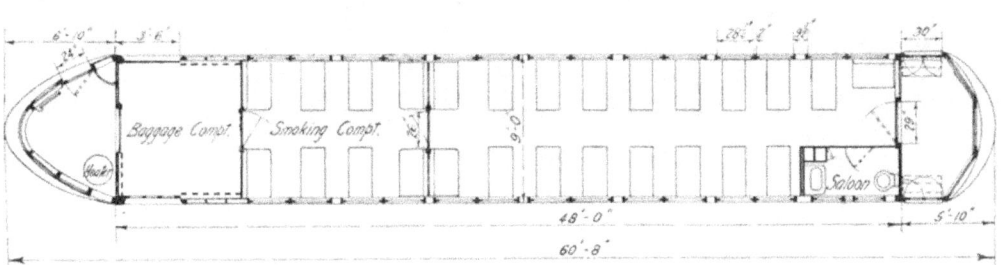

Fig. 159—Floor Plan of Combination Interurban Car Shown in Fig. 158
Jewett Car Company, Builder

Fig. 160—Single-End, Combination Passenger, Smoking and Baggage Interurban Car
Cincinnati Car Company, Builder

Fig. 161—Open Trail Car; Lehigh Valley Transit Company
The J. G. Brill Company, Builder

Fig. 162—Open Trail Car; Colorado Railway, Light & Power Company
The J. G. Brill Company, Builder

Fig. 163—Open Trail Car with Canvas Canopy
The J. G. Brill Company, Builder

INTERURBAN CARS, Parlor, Observation and Private Cars

Fig. 164—Two-Compartment, Semi-Convertible, Observation Car; Lewiston, Augusta & Waterville Street Railway
The J. G. Brill Company, Builder

Fig. 165—View of Interior and Observation Platform of Car Shown in Fig. 164
The J. G. Brill Company, Builder

Fig. 166—Interior of Observation Compartment of Private Car Shown in Fig. 167
Niles Car & Manufacturing Company, Builder

Fig. 167—Private Car; Northern Ohio Traction & Light Company
Niles Car & Manufacturing Company, Builder

(48)

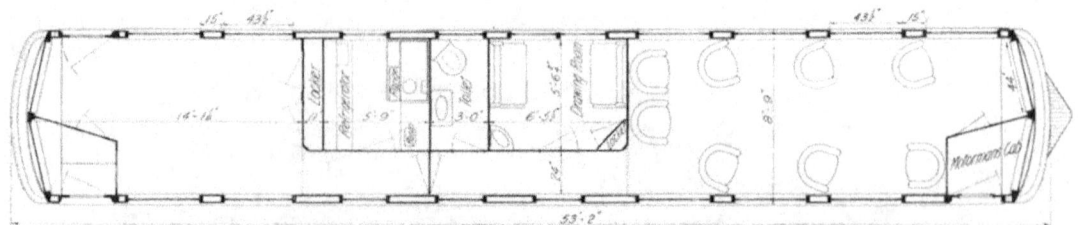

Fig. 168—Floor Plan of Private Car Shown in Figs. 166-167
Niles Car & Manufacturing Company, Builder

Fig. 169—Single-End, Interurban Parlor Car; Cleveland, Southwestern & Columbus Railway
Niles Car & Manufacturing Company, Builder

Fig. 170—Interior of Smoking Compartment of Car Shown in Fig. 169
Niles Car & Manufacturing Company, Builder

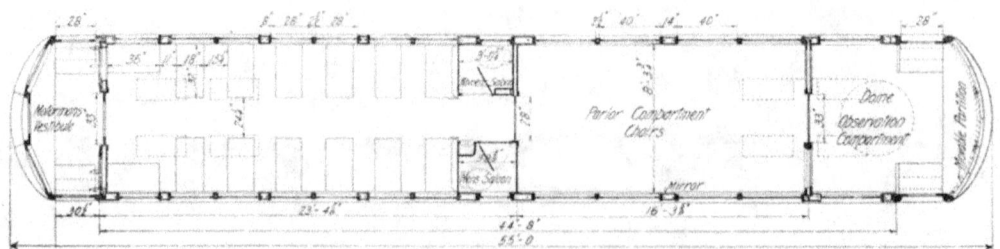

Fig. 171—Floor Plan of Observation Parlor Car; Puget Sound Electric Railway
St. Louis Car Company, Builder

INTERURBAN CARS, Parlor, Observation and Private Cars

Fig. 172—Observation Parlor Trail Car; Coeur D'Alene & Spokane Railway
The J. G. Brill Company, Builder

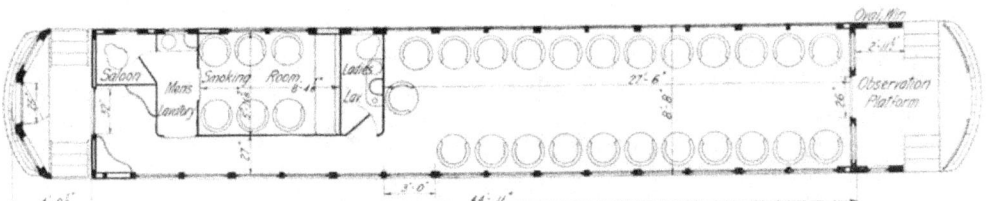

Fig. 173—Floor Plan of Parlor Trail Car Shown in Fig. 172
The J. G. Brill Company, Builder

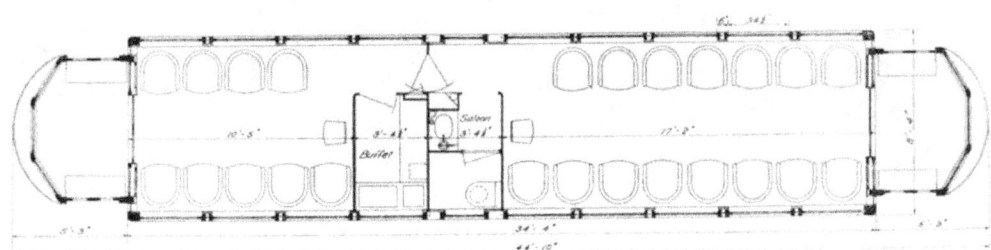

Fig. 174—Floor Plan of Buffet Parlor Car
Barney & Smith Car Company, Builder

(Interior view of this car is shown in Fig. 182.)

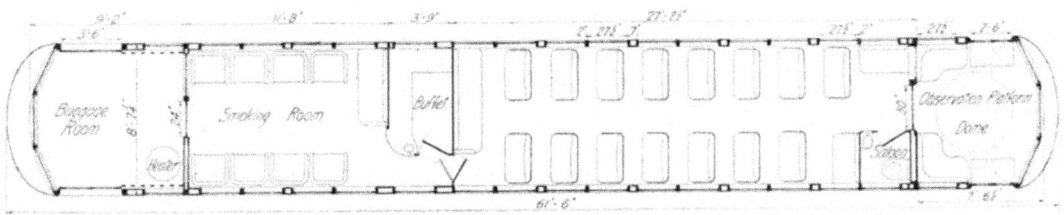

Fig. 175—Floor Plan of Observation Buffet Car; Ft. Wayne & Wabash Valley Traction Company
Cincinnati Car Company, Builder

(50)

INTERURBAN CARS, Parlor, Observation and Private Cars

Fig. 176—Officers' Private Car; Illinois Traction System
The J. G. Brill Company, Builder

Fig. 177—Observation Room of Private Car Shown in Fig. 176

Fig. 178—Dining Room of Private Car Shown in Fig. 176

The J. G. Brill Company, Builder

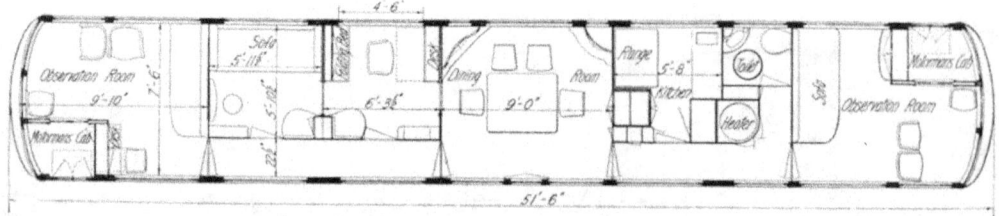

Fig. 179—Floor Plan of Private Car; Milwaukee Electric Railway & Light Company
St. Louis Car Company, Builder

Fig. 180—Café Parlor Car; Aurora, Elgin & Chicago Railroad
Niles Car & Manufacturing Company, Builder

Fig. 181—Interior of Café Parlor Car Shown in
Fig. 180
Niles Car & Manufacturing Company, Builder

Fig. 182—Interior of Buffet Parlor Car
Barney & Smith Car Company, Builder
(Floor plan of this car is shown in Fig. 174.)

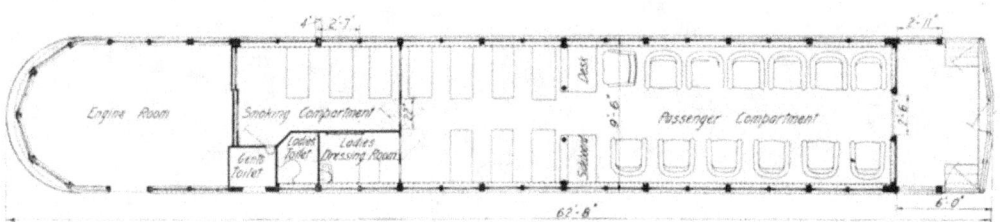

Fig. 183—Floor Plan of Strang Gas-Electric Parlor Car
The J. G. Brill Company, Builder

INTERURBAN CARS, Gas-Electric

Fig. 184—Strang Gas-Electric Parlor Car
The J. G. Brill Company, Builder

Fig. 185—Interior of Strang Gas-Electric Parlor Car
The J. G. Brill Company, Builder

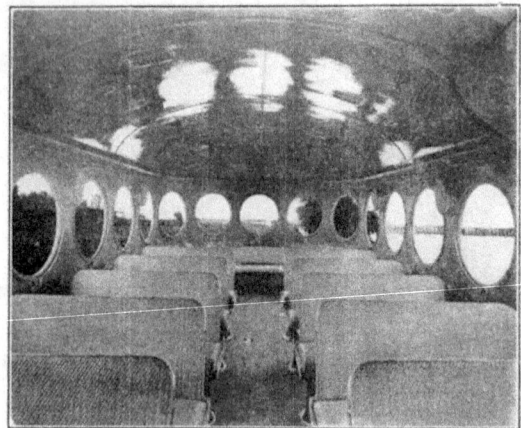

Fig. 186—Interior of Gasoline Motor Car Shown in
Fig. 187
McKeen Motor Car Company, Builder

Fig. 187—55-Foot, All-Steel, Gasoline Motor Car with Center Side Entrance
McKeen Motor Car Company, Builder

INTERURBAN CARS, Express and Freight

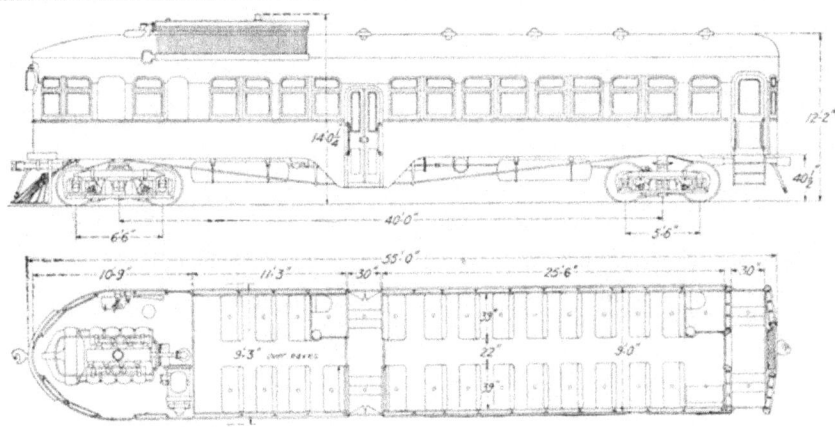

Fig. 188—Elevation and Floor Plan of Gas-Electric Interurban Car
General Electric Company, Builder

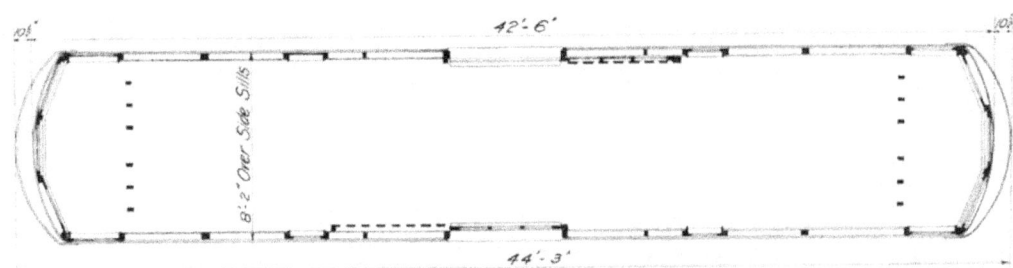

Fig. 189—Floor Plan of Double-End, Motor Express Car
American Car & Foundry Company, Builder

Fig. 190—Double-End, Motor Express Car with Monitor Deck Roof
The J. G. Brill Company, Builder

INTERURBAN CARS, Express and Freight

Fig. 191—Double-End, Motor Express Car with Arch Roof
The J. G. Brill Company, Builder

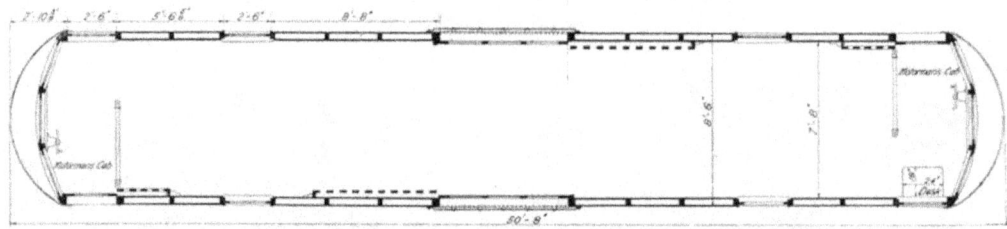

Fig. 192—Floor Plan of Double-End, Motor Express Car; Illinois Traction System
American Car & Foundry Company, Builder

Fig. 193—Freight and Express Trail Car with Arch Roof
Niles Car & Manufacturing Company, Builder

(Framing of this car is shown in Figs. 372-373.)

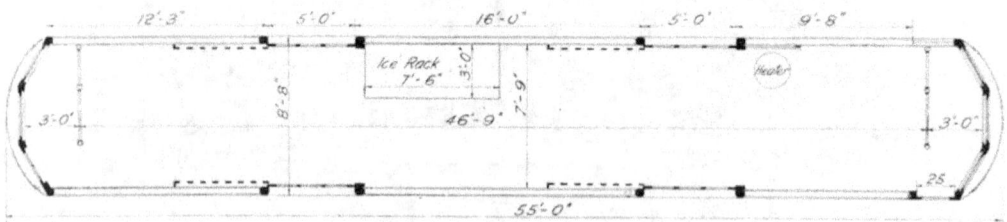

Fig. 194—Floor Plan of Motor Express and Baggage Car Shown in Fig. 195
Barney & Smith Car Company, Builder

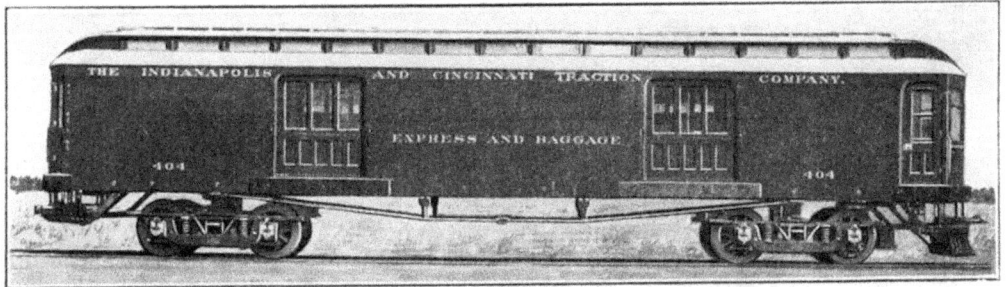

Fig. 195—Express and Baggage Motor Car with Monitor Deck Roof
Barney & Smith Car Company, Builder

Fig. 196—Interior of Express and Baggage Car Shown in Fig. 195
Barney & Smith Car Company, Builder

Fig. 197—Interior of Express Motor Car Shown in Fig. 198
The J. G. Brill Company, Builder

Fig. 198—Double-End, Express Motor Car with Monitor Deck Roof
The J. G. Brill Company, Builder

Fig. 199—Motor Express Car with Monitor Deck Roof
Niles Car & Manufacturing Company, Builder

Fig. 200—Motor Express Car with Monitor Deck Roof
The J. G. Brill Company, Builder

Fig. 201—Refrigerator Trail Car with Ice Boxes and Monitor Deck Roof
American Car & Foundry Company, Builder

Fig. 202—Double-End, Elevated Motor Car; Manhattan Elevated Railroad
The J. G. Brill Company, Builder

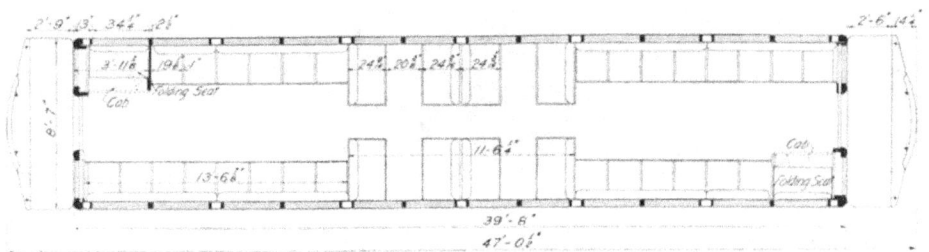

Fig. 203—Floor Plan of Manhattan Elevated Double-End Motor Car Shown in Fig. 202
The J. G. Brill Company, Builder

(Framing of this car is shown in Figs. 376-380.)

Fig. 204—Interior of Elevated Motor Car Shown in Fig. 206

Fig. 205—Vestibule of Elevated Motor Car Shown in Fig. 206

The J. G. Brill Company, Builder

Fig. 206—Double-End, Elevated Motor Car; Chicago & Oak Park Elevated Railroad
The J. G. Brill Company, Builder

Fig. 207—Interior of Suburban Steel Motor Car
Shown in Fig. 208
Standard Steel Car Company, Builder

Fig. 208—Double-End, All-Steel, Suburban Passenger Coach; New York, New Haven & Hartford Railroad
Standard Steel Car Company, Builder

ELEVATED AND SUBWAY CARS

Fig. 209—All-Steel, Double-End, Subway Motor Car with Center Side Doors
Pressed Steel Car Company, Builder

Fig. 210—End View of Subway Motor Car Shown in Fig. 209

Fig. 211—Interior View of Subway Motor Car Shown in Fig. 209

Pressed Steel Car Company, Builder

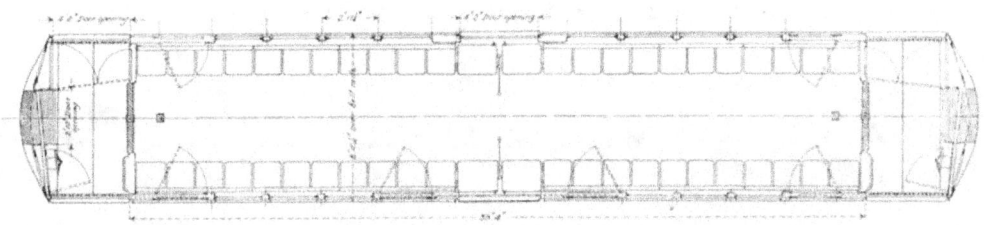

Fig. 212—Floor Plan of All-Steel, Double-End, Subway Motor Car Shown in Figs. 209-211
Pressed Steel Car Company, Builder

(Framing of this car is shown in Figs. 392-398.)

(60)

SNOW SWEEPERS AND PLOWS

Fig. 213—Single-Truck, Long-Broom Sweeper
The J. G. Brill Company, Builder

Fig. 214—Single-Truck, Long-Broom Sweeper
McGuire-Cummings Manufacturing Company, Builder

(Framing of this sweeper is shown in Figs. 407-408.)

Fig. 215—Baggage Car with Detachable Shear Plows on Each End
The J. G. Brill Company, Builder

Fig. 216-218   SNOW SWEEPERS AND PLOWS

Fig. 216—Baggage and Express Car with Nose Plows Attached to Each End
Russell Car & Snow Plow Company, Builder

Fig. 217—Double-Truck, Double-End, Elevating Wing, Shear Plow
Cincinnati Car Company, Builder

(Framing of this plow is shown in Figs. 394-402.)

Fig. 218—Double-Truck, Double-End, Nose Plow
The J. G. Brill Company, Builder

(Framing of this plow is shown in Figs. 403-404.)

Fig. 219—Single-Truck, Double-End, Shear Plow
McGuire-Cummings Manufacturing Company, Builder

Fig. 220—Single-Truck, Double-End, Shear Plow
The J. G. Brill Company, Builder
(Framing of this plow is shown in Figs. 405-406.)

Fig. 221—Single-Truck, Double-End, Nose Plow
The J. G. Brill Company, Builder

Fig. 222—Single-Truck, Single-End, Sprinkler Car with Enclosed Tank; Detroit United Railway
Built in Company's Shops

Fig. 223—Single-Truck, Centrifugal Sprinkler Car with Enclosed Tank
The J. G. Brill Company, Builder

(Framing of this sprinkler is shown in Figs. 419-421.)

SPRINKLERS

Fig. 224—Single-Truck, Centrifugal Sprinkler with Open Tank
The J. G. Brill Company, Builder

Fig. 225—Combined Sprinkler, Snow Plow and Line Car
McGuire-Cummings Manufacturing Company, Builder
(Framing of this car is shown in Figs. 415-418.)

Fig. 226—Double-Truck, 4,000-Gal., Pneumatic Sprinkler; Chicago Railways
McGuire-Cummings Manufacturing Company, Builder
(Framing of this sprinkler is shown in Figs. 422-425.)

Fig. 227—Motor Flat Car with End Cabs and Center Trolley Stand
The J. G. Brill Company, Builder

Fig. 228—Motor Flat Car with Center Trolley Stand
The J. G. Brill Company, Builder

Fig. 229—Motor Flat Car with Center Cab
The J. G. Brill Company, Builder

Fig. 230—Motor Coal and Ash Car with Cab
St. Louis Car Company, Builder

Fig. 231—Coal and Ash Trail Car with Roof and Drop Sides
The J. G. Brill Company, Builder

Fig. 232—Coal and Ash Trail Car with Hopper Bottom and Drop Sides
The J. G. Brill Company, Builder

Fig. 233—Single-Truck, All-Steel, Motor Coal Car with Drop Sides
McGuire-Cummings Manufacturing Company, Builder

Fig. 234—Single-Truck Crane Car with Roof and Open Sides
The J. G. Brill Company, Builder

Fig. 235—Double-Truck Crane Car with Motor-Driven Pillar Crane
Boston Elevated Railway

Fig. 236—Double-Truck Crane Car with Motor-Driven Cranes at Each End
Metropolitan Street Railway, New York

Fig. 237—Single-Truck Crane Car
Detroit United Railway

Fig. 238—Trailer Wrecking Car for Elevated Lines
Boston Elevated Railway

Fig. 239—Double-Truck Motor Crane Car; The Connecticut Company
McGuire-Cummings Manufacturing Company, Builder

Fig. 240—Line Car for Interurban Service
Cleveland, Southwestern & Columbus Railway

Fig. 241—Line Car with Extension Platform
United Railways of St. Louis

Fig. 242—Interior of Line Car Shown in Fig. 43
Washington Water Power Company

Fig. 243—Double-Truck Line Car with Extension Platform
Washington Water Power Company

Fig. 244—Single-Truck Trailer Line-Construction Car
The J. G. Brill Company, Builder

Fig. 245—Sub-Station Car; Chicago, South Bend & Northern Indiana Railway
Cincinnati Car Company, Builder

(Framing of this car is shown in Figs. 430-433.)

Fig. 246—Trailer Type Gasoline Weed-Burner Car; Illinois Traction System
Commonwealth Steel Company, Builder

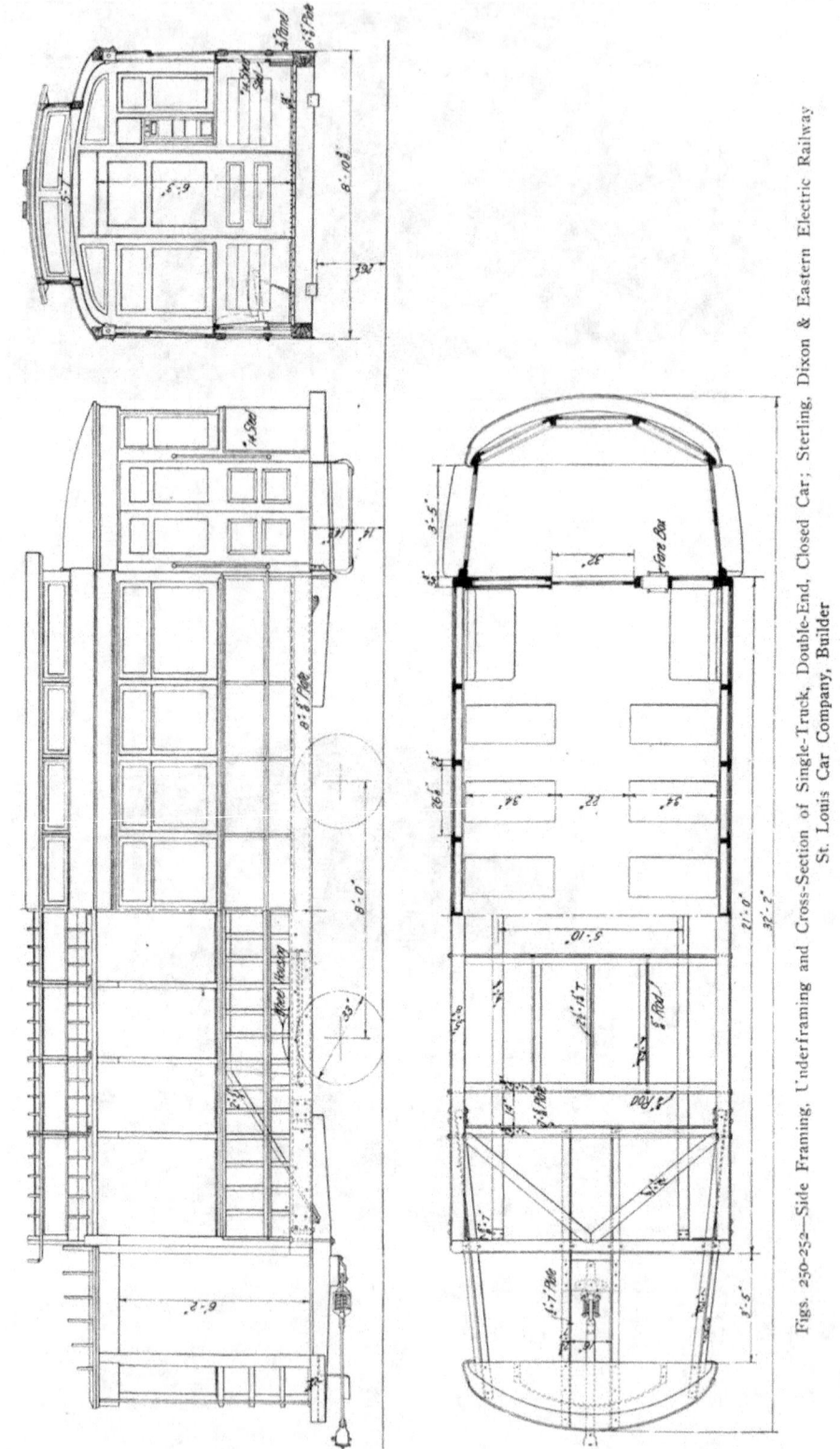

Figs. 250-252—Side Framing, Underframing and Cross-Section of Single-Truck, Double-End, Closed Car; Sterling, Dixon & Eastern Electric Railway. St. Louis Car Company, Builder

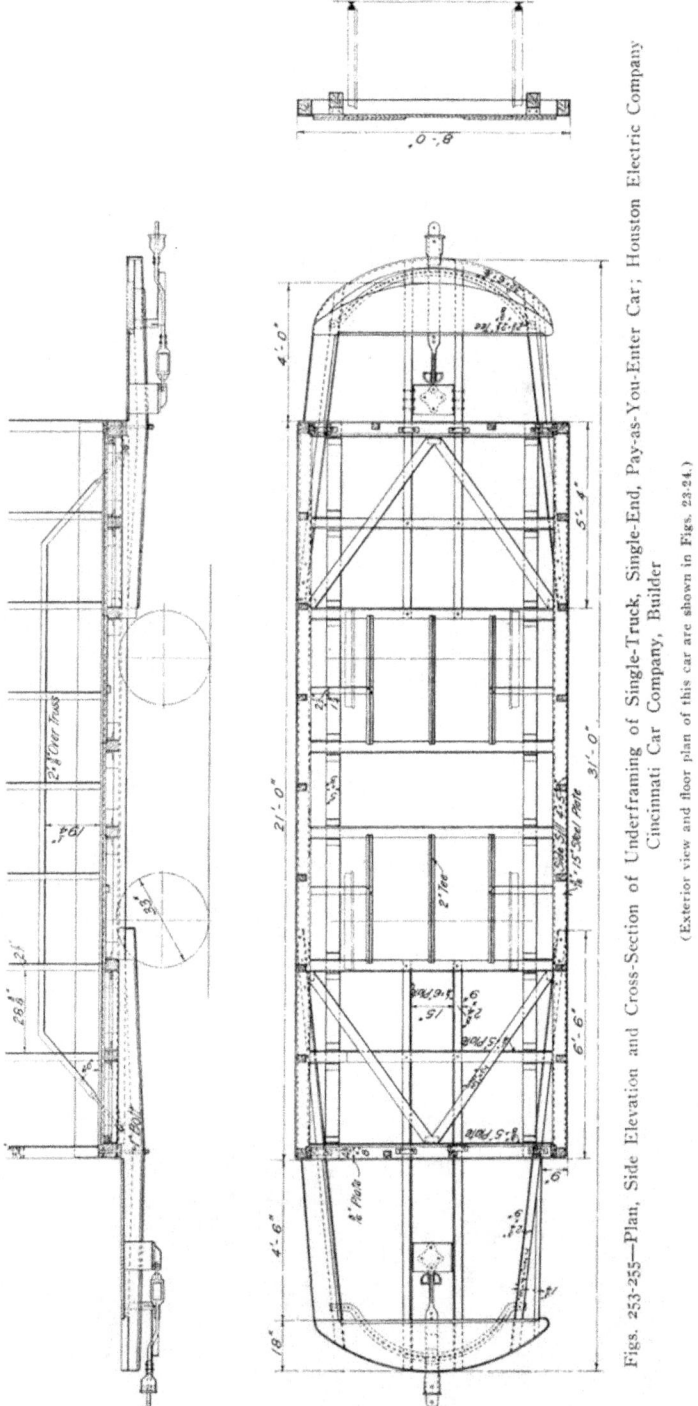

Figs. 253-255—Plan, Side Elevation and Cross-Section of Underframing of Single-Truck, Single-End, Pay-as-You-Enter Car; Houston Electric Company Cincinnati Car Company, Builder

(Exterior view and floor plan of this car are shown in Figs. 23, 24.)

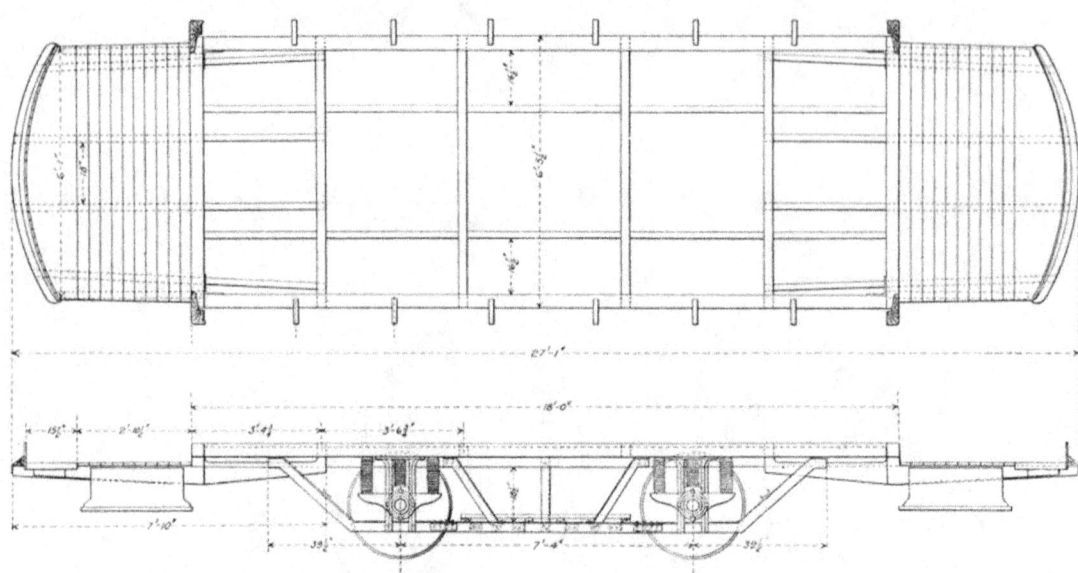

Figs. 256-257—Plan and Side Elevation of Underframing of Single-Truck, Double-End, Storage Battery Car; Third Avenue Railroad, New York
Built in Company's Shops

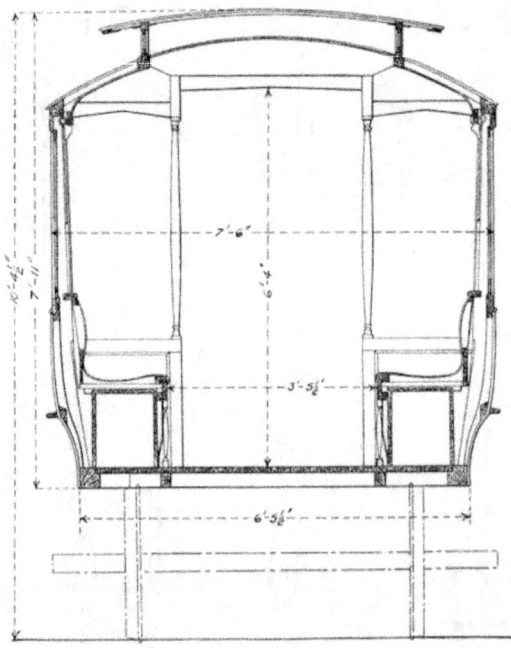

Fig. 258—Cross-Section of Third Avenue Railroad Single-Truck, Storage Battery Car Shown in Figs. 256-257

CAR BODY FRAMING, Single-Truck, City

Numbers Refer to List of Names of Parts Below

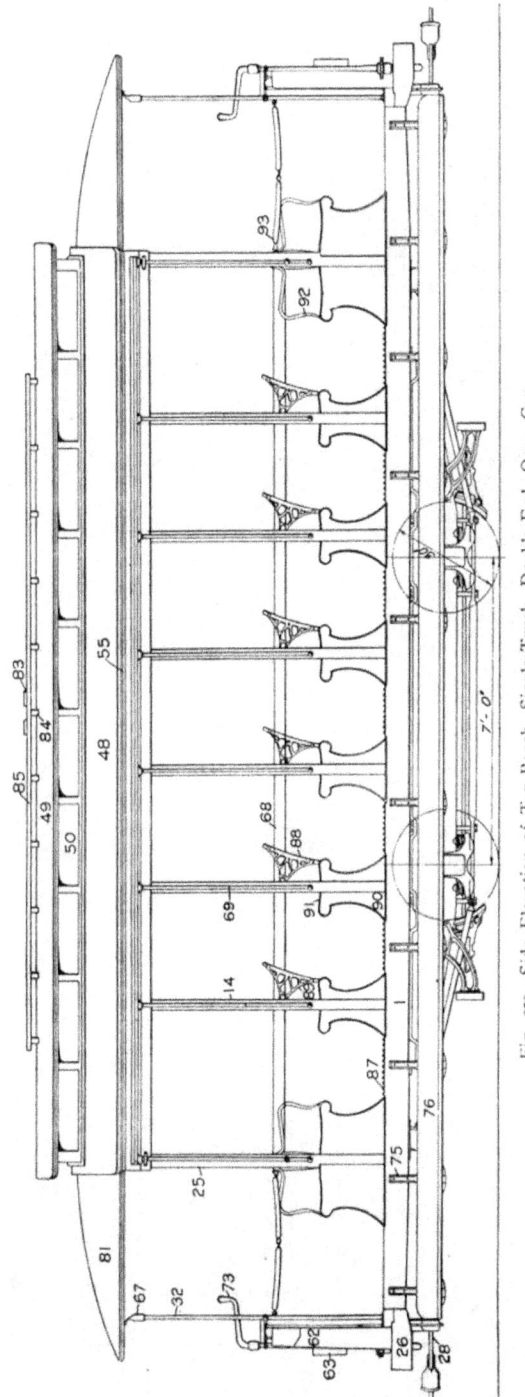

Fig. 259—Side Elevation of Ten-Bench, Single-Truck, Double-End, Open Car
The J. G. Brill Company, Builder

(Exterior view and floor plan of this car are shown in Figs. 31-32.)

List of Names of Parts of Car Bodies

1. Side Sill
2. Center Sill
3. Body Bolster
4. Body Truss Rod
5. Body Truss Rod Queen Post
6. Needlebeam
7. Overhang Truss Rod Strut
8. Overhang Truss Rod
9. Overhang Truss Rod Anchor
10. Pilot Knee
11. Brace
12. Sill and Plate Rod
13. Intermediate Window Post
14. Pier Post
15. Belt Rail
16. Side Plate
17. Deck Sill
18. Deck Plate
19. Upper Deck Carline
20. Compound Carline
21. Lower Deck Carline
22. Hood Side Piece
23. Hood Plate
24. Hood Carline
25. Body Corner Post
26. Bumper
27. Coupler Head
28. Drawbar
29. Drawbar Carry Iron
30. Pilot
31. Draft Spring
32. Vestibule Corner Post
33. Vestibule Center Post
34. Vestibule Belt Rail
35. Side Rib
36. Sheathing Lining
37. Vestibule Rib
38. Vestibule Hood Bow
39. Vestibule Door Lintel
40. Pilot Brace
41. Floor Strips
42. Floor Boards
43. Floor Nailing Strips
44. Inside Lining
45. Inside Window Sill
46. Bottom Window Sash
47. Top Window Sash
48. Lower Deck Roof
49. Upper Deck Roof
50. Deck Sash
51. Advertising Rack Rail
52. Deck Apron
53. Upper Deck Headlining
54. Lower Deck Headlining
55. Eaves Fascia Board
56. Letter Board
57. Deck Sill Molding
58. Window Post
59. Pier Post Pilaster
60. Outside Window Sill
61. Deck Plate Molding
62. Dasher or Dash
63. Headlight
64. Dasher Rail
65. Dasher Rail Cap
66. Dasher Post
67. Platform Corner Post Bracket
68. Guard Rail
69. Grab Handle
70. Grab Handle Bracket
71. Platform Sill
72. Brake Shaft
73. Brake Handle
74. Brake Ratchet Wheel
75. Running Board Bracket
76. Running Board Riser
77. Running Board
78. End Bulkhead Sash
79. End Bulkhead Post
80. End Bulkhead Upper Sash
81. Platform Hood
82. Deck End Sash

(76)

CAR BODY FRAMING, Single-Truck, City — Figs. 260-262

Numbers Refer to Accompanying List of Names of Parts

List of Names of Parts of Car Bodies (Cont.)

83. Trolley Base Blocks
84. Trolley Board Cleats
85. Trolley Board
86. Guard Rail Latch
87. Aisle Floor Strips
88. Seat Back
89. Seat Back Arm
90. Seat End Panel
91. Seat Bottom
92. Seat End Bracket
93. Platform Guard Chain
94. Seat Back Top Rail
95. Seat Back Bottom Rail
96. Seat Back Mullion
97. Foot Rest
98. Body Side Bearing
99. Curtain Roller
100. Side Sill Step
101. Body Bolster Top Plate
102. Body Bolster Bottom Plate
103. Intermediate Sill
104. Center Sill Filler
105. Side Sill Filler
106. Sill Tie Rod
107. Sheathing
108. Side Sill Plate
109. Transverse Floor Timber
110. Trap Door Beam

List of Names of Parts of Car Bodies (Cont.)

111. Corner Brace
112. Sand Box
113. Sand Valve
114. Sand Spout
115. Bridging
116. Crown Piece
117. End Sill
118. Diagonal Floor Timber
119. Center Sill Blocking
120. Platform Step
121. Platform Sill Clamp
122. Compression Beam
123. Compression Beam Brace
124. Counter Brace
125. Auxiliary Compression Beam Brace
126. Truss Plank
127. Body Truss Rod Anchor
128. Fender Rail
129. Side Panel
130. Seat Stand
131. End Panel
132. Door Sheave Panel
133. Top Door Rail
134. Middle Door Rail
135. Door Stile
136. Bottom Door Rail
137. Door Panel

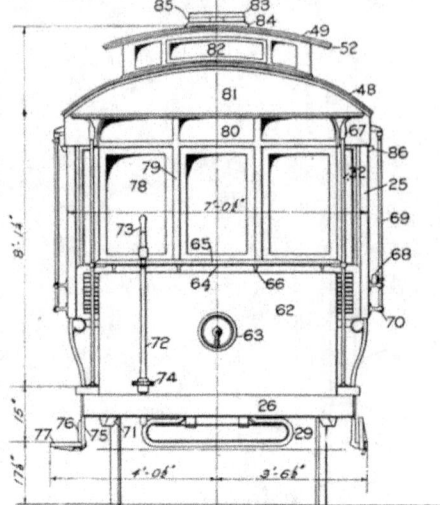

Fig. 260—End Elevation of Ten-Bench Open Car Shown in Fig. 259
The J. G. Brill Company, Builder

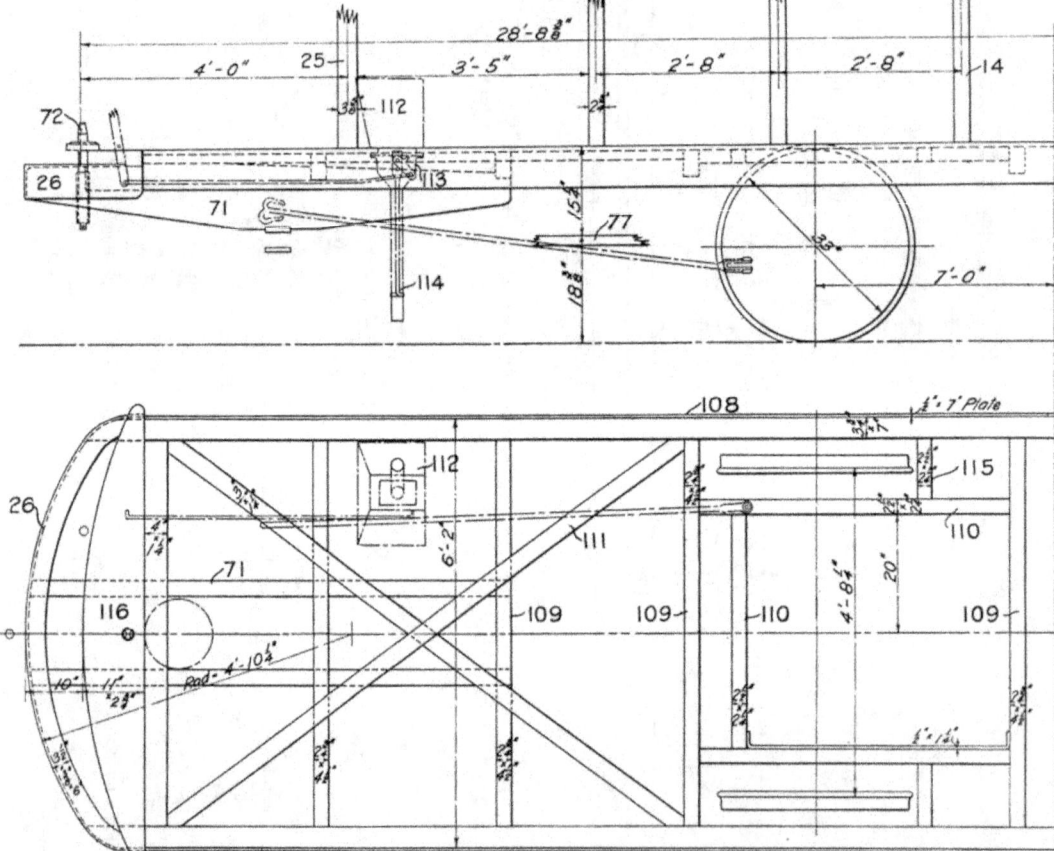

Figs. 261-262—Plan and Side Elevation of Underframing of Ten-Bench, Single-Truck, Open Car Shown in Fig. 259
The J. G. Brill Company, Builder

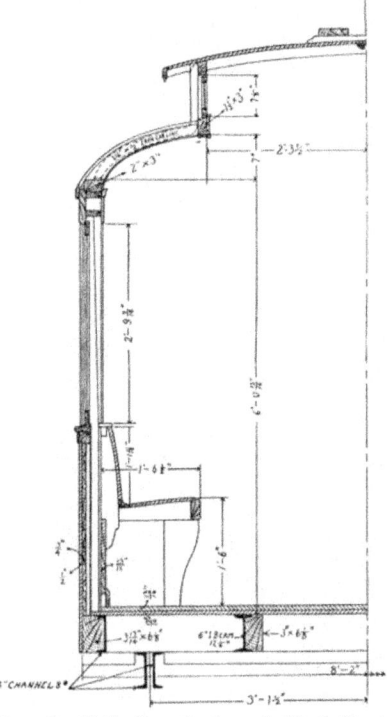

Fig. 263—Half Cross-Section of Single-Truck,
Closed City Car with Longitudinal Seats
American Car & Foundry Company, Builder

Fig. 263a—Half Cross-Section of Light
Storage Battery Car Body
J. P. Sjoberg & Co., Builders

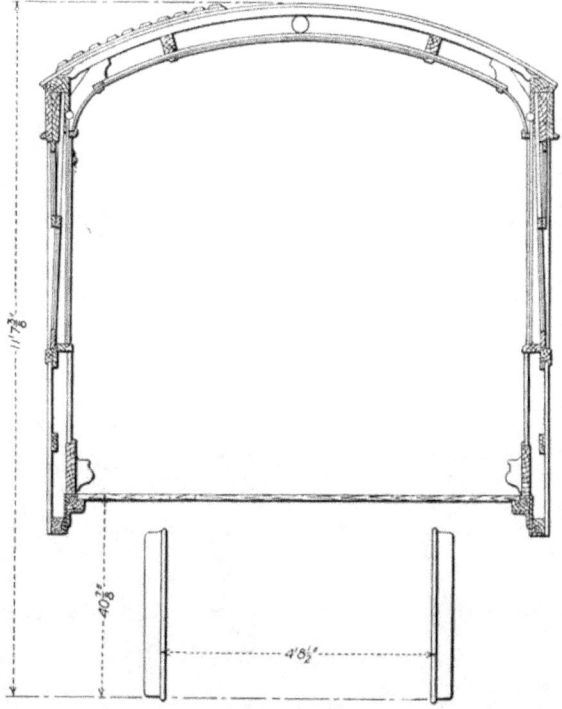

Fig. 264—Cross-Section of Arch Roof, Semi-Convertible,
Double-Truck, City Car
The J. G. Brill Company, Builder

(Exterior and interior views and floor plan of this car are shown in Figs. 77-79.)

CAR BODY FRAMING, Double-Truck, City Figs. 265-270

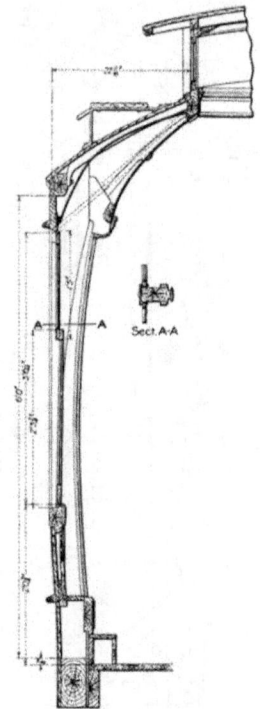

Fig. 265—Section Through Side of Standard Semi-Convertible Car
The J. G. Brill Company, Builder

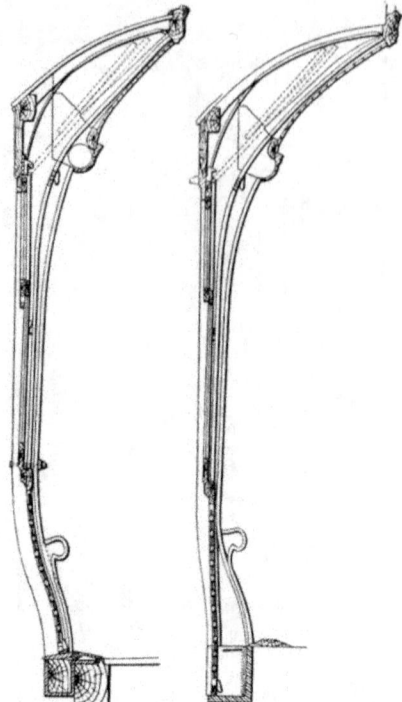

Figs. 266-267—Sections Through Side of Convertible Car with Plain Sills and Narragansett Type Sills
The J. G. Brill Company, Builder

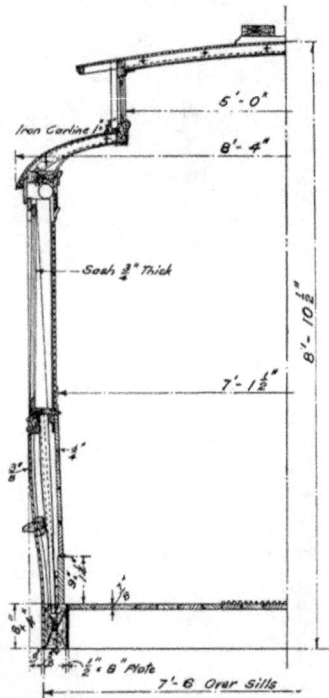

Fig. 268—Half Cross-Section of Standard Closed Car

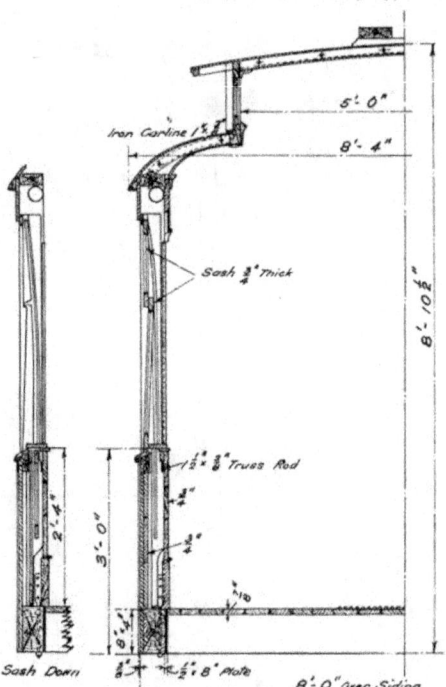

Figs. 269-270—Sections Through Side of Standard Semi-Convertible Car

American Car & Foundry Company, Builder

Figs. 271-273 — CAR BODY FRAMING, Double-Truck, City

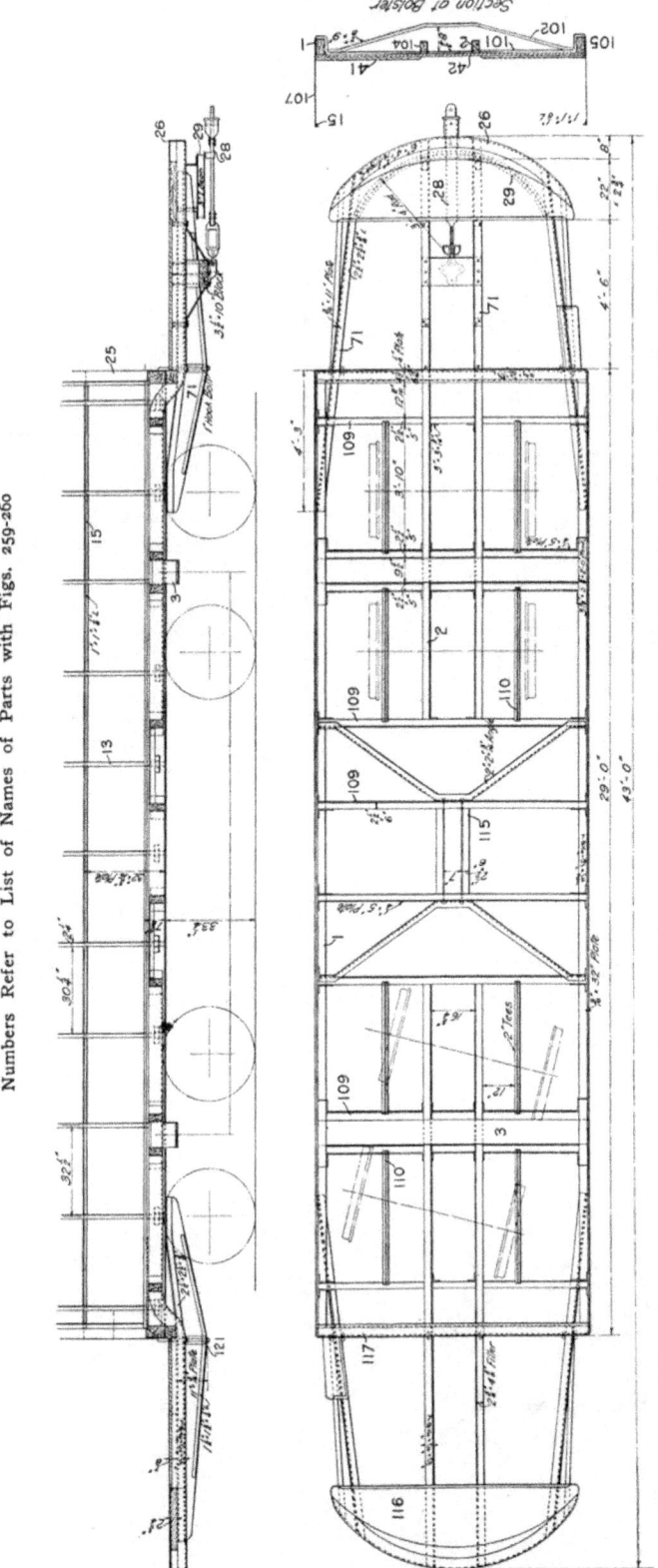

Figs. 271-273.—Plan, Side Elevation and Cross-Section of Steel Underframe for Double-Truck, Double-End, Closed, Pay-as-You-Enter Car; Buffalo & Lackawanna Traction Company
Cincinnati Car Company, Builder

Numbers Refer to List of Names of Parts with Figs. 259-260

(80)

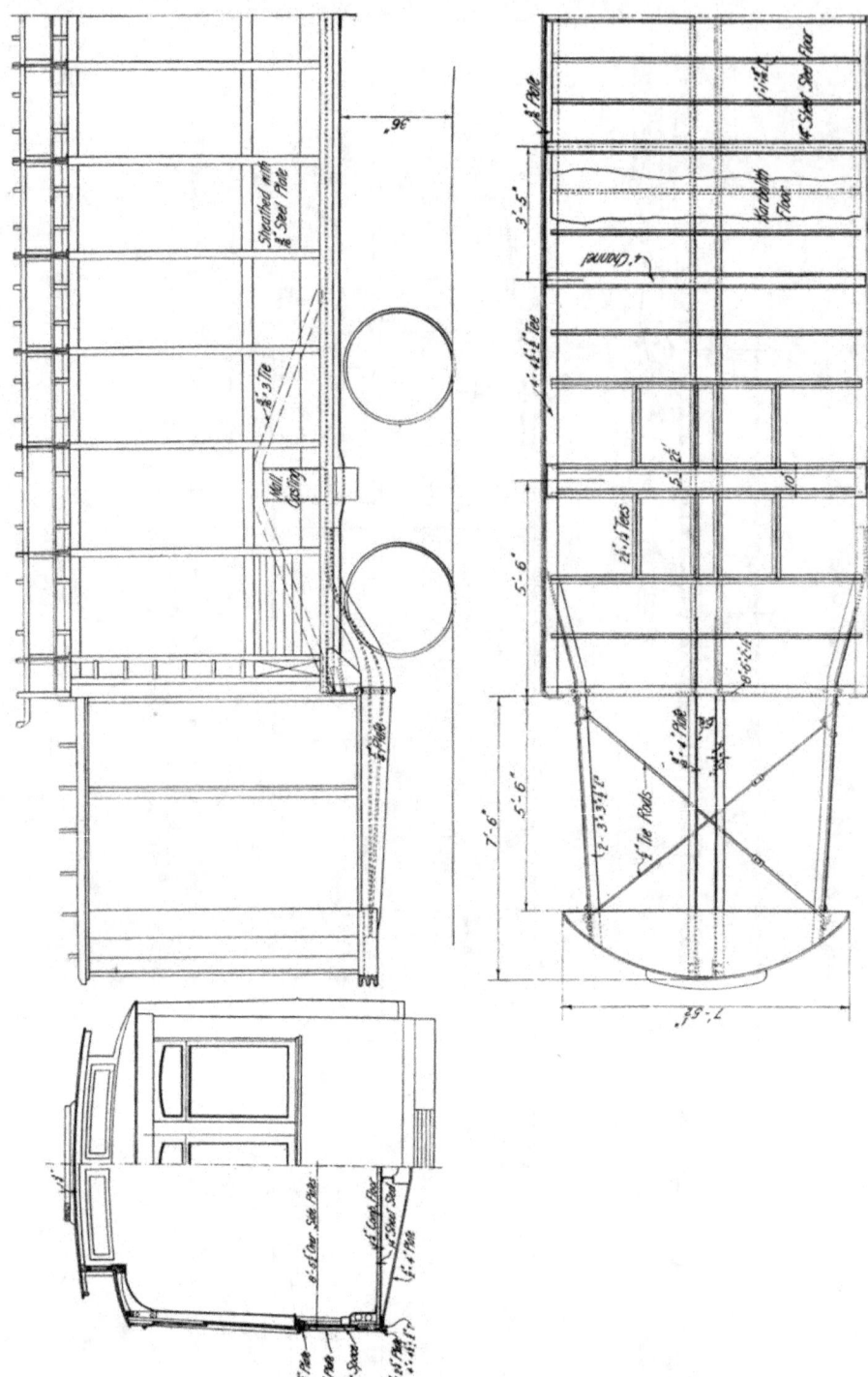

Figs. 274-276—Plan, Side Elevation and Cross-Section of Framing of Double-Truck, Semi-Steel, Closed, Pay-as-You-Enter Car; Milwaukee Electric Railway & Light Company
St. Louis Car Company, Builder

(Floor plan of this car is shown in Fig. 47.)

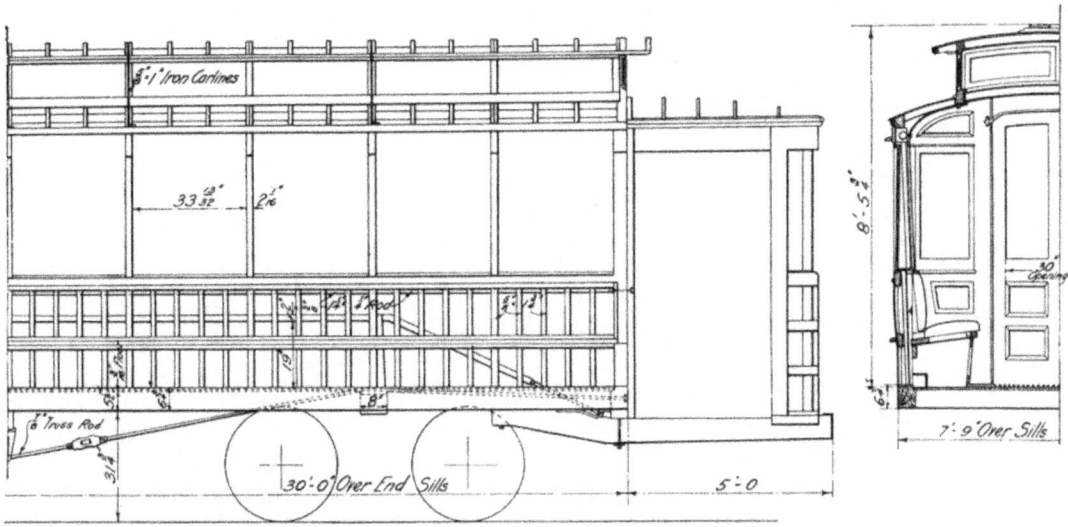

Figs. 277-278—Half Side Elevation and Cross-Section of Double-Truck, Closed Car; Yonkers Railroad
St. Louis Car Company, Builder

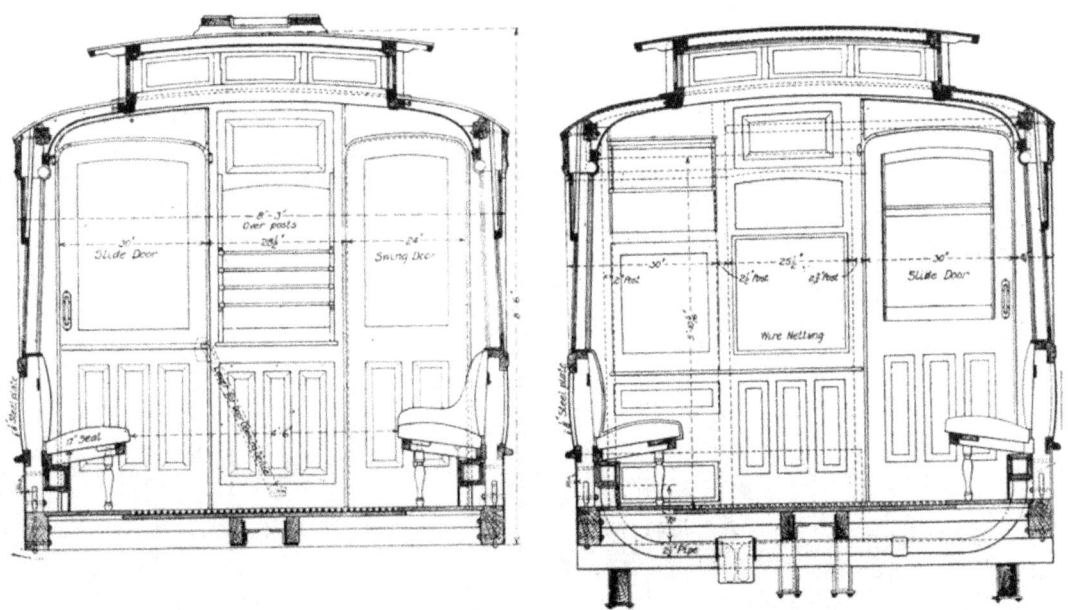

Figs. 279-280—Cross-Sections of Single-End, Double-Truck, Closed Prepayment Car; Public Service Railway
Cincinnati Car Company, Builder

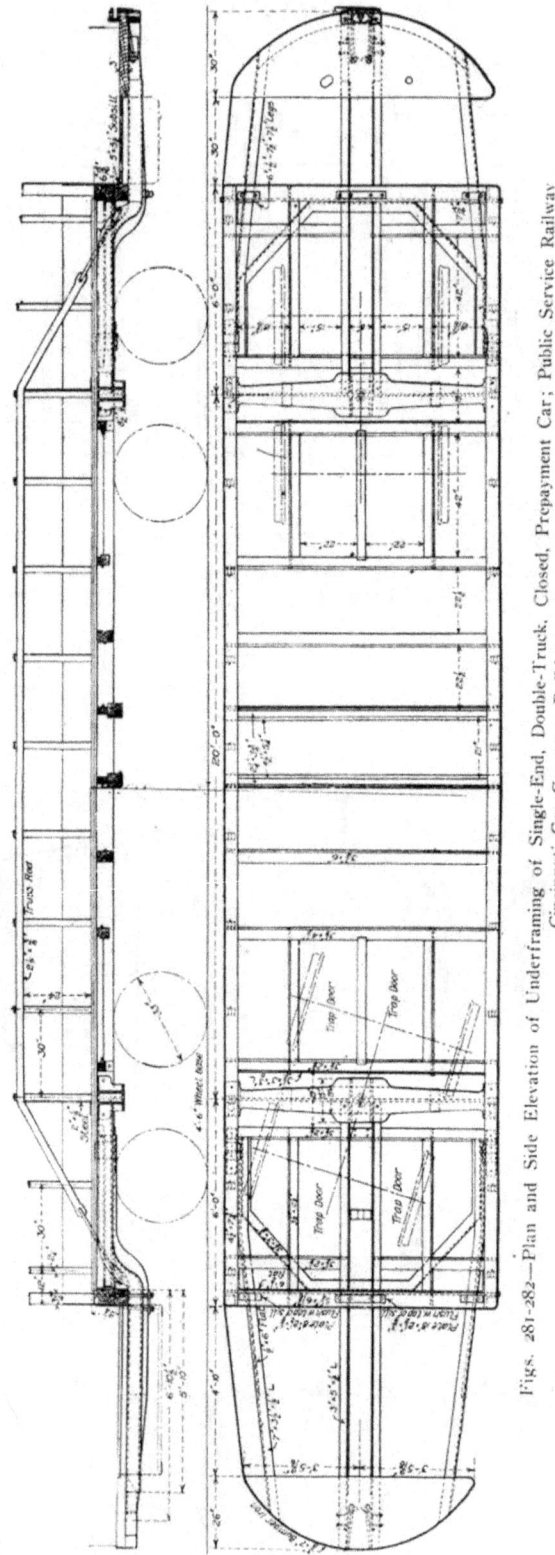

Figs. 281-282.—Plan and Side Elevation of Underframing of Single-End, Double-Truck, Closed, Prepayment Car; Public Service Railway Cincinnati Car Company, Builder

(Floor plan of this car is shown in Fig. 55.)

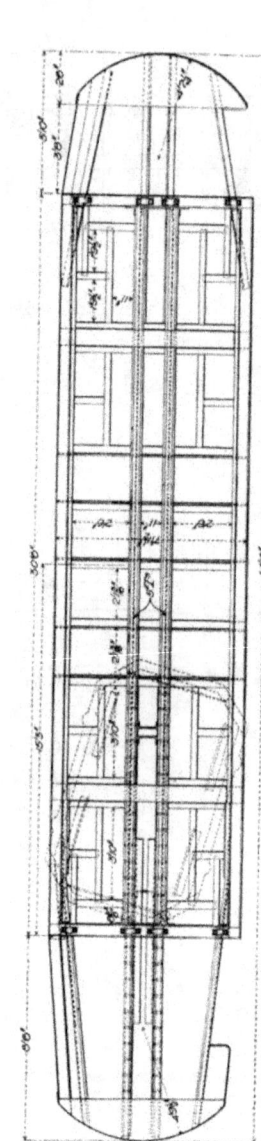

Fig. 283.—Plan of Underframing of Single-End, Double-Truck, Closed Car with Long Rear Platform St. Louis Car Company, Builder

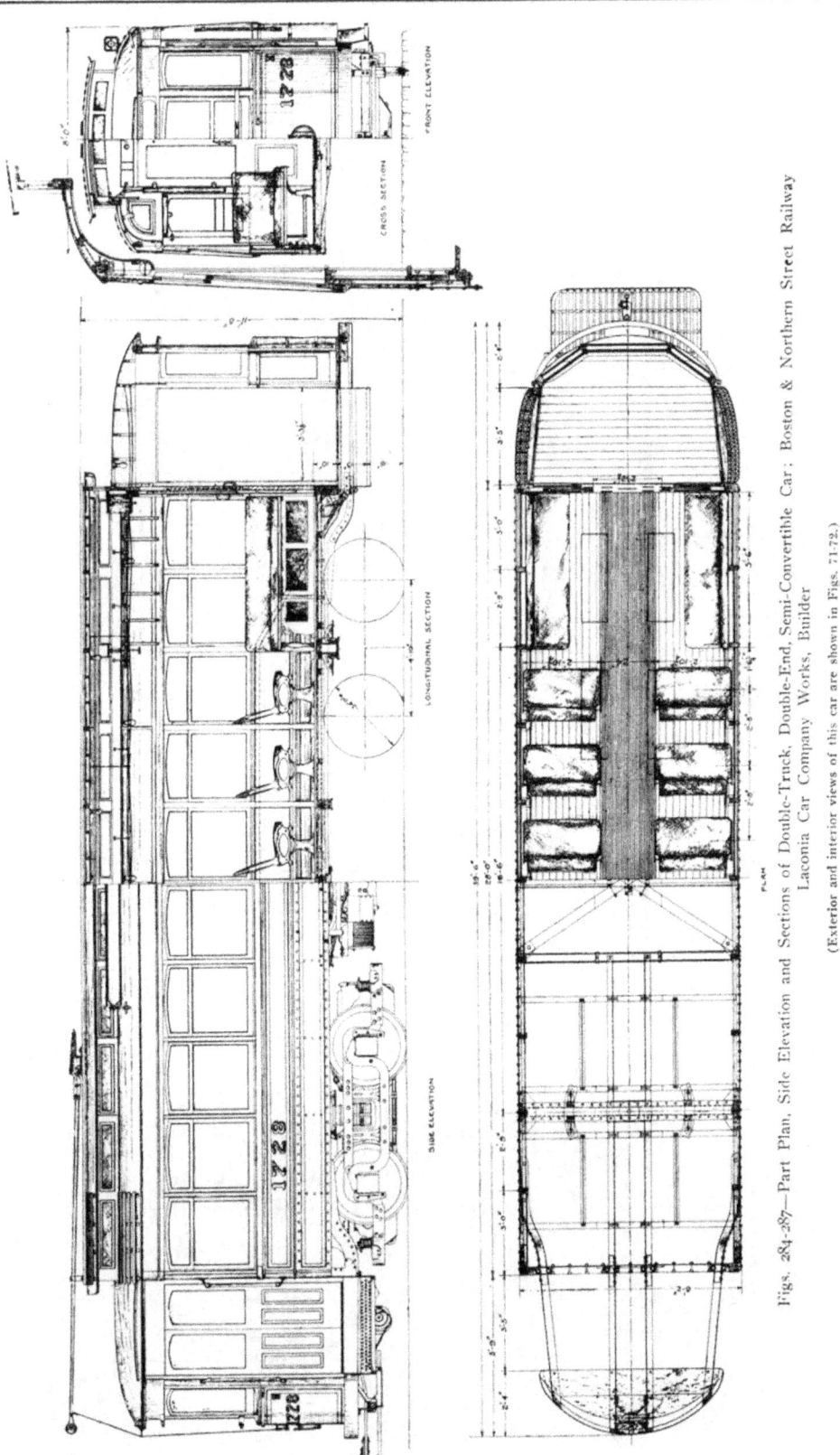

Figs. 284-287—Part Plan, Side Elevation and Sections of Double-Truck, Double-End, Semi-Convertible Car; Boston & Northern Street Railway Laconia Car Company Works, Builder

(Exterior and interior views of this car are shown in Figs. 71-72.)

CAR BODY FRAMING, Double-Truck, City — Figs. 288-289

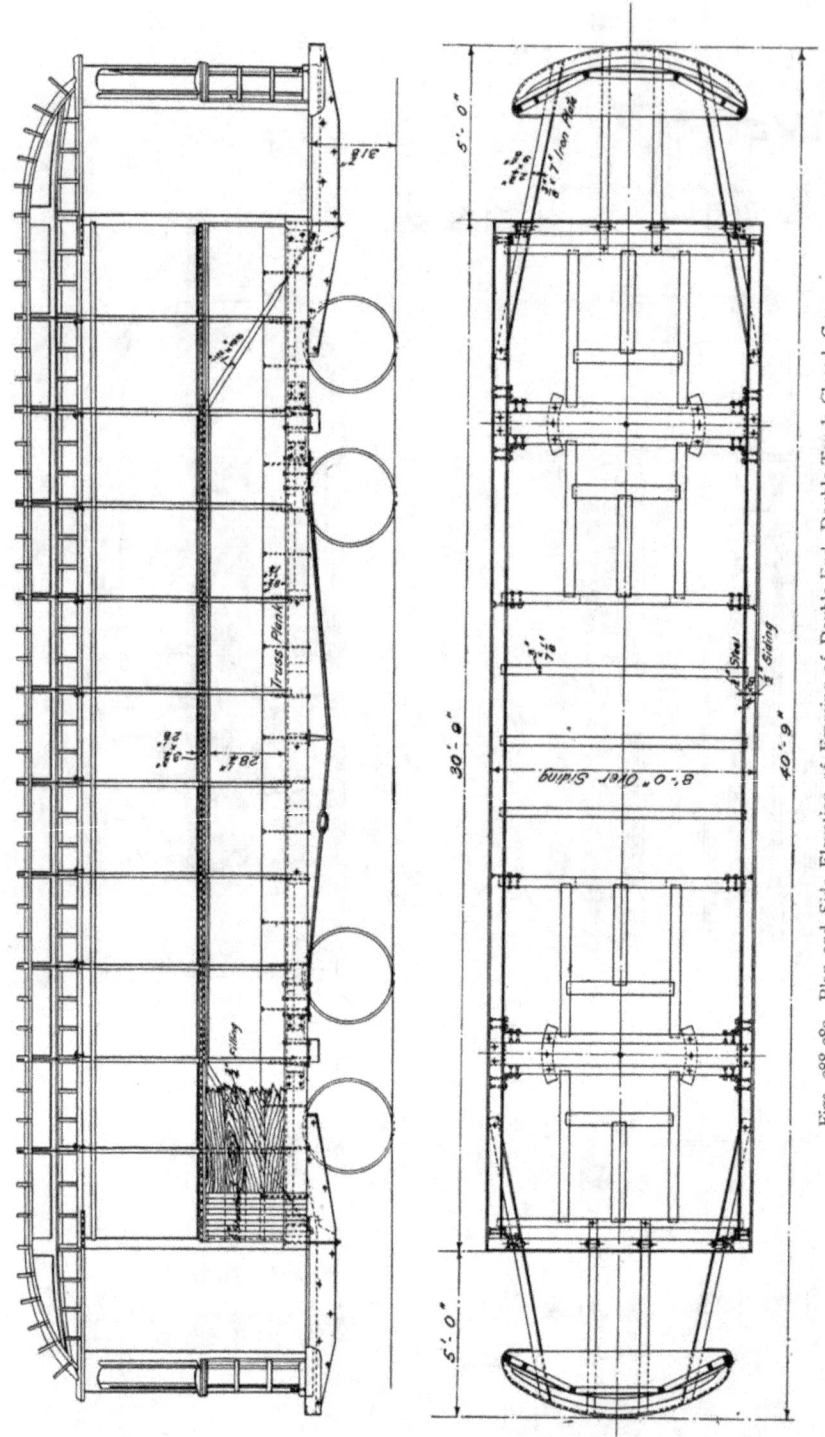

Figs. 288-289.—Plan and Side Elevation of Framing of Double-End, Double-Truck Closed Car American Car & Foundry Company, Builder (Exterior view of this car is shown in Fig. 87.)

CAR BODY FRAMING, Double-Truck, City

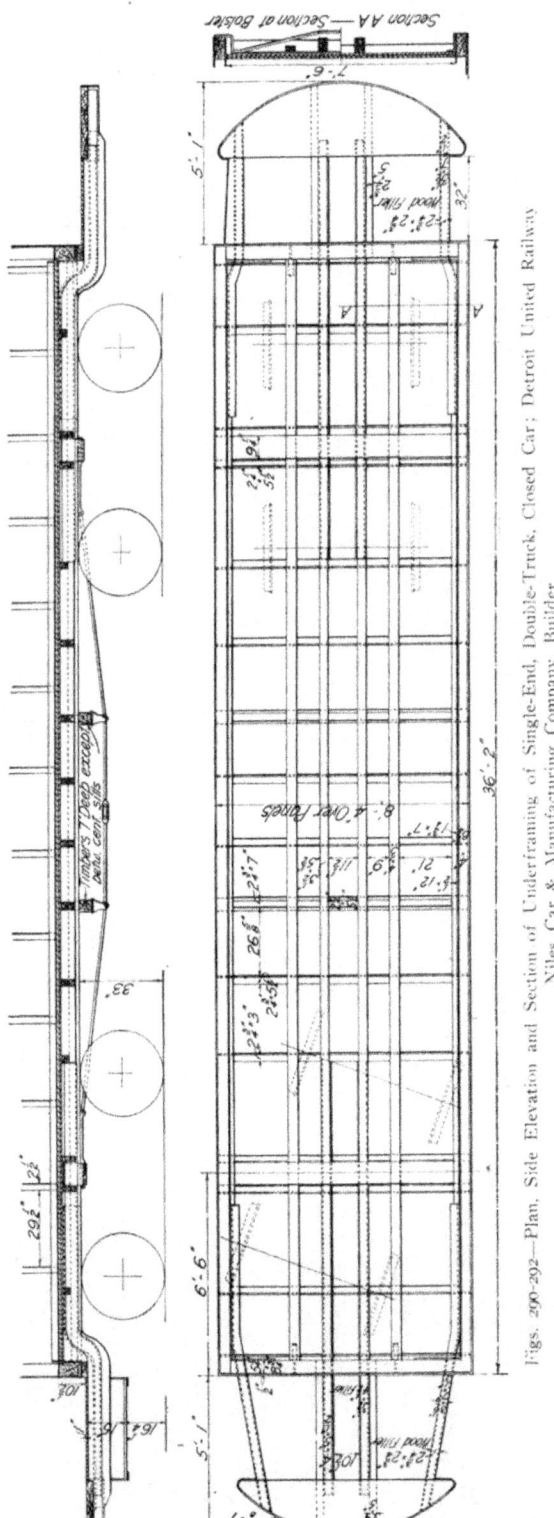

Figs. 290-292—Plan, Side Elevation and Section of Underframing of Single-End, Double-Truck, Closed Car; Detroit United Railway
Niles Car & Manufacturing Company, Builder

(Exterior view and floor plan of this car are shown in Figs. 100-101.)

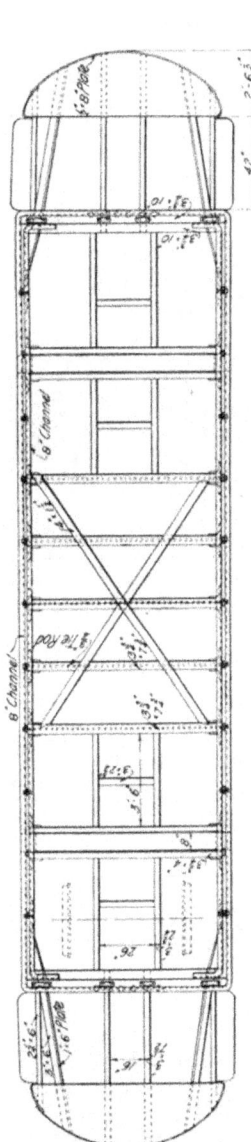

Fig. 293—Plan of Underframing of Double-End, Double-Truck, Closed Car; Schenectady Railway
St. Louis Car Company, Builder

(Floor plan of this car is shown in Fig. 102.)

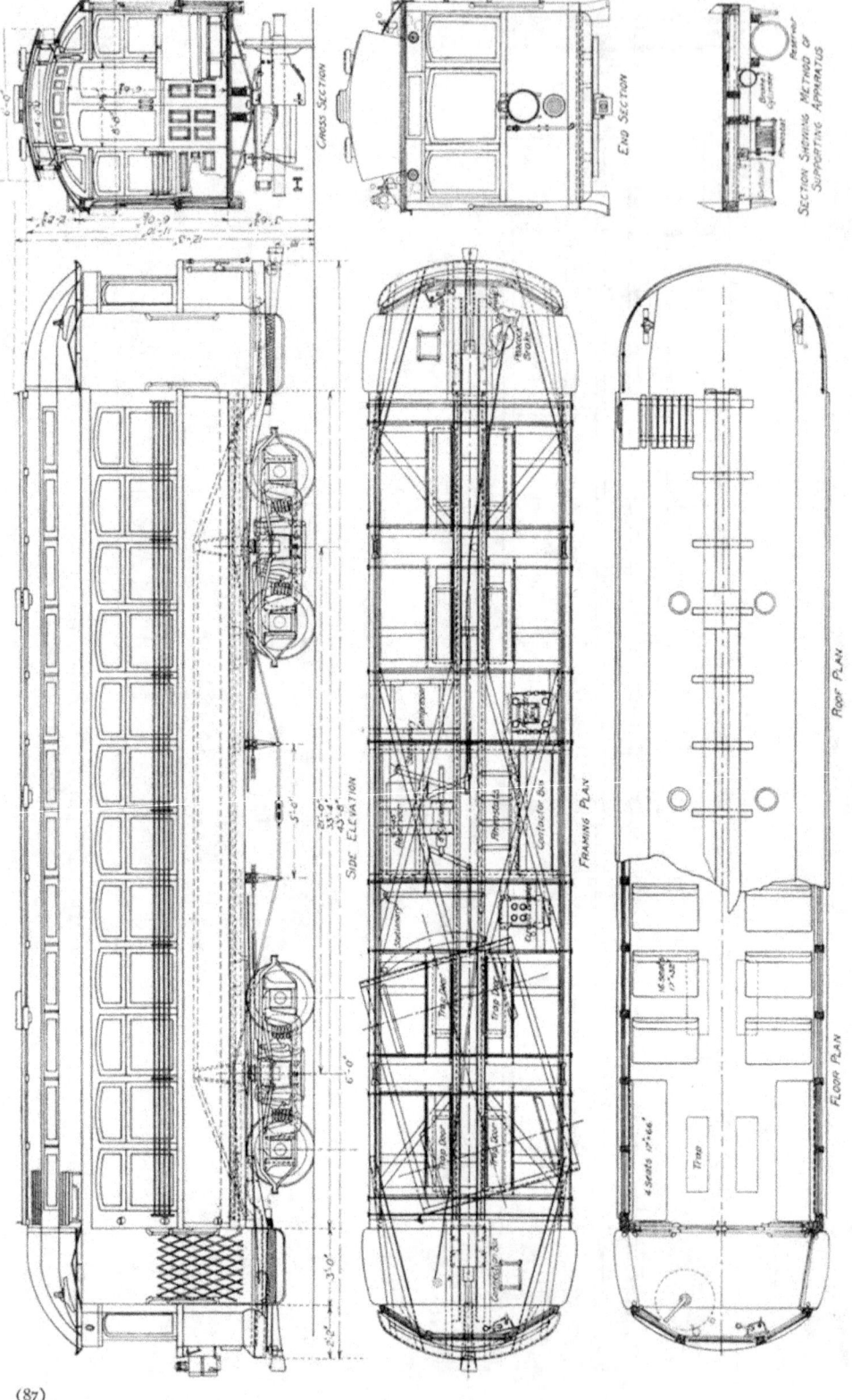

Figs. 294-299.—Plan, Elevations and Sections of Framing of Double-End, Double-Truck, Semi-Convertible Car; Mexico City Tramway. St. Louis Car Company, Builder

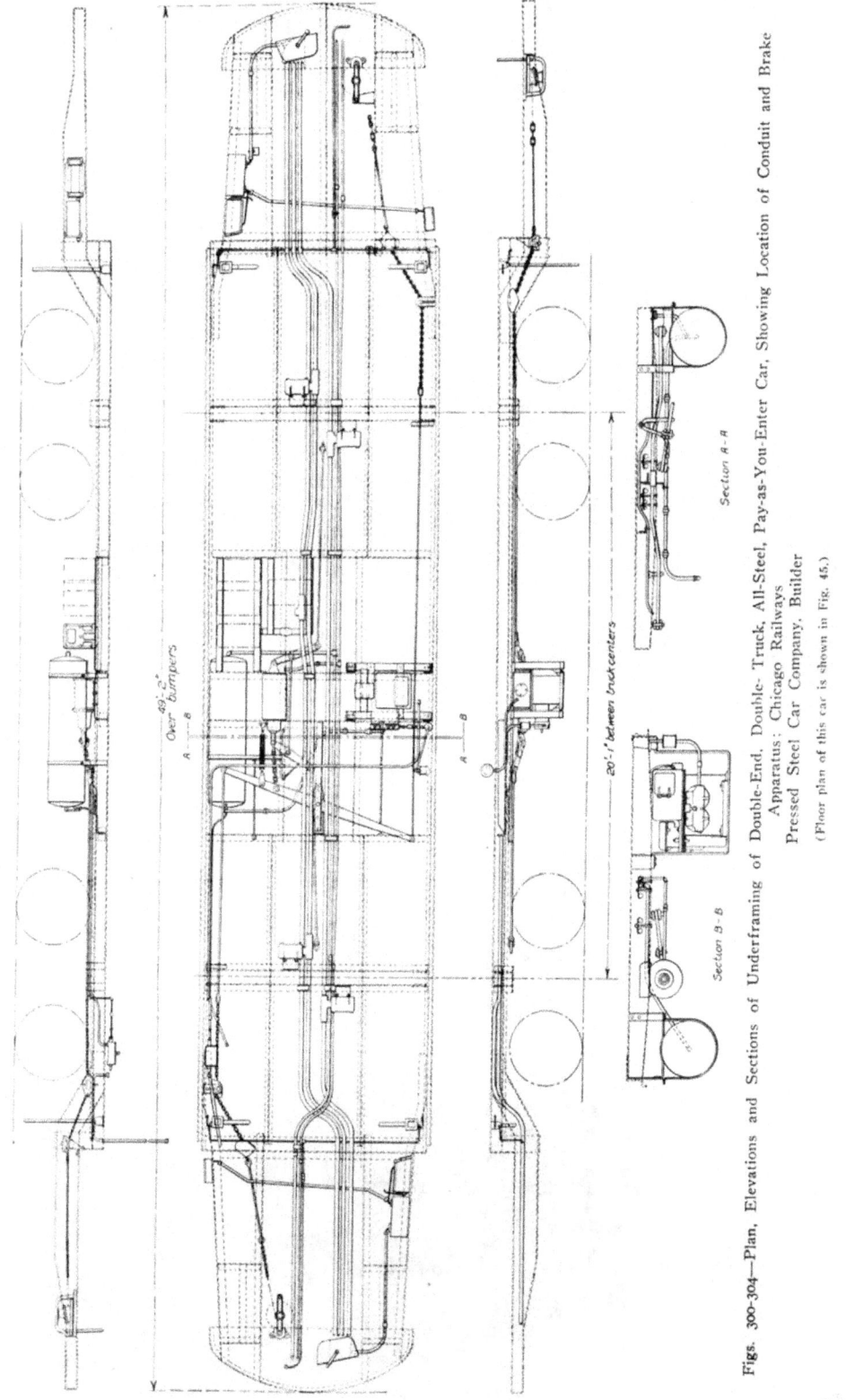

Figs. 300-304—Plan, Elevations and Sections of Underframing of Double-End, Double-Truck, All-Steel, Pay-as-You-Enter Car, Showing Location of Conduit and Brake Apparatus: Chicago Railways Pressed Steel Car Company, Builder

(Floor plan of this car is shown in Fig. 45.)

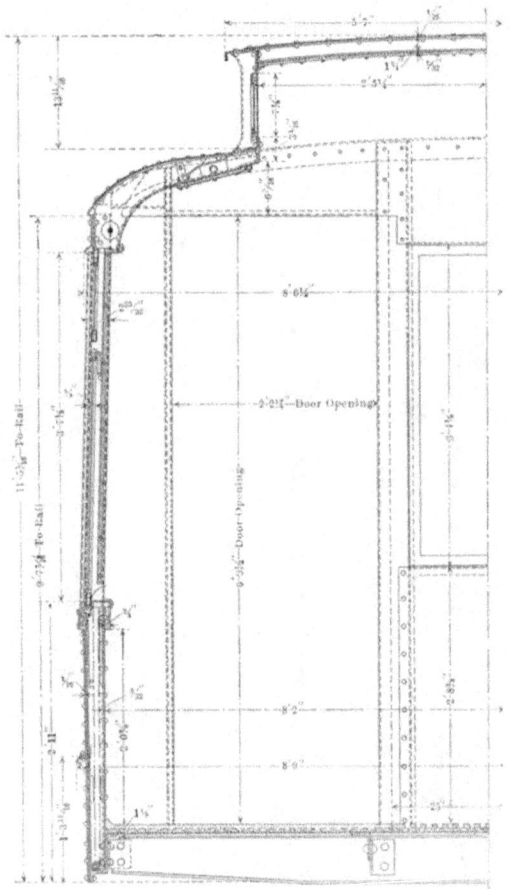

Fig. 305—Half Cross-Section of All-Steel, Pay-as-You-Enter Car; Chicago Railways
Pressed Steel Car Company, Builder

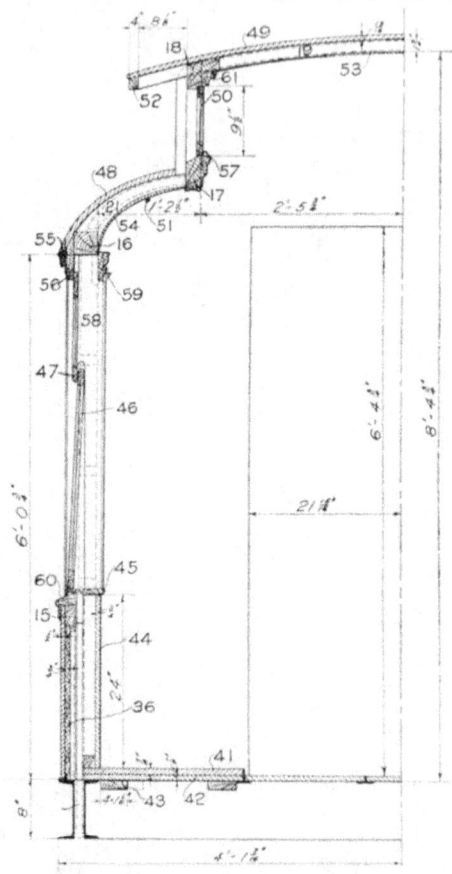

Fig. 306—Half Cross-Section of Semi-Convertible Car; Louisville & Northern Ry. & Lt. Co.
American Car & Foundry Company, Builder

Fig. 307—Brill Convertible Car with Narragansett Type Sills
The J. G. Brill Company, Builder

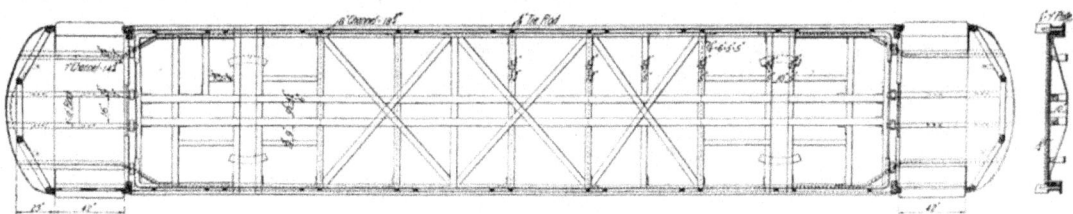

Figs. 309-310—Plan and Cross-Section of Underframing of Double-End, Double-Truck, Closed Car; Southern Michigan Railway
St. Louis Car Company, Builder

(Exterior view of this car is shown in Fig. 118.)

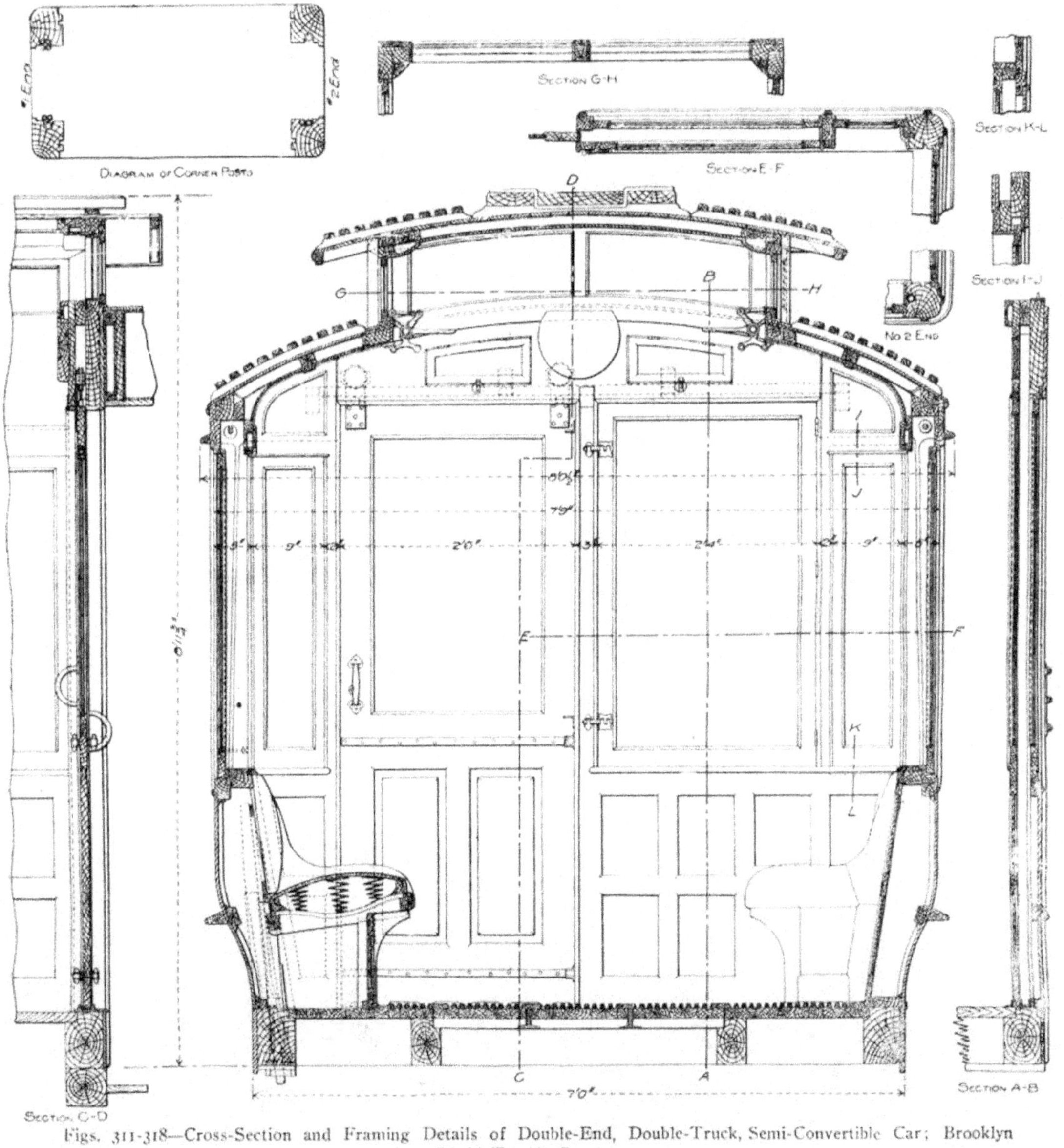

Figs. 311-318—Cross-Section and Framing Details of Double-End, Double-Truck, Semi-Convertible Car; Brooklyn Rapid Transit Company
The J. G. Brill Company, Builder

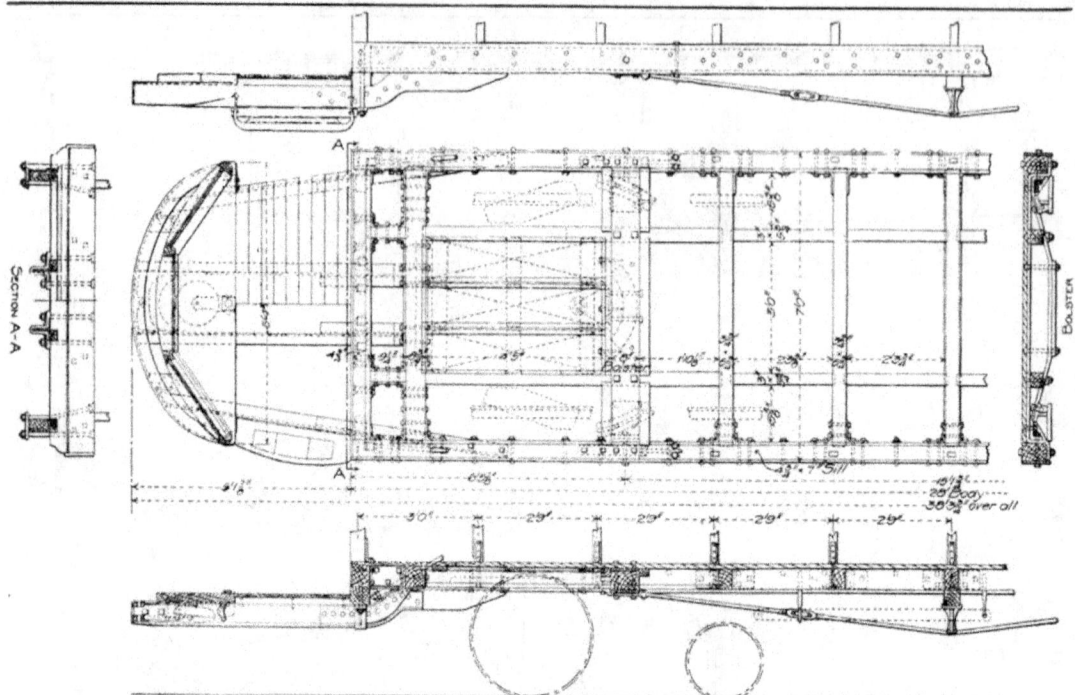

Figs. 319-323—Plan, Elevations and Sections of Underframing of Double-End, Double-Truck, Semi-Convertible Car; Brooklyn Rapid Transit Company
The J. G. Brill Company, Builder

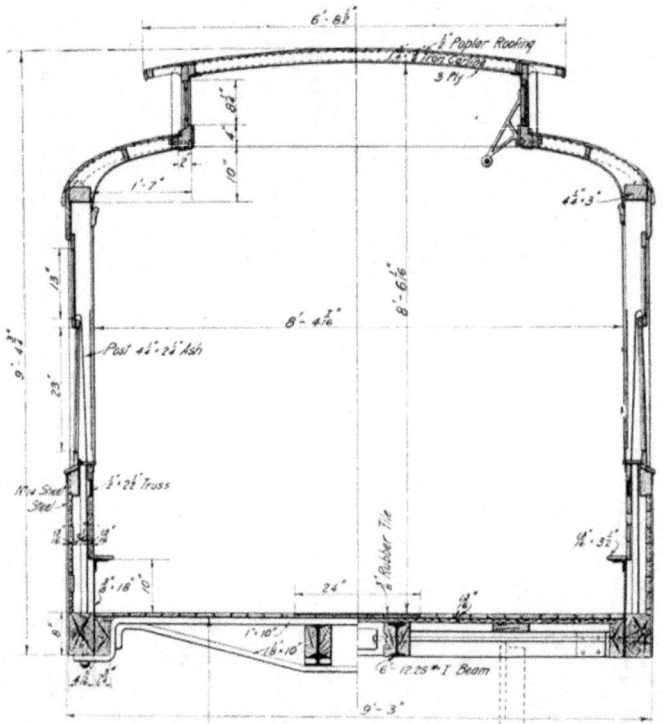

Fig. 324—Cross-Section of Single-End, Double-Truck, Closed, Pay-as-You-Enter Car; Illinois Traction System
The J. G. Brill Company, Builder

(Floor plan and interior view of this car are shown in Figs. 49-50.)

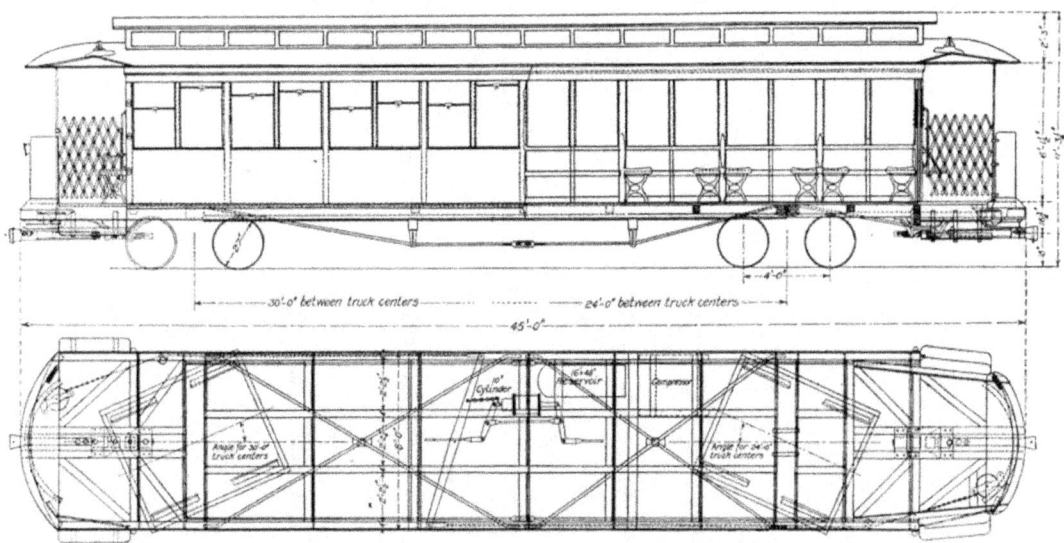

Figs. 325-326—Plan and Elevation of Framing of Double-End, Double-Truck, Semi-Convertible Trail Car; Mexico City Tramway
Built in Company's Shops

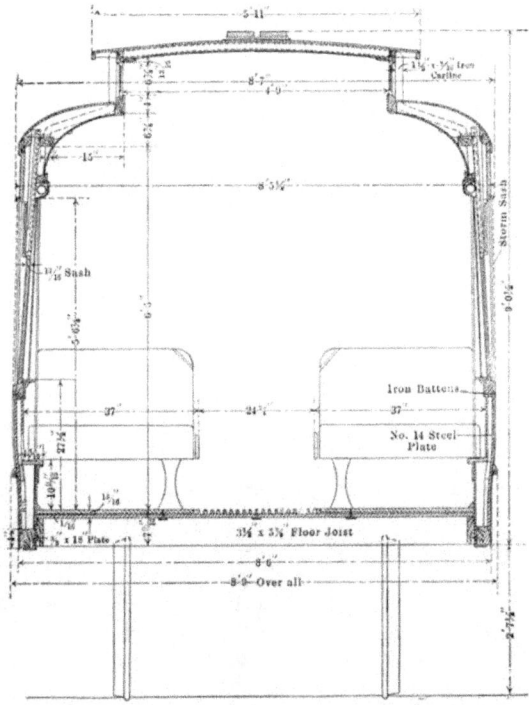

Fig. 327—Cross-Section of Double-End, Double-Truck Pay-as-You-Enter, Closed Car; Chicago Railway
The Pullman Company, Builder

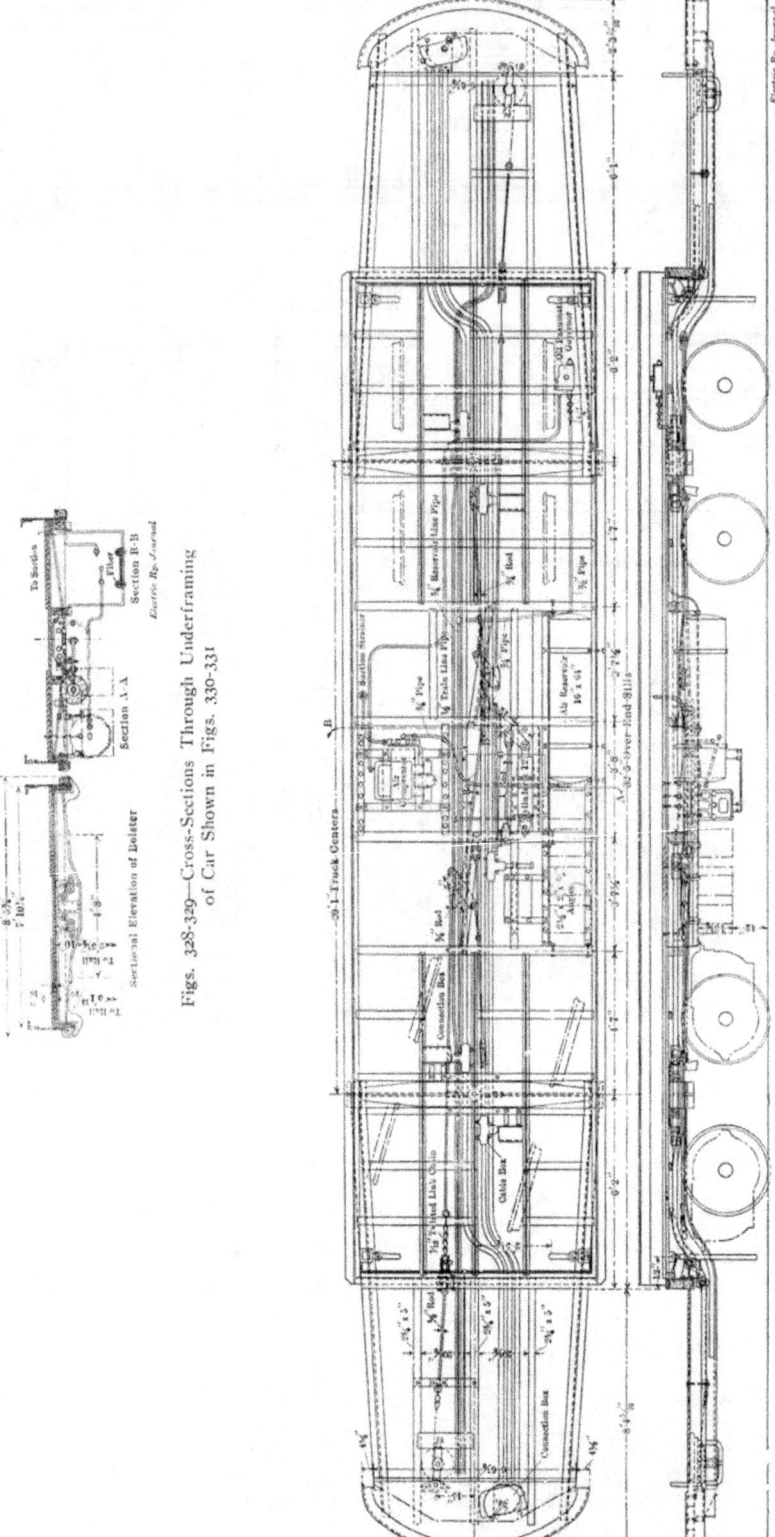

Figs. 328-329—Cross-Sections Through Underframing of Car Shown in Figs. 330-331

Figs. 330-331—Plan and Longitudinal Section of Underframing of Double-End, Double-Truck, Pay-as-You-Enter, Closed Car, Showing Location of Conduit and Air Brake Apparatus; Chicago Railways The Pullman Company, Builder

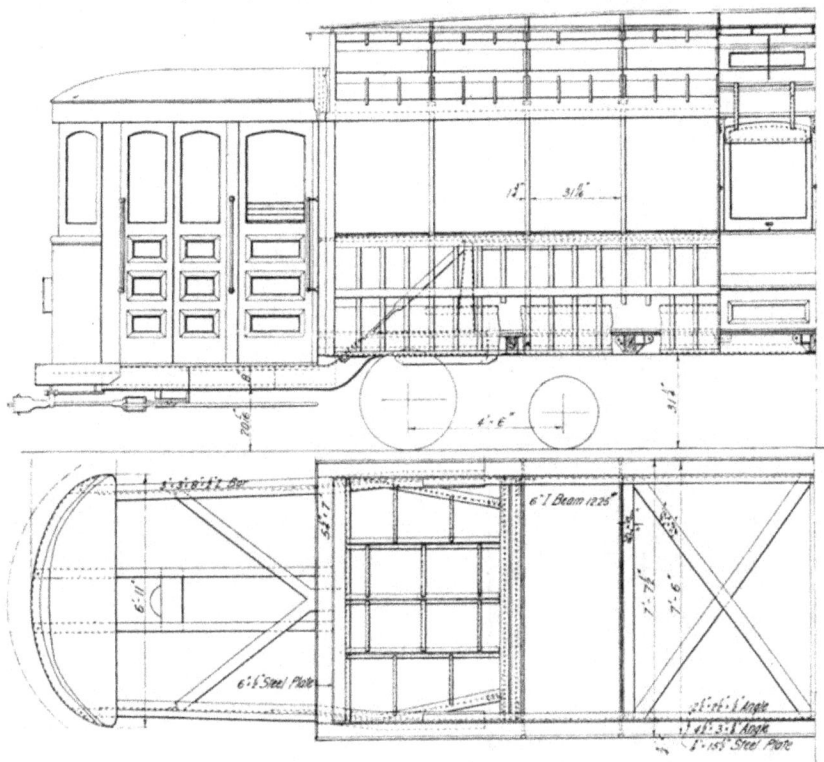

Figs. 332-333—Half Plan and Side Elevation of Framing of Double-End, Double-Truck, Pay-as-You-Enter, Closed Car: St. Joseph Railway, Light, Heat & Power Company
St. Louis Car Company, Builder

(Floor plan of this car is shown in Fig. 46.)

Numbers Refer to List of Names of Parts with Figs. 259-260

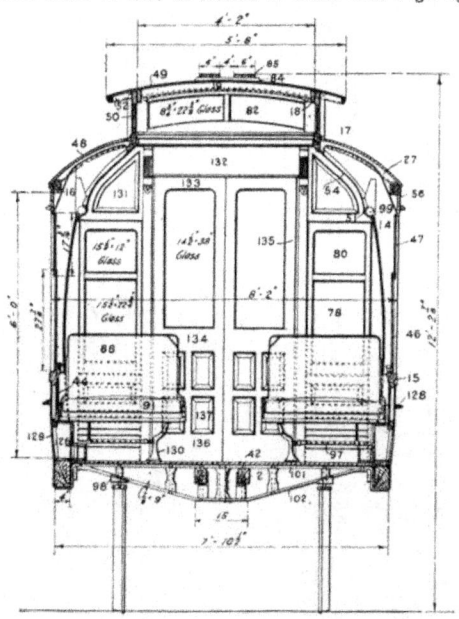

Fig. 334—Cross-Section of Standard, Double-Truck, Semi-Convertible Car
The J. G. Brill Company, Builder

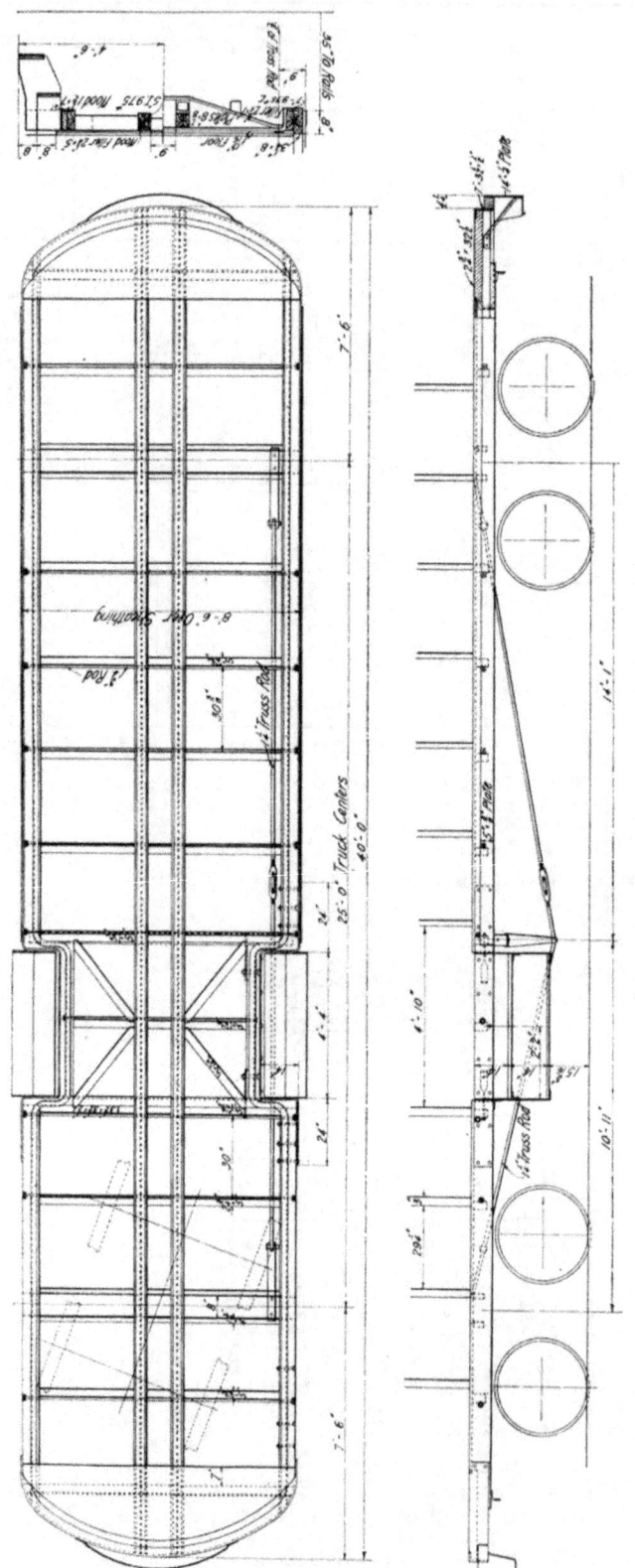

Figs. 335-337—Plan, Elevation and Cross-Section of Underframing of Single-End, Double-Truck, Combination Open and Closed Car with Center Side Entrance; Seattle Electric Company
St. Louis Car Company, Builder

(Exterior view and floor plan of this car are shown in Figs. 84-85.)

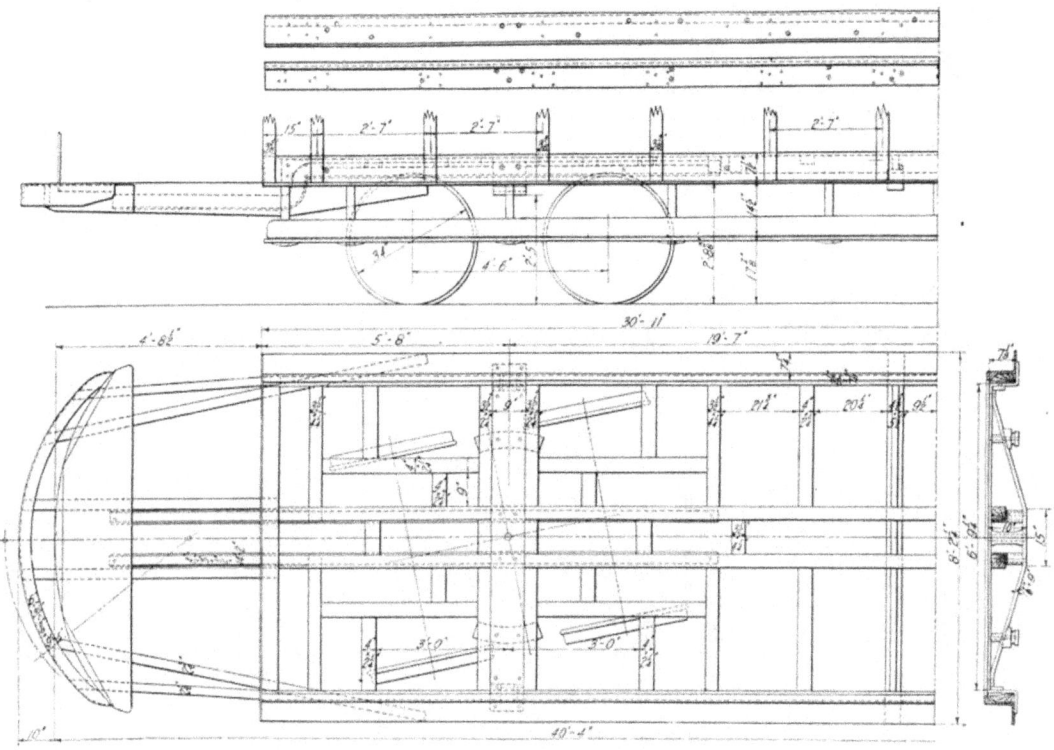

Figs. 338-340—Half Plan, Elevation and Cross-Section of Underframing of Double-End, Double-Truck, Convertible Car; Hanover & McSherrystown Street Railway
The J. G. Brill Company, Builder

Numbers Refer to List of Names of Parts with Figs. 259-260

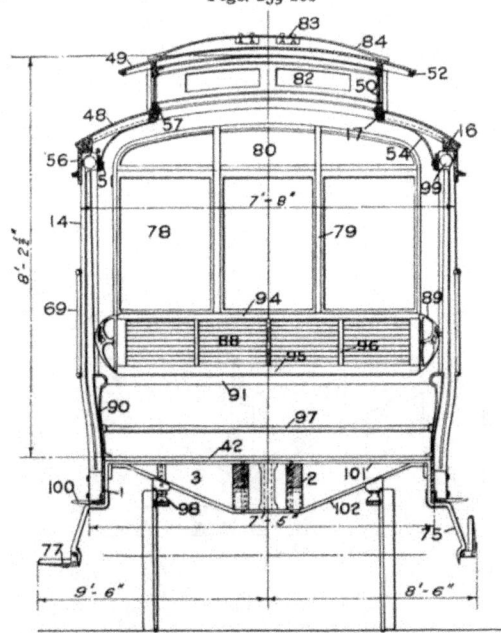

Fig. 341—Cross-Section of Standard, Double-Truck, Narragansett Type Fourteen-Bench Open Car
The J. G. Brill Company, Builder

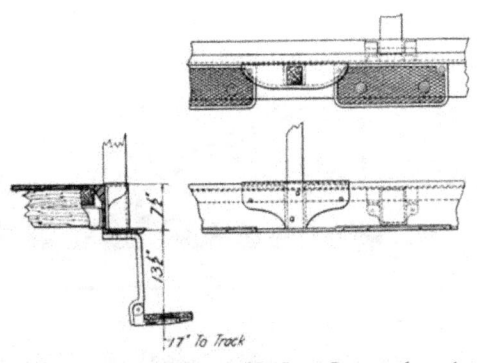

Figs. 342-344—Details of Sill Step Construction of Narragansett Type Open Cars
The J. G. Brill Company, Builder

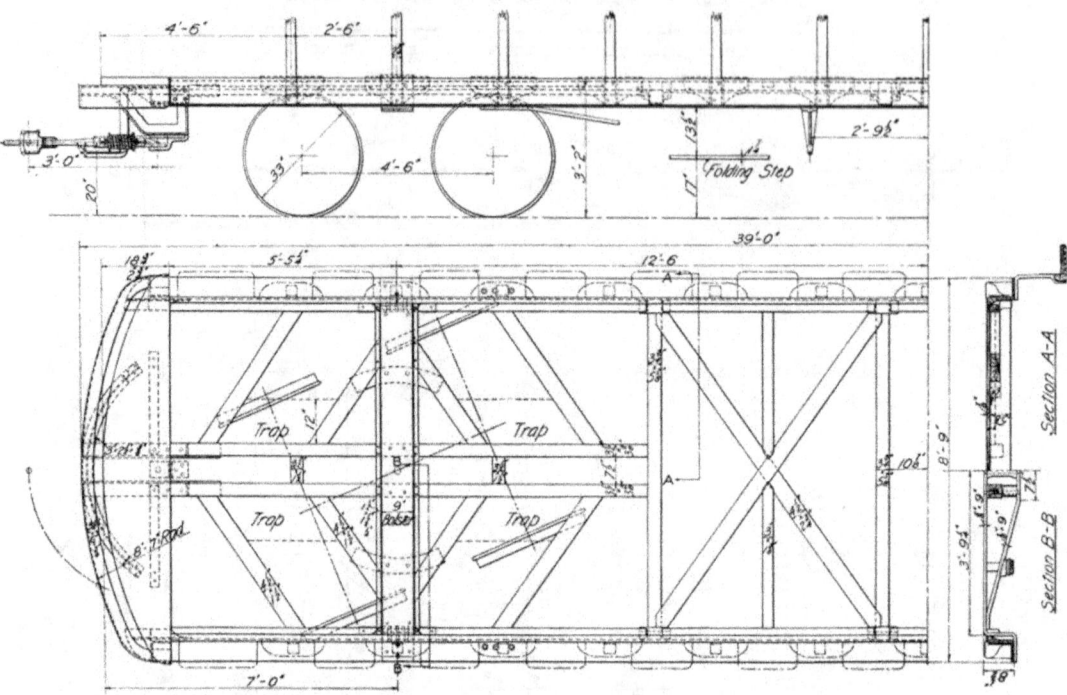

Figs. 345-347—Half Plan, Elevation and Cross-Section of Underframing of Double-End, Double-Truck, Thirteen-Bench, Narragansett Type Open Car; Conestoga Traction Company
The J. G. Brill Company, Builder

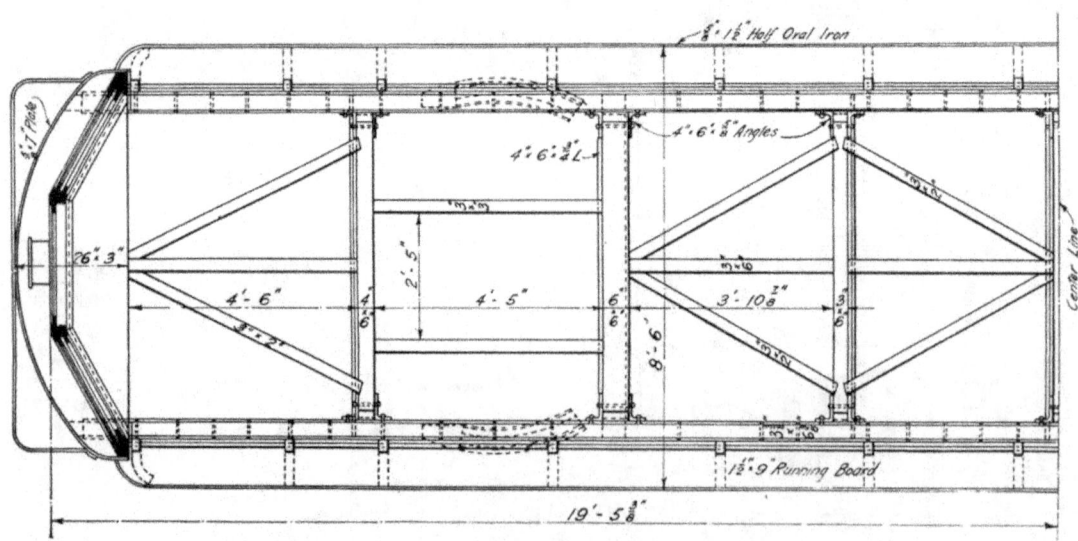

Fig. 348—Half Plan of Underframing of Double-End, Double-Truck, Twelve-Bench Open Car
St. Louis Car Company, Builder

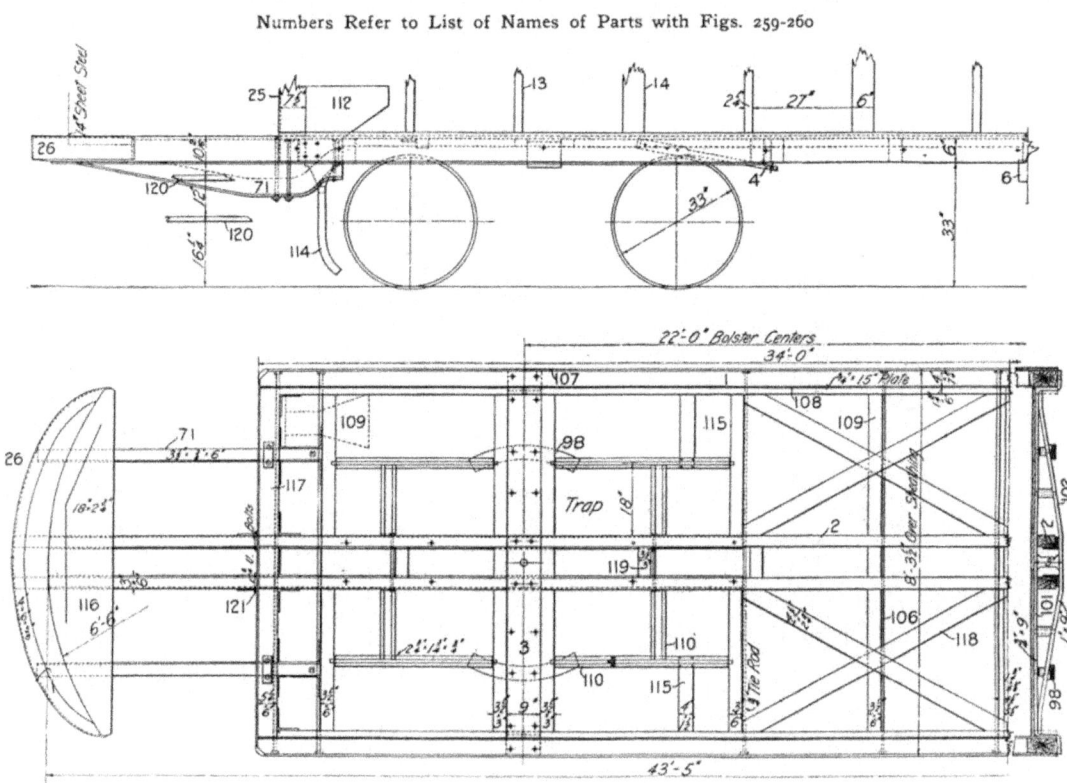

Figs. 349-351—Half Plan, Elevation and Cross-Section of Underframing of Double-End Interurban Car;
Emigration Canyon Railroad
The J. G. Brill Company, Builder

(Exterior view and floor plan of this car are shown in Figs. 106-107.)

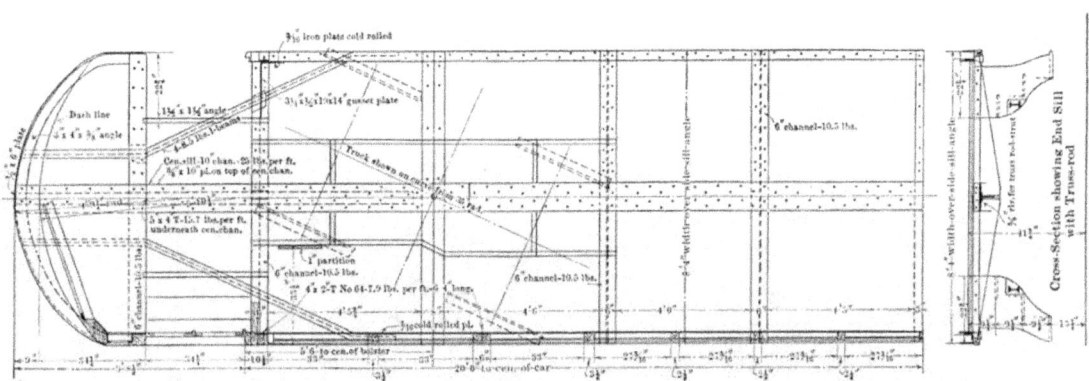

Figs. 352-353—Plan and Cross-Section of Steel Underframing of Double-End, Interurban Car;
Milwaukee Electric Railway & Light Company
St. Louis Car Company, Builder

CAR BODY FRAMING, Interurban

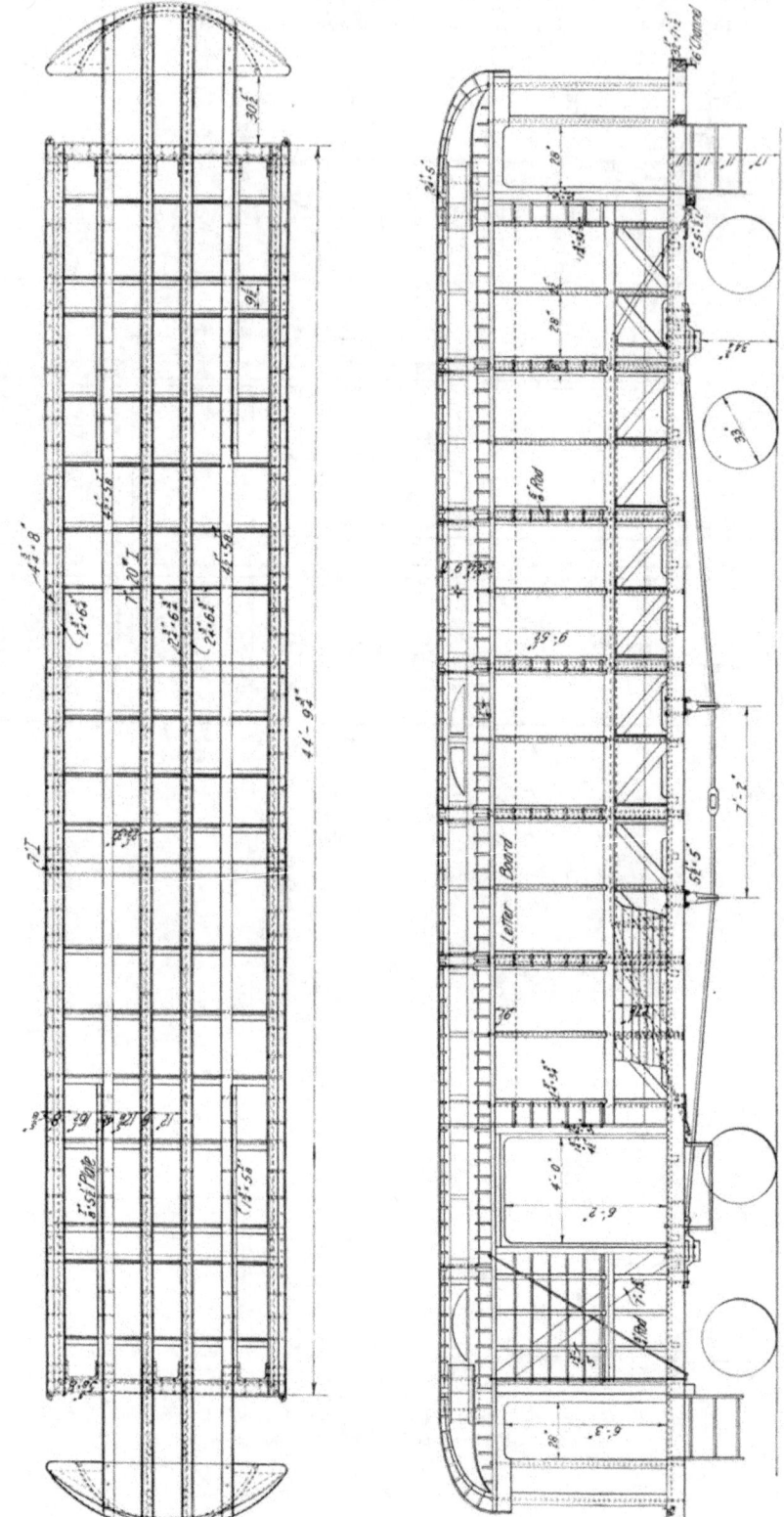

Figs. 354-355—Plan and Elevation of Framing of Single-End Interurban Car with Baggage Compartment; Puget Sound Electric Railway. St. Louis Car Company, Builder

CAR BODY FRAMING, Interurban

Numbers Refer to List of Names of Parts with Figs. 259-260

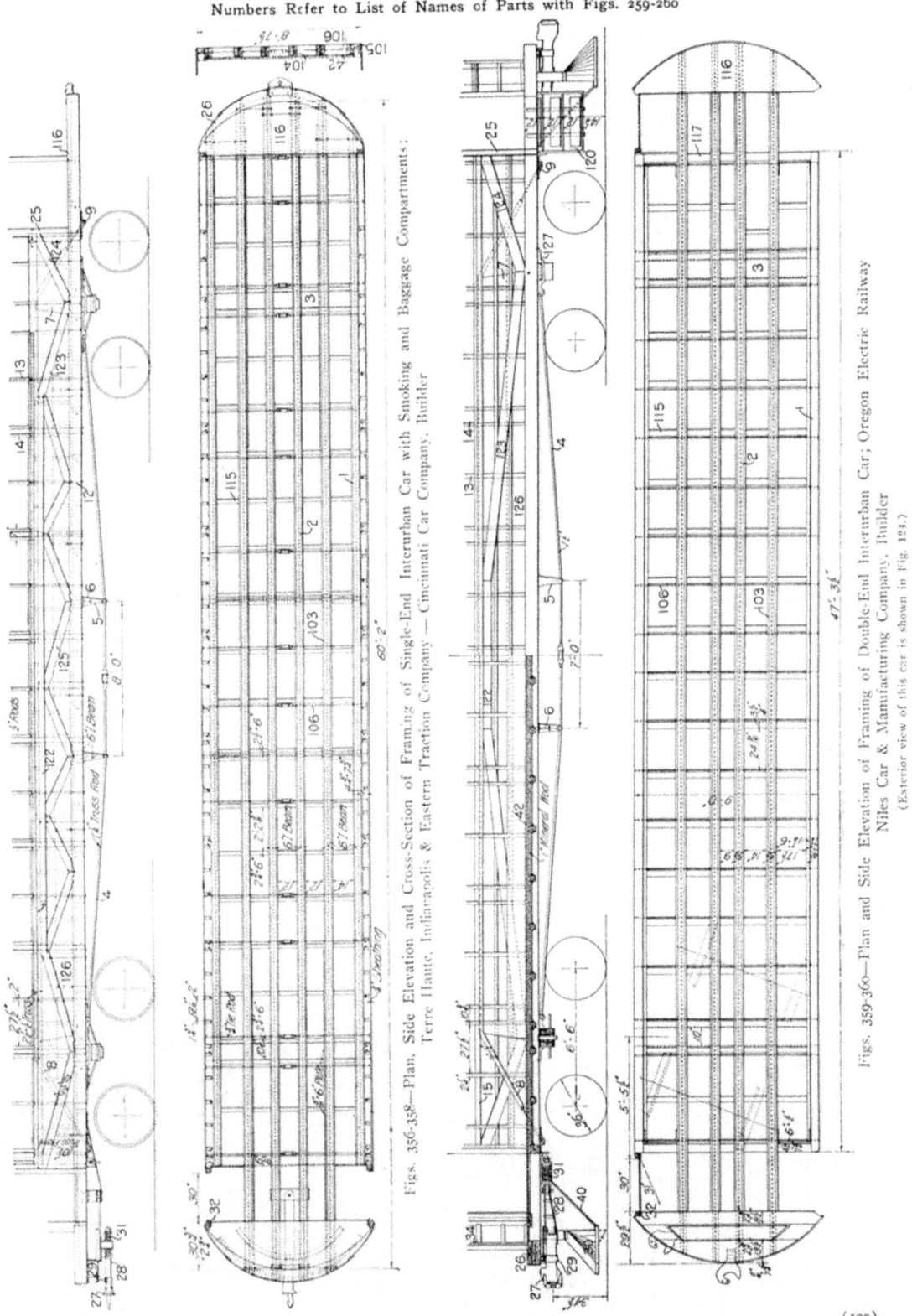

Figs. 356-358.—Plan, Side Elevation and Cross-Section of Framing of Single-End Interurban Car with Smoking and Baggage Compartments; Terre Haute, Indianapolis & Eastern Traction Company.—Cincinnati Car Company, Builder

Figs. 359-360.—Plan and Side Elevation of Framing of Double-End Interurban Car; Oregon Electric Railway Niles Car & Manufacturing Company, Builder
(Exterior view of this car is shown in Fig. 124.)

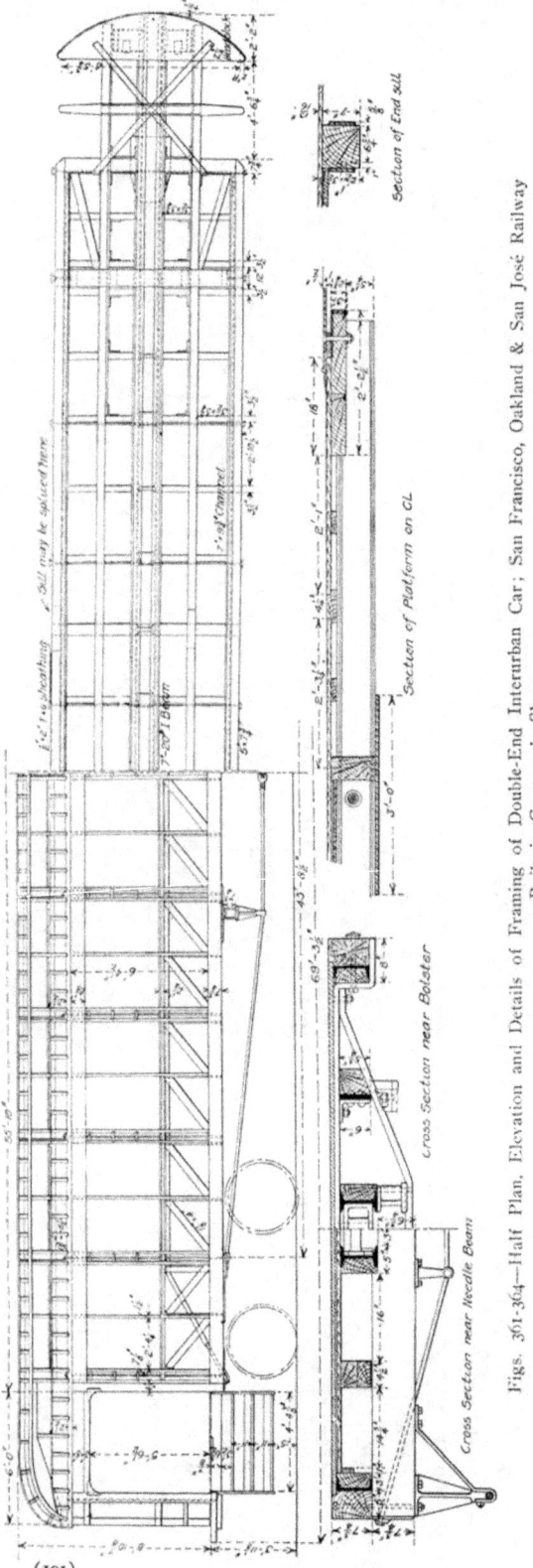

Figs. 361-364—Half Plan, Elevation and Details of Framing of Double-End Interurban Car; San Francisco, Oakland & San José Railway Built in Company's Shops

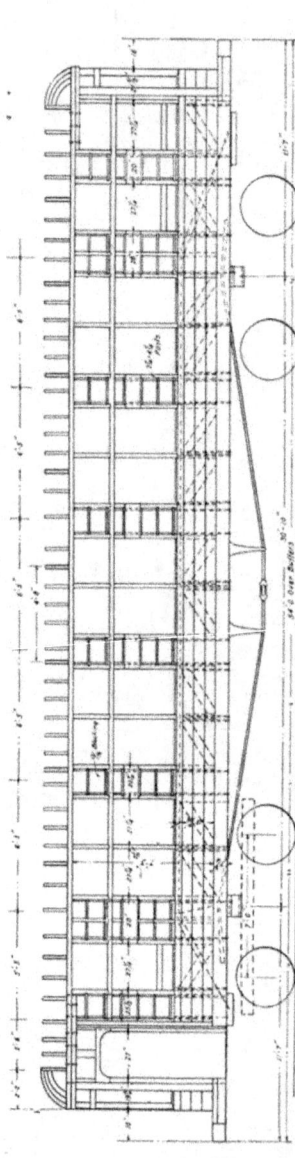

Fig. 365—Side Elevation of Framing of Ten-Section Trailer Sleeping Car; Illinois Traction System American Car & Foundry Company, Builder

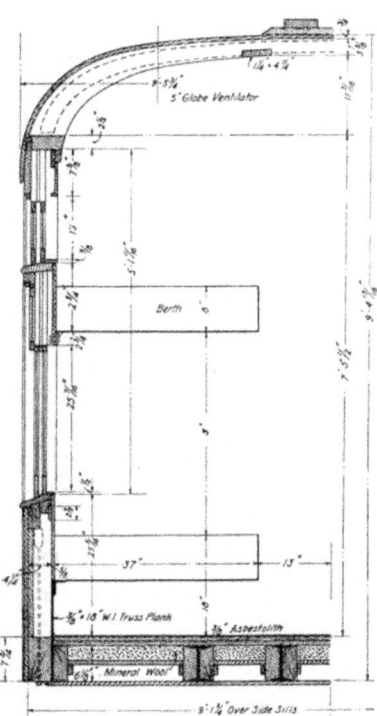

Fig. 366—Half Cross-Section of Sleeping Car; Illinois Traction System
American Car & Foundry Company, Builder

Numbers Refer to List of Names of Parts with Figs. 259-260

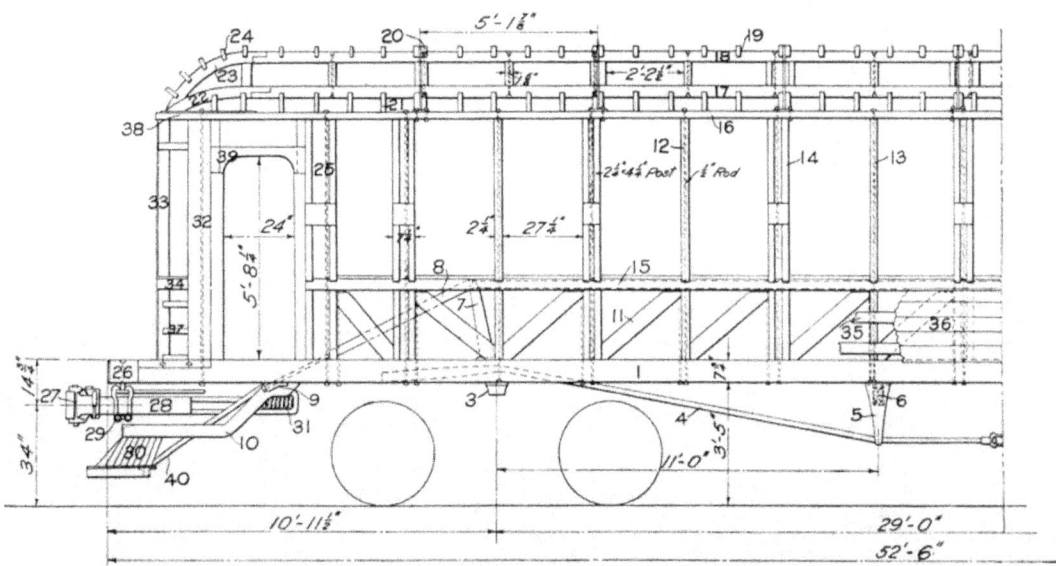

Fig. 367—Half Side Elevation of Framing of Single-End Interurban Car with Baggage and Smoking Compartment; Illinois Traction System
American Car & Foundry Company, Builder

(Exterior view of this car is shown in Fig. 144.)

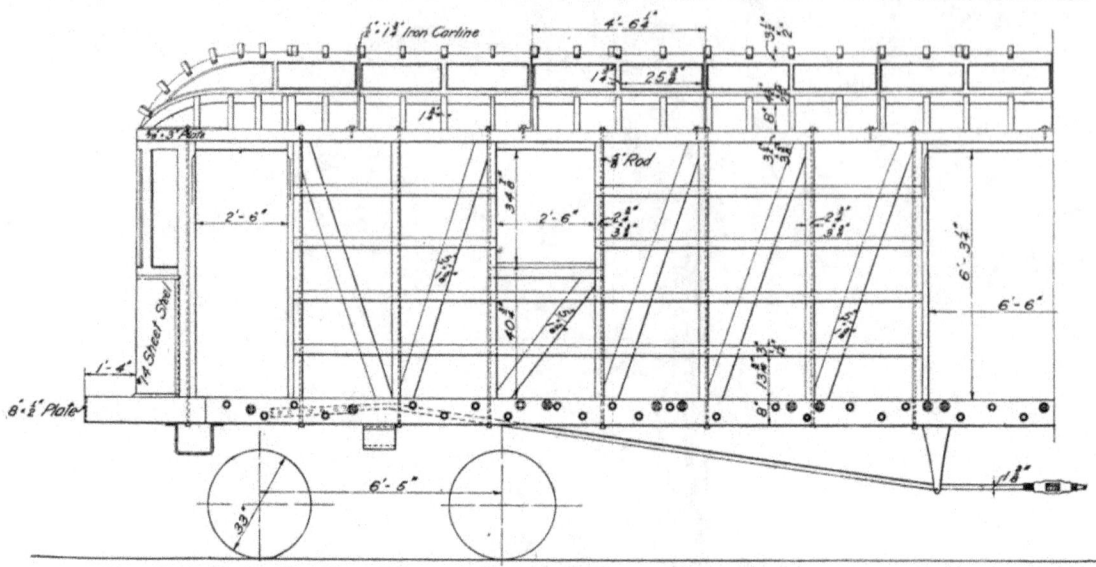

Fig. 368—Half Side Elevation of Framing of Motor Baggage and Express Car; Illinois Traction System
American Car & Foundry Company, Builder

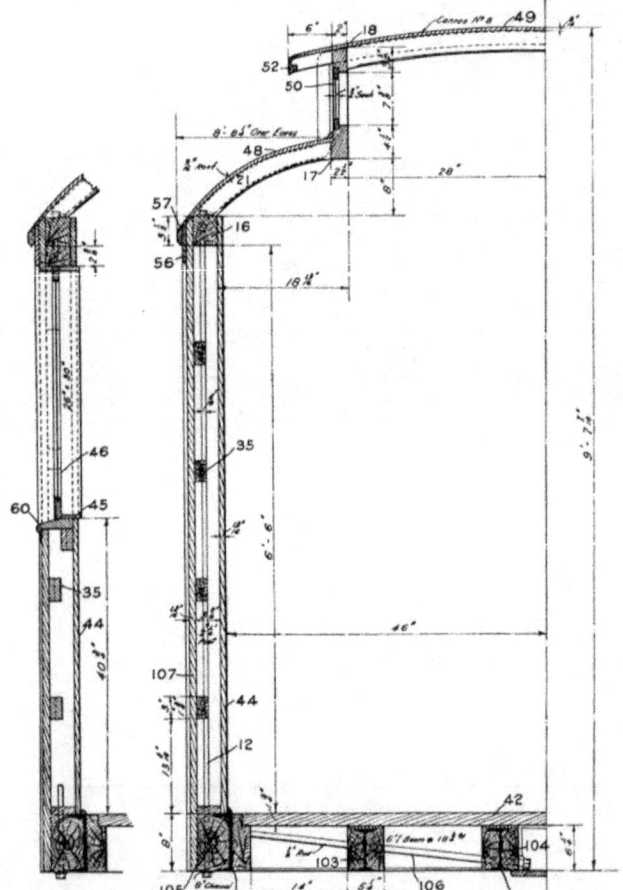

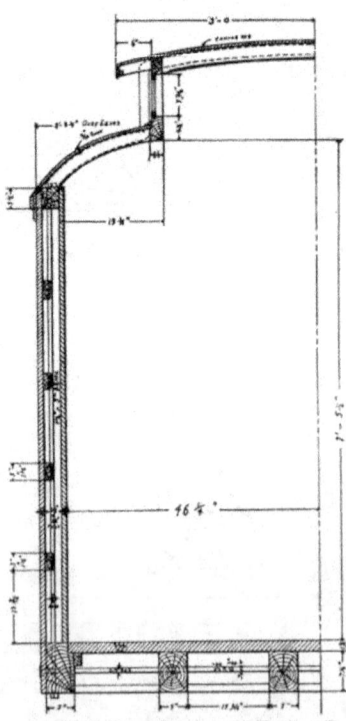

Numbers Refer to List of Names of Parts with Figs. 259-260

Figs. 369-370—Cross-Section of Motor Baggage and Express Car;
Illinois Traction System
American Car & Foundry Company, Builder

Fig. 371—Half Cross-Section of Trailer Express Car; Illinois Traction System
American Car & Foundry Company, Builder

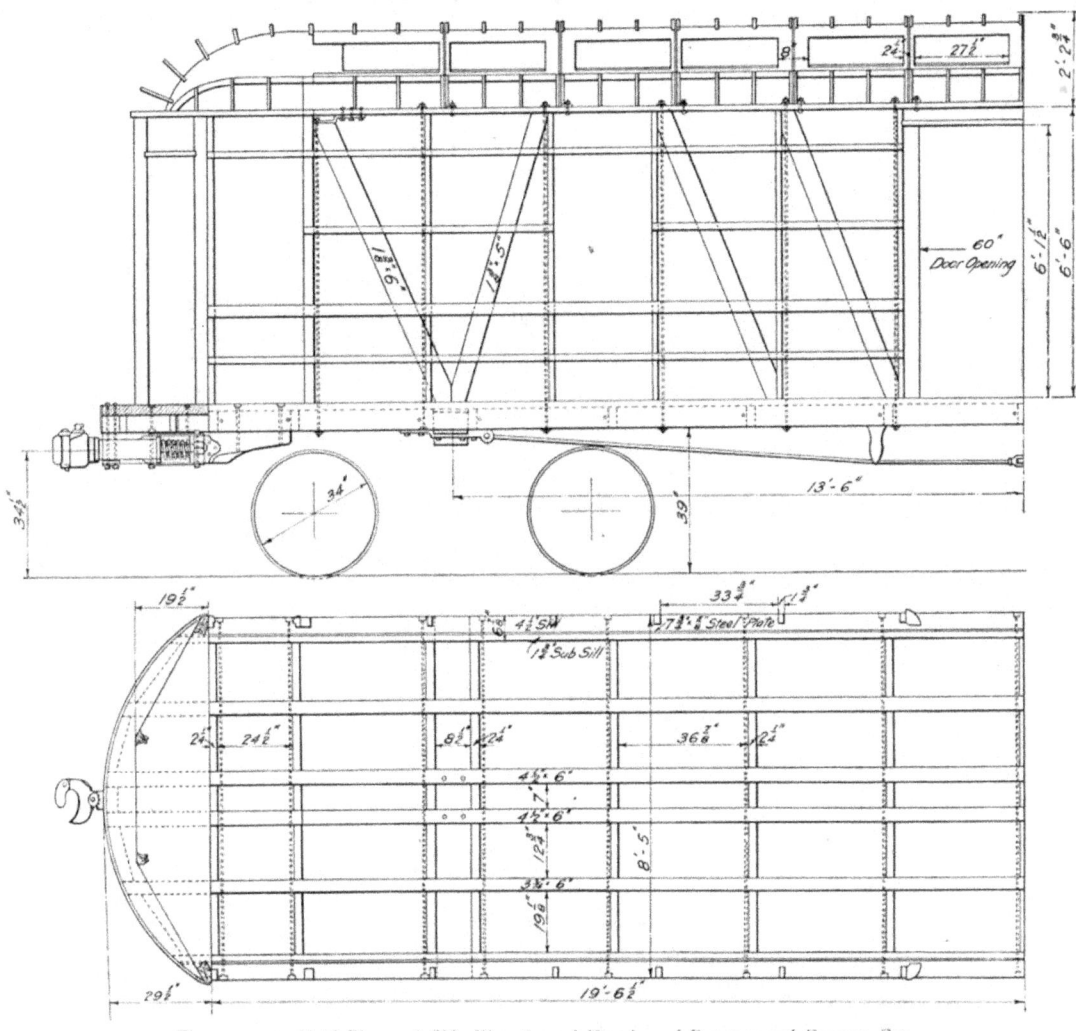

Figs. 372-373—Half Plan and Side Elevation of Framing of Baggage and Express Car
Niles Car & Manufacturing Company, Builder

(Exterior view of this car is shown in Fig. 193.)

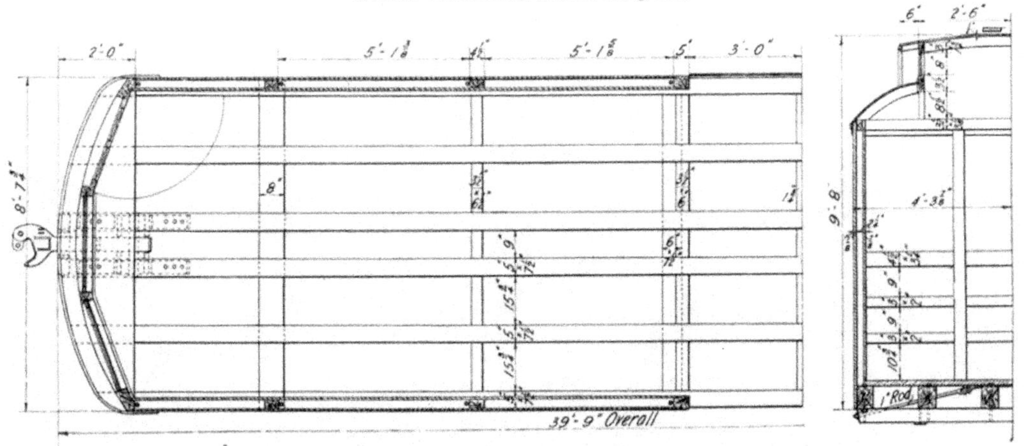

Figs. 374-375—Half Plan and Cross-Section of Framing of Express Car
St. Louis Car Company, Builder

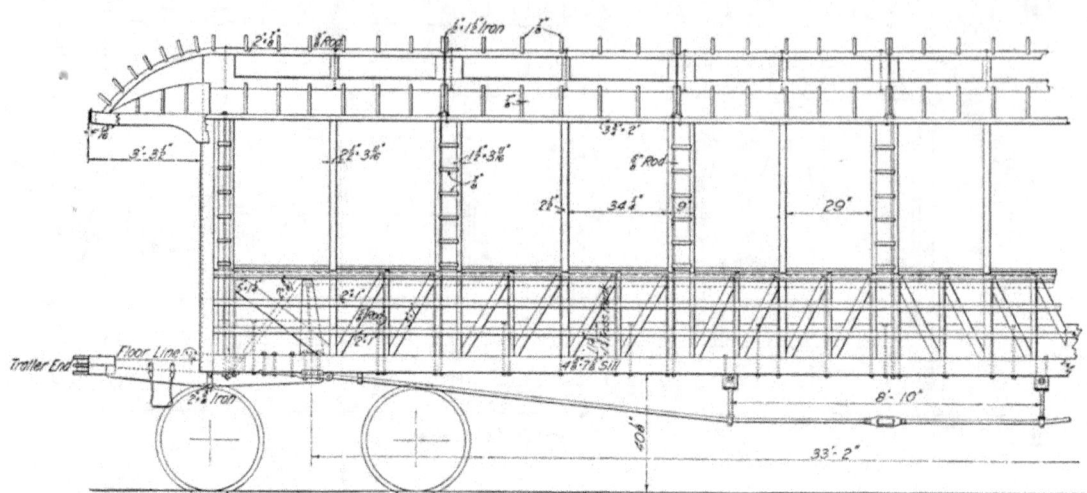

Fig. 376—Half Side Elevation of Framing of Elevated Motor Car; Interborough Rapid Transit Company
The J. G. Brill Company, Builder

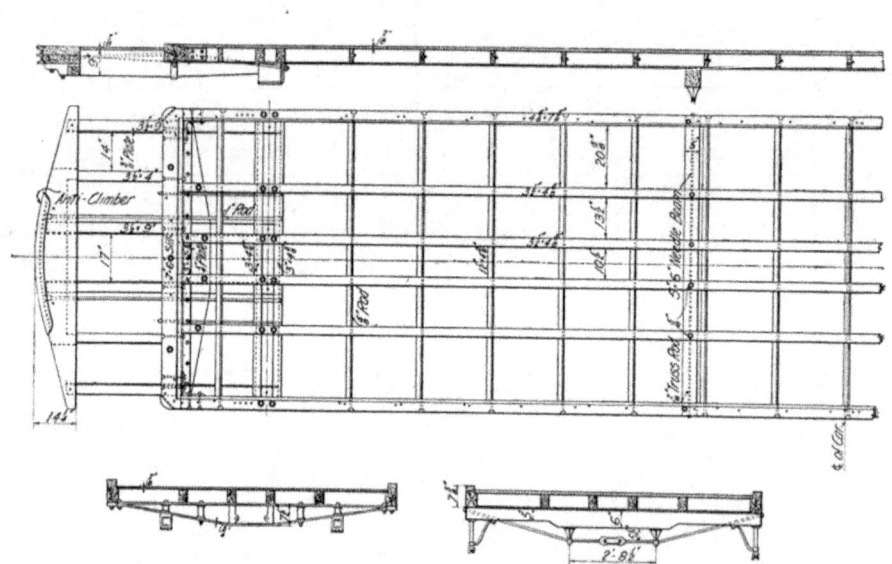

Figs. 377-380—Half Plan and Sections of Underframing of Elevated Motor Car;
Interborough Rapid Transit Company
The J. G. Brill Company, Builder

(Floor plan and exterior view of this car are shown in Figs. 202-203.)

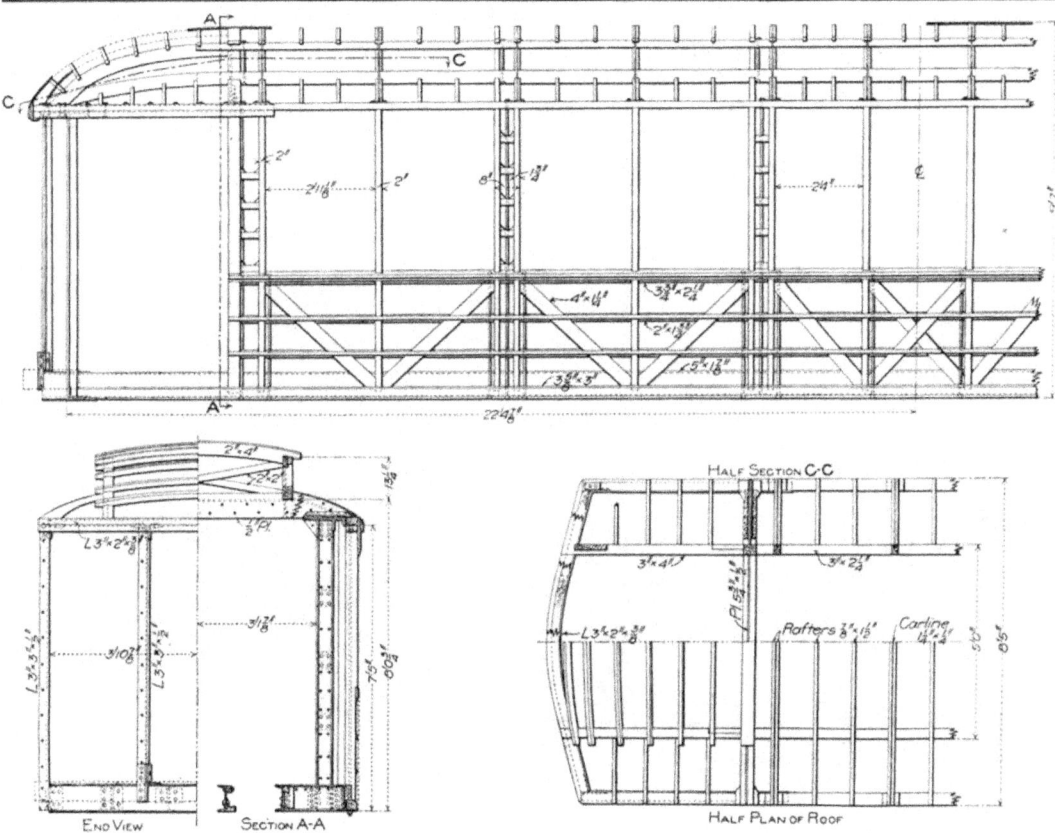

Figs. 381-383—Half Side Elevation, Roof Plan and End Elevation of Framing of Elevated Trailer Car; Northwestern Elevated Railway—American Car & Foundry Company, Builder

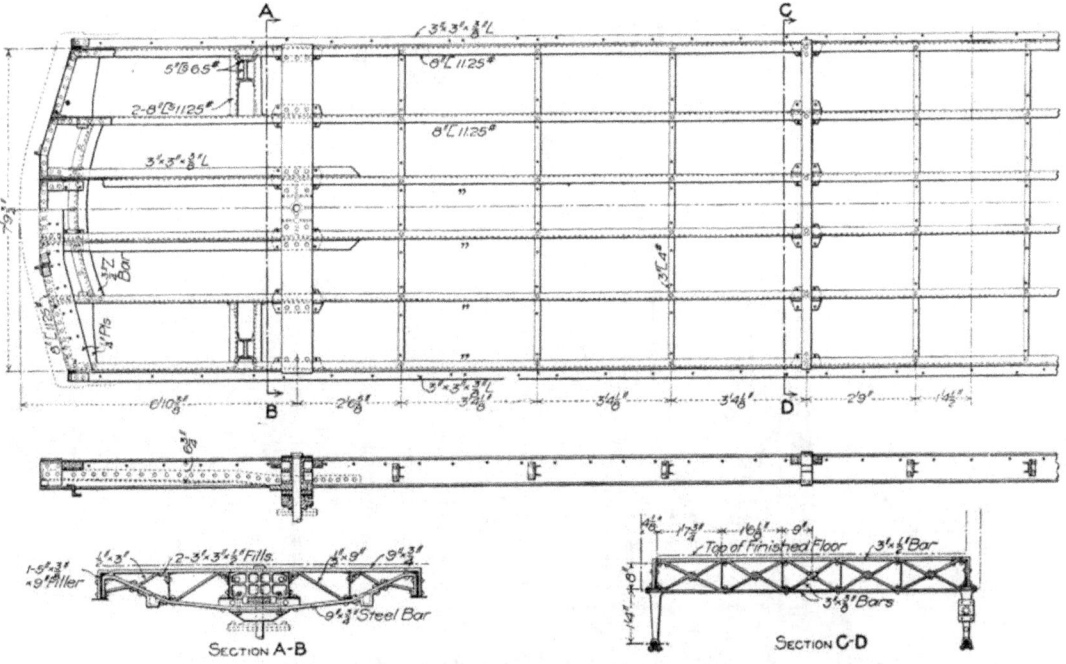

Figs. 384-387—Half Plan and Sections of Steel Underframing of Elevated Trailer Car; Northwestern Elevated Railway—American Car & Foundry Company, Builder

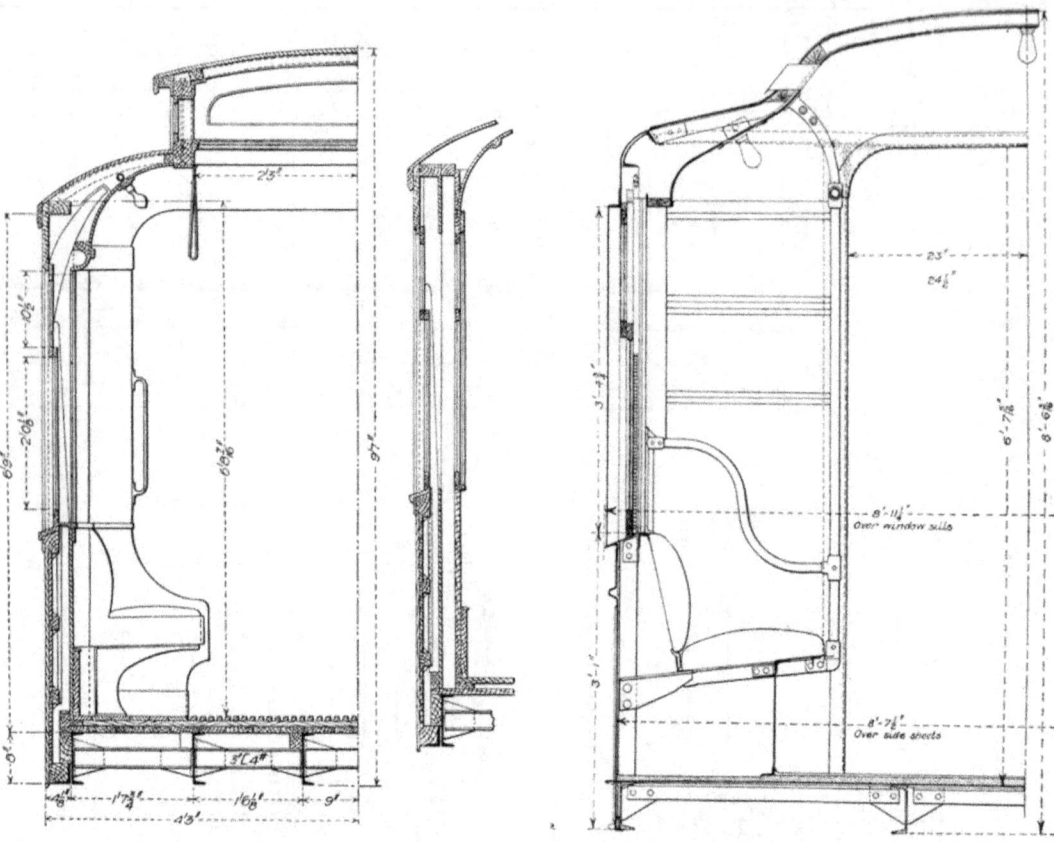

Figs. 388-389—Cross-Sections of Elevated Trailer Car; Northwestern Elevated Railway
American Car & Foundry Company, Builder

Fig. 390—Half Cross-Section of All-Steel Subway Car; Hudson & Manhattan Railroad
Pressed Steel Car Company, Builder

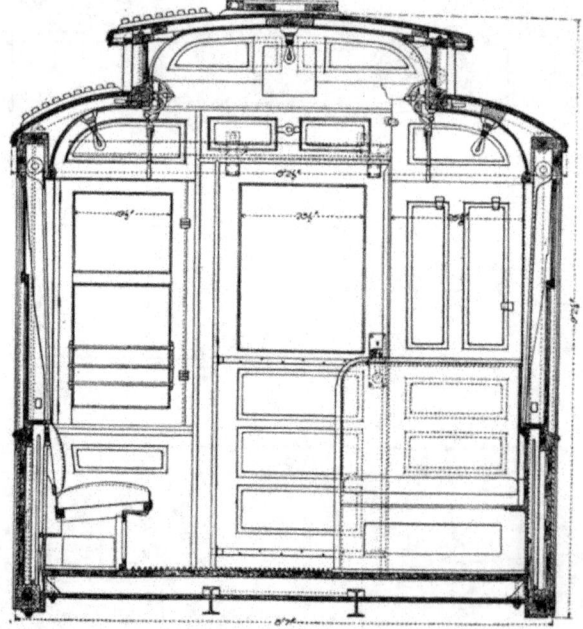

Fig. 391—Cross-Section of Elevated Motor Car; Brooklyn Rapid Transit Company
Jewett Car Company, Builder

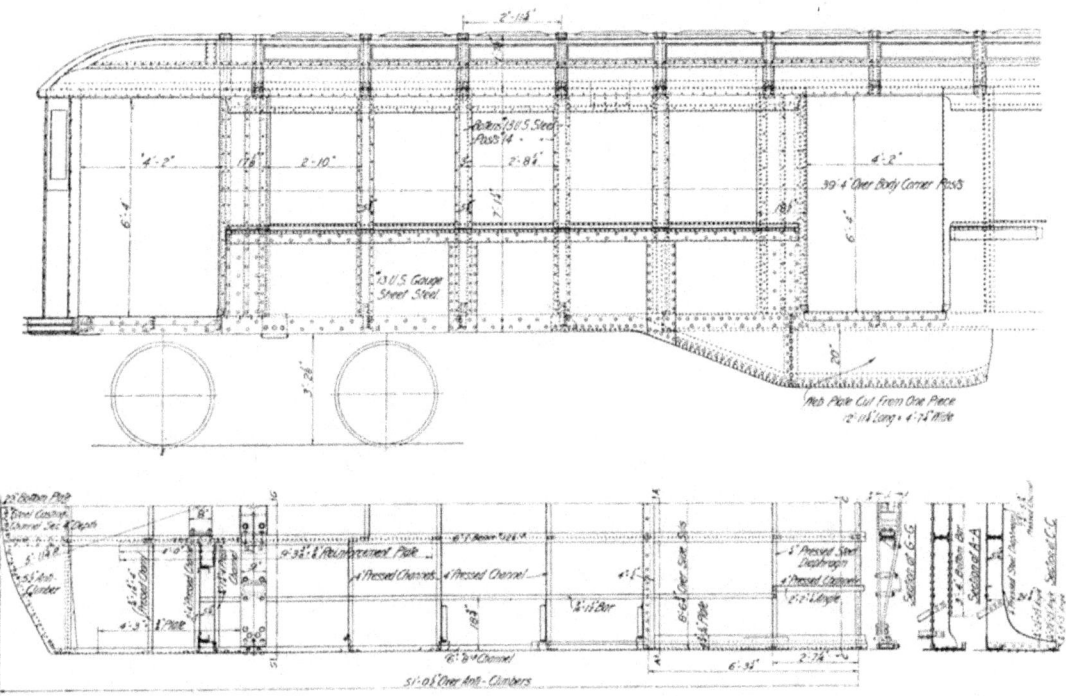

Figs. 392-396—Half Plan, Side Elevation and Sections of Framing of All-Steel Subway Motor Car, with Center Side Doors: Interborough Rapid Transit Company
Pressed Steel Car Company, Builder

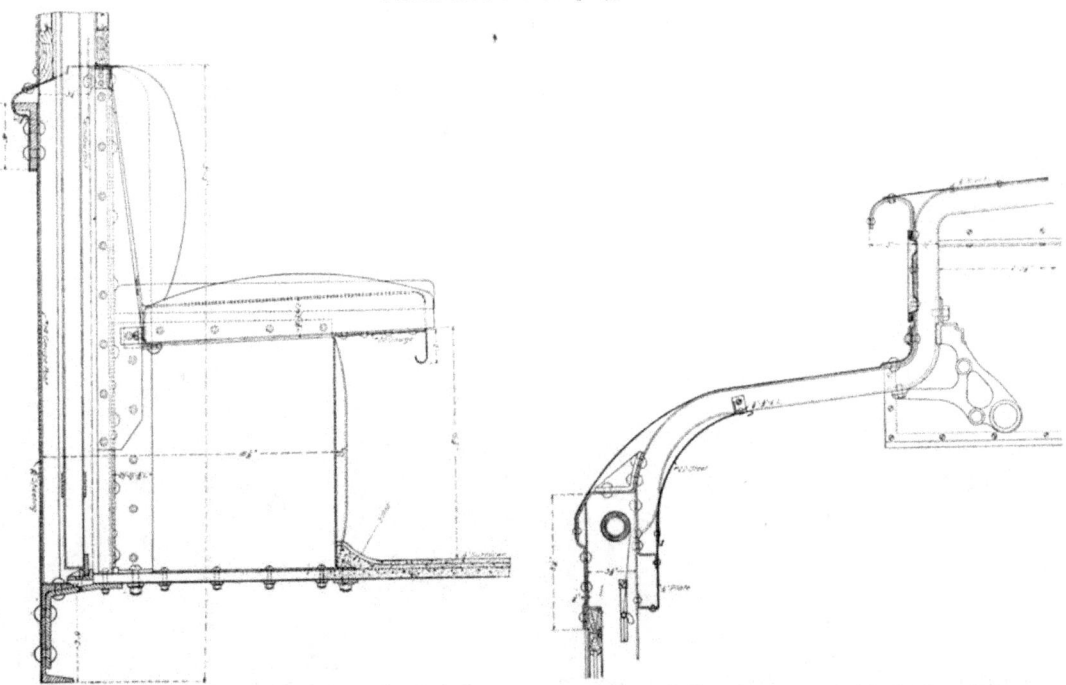

Fig. 397—Section through Floor and Side of Steel Subway Car

Fig. 398—Section through Roof of Steel Subway Car

Pressed Steel Car Company, Builder

(Exterior and interior views and floor plan of this car are shown in Figs. 209-212.)

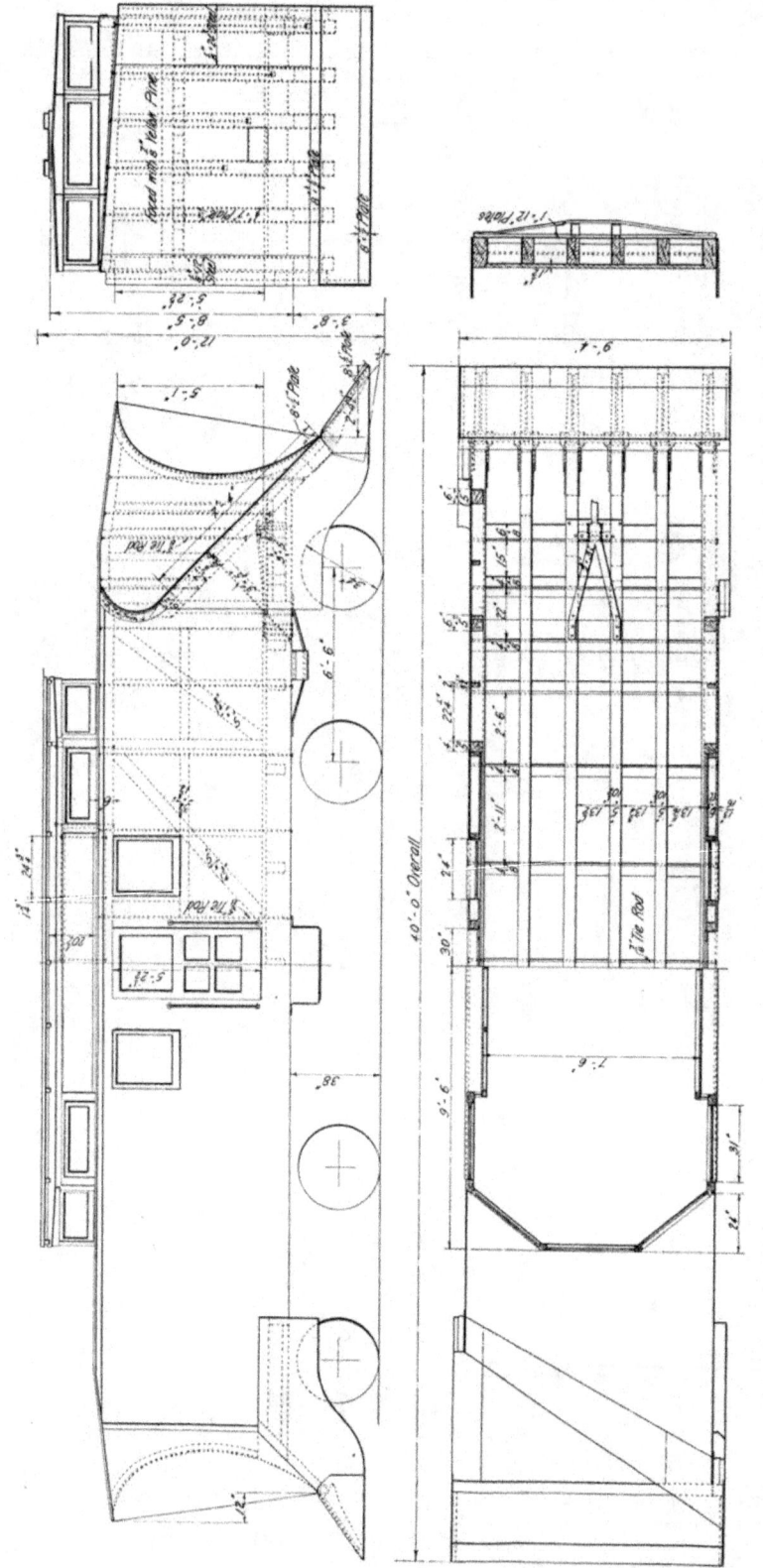

Figs. 399-402—Plan, Elevations and Sections of Framing of Double-Truck, Double-End, Shear Plow; Buffalo & Lake Erie Traction Company Cincinnati Car Company, Builder
(Exterior view of this plow is shown in Fig. 217.)

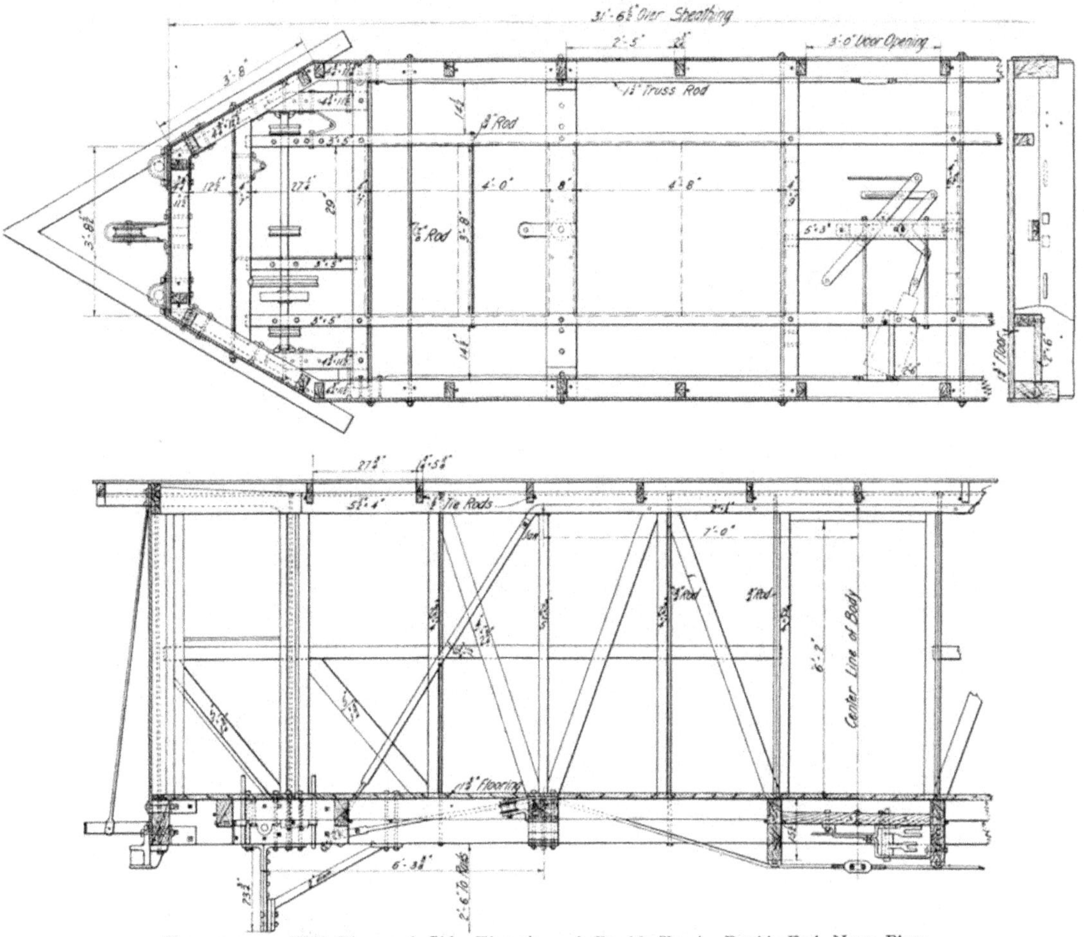

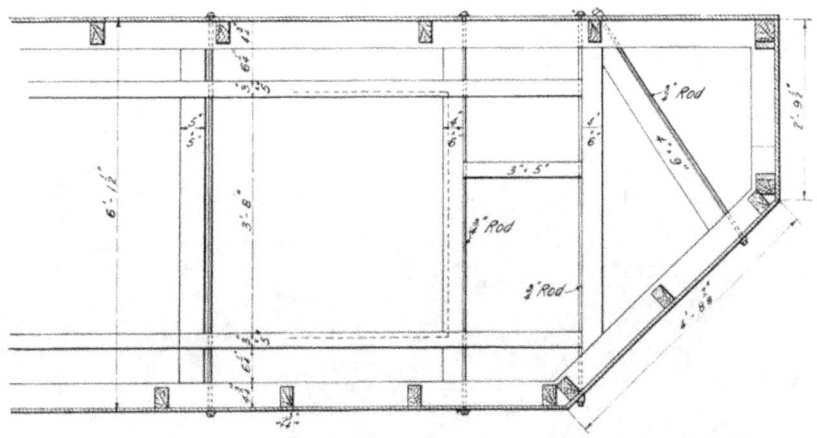

Figs. 403-404—Half Plan and Side Elevation of Double-Truck, Double-End Nose Plow
The J. G. Brill Company, Builder

(Exterior view of this plow is shown in Fig. 218.)

Fig. 405—Part Plan of Underframing of Single-Truck, Double-End Shear Plow
The J. G. Brill Company, Builder

(Exterior view of this plow is shown in Fig. 220.)

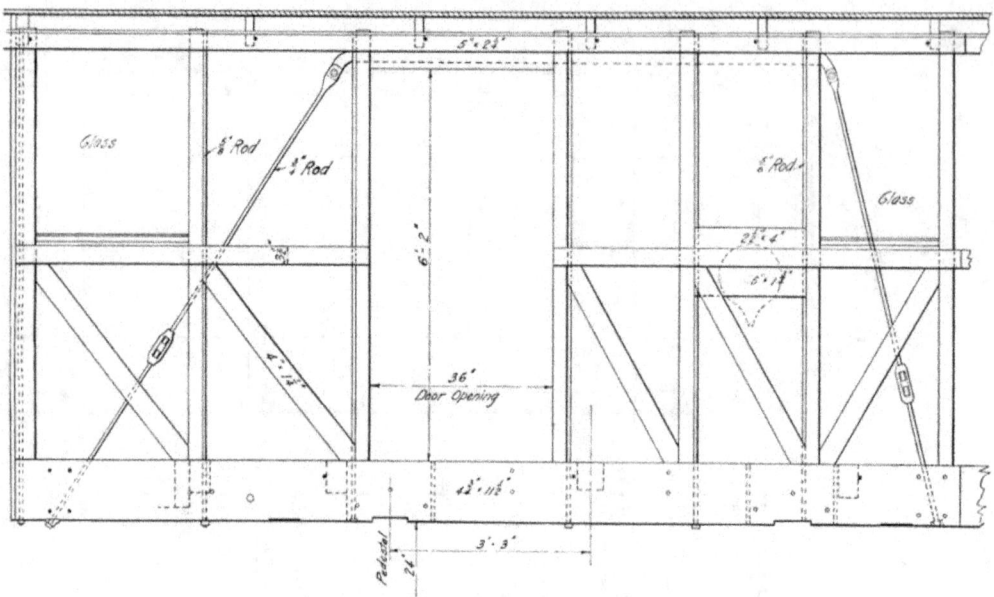

Fig. 406—Side Framing of Single-Truck, Double-End Shear Plow
The J. G. Brill Company, Builder

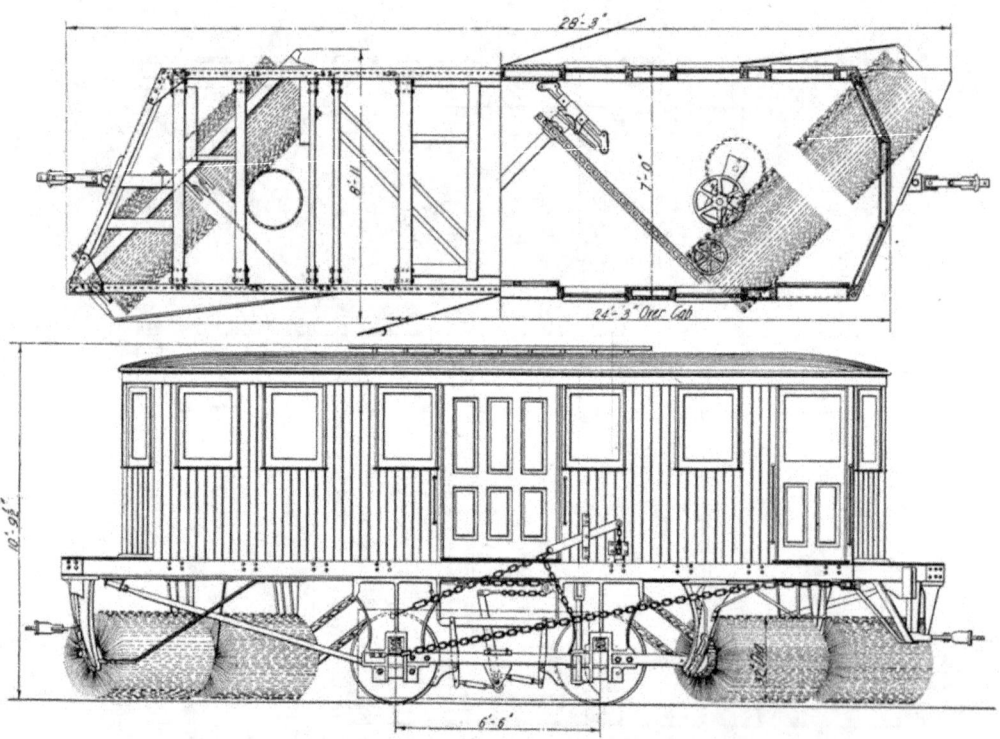

Figs. 407-408—Plan and Side Elevation of Single-Truck, Double-End, Long-Broom Snow Sweeper
McGuire-Cummings Manufacturing Company, Builder

(Exterior view of this sweeper is shown in Fig. 214.)

CAR BODY FRAMING, Snow Plow

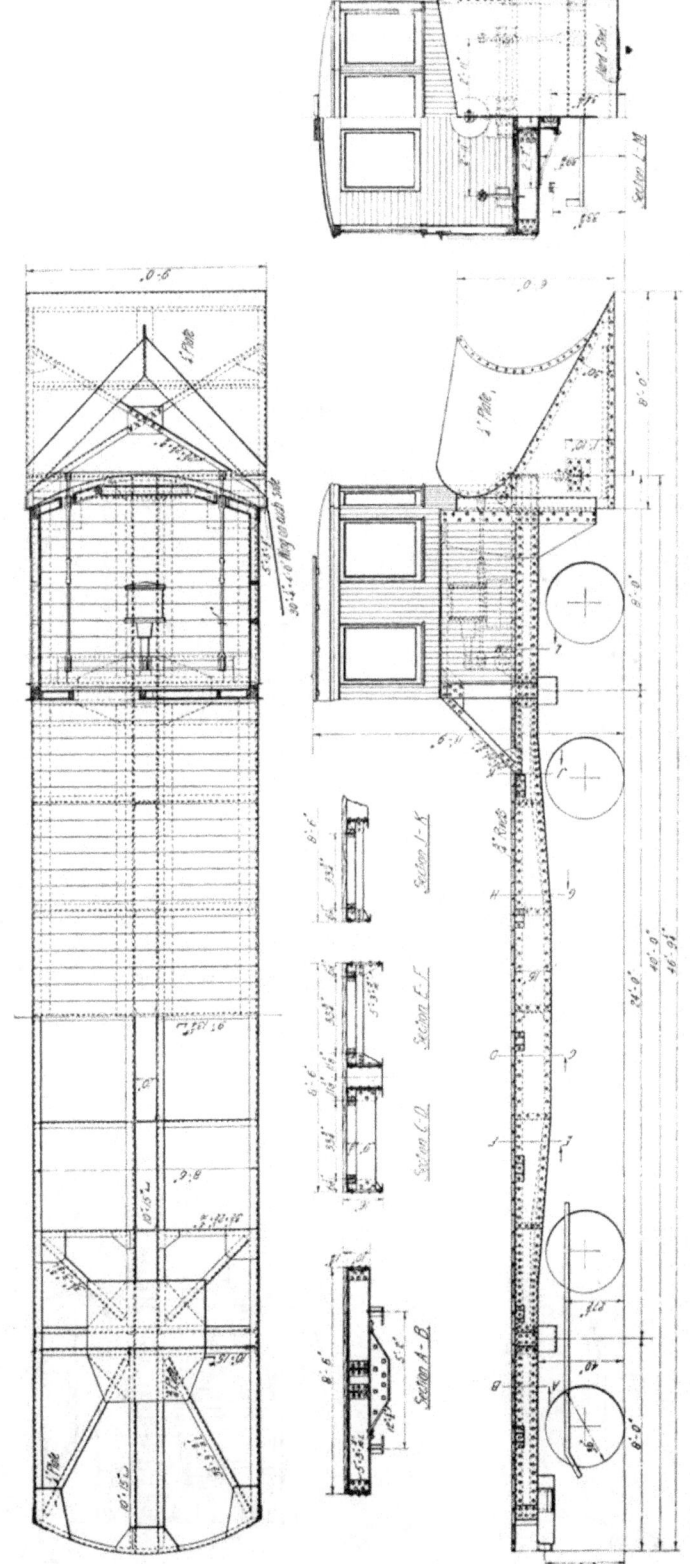

Figs. 409-414—Plan, Elevations and Details of Framing of Steel Underframe Motor Flat Car with Detachable Nose Plow; Buffalo, Lockport & Rochester Railway. McGuire-Cummings Manufacturing Company, Builder

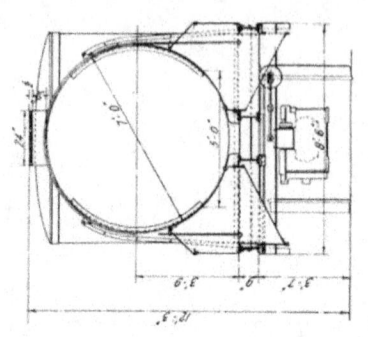
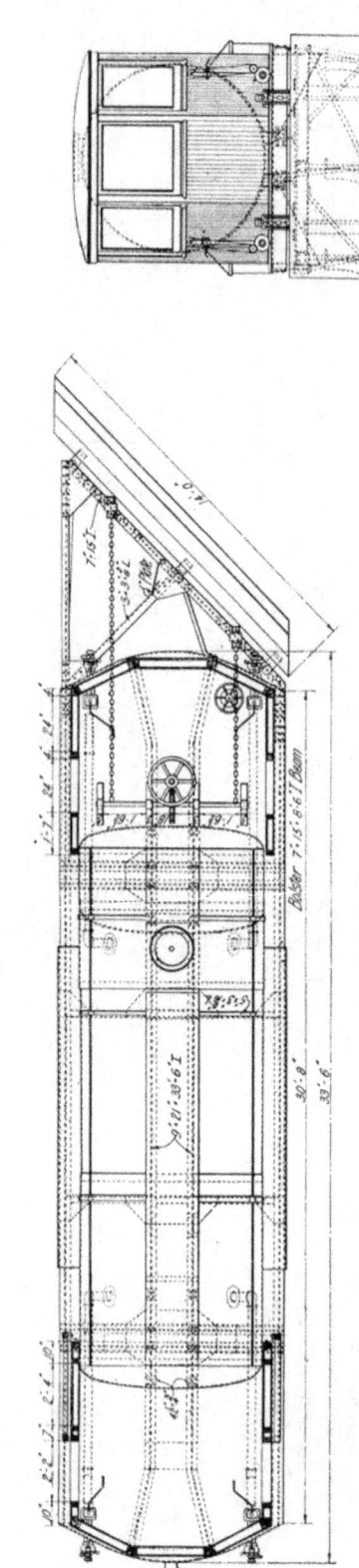
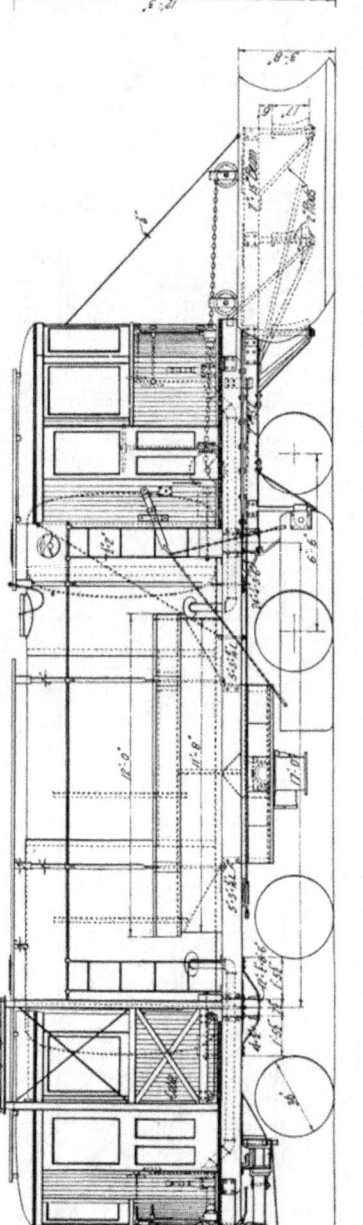

Figs. 415-418—Plan, Elevations and Section of Combination Sprinkler and Line Car with Detachable Shear Plow; Peoria Railway Terminal Company. McGuire-Cummings Manufacturing Company, Builder

(Exterior view of this car is shown in Fig. 225.)

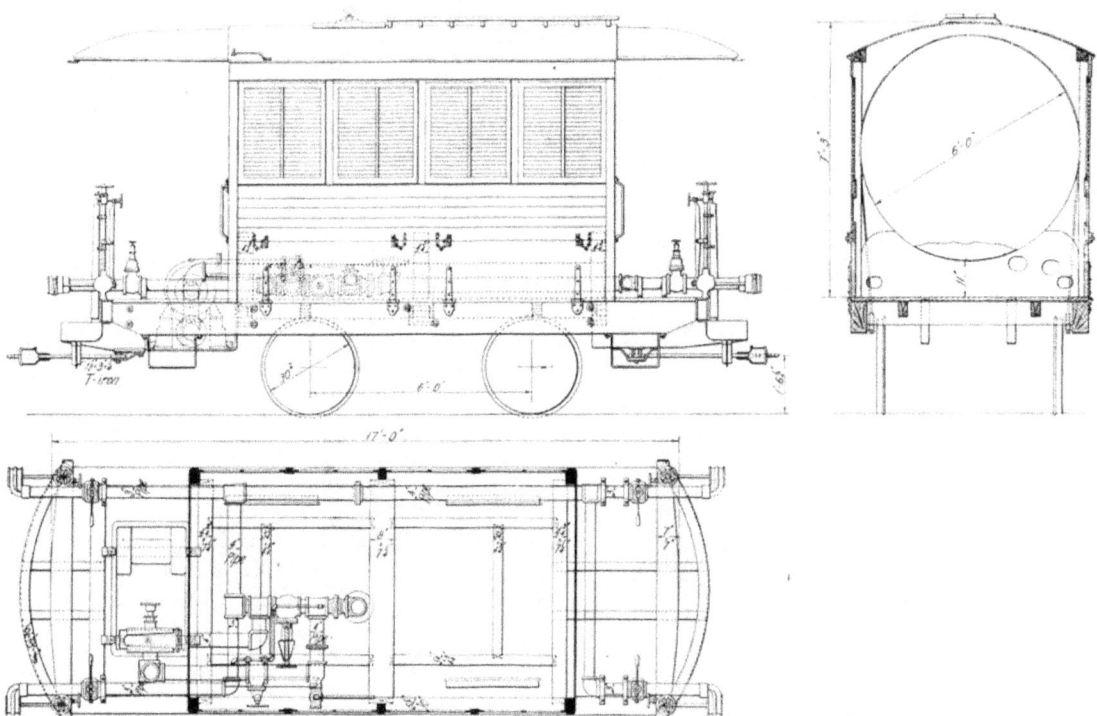

Figs. 419-421—Plan, Elevation and Section of 2,480-Gallon, Single-Truck, Centrifugal Sprinkler with Covered Tank
The J. G. Brill Company, Builder

(Exterior view of this sprinkler is shown in Fig. 223.)

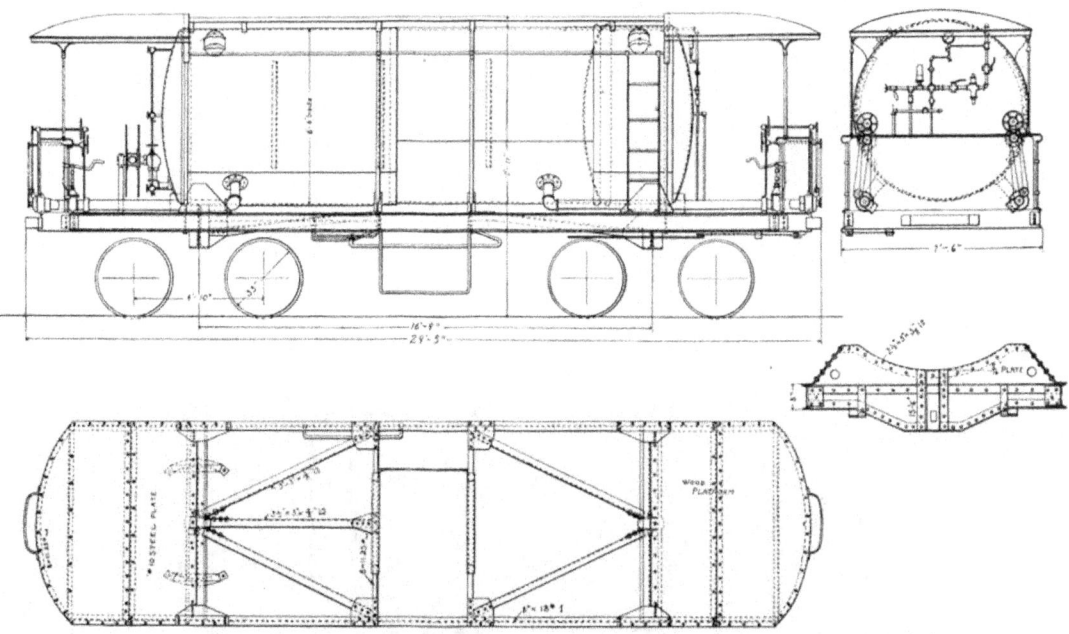

Figs. 422-425—Plan and Side and End Elevations of Double-Truck, 4,000-Gallon Pneumatic Sprinkler; Chicago Railways
McGuire-Cummings Manufacturing Company, Builder

(Exterior view of this sprinkler is shown in Fig. 226.)

CAR BODY FRAMING, Sprinkler

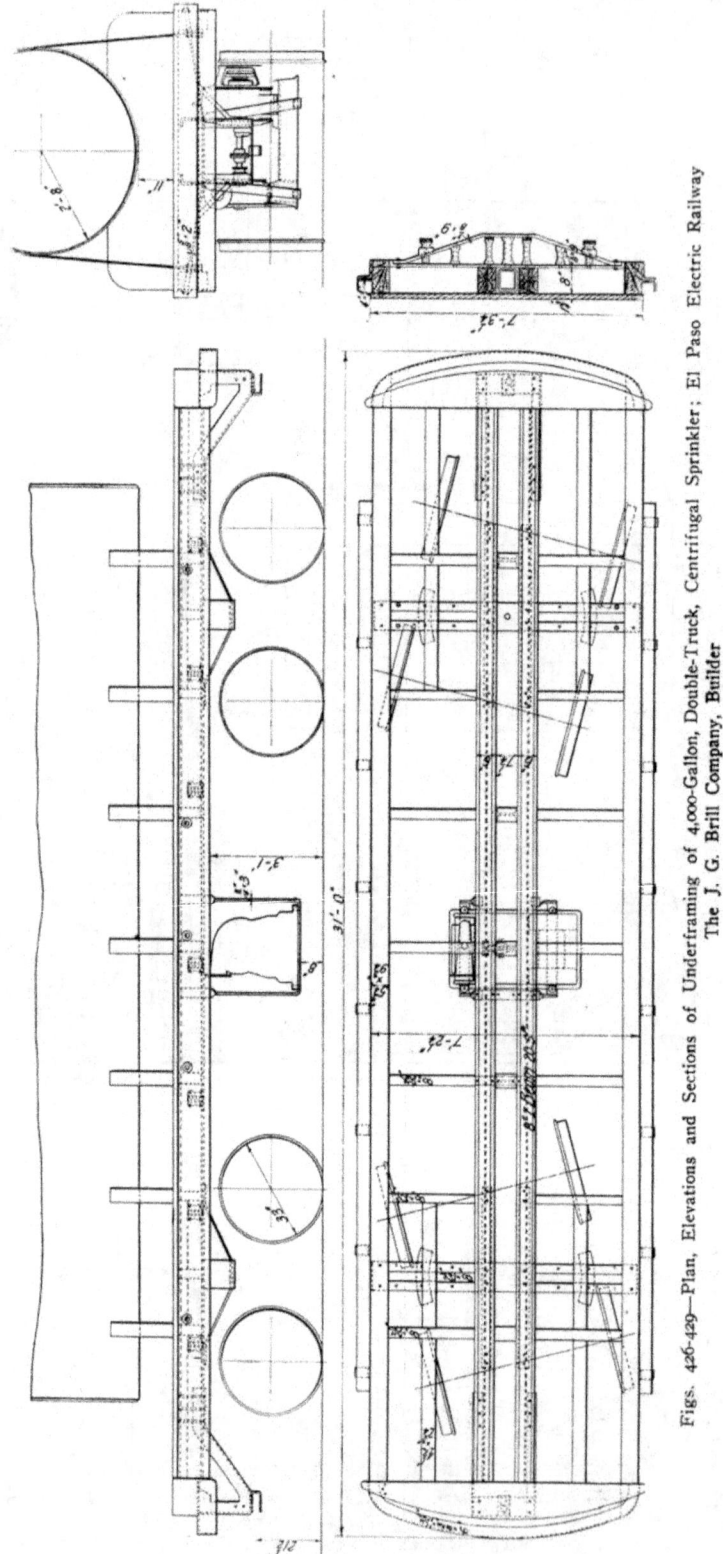

Figs. 426-429—Plan, Elevations and Sections of Underframing of 4,000-Gallon, Double-Truck, Centrifugal Sprinkler; El Paso Electric Railway. The J. G. Brill Company, Builder

CAR BODY FRAMING, Substation Car

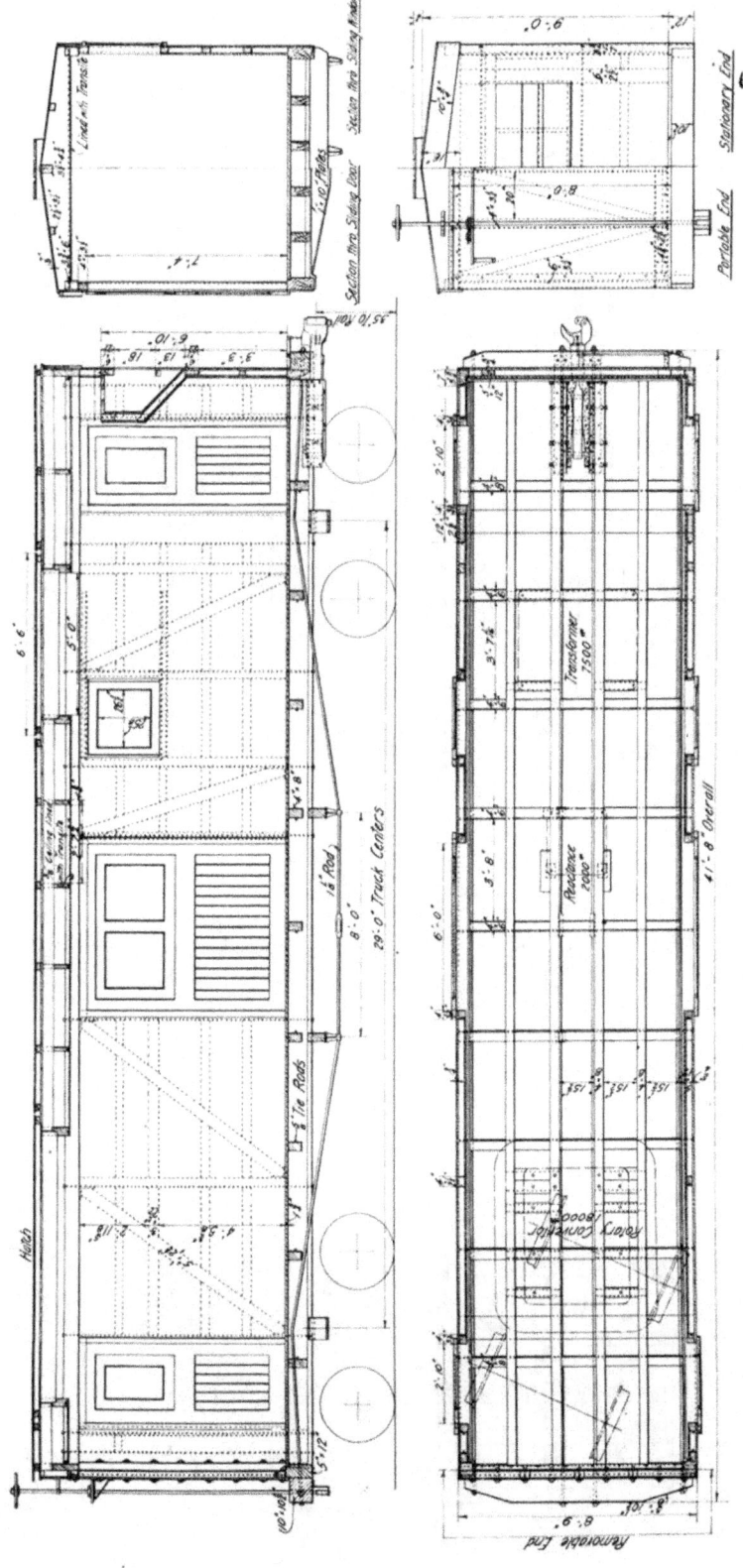

Figs. 430-433—Plan, Sections and End Elevation of Framing of Portable Substation Car; Chicago, South Bend & Northern Indiana Railway. Cincinnati Car Company, Builder

(Exterior view of this car is shown in Fig. 245.)

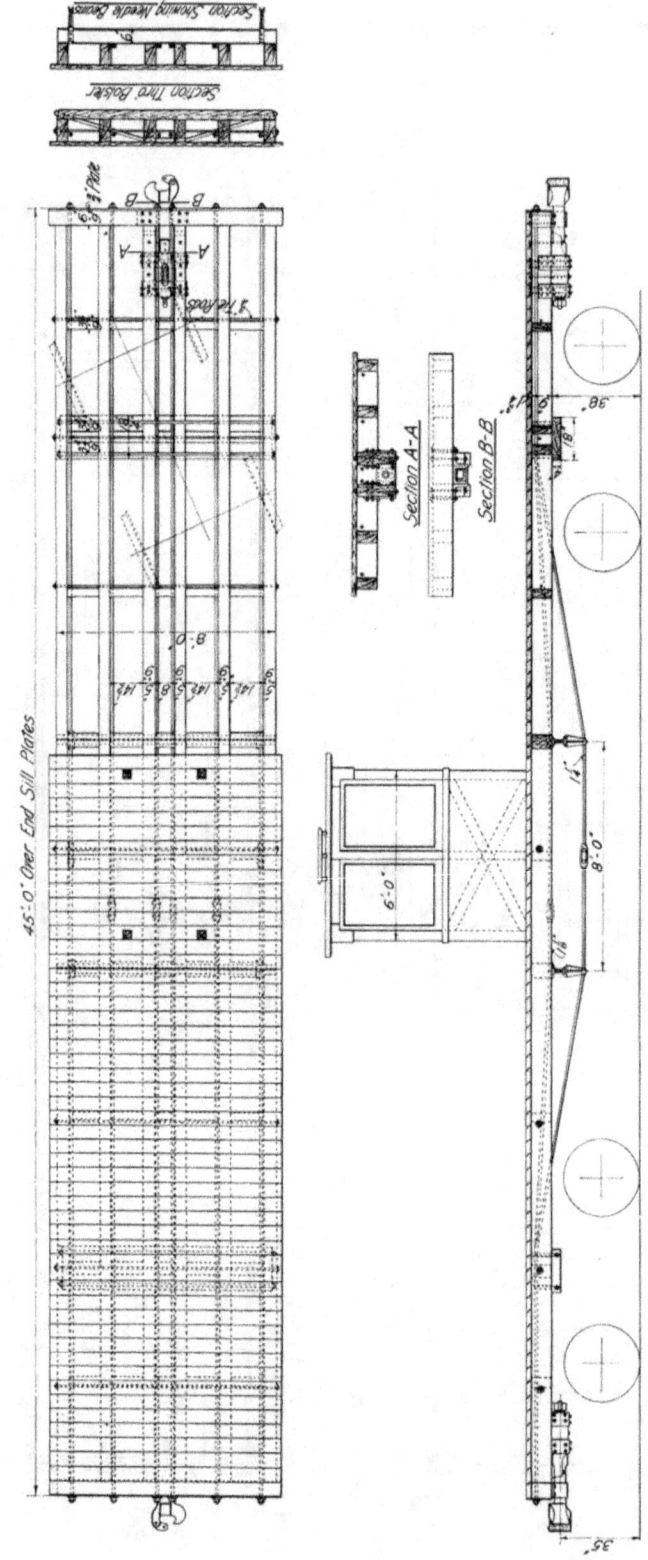

Figs. 434-439—Plan, Elevation and Sections of Motor Flat Car with Center Cab; Muncie & Portland Traction Company
Cincinnati Car Company, Builder

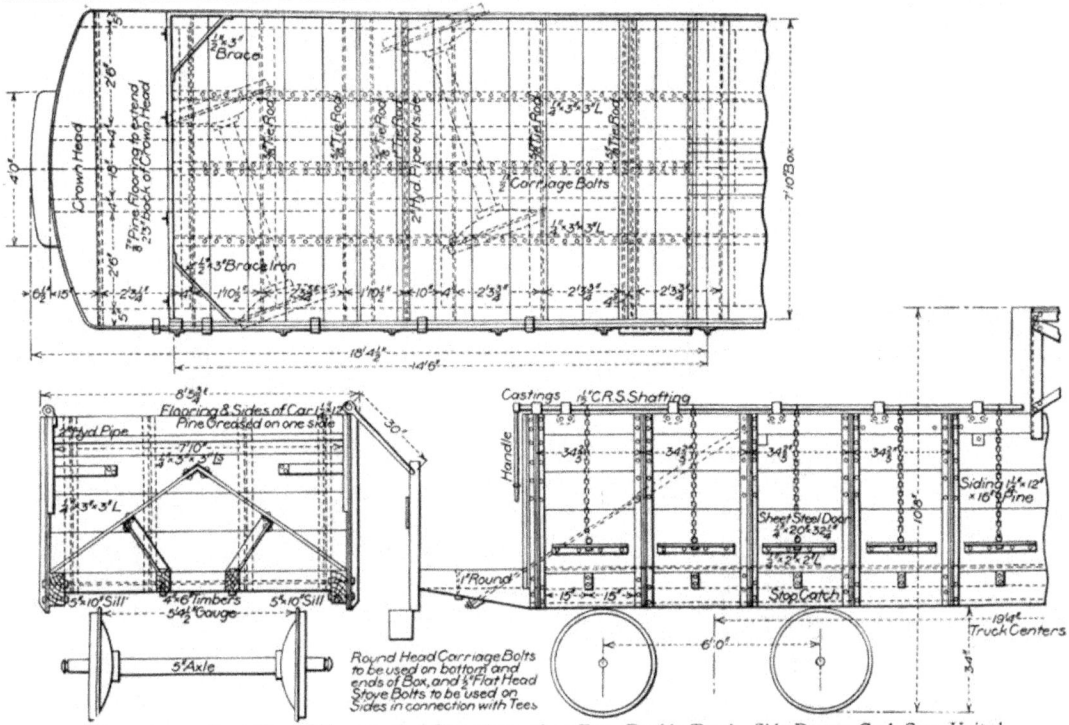

Figs. 440-442—Part Plan, Side and End Elevations of 15-Ton, Double-Truck, Side-Dump, Coal Car; United Railways & Electric Company, Baltimore, Md.
Built in Company's Shops

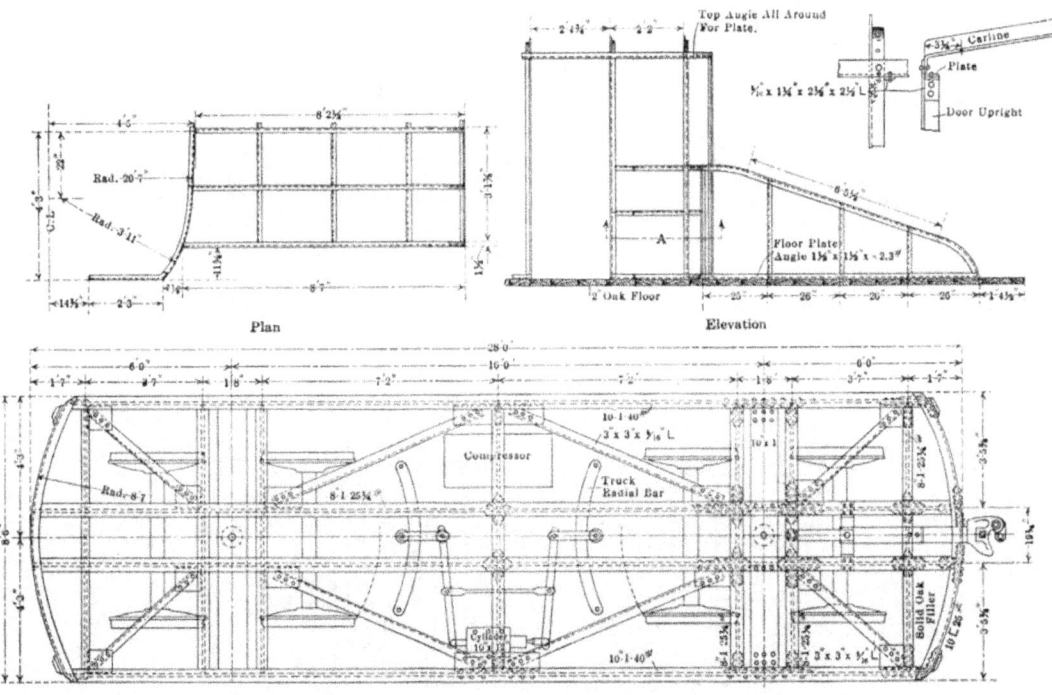

Figs. 443-447—Plan and Details of Cab Framing of 40-Ton Electric Locomotive; Chicago City Railway
Built in Company's Shops

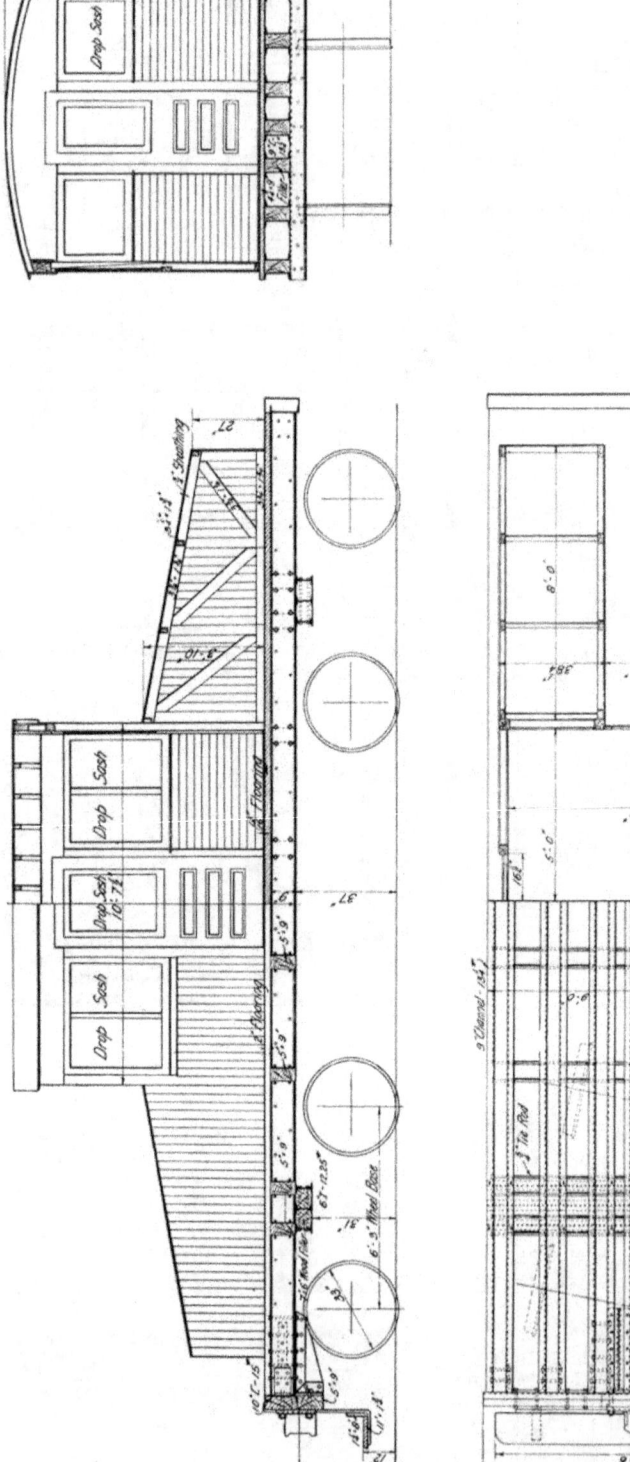

Figs. 448-450—Plan, Elevation and Cross-Section of Double-Truck Electric Switching Locomotive; Sapulpa Interurban Railway
St. Louis Car Company, Builder

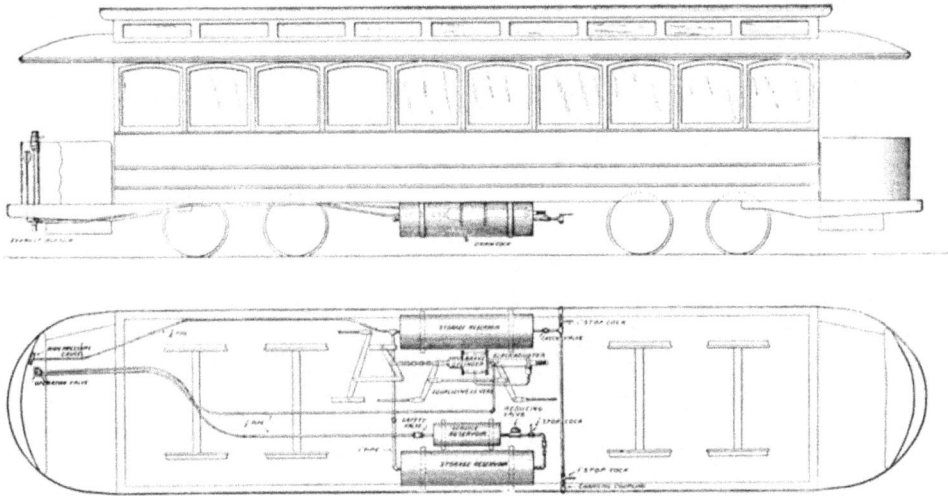

Figs. 451-452—Diagram of Storage Air Brake Equipment, Straight-Air Type, for Single Car

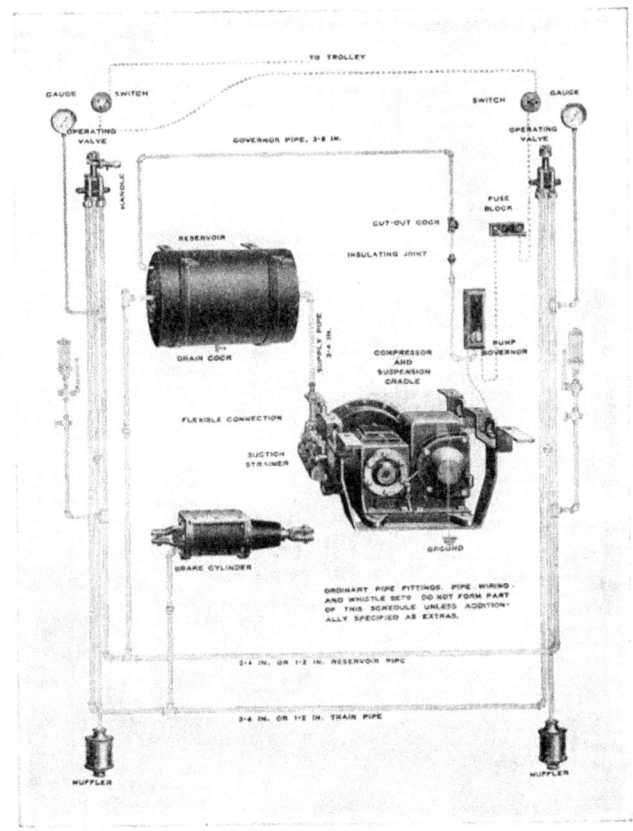

Fig. 453—Diagram of Straight-Air Brake Equipment, Schedule SM-3, for Single-Motor Car

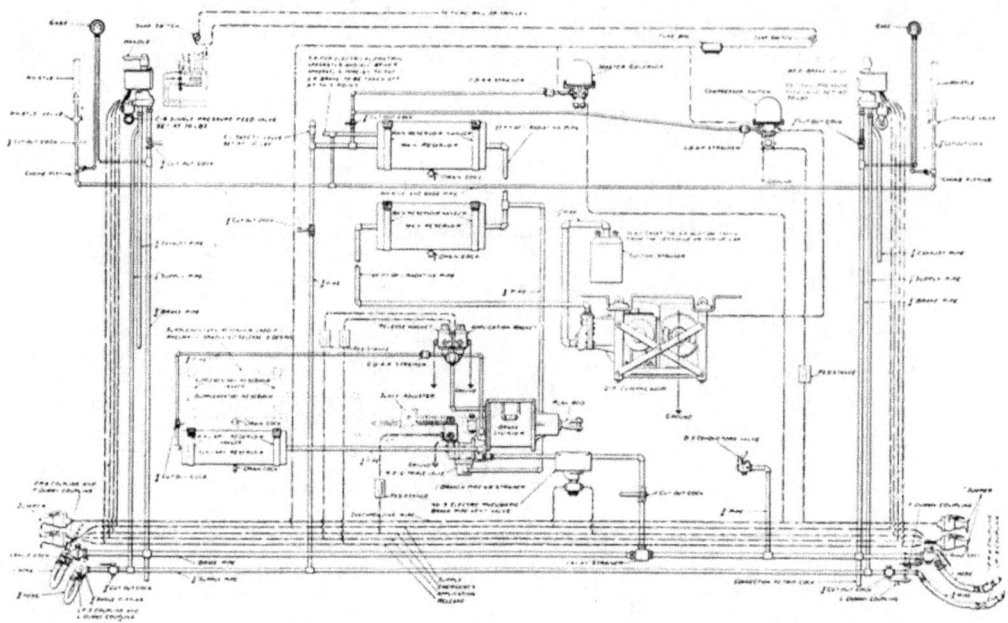

Fig. 454—Diagram of Electro-Pneumatic Brake Equipment, Schedule AMR-5-E, for High-Speed Electric Trains of Any Length

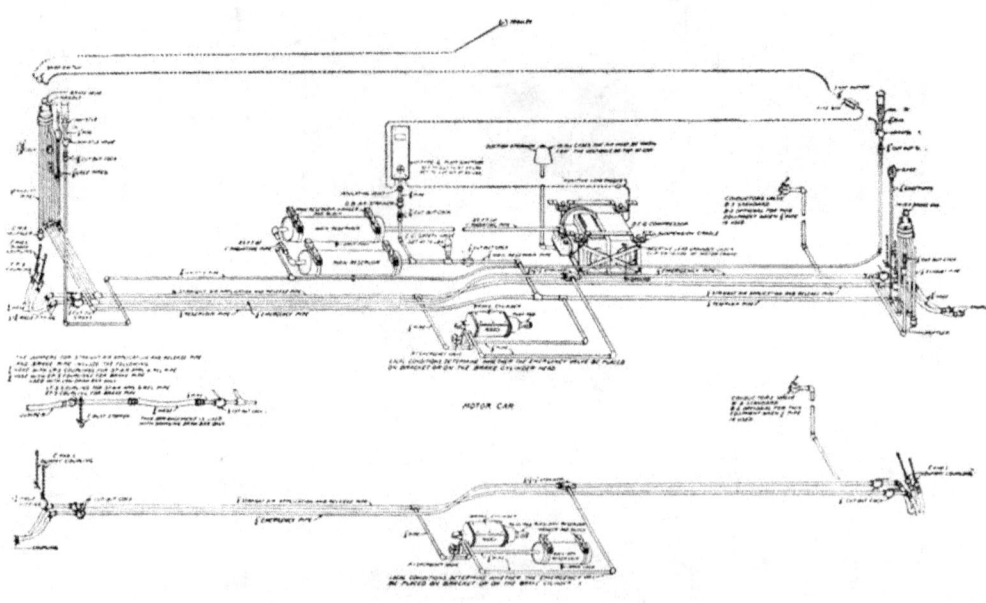

Fig. 455—Diagram of Straight-Air Brake Equipment with Emergency Feature, Schedule SME, for Motor Car and Trailer

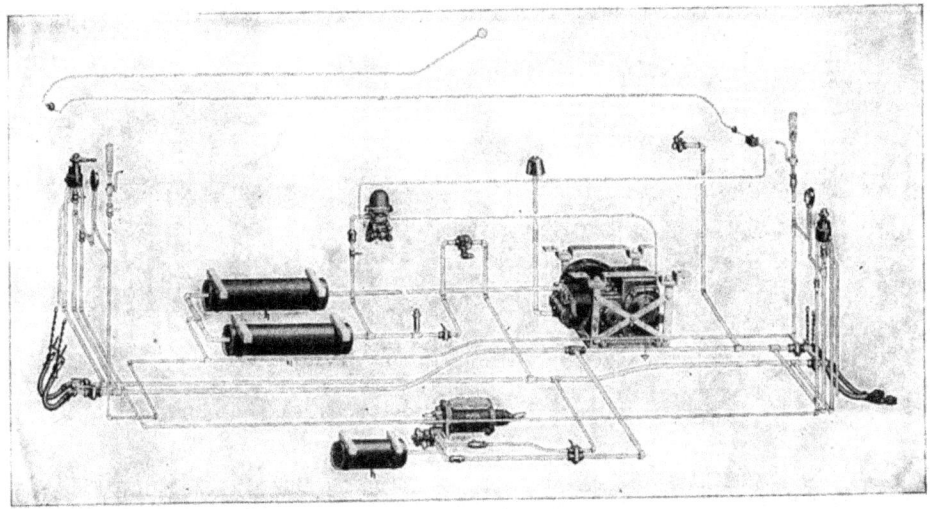

Fig. 456—Diagram of Automatic Air-Brake Equipment, Schedule AMM, for Electric Trains of Any Length

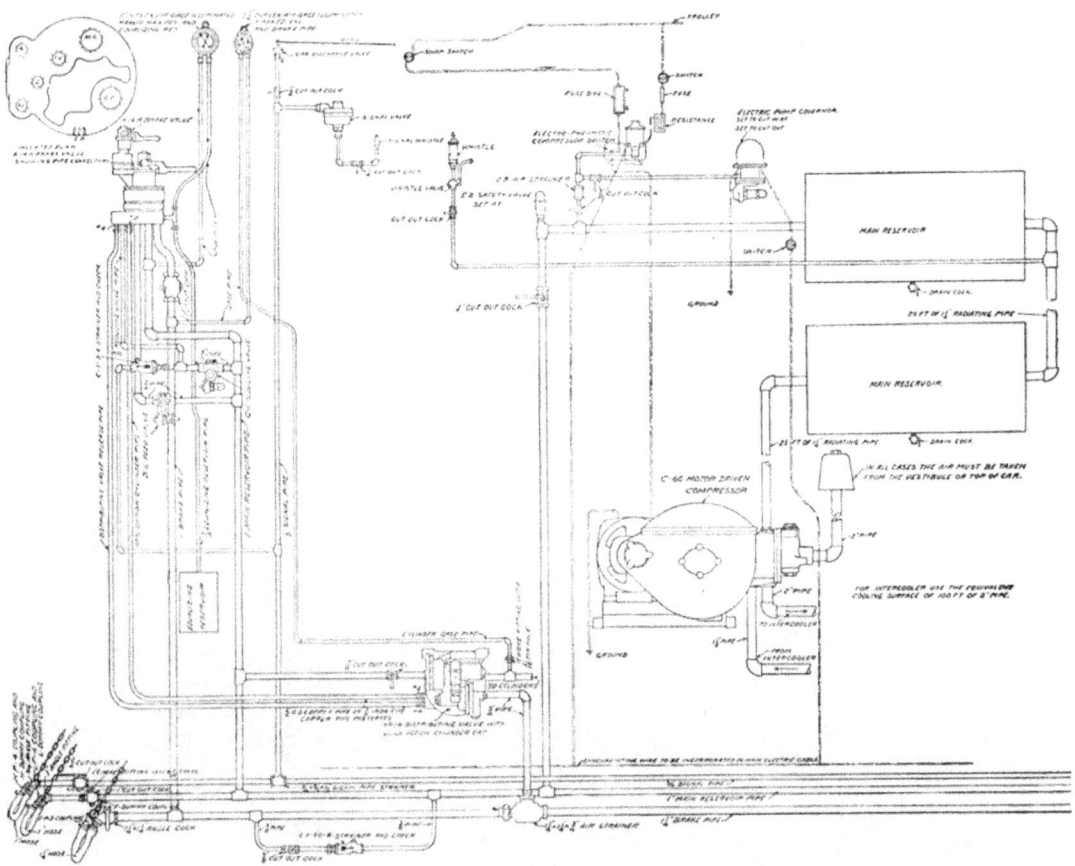

Fig. 457—Diagram of Combined Automatic and Independent Straight-Air Brake Equipment, Schedule EL, for Electric Locomotives

CAR BODY DETAILS, Air Brakes, Westinghouse

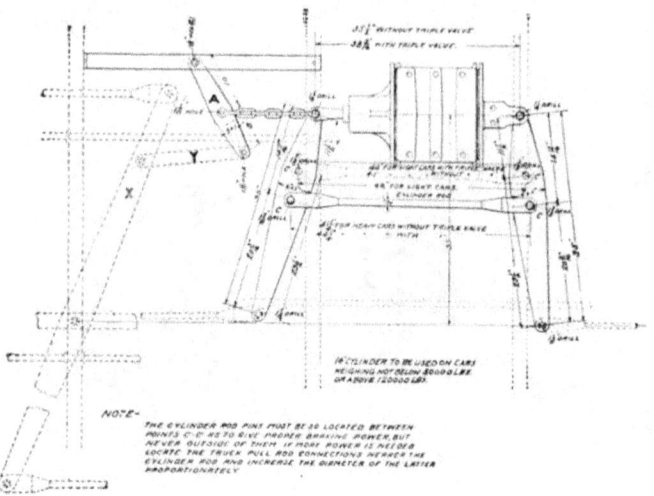

Fig. 458—Arrangement of Cylinder and Hand-Brake Levers for Car Equipped with 14-in. Brake Cylinder

Fig. 460—Air Compressor Switch Used with Governor Synchronizing System

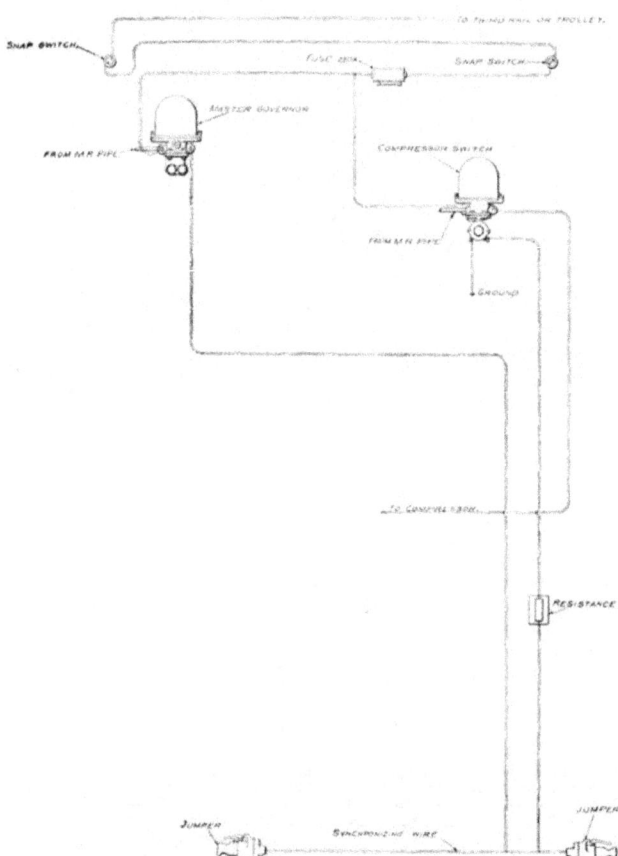

Fig. 459—Diagram of Connections for Air Compressor Governor Synchronizing System for Electric Trains Consisting of More than One Motor Car

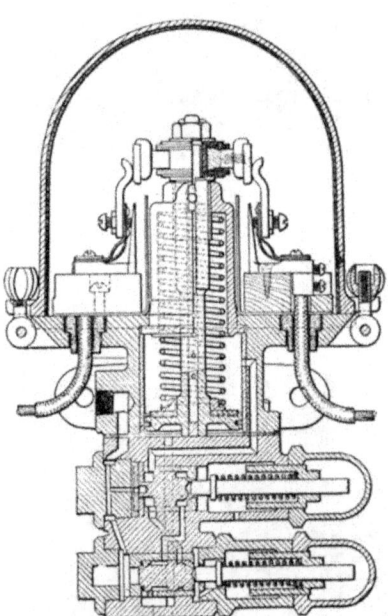

Fig. 461—Electro-Pneumatic Master Governor Used with Governor Synchronizing System

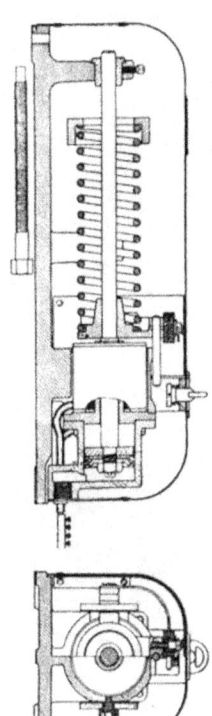

Fig. 464—Air Compressor Governor, Type J, with Cover Removed

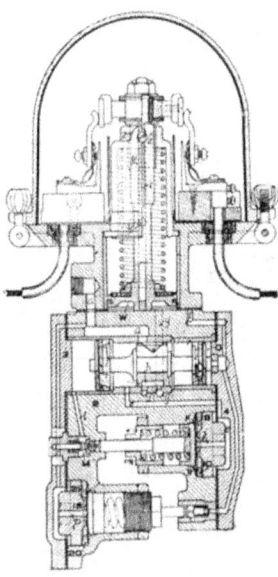

Fig. 465—Section Through Air Compressor Governor, Type J

Figs. 462-463—Air Compressor Governor, Type G

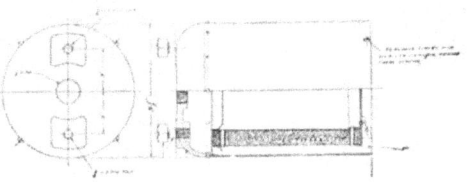

Fig. 466—Air Strainer for Intake of Motor-Driven Air Compressor

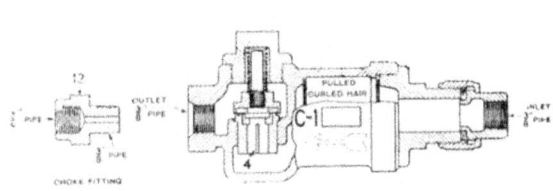

Figs. 467-468—Combined Air Strainer and Check Valve

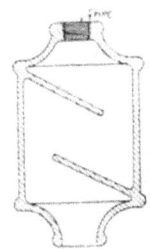

Fig. 469—Exhaust Muffler

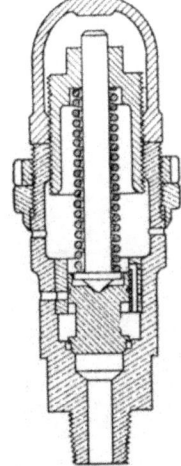

Fig. 470—Safety Valve, Type E-3, with Adjustable Blowdown

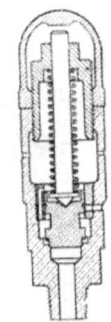

Fig. 471—Safety Valve, Type E-1, without Adjustable Blowdown

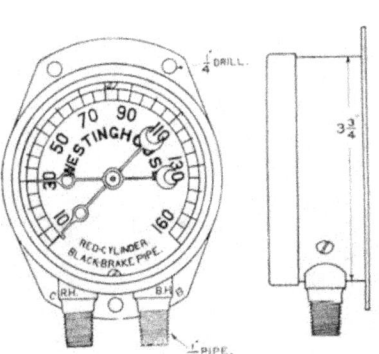

Figs. 472-473—Duplex Air Gage

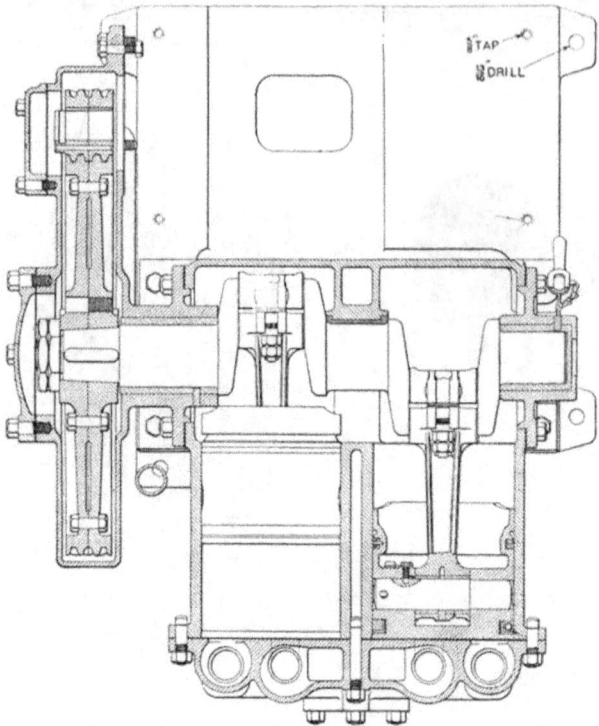

Fig. 476—Motor-Driven Air Compressor, Type D

Fig. 474—Sectional Plan View of Type D Motor-Driven Air Compressor

Fig. 477—Enclosed Fuse Box for Air Compressor Motor Circuit

Fig. 478—Open Fuse Block

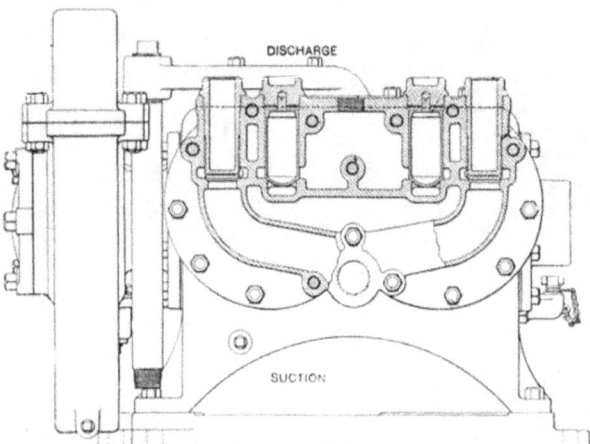

Fig. 475—Sectional End Elevation of Type D Motor-Driven Air Compressor

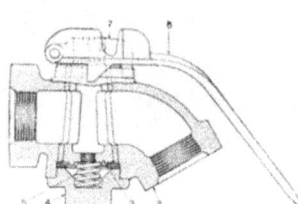

Fig. 479—Self-Locking Angle Cock

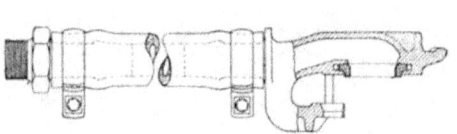

Fig. 480—Air Hose and Coupling

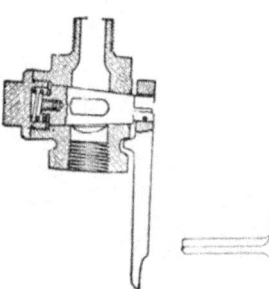
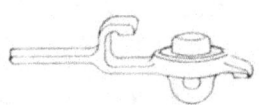

Fig. 481—Reservoir Drain Cock

Fig. 482—Dummy Hose Coupling

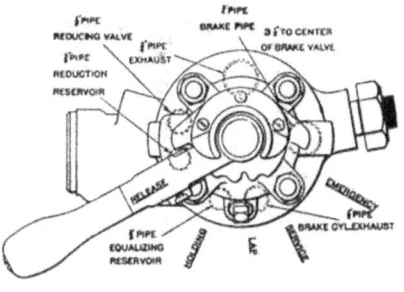

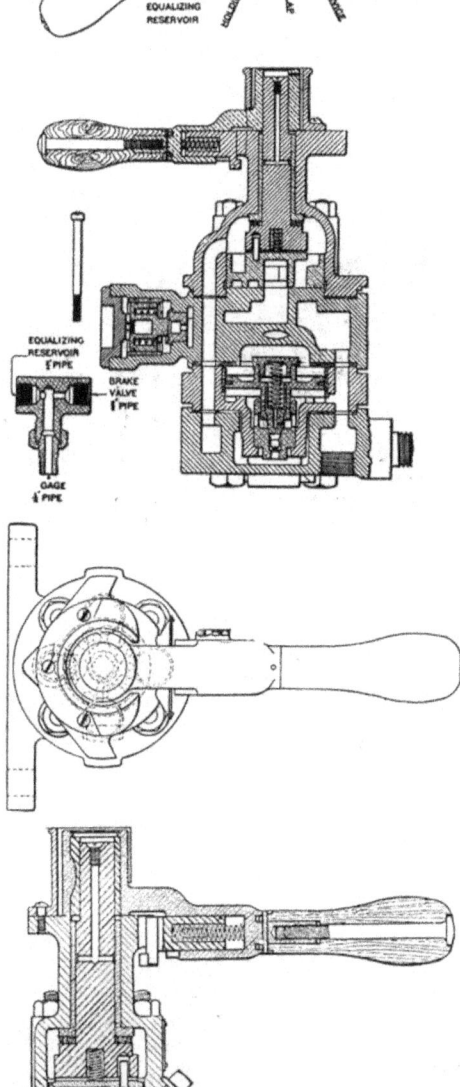

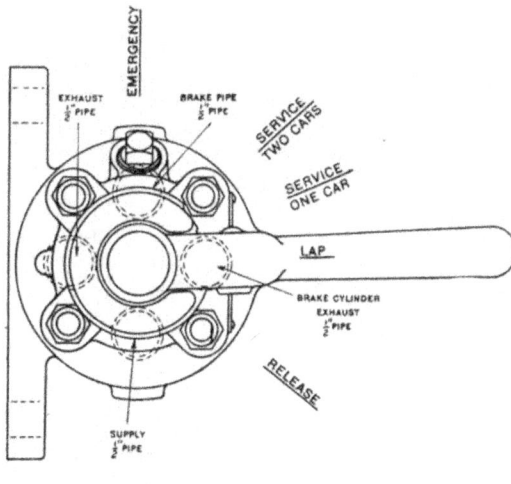

Figs. 483-484—Motorman's Brake Valve, Type M-19-C, for Automatic Air Brake Equipments on Trains of any Length. Has Collapsible Type of Equalizing Piston and Combined Direct and Equalized Brake Pipe Discharge

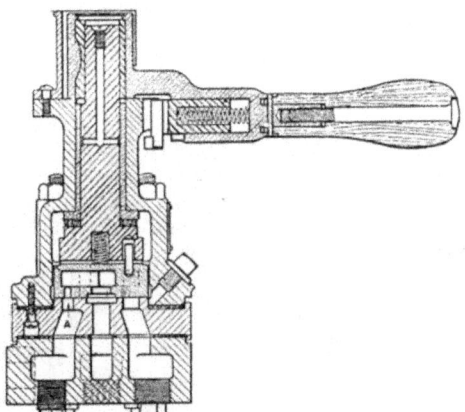

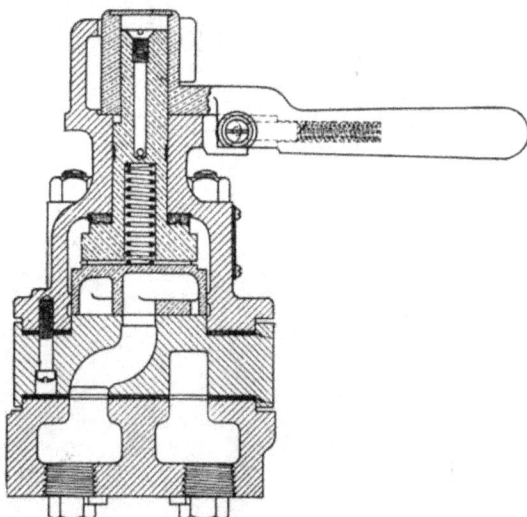

Figs. 485-486—Motorman's Brake Valve, Type SX-2, for Straight-Air Brake Equipments

Figs. 478-488—Motorman's Brake Valve, Type M-18, for Semi-Automatic Brake Equipments

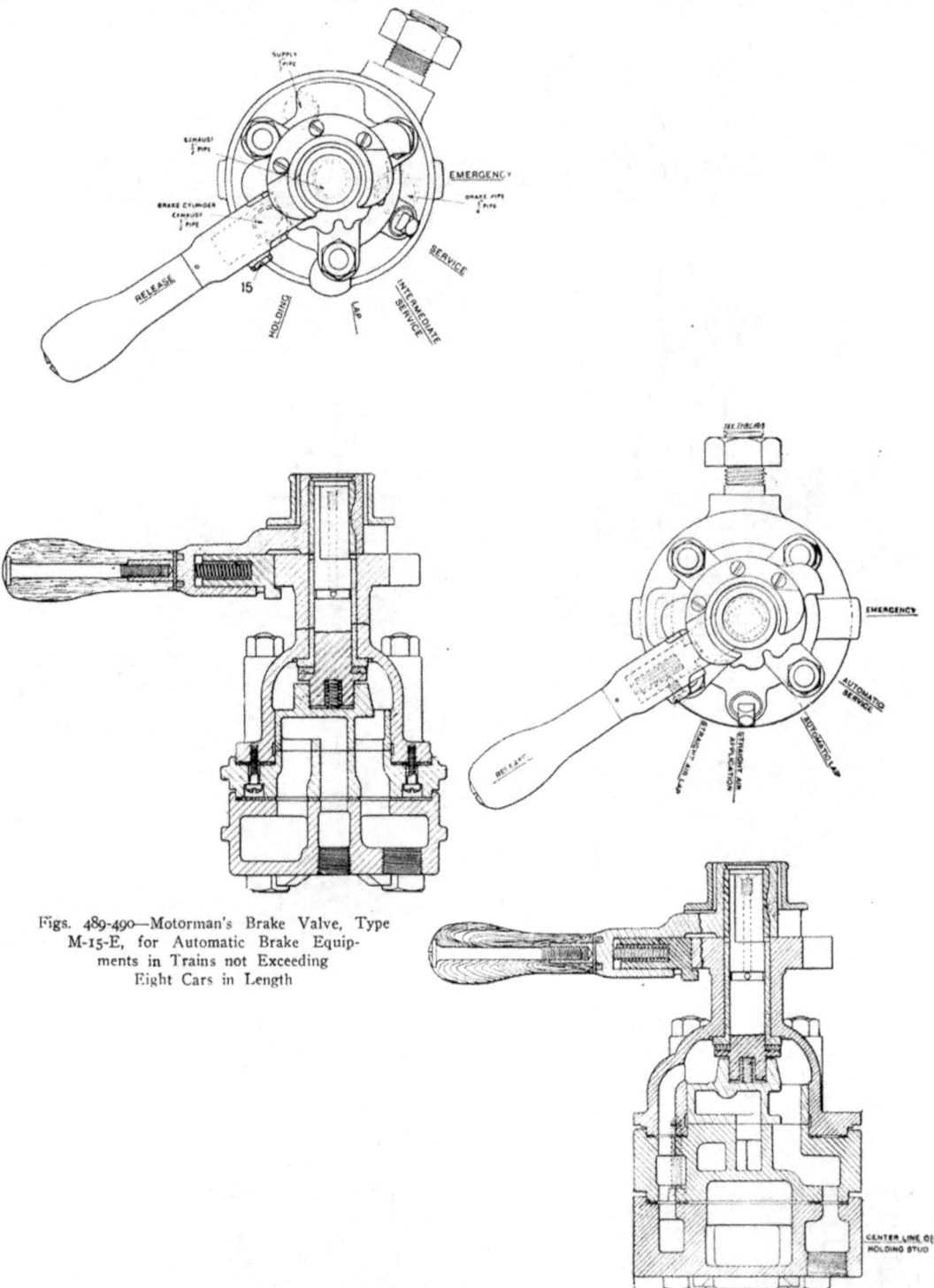

Figs. 489-490—Motorman's Brake Valve, Type M-15-E, for Automatic Brake Equipments in Trains not Exceeding Eight Cars in Length

Figs. 491-492—Motorman's Brake Valve, Type M-22, for Combined Automatic and Straight-Air Brake Equipments, Schedule AMM

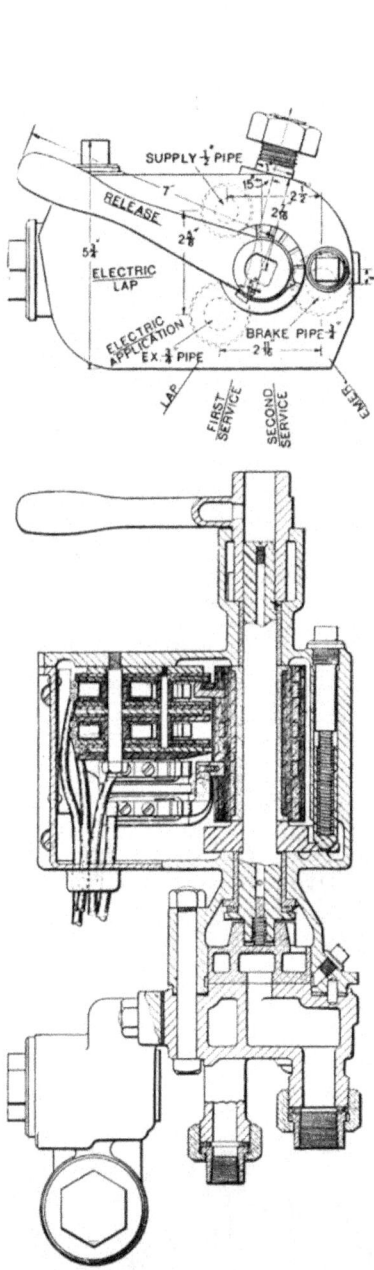

Figs. 493-494—Motorman's Brake Valve, Type ME-21, for Electro-Pneumatic Brake Equipments

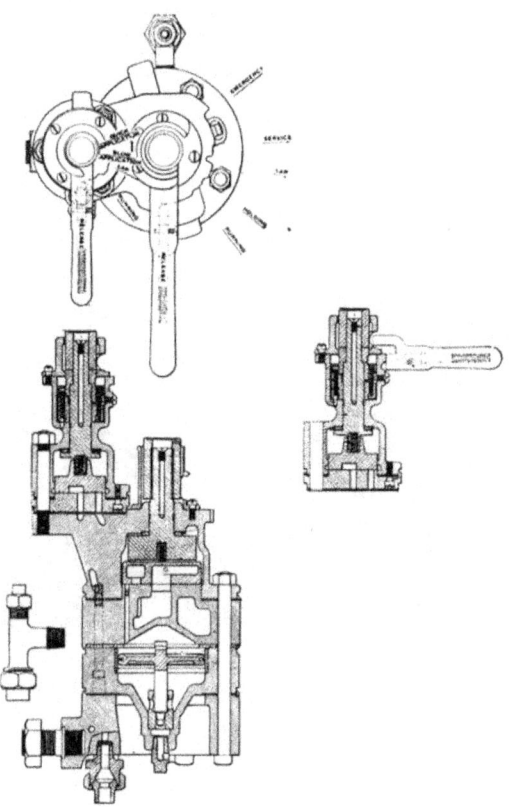

Figs. 495-497—Motorman's Brake Valve, Type K-14-A, for Combined Automatic and Straight-Air Electric Locomotive Brake Equipments

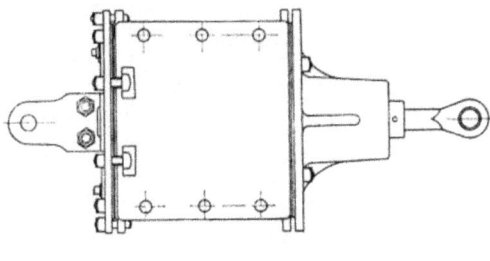

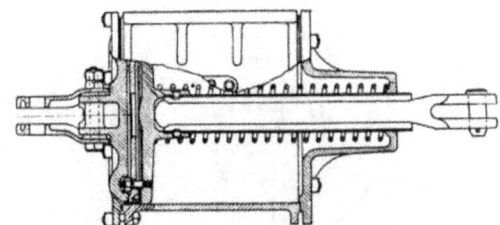

Figs. 498-499—Brake Cylinder, Type S, for Straight-Air Brake Equipments or for Automatic Brake Equipments when Triple Valve is Mounted on a Bracket

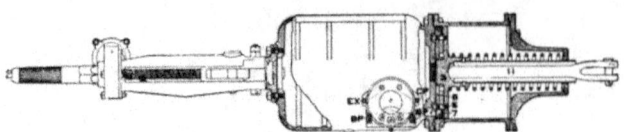

Fig. 500—Combined Brake Cylinder and Auxiliary Reservoir, Type T, with Automatic Slack Adjuster

Fig. 501—Single-Pressure Feed Valve, Type C-6

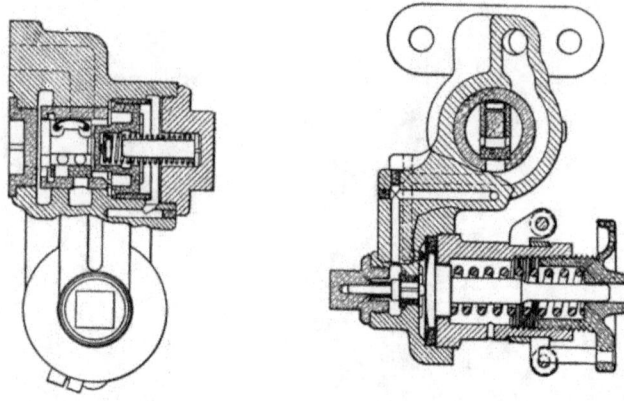

Figs. 502-503—Sectional Views of Double-Pressure Feed Valve, Type B-6

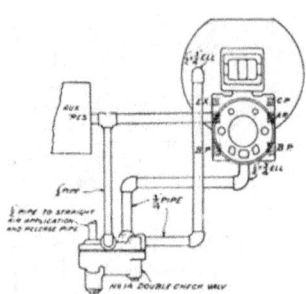

Fig. 504—Diagram of Connections Between Brake-Cylinder Head and Double Check Valve of Combined Automatic and Straight-Air Brake Equipments, Schedule AMM

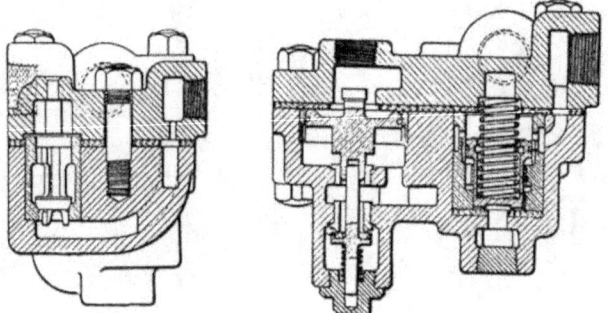

Figs. 505-506—Sections of No. 14 Double Check Valve Used with Combined Automatic and Straight-Air Brake Equipments, Schedule AMM

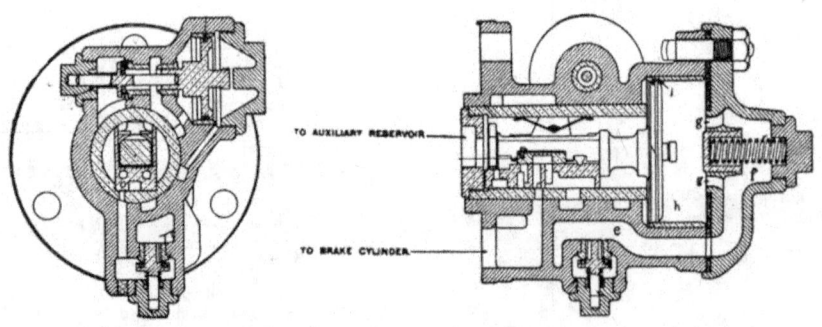

Figs. 507-508—Triple Valve, Type M, Used with Automatic Air Brake Equipment, Schedule AMM

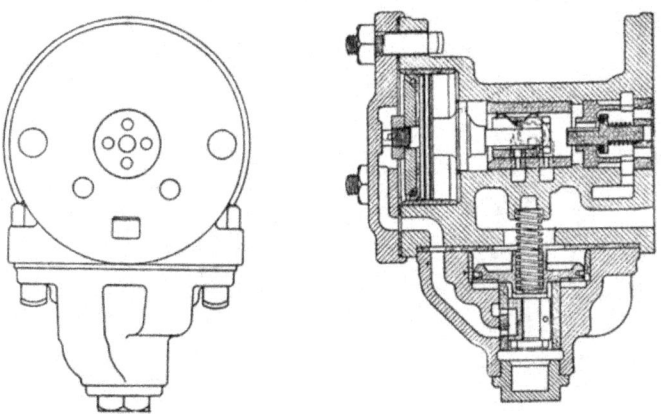

Figs. 509-510—Emergency Valve, Type D, Used with Straight-Air Brake Equipments Having Automatic Emergency Features

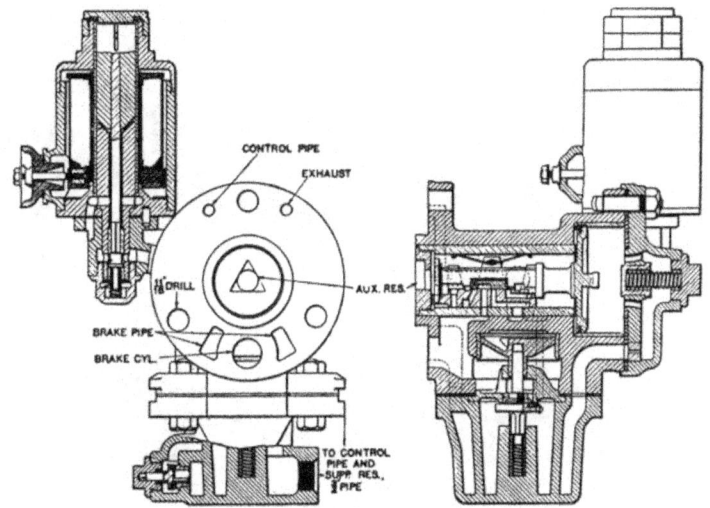

Figs. 511-512—Triple Valve, Type R-C, Used with Electro-Pneumatic Brake Equipments

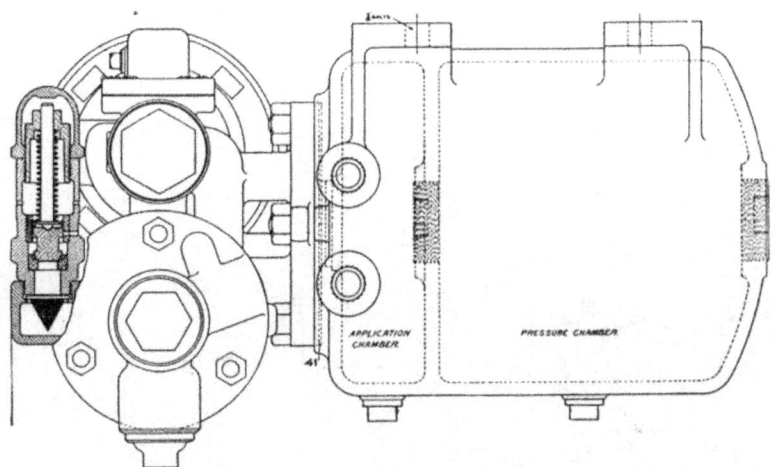

Fig. 513—Side View of No. 14 Distributing Valve and Double Compartment Reservoir, Used with Electric Locomotive Equipments

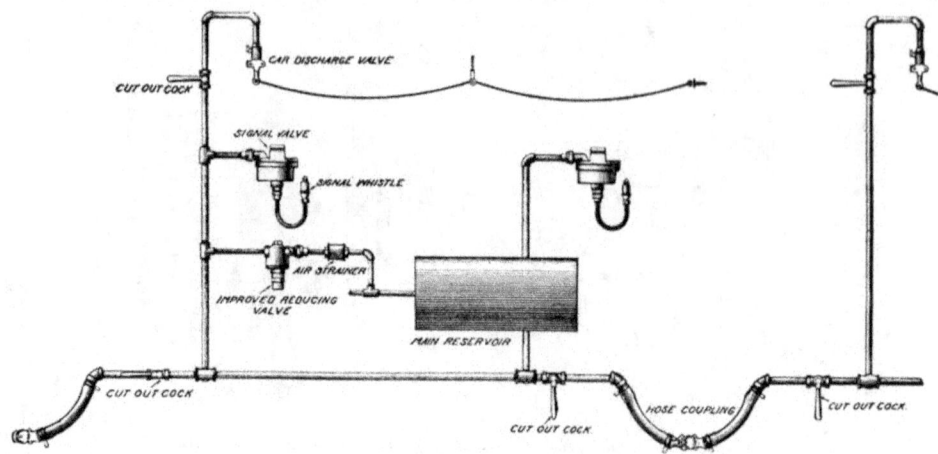

Fig. 514—Diagram of Pneumatic Train Signal Equipment

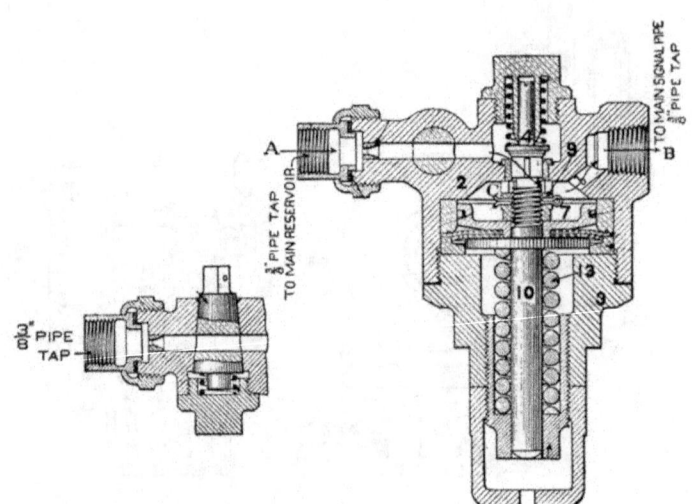

Figs. 515-516—Reducing Valve for Pneumatic Train Signal Equipments

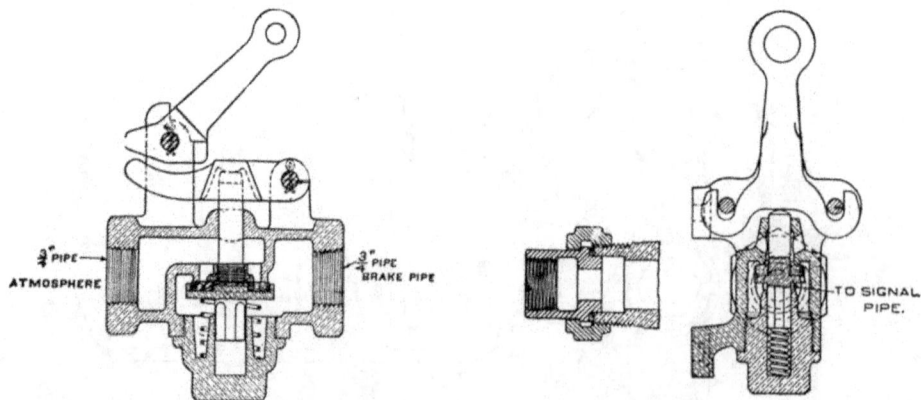

Fig. 517—Conductor's Valve, Type B-3, for Pneumatic Train Signal Equipments

Figs. 518-519—Car Discharge Valve for Pneumatic Train Signal Equipments

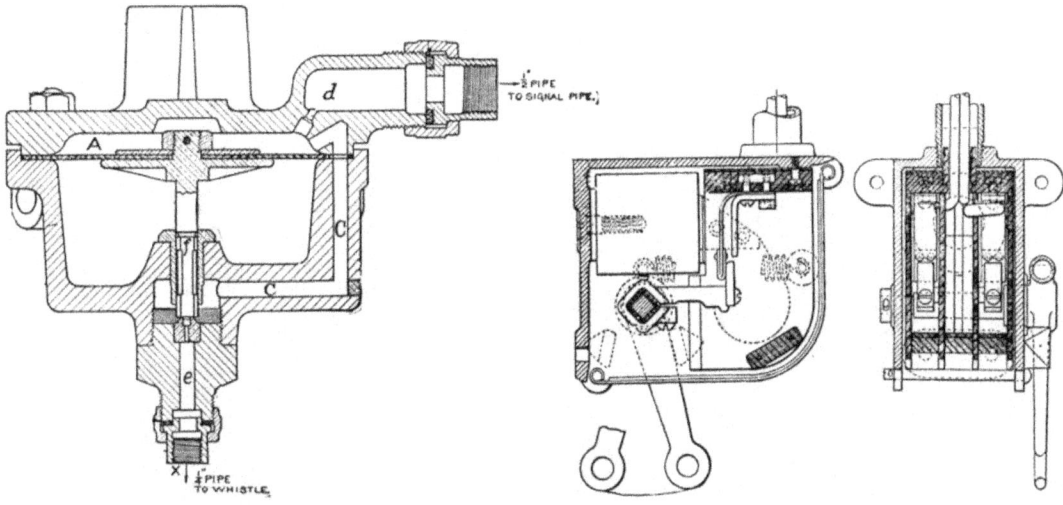

Fig. 520—Signal Valve for Pneumatic Train Signal Equipments

Figs. 521-522—Conductor's Switch for Electro-Pneumatic Train Signal Equipments

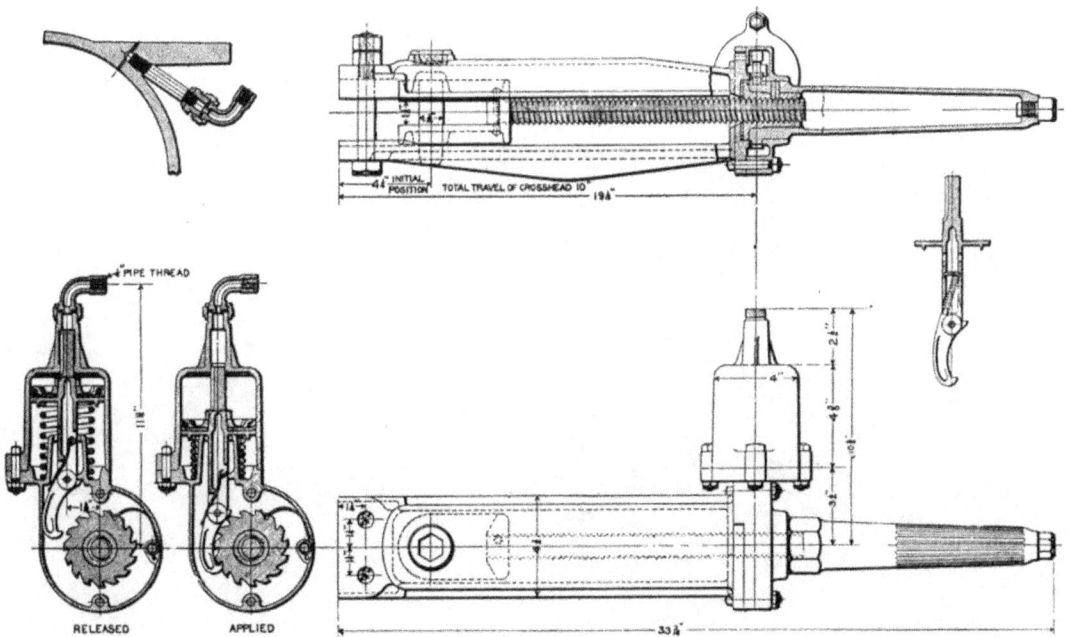

Figs. 523-528—Automatic Brake Slack Adjuster
American Brake Company

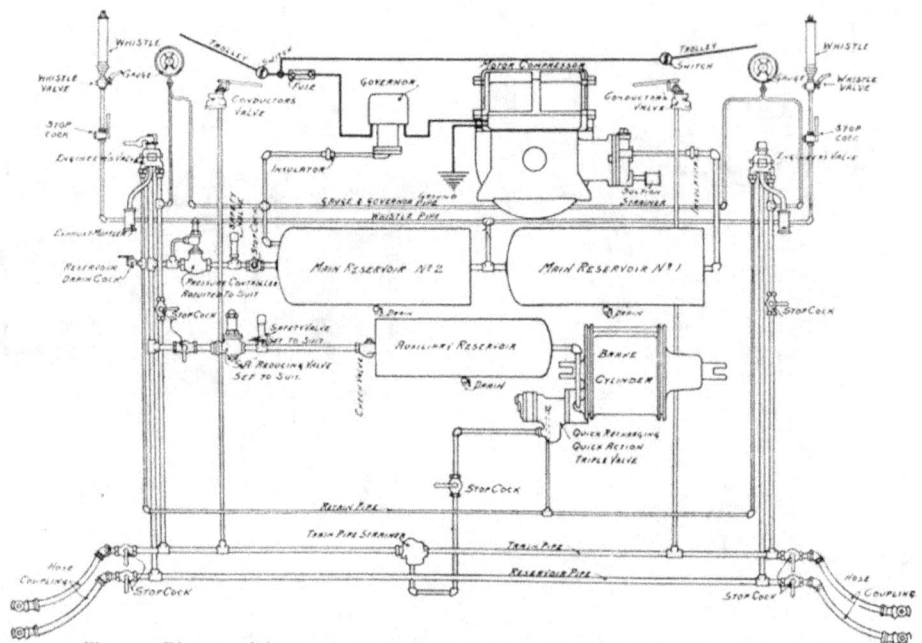

Fig. 529—Diagram of Automatic Air Brake Equipment with Quick-Recharging, Quick-Action, Triple Valve, for Trains of Any Number of Cars
Allis-Chalmers Company

Fig. 530—Motor-Driven Air Compressor, Type AA-6

Allis-Chalmers Company

Fig. 531—Air Compressor Governor, Type OB

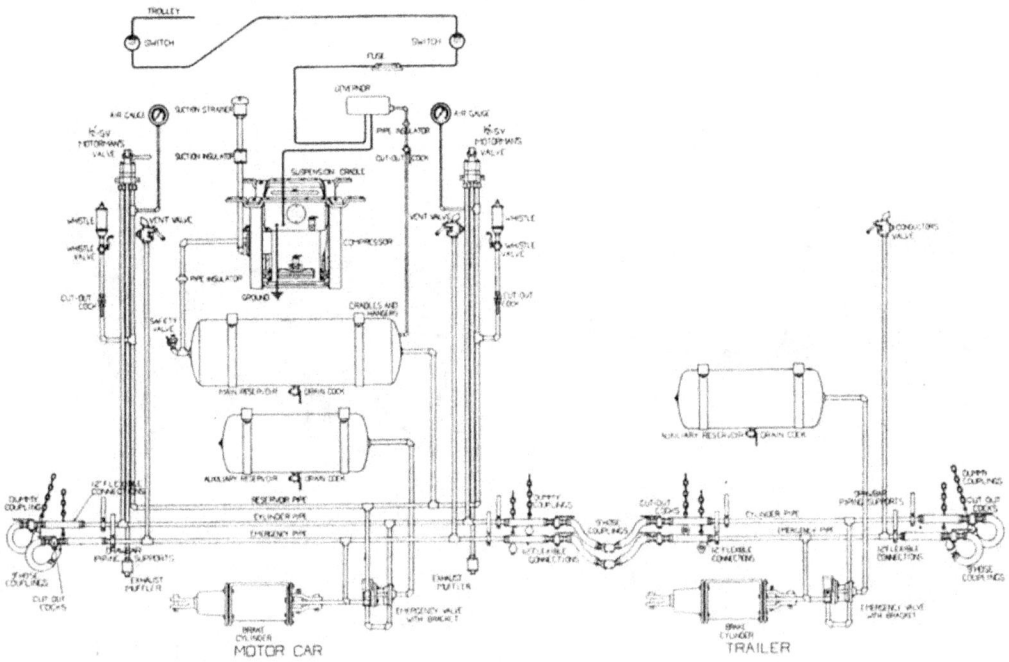

Fig. 532—Diagram of National, Type A, Emergency Straight-Air Brake Equipment for Motor Car and Trailer

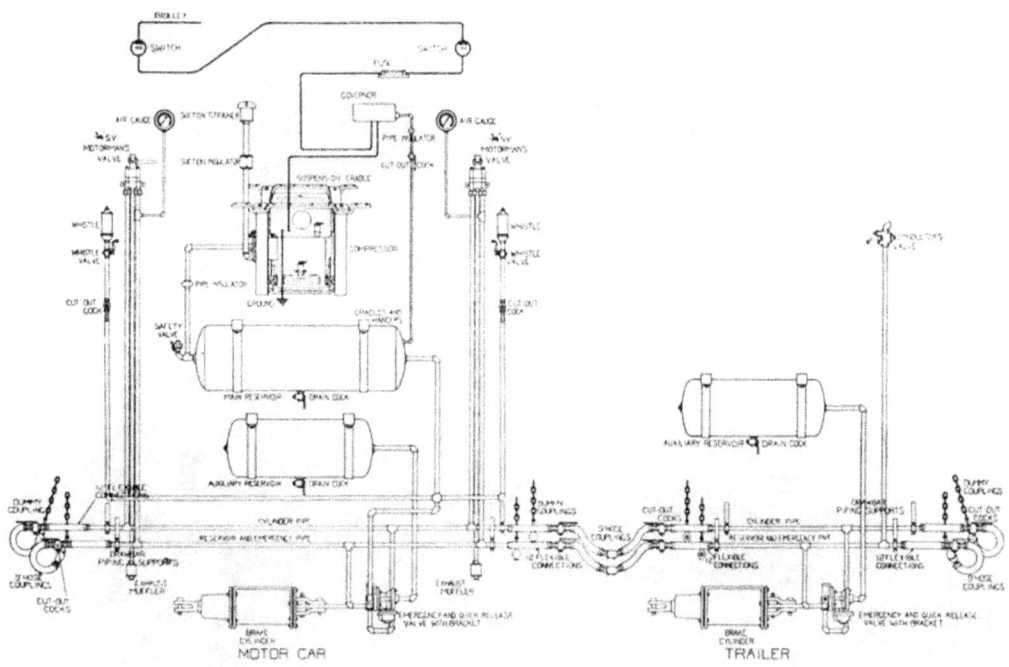

Fig. 533—Diagram of National, Type B, Emergency Straight-Air Brake Equipment for Motor Car and Trailer
National Brake & Electric Company

CAR BODY DETAILS, Air Brakes, National

Fig. 534—Motor-Driven Air Compressor, Type CC-3; Capacity, 35 cubic feet

Fig. 535—Motor-Driven Air Compressor, Type A-1; Capacity, 11 cubic feet

Fig. 536—Air Compressor Governor, Type R

Fig. 537—Air Compressor Governor, Type A

Fig. 538—Air Compressor Governor, Type N

Fig. 539—Emergency Valve, Type C

National Brake & Electric Company

Fig. 540—Emergency Valve, Type A

Fig. 541—Emergency Valve, Type B

Fig. 542—Motorman's Brake Valve; Piston Valve Type

Fig. 543—Motorman's Brake Valve; Slide Valve Type

National Brake & Electric Company

Fig. 544—Motor-Driven Air Compressor, Type CP-27

Fig. 545—Motor-Driven Air Compressor, Type CP-27, Dismantled

General Electric Company

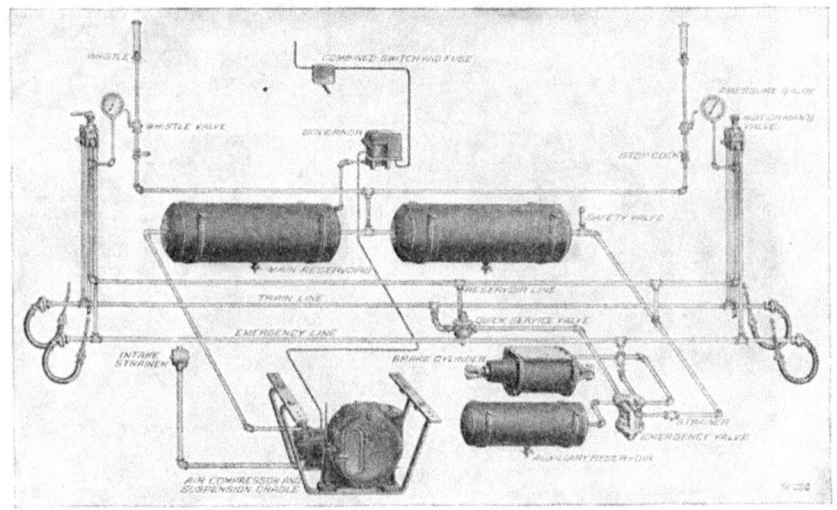

Fig. 546—Diagram of Emergency Straight-Air Brake Equipment for Motor Car and Trailer

Fig. 547—Air Compressor Governor, Exterior View

Fig. 548—Air Compressor Governor, Interior View

Fig. 549—Motorman's Brake Valve

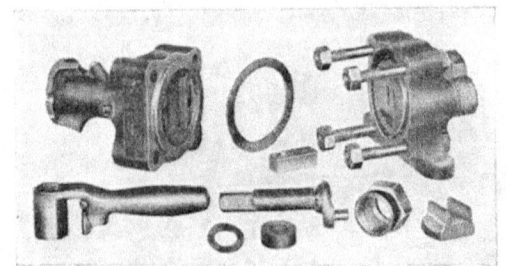

Figs. 550-559—Parts of Motorman's Brake Valve

CAR BODY DETAILS, Air Brake Accessories

Fig. 560—Emery Lubricator for Air Brake Cylinders
Emery Pneumatic Lubricator Co.

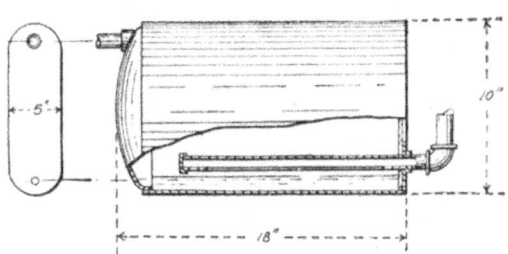

Fig. 561—Spencer Air Purifier for Air Brake Compressor Supply
Spencer Air Purifier Company

Fig. 562—Air Whistle Valve
Ohio Brass Company

Fig. 563—Air Whistle Valve
Electric Service Supplies Company

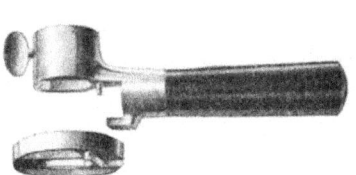

Fig. 564—Handle for Motorman's Brake Valve, Equipped with Automatic Lock
W. R. Kerschner

Fig. 565—Automatic Brake Valve Lock

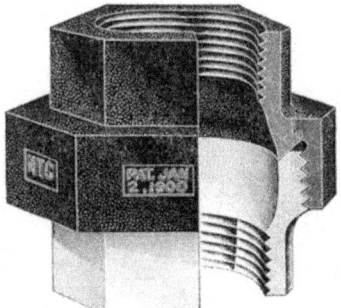

Fig. 566—Kewanee Union for Air Brake Piping

Fig. 567—Kewanee Flange Union for Air Brake Piping

National Tube Company

CAR BODY DETAILS, Brakes, Hand

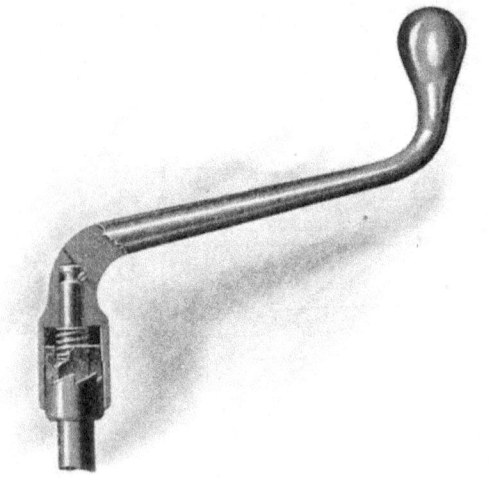

Fig. 568—Ratchet Brake Handle
The J. G. Brill Company

Fig. 569—Gravity Ratchet Brake Handle
Adams & Westlake Company

Fig. 570—Sectional View of Gravity Ratchet Brake Handle
A. & W. Co.

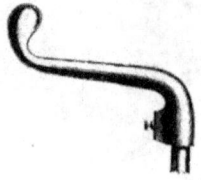

Fig. 571—Kling's Ratchet Brake Handle
Dayton Mfg. Co.

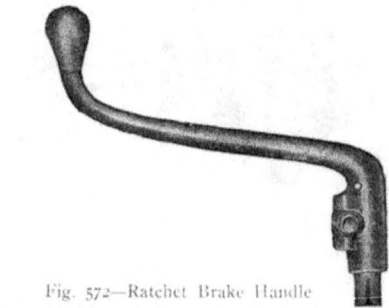

Fig. 572—Ratchet Brake Handle
Columbia Machine Works & Malleable Iron Company

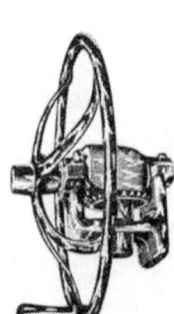

Fig. 573—Ratchet Wheel Brake
Dayton Mfg. Co.

Fig. 574—Wheel Brake and Staff
Dayton Mfg. Co.

Fig. 575—Geared Ratchet Wheel Brake
The J. G. Brill Co.

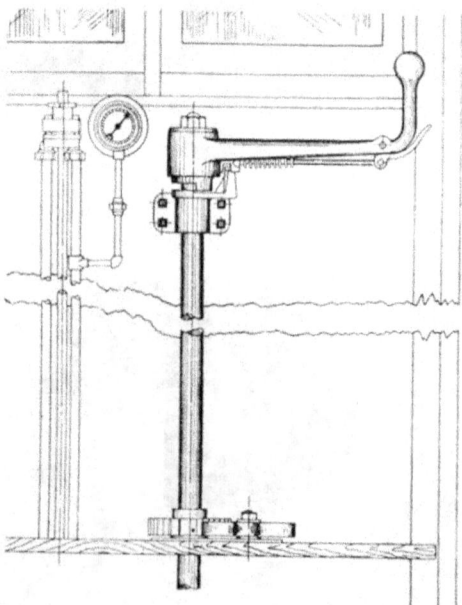

Fig. 576—Lindstrom Ratchet Brake Handle
Dayton Manufacturing Company

(139)

Fig. 577—Giant Geared Brake
Sterling-Meaker Company

Figs. 578-579—Sterling Safety Brake
Sterling-Meaker Company

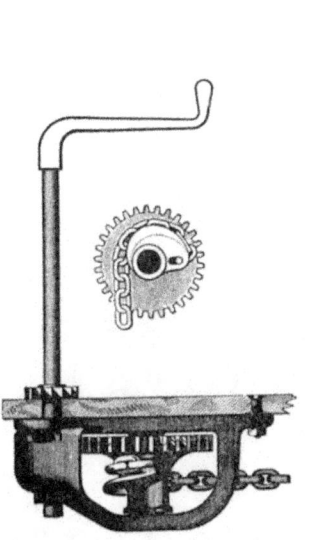

Figs. 580-581—Peacock Geared Brake

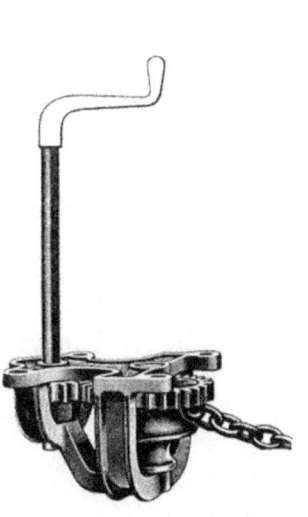

Fig. 582—Tiger Brake
National Brake Company

Fig. 583—Ackley Adjustable Brake

Fig. 584—Winding Drum

Fig. 585—Frame and Gears

Fig. 586—Roller Bearing and Brake Shaft Pinion

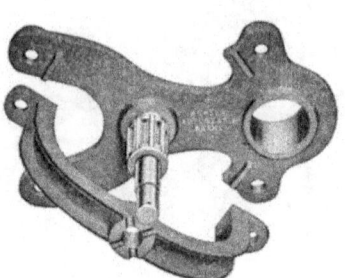

Fig. 587—Adjustable Yoke

Figs. 584-587—Parts of Ackley Adjustable Brake
National Brake Company

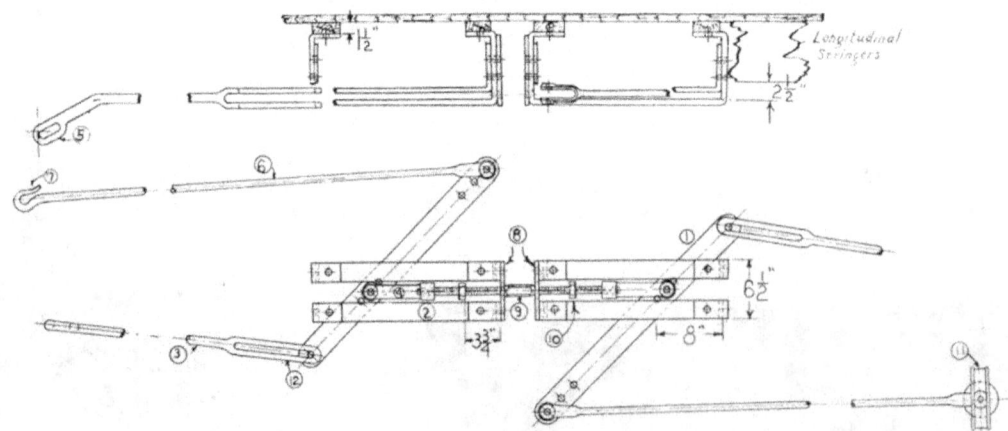

Figs. 588-589—Equalizing Brake Rigging for Hand Brakes of Double-Truck Cars
The J. G. Brill Company

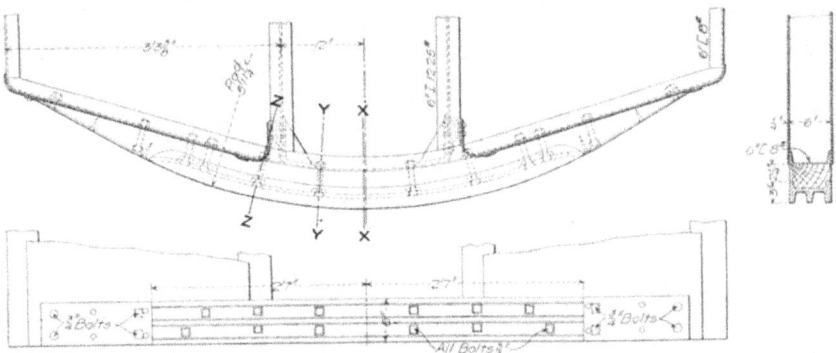

Figs. 590-592—Hedley Rolled-Steel Anti-Climber Applied to Platform End Sill of Subway Car
Whipple Supply Company

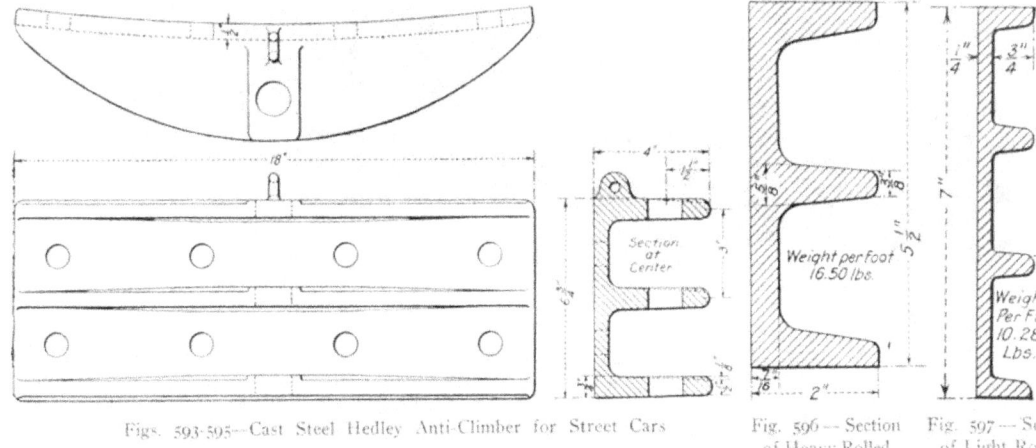

Figs. 593-595—Cast Steel Hedley Anti-Climber for Street Cars   Fig. 596—Section of Heavy Rolled Anti-Climber   Fig. 597—Section of Light Rolled Anti-Climber

Whipple Supply Company

Fig. 598—Brill Angle-Iron Bumper
The J. G. Brill Company

Fig. 599—High Capacity Draft Gear Adapted for Westinghouse Automatic Coupler as Applied to Interborough Subway Cars
Forsyth Bros. Company

Fig. 600—High Capacity Draft Gear Housed in Swinging Pocket with Westinghouse Automatic Coupler as Applied to Interborough Subway Cars
Forsyth Bros. Company

Fig. 601—Self-Centering, Radial Drawbar with M. C. B. Type Coupler Head and Remote Disconnecting Levers
Jewett Car Company

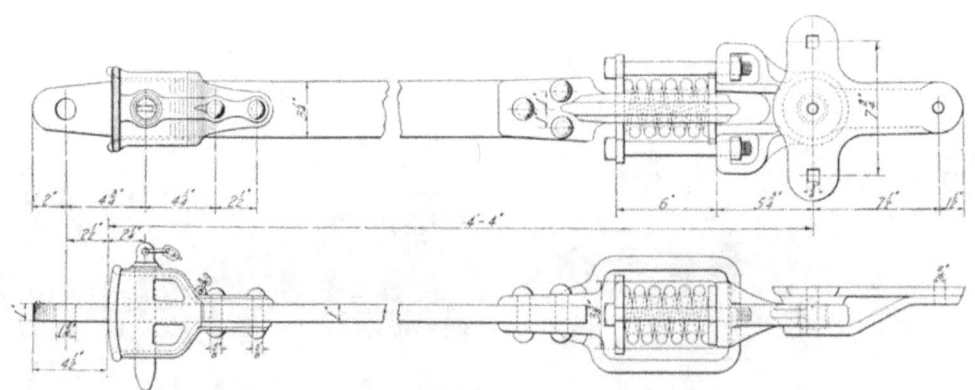

Figs. 602-603—Standard Drawbar and Attachment for City Cars
St. Louis Car Company

Fig. 605—Washburn, Type K, Coupler and Radial Attachment

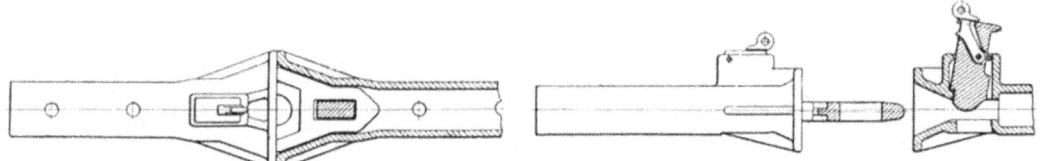

Figs. 606-607—Plan and Side View of Washburn, Type K, Link and Pin Automatic Coupler

Fig. 608—Washburn M. C. B. Type Coupler and Radial Attachment

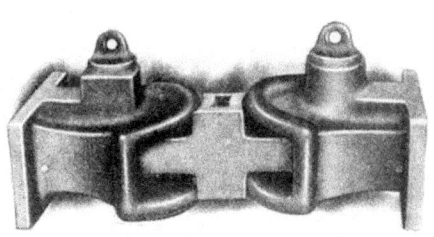

Fig. 609—Washburn, Type M, Link and Pin Drawbar Heads

E. C. Washburn

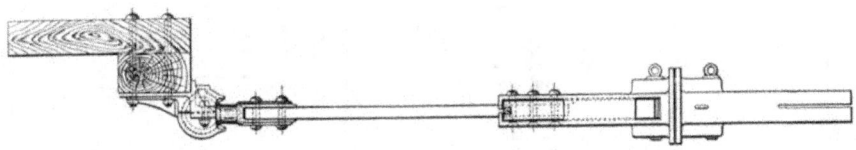

Fig. 610—Van Dorn Radial Drawbar, No. 166, for Light City Cars
W. T. Van Dorn Company

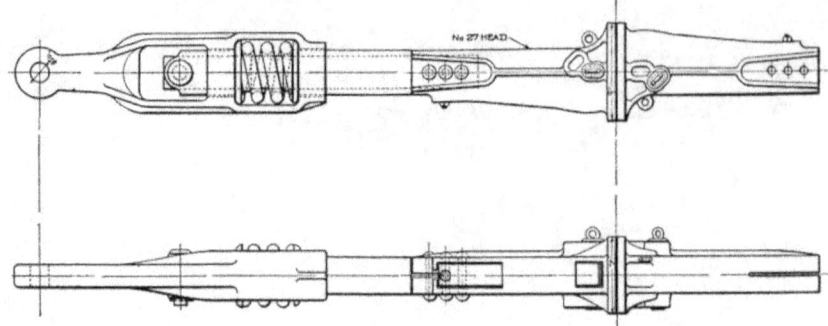

Figs. 611-612—Van Dorn Coupler and Attachment, No. 27, Standard for City and Interurban Cars
W. T. Van Dorn Company

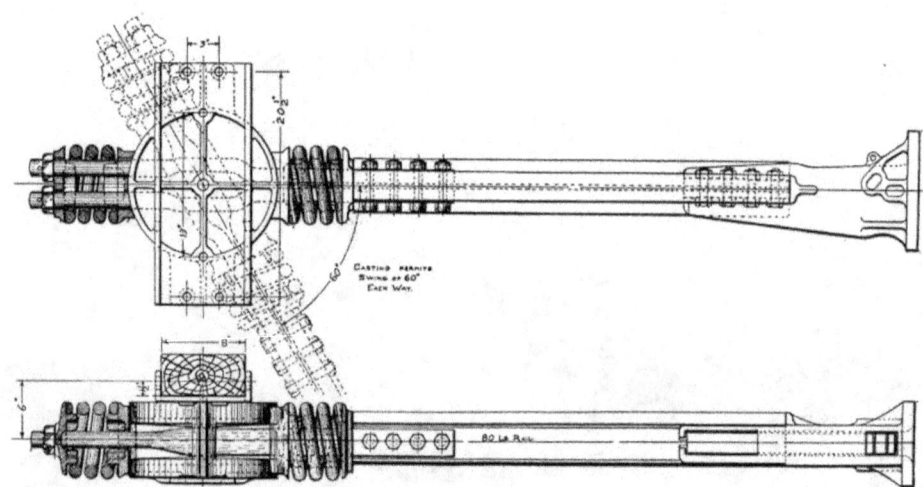

Figs. 613-614—Van Dorn Coupler and Attachment, No. 131, for Heavy Elevated and Interurban Cars
W. T. Van Dorn Company

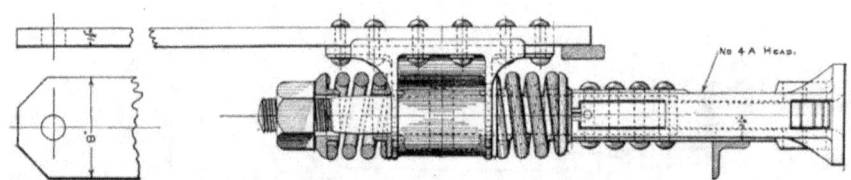

Fig. 615—Van Dorn Coupler and Attachment, No. 133, for Heavy Subway and Elevated Cars
W. T. Van Dorn Company

CAR BODY DETAILS, Couplers and Draft Gear

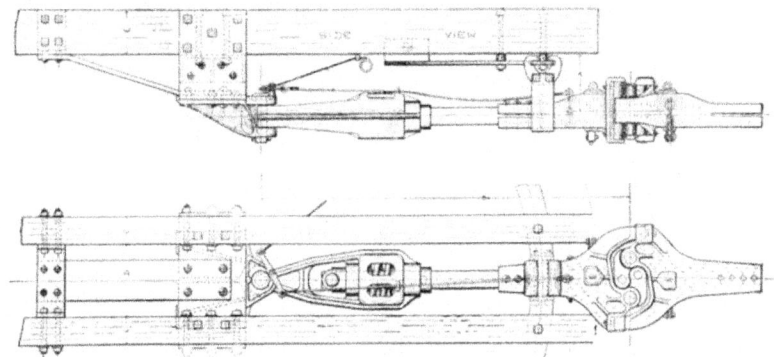

Figs. 616-617—Van Dorn, M. C. B. Type, Coupler and Radial Drawbar Attachment
for Interurban Cars
W. T. Van Dorn Company

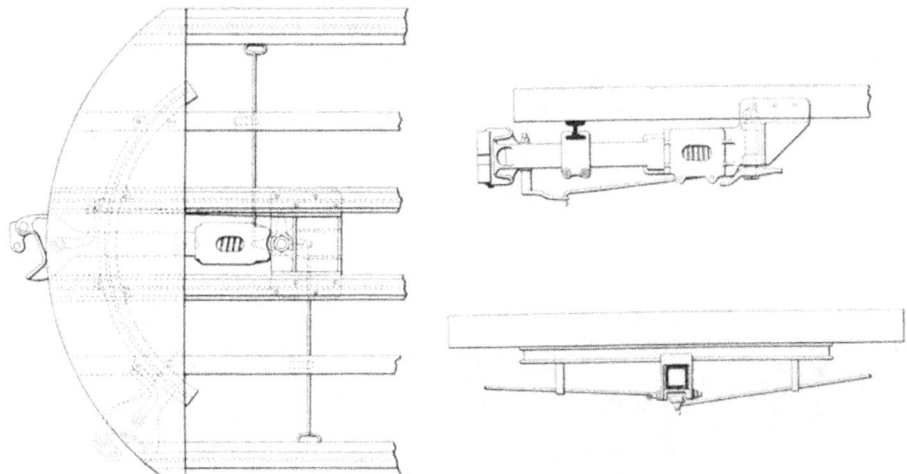

Figs. 618-620—Application of Janney Radial Coupler and Draft Gear to Platform of Interurban Car
McConway & Torley Company

Fig. 621—Tomlinson Automatic Radial Coupler with Drop Draft Gear for
City and Light Interurban Cars
Ohio Brass Company

CAR BODY DETAILS, Couplers and Draft Gear   Figs. 622-628

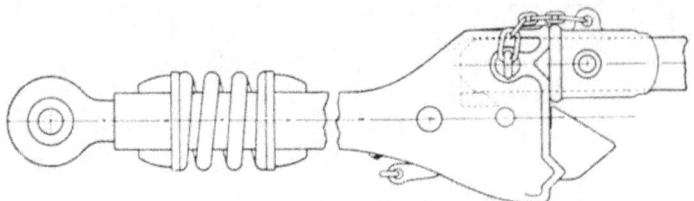

Fig. 622—Tomlinson Coupler Coupled with Standard Pocket Coupler

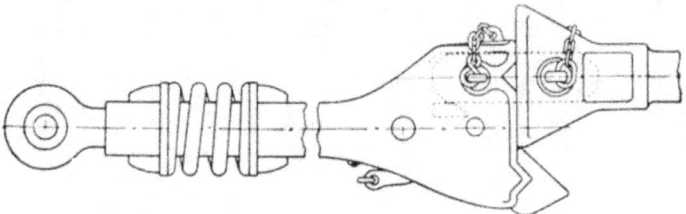

Fig. 623—Tomlinson Coupler Coupled with Brill Coupler

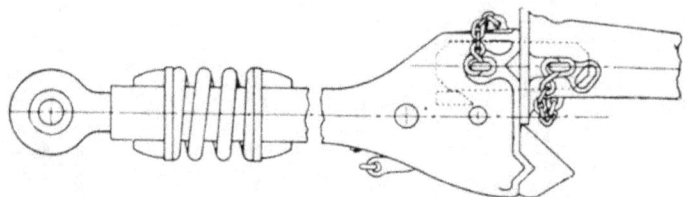

Fig. 624—Tomlinson Coupler Coupled with Van Dorn Coupler

Fig. 625—Tomlinson Coupler Head for Attachment to Channel Bar Draft Stem

Fig. 626—Channel Bar Draft Stem with Vertical Eye for Tomlinson Coupler

Fig. 627—Tomlinson Coupler for City Cars

Fig. 628—Spring Drawbar Carrier

Ohio Brass Company

Fig. 629—Exterior View of Drawbar Anchorage

Fig. 630—Section Through Drawbar Anchorage

Ohio Brass Company

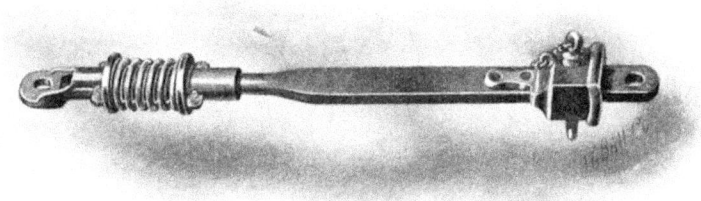
Fig. 631—Brill Radial Drawbar
The J. G. Brill Company

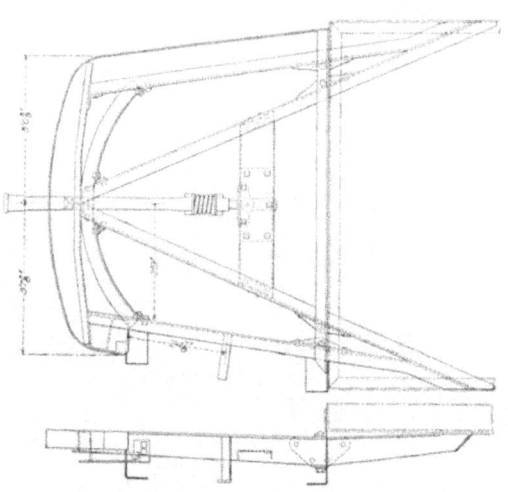
Figs. 632-633—Attachment of Drawbar to Rear Platform Framing of Pay-as-You-Enter Cars of United Railways of St. Louis

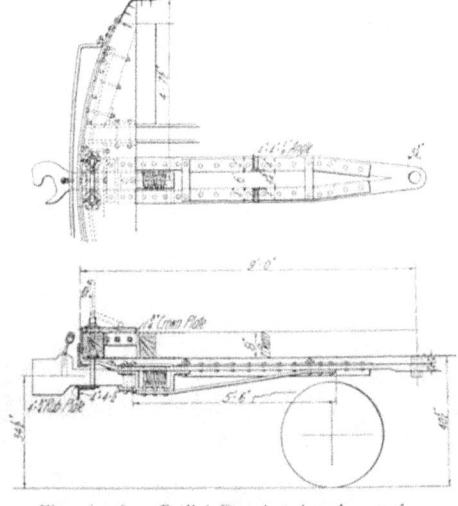
Figs. 634-635—Radial Drawbar Attachment for M. C. B. Coupler Head
St. Louis Car Co.

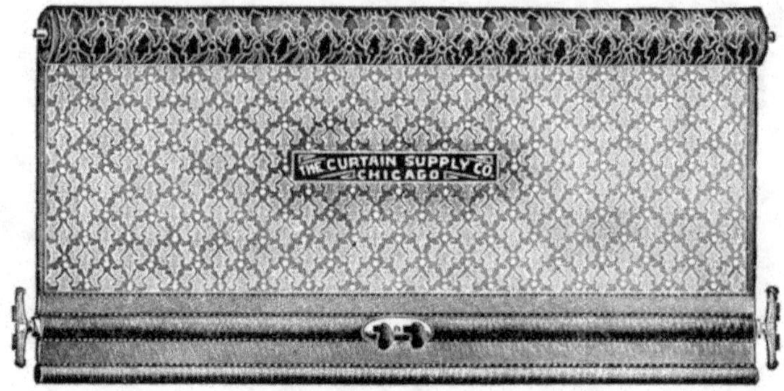

CAR BODY DETAILS, Curtain Fixtures   Figs. 636-640

Fig. 636—Car Curtain with No. 88 Ring Fixture

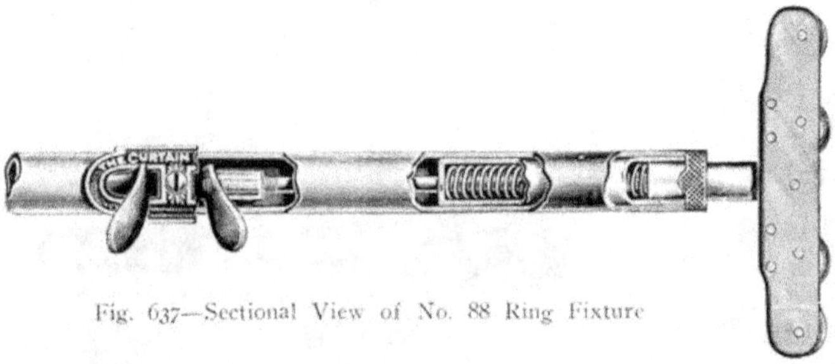

Fig. 637—Sectional View of No. 88 Ring Fixture

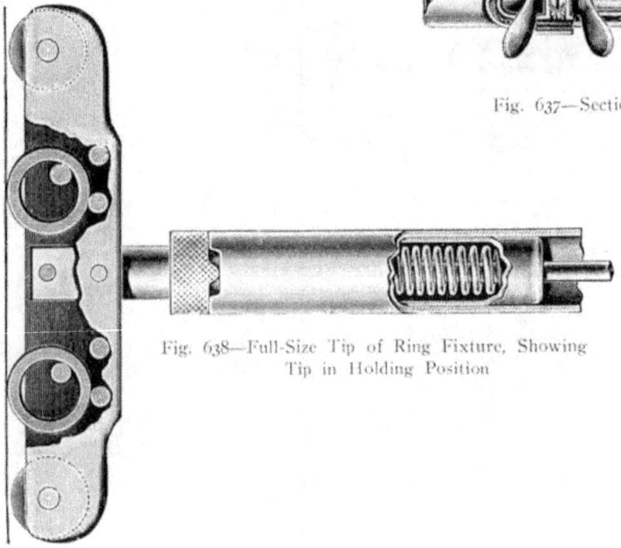

Fig. 638—Full-Size Tip of Ring Fixture, Showing Tip in Holding Position

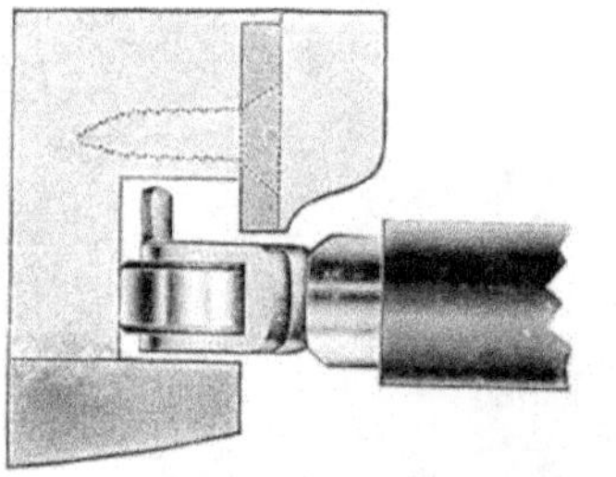

Fig. 639—Sectional View of Post, Showing Steel Strip Placed Underneath Stop to Form Closed Groove for No. 89 Ring Fixture

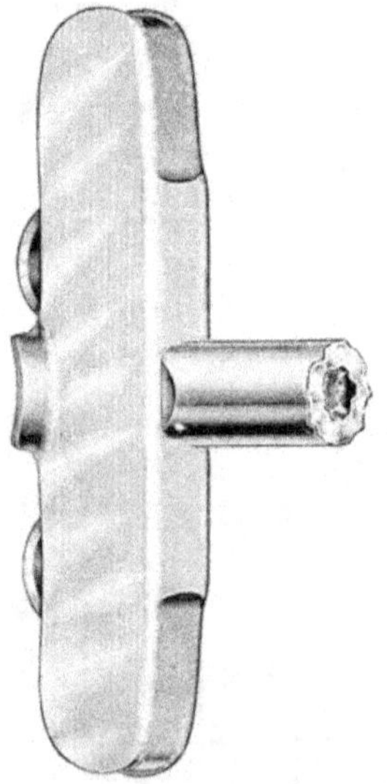

Fig. 640—Full-Size Tip of No. 89 Ring Fixture, Showing Flange Adapted to Work in Closed Groove

Curtain Supply Company

(149)

CAR BODY DETAILS, Curtain Fixtures

Fig. 641—Rex All-Metal Car Curtain Roller

Fig. 642—Section View of Rex Curtain Roller, Showing Extension Plug

Fig. 643—Method of Forming Groove and Seaming Barrel of Rex Curtain Roller

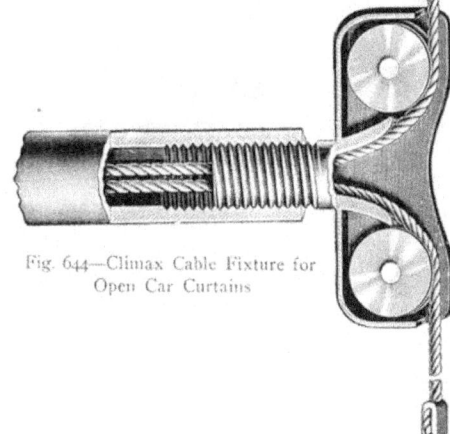

Fig. 644—Climax Cable Fixture for Open Car Curtains

Fig. 645—Open Car Curtain with Acme or Climax Cable Fixtures

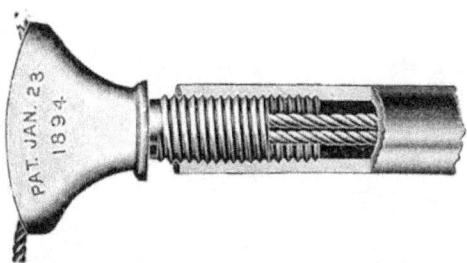

Fig. 646—Acme Cable Fixture for Open Car Curtains
Curtain Supply Company

CAR BODY DETAILS, Destination Signs — Figs. 647-658

Fig. 647—Hartshorn Tin Curtain Roller

Figs. 648-649—
Curtain Roller
Brackets

Figs. 650-651—
Curtain Roller
Brackets

Stewart Hartshorn Company

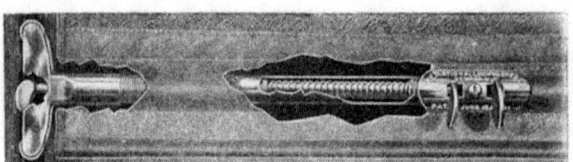

Fig. 652—National Cam Curtain Fixture
National Lock Washer Company

Fig. 653—Protected Groove Curtain Fixture
National Lock Washer Company

Fig. 654—Craighead Day and Night Destination Sign
Craighead Engineering Company

Fig. 655—Eclipse Destination Sign
Eclipse Railway Supply Company

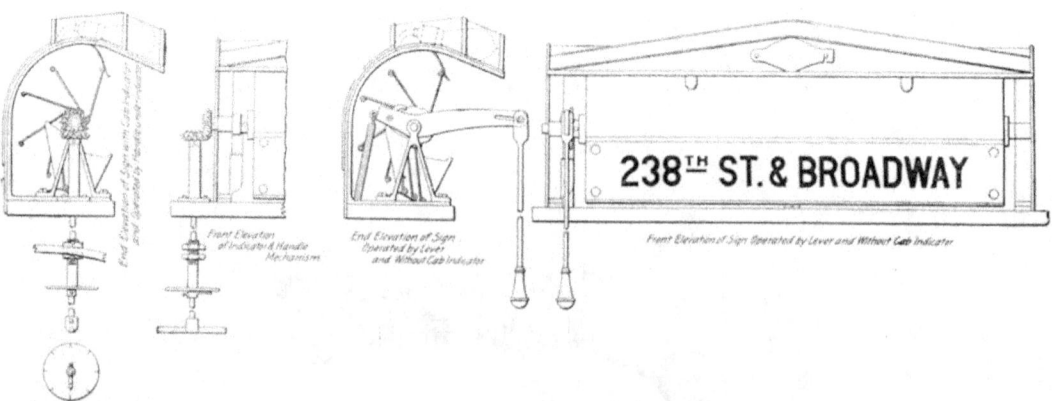

Figs. 656-658—Sterling Destination Sign
Sterling-Meaker Company

(151)

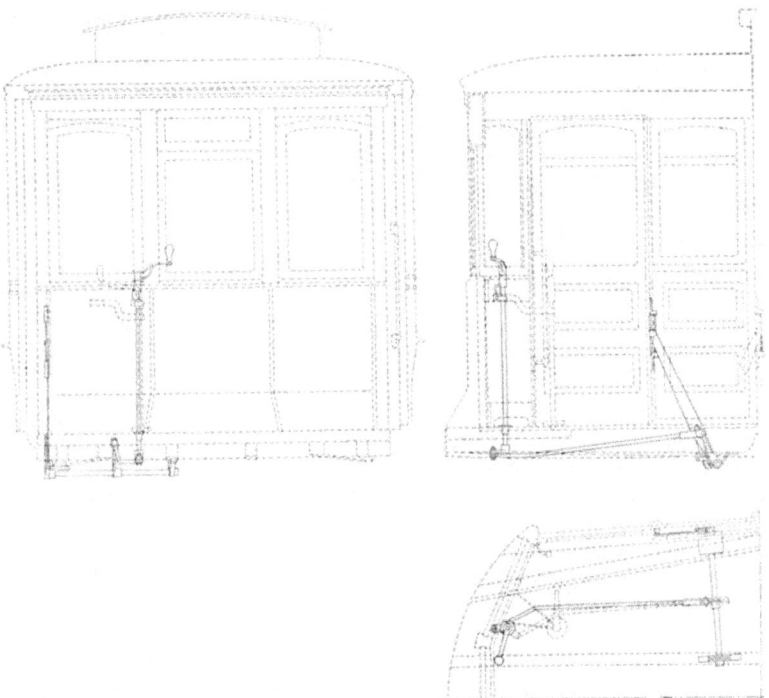

Figs. 659-661—Voight Mechanical Door Operating Mechanism for Front Exit Door of Prepayment Cars
George W. Voight

Fig. 662—Door Operating Mechanism for Front Exit Doors of Pay-as-You-Enter Cars
United Railways of St. Louis

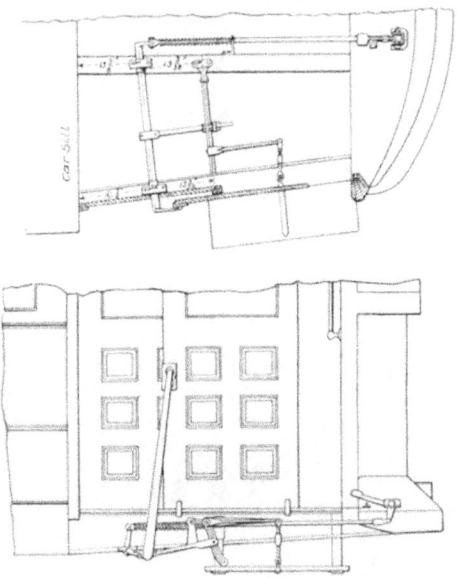

Figs. 663-664—Door and Folding Step Mechanism for Front Exit Doors of Pay-as-You-Enter Cars
Third Avenue Railroad, New York

CAR BODY DETAILS, Door Operating Devices

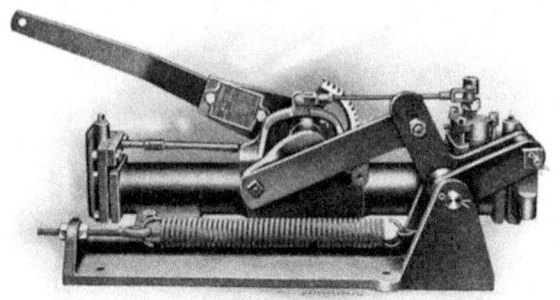

Fig. 665—Pneumatic Engine for Operating Sliding Doors and Folding Steps of Pay-Within Cars

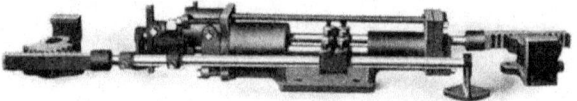

Fig. 666—Pneumatic Engine for Operating Folding Doors of Pay-Within Cars

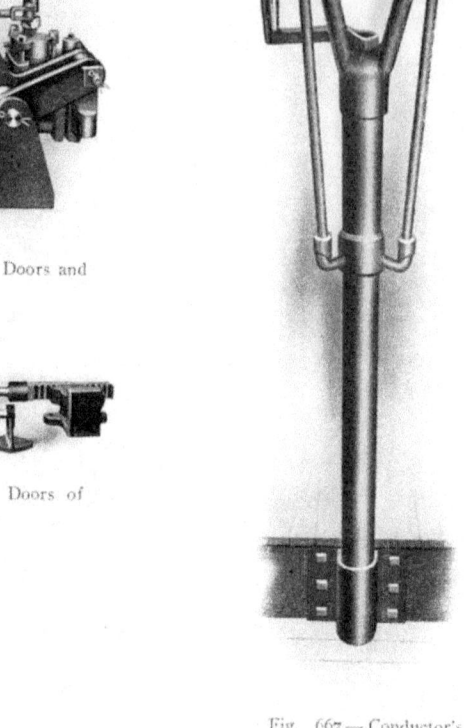

Fig. 667—Conductor's Control Stand for Pay-Within Car with Manually Operated Door

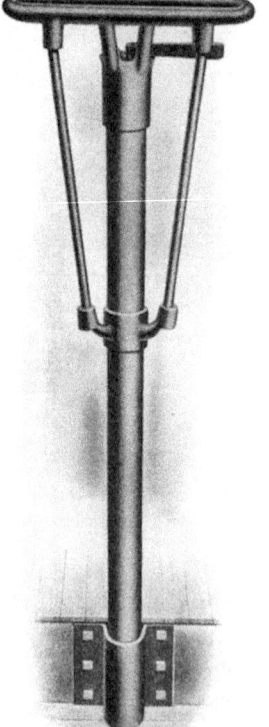

Fig. 668—Conductor's Control Stand for Pay-Within Car with Pneumatically Operated Door

Fig. 669—Pneumatic Engine for Operating Sliding Door with Safety Shoe

Fig. 670—Electrically-Controlled Pneumatic Engine for Operating Sliding Door

National Pneumatic Company

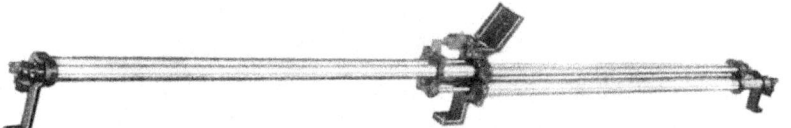

Fig. 671—Pneumatic Cylinder for Operating Sliding Door, with Contact for
Automatic Door Signal
Consolidated Car Heating Company

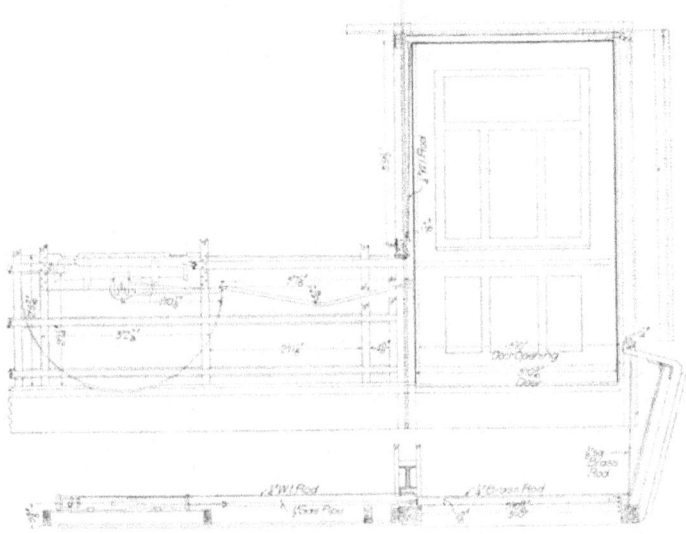

Figs. 672-673—Osmer Pneumatic Door Operating Device for Sliding Doors
Northwestern Elevated Railroad, Chicago

Fig. 677—Two-Speed Double Sliding Door
Mechanism, No. 71
J. L. Howard & Company

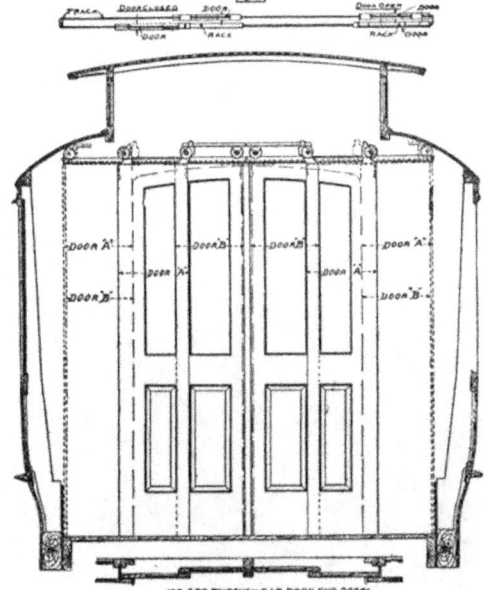

Figs. 674-676—Mutually-Operating Door Mechanism
for Four-Part Sliding End Doors
Jewett Car Company

Fig. 678—Double Sliding Door Mechanism, No. 63
J. L. Howard & Company

Fig. 679—Double Sliding Door Mechanism, No. 61
J. L. Howard & Company

Fig. 680—Brill Mutually-Operating Door Mechanism
The J. G. Brill Company

Figs. 681-688—Parts of Agard Vestibule Door Fixture
J. L. Howard & Company

Fig. 689—Brill Vestibule Door Controller
The J. G. Brill Company

Fig. 690—Brill Folding Platform Gate
The J. G. Brill Company

CAR BODY DETAILS, Doors, Metal

Fig. 691—Forsyth One-Piece Metal Door for Interborough Subway Cars

Fig. 692—Forsyth Metal Sash for Chicago Railways

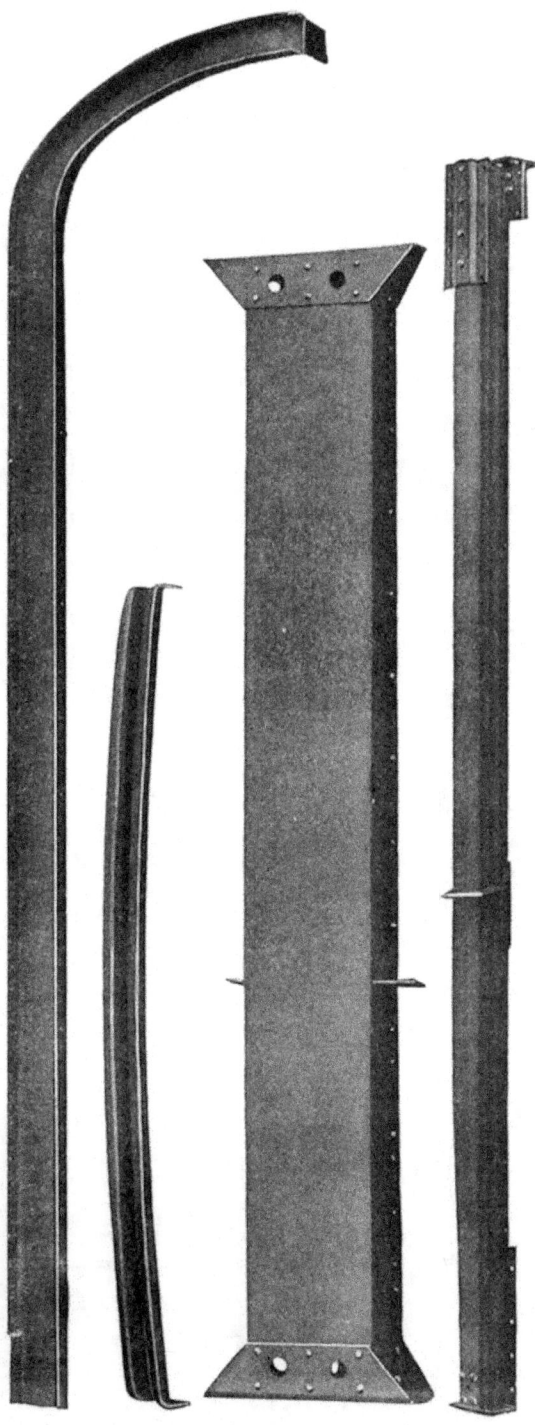

Figs. 693-696—Pressed Steel Posts, Carlines, etc., for Electric Cars

Forsyth Bros. Company

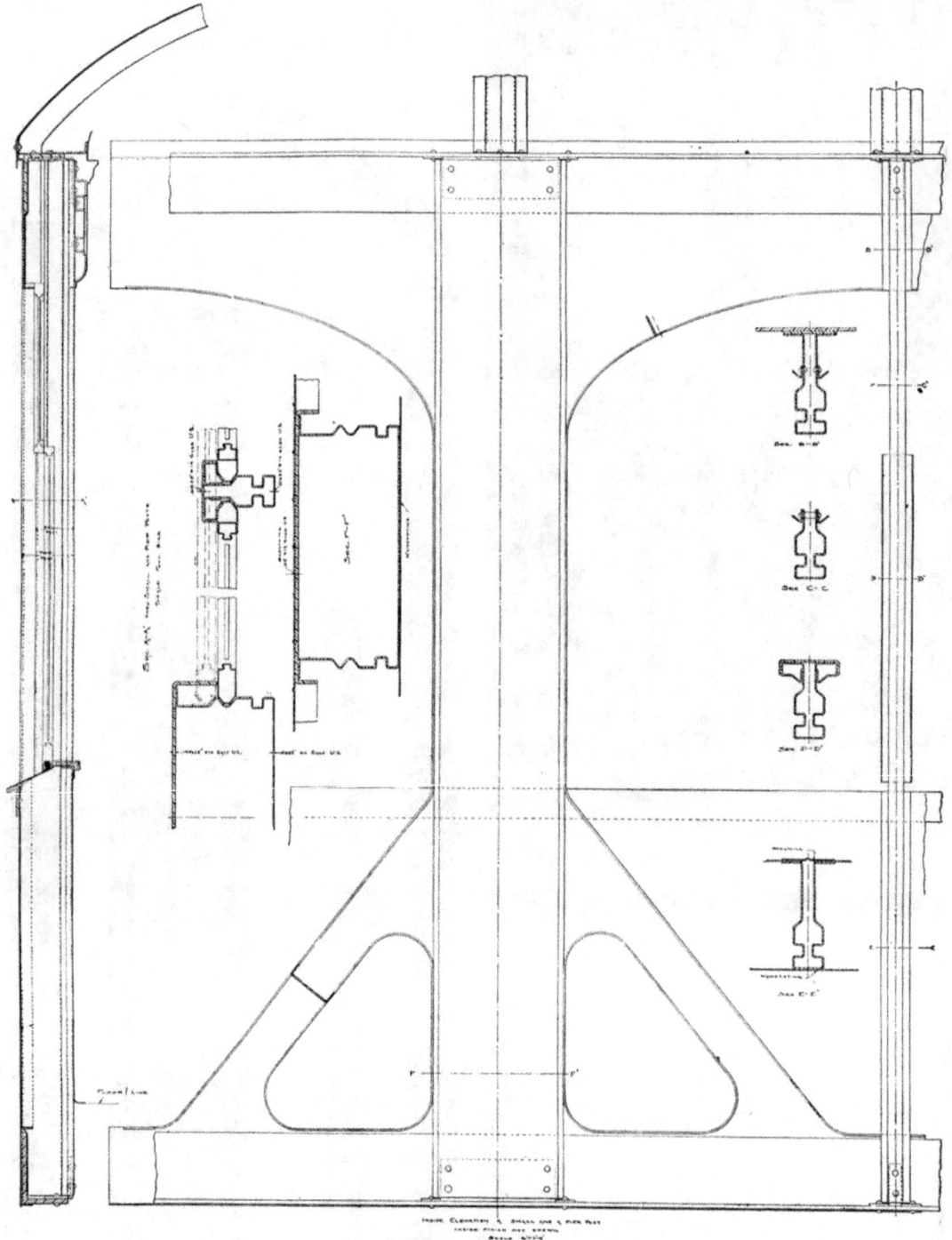

Figs. 697-704—Details of Brinkerhoff Pressed Steel Car Side Construction
Forsyth Bros. Company

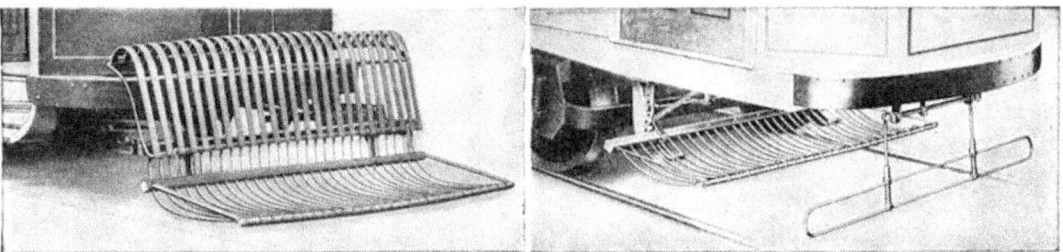

Fig. 705—Providence Fender   Fig. 706—Providence Wheelguard Attached to Body Framing

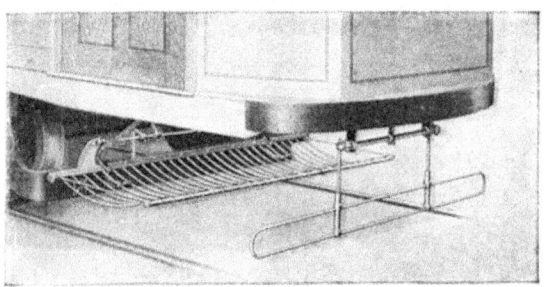

Fig. 707—Providence Wheelguard Attached to Truck
End Piece
Consolidated Car Fender Company

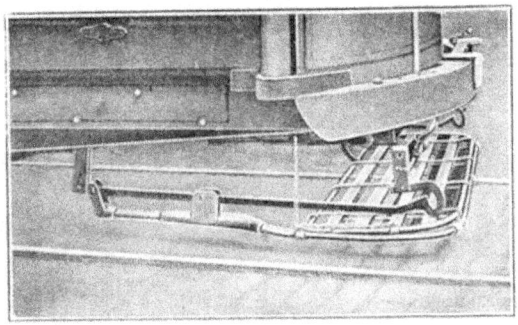
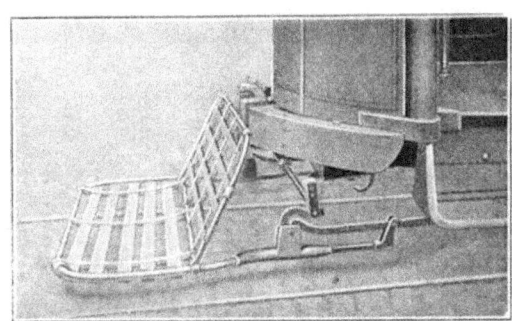

Fig. 708—Berg Sliding Fender Under Car   Fig. 709—Berg Sliding Fender Ready for Service
Sterling-Meaker Company

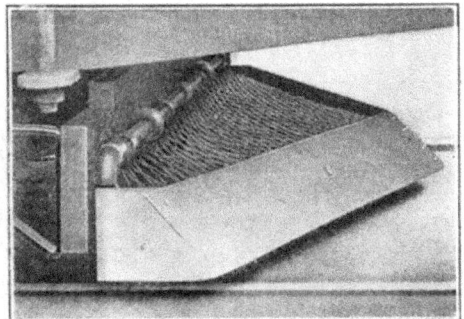

Fig. 710—Berg Folding Fender   Fig. 711—Sterling Wheelguard, No. 1
Sterling-Meaker Company

(158)

CAR BODY DETAILS, Fenders and Wheelguards

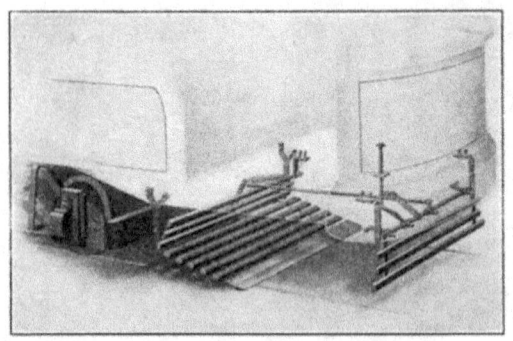

Fig. 712—"H-B" Universal Life Guard, Dropped

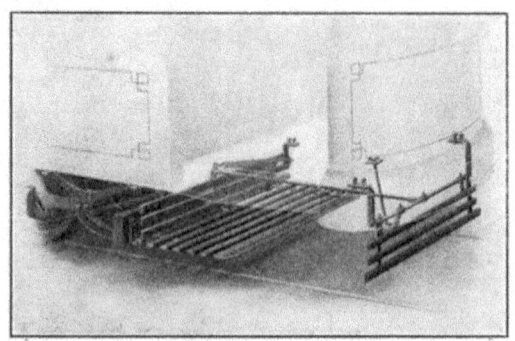

Fig. 713—"H-B" Universal Life Guard, Raised

Wonham, Sanger & Bates

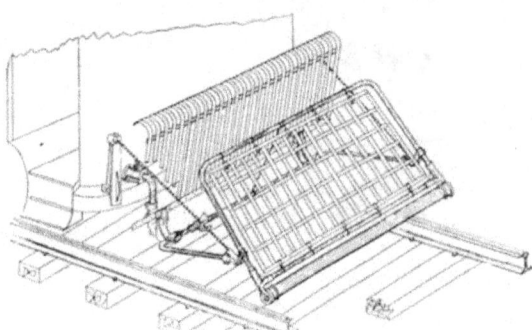

Fig. 714—Eclipse Life Guard
Eclipse Railway Supply Company

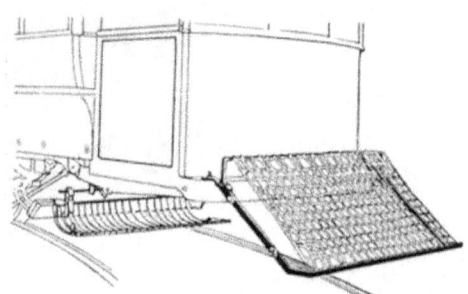

Fig. 715—Clark Fender and Wheelguard
Ira P. Clark

Fig. 716—Clark Wheelguard Applied to Truck
Ira P. Clark

Fig. 717—Parmenter Fender and Wheelguard
Parmenter Fender & Wheel Guard Company

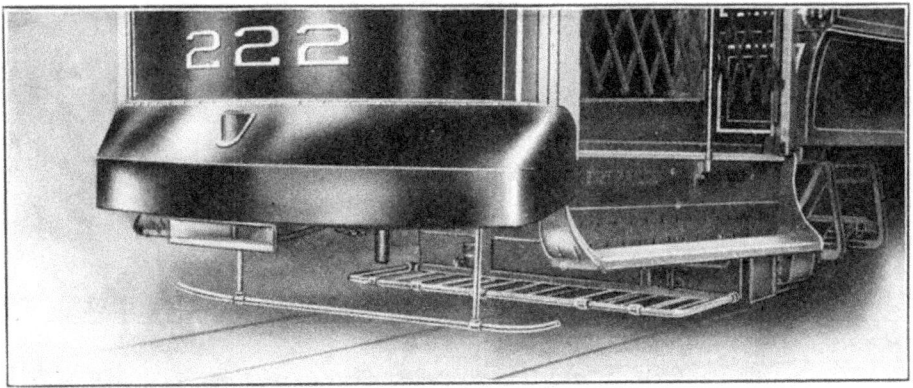

Fig. 718—Parmenter Wheelguard
Parmenter Fender & Wheel Guard Company

Fig. 719—Philadelphia Safety Car Fender
Electric Service Supplies Company

CAR BODY DETAILS, Hardware, Basket Racks, Bells

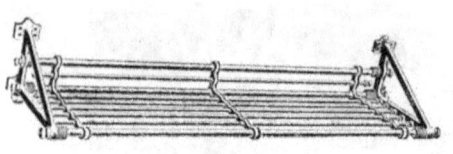

Fig. 720—Rex Rod Basket Rack
Dayton Manufacturing Company

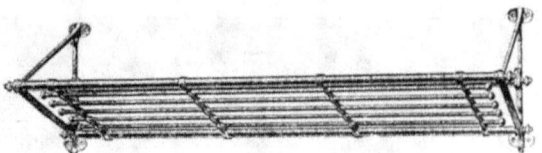

Fig. 721—Rod Basket Rack
Adams & Westlake

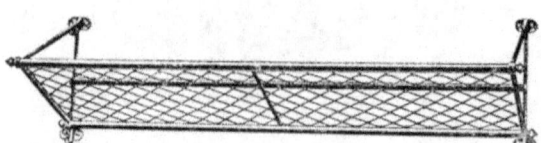

Fig. 722—Wire Basket Rack
Adams & Westlake

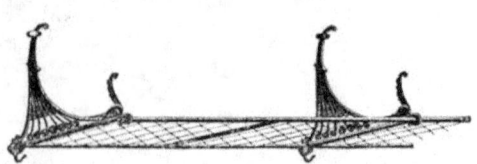

Fig. 723—Wire Basket Rack
Dayton Manufacturing Company

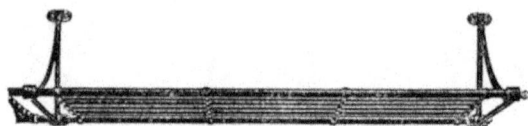

Fig. 724—Removable Rod Bottom Basket Rack
Adams & Westlake

Fig. 725—Cast Basket Rack
Dayton Manufacturing Company

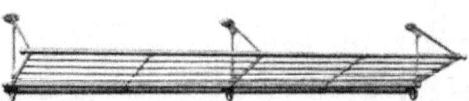

Fig. 726—Rod Basket Rack

Fig. 727—Rod Basket Rack

J. L. Howard & Company

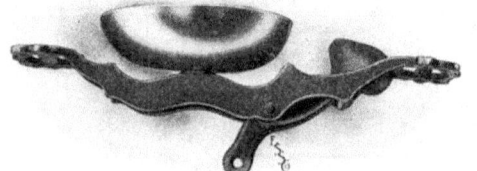

Fig. 728—Standard Type Signal Bell

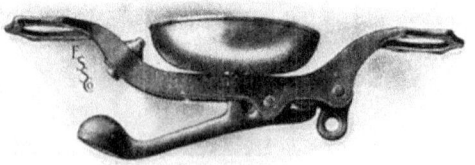

Fig. 729—Improved Type Signal Bell

Electric Service Supplies Company

Figs. 730-731—Conductors' Signal Bells
J. L. Howard & Company

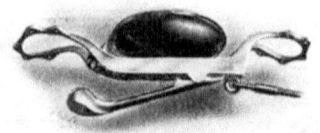

Fig. 732—Retriever Signal Bell
The J. G. Brill Co.

CAR BODY DETAILS, Hardware, Bells

Figs. 733-734—Conductors' Signal Bells
Dayton Manufacturing Company

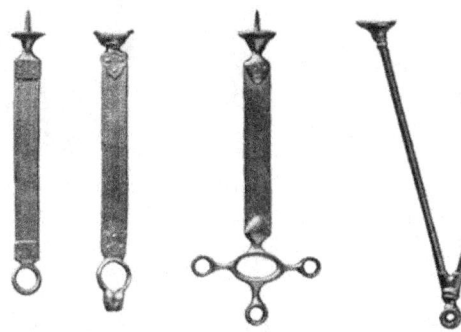

Figs. 735-738—Strap and Rod Bell Cord Hangers
J. L. Howard & Company

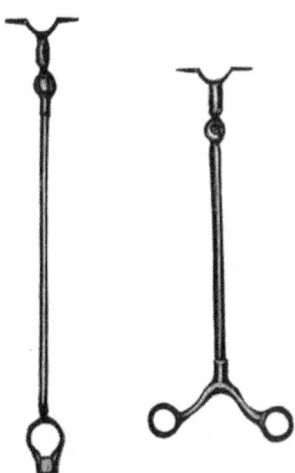

Figs. 739-740—Rod Bell Cord Hangers
The J. G. Brill Company

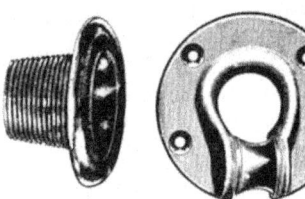

Figs. 741-742—Bell Cord Bushings
Adams & Westlake

Fig. 743—Bell Cord Fastener
D. M. Co.

Fig. 744—Bell Cord Hook
D. M. Co.

Fig. 745—Bell Cord Anchor
A. & W.

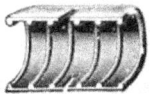 

Figs. 746-747—Keystone Cord Connectors

Fig. 748—Bell Cord Hook
Samson Cordage Works

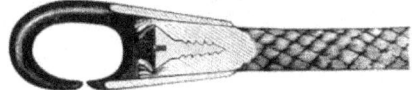

Fig. 749—Bell Cord Hook, Screw Fastening

Fig. 750—Samson Spot Bell Cord

Fig. 751—Plain Samson Bell Cord

Fig. 752—Samson Wire Center Bell Cord
Samson Cordage Works

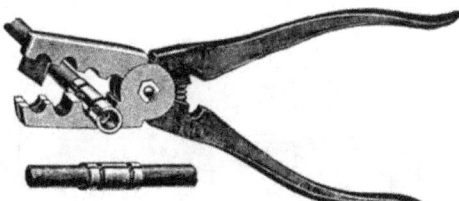

Figs. 753-754—Bay State Cord Connector and Pliers
C. N. Wood Company

(162)

CAR BODY DETAILS, Hardware, Doors

Figs. 802-803—Double Sliding Door Lock and Keeper

Figs. 804-805—Double Sliding Door Lock and Keeper
Adams & Westlake Company

Figs. 806-807—Double Sliding Door Lock and Keeper

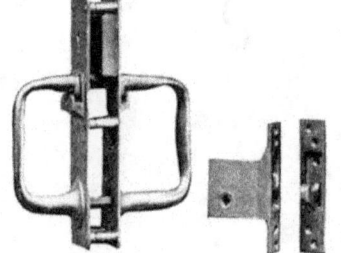
Figs. 808-814—Double Sliding Door Locks
J. L. Howard & Company

Figs. 815-820—Sliding Door Locks and Keepers
J. L. Howard & Company

Figs. 821-822—Sliding Door Lock and Keeper
Adams & Westlake

Figs. 823-824—Baggage Car Sliding Door Latch
Dayton Manufacturing Company

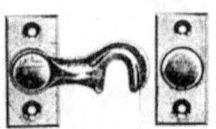
Figs. 825-826—Sliding Door Catch and Button
A. & W.

Figs. 827-829—Sliding Door Catch and Keepers
D. M. Co.

Figs. 830-831—Sliding Door Catch and Keeper
D. M. Co.

Fig. 832—Sliding Door Bumper
A. & W.

Figs. 833-834—Sliding Door Rollers
Dayton Manufacturing Company

Fig. 835—Sliding Door Roller
A. & W.

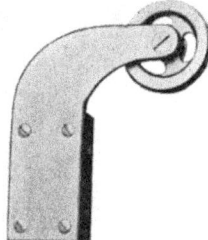

Fig. 836—Sliding Door Corner Roller
Adams & Westlake

Figs. 837-839—Sliding Door Sheaves
J. L. Howard & Company

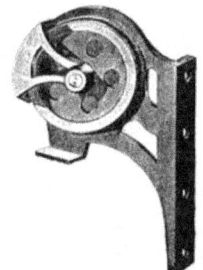
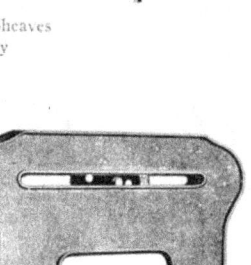

Figs. 840-843—Sliding Door Sheaves
Adams & Westlake and Dayton Manufacturing Company

Fig. 844—Baggage Car Sliding Door Sheave
Dayton Manufacturing Company

Fig. 849—Sliding Door Flush Handle
J. G. Brill Co

Figs. 845-848—Sliding Door Handles
Adams & Westlake and Dayton Manufacturing Company

Figs. 850-852—Sliding Door Handles
The J. G. Brill Company

CAR BODY DETAILS, Hardware, Hand-Strap Pole Fixtures   Figs. 853-871

Figs. 853-856—Hand-Strap Pole Brackets
The J. G. Brill Company

Figs. 857-860—Hand-Strap Pole Brackets
The J. G. Brill Company

Figs. 861-863—Hand-Strap Pole Brackets
J. L. Howard & Company

Fig. 864—Hand-Strap
Pole Bracket
D. M. Co.

  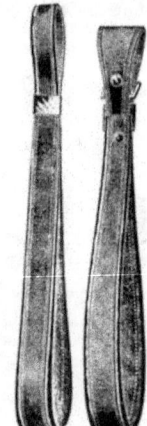

Fig. 865—Hand-Strap Pole Bracket
Adams & Westlake

Fig. 866—Hand-Strap Pole
Bracket
D. M. Co.

Figs. 868-869—Leather
Hand Straps
A. & W.

  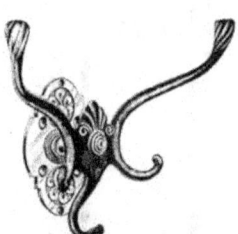

Fig. 867—Hand-Strap Pole Bracket
Adams & Westlake

Fig. 870—Coat
Hook
D. M. Co.

Fig. 871—Coat and Hat
Hook
A. & W.

(167)

Fig. 872—Three-Light Cluster and Reflector for Deck Lights

Fig. 873—Keyless Lamp Socket for Cluster

Fig. 874—Keyless Lamp Socket and Base

Figs. 875-877—Keyless Lamp Sockets and Bases

Fig. 878—Three-Way Snap Switch for Lighting Circuit

Fig. 879—Extra Heavy Lighting Switch and Cut-Out

General Electric Company

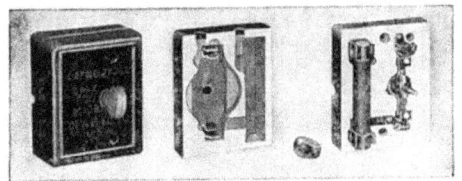   

Figs. 880-882—Lighting Switch and Cut-Out
General Electric Company

Figs. 883-885—Snap Switches for Car Lighting Circuits
Hart & Hegeman

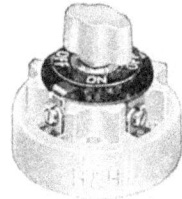  

Fig. 886—Snap Switch

Figs. 887-888—Car Lighting Switch
Hart & Hegeman

Figs. 889-890—Car Lighting Switch
Electric Service Supplies Co.

Fig. 891—Battery Charging

Fig. 892—Battery Supplying Lights

Figs. 891-892—Battery Relay and Charging Switch, No. 275B
Consolidated Car-Heating Company

CAR BODY DETAILS, Hardware, Lighting Fixtures

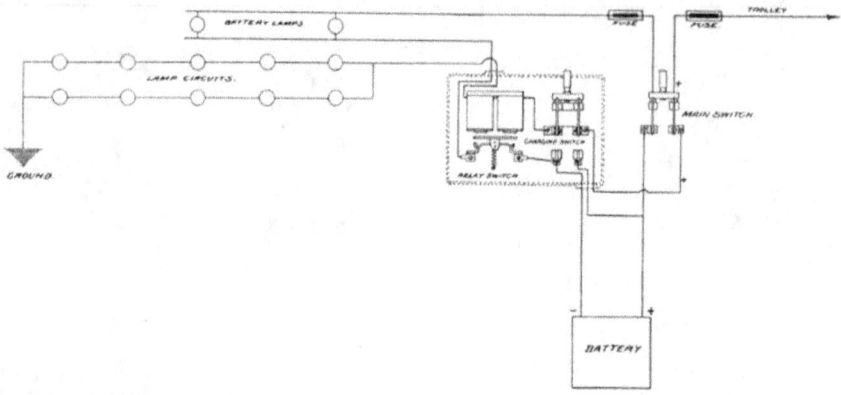

Fig. 893—Wiring Diagram of Connections for Supply of Current for Auxiliary Lights from Storage Battery Using Battery Relay and Charging Switch Shown in Figs. 891-892
Consolidated Car-Heating Company

Fig. 894—Car Lighting Switch, No. 204V
Consolidated Car Heating Co.

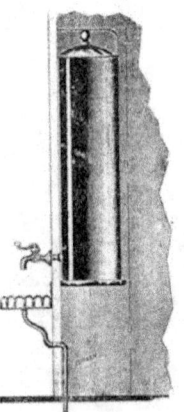

Fig. 895—Water Cooler
D. M. Co.

Fig. 896—Eckert Water Closet
Dayton Manufacturing Co.

Fig. 897—Standard Improved Dry Closet
Dayton Manufacturing Co.

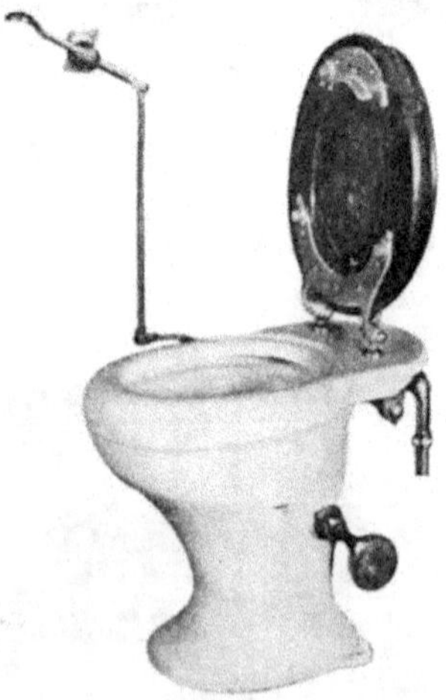

Fig. 898—Duner Flush Closet with Wall Pull
Duner Co.

Figs. 899-902—Body and Post Metal Grab Handles
The J. G. Brill Company

Fig. 903—Post Grab Handle Sockets
A. & W.

Figs. 904-910—Post Grab Handle Sockets
The J. G. Brill Company

Figs. 914-916—Roof Grab Handles
The J. G. Brill Company

Figs. 911-913—Single and Double-Metal Post Grab Handles
The J. G. Brill Company

Figs. 917-918—Trolley Steps
J. G. Brill Company

Figs. 919-920—Trolley Steps
J. L. Howard & Company

CAR BODY DETAILS, Hardware, Platform — Figs. 921-928

Fig. 921—Ribbed Type Metal Vestibule Trap Door,
Suitable for Low Station Platforms
O. M. Edwards Company

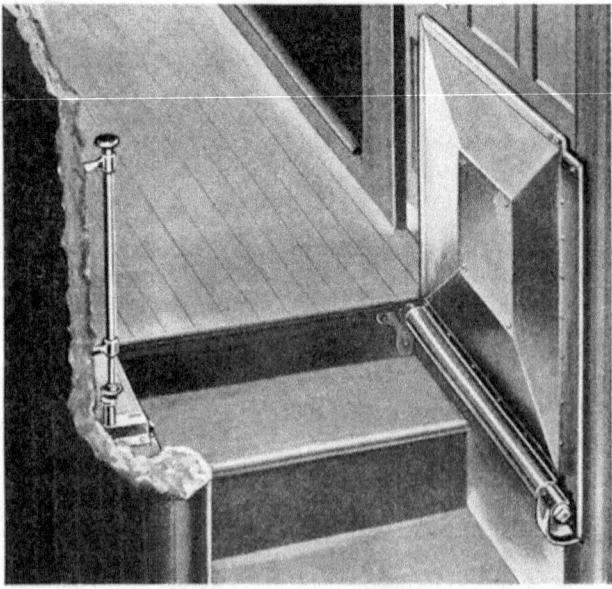

Fig. 922—Smooth Bottom Type Metal Vestibule Trap Door,
Suitable for High Station Platforms
O. M. Edwards Company

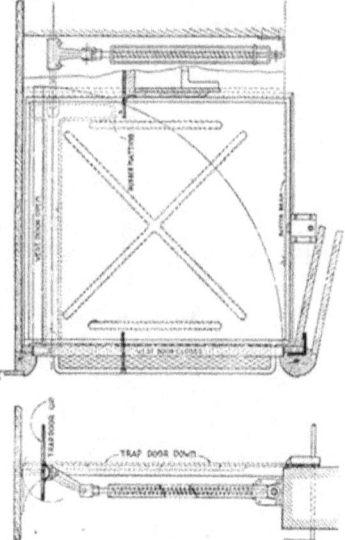

Figs. 923-924—National Steel Trap Door
for High Station Platforms
General Railway Supply Company

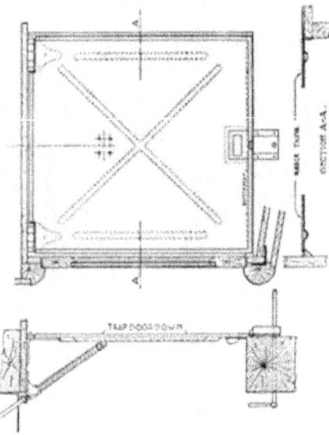

Figs. 925-926—National Steel Trap Door
for Low Station Platforms
General Railway Supply Company

Fig. 927—Section Through American Mason Safety
Step Tread
American Mason Safety Tread Company

Fig. 928—Universal Safety Step Tread
Universal Safety Tread Company

Fig. 929—Stanwood Safety Step Tread
Quincy, Manchester, Sargent Co.

Fig. 930—Brill Platform Step
The J. G. Brill Co.

Fig. 931—Hood Socket for Dasher Corner Post
A. & W.

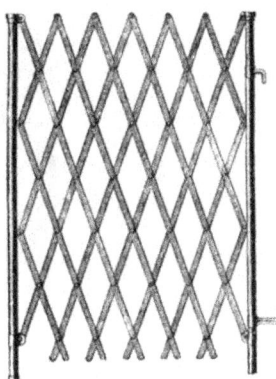

Fig. 934—Folding Platform Gate
Dayton Manufacturing Co.

Fig. 935—Vestibule Center Sash Adjuster
The J. G. Brill Company

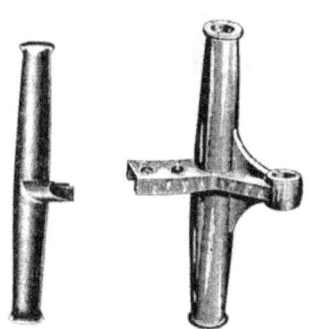

Figs. 932-933—Dasher Corner Post Brackets
A. & W.

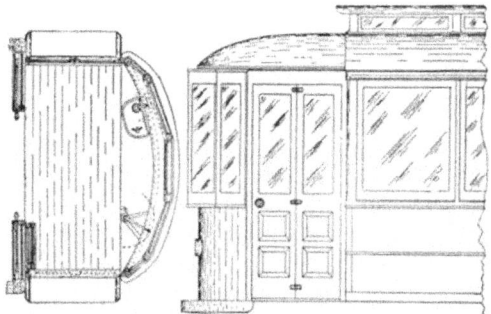

Figs. 936-937—Portable Vestibule
J. P. Sjoberg & Company

Fig. 938—Brill Portable Vestibule
The J. G. Brill Company

CAR BODY DETAILS, Hardware, Platform   Figs. 939-949

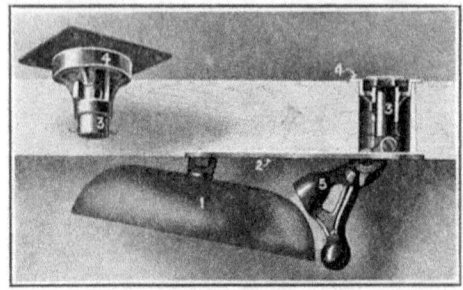

Fig. 939—Dedenda Platform Gong
The J. G. Brill Company

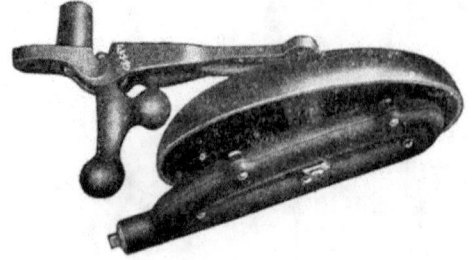

Fig. 940—Keystone Pneumatic Gong Ringer
Electric Service Supplies Company

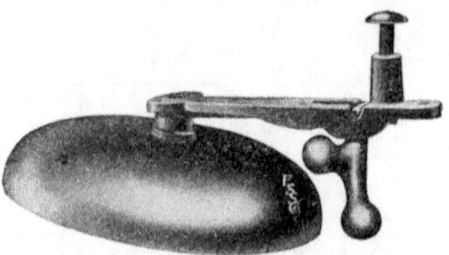

Fig. 941—Single-Stroke Platform Gong
Electric Service Supplies Company

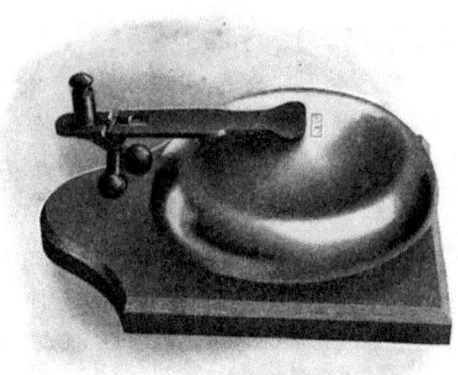

Fig. 944—Shelby Platform Gong
National Tube Company

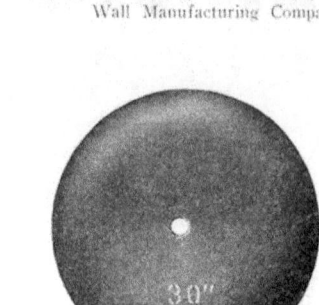

Fig. 942—Foot Gong   Fig. 943—Roof Gong
Wall Manufacturing Company

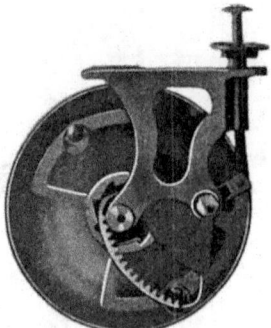

Fig. 945—Shelby Seamless   Fig. 946—Vertical Multiple-   Fig. 947—Horizontal Multiple-
Gong   Stroke Gong   Stroke Gong
National Tube Company   Adams & Westlake Company

Fig. 948—Single-Stroke Gong   Fig. 949—Dayton Multi-Stroke
                                         Gong
Dayton Manufacturing Company

CAR BODY DETAILS, Hardware, Windows

Fig. 952—Universal Gravity Wedge Sash Lock
McCord Mfg. Company

Fig. 953—Section Through Sash Equipped with Universal Weather Strips and Gravity Sash Lock
McCord Mfg. Company

Fig. 950—Cast Rack for Universal Gravity Wedge Sash Lock
McCord Mfg. Company

Fig. 951—Pressed Rack for Universal Gravity Wedge Sash Lock

Figs. 954-955—Universal Top and Bottom Weather Strips for Car Windows
McCord Mfg. Company

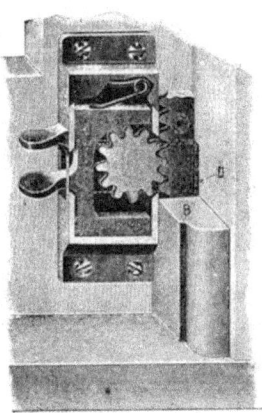

Fig. 956—Raymond Sash Lock and Ratchet
Dayton Manufacturing Co.

Fig. 957—Ratchet Sash Lock
J. L. Howard & Co.

Fig. 958—Plain Sash Lock

Fig. 959—Ulin Sash Lock and Ratchet
Dayton Manufacturing Company

Fig. 960—Sash Lock with Corner Plate
A. & W.

Fig. 961—Center Operating Device for
Drop Sash
O. M. Edwards Company

Fig. 962—Double Sash Locks Applied to
Drop Sash
O. M. Edwards Company

Fig. 963—Application of Type 13-O Sash
Locks with Three-Notch Stops to
Lift Sash. Sash Lowered
O. M. Edwards Co.

Fig. 964—Application of Type 13-O Sash
Locks with Three-Notch Stops
to Lift Sash. Sash Raised
O. M. Edwards Co.

Figs. 965-985 — CAR BODY DETAILS, Hardware, Window

Figs. 966-967—Pinch Handle Sash Locks
Adams & Westlake

Figs. 968-969—Sash Locks for Semi-Convertible Sashes
The J. G. Brill Company

Figs. 970-971—Sash Locks for Drop Sashes
The J. G. Brill Company

Fig. 965—Sash Lock, Type 13-O, with Corrugated Stop Bar
O. M. Edwards Company

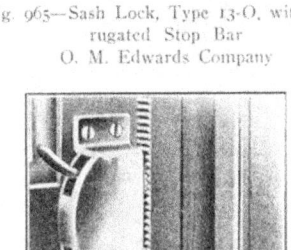 

Fig. 973—National Ratchet Sash Lock

Fig. 974—National Sash Balance Fixture

National Lock Washer Company

Fig. 974—Sash Catch for Semi-Convertible Car
J. G. Brill Co.

Figs. 975-981—Window Catches and Keepers
The J. G. Brill Company

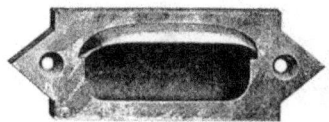  

Figs. 982-983—Sash Lifts
Dayton Manufacturing Company

Figs. 984-985—Sash Lifts
Adams & Westlake Company

(176)

CAR BODY DETAILS, Hardware, Window — Figs. 986-1013

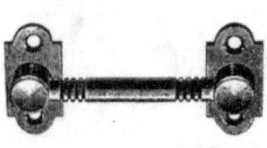    

Figs. 986-989—Bar and Hook Sash Lifts
Adams & Westlake and Dayton Manufacturing Company

Figs. 990-991—Leather Sash Lift Plates
Dayton Manufacturing Co.

Figs. 992-993—Leather Sash Lifts
Adams & Westlake

Figs. 994-995—Sash Anti-Rattling Springs
Adams & Westlake

 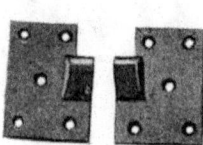  

Fig. 996—Sash Flap Lift

Figs. 997-1000—Sash Corner Plates
The J. G. Brill Company

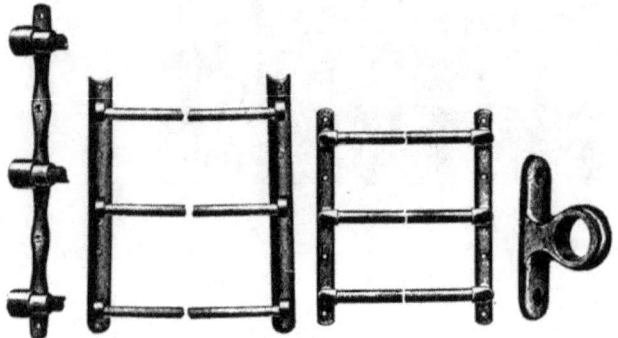
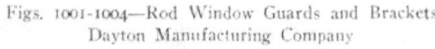

Figs. 1001-1004—Rod Window Guards and Brackets
Dayton Manufacturing Company

 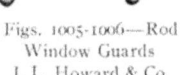 

Figs. 1005-1006—Rod Window Guards
J. L. Howard & Co.

Figs. 1007-1008—Rod Window Guard Brackets
J. G. Brill Co

Figs. 1010-1011—Deck Sash Pulls
Dayton Manufacturing Co.

Fig. 1009—Removable Wire Screen Window Guard
Adams & Westlake Company

Figs. 1012-1013—Deck Sash Pivots
Adams & Westlake

(177)

Figs. 1014-1015—Deck Sash Pivots
Dayton Manufacturing Co.

Figs. 1016-1018—Deck Sash Catches
Adams & Westlake

Fig. 1019—Continuous Deck Sash Opener
Adams & Westlake Company

 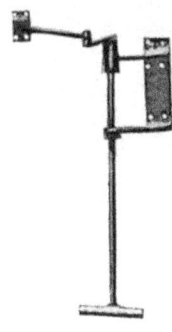  

Fig. 1020—Single Deck Sash Opener A. & W.

Fig. 1021—Single Deck Sash Opener J. G. Brill Co.

Fig. 1022—Double Deck Sash Opener J. G. Brill Co.

Fig. 1023—Double Deck Sash Opener J. G. Brill Co.

Fig. 1024—Single Deck Sash Opener D. M. Co.

Fig. 1025—Continuous Deck Sash Opener D. M. Co.

Fig. 1026—Deck Sash Ratchet A. & W.

Fig. 1027—Universal Deck Sash Ratchet McCord Mfg. Company

CAR BODY DETAILS, Headlights and Marker Lamps — Figs. 1051-1061

Fig. 1051—Imperial Luminous Arc Headlight with Fresnel Lens and No Reflector

Fig. 1052—Imperial Combination Luminous Arc and Incandescent Headlight with Plain Glass Door and Reflector

Fig. 1053—Carbon Arc and Incandescent Headlight with Plain Glass Door and Reflector

Fig. 1054—Carbon Arc Headlight with Grid Door and Reflector

Figs. 1055-1056—Incandescent Dasher Headlight with Grid Door

Figs. 1057-1058—Incandescent Dasher Headlight, Flush Pattern, with Fresnel Lens

Crouse-Hinds Company

Fig. 1059—Square Body Marker Tail Lamp

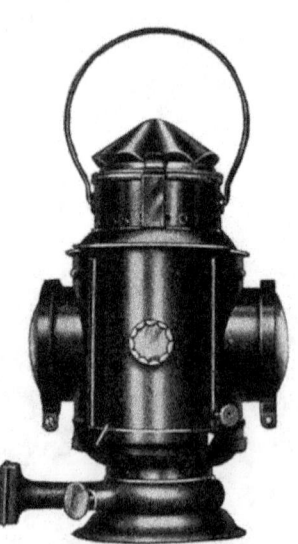

Fig. 1060—Round Body Route Signal or Marker Tail Lamp

Dressel Railway Lamp Works

Fig. 1061—Square Body Tail Lamp for Attachment to Dasher

CAR BODY DETAILS, Headlights and Marker Lamps

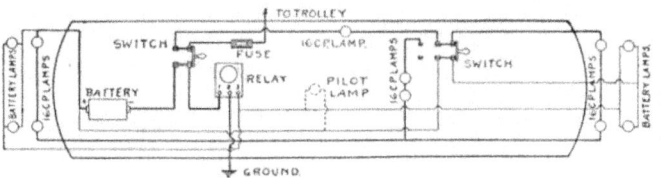

Fig. 1062—Wiring Diagram of Signal Lamps for Single-End Car with Two Red Tail Lights and Two Classification Lights

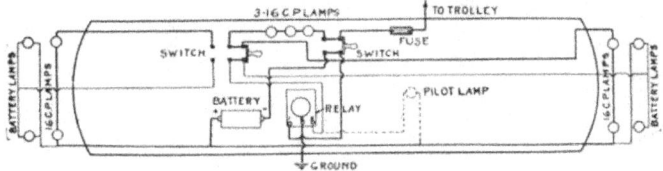

Fig. 1063—Wiring Diagram of Signal Lamps for Double-End Car with Two Red Tail Lights at Each End

Fig. 1064—Duplex Tri-Color Lantern for Car Signal System

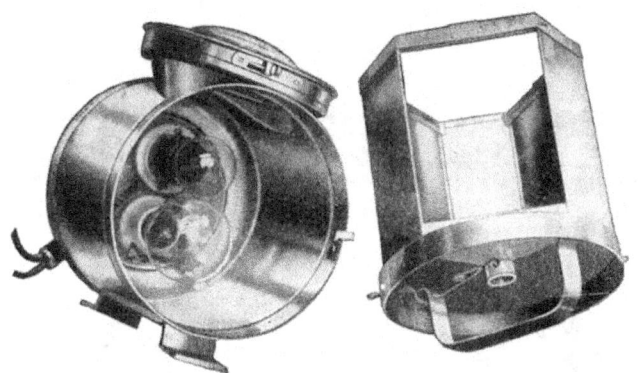

Figs. 1065-1066—Interior Construction of Duplex Tri-Color Lantern for Car Signal System
Ohio Brass Company

Fig. 1067—Relay for Car Signal System
Ohio Brass Company

Fig. 1068—Electric Tail Lamp

Fig. 1069—Electric Destination Marker Lamp

Lintern Car Signal Company

CAR BODY DETAILS, Headlights and Marker Lamps — Figs. 1070-1081

Fig. 1070—One-Light Marker Lamp

Fig. 1071—Three-Light Marker Lamp

Fig. 1072—Exterior of Electric Deck Signal Marker Lamp

Fig. 1073—Interior of Electric Deck Signal Marker Lamp

Peter Gray & Sons

Fig. 1074—One-Light Marker Lamp

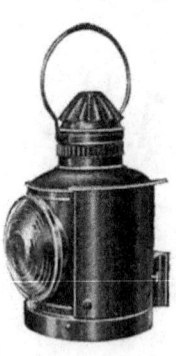

Fig. 1075—One-Light Marker Lamp

Peter Gray & Sons

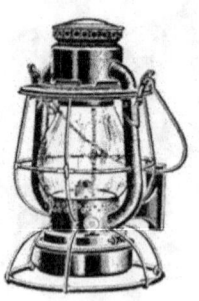

Fig. 1076—Vesta Tail Lamp

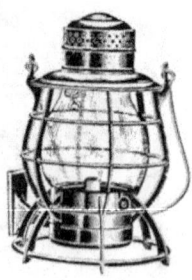

Fig. 1077—Steel-Clad Tail Lamp

R. E. Dietz Company

Fig. 1078—Classification Lamp, No. 77

Fig. 1079—Marker Lamp, No. 78

Fig. 1080—Marker Lamp, No. 83

Fig. 1081—Steel-Clad Tail Lantern, No. 11

Adams & Westlake Company

(183)

CAR BODY DETAILS, Headlights and Marker Lamps

Fig. 1082—Tin Tail Lamp, No. 24

Fig. 1083—Automatic Classification Lamp, Lamp, No. 187½

Fig. 1084—Steel Tail or Classification Lamp, No. 183

Fig. 1085—Automatic Marker Lamp, No. 205

Fig. 1086—Steel Tail Lamp, No. 208

Fig. 1087—Square Body Tin Tail Lamp, No. 19

Fig. 1088—Square Body Tin Tail Lamp, No. 22

Fig. 1089—Square Body Tail Lamp, No. 60

Fig. 1090—Platform Tail Lamp, No. 15

Fig. 1091—Combination Day and Night Corner Marker Lamp

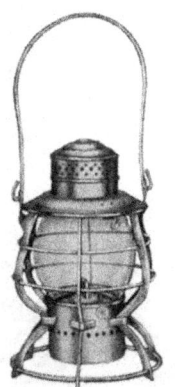

Fig. 1092—Steel Guard Railroad Lantern

Fig. 1093—Double Wire Guard Railroad Lantern

Adams & Westlake Company

CAR BODY DETAILS, Heaters, Hot Water

Fig. 1094—Forced Ventilation Hot Air Car Heater
The Peter Smith Heater Co.

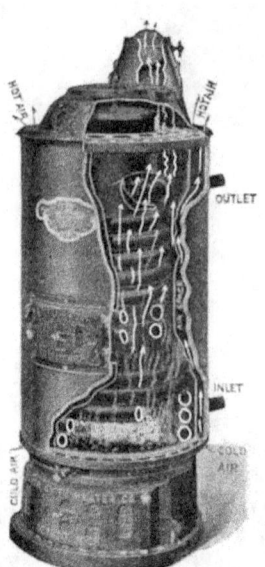

Fig. 1095—Hot Water Car Heater
The Peter Smith Heater Co.

Fig. 1096—Mighty Midget Hot Water Car Heater
Wm. C. Baker

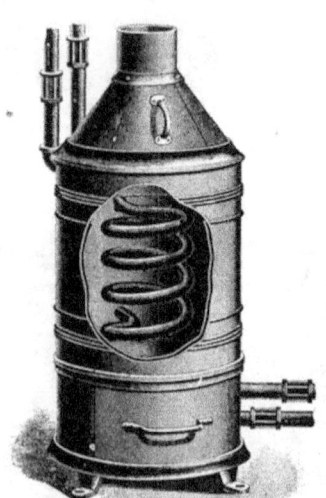

Fig. 1097—Single Coil, Hot Water Car Heater
William C. Baker

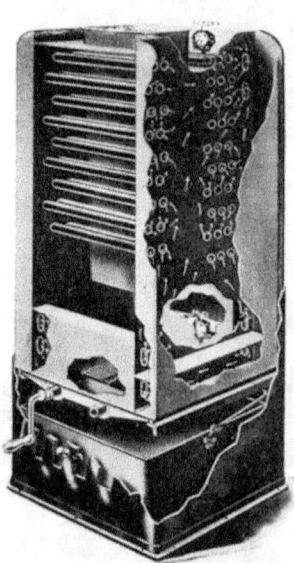

Fig. 1098—Sectional View of Cooper Pressed Steel Hot Water Car Heater

Fig. 1099—Exterior View of Cooper Pressed Steel Hot Water Car Heater

The Cooper Heater Company

CAR BODY DETAILS, Heaters, Stoves

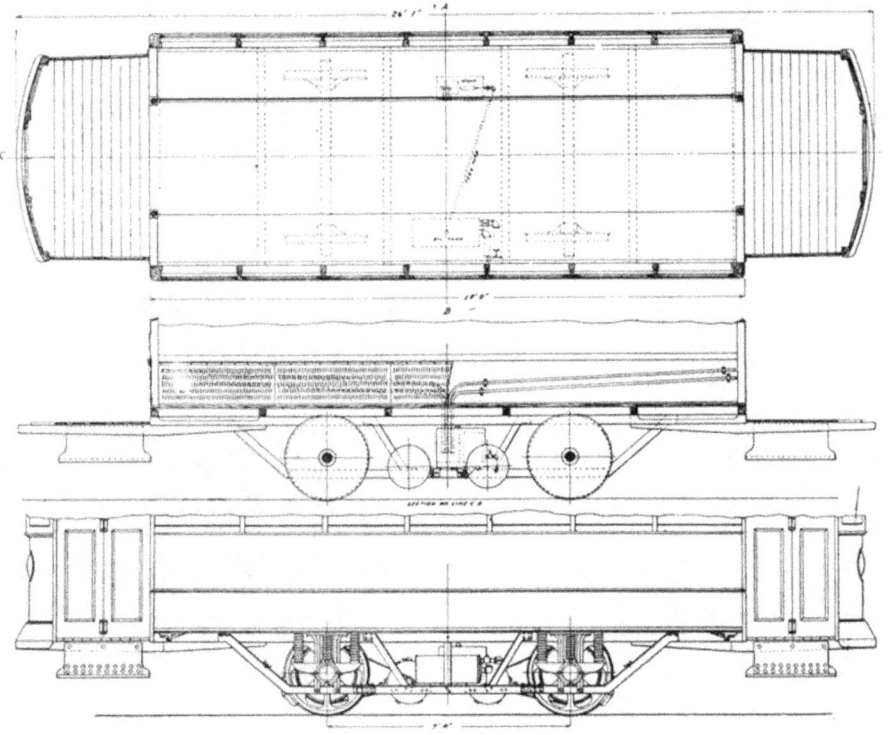

Figs. 1100-1102—Gold Oil-Vacuum System of Heating for Street Cars
Gold Car Heating & Lighting Company

Fig. 1103—New Columbia Car Stove.
Floor Type

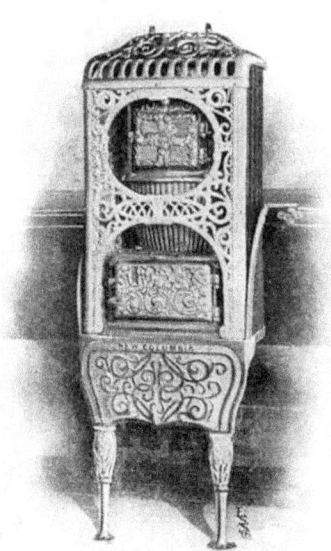

Fig. 1104—New Columbia Car
Stove. Seat Type

Electric Service Supplies Company

Fig. 1105—Jewell Car Stove
Detroit Stove Works

Fig. 1106—Hot Air Car Heater
Detroit Stove Works

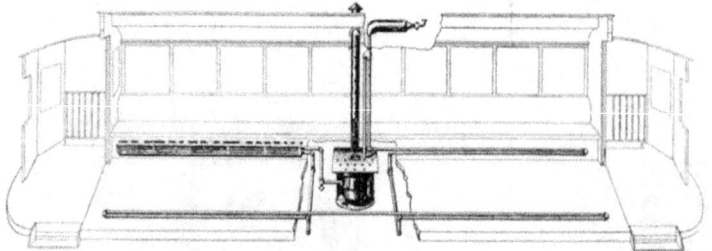

Fig. 1107—Gold's Sealed Jet Accelerator System of Hot Water Heating for **Electric Cars**
Gold Car Heating & Lighting Company

Fig. 1108—Three-Degree Car Heater Switch
Hart & Hegeman Mfg. Company

Fig. 1109—Knife Switch for Electric Heaters

Fig. 1110—Three-Degree Snap Switch for Electric Heaters
Gold Car Heating & Lighting Company

Fig. 1111—Interior View of Three-Degree Snap Switch

CAR BODY DETAILS, Heaters, Electric

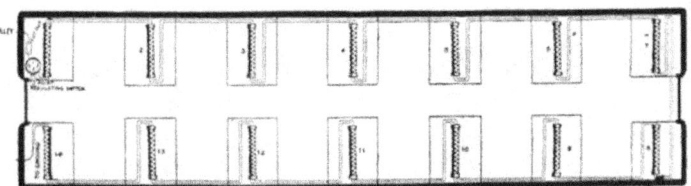

Fig. 1112—Diagram of Installation of Cross-Seat Electric Heater Equipment

Figs. 1113-1114—One-Degree Cross-Seat Heater

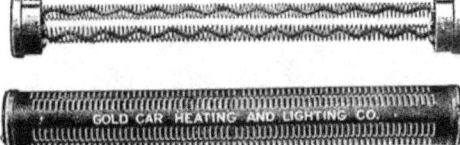

Figs. 1115-1116—Standard Three-Degree Cross-Seat Heater

Fig. 1117—Resistance Coil for Electric Heater

Fig. 1118—Ventilated Core Heater, No. 120E

Fig. 1119—Method of Winding Ventilated Porcelain Core Heater Coil

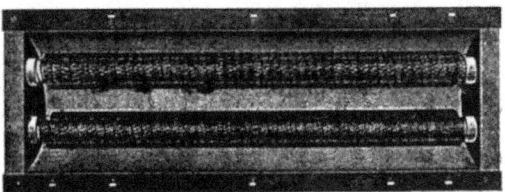

Fig. 1120—Interior View of Ventilated Core, Panel Type Heater, No. 118E

Fig. 1121—Diagram of Installation of Panel Type Electric Car Heaters

Fig. 1122—Interior View of Ventilated Core, Truss Plank Type Heater, No. 119E

Fig. 1123—Ventilated Core, Longitudinal Seat Type Heater, No. 121E

Fig. 1124—Heater for Attachment to Seat Riser

Gold Car Heating & Lighting Company

CAR BODY DETAILS, Heaters, Electric — Figs. 1125-1136

Fig. 1125—Exterior View of Two-Degree, Panel Type Heater

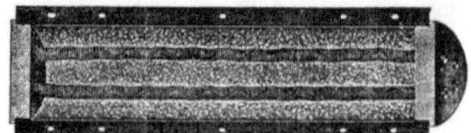

Fig. 1126—Exterior View of Two-Degree, Panel Type Heater

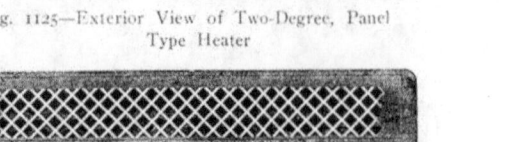

Fig. 1127—Exterior View of Three-Degree, Panel Type Heater

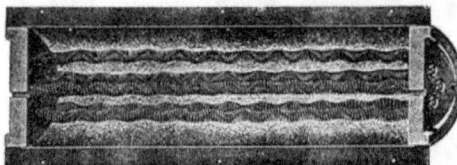

Fig. 1128—Interior View of Three-Degree, Panel Type Heater

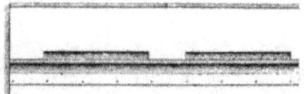

Figs. 1129-1131—Method of Mounting Panel Type Heaters and Deflectors

Gold Car Heating & Lighting Company

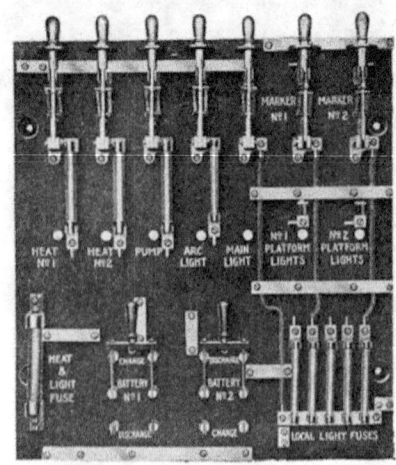

Fig. 1132—Switchboard for Subway and Elevated Cars, No. 201

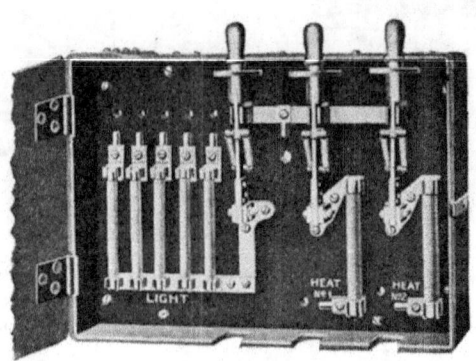

Fig. 1133—Switchboard for Heaters and Lights, No. 213VH

Figs. 1134-1135—Jumper and Socket for Heater Train Line, No. 174

Fig. 1136—Automatic Open Circuiting Cab Heater Switch, No. 248

(189) Consolidated Car-Heating Company

CAR BODY DETAILS, Heaters, Electric

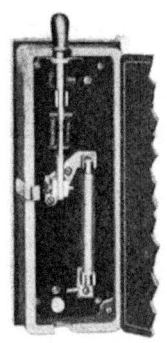

Fig. 1137—Single Quick-Break Knife Switch, No. 213S

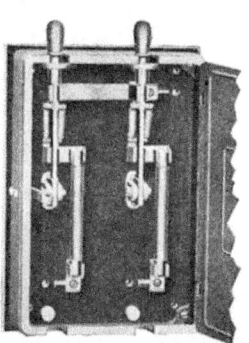

Fig. 1138—Double Quick-Break Knife Switch, No. 213

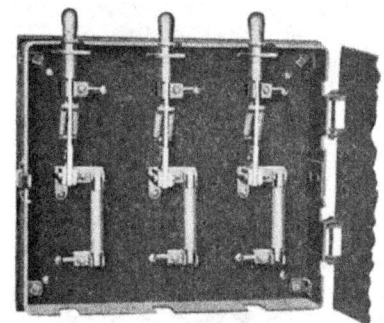

Fig. 1139—Triple Quick-Break Knife Switch, No. 213Z

Fig. 1140—Interior View of Double-Pole Switch for 1200-Volt Heater Equipments, No. 313

Fig. 1141—Exterior View of Double-Pole Switch for 1200-Volt Heater Equipments, No. 313

Fig. 1142—Cab Heater Switch, No. 266. Cover On

Fig. 1143—Cab Heater Switch, No. 266. Cover Off

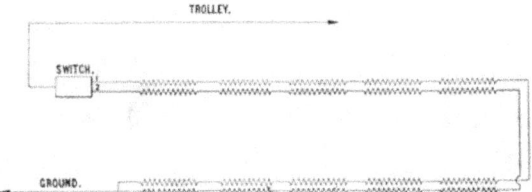

Fig. 1144—Wiring Diagram for Ten-Heater Equipment

Fig. 1145—Double-Coil Cross-Seat Heater, No. 192 W5

Consolidated Car-Heating Company

CAR BODY DETAILS, Heaters, Electric

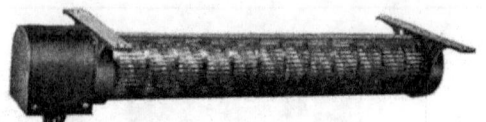

Fig. 1146—Double-Coil Cross-Seat Heater with Junction Box, No. 217RJ

Fig. 1147—Single-Coil Cross-Seat Heater, No. 192

Fig. 1148—Double-Coil, All-Steel Cross-Seat Heater, No. 392

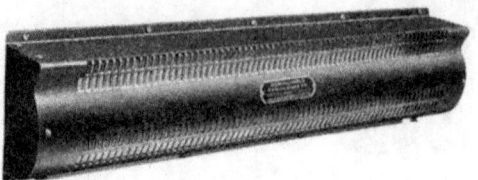

Fig. 1149—Single-Coil, All-Steel Truss Plank Heater, No. 393

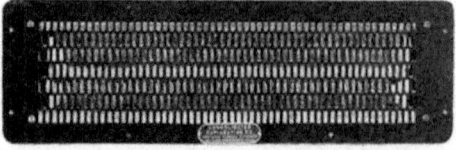

Fig. 1150—Double-Coil, All-Steel Panel Heater, No. 346

Fig. 1151—Single-Coil Panel Heater, No. 221

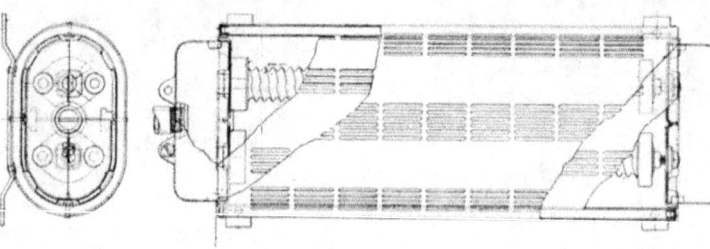

Figs. 1152-1153—Double-Coil, Cross-Seat Heater, No. 392T, for 1200 Volts

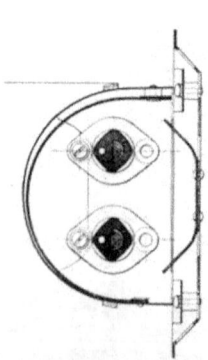

Fig. 1154—Section Through Double-Coil Panel Heater, No. 346T, for 1200 Volts

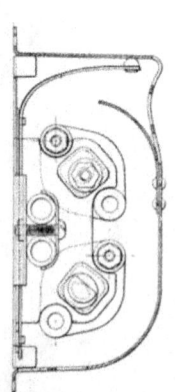

Fig. 1155—Section Through Double-Coil Truss Plank Heater, No. 303T, for 1200 Volts

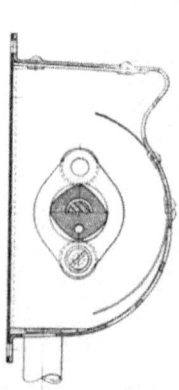

Fig. 1156—Section Through Single-Coil Truss Plank Heater, No. 393T, for 1200 Volts

Fig. 1157—Portable Vestibule or Cab Heater, No. 222

Consolidated Car-Heating Company

Figs. 1158-1165 CAR BODY DETAILS, Registers and Fare Boxes

Fig. 1158—International Single Register

Fig. 1159—International Double Register

International Register Company

Fig. 1160—Ohmer Indicating, Recording and Printing Register

Ohmer Fare Register Co.

Fig. 1161—Sterling Single Register with Separate Direction Indicator

Fig. 1162—Sterling Single Register

Sterling Fare Register Company

Fig. 1163—Sterling Double Register

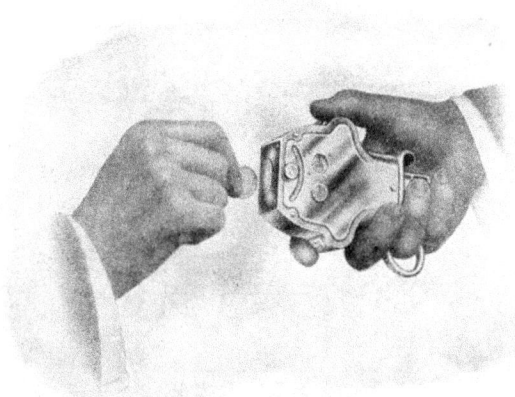

Fig. 1164—Method of Inserting Coin in Rooke Portable Register

Rooke Automatic Register Company

Fig. 1165—Rooke Portable Register

(192)

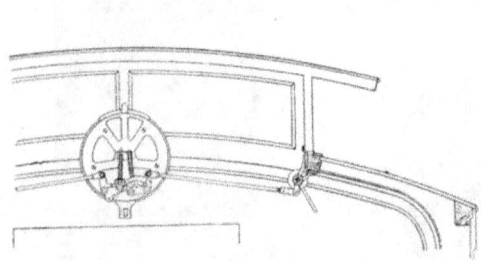
Fig. 1166—Rod Connections for Double Register Back, with Register Rod Mounted Under Deck Sill of Closed Car

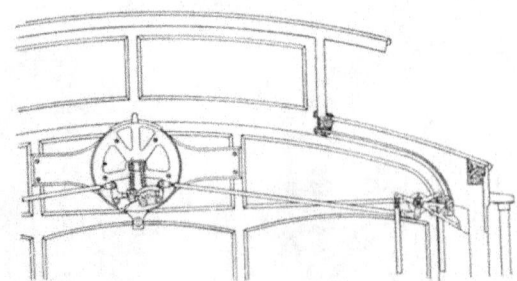
Fig. 1167—Rod Connections for Double Register Back, with Register Rod Mounted Under Side Plate of Open Car

International Register Company

Fig. 1168—Single Register Cord Back

Fig. 1169—Single Register Rod Back
International Register Company

Fig. 1170—Double Register Cord Back

Figs. 1171-1174—Square and Round Register Rod Handles
International Register Company

Fig. 1175—Square Register Rod Removable Handle
Sterling Fare Register Co.

Figs. 1176-1177—Single and Double Register Rod Strap Handles
International Register Company

Figs. 1178-1197   CAR BODY DETAILS, Registers and Fare Boxes

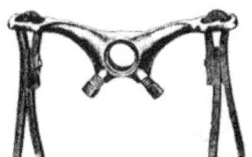

Fig. 1178—Double Strap Handle
Sterling Fare Register Co.

Figs. 1179-1180—Register Rod Cranks

Fig. 1181—Register Rod Coupling

Fig. 1182—Register Rod Bracket

International Register Company

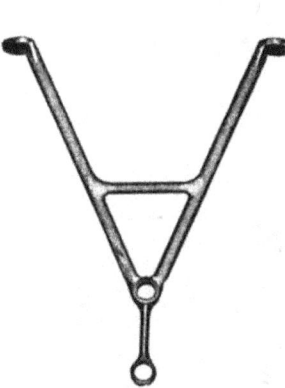

Fig. 1183—Register Rod Center Bracket
Sterling Fare Register Co.

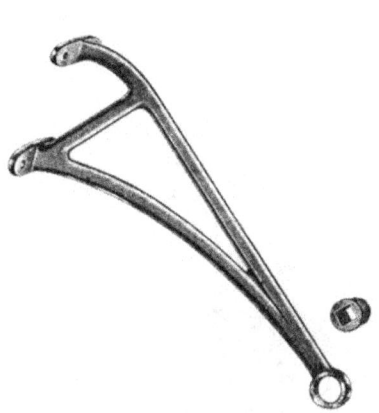

Figs. 1184-1187—Register Rod Brackets and Bushings for Square Rods
International Register Company

Figs. 1188-1189—Adjustable Register Rod Bracket and Bushing

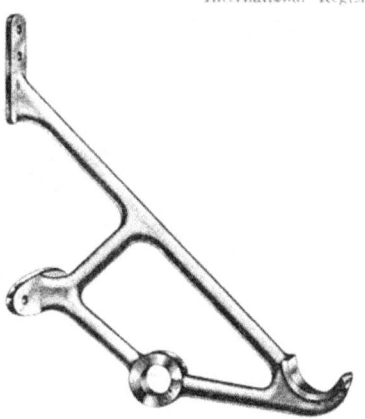

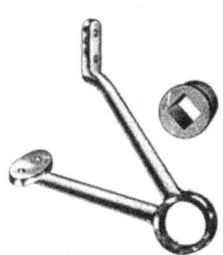

Figs. 1190-1192—Register Rod Brackets and Bushings
International Register Company

Figs. 1193-1196—Register Cord Guides

Fig. 1197—Register Cord Pull for Double Register

International Register Company

(194)

CAR BODY DETAILS, Registers and Fare Boxes — Figs. 1198-1202

Fig. 1198—Brill Portable Fare Box, No. 4A

Fig. 1199—Brill Nickel-Separating Fare Box, No. 5A

Fig. 1200—Brill Single-Compartment-Till, Stationary Fare Box, No. 1A

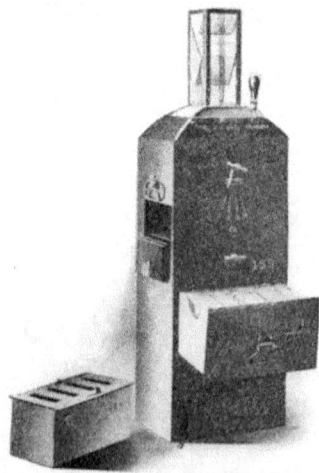

Fig. 1201—Brill Four-Compartment-Till, Stationary Fare Box, No. 2

Fig. 1202—Brill Narrow Four-Compartment-Till, Stationary Fare Box, No. 3

The J. G. Brill Company

Figs. 1203-1207 CAR BODY DETAILS, Registers and Fare Boxes

Fig. 1203—Johnson Fare Box
Johnson Fare Box Co.

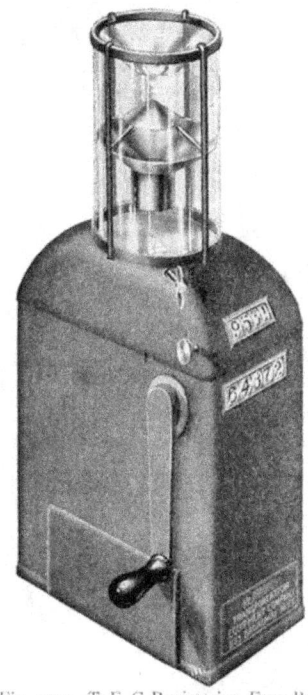

Fig. 1204—T E C Registering Fare Box
Transportation Equipment Co.

Fig. 1205—Coleman Fare Box, No. 2
Coleman Fare Box Co.

Fig. 1206—Coleman Fare Box, No. 1
Coleman Fare Box Company

Fig. 1207—Registering Fare Box
Recording Register & Fare Box Company

CAR BODY DETAILS, Sanders, Pneumatic — Figs. 1208-1214

Fig. 1208—Auxiliary Sander Valve

Fig. 1209—Removable Handle for Auxiliary Sander Valve

Fig. 1210—Independent Sander Valve

Fig. 1211—Sand Trap, Type B, for Pneumatic Sander

Fig. 1212—Top for Sand Trap

Nichols-Lintern Company

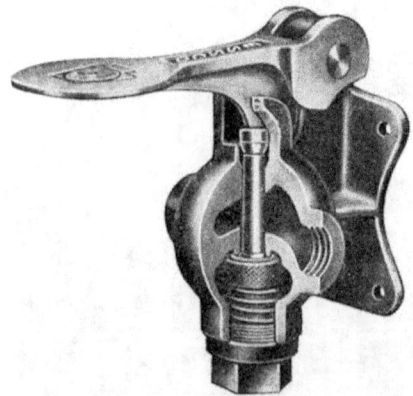

Fig. 1213—Keystone Pneumatic Sander Valve, Single

Fig. 1214—Keystone Pneumatic Sander and Gong Ringer Valve Combined

Electric Service Supplies Company

CAR BODY DETAILS, Sanders, Pneumatic

Fig. 1215—Keystone Pneumatic Sander Valve, Floor Type

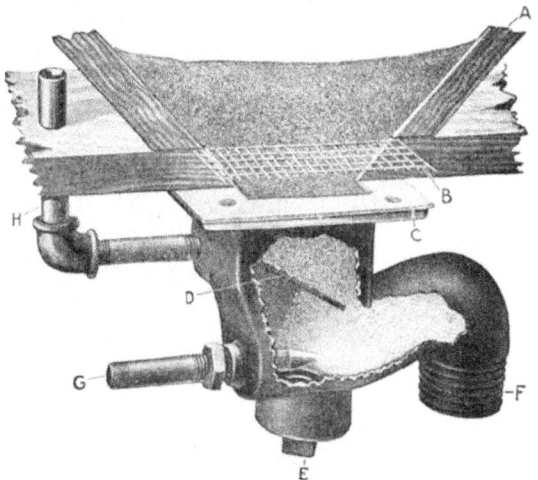

Fig. 1216—Keystone Pneumatic Sander Trap and Hopper

Fig. 1217—Exterior View of Keystone Pneumatic Sander Trap

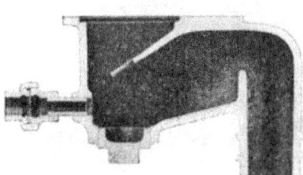

Fig. 1218—Sectional View of Keystone Pneumatic Sander Trap

Electric Service Supplies Company

Fig. 1219—Pneumatic Sander Valve; Diaphragm Type

Fig. 1220—Independent Sander Valve

Fig. 1221—Exterior View of Pneumatic Sander Trap

Fig. 1222—Sectional View of Pneumatic Sander Trap

Ohio Brass Company

CAR BODY DETAILS, Sanders, Mechanical

Fig. 1223—Brill "Dumpit" Sand Box
The J. G. Brill Company

Fig. 1224—Mechanical Tilting Sander, Type 10
Electric Service Supplies Company

Fig. 1225—M-B Sand Box
Western Electric Co.

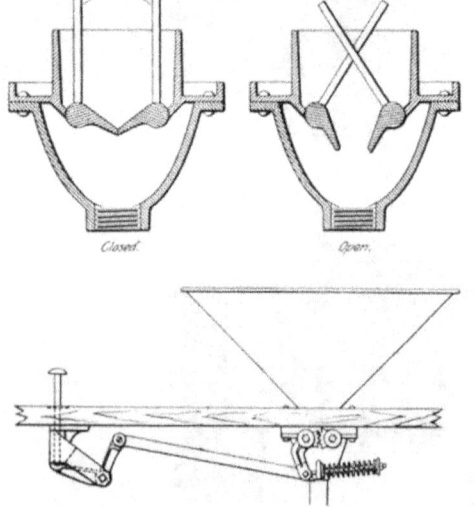

Figs. 1226-1228—Sterling Sand Box
Sterling-Meaker Company

Fig. 1229—Mechanical Gate Sander, Type 7
Electric Service Supplies Company

CAR BODY DETAILS, Sanders, Mechanical

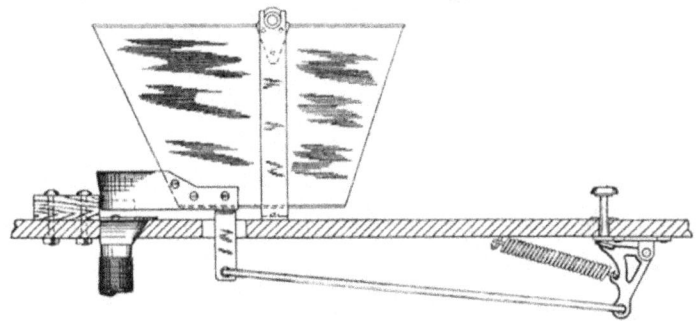

Fig. 1230—Ham Sander, No. 10
Ham Sand Box Company

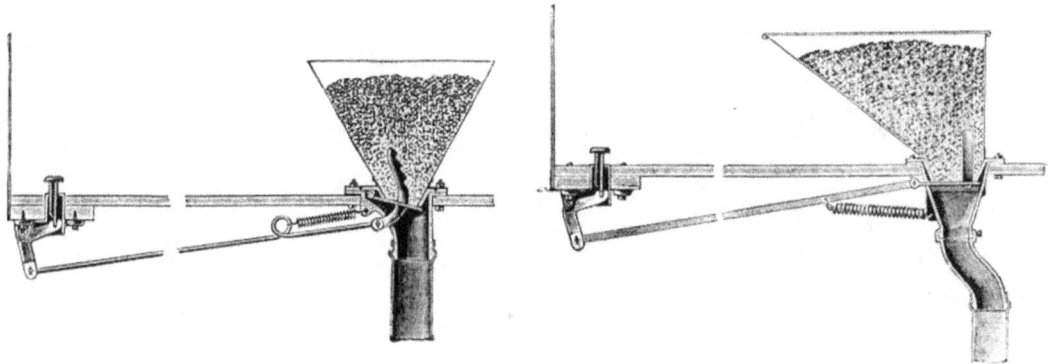

Fig. 1231—De Witt Sand Box

Fig. 1232—Common Sense Sand Box

De Witt Sand Box Company

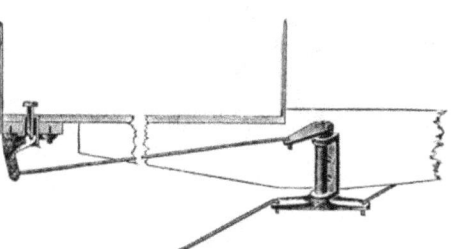

Fig. 1233—Method of Connecting Two De Witt Sand Boxes at Same End of Car

Fig. 1234—Signal Push Button

Fig. 1235—Monitor Type Electric Signal Bell
Electric Service Supplies Company

Fig. 1236—Electric Signal Buzzer

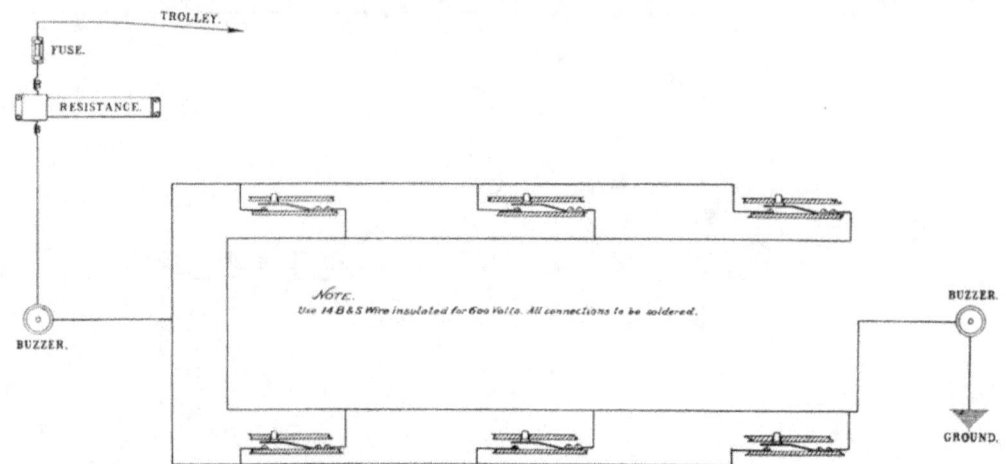

Fig. 1237—Wiring Diagram for Installation of Push Button Buzzer Signal System for Single Car

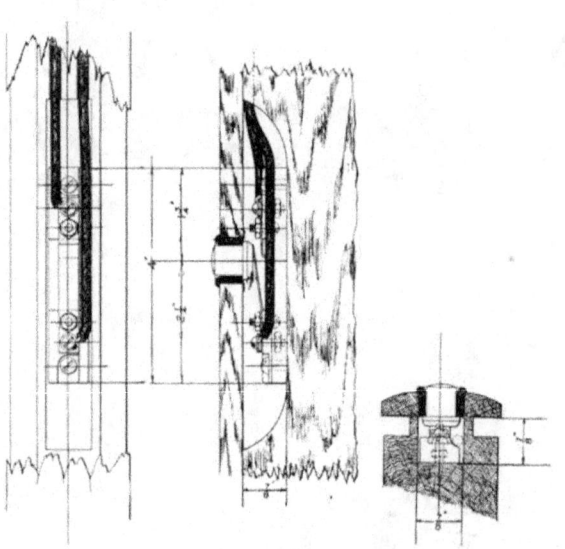

Figs. 1238-1240—Push Button, No. 233D, for Wooden Post

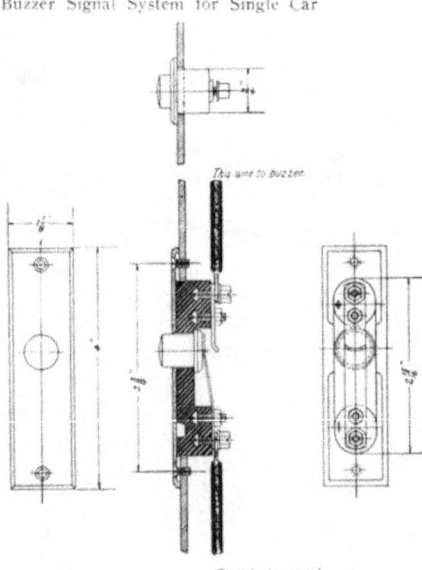

Figs. 1241-1244—Push Button, No. 233F, for Steel Post

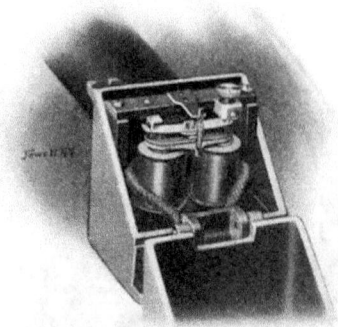

Fig. 1245—Interrupter for Buzzer Signal System

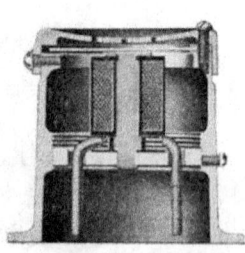

Fig. 1246—Sectional View of Buzzer, No. 233K

Fig. 1247—Fuse Box, No. 233H, for Buzzer Signal System

Consolidated Car-Heating Company

CAR BODY DETAILS, Signal Systems

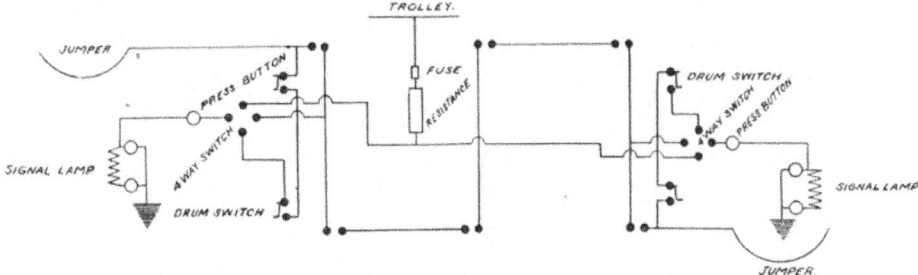

Fig. 1248—Diagram of Train Starting Signal System with Lamp Signal

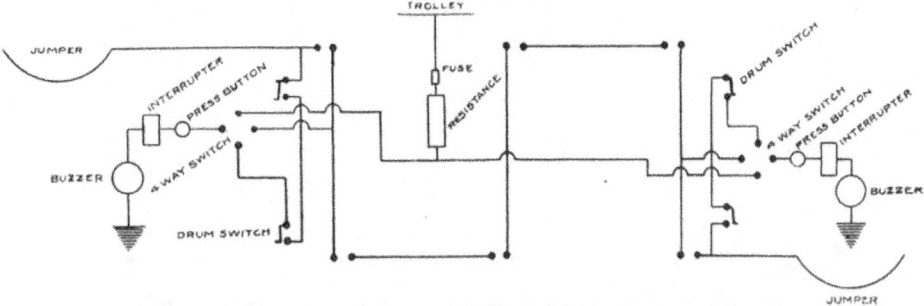

Fig. 1249—Diagram of Train Starting Signal System with Buzzer Signal

Fig. 1250—Clip Type, 850-Ohm Resistance Unit, No. 282E, for Signal System

Fig. 1251—Resistance Unit, No. 256R, for Train Signal System

Figs. 1252-1253—Lamp Signal and Box, No. 256C, for Train Signal System

Fig. 1254—Vestibule Snap Switch for Train Signal System

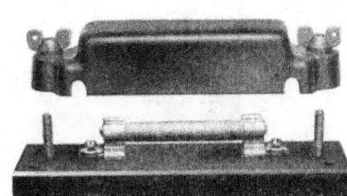

Figs. 1255-1256—Fuse and Box, No. 256F, for Train Signal System

Fig. 1257—Switch on End Cars

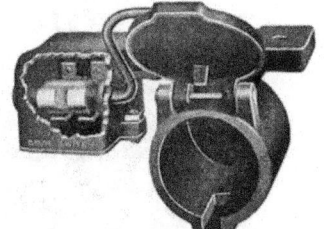

Fig. 1258—Switch on Intermediate Cars

Figs. 1257-1258—Drum Switch, No. 290, for Train Signal System

Consolidated Car-Heating Company

CAR BODY DETAILS, Seats

Fig. 1259—Wheeler Car Seat; High Head Roll, Detachable Leather Back; No. 55AGF

Fig. 1260—Universal Car Seat, Wheeler Reversing Type; Pressed Steel Pedestal and End Plates, No. 325AGF

Fig. 1261—Universal Car Seat, Wheeler Reversing Type; Pressed Steel Pedestal, Single Foot Rest, No. 327SC

Fig. 1262—Turnover Back Car Seat, No. 99

Fig. 1263—Universal Non-Reversible Seat, No. 3SC

Fig. 1264—Universal Car Seat, Wheeler Reversing Type; Slat Seat and Back, No. 327SB

Fig. 1265—Double-Revolving Car Seat, No. 97B

Figs. 1266-1267—Adjustable Folding Motorman's Seat

Heywood Bros. & Wakefield Company

CAR BODY DETAILS, Seats

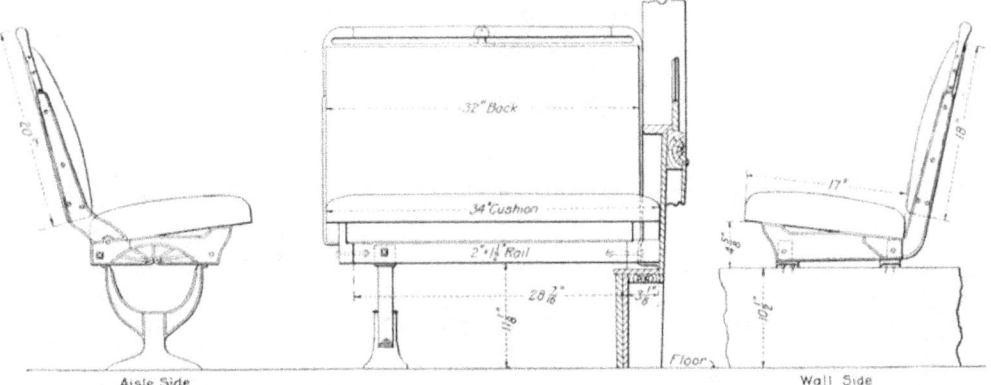

Figs. 1268-1270—Stationary Car Seat
St. Louis Car Company

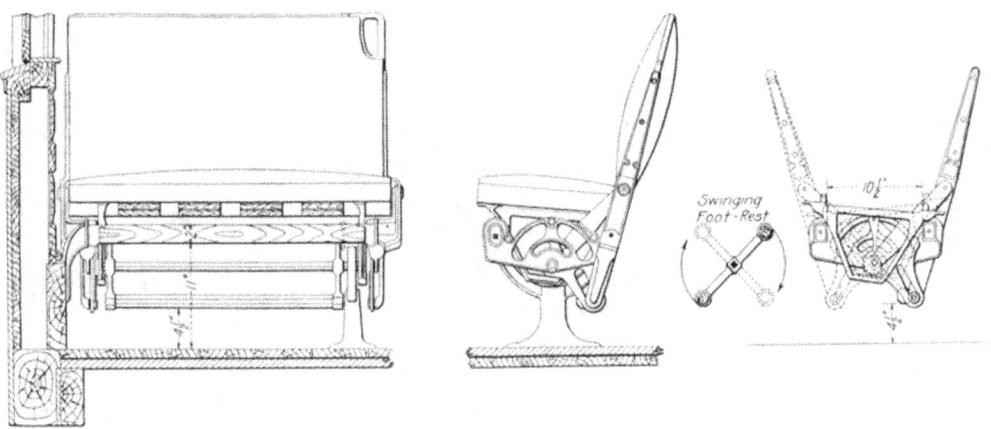

Figs. 1271-1274—Reversible Car Seat with Swinging Foot Rest
St. Louis Car Company

Fig. 1275—Stationary Back Car Seat, No. 35½

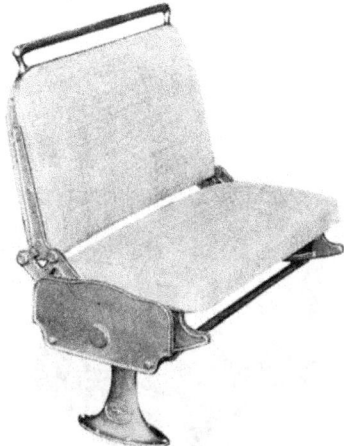

Fig. 1276—Movable Back Car Seat, No. 60

Fig. 1277—Reversible Back Car Seat No. 47

Scarritt-Comstock Furniture Company

CAR BODY DETAILS, Seats — Figs. 1278-1286

Fig. 1278—Walkover Car Seat, No. 99-F, Upholstered in Rattan

Fig. 1279—Walkover Car Seat, No. 199-B, Upholstered in Plush

Fig. 1280—Stationary Seat, No. 770-CE, for Single-End Cars, Upholstered in Rattan

Fig. 1281—Walkover Car Seat, No. 80½, with Double Movable Foot Rest

Fig. 1282—Walkover Slat Seat, No. 199-A, with Pressed Steel Oval Pedestal

Fig. 1283—Walkover Seat, No. 99-EE, for Interurban Cars, Upholstered in Leather

Fig. 1284—All-Steel Walkover Seat, No. 200, for Steel Cars

Fig. 1285—Stationary Seat, No. 11-A, for Single-End Cars

Hale & Kilburn Manufacturing Company

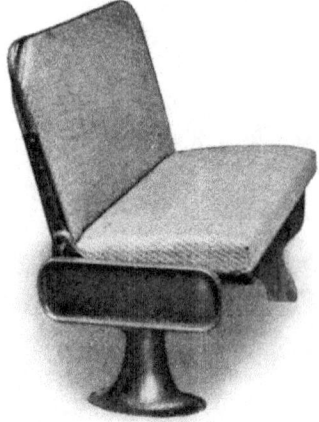

Fig. 1286—Walkover Car Seat, No. 199-A, Upholstered in Rattan

Fig. 1287—Reversible Slat Seat with Movable Foot Rest

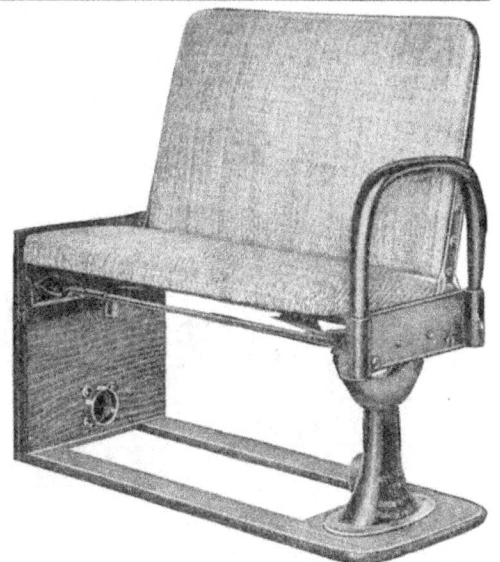

Fig. 1288—Reversible Rattan Seat, with Pipe Arm Rest

Fig. 1289—High Back Reversible Plush Seat for Interurban Cars

Fig. 1290—Reversible Rattan Seat, with Movable Foot Rest

Ford & Johnson Company

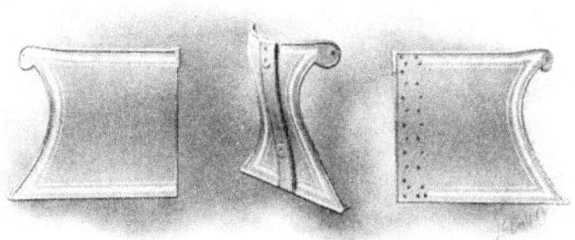

Figs. 1291-1293—Curved Seat End Panels for Open Cars
The J. G. Brill Company

CAR BODY DETAILS, Seats

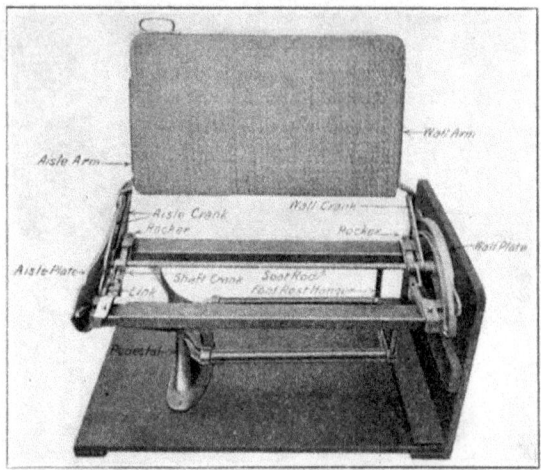

Fig. 1294—Names of Parts of Winner Car Seat

Fig. 1295—Winner Car Seat, with Shifting Cushion and Double Foot Rest

Fig. 1296—Winner Car Seat, with Self-Adjusting Foot Rests

Fig. 1297—Winner Car Seat, with Shifting Cushion and Double Foot Rest

Fig. 1298—Winner Car Seat, with Stationary Back for Single-End Cars

Fig. 1299—Winner Car Seat, with Wooden Arm Rest

Fig. 1300—Winner Car Seat, with Spindle Back

Fig. 1301—Winner Car Seat, with Slat Seat and Back

The J. G. Brill Company

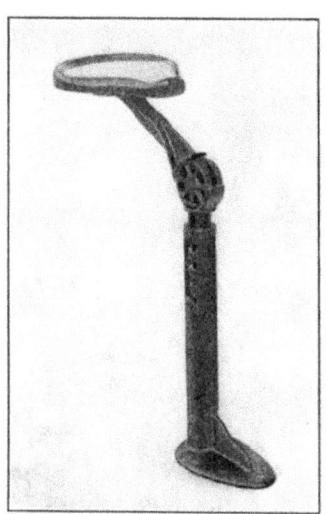
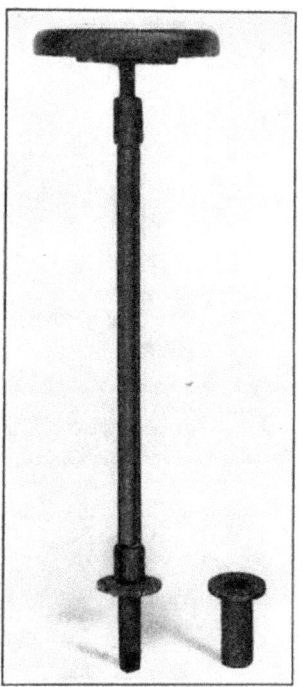

Fig. 1302—Adjustable Motorman's Seat

Figs. 1303-1304—Revolving Motorman's Seat and Floor Bushing

The J. G. Brill Company

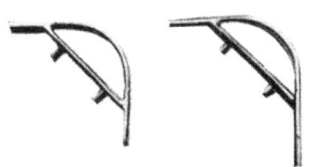  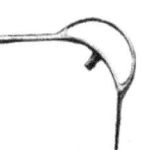  

Figs. 1305-1310—Seat Back Corner Handles
The J. G. Brill Company

Figs. 1312-1314—Seat Back Bumpers
Elastic Tip Company

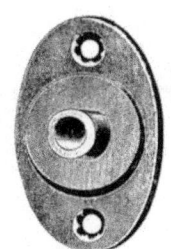

Fig. 1311—Curved Seat Arm for Open Car Seats
J. G. Brill Company

Figs. 1315-1316—Seat Arm Pivots
Adams & Westlake Company

Figs. 1317-1318—Seat Back Bumper Plates

Fig. 1319—Root Spring Scraper, No. 1
Root Spring Scraper Company

Fig. 1320—Root Spring Scraper, No. 5, with Center Blades
Root Spring Scraper Company

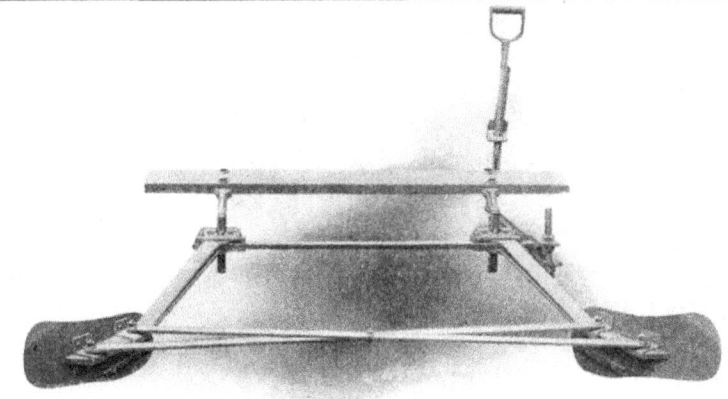

Fig. 1321—Brill Track Scraper
The J. G. Brill Company

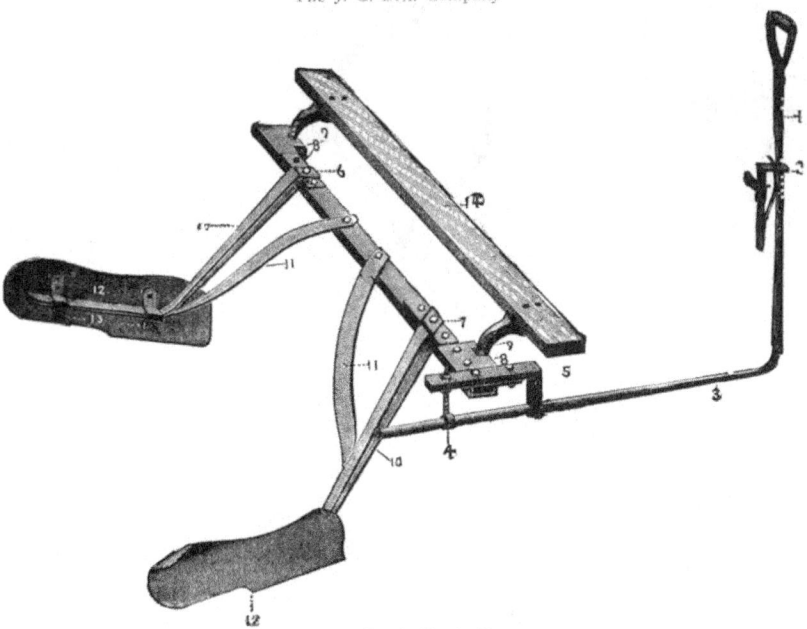

Fig. 1322—Clark Track Scraper
Van Dorn & Dutton Company

Fig. 1323—Adjustable Track Brush Holder
Ohio Brass Company

Fig. 1324—Ice Leveler Applied to Work Car
Gifford-Wood Company

Fig. 1325—Earll Trolley Retriever, No. 5, with Emergency Release

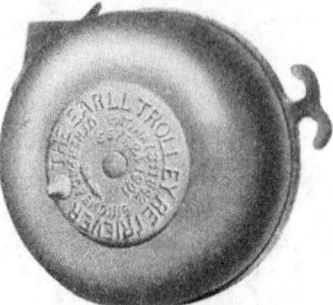

Fig. 1326—Earll Trolley Retriever, No. 4, without Emergency Release
Lord Manufacturing Company

Fig. 1327—Interior of Earll Trolley Retriever, No. 4

Fig. 1328—Interior of Earll Trolley Retriever, No. 5

Fig. 1329—Trolley Retriever or Catcher Socket

Fig. 1330—Interior of Earll Trolley Catcher, No. 7

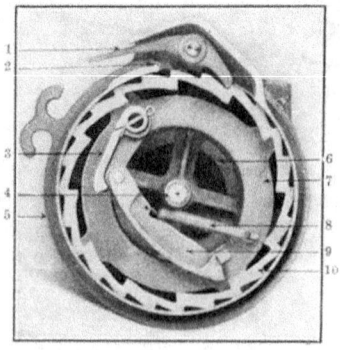

Fig. 1331—Interior of Earll Trolley Catcher, No. 8

Names of Parts of Fig. 1331

1. Release Lever
2. Brake
3. Check Pawl
4. Shaft
5. Back
6. Tension Spring
7. Drum
8. Centrifugal Pawl Spring
9. Centrifugal Pawl
10. Ratchet Ring

Fig. 1332—Ridlon Trolley Catcher
Frank Ridlon Company

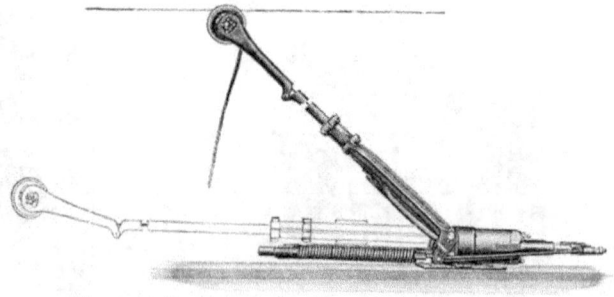

Fig. 1333—Prentiss Trolley Base with Pneumatic Retriever
A. L. Prentiss & Company

CAR BODY DETAILS, Trolley Catchers and Retrievers

Figs. 1334-1336—Front, Back and Interior Views of Wilson Trolley Catcher
Wilson Trolley Catcher Company

Fig. 1337—Wilson Trolley Retriever
Wilson Trolley Catcher Co.

Fig. 1338—Ideal Trolley Catcher
Trolley Supply Company

Fig. 1339—Knutson Trolley Retriever

Fig. 1340—Perry Ventilator Applied to Curved Roof Car

Perry Ventilator Corporation

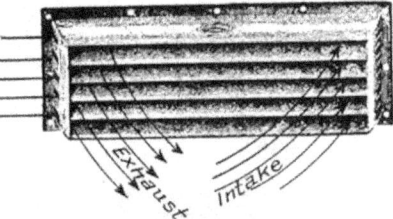

Fig. 1341—Exterior View of Perry Deck Sash Ventilator, Showing Direction of Air Currents

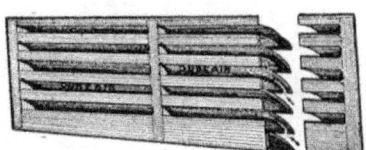

Fig. 1342—Interior View of Perry Deck Sash Ventilator

CAR BODY DETAILS, Ventilators

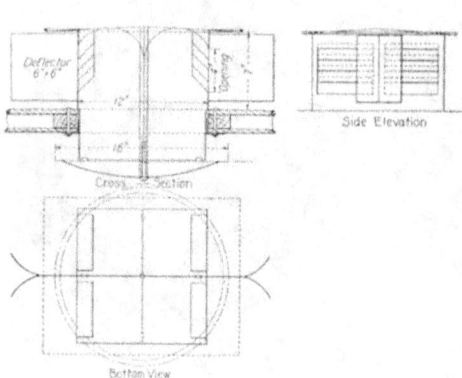

Figs. 1343-1345—Automatic Ventilator Applied on Center Line of Arch Roof Car

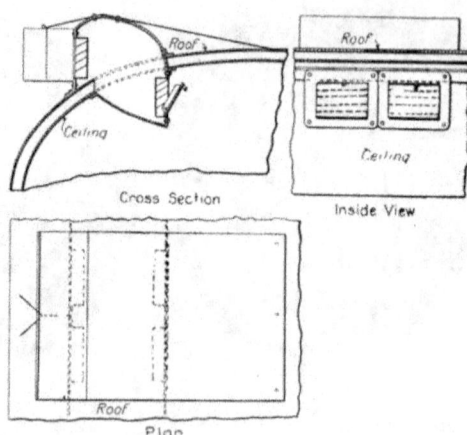

Figs. 1346-1348—Automatic Ventilator Applied on Side of Arch Roof Car

Automatic Ventilator Company

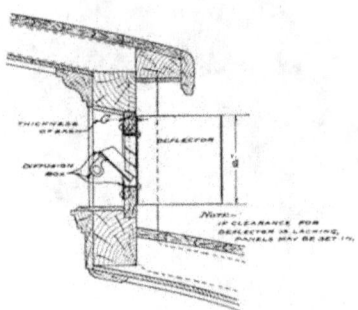

Fig. 1349—Automatic Ventilator Applied to Deck Sash Opening
Automatic Ventilator Company

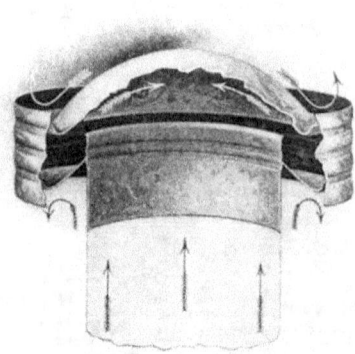

Fig. 1351—Globe Ventilator
Globe Ventilator Co.

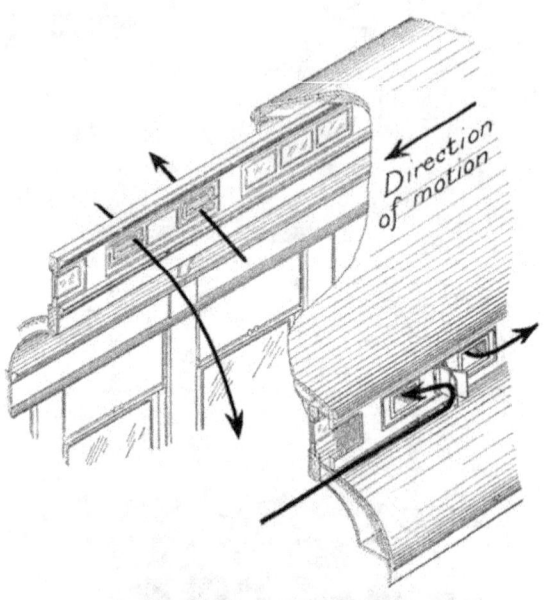

Fig. 1350—Diagram Showing Direction of Intake and Exhaust Air Currents Through Automatic Ventilators Applied to Deck Sash Openings
Automatic Ventilator Co.

CAR BODY DETAILS, Ventilators

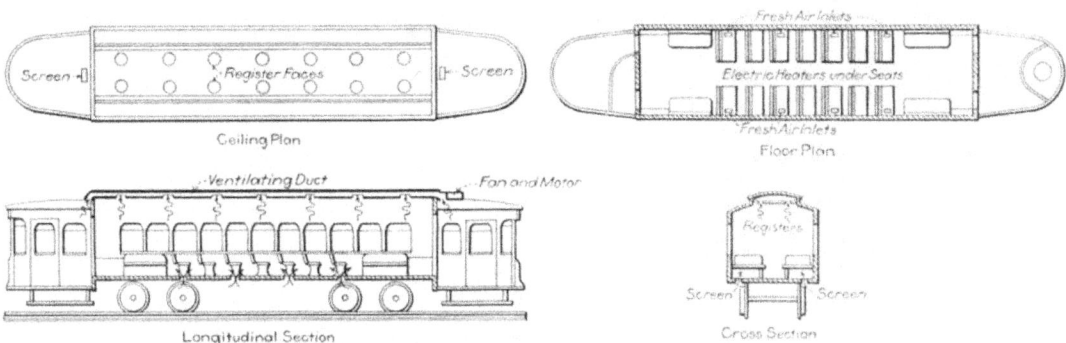

Figs. 1352-1355—Diagrammatic Views Showing Principle of Cooke System of Forced Ventilation for Electric Railway Cars

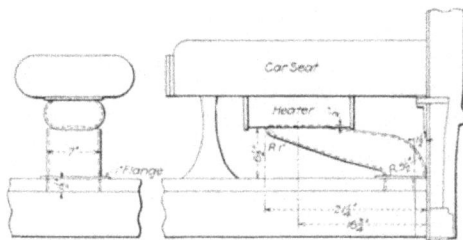

Figs. 1356-1357—Details of Fresh Air Intake Flues Under Seats

Fig. 1358—Exhaust Fan and Motor Mounted on Vestibule Hood

Fig. 1359—Interior View of Car Showing Exhaust Registers in Ceiling

Vacuum Car Ventilating Company

CAR BODY DETAILS, Ventilators

Fig. 1360—Phantom View of Garland Ventilator

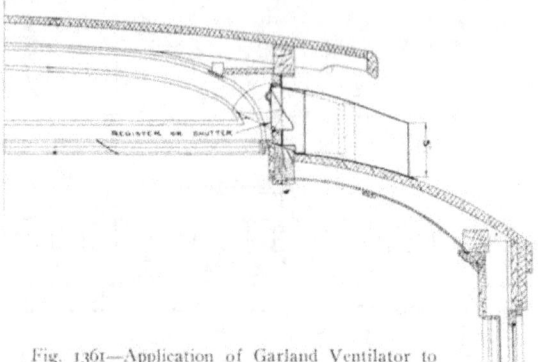

Fig. 1361—Application of Garland Ventilator to Monitor Deck Roof

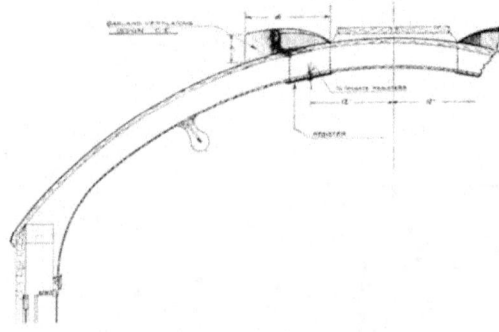

Fig. 1362—Application of Garland Ventilator to Side of Elliptical Roof with Inside Ceiling

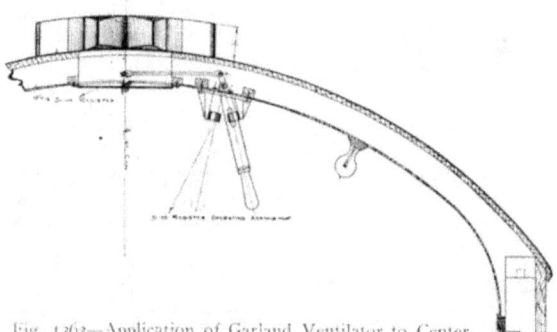

Fig. 1363—Application of Garland Ventilator to Center Line of Elliptical Roof, Showing Slide Register Operated from Ends of Car

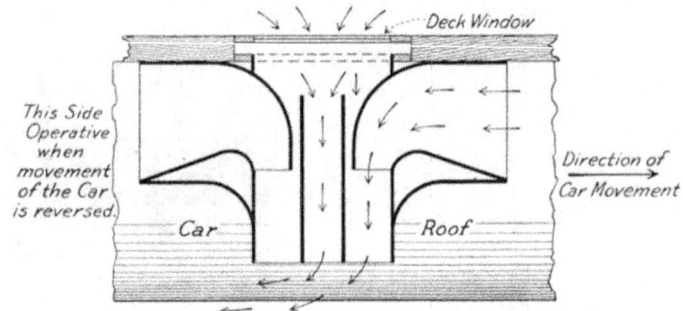

Fig. 1364—Diagram of Air Currents in Garland Ventilator

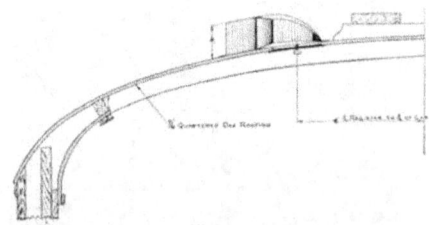

Fig. 1365—Application of Garland Ventilator to Side of Elliptical Roof Without Inside Ceiling

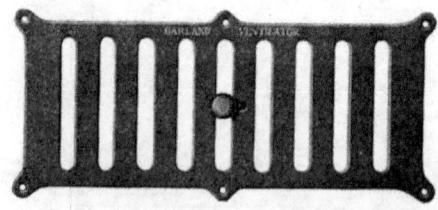

Fig. 1366—Register for Garland Ventilator

Burton W. Mudge & Company

Fig. 1367—Brill No. 27-M. C. B. High-Speed Interurban Truck
The J. G. Brill Company

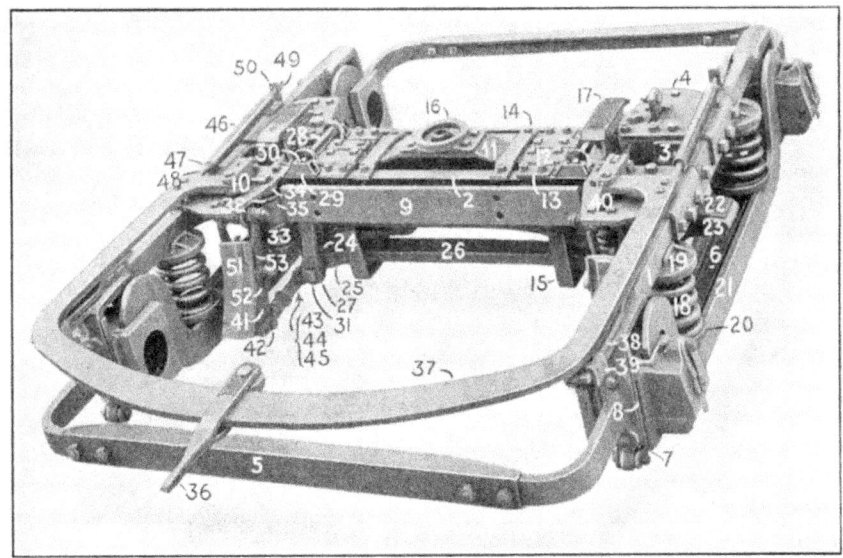

Fig. 1368—Frame and Details of Brill No. 27-M. C. B. Truck

Names of Parts of Fig. 1368

1. Side Frame
2. Transom
3. Transom Corner Bracket
4. Transom Gusset Plate
5. End Frame
6. Pedestal Tie Bar
7. Pedestal Cap
8. Pedestal Gib or Wear Plate
9. Motor Suspension Bar
10. Motor Suspension Bar Bolt
11. Bolster
12. Bolster Chafing Plate
13. Transom Chafing Plate
14. Transom Tie Bar
15. Spring Plank Safety Hanger
16. Truck Center Plate
17. Side Bearing Wear Plate
18. Equalizer Spring
19. Equalizer Spring Cap
20. Equalizer Spring Seat
21. Equalizer or Equalizing Bar
22. Bolster Spring
23. Bolster Spring Scroll
24. Bolster Spring Seat
25. Bolster Spring Seat Rocker
26. Spring Plank
27. Swing Link or Bolster Hanger
28. Swing Link Pin (Top)
29. Swing Link Pin Pivot
30. Swing Link Pin Bearing
31. Swing Link Pin (Bottom)
32. Motor Suspension Spring (Top)
33. Motor Suspension Spring (Bottom)
34. Motor Suspension Spring Cap
35. Motor Suspension Spring Seat
36. Brake Rod
37. Radius Bar
38. Radius Bar Wear Plate
39. Radius Bar Guide
40. Radius Bar Clevis
41. Live Lever
42. Brake Turnbuckle End
43. Brake Turnbuckle
44. Brake Turnbuckle Lock
45. Brake Turnbuckle Lock Spring
46. Brake Release Spring
47. Brake Release Spring Casting
48. Brake Release Spring Hook Bolt
49. Brake Release Spring Nut
50. Brake Release Spring Clip
51. Brake Shoe
52. Brake Head
53. Brake Hanger

TRUCKS, General Views; Brill

Fig. 1369—Brill No. 27-F Short Wheelbase Truck for Outside-Hung Motors
The J. G. Brill Company

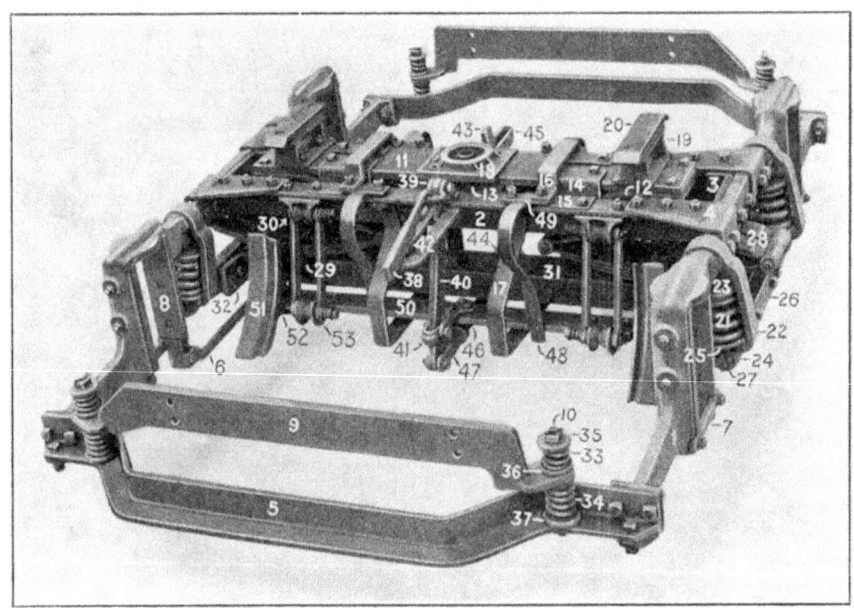

Fig. 1370—Frame and Details of Brill No. 27-F Truck

Names of Parts of Fig. 1370

1. Side Frame
2. Transom
3. Transom Corner Bracket
4. Transom Gusset Plate
5. End Frame
6. Pedestal Tie Bar
7. Pedestal Cap
8. Pedestal Gib or Wear Plate
9. Motor Suspension Bar
10. Motor Suspension Bar Bolt
11. Bolster Top Plate
12. Bolster Bottom Plate
13. Bolster Filling Casting
14. Bolster Chafing Plate
15. Transom Chafing Plate
16. Transom Tie Bar
17. Brake Beam Safety Hanger
18. Truck Center Plate
19. Side Bearing
20. Side Bearing Wear Plate
21. Equalizer Spring
22. Equalizer Spring Link
23. Equalizer Spring Cap
24. Equalizer Spring Eye-Bolt
25. Equalizer Spring Seat
26. Equalizer or Equalizing Bar
27. Equalizer Nut
28. Bolster Spring
29. Bolster Spring Seat
30. Bolster Spring Cap
31. Spring Plank
32. Spring Plank Carrier
33. Motor Suspension Spring (Top)
34. Motor Suspension Spring (Bottom)
35. Motor Suspension Spring Cap
36. Motor Suspension Spring Seat (Top)
37. Motor Suspension Spring Seat (Bottom)
38. Brake Rod
39. Brake Rod Clevis
40. Live Lever
41. Live Lever Fulcrum
42. Live Lever Guide
43. Dead Lever
44. Dead Lever Fulcrum
45. Dead Lever Guide
46. Bottom Truck Connection
47. Bottom Truck Connection Jaw
48. Brake Release Spring
49. Brake Release Spring Clip
50. Brake Beam
51. Brake Shoe
52. Brake Head
53. Brake Hanger

TRUCKS, General Views; Brill

Fig. 1371—Brill, No. 27-G, Short Wheelbase Truck for Outside-Hung Motors
The J. G. Brill Company

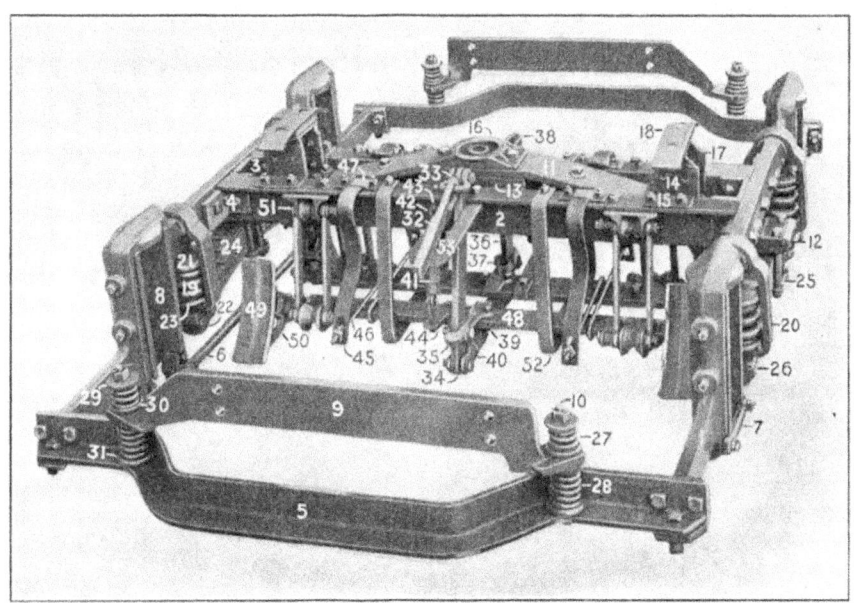

Fig. 1372—Frame and Details of Brill, No. 27-G, Truck

Names of Parts of Fig. 1372

1. Side Frame
2. Transom
3. Transom Corner Bracket (Inside)
4. Transom Corner Bracket (Outside)
5. End Frame
6. Pedestal Tie Bar
7. Pedestal Cap
8. Pedestal Gib or Wear Plate
9. Motor Suspension Bar
10. Motor Suspension Bar Bolt
11. Bolster Top Plate
12. Bolster Bottom Plate
13. Bolster Filling Casting
14. Bolster Chafing Plate
15. Transom Chafing Plate
16. Truck Center Plate
17. Side Bearing
18. Side Bearing Wear Plate
19. Equalizer Spring
20. Equalizer Spring Link
21. Equalizer Spring Cap
22. Equalizer Spring Bolt
23. Equalizer Spring Seat
24. Bolster Spring
25. Bolster Spring Seat
26. Bolster Spring Seat Rocker
27. Motor Suspension Spring (Top)
28. Motor Suspension Spring (Bottom)
29. Motor Suspension Spring Cap
30. Motor Suspension Spring Seat (Top)
31. Motor Suspension Spring Seat (Bottom)
32. Brake Rod
33. Brake Rod Clevis
34. Live Lever
35. Live Lever Fulcrum
36. Dead Lever
37. Dead Lever Fulcrum
38. Dead Lever Guide
39. Bottom Truck Connection
40. Bottom Truck Connection Jaw
41. Brake Beam Adjusting Spring
42. Brake Beam Adjusting Spring Eye
43. Brake Beam Adjusting Spring Hook Bolt
44. Brake Beam Adjusting Spring Clip
45. Brake Release Spring
46. Brake Release Spring Hook Bolt
47. Brake Release Spring Clip
48. Brake Beam
49. Brake Shoe
50. Brake Head
51. Brake Hanger
52. Brake Beam Safety Hanger
53. Live Lever Guide

TRUCKS, General Views; Brill Figs. 1373-1374

Fig. 1373—Brill Single-Motor Truck, No. 39-E
The J. G. Brill Company

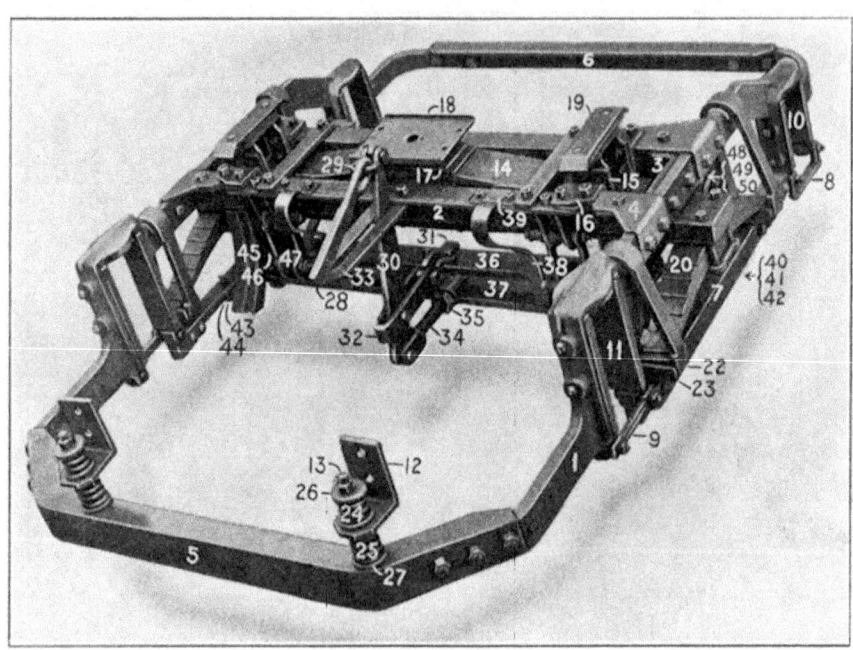

Fig. 1374—Frame and Details of Brill Single-Motor Truck, No. 39-E

Names of Parts of Fig. 1374

1. Side Frame
2. Transom
3. Transom Corner Bracket
4. Transom Gusset Plate
5. End Frame (Motor End)
6. End Frame (Trail End)
7. Pedestal Tie Bar
8. Pedestal Cap (Trail)
9. Pedestal Cap (Motor)
10. Pedestal Gib (Trail)
11. Pedestal Gib (Motor)
12. Motor Suspension Bracket
13. Motor Suspension Bracket Bolt
14. Bolster
15. Bolster Chafing Plate
16. Transom Chafing Plate
17. Truck Center Plate
18. Body Center Plate
19. Side Bearing Wear Plate
20. Bolster Spring
21. Bolster Spring Link
22. Bolster Spring Seat Rocker
23. Bolster Spring Seat
24. Motor Suspension Spring (Top)
25. Motor Suspension Spring (Bottom)
26. Motor Suspension Spring Cap
27. Motor Suspension Spring Seat
28. Brake Rod
29. Brake Rod Clevis
30. Live Lever
31. Live Lever Fulcrum Jaw
32. Live Lever Fulcrum
33. Live Lever Guide
34. Bottom Truck Connection
35. Bottom Truck Connection Adjusting Nut
36. Brake Beam (Driving Wheel)
37. Brake Beam (Trail Wheel)
38. Brake Beam Release Spring (Driving Wheel)
39. Brake Beam Release Spring Clip (Driving Wheel)
40. Brake Beam Release Spring (Trail Wheel)
41. Brake Beam Release Spring Bolt (Trail Wheel)
42. Brake Beam Release Spring Cap (Trail Wheel)
43. Brake Beam Slide
44. Brake Beam Slide Wear Plate
45. Brake Shoe (Driving Wheel)
46. Brake Head (Driving Wheel)
47. Brake Hanger (Driving Wheel)
48. Brake Shoe (Trail Wheel)
49. Brake Head (Trail Wheel)
50. Brake Hanger (Trail Wheel)

TRUCKS, General Views; Brill

Fig. 1375—Brill Single-Motor Truck, No. 22
The J. G. Brill Company

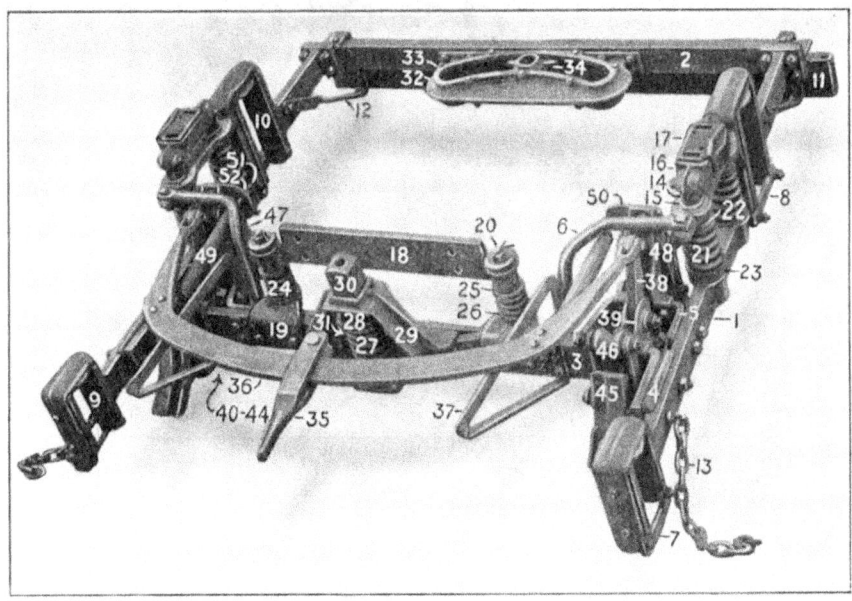

Fig. 1376—Frame and Details of Brill Single-Motor Truck, No. 22

Names of Parts of Fig. 1376

1. Side Frame
2. End Frame
3. Cross Bar
4. Cross Bar Carrier
5. Brake Hanger Carrier
6. Spring Post Frame Extension Brace
7. Pedestal Cap (Trail)
8. Pedestal Cap (Motor)
9. Pedestal Gib (Trail)
10. Pedestal Gib (Motor)
11. Wheelguard
12. Wheelguard Bracket
13. Safety Chain
14. Body Spring Post
15. Body Spring Post Bushing
16. Side Bearing
17. Side Bearing Wear Plate
18. Motor Suspension Bar
19. Motor Suspension Spring Bracket
20. Motor Suspension Bar Bolt
21. Body Spring
22. Body Spring Cap
23. Body Spring Seat
24. Motor Suspension Spring
25. Motor Suspension Spring Cap
26. Motor Suspension Spring Seat
27. Compression Spring
28. Compression Spring Cap
29. Compression Spring Bracket
30. Compression Block
31. Compression Spring Post
32. Radial Casting
33. Radial Casting Plate
34. Radial Block
35. Brake Rod
36. Radius Bar
37. Radius Bar Slide
38. Live Lever
39. Live Lever Fulcrum
40. Bottom Truck Connection (Driving Wheel)
41. Bottom Truck Connection (Trail Wheel)
42. Brake Link
43. Bottom Truck Connection Nut
44. Bottom Truck Connection Jamb Nut
45. Brake Shoe (Trail Wheel)
46. Brake Hanger (Trail Wheel)
47. Brake Shoe (Driving Wheel)
48. Brake Hanger (Driving Wheel)
49. Brake Release Spring
50. Brake Release Spring Holder
51. Brake Release Spring Bolt
52. Brake Release Spring Nut

Fig. 1377—Brill Single Truck, No. 21-E
The J. G. Brill Company

Fig. 1378—Frame and Details of Brill Single Truck, No. 21-E

Names of Parts of Fig. 1378

1. Side Frame
2. End Frame
3. Diagonal Brace
4. Top Chord
5. Spring Post Stay
6. Body Spring Post
7. Spring Post Stay Lug
8. Motor Suspension Bar
9. Motor Suspension Bar Bolt
10. Wheelguard
11. Wheelguard Bracket
12. Body Spring
13. Body Spring Cap
14. Body Spring Seat
15. Motor Suspension Spring (Top)
16. Motor Suspension Spring (Bottom)
17. Motor Suspension Spring Cap
18. Motor Suspension Spring Seat
19. Body End Spring
20. Body End Spring Cap
21. Body End Spring U-Bolt
22. Brake Rod
23. Brake Beam
24. Brake Lever
25. Equalizing Lever
26. Equalizing Lever Casting
27. Equalizing Lever Fulcrum
28. Brake Lever Casting
29. Brake Lever Stud
30. Brake Beam Fulcrum
31. Brake Hanger
32. Brake Release Spring

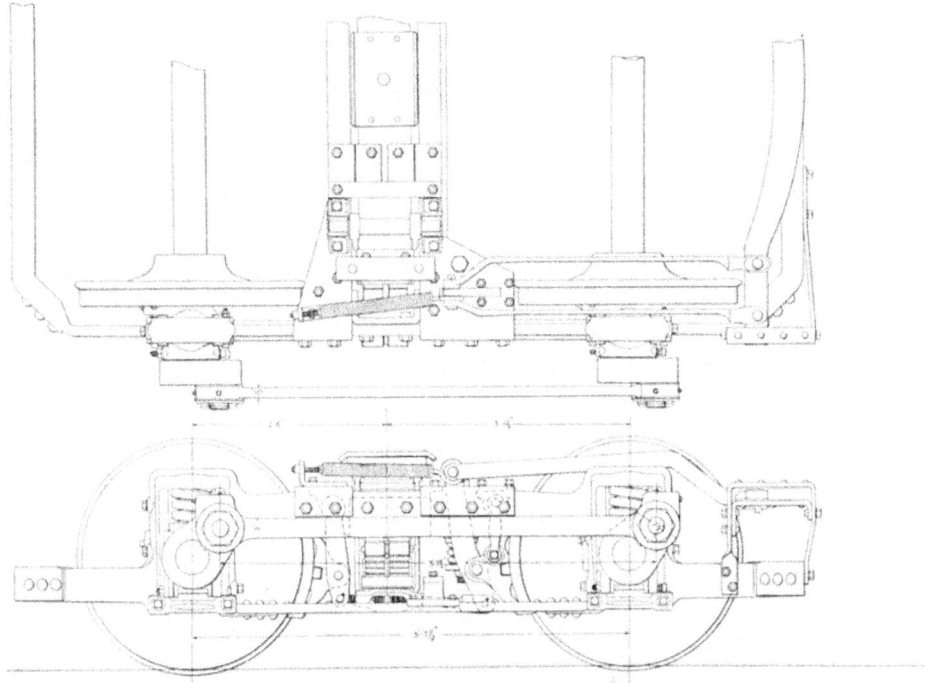

Figs. 1379-1380—Half Plan and Side Elevation of Brill Special Truck with Side Rods; Pittsburg Railways
The J. G. Brill Company

Fig. 1381—Brill No. 27-E, High-Speed Interurban Truck
The J. G. Brill Company

Fig. 1382—Brill Diamond Arch Bar Motor Truck, No. 50, for Work and Freight Cars
The J. G. Brill Company

Fig. 1383—Brill Diamond Arch Bar Trailer Truck, No. 57, for Work and Freight Cars
The J. G. Brill Company

Fig. 1384—Brill Cast Steel Side Frame Motor Truck, No. 23
The J. G. Brill Company

TRUCKS, General Views; Baldwin

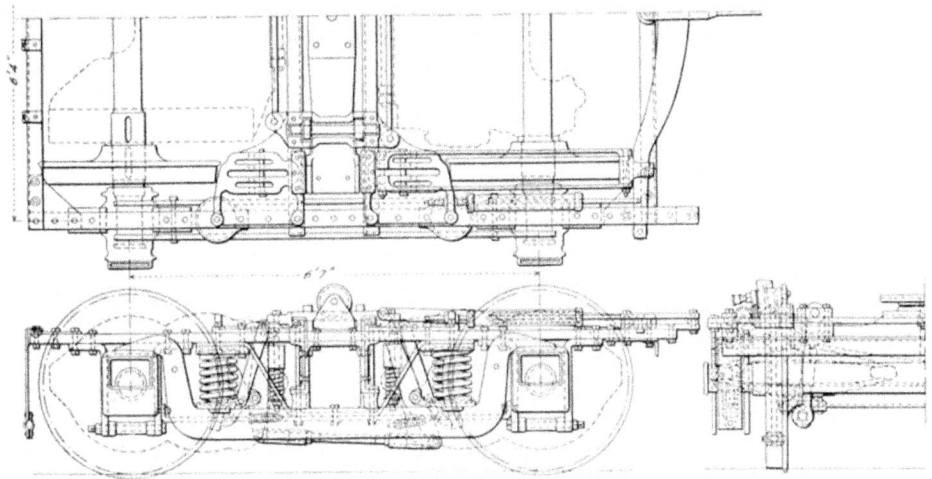

Figs. 1385-1387—Baldwin M. C. B. Type, High-Speed Interurban Truck, No. 78-25-A
Baldwin Locomotive Works

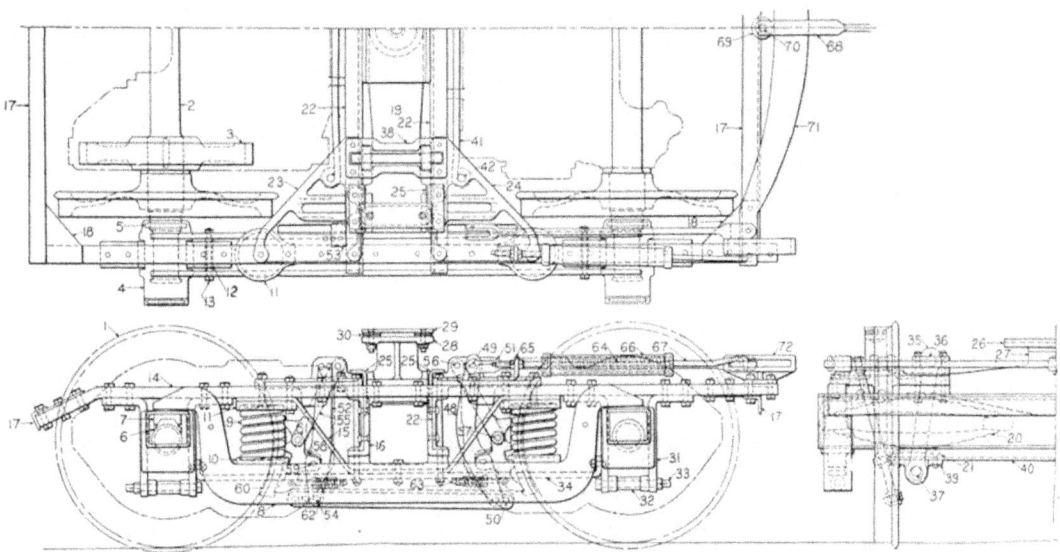

Figs. 1388-1390—Baldwin M. C. B. Type, High-Speed Interurban Truck
Baldwin Locomotive Works

Names of Parts of Figs. 1388-1390

1. Wheel
2. Axle
3. Gear
4. Journal Box
5. Dust Guard
6. Journal Bearing
7. Journal Bearing Wedge
8. Equalizer or Equalizing Bar
9. Equalizer Spring
10. Equalizer Spring Seat
11. Equalizer Spring Cap
12. Equalizer Separator
13. Equalizer Separator Bolt
14. Side Frame
15. Side Frame Truss or Arch Bar
16. Column or Frame Filler
17. End Frame
18. End Frame Gusset Plate
19. Bolster
20. Bolster Spring
21. Bolster Spring Seat
22. Transom
23. Transom Gusset (Front)
24. Transom Gusset (Back)
25. Transom Chafing Plate
26. Body Center Plate
27. Truck Center Plate
28. Side Bearing
29. Side Bearing Wear Plate
30. Side Bearing Shims
31. Pedestal
32. Pedestal Cap
33. Pedestal Bolt
34. Pedestal Tie Bar
35. Swing Link Bolster Hanger
36. Swing Link Pin (Top)
37. Swing Link Pin (Bottom)
38. Swing Link Pin Bearing (Top)
39. Swing Link Pin Bearing (Bottom)
40. Spring Plank
41. Motor Suspension Bar
42. Motor Suspension Bar Bolt

Names of Parts of Figs. 1388-1390 (Continued)

43. Motor Suspension Spring
44. Motor Suspension Spring Washer
45. Brake Turnbuckle
46. Brake Turnbuckle End
47. Brake Turnbuckle End
48. Live Lever
49. Live Lever Pin (Top)
50. Live Lever Pin (Bottom)
51. Live Lever Brake Rod
52. Dead Lever
53. Dead Lever Stop
54. Dead Lever Pin (Bottom)
55. Brake Hanger
56. Brake Hanger Pin (Top)
57. Brake Hanger Pin (Bottom)
58. Brake Head
59. Brake Head Pin
60. Brake Shoe
61. Brake Shoe Key
62. Brake Shoe Adjusting Spring
63. Brake Shoe Spring Rod
64. Brake Release Spring
65. Brake Release Spring Fulcrum
66. Brake Release Spring Casing
67. Brake Release Spring Rod
68. Brake Rod Jaw
69. Brake Rod Roller
70. Brake Rod Roller Pin
71. Radius Bar
72. Radius Bar Guide

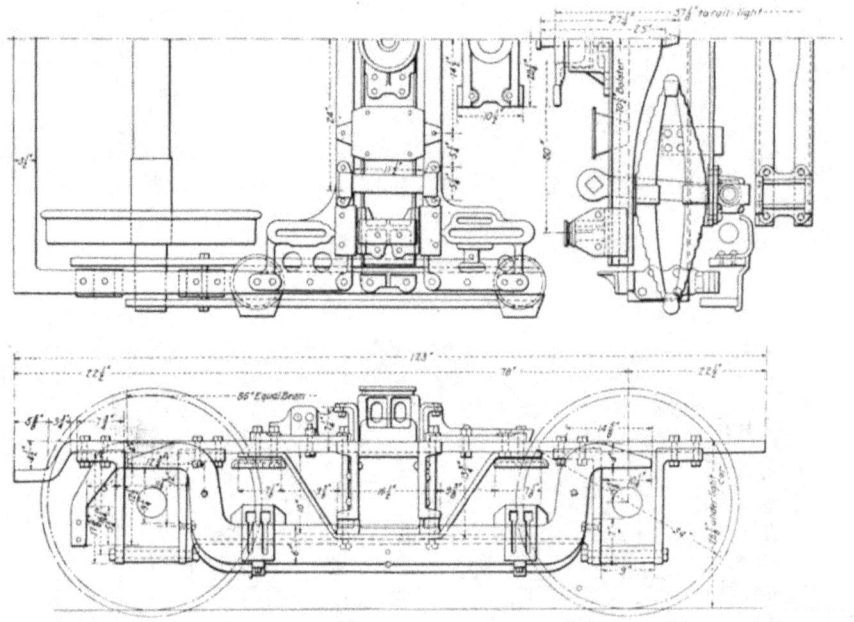

Figs. 1391-1393—Baldwin M. C. B. Type High-Speed Interurban Truck, No. 78-30-S;
Hudson & Manhattan Railroad
Baldwin Locomotive Works

Fig. 1394—Baldwin M. C. B. Type Light Interurban Truck Without End Frames
Baldwin Locomotive Works

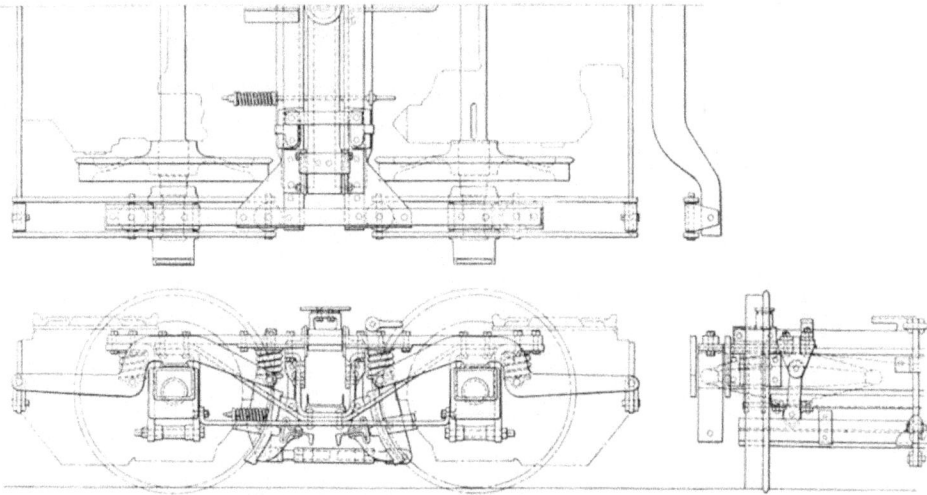

Figs. 1395-1397—Baldwin Type F Short Wheelbase Truck
Baldwin Locomotive Works

Fig. 1398—Frame of Baldwin Type E Truck
Baldwin Locomotive Works

Fig. 1399—Baldwin Type C Diamond Arch Bar Freight Trailer Truck
Baldwin Locomotive Works

TRUCKS, General Views; McGuire-Cummings — Figs. 1400-1402

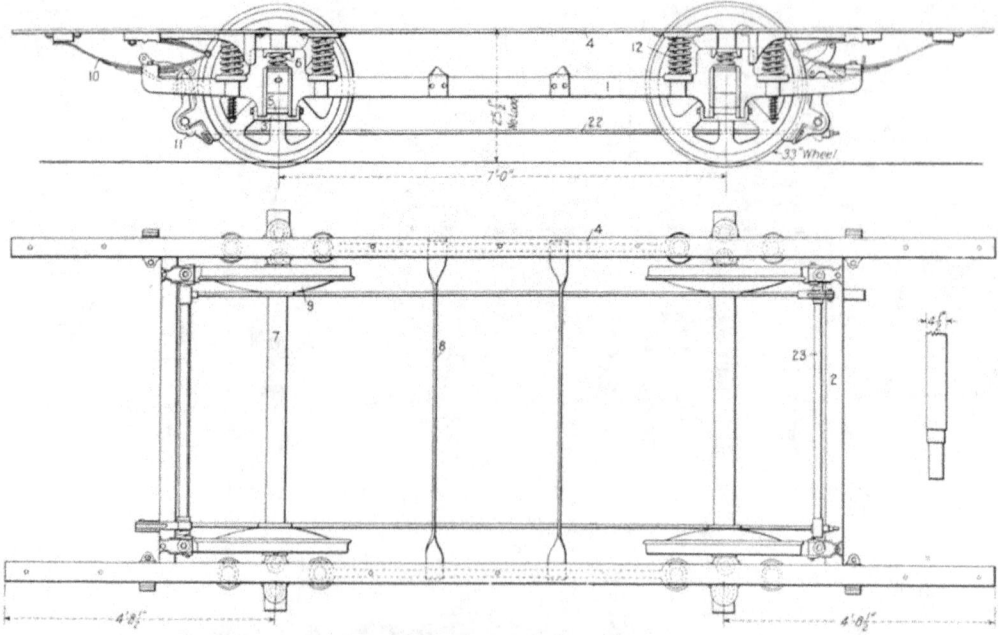

Figs. 1400-1401—Columbian Solid Steel Single Truck
McGuire-Cummings Manufacturing Company

Names of Parts of Figs. 1400-1401

1. Side Frame
2. End Frame
3. Pedestal Cap
4. Top Chord
5. Pedestal Bolt
6. Pedestal Spring
7. Axle
8. Motor Suspension Bar
9. Wheel
10. Body End Spring
11. Brake Head
12. Body Spring
22. Brake Rod
23. Brake Beam

Fig. 1402—Cast Steel Side Frame Motor Truck for Elevated Cars
McGuire-Cummings Manufacturing Company

Fig. 1403—Heavy M. C. B. Type Truck for High-Speed Interurban Service
McGuire-Cummings Manufacturing Company

Fig. 1404—Standard M. C. B. Type Truck, No. 20-A
McGuire-Cummings Manufacturing Company

Fig. 1405—Light M. C. B. Type Truck, No. 10-A
McGuire-Cummings Manufacturing Company

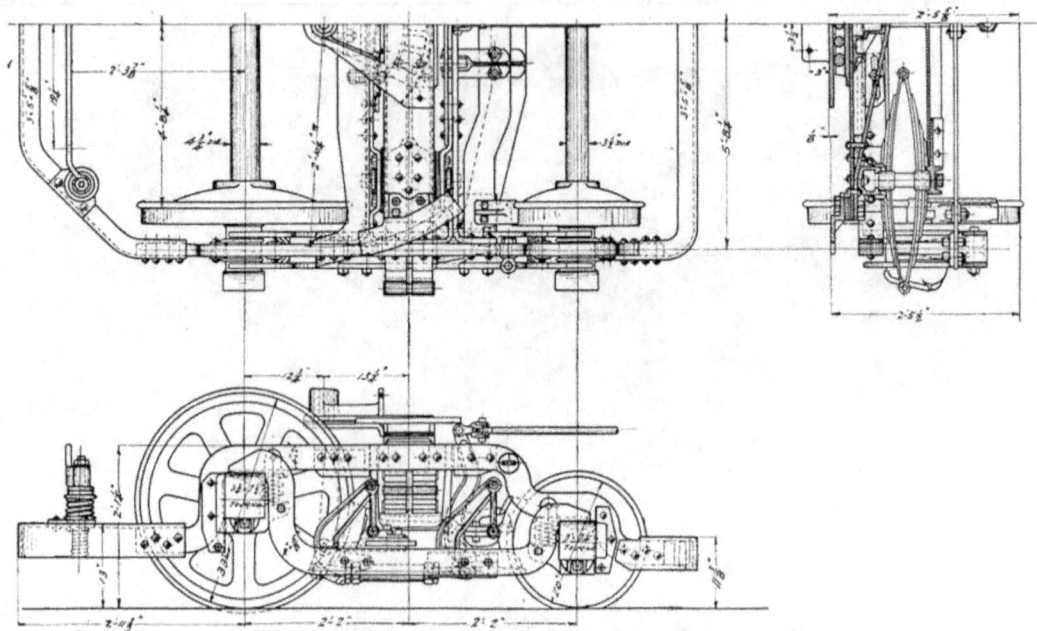

Figs. 1406-1408—Standard Maximum Traction Truck, No. O-45
Standard Motor Truck Company

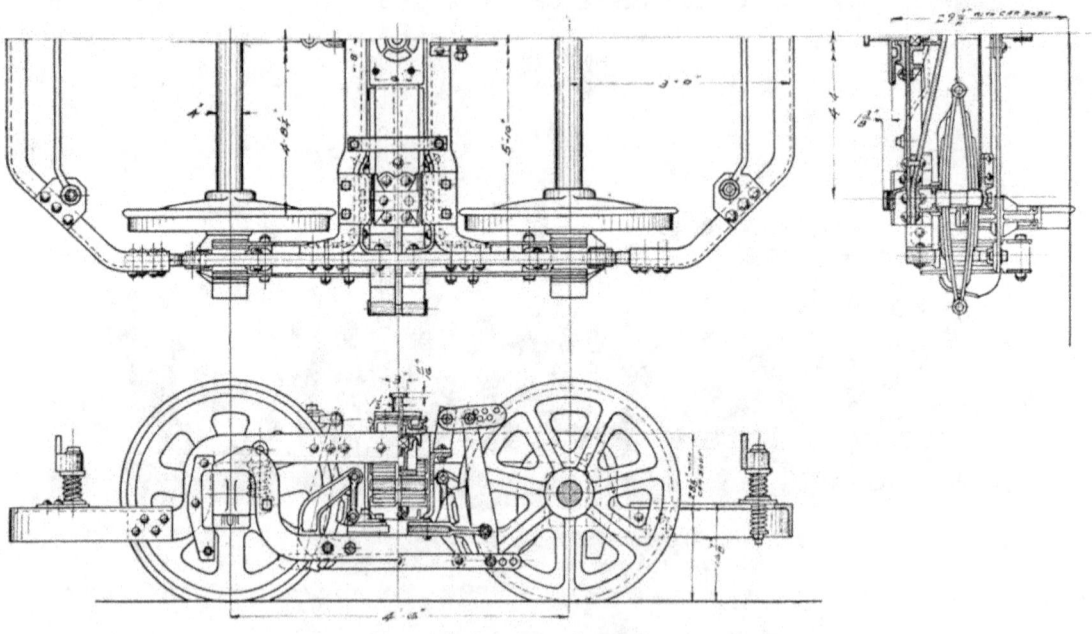

Figs. 1409-1411—Standard Short Wheelbase Truck, No. O-50
Standard Motor Truck Company

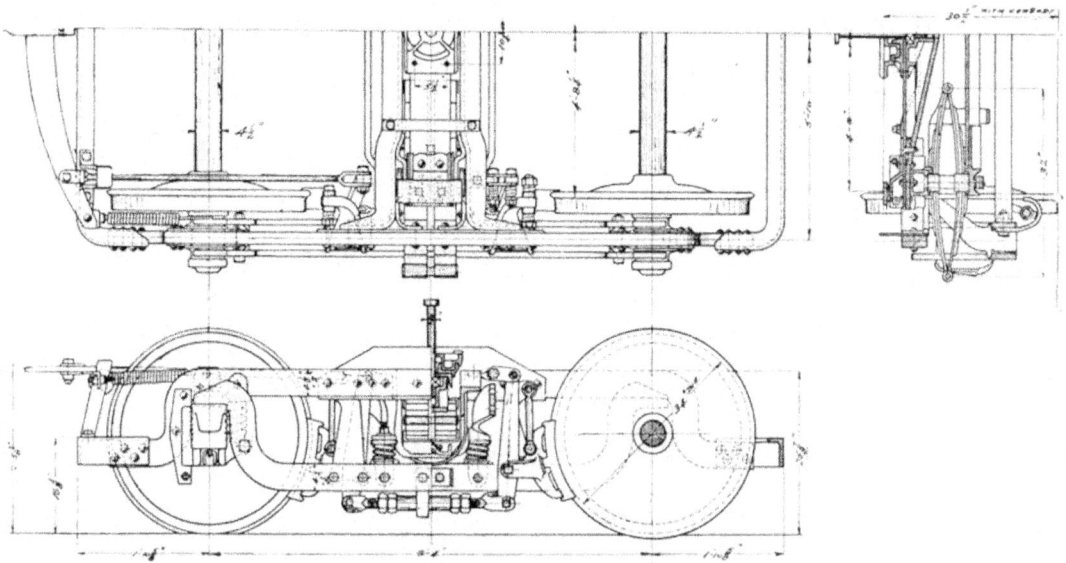

Figs. 1412-1414—Standard City and Suburban Truck, No. C-50
Standard Motor Truck Company

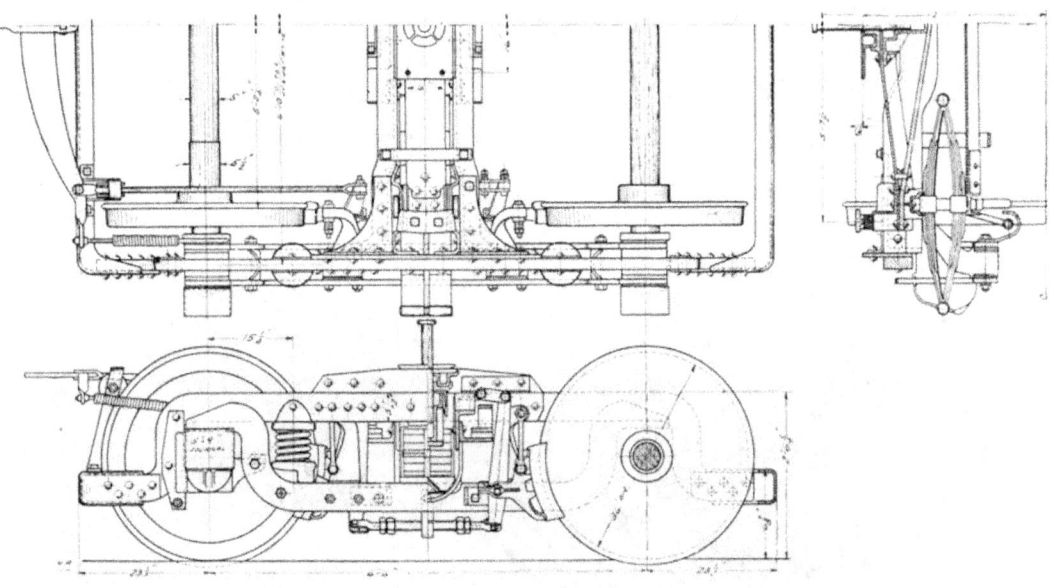

Figs. 1415-1417—Standard High-Speed Interurban Truck, No. C-60
Standard Motor Truck Company

TRUCKS, General Views; Standard, Barber, Jewett

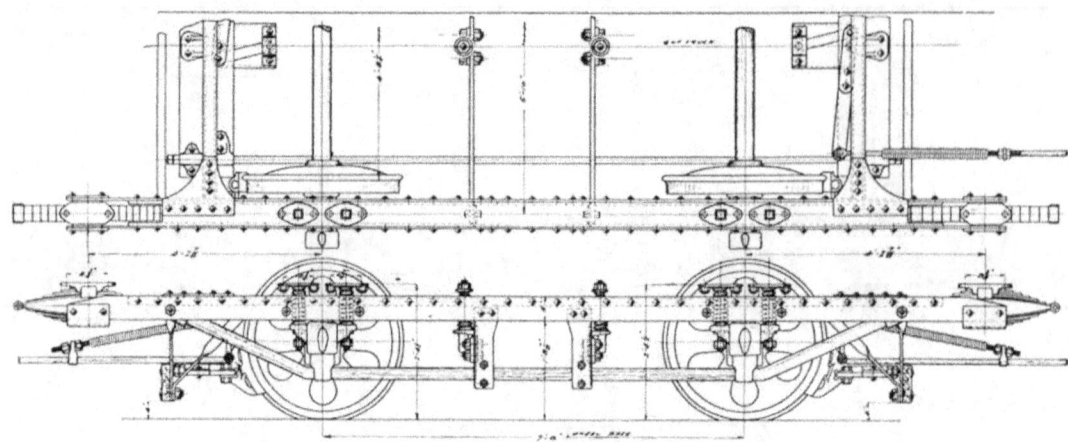

Figs. 1418-1419—Standard Long Spring Base Single Truck, No. C-35
Standard Motor Truck Company

Fig. 1420—Barber Single Truck
Barber Car Company

Fig. 1421—Jewett Short Wheelbase City and Suburban Truck
Jewett Car Company

Fig. 1422—Warner Non-Parallel Axle, Long Wheelbase, Single Truck
St. Louis Car Company

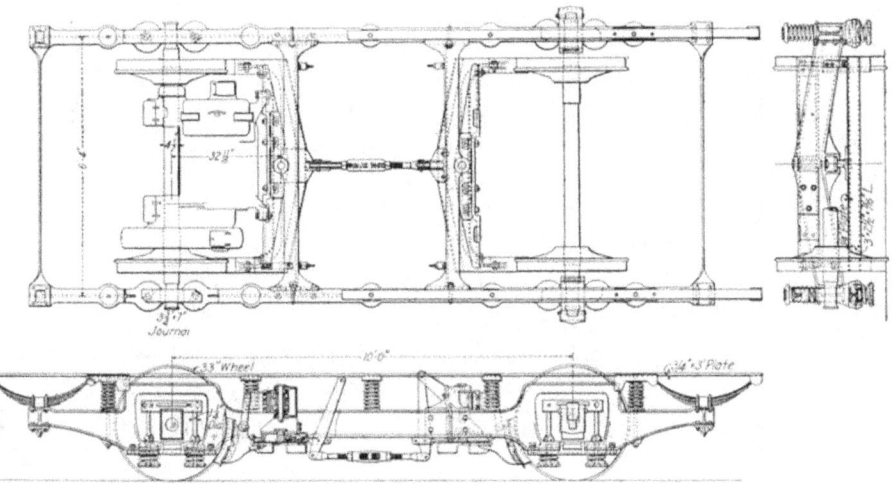

Figs. 1423-1425—Plan, Side and End Elevations of Warner Non-Parallel Axle, Single Truck
St. Louis Car Company

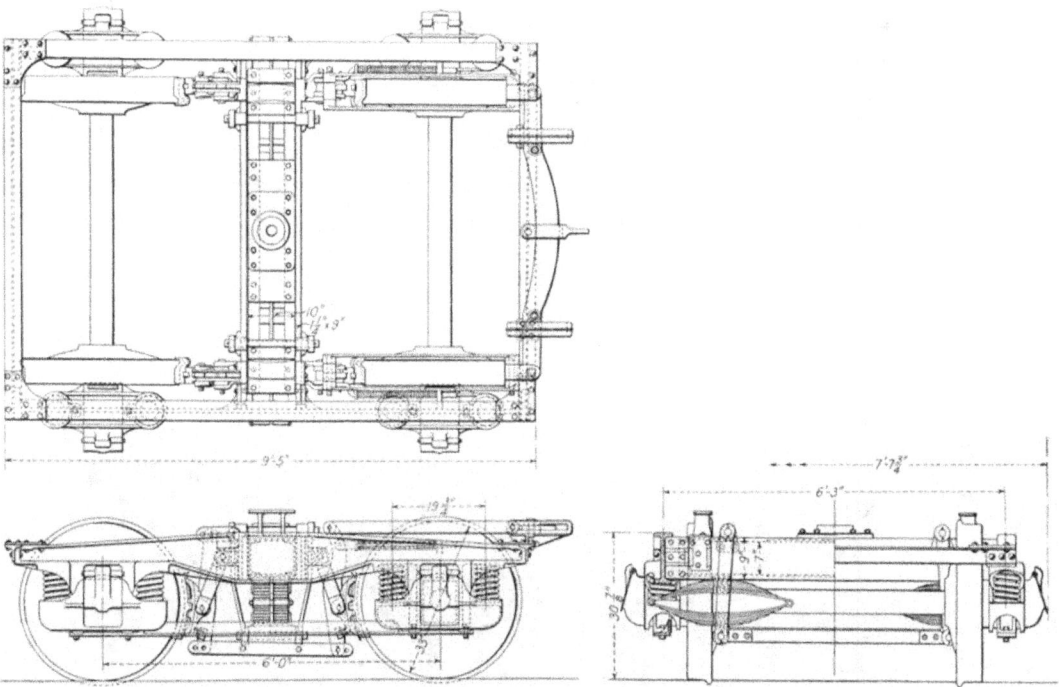

Figs. 1426-1428—Cast Steel Side Frame Trailer Truck for Elevated Cars
St. Louis Car Company

TRUCKS, General Views; St. Louis — Figs. 1429-1436

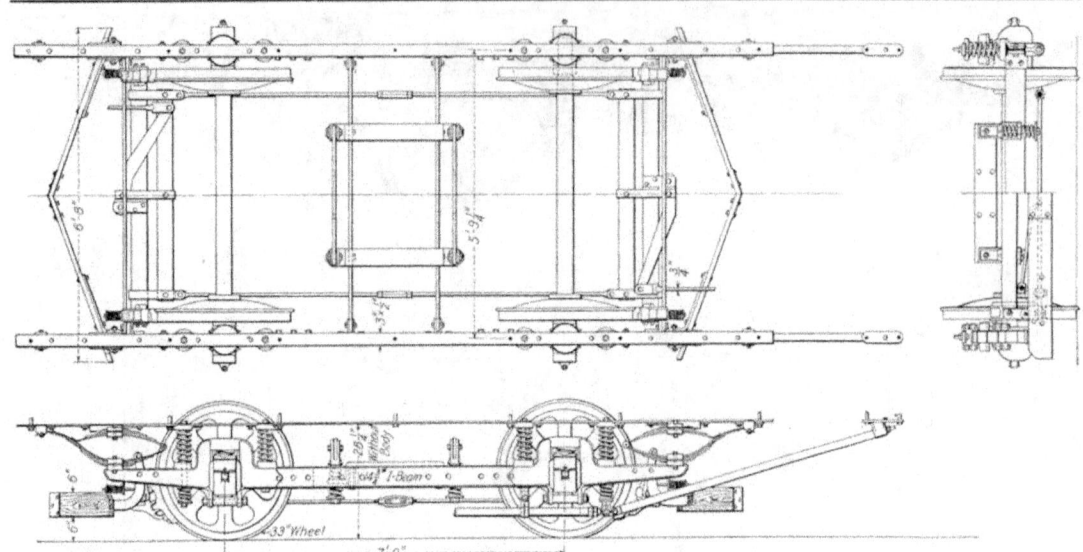

Figs. 1429-1431—St. Louis Single Truck, No. 9
St. Louis Car Company

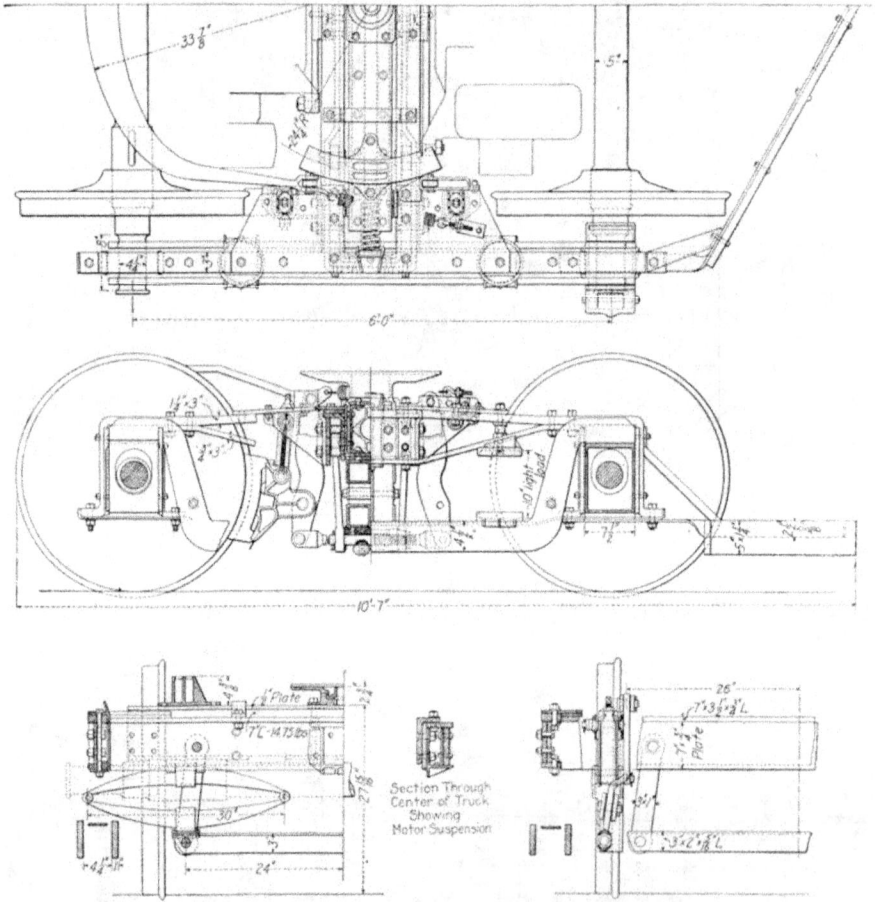

Figs. 1432-1436—St. Louis M. C. B. Type Truck, No. 23-M. C.
St. Louis Car Company

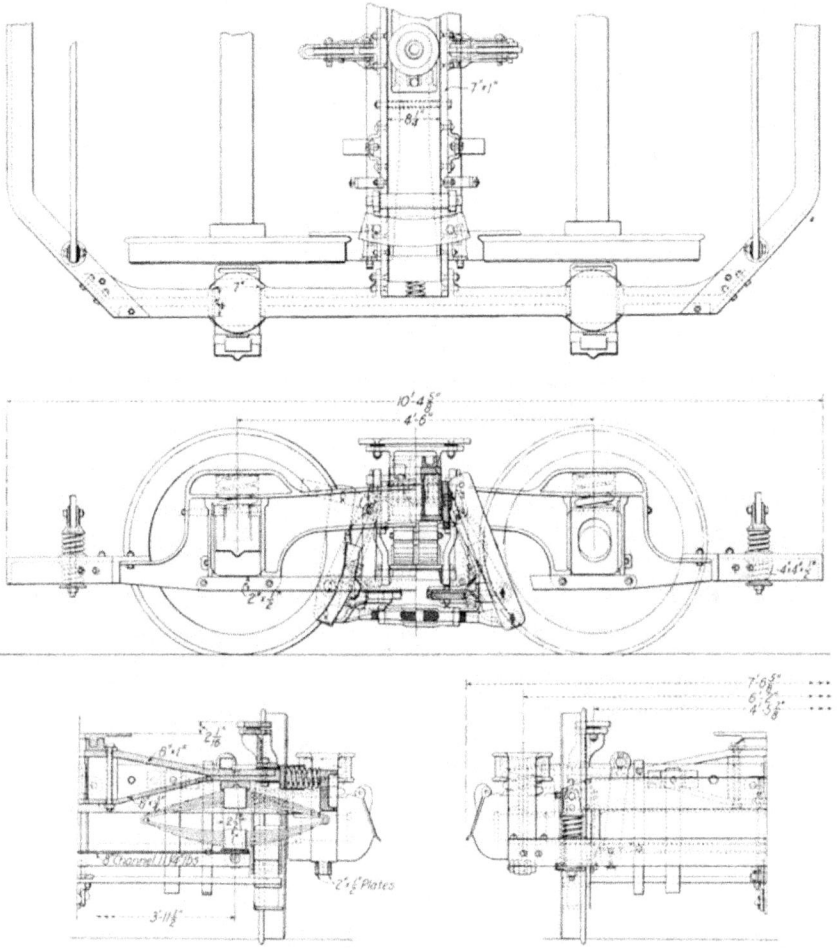

Figs. 1437-1440—Cast Steel Side Frame Truck, No. 47
St. Louis Car Company

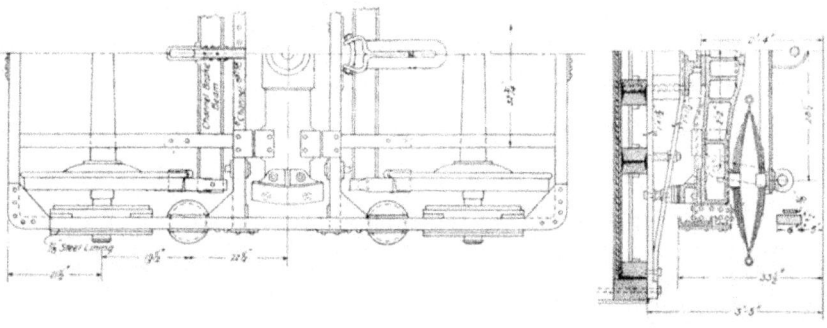

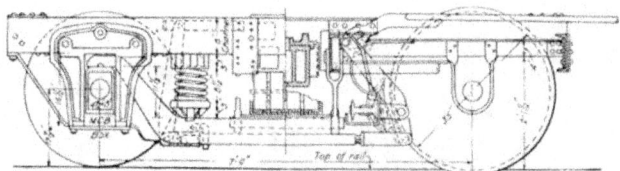

Figs. 1441-1443—All-Steel M. C. B. Type Trailer Truck
American Car & Foundry Company

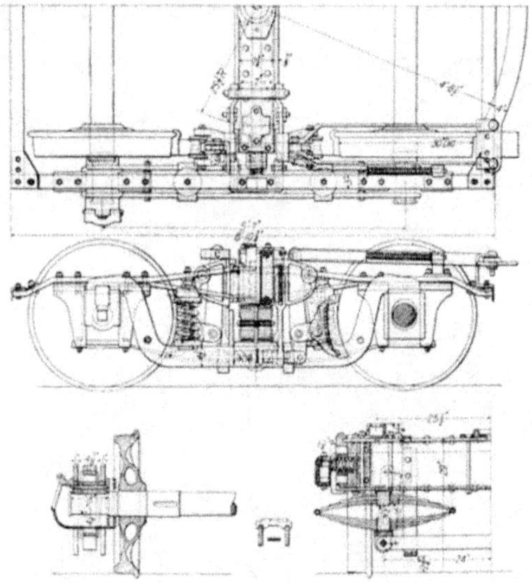

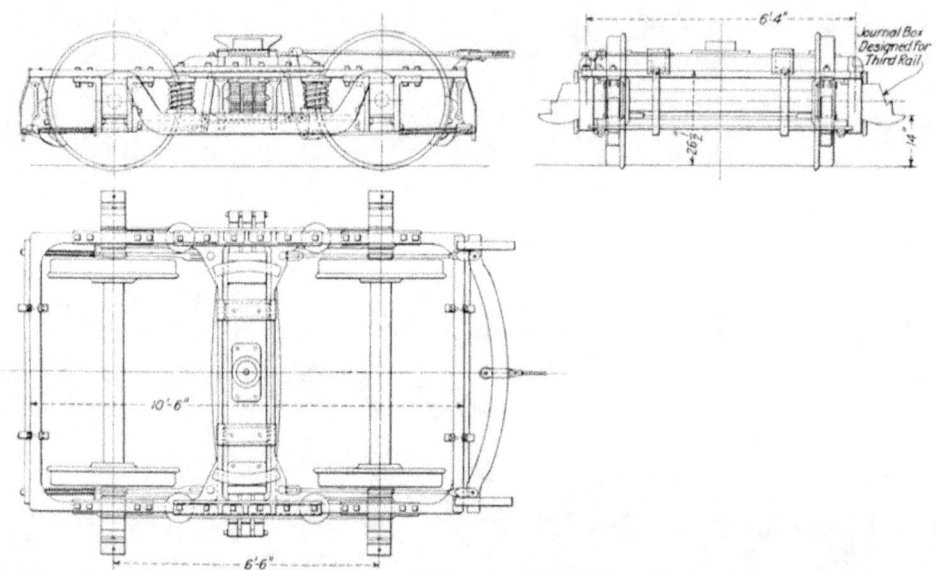

Figs. 1444-1447—St. Louis M. C. B. Type Truck, No. 23
St. Louis Car Company

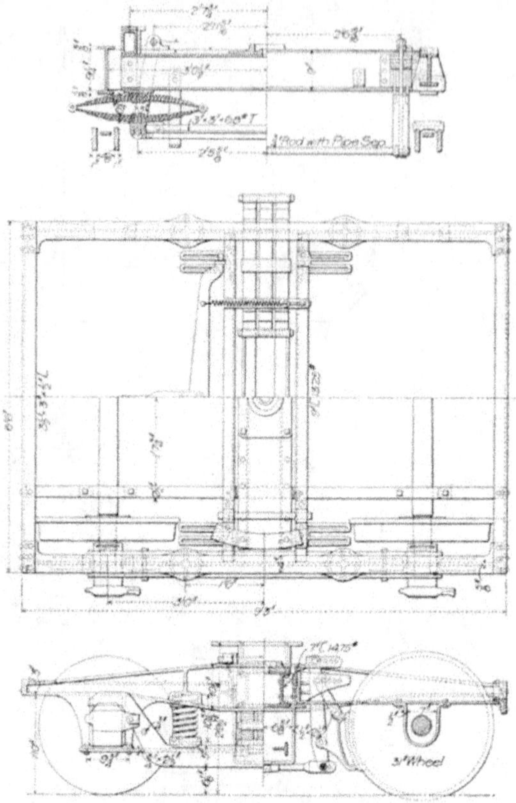

Figs. 1448-1450—Cast Steel Side Frame M. C. B. Type Trailer Truck
American Car & Foundry Company

Figs. 1451-1453—High-Speed M. C. B. Type Interurban Motor Truck
American Car & Foundry Company

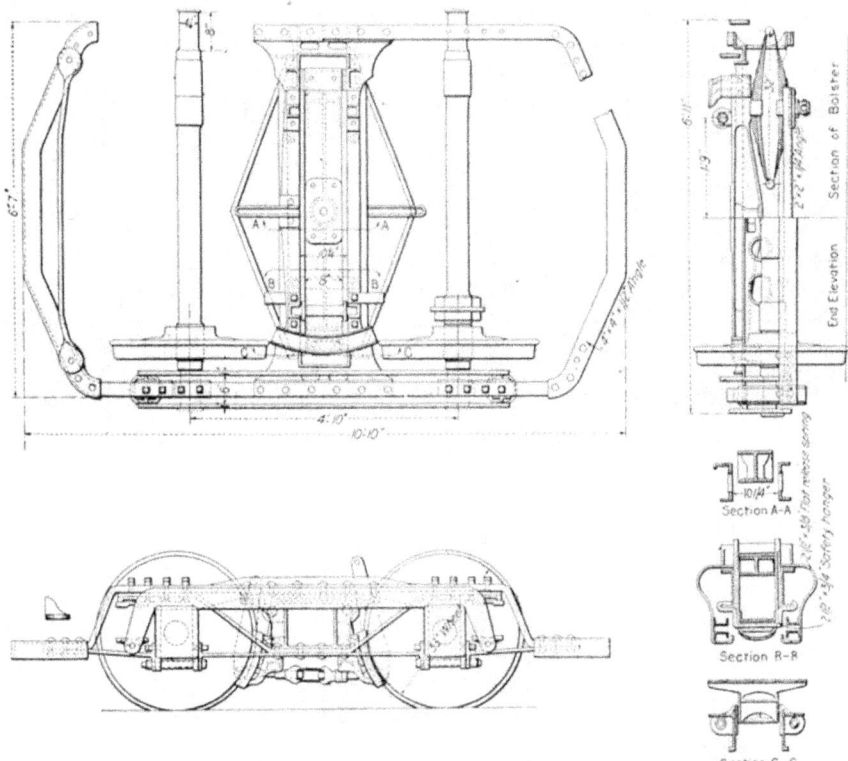

Figs. 1454-1459—Cast Steel Frame Equalized Truck; Chicago Railways
Commonwealth Steel Company

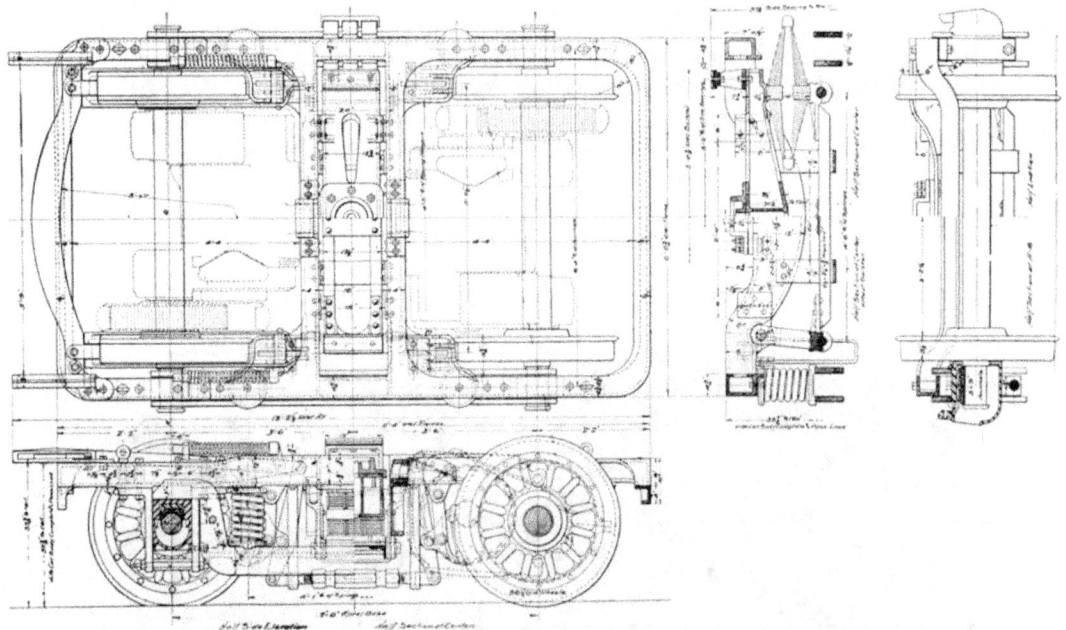

Figs. 1460-1463—Cast Steel Frame M. C. B. Type Motor Truck for High-Speed Service
Commonwealth Steel Company

Fig. 1464—Single Truck, Type G
Barney & Smith Car Company

Fig. 1465—Maximum Traction Truck, Type I
Barney & Smith Car Company

Fig. 1466—Steel Plate Side Frame Interurban Truck, Type J
Barney & Smith Car Company

Fig. 1467—Taylor Extra Heavy Single Truck

Fig. 1468—Taylor Short Wheelbase Double Truck

Fig. 1469—Taylor Double Truck, Type H. L. B.

Fig. 1470—Taylor Quadruple M. C. B. Type Truck
Taylor Electric Truck Company

Fig. 1471—Taylor Double M. C. B. Type Truck
Taylor Electric Truck Company

Fig. 1472—Curtis Forged Steel Truck, No. CI-158-72, for City Service
Curtis Motor Truck Company

Fig. 1473—Curtis Forged Steel Truck, No. J-669-84, for Interurban Service
Curtis Motor Truck Company

TRUCK DETAILS, Brakes

Fig. 1474—Bradshaw Wrecking Skid
Lord Manufacturing Company

Fig. 1475—Brake Rigging for Maximum Traction Truck
Columbia Machine Works and Malleable Iron Co.

Fig. 1476—Application of Brill Half-
Ball Brake Hanger

Figs. 1477-1478—Brill Half-Ball Brake
Hanger

The J. G. Brill Company

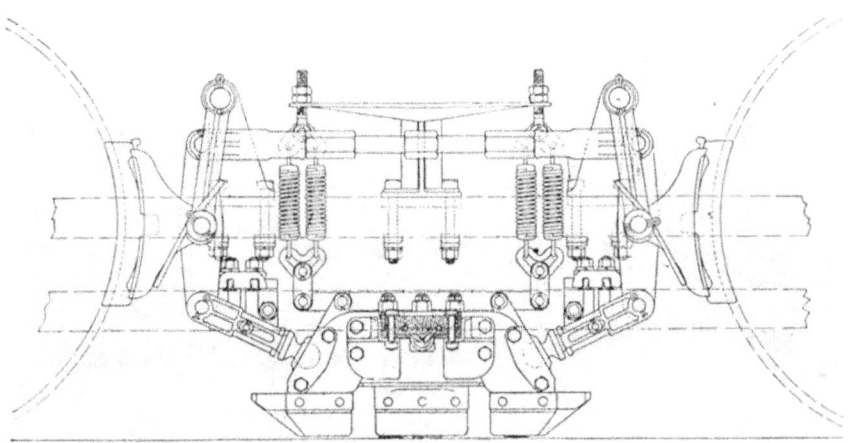

Fig. 1479—Westinghouse Magnetic Track Brake
Westinghouse Air Brake Company

TRUCK DETAILS, Brakes

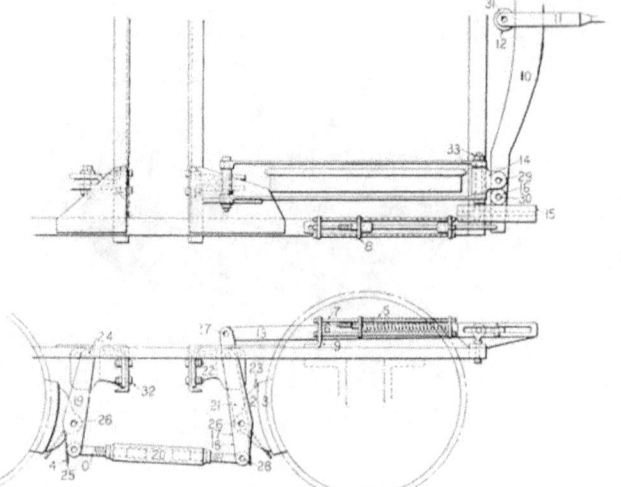

Figs. 1480-1481—Brake Rigging for Baldwin M. C. B. Type Truck
Baldwin Locomotive Works

Names of Parts of Figs. 1480-1481

0. Brake Turnbuckle End
2. Brake Head
3. Brake Shoe
4. Brake Shoe Spring
5. Brake Release Spring
6. Brake Release Spring Stem
7. Brake Release Spring Rod
8. Brake Release Spring Seat
9. Brake Release Spring Fulcrum
10. Radius Bar
11. Brake Rod Jaw
12. Brake Rod Roller
13. Live Lever Brake Rod
14. Live Lever Brake Rod Jaw
15. Radius Bar Guide
16. Radius Bar Guide Roller
17. Live Lever (Inside)
18. Live Lever (Outside)
19. Dead Lever
20. Brake Turnbuckle
21. Brake Hanger
22. Brake Hanger Bracket
23. Brake Shoe Key
24. Dead Lever Pin (Top)
25. Dead Lever Pin (Bottom)
26. Brake Head Pin
27. Live Lever Pin (Top)
28. Live Lever Pin (Bottom)
29. Live Lever Brake Rod Pin
30. Radius Bar Guide Roller Pin
31. Brake Rod Roller Pin
32. Brake Hanger Bracket Bolts
33. Live Lever Brake Rod Jaw Bolt

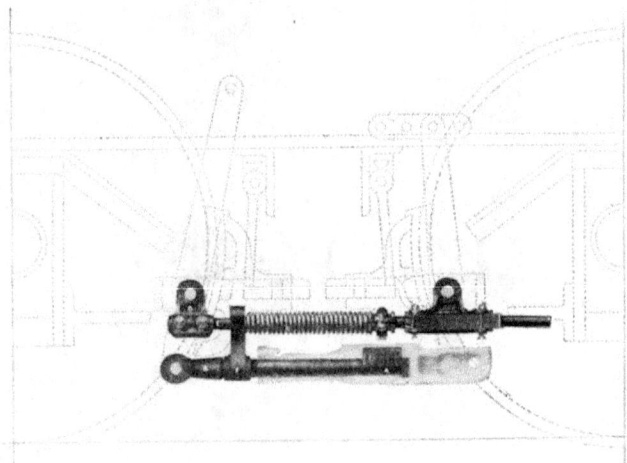

Fig. 1482—Sauvage Shim Slack Adjuster
Standard Coupler Company

Fig. 1483—Mechanical Slipper Track Brake
McGuire-Cummings Manufacturing Company

TRUCK DETAILS, Brake Shoes

Fig. 1484—Plain Gray Iron Brake Shoe

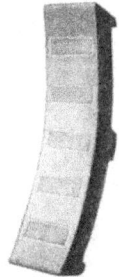
Fig. 1485—Congdon Brake Shoe

Fig. 1486—Special "Electric" Brake Shoe

Fig. 1487—Streeter Brake Shoe

Fig. 1488—"U" Brake Shoe

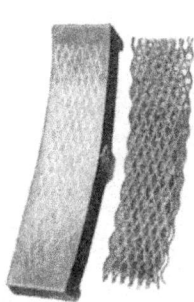
Figs. 1489-1490—"Diamond-S" Brake Shoe and Expanded Metal Insert

Fig. 1491—Steel Back Reinforcement for Brake Shoes

Fig. 1492—New Steel Back Brake Shoe

Fig. 1493—Steel Back Brake Shoe, Broken but Good for Service

Fig. 1494—Steel Back Brake Shoe, Worn Out

Fig. 1495—Steel Back Reinforcement for Flanged Brake Shoes

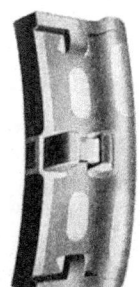
Fig. 1496—Steel Back Flanged Brake Shoe

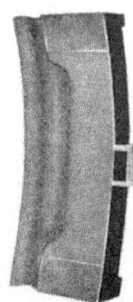
Fig. 1497—Special "Electric" Flanged Brake Shoe

Fig. 1498—Streeter Flanged Brake Shoe

Fig. 1499—"Diamond-S" Flanged Brake Shoe

American Brake Shoe & Foundry Company

TRUCK DETAILS, Brake Shoes and Center Plates — Figs. 1500-1517

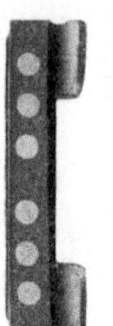

Fig. 1500—Steel Back Brake Shoe and Head
Railway Materials Company

Fig. 1501—Steel Back Flanged Brake Shoe

Figs. 1502-1503—Front and Back Views of Philadelphia Insert Brake Shoe
Philadelphia Brake Shoe Company

Fig. 1504—Wheel Truing Brake Shoe
Wheel Truing Brake Shoe Company

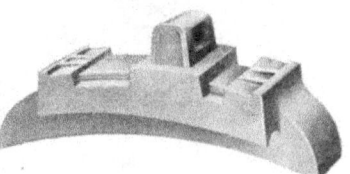

Figs. 1505-1506—Steel Lug Flanged Brake Shoe

Figs. 1507-1508—Steel Lug Plain Brake Shoe
Lancaster Iron Works

Fig. 1509—Armbrust Brake Shoe
Love Brake Shoe Company

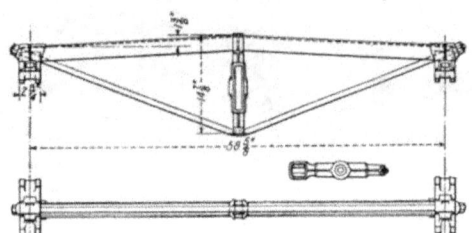

Figs. 1510-1512—Vanderbilt Trussed Brake Beam; Light Pattern

Fig. 1516—Baltimore Ball-Bearing Center Plate

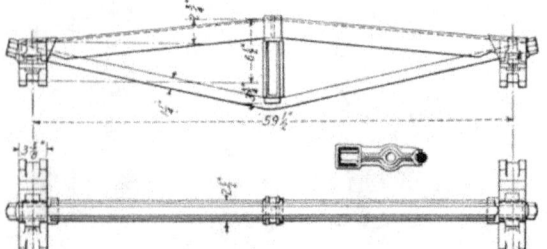

Figs. 1513-1515—Vanderbilt Trussed Brake Beam; Heavy Pattern
Buffalo Brake Beam Company

Fig. 1517—Section Through Baltimore Ball-Bearing Center Plate
The T. H. Symington Company

Fig. 1518—Cincinnati Tool-Steel Gear and Pinion
Whipple Supply Company

Fig. 1519—Solid Spoke Gear
The Falk Company

Fig. 1520—Four-Bolt Split Gear
E. W. Bliss & Company

Fig. 1521—Solid Spoke Gear
E. W. Bliss & Company

Fig. 1522—Solid Spoke Gear
E. W. Bliss & Company

Fig. 1523—Four-Bolt Split Gear
Van Dorn & Dutton Company

Fig. 1524—Solid Spoke Gear

Fig. 1525—Eight-Bolt Split Gear
Van Dorn & Dutton Company

Fig. 1526—Solid Four-Spoke Gear

(244)

TRUCK DETAILS, Gears

Fig. 1527—Steel-Tired Gear

Fig. 1528—Armature Pinion

Fig. 1529—Solid Spoke Gear

Fig. 1530—Four-Bolt Split Gear

General Electric Company

Fig. 1531—Gear End

Fig. 1532—Commutator End

Fig. 1533—Gear Mounted on Hollow Quill

Fig. 1534—Driving Spokes

Figs. 1531-1534—Quill Drive for Trucks of Suburban Motor Cars; New York, New Haven & Hartford Railroad

Westinghouse Electric & Manufacturing Company

TRUCK DETAILS, Gear Cases

Fig. 1535—Welded Steel Gear Case

Fig. 1536—Parts of Welded Steel Gear Case

Westinghouse Electric & Manufacturing Company

Fig. 1537—Sectional View of Lyon Reinforced Steel Gear Case
Electric Service Supplies Company

Fig. 1539—Malleable Iron Gear Case
General Electric Co.

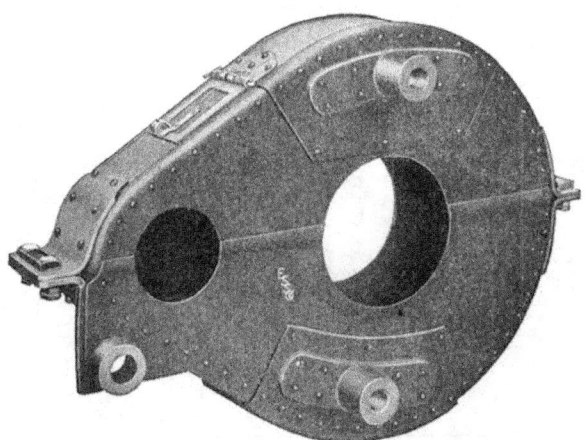

Fig. 1538—Lyon Reinforced Steel Gear Case for G. E.-216 Motor
Electric Service Supplies Company

Fig. 1540—Columbia Sheet Steel Gear Case
Columbia Machine Works & Malleable Iron Company

TRUCK DETAILS, Bolsters and Journal Boxes

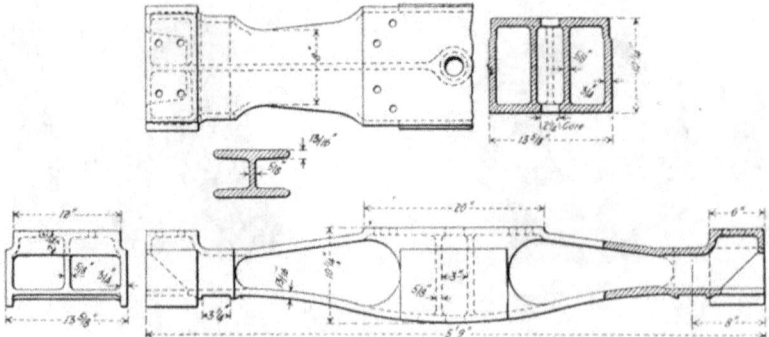

Figs. 1541-1545—Cast Steel, One-Piece Truck Bolster

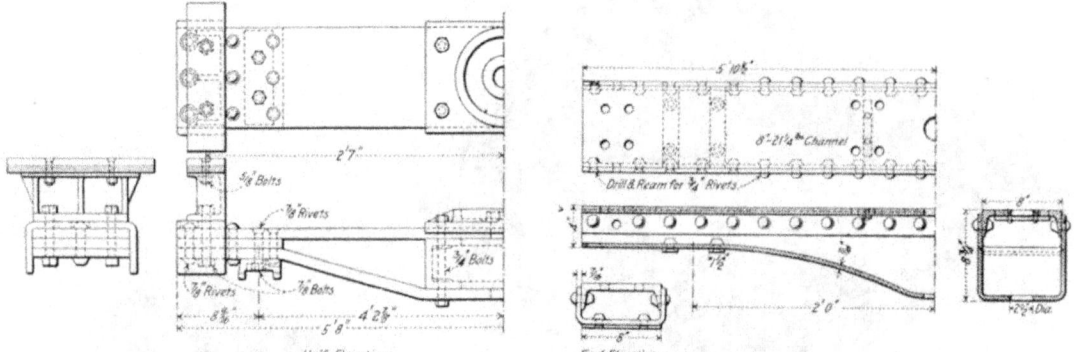

Figs. 1546-1548—Built-Up Steel Truck Bolster   Figs. 1549-1552—Pressed Steel Truck Bolster

Figs. 1553-1554—Brill M. C. B. Type Journal Box
The J. G. Brill Company

TRUCK DETAILS, Journal Boxes

Fig. 1555—McCord Journal Box for Arch Bar Truck

Fig. 1556—Section Through McCord Journal Box, Showing National Equalizing Wedge

Fig. 1557—McCord Journal Box for Pedestal Truck; Chicago Railways Standard

Fig. 1558—McCord Journal Box for Pedestal Truck with Inserted Steel Wear Plates

Fig. 1559—Top View of National Equalizing Wedge

Fig. 1560—Bottom View of National Equalizing Wedge

McCord & Company

TRUCK DETAILS, Journal Boxes

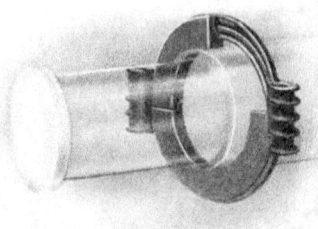

Fig. 1561—McCord Metal Dust Guard, Assembled on Axle

Fig. 1562—McCord Metal Dust Guard, Dismantled

McCord & Company

Fig. 1563—Symington M. C. B. Type Journal Box

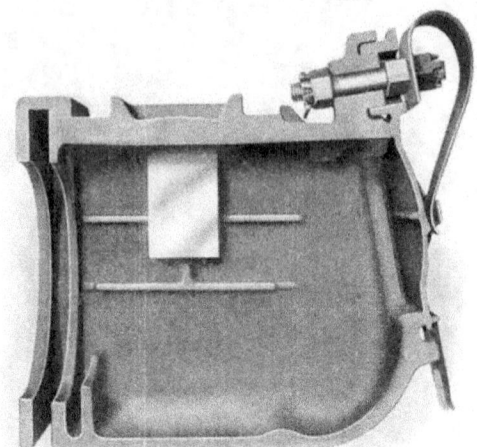

Fig. 1564—Section Through Symington M. C. B. Type Journal Box

The T. H. Symington Company

Fig. 1565—Symington Journal Box for Street Cars

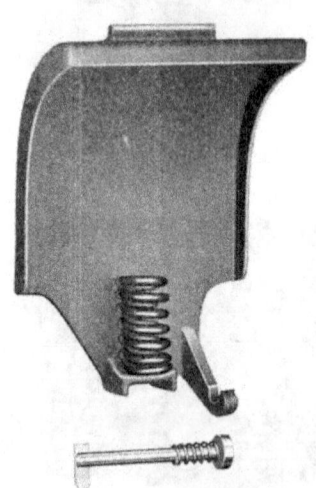

Figs. 1566-1567—Lid and Locking Pin for Street Car Journal Box

The T. H. Symington Company

Figs. 1568-1593   TRUCK DETAILS, Springs

Fig. 1568—Armstrong Journal Oiler
Armstrong Oiler Company

Figs. 1569-1570—Double Coil Equalizer Springs
Standard Steel Works Company

Fig. 1571—Single Half-Elliptic Spring
Standard Steel Works Company

Fig. 1572—Triple Full-Elliptic Spring, Sectional Type   Fig. 1573—Double Full-Elliptic Spring, Sectional Type
Standard Steel Works Company

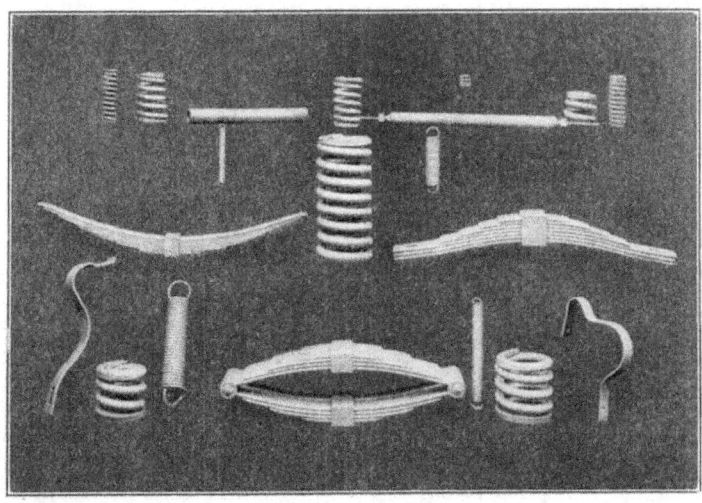

Figs. 1574-1593—Types of Car and Truck Springs
The J. G. Brill Company

(250)

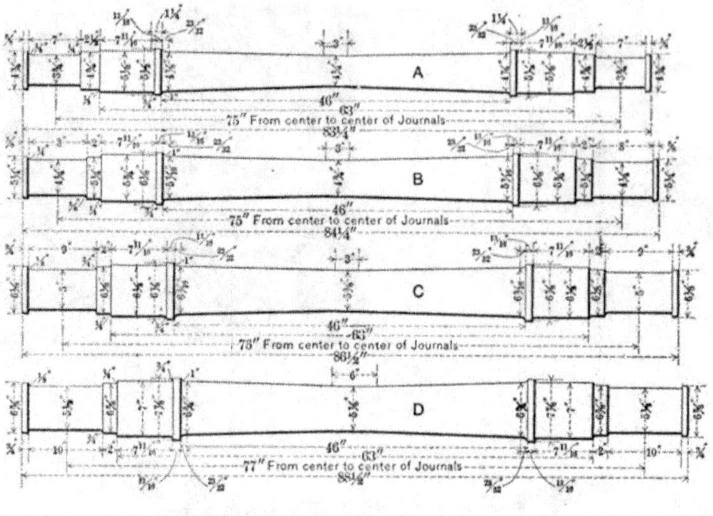

Type	Journals	Diameter of Center	Diameter of Wheel Fit	Distance Between Hubs	Centers of Journals	Maximum Capacity	Approximate Weight
	Inches	Inches	Inches	Inches	Inches	Pounds	Pounds
A	3¾ x 7	4¼	5⅛	48⅛	75	15,000	420
B	4¼ x 8	4¾	5¾	48⅛	75	22,000	520
C	5 x 9	5⅛	6½	48⅛	76	31,000	680
D	5½ x 10	5⅛	7	48⅛	77	38,000	830

Figs. 1594-1597—Standard M. C. B. Type Trailer Axles

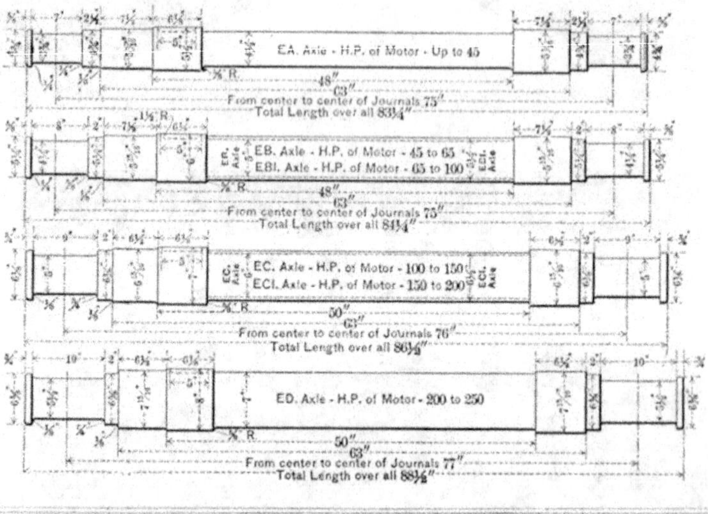

Type	Journals	Diameter of Motor Fit	Diameter of Gear Fit	Diameter of Wheel Fit	Distance Between Hubs	Centers of Journals	Maximum Capacity	Length of Gear Seat	Approximate Weight.
	Inches	Inches	Inches	Inches	Inches	Inches	Pounds	Inches	Pounds
EA	3¾ x 7	4½	5½	5 7/16	48	75	15,000	6¼	450
EB	4¼ x 8	5	6	5 15/16	48	75	19,000	6¼	530
EB1	4¼ x 8	5½	6	5 15/16	48	75	22,000	6¼	580
EC	5 x 9	6	7	6 15/16	50	76	27,000	6¼	750
EC1	5 x 9	6½	7	6 15/16	50	76	31,000	6¼	820
ED	5½ x 10	7	8	7 15/16	50	77	38,000	6¼	1050

Figs. 1598-1601—American Electric Railway Engineering Association Standard Motor Axles

TRUCK DETAILS, Wheels; Cast Iron

Figs. 1602-1603—Channel Spoke Cast Iron Wheel
Griffin Wheel Company

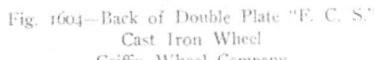

Fig. 1604—Back of Double Plate "F. C. S."
Cast Iron Wheel
Griffin Wheel Company

Fig. 1605—Front of Double Plate "F. C. S."
Cast Iron Wheel
Griffin Wheel Company

Figs. 1606-1608—Reinforced Spoke Cast Iron Wheels
Atlanta Car Wheel & Manufacturing Company

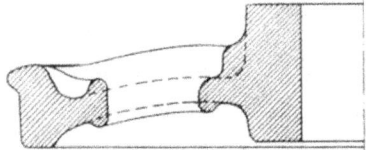

33" CURVED ARM CHANNEL SPOKE WHEEL

33" F.C.S. WHEEL
PATENT APPLIED FOR

WEIGHT OF CAR	CITY SERVICE 2½" TREAD		LIGHT INTERURBAN SERV. 3" TREAD		WEIGHT OF CAR	SIZE OF AXLE A.S.R.R. STD	HEAVY INTERURBAN SERVICE 3½" TREAD	HEAVY INTERURBAN SERVICE M.C.B. FL.&TR.
	SPOKE	F.C.S.	SPOKE	F.C.S.			F.C.S.	F.C.S.
32000	440		490		55000	E.B.	640	670
36000	460		510		60000	E.B.	660	690
40000	480		530	510	65000	E.B.-1	680	710
44000	500	480	550	530	70000	E.B.-1	700	730
48000	520	500	570	550	75000	E.C.	720	750
52000	540	520	590	570	80000	E.C.	740	770
56000	560	540	610	590	85000	E.C.-1		790
60000	580	560		610	90000	E.C.-1		810
64000	600	580		630	95000	E.D.		830
68000	620	600		650	100000	E.D.		850

Figs. 1609-1610—Recommended Weights of Cast Iron Wheels for Different
Weights of Cars
Griffin Wheel Company

Figs. 1611-1614—Cast Steel Spoke Wheels
Lobdell Car Wheel Company

Figs. 1615-1616—Steel Tired Wheel with Cast Iron Spoke Center and
Bolted Fastening
Midvale Steel Company

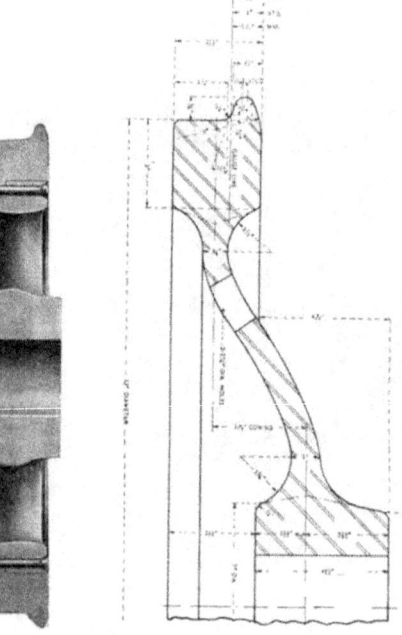

Fig. 1617—Section of Typical Solid
Rolled and Forged Steel Wheel
Carnegie Steel Company

Figs. 1618-1620—Solid Rolled and Forged Steel Wheels
Carnegie Steel Company

TRUCK DETAILS, Wheels; Steel Tired

Figs. 1621-1622—Steel Tired Wheel with Cast Iron or Cast Steel Spoke Center, Tire Held by Shrinkage and Bolts

Figs. 1623-1624—Steel Tired Wheel with Cast Iron Double Plate Center, Tire Held by Shrinkage and Bolts

Figs. 1625-1626—Steel Tired Wheel with Cast Steel Single Plate Center, Tire Held by Shrinkage and Bolts

Figs. 1627-1628—Steel Tired Wheel with Cast Iron or Cast Steel Spoke Center, Tire Held by Double Lip Retaining Rings and Rivets

Figs. 1629-1630—Steel Tired Wheel with Cast Iron Double Plate Center, Tire Held by Double Lip Retaining Rings and Rivets

Figs. 1631-1632—Steel Tired Wheel with Cast Steel Single Plate Center, Tire Held by Double Lip Retaining Rings and Rivets

Standard Steel Works Company

TRUCK DETAILS, Wheels; Steel Tired — Figs. 1633-1644

Figs. 1633-1634—Steel Tired Wheel with Cast Iron or Cast Steel Spoke Center, Tire Held by Shrinkage and Shoulder

Figs. 1635-1636—Solid Rolled Steel Wheel

Standard Steel Works Company

Fig. 1637—Taylor Malleable Iron Spoke Center Steel Tired Wheel
Taylor Electric Truck Company

Figs. 1638-1640—Steel Tired Wheels with Double Plate Cast Iron Centers, Tires Held by Gibson Retaining Rings
National Car Wheel Company

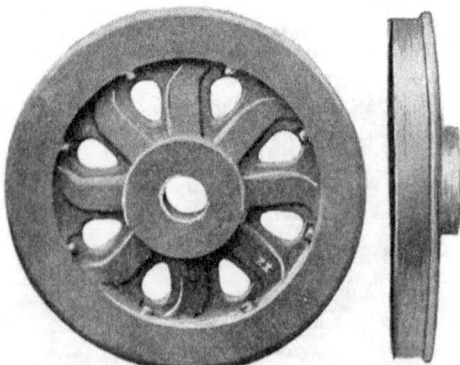

Figs. 1641-1642—Steel Tired Wheel with Heavy Spoke Cast Iron Center, Tire Held by Shrinkage
National Car Wheel Company

Figs. 1643-1644—Steel Tired Wheel with Double Plate Cast Iron Center, Tire Held by Bolted Fastening
Railway Steel-Spring Company

(255)

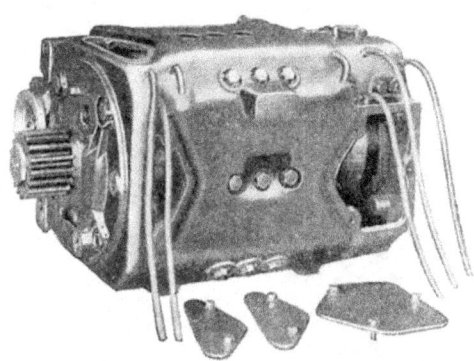

Fig. 1645—Front View of G. E.-207 Commutating Pole, Box Frame Motor

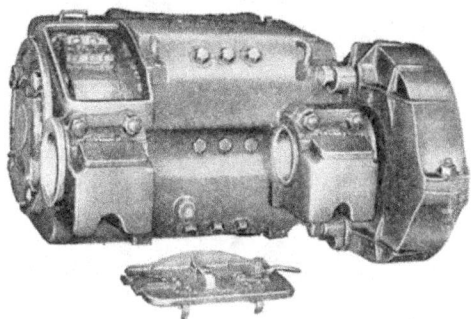

Fig. 1646—Rear View of G. E.-207 Commutating Pole, Box Frame Motor

Fig. 1647—Front View of G. E.-205 Commutating Pole, Box Frame Motor

Fig. 1648—Rear View of G. E.-205 Commutating Pole, Box Frame Motor

Fig. 1649—G. E.-219 Commutating Pole, Split Frame Motor, with Lower Half of Frame Dropped and Armature Ready for Removal

Fig. 1650—Brush Holder for G. E.-216 Motor

Fig. 1651—Commutator Construction of G. E.-216 Motor

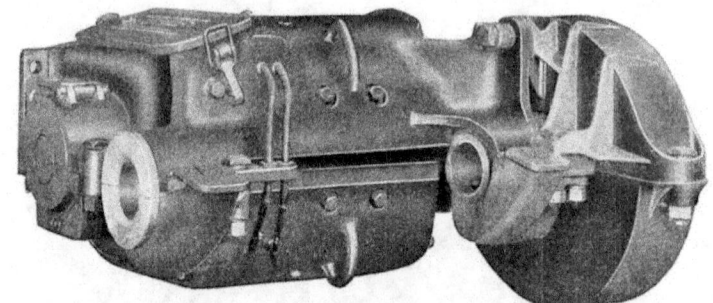

Fig. 1652—Rear View of G. E.-219 Commutating Pole, Split Frame Motor and Gear Case

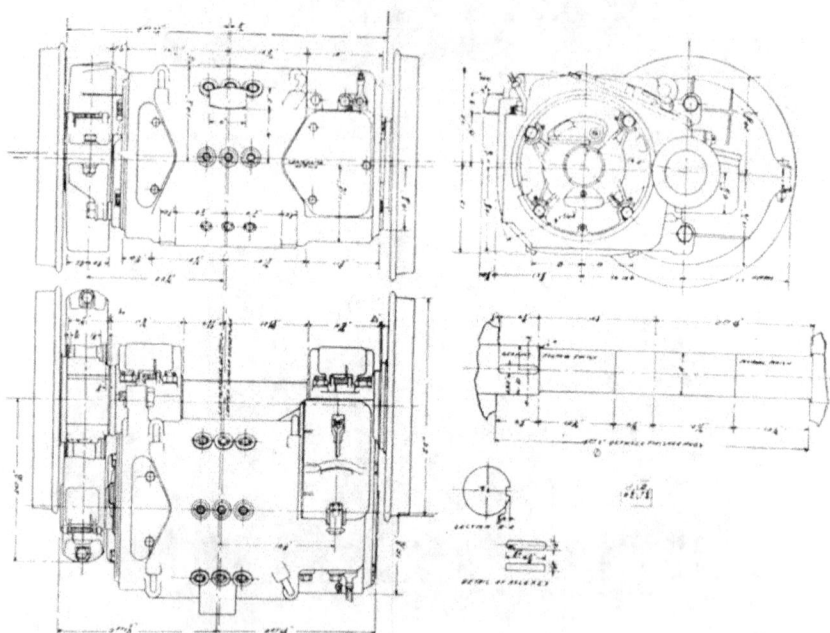

Figs. 1653-1656—Plan, Side and End Elevations of G. E.-207 Commutating Pole Box Frame Motor

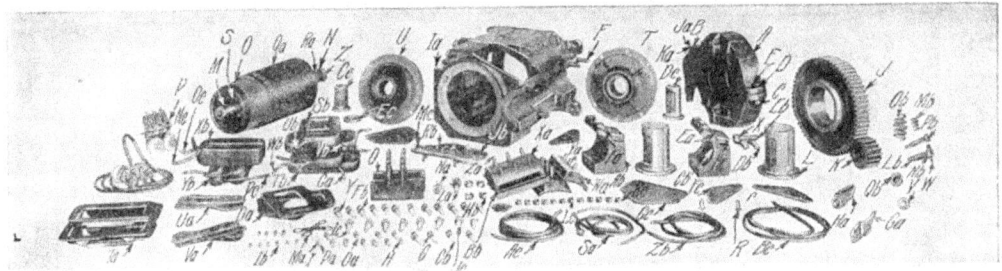

Fig. 1657—Parts of G. E.-207, Commutating Pole, Box Frame Motor
General Electric Company

Names of Parts of Fig. 1657

A. Gear Case
B. Gear Case Oil Hole Lid
C. Gear Case Bolt
D. Gear Case Bolt Lock Washer
E. Gear Case Bolt Nut
F. Axle Cap Stud
G. Lock Washer
H. Lock Washer
I. Lock Washer
J. Gear
K. Pinion
L. Axle Bearing Lining
M. Armature Shaft
N. Pinion Nut
O. Commutator
P. Brush Holder
Q. Commutating Pole Piece
R. Cable Bushing
S. Armature Thrust Collar
T. Frame Head (Pinion End)
U. Frame Head (Commutator End)
V. Washer
W. Spring Cotter
X. Lock Washer
Y. Lock Washer
Z. Lock Washer
Ba. Ground Cable Terminal
Ca. Field Coil Lead Terminal
Da. Exciting Field Coil Pad
Ea. Oil Well Lid Spring
Fa. Oil Well Lid Hinge Pin
Ga. Frame Head Cover (Pinion End)
Ha. Frame Head Cover (Commutator End)
Ia. Magnet Frame
Ja. Gear Case Oil Hole Lid Spring
Ka. Gear Case Oil Hole Lid Hinge Pin
La. Axle Cap Bolt
Ma. Axle Cap Stud Lock Washer Plate
Na. Axle Cap Bolt Lock Washer Plate
Oa. Frame Head Cover Bolt
Pa. Ground Terminal Bolt
Qa. Armature, Complete
Ra. Pinion Key
Sa. Ground Cable
Ta. Exciting Field Coil Flange
Ua. Commutating Field Coil Flange
Va. Commutating Field Coil Spring Pad
Wa. Laminated Pole Piece (Axle Side)
Xa. Laminated Pole Piece
Ya. Laminated Pole Piece Stud (Axle Side)
Za. Laminated Pole Piece Stud
Ab. Axle Bearing Cap (Pinion End)
Bb. Axle Bearing Cap (Commutator End)
Cb. Axle Bearing Cap Dowel Pin
Db. Gear Case Suspension Bolt
Eb. Gear Case Suspension Bolt
Fb. Commutating Pole Piece Bolt
Gb. Brush Holder Support Bolt
Hb. Axle Cap Stud Nut
Ib. Cable Terminal Connector
Jb. Top Magnet Frame Cover Cam
Lb. Frame Head Cover Spring Bolt (Pinion End)
Mb. Frame Head Cover Spring (Pinion End)
Nb. Frame Head Bolt Nut (Pinion End)
Ob. Frame Head Cover Spring (Commutator End)
Pb. Frame Head Cover Spring Bolt (Commutator End)
Qb. Frame Head Bolt Washer (Commutator End)
Rb. Magnet Frame Cover (Top)
Sb. Exciting Field Coil (Side)
Tb. Exciting Field Coil (Top and Bottom)
Ub. Side Exciting Field Coil Lead
Vb. Side Exciting Field Coil Lead
Wb. Top and Bottom Exciting Field Coil Leads
Xb. Commutating Field Coil (Top Axle Side)
Yb. Commutating Field Coil (Bottom Axle Side)
Zb. Commutating Field Coil Cable
Ac. Exciting Field Coil Cable
Bc. Exciting Field Coil Cable
Cc. Armature Bearing Lining (Pinion End)
Dc. Armature Bearing Lining (Commutator End)
Ec. Armature Bearing Lining Cover (Pinion End)
Fc. Magnet Frame Ventilating Cover (Pinion End)
Gc. Magnet Frame Ventilating Cover (Commutator End)
Hc. Axle Bearing Cap Oil Well Lid
Ic. Frame Head Bolt (Commutator End)
Jc. Frame Head Bolt (Pinion End)
Kc. Exciting Pole Piece Stud Nut (Axle Side)
Lc. Exciting Pole Piece Stud Nut
Mc. Magnet Frame Cover Spring
Nc. Commutating Field Coil Lead (Top Axle Side)
Oc. Commutating Field Coil Lead (Top Axle Side)
Pc. Commutating Field Coil Lead (Bottom Axle Side)

Fig. 1658—Westinghouse No. 101-B2 Split Frame Direct-Current Motor
Westinghouse Electric & Manufacturing Company

(258)

MOTORS, Westinghouse

Fig. 1660—Exterior View of Westinghouse No. 93a Split Frame Direct-Current Motor

Fig. 1659—Interior View of Westinghouse No. 93a Split Frame Direct-Current Motor

Fig. 1661—Armature and Bearings of Westinghouse No. 93a Split Frame Direct-Current Motor

Names of Parts of Motors, Figs. 1659-1661

1. Field Pole Piece
3. Frame (Bottom Half)
3a. Frame (Top Half)
5. Commutator
6. Motor Leads
7. Armature Bearing Oil Well Lid.
8. Armature Shaft
9. Frame Bail
10. Armature Bearing Housing
11. Axle Bearing Oil Well Lid
12. Axle Bearing Cap
13. Brush
14. Field Coil
15. Gear Case Support
16. Armature Core
17. Armature Band Wire
18. Armature Band Wire Clip
19. Armature Bearing Oil Well
20. Armature End Plate
21. Armature Coil in Slot
22. Pole Piece Bolts
23. Axle Bearing Cap Bolts
24. Inspection Lid (Commutator End)
25. Axle Bearing
26. Frame Bolt Holes

Fig. 1662—Westinghouse No. 303a Standard Interpole, Direct-Current Motor for Heavy Interurban Service

Fig. 1663—Westinghouse, No. 306c, Box Frame, Interpole, Direct-Current Motor for Heavy City Service

Fig. 1664—Westinghouse, No. 305, Split Frame, Interpole, Direct-Current Motor for Heavy City or Light Interurban Service

Fig. 1665—Westinghouse, No. 306, Split Frame, Interpole, Direct-Current Motor for Heavy City Service; Lower Field Down for Inspection

Fig. 1666—Westinghouse, No. 310, Box Frame, Interpole, Direct-Current Motor for Heavy City and Light Interurban Service

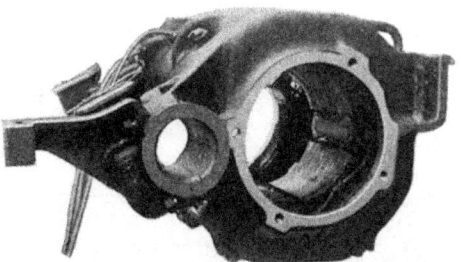

Fig. 1667—Westinghouse, No. 310, Box Frame, Interpole, Direct-Current Motor, with Armature Removed

MOTORS, Westinghouse

Fig. 1668—Westinghouse, No. 132-A, Standard, 25-Cycle, Single-Phase, A. C.-D. C. Box Frame Motor for Interurban Service; Pinion End

Fig. 1669—Westinghouse, No. 132-A, Standard, 25-Cycle, Single-Phase, A. C.-D. C. Box Frame Motor for Interurban Service; Commutator End

Fig. 1670—Westinghouse, No. 156, Standard, 25-Cycle, Single-Phase, A. C.-D. C. Box Frame Railway Motor for Heavy Interurban Service

Fig. 1671—Field of Westinghouse, No. 156, Box Frame, A. C.-D. C. Motor, Showing Brush Holders

Fig. 1672—Armature Bearing Housing for Box Frame Motor

Fig. 1673—Axle Cap and Oil Well for Box Frame Motor

Figs. 1674-1675—Armature Bearings

Figs. 1676-1677—Brush Holders for Westinghouse, No. 101B-2, Motor

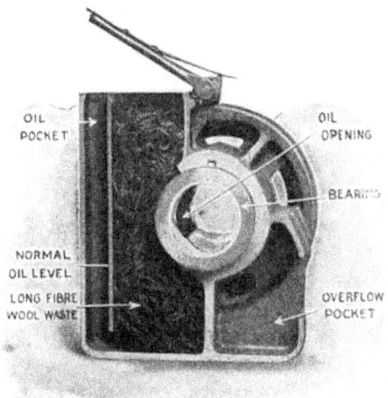

Fig. 1678—Section through Armature Bearing Housing of Split Frame Motor. Showing Oil Filtering Lubrication

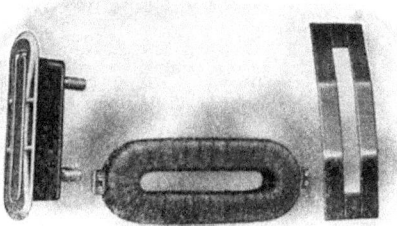

Figs. 1679-1681—Interpole Coil, Pole Piece and Cushion Spring

Figs. 1682-1683—Complete Field Pole and Interpole

Figs. 1684-1687—Main Field Pole Piece, Coil and Clamps

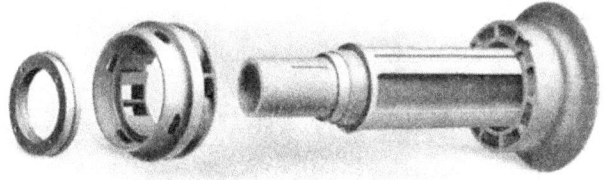

Figs. 1688-1690—Armature Spider, End Plate and Ring Nut

Figs. 1691-1692—Armature Spider and Ring Key Type End Plate

Fig. 1693—Armature Core on Spider

Fig. 1694—Bolted Type Commutator, Rear View

Fig. 1695—Bolted Type Commutator, Front View

Fig. 1696—Armature Core and Commutator Assembled on Spider

Fig. 1697—Armature Core and Commutator Mounted on Shaft

Fig. 1698—Armature Core and Commutator of Standard Interpole Motor

Fig. 1699—Armature and Insulation in Place Ready for Winding

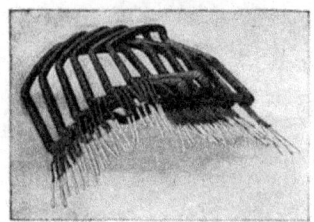

Fig. 1700—Wire-Wound Armature Coils

Fig. 1701—Connecting Lower Leads of Armature Coils to Commutator Segments

Fig. 1702—Connecting Upper Leads of Armature Coils to Commutator Segments

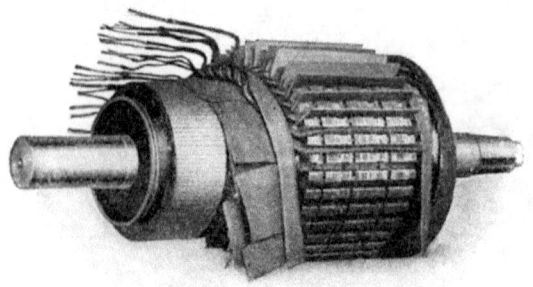

Fig. 1703—Insulating Coil Ends

Fig. 1704—Completed Armature

Fig. 1705—Method of Ventilating Two Westinghouse, No. 308, Motors with Motor-Driven Blower Set
Westinghouse Electric & Manufacturing Company

Fig. 1706—Exterior View of Allis-Chalmers, No. 301, Split Frame, Direct-Current Motor, 40 hp.

Fig. 1708—Exterior View of Allis-Chalmers, No. 501, Split Frame, Interpole, Direct-Current Motor, 50 hp.

Fig. 1707—Interior View of Allis-Chalmers, No. 301, Split Frame, Direct-Current Motor

Fig. 1709—Interior View of Allis-Chalmers, No. 501, Split Frame, Interpole, Direct-Current Motor

Allis-Chalmers Company

MOTOR DETAILS

Fig. 1710—Fowler Brush Holder
Par Sill Metal Company

Fig. 1711—Economy Oil
Cup for Armature
Bearings
Economy Oil Cup Co.

Fig. 1712—Triple Wrapped Cotton
Insulated Magnet Wire

Fig. 1713—Single Wrapped Cotton
Insulated Magnet Wire
Electric Cable Company

Fig. 1714—Cotton and Asbestos Paper
Insulated Magnet Wire

TABLE OF WEIGHTS AND HORSEPOWER OF WESTINGHOUSE RAILWAY MOTORS AND CONTROL APPARATUS

DIRECT CURRENT, NON-INTERPOLE MOTORS

Trade Name	H. P.	No. of Motors	Type of Control	Weight of Control	Weight of Motor Including Gear and Gear Case	Total Weight of Equipment
12-A	25	2	K-10	1,000	2,260	5,400
	25	4	K-12	1,340		10,100
69	30	2	K-10	1,000	1,950	4,900
	30	4	K-12	1,200		9,100
49	35	2	K-10	1,050	1,925	4,900
	35	4	K-28	1,600		9,300
92-A	35	2	K-10	1,040	2,265	5,570
	35	4	K-28	1,440		10,560
38-B	40	2	K-10	1,040	2,380	5,816
	40	4	K-28	1,440		10,960
68-C	40	2	K-10	1,050	2,280	5,600
	40	4	K-28	1,440		10,560
101	40	2	K-10	1,050	2,645	6,340
	40	4	K-28	1,440		12,020
101-C	40	2	K-10	1,140	2,730	6,600
	40	4	K-28	1,580		12,500
93-A	50	2	K-11	1,200	3,440	8,080
	50	4	K-14	2,400		16,360
56	55	2	K-11	1,200	3,000	7,200
	55	4	K-14	2,400		14,400
112	75	2	M. U.	1,125	3,440	8,065
	75	4	M. U.	2,400		16,260
76	75	2	M. U.	1,770	3,840	9,450
	75	4	M. U.	3,640		19,000
85	75	2	M. U.	1,770	4,500	10,770
	75	4	M. U.	3,640		21,640
121	90	2	M. U.	1,770	4,300	10,370
	90	4	M. U.	3,640		20,840
119	125	2	M. U.	1,770	4,680	11,130
	125	4	M. U.	2,640		22,360
113	200	2	M. U.	Special	6,550	18,800
	200	4	M. U.	Special		

ADDITIONAL DIRECT CURRENT MOTORS, NON-INTERPOLE

Trade Name	H. P.	No. of Motors	Type of Control	Weight of Control	Weight of Motor Including Gear and Gear Case	Total Weight of Equipment
101-B2	40	2	K-10-A	1,140	2,825	6,790
	40	4	K-28-B	1,580		12,880
101-D2	50	2	K-36-B	1,130	2,825	6,780
	50	4	K-35-D	2,080		13,580
93-A2	60	2	K-36-B	1,130	3,440	8,010
	60	4	K-34-D	2,240		16,000
112-B	75	2	K-35-D	1,480	2,440	8,360
	75	4	K-34-D	2,240		16,000
121-A	90	2	K-35-D	1,480	4,250	9,980
	90	4	K-34-D	2,240		19,240
114	160	2	M. U.	Special	5,300	Special
	160	4	M. U.	Special		Special

DIRECT CURRENT INTER-POLE MOTORS

Trade Name	H.P. 600 V.	H.P. 500 V.	No. of Motors	Type of Control	Weight of Control	Weight of Motor Including Gear and Gear Case	Total Weight of Equipment
312	50	40	2	K-10-A	1,140	2,670	6,480
	50	40	4	K-28-B	1,580		12,260
307	50	40	2	K-36-B	1,130	2,850	6,830
	50	40	4	K-35-4	2,080		13,480
319-B	50	40	2	K-36-B	1,130	2,740	6,610
	50	40	4	K-35-D	2,080		13,040
306	60	50	2	K-36-B	1,130	2,850	6,815
	60	50	4	K-35-D	2,080		13,480
316	60	50	2	K-36-B	1,130	3,170	7,470
	60	50	4	K-35-D	2,080		14,760
305	75	60	2	K-36-B	1,130	3,550	8,230
	75	60	4	K-34-D	2,240		16,440
310	75	60	2	K-36-B	1,130	3,440	8,010
	75	60	4	K-34-D	2,240		16,000
304	90	75	2	K-35-D	2,080	3,550	9,180
	90	75	4	K-34-D	2,240		16,440
317	90	75	2	K-35-D	2,080	3,550	9,180
	90	75	4	K-34-D	2,240		16,440
303-A	110		2	M. U.	Special	4,000	Special
	110		4	M. U.	Special		Special
302	140		2	M. U.	Special	4,600	Special
	140		4	M. U.	Special		Special
301-B	175		2	M. U.	Special	5,520	Special
	175		4	M. U.	Special		Special
300-B	220		2	M. U.	Special	6,400	Special

ALTERNATING CURRENT, SINGLE-PHASE RAILWAY MOTORS FOR MOTOR CARS

Trade Name	H.P.	No. of Motors	Type of Control	Weight of Control	Weight of Motor Including Gear and Gear Case
135-B	75	4	M. U.	Special	4,500
132	100	4	M. U.	Special	5,100
132-A	100	4	M. U.	Special	5,300
133	150	4	M. U.	Special	6,090
148-A	125	4	M. U.	Special	6,100
156	150	4	M. U.	Special	7,500

ALTERNATING CURRENT, SINGLE-PHASE RAILWAY MOTORS FOR LOCOMOTIVES

Trade Name	H.P.	No. of Motors	Type of Control	Weight of Control	Weight of Motor Including Gear and Gear Case
130	250	4	M. U.	Special	16,400
137	240	3	M. U.	Special	15,700
151	175	4	M. U.	Special	10,400
403	310	4	M. U.	Special	19,860

MOTOR DETAILS

TABLE OF WEIGHTS AND HORSEPOWER OF GENERAL ELECTRIC RAILWAY MOTORS AND CONTROL APPARATUS

Trade Name.	H.P. at 500 Volts.	No. of Motors.	Type of Control.	Weight of Control, Lbs.	Weight of Motor Including Gear and Case, Lbs.	Total Weight of Equipment.
GE-800	25	2	K-10	960	1,950	4,860
		4	K-12	1,265		9,065
GE-54	25	2	K-10	960	1,900	4,760
		4	K-12	1,265		8,865
GE-60	25	2	K-10	960	1,700	4,360
		4	K-12	1,265		8,065
GE-1,000	35	2	K-10	960	2,185	5,330
		4	K-28	1,460		10,200
GE-78	35	2	K-10	960	2,580	6,120
		4	K-28	1,460		11,780
GE-58	35	2	K-10	960	2,225	5,410
		4	K-28	1,460		10,360
GE-67	40	2	K-10	960	2,450	5,860
		4	K-28	1,460		11,260
GE-70	40	2	K-10	960	2,750	6,460
		4	K-28	1,460		12,460
GE-80	40	2	K-10	960	2,850	6,660
		4	K-28	1,460		12,860
GE-53	45	2	K-11	1,050	2,850	6,750
		4	K-14	2,265		13,665
GE-57	50	2	K-11	1,050	3,030	7,110
		4	K-14	2,265		14,385
		4	M. U.	2,625		14,745
GE-90	50	2	K-11	1,050	2,900	6,850
		4	K-14	2,265		13,865
		4	M. U.	2,625		14,225
GE-87	60	2	M. U.	2,290	3,380	9,050
		4	M. U.	2,625		16,145
GE-74	65	2	M. U.	2,290	3,535	9,360
		4	M. U.	2,785		16,925
GE-73	75	2	M. U.	2,305	4,100	10,505
		4	M. U.	3,120		19,520
GE-66	125	2	M. U.	2,715	4,400	11,515
		4	M. U.	3,670		21,270
GE-55	160	2	M. U.	3,245	5,420	14,085
		4	M. U.	5,840		27,520
GE-76	160	2	M. U.	3,245	5,170	13,585
		4	M. U.	5,840		26,520
GE-69	200	2	M. U.	3,320	6,250	15,820
		4	M. U.	6,000		31,000
GE-81	30	2	K-10	960	1,996	4,952
		4	K-12	1,265		9,249
*GE-202	40	2	K-10	960	2,745	6,450
		4	K-28	1,460		12,440
*GE-204	65	2	M. U.	2,290	3,385	9,060
		4	M. U.	2,785		16,325
*GE-205	90	2	M. U.	2,550	3,925	10,400
		4	M. U.	3,420		19,120
*GE-207	140	2	M. U.	2,715	5,160	13,035
		4	M. U.	5,370		26,850
*GE-208	200	2	M. U.	3,320	6,380	16,080
		4	M. U.	6,000		31,520
*GE-210	60	2	M. U.	2,290	3,380	9,050
		4	M. U.	2,625		16,145

* These motors are equipped with commutating poles.

CLASSIFICATION OF RAILWAY CONTROLLERS

Series Parallel Controllers

Title	Motors No.	Capacity	No. Points	Special Features, Etc.
K-2-A	2	40 hp	5 series / 4 parallel	For motors using loop or shunted field
K-2-B	2	40 hp	5 series / 4 parallel	For motors using loop or shunted field (emergency reverse)
K-4-A	4	30 hp	5 series / 4 parallel	For motors using loop or shunted field
K-6-A	2	80 hp	6 series / 5 parallel	Superseded for general use by K-28-B
	4	40 hp		
K-7-A	4	30 hp	5 series / 4 parallel	K-12-A adapted to non-grounded return system
K-8-A	2	60 hp	5 series / 4 parallel	K-9-A with increased capacity
K-9-A	2	40 hp	5 series / 4 parallel	K-10-A adapted to non-grounded return system
K-9-B	2	40 hp	5 series / 4 parallel	Emergency reverse
K-10-A	2	40 hp	5 series / 4 parallel	
K-10-D	2	40 hp	5 series / 4 parallel	Emergency reverse
K-10-H	2	40 hp	5 series / 4 parallel	Includes contacts for operating auxiliary contactors
K-11-A	2	60 hp	5 series / 4 parallel	K-10-A with increased capacity
K-11-C	2	60 hp	5 series / 4 parallel	Emergency reverse
K-11-H	2	60 hp	5 series / 4 parallel	Includes contacts for operating auxiliary contactors
K-12-A	4	30 hp	5 series / 4 parallel	Similar to K-11 but for 4 motors
K-12-D	4	30 hp	5 series / 4 parallel	Includes contacts for operating auxiliary contactors
K-13-A	2	125 hp	7 series / 6 parallel	Superseded for general use by K-34-A
K-14-A	4	60 hp	7 series / 6 parallel	Superseded for general use by K-34-A
K-14-E	4	60 hp	7 series / 6 parallel	Includes contacts for operating auxiliary contactors
K-27-A	2	60 hp	4 series / 4 parallel	For use on non-grounded return system
K-28-B	4	40 hp	5 series / 5 parallel	
	2	80 hp		
K-28-E	4	40 hp	5 series / 5 parallel	K-28-B adapted for conduit wiring
	2	80 hp		
K-28-F	4	50 hp	5 series / 5 parallel*	Has extra heavy wiring and includes contacts for operating auxiliary contactors
K-28-J	4	50 hp	5 series / 5 parallel*	K-28-F adapted for conduit wiring
K-29-A	4	40 hp	6 series / 5 parallel	For non-grounded return, similar to K-6
K-31-A	4	30 hp	4 series / 4 parallel	Similar to K-27 but for 4 motors
K-32-A	2	40 hp	4 series / 4 parallel	K-27 with decreased capacity
K-34-A	4	75 hp	6 series / 4 parallel	For systems in which the voltage peaks reach over 600 volts
	2	150 hp		
K-35-A	4	50 hp	5 series / 3 parallel	For systems in which the voltage peaks reach over 600 volts
	2	100 hp		
K-36-A	2	60 hp	4 series / 4 parallel	For systems in which the voltage peaks reach over 600 volts
L-2-A	2	175 hp	4 series / 4 parallel	
L-3-A	4	150 hp	8 series / 7 parallel	
L-4-A	4	100 hp	4 series / 4 parallel	

Electric Brake Controllers

Title	Motors No.	Capacity	No. Points	Special Features, Etc.
B-8-B	4	60 hp	6 series / 5 parallel / 7 brake	Has separate braking handle
B-13-A	2	40 hp	5 series / 4 parallel / 7 brake	For use with disc brakes
B-18-C	2	40 hp	4 series / 4 parallel / 6 brake	For use with magnetic track brake
B-19-A	4	40 hp	5 series / 4 parallel / 7 brake	Has separate braking handle
B-23-A	2	60 hp	5 series / 4 parallel / 7 brake	B-13 with increased capacity
B-35-B	2	50 hp	4 series / 4 parallel / 6 brake	B-18-C with increased capacity

Rheostatic Controllers

Title	Motors No.	Capacity	No. Points	Special Features, Etc.
R-17-A	1	50 hp	6 forward / 6 reverse	
R-19-A	2	50 hp	6 forward / 6 reverse	

* When used with auxiliary contactor equipment.

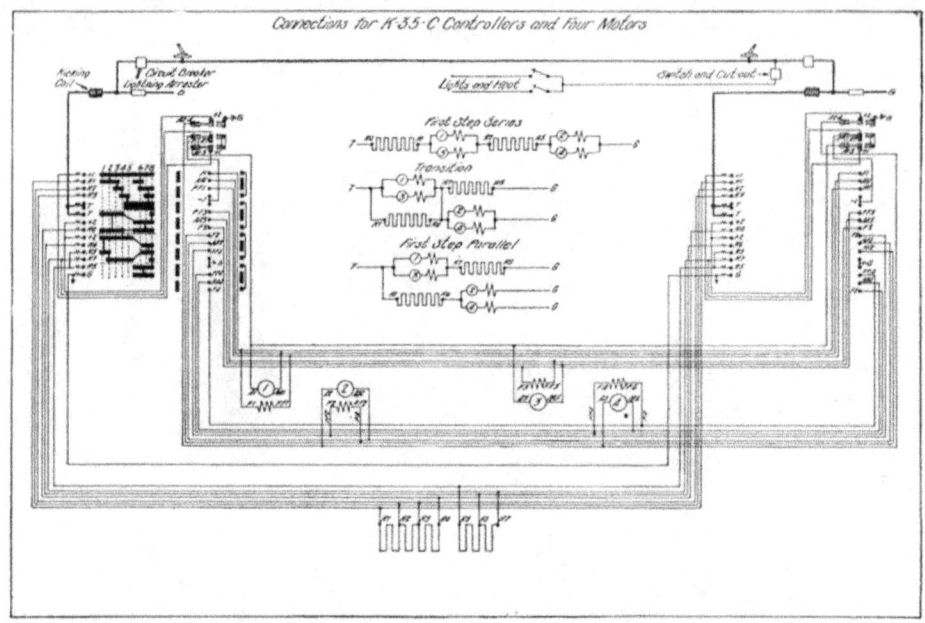

Fig. 1715—Diagram of Connections for Double-End Equipment of K-35-C Controllers and Four Motors

Figs. 1715-1716—Series-Parallel Platform Controller, No. K-36-B, with Cover Removed and Arc Deflector Opened

Figs. 1717-1718—Series-Parallel Platform Controller, No. K-35, with Cover Removed and Arc Deflector Opened

General Electric Company

Figs. 1719-1720—Series-Parallel Controller, Type S-4, for Four 40-hp. Motors
Allis-Chalmers Company

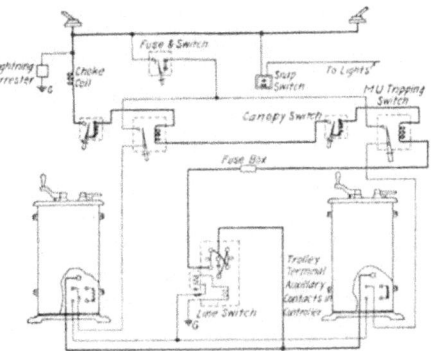

Fig. 1721—Diagram of Connections for Auxiliary Contactor Equipment for Hand-Operated Series-Parallel Controllers

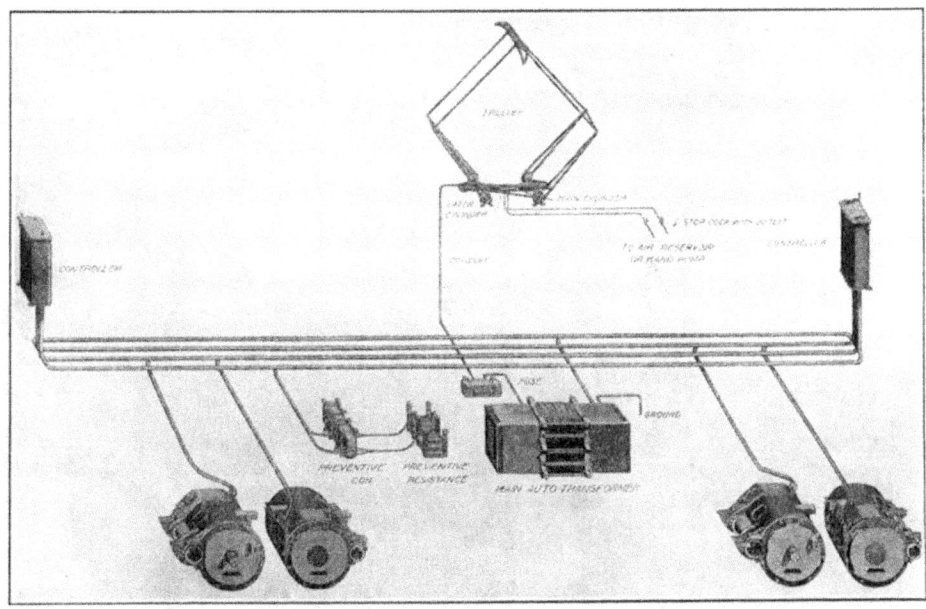

Fig. 1722—Diagram of Hand-Operated Control for Four-Motor Single-Phase Equipments
Westinghouse Electric and Manufacturing Company

CONTROL APPARATUS

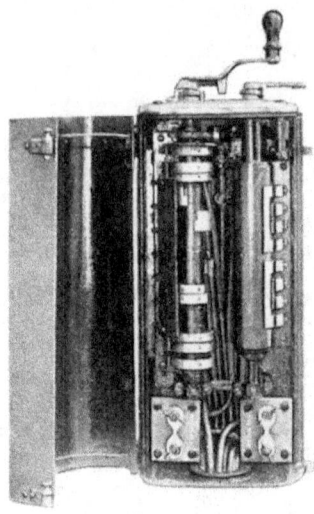

Fig. 1723—Hand-Operated Controller, Type 224, for Two 50-hp. Single-Phase Motors

Fig. 1724—Hand-Operated Controller, Type 451, for Four 50-hp. or Two 100-hp. Single-Phase Motors

Westinghouse Electric and Manufacturing Company

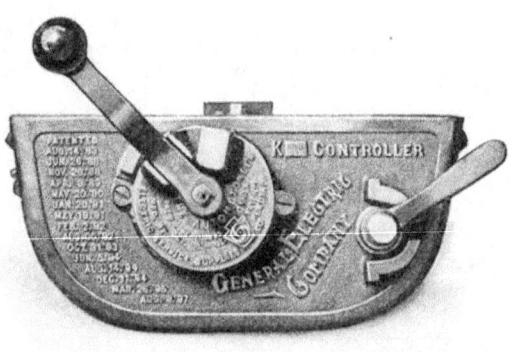

Fig. 1725—Automotoneer, Type JA, Applied to Controller

Fig. 1726—Automotoneer, Type JC

Figs. 1727-1728—Automotoneer, Type JA, Dismantled

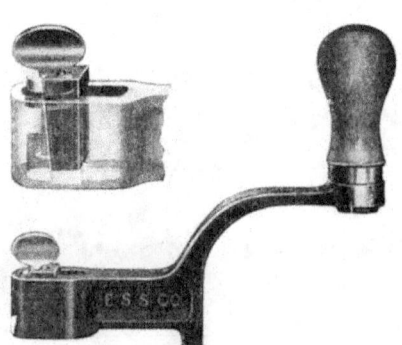

Figs. 1729-1730—Lock-On Controller Handle.

Electric Service Supplies Company

Fig. 1731—Duo Controller Contact Finger
Lord Electric Company

Fig. 1732—Controlator, Applied to Controller
Lord Manufacturing Company

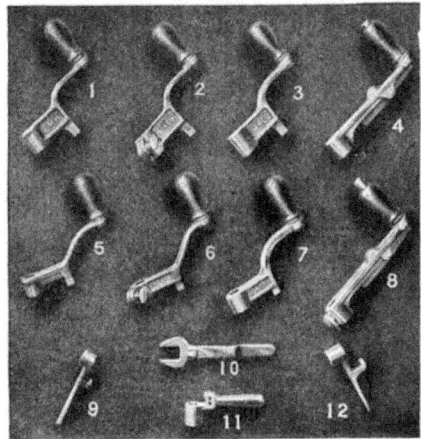

Figs. 1733-1743—Types of Controller and Reverse Handles
Columbia Machine Works and Malleable Iron Company

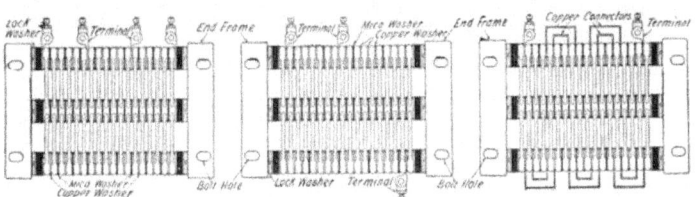

Figs. 1744-1746—Grid Resistor Connections

Fig. 1747—Grid Resistor Unit

Westinghouse Electric and Manufacturing Company

Fig. 1748—Assembled Grid Resistor
Westinghouse Electric & Manufacturing Company

Fig. 1749—Grid Resistance, Type RG
General Electric Company

(270)

CONTROL APPARATUS

Fig. 1750—Spiral Grid Resistance
W. R. Kerschner

Fig. 1751—Motor Circuit Switch, Type MS-8, with Cover Removed
General Electric Company

Fig. 1752—Automatic Circuit Breaker, Capacity 60 to 200 amp.

Figs. 1753-1754—Automatic Circuit Breaker, Capacity 400 to 500 amp.

Westinghouse Electric and Manufacturing Company

Figs. 1755-1757—Automatic Circuit Breaker, Type MR
General Electric Company

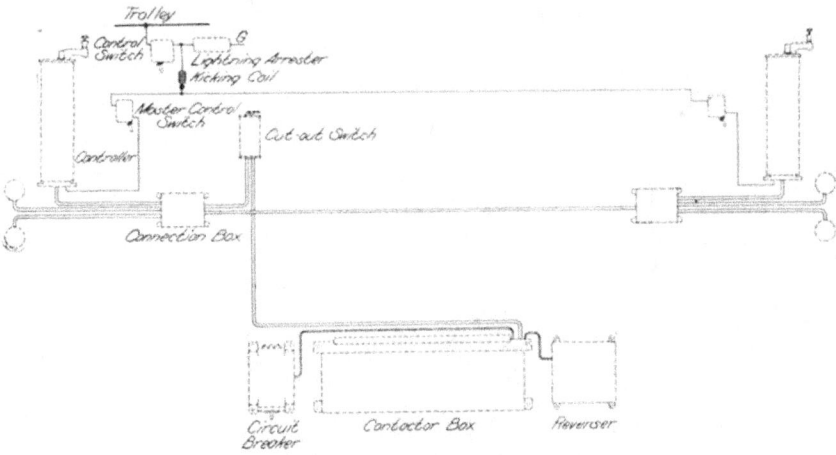

Fig. 1758—Diagram of Control Wiring for General Electric, Type M, Non-Automatic Multiple-Unit Control

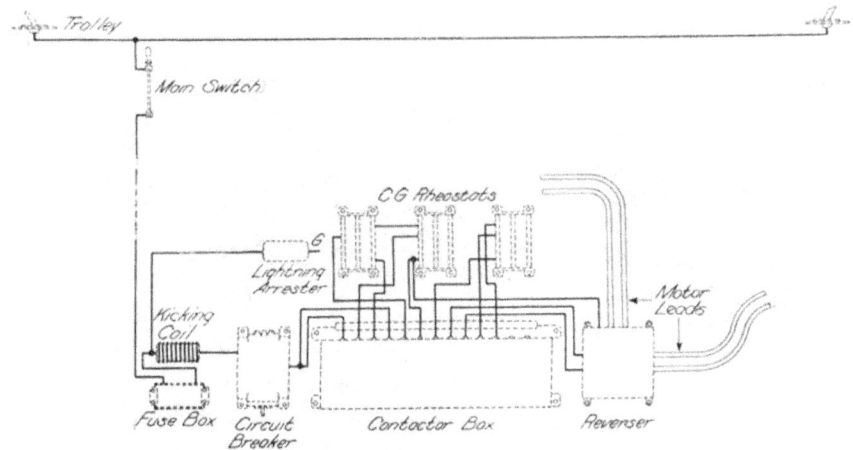

Fig. 1759—Diagram of Motor Wiring for General Electric, Type M, Non-Automatic Multiple-Unit Control

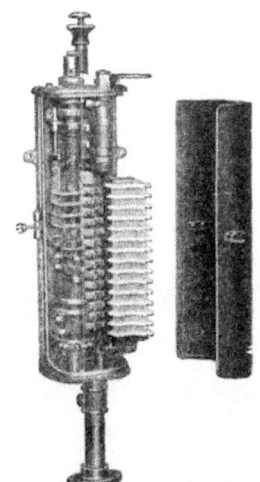

Fig. 1760—Master Controller for Type M, Non-Automatic Multiple-Unit Control

Fig. 1761—Master Controller for Type M, Automatic, Multiple-Unit Control

Fig. 1762—Reverser for Type M, Multiple-Unit Control

General Electric Company

CONTROL APPARATUS

Figs. 1763-1772

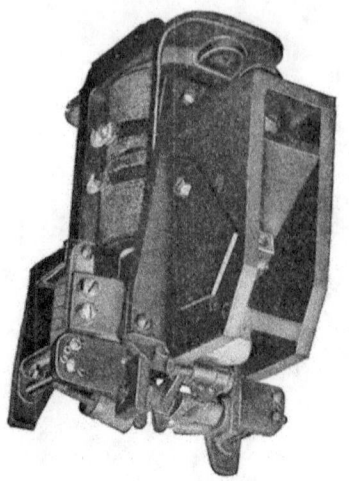

Fig. 1763—Circuit Breaker for Type M Control

Fig. 1764—Contactor for Type M Control

Fig. 1765—Train Line Control Wire Jumper for Type M Control

Fig. 1766—Coupler Socket for Train Line Control Wire Jumper

Fig. 1767—Dynamotor, Type CDM-13, for 1,200-Volt Equipment Control Circuits

General Electric Company

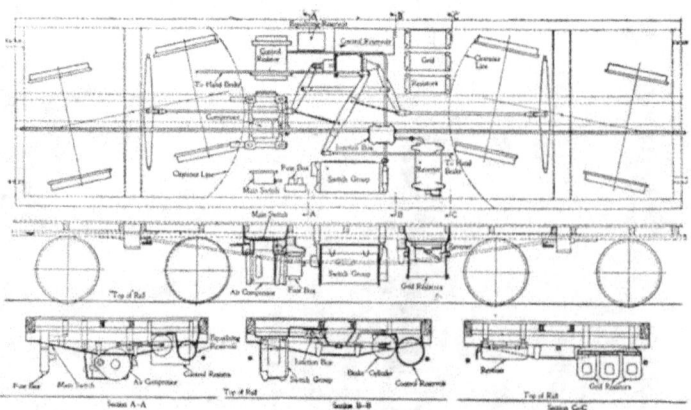

Figs. 1768-1772—General Arrangement of Apparatus Under Car for Westinghouse, Type HL, Electro-Pneumatic Unit-Switch Control

Westinghouse Electric & Manufacturing Company

CONTROL APPARATUS

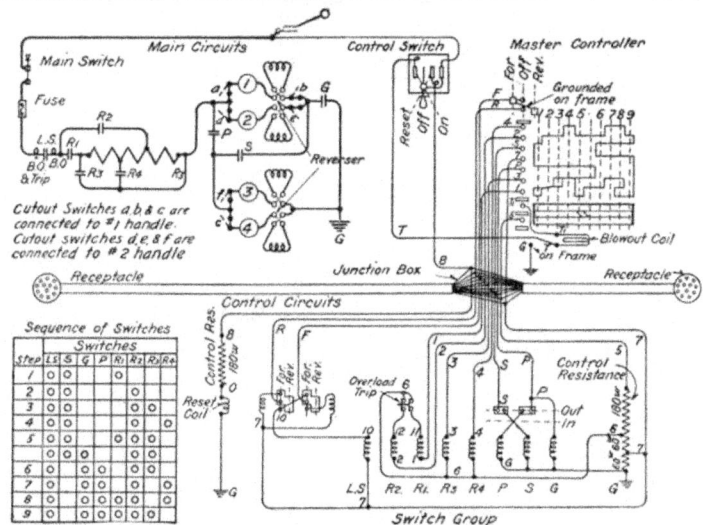

Fig. 1773—Diagram of Motor and Control Wiring for Type H. L., Hand-Operated Electro-Pneumatic Unit-Switch Control

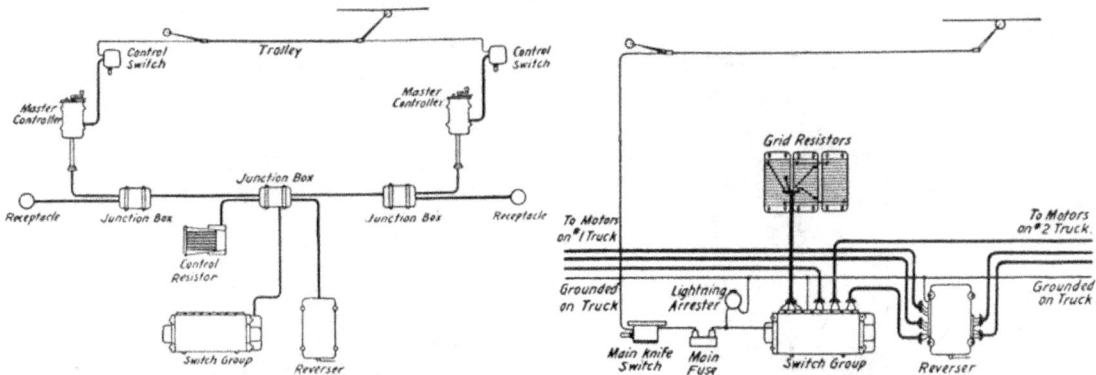

Fig. 1774—Diagram of Control Wiring for Type H. L., Hand-Operated Unit-Switch Control

Fig. 1775—Diagram of Motor Wiring for Type H. L., Hand-Operated Unit-Switch Control

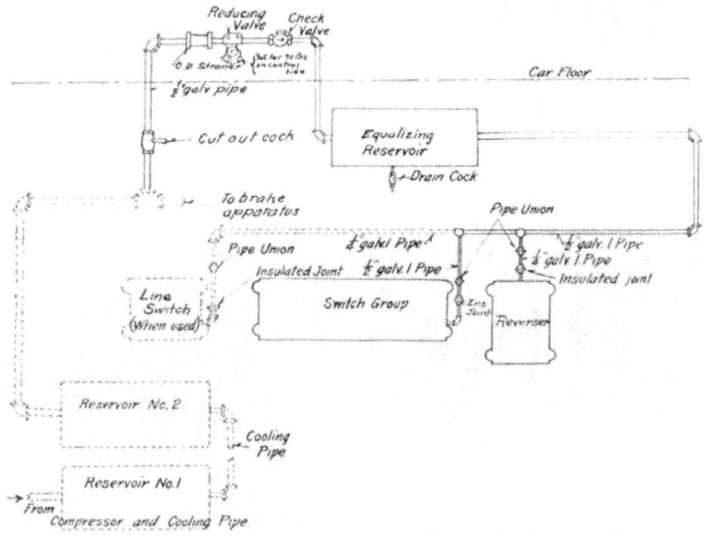

Fig. 1776—Diagram of Piping for Type H. L., Electro-Pneumatic Unit-Switch Control

Westinghouse Electric & Manufacturing Company

CONTROL APPARATUS

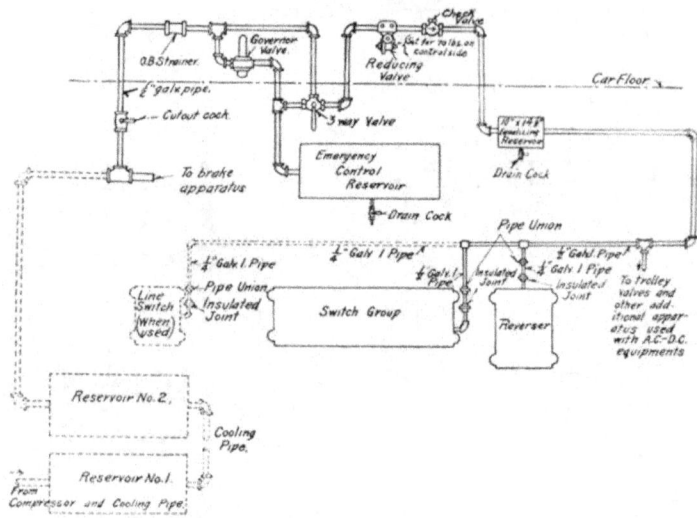

Fig. 1777—Diagram of Piping with Emergency Control Reservoir for Type H. L., Electro-Pneumatic Unit-Switch Control

Fig. 1778—Master Controller for Type H. L. Control, Closed

Fig. 1779—Master Controller for Type H. L. Control

Figs. 1780-1781—Control Resistor and Cover

Fig. 1782—Reverser for Type H. L. Control, Cover Removed

Westinghouse Electric & Manufacturing Company

CONTROL APPARATUS

Fig. 1783—Line Switch for Type H. L. Control

Fig. 1784—Line Switch with Cover Removed

Fig. 1785—Sectional View of Electro-Pneumatic Unit Switch

Fig. 1786—Cylinder and Magnet Valve of Unit Switch

Fig. 1787—Section Through Arc Box of Unit Switch

Fig. 1788—Control Switch for Type H. L. Control

Fig. 1789—Battery Charging Relay for Type H. B. Control

Fig. 1790—Storage Battery for Supplying Current to Control Circuits of Type H. B. Control

Westinghouse Electric & Manufacturing Company

CONTROL APPARATUS

Fig. 1791—Train Line Junction Box Used with Type H. L. Control

Fig. 1792—Dashboard Type, 12-Point Train Line Receptacle

Fig. 1793—12-Wire Train Line Jumper

Fig. 1794—Four-Point Bus Line Receptacle

Fig. 1795—Master Controller for Type AB Electro-Pneumatic Multiple-Unit Control

Fig. 1796—Limit Switch for Automatic Multiple-Unit Control

Fig. 1797—Bridging Relay for Automatic Multiple-Unit Control

Westinghouse Electric & Manufacturing Company

CONTROL APPARATUS

Fig. 1798—Electro-Pneumatic Switch Group for Multiple-Unit Control, Cover Removed

Fig. 1799—Electro-Pneumatic Switch Group for Multiple-Unit Control, Cover On

Fig. 1800—Reverser, No. 284, for Electro-Pneumatic Multiple-Unit Control, Cover Removed

Fig. 1801—Reverser, No. 284, for Electro-Pneumatic Multiple-Unit Control, Cover On

Fig. 1802—Master Controller for Multiple-Unit Control for Single-Phase Equipments

Fig. 1803—Oil Insulated Auto-Transformer for Single-Phase Equipments

Westinghouse Electric & Manufacturing Company

MISCELLANEOUS ELECTRICAL EQUIPMENT, Fuses   Figs. 1804-1814

Fig. 1804—High-Capacity Car Fuse Box

Fig. 1805—Low-Capacity Car Fuse Box

Westinghouse Electric & Manufacturing Company

Fig. 1806—Car Fuse Box
General Electric Company

Fig. 1807—Enclosed Fuse and Base, Spring Contact Type

Fig. 1808—Enclosed Fuse and Metal Box

Figs. 1809-1810—Interborough Type Third-Rail Shoe Fuse with Bolted Contacts

D. & W. Fuse Company

Fig. 1811—Enclosed Fuse and Box, Knife Contact Type

Fig. 1812—Enclosed Fuse and Box, Set Screw Contact Type

D. & W. Fuse Company

Fig. 1813—Noark Enclosed Fuse and Box

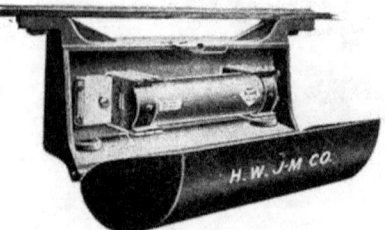
Fig. 1814—Noark Enclosed Fuse and Box

H. W. Johns-Manville Company

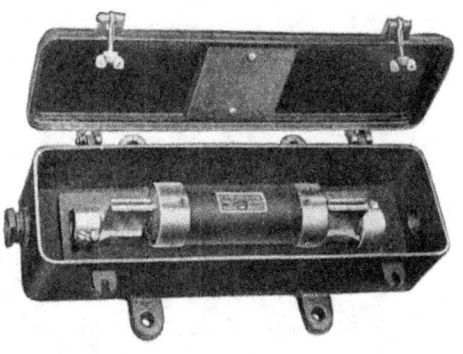

Fig. 1815—Noark Car Fuse Box; 600 Volts, 201-400 Amperes
H. W. Johns-Manville Company

Fig. 1816—Westinghouse Multi-Path Car Type Lightning Arrester
Westinghouse Elec. & Mfg. Co.

Figs. 1817-1819—Car Lightning Arrester, D-2, Type M
General Electric Company

Figs. 1820-1821—Garton-Daniels Car Type Lightning Arrester in Metal Box

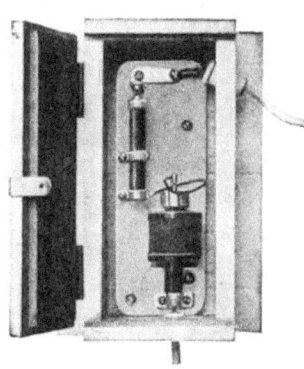

Fig. 1822—Garton-Daniels Car Type Lightning Arrester in Wooden Box
Electric Service Supplies Company

Fig. 1823—M.-G. Car Lightning Arrester
Lord Manufacturing Co

Fig. 1824—Shaw Lightning Arrester
Lord Mfg. Co.

Fig. 1825—Kicking Coil for Garton-Daniels Lightning Arrester
Electric Service Supplies Company

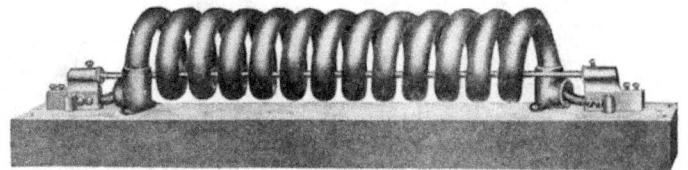

Fig. 1826—Kicking Coil for M.-G. Lightning Arrester
Lord Manufacturing Company

MISCELLANEOUS ELECTRICAL EQUIPMENT, Coasting Register, Current Meter   Figs. 1827-1832

Fig. 1827—Coasting Register Mounted in Car

Fig. 1828—Interior of Coasting Register

Fig. 1829—Motorman's Recording Key

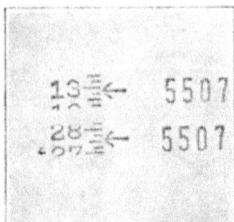

Fig. 1830—Sample of Record Strip

Railway Improvement Company

Fig. 1831—Exterior of "C.-H." Special Ampere-Hour Car Meter

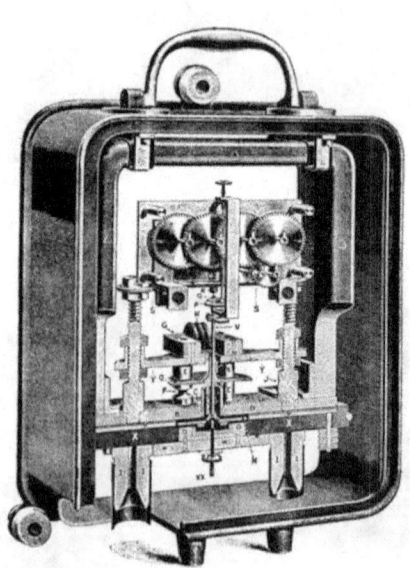

Fig. 1832—Interior of "C.-H." Ampere-Hour Car Meter

Wonham, Sanger & Bates

Fig. 1833—Group of Cells of Gould Pasted Type Storage Battery for Traction Use
Gould Storage Battery Company

Fig. 1834—Sectional View of Gould Pasted Type Storage Battery Cell

Fig. 1835—Car Telephone with Connection Jack and Wire Reel

Fig. 1836—Portable Car Telephone

Fig. 1837—Stationary Car Telephone

Stromberg-Carlson Telephone Manufacturing Company

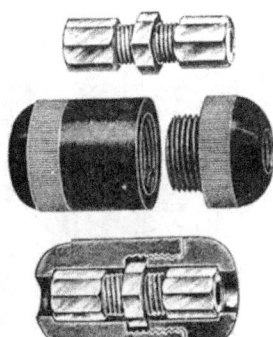

Fig. 1838—Base of National Metal Molding

Fig. 1839—Cap of National Metal Molding

National Metal Molding Company

Fig. 1840—National Metal Molding Assembled
National Metal Molding Co.

Fig. 1841—Dossert Connector
Dossert & Company

Figs. 1842-1844—Insulated Dossert Connector for Junction Boxes
Dossert & Company

Fig. 1845—Metal Conduit in Roof Framing with Condulet Outlets for Deck Lamps

Fig. 1846—Main Motor Cable Conduit, Showing Four-Way Condulet Outlet for Motor Leads

Fig. 1847—Main Motor Cable Conduit Under Floor of Car

Fig. 1848—Conduits Leading from Condulet Junction Box Under Platform Controller

Fig. 1849—Condulet Outlet for Seven Cables Leading to Motor Resistance Grids

Crouse-Hinds Company

THIRD-RAIL SHOES

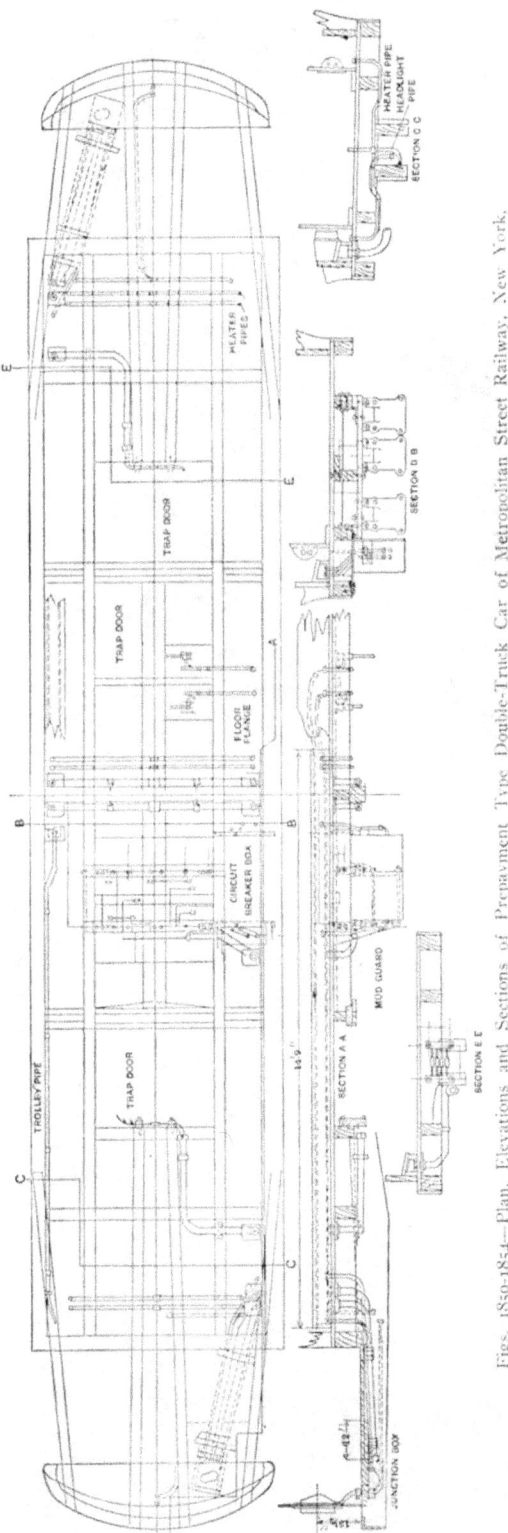

Figs. 1850-1854—Plan, Elevations and Sections of Prepayment Type Double-Truck Car of Metropolitan Street Railway, New York. Showing Method of Running Wiring in Pipe Conduit and Cable Boxes

Figs. 1857-1858—Slipper Type Third-Rail Shoe for Underrunning Third Rail; Capacity, 800 Amperes
General Electric Company

Figs. 1855-1856—Slipper Type Third-Rail Shoe for Overrunning Third Rail; Capacity, 2,000 Amperes
General Electric Company

TROLLEYS

Figs. 1859-1860—Slipper Type Third-Rail Shoe for Overrunning Third Rail; Capacity, 800 Amperes
General Electric Company

Fig. 1861—Gravity Type Third-Rail Shoe for Overrunning Third Rail
General Electric Company

Fig. 1862—Pneumatically-Operated Third-Rail Shoe for Underrunning Third Rail
Westinghouse Electric & Manufacturing Company

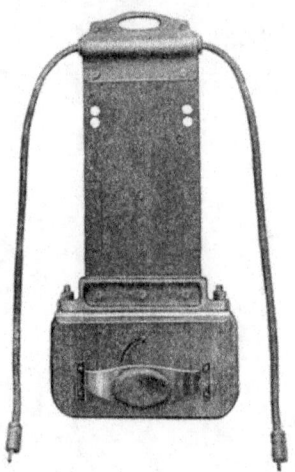

Fig. 1863—Conduit Plow
General Electric Co.

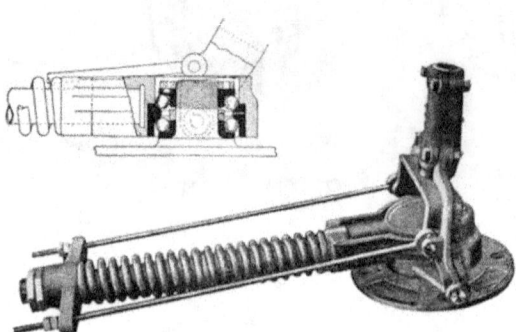

Figs. 1864-1865—Union Standard Trolley Base, No. 11
R. D. Nuttall Company

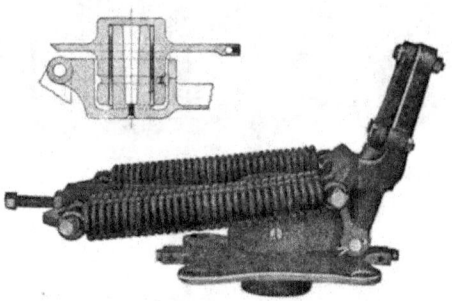

Figs. 1866-1867—Union Standard Trolley Base, No. 13
R. D. Nuttall Company

Fig. 1868—Union Standard Trolley Base, No. 5
R. D. Nuttall Company

TROLLEYS

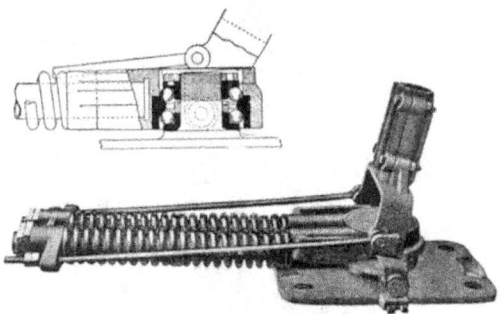

Figs. 1869-1870—Union Standard Trolley Base, No. 10
R. D. Nuttall Company

Fig. 1871—National Ball and Roller-Bearing Trolley Base, No. 2
Trolley Supply Company

Fig. 1873—Bayonet Detachable Trolley Pole Clamp
Bayonet Trolley Harp Company

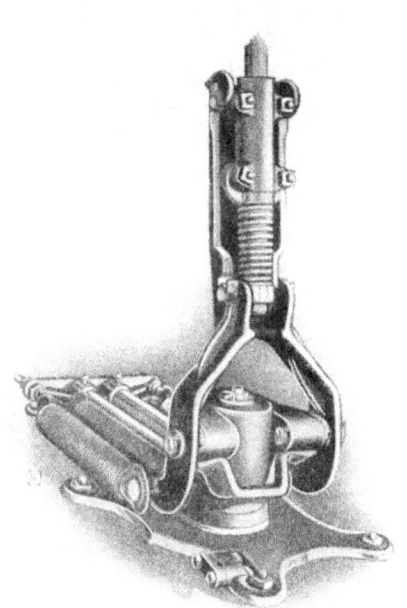

Fig. 1872—Bayonet Roller-Bearing Trolley Base
Bayonet Trolley Harp Company

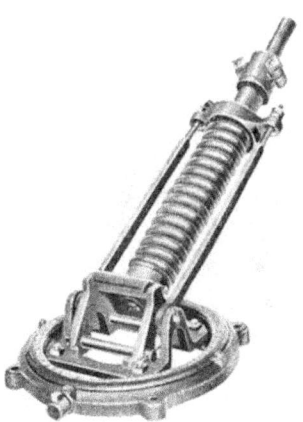

Fig. 1874—Holland Ball-Bearing Trolley Base, No. 3
Holland Trolley Supply Company

Fig. 1875—Pantograph Trolley, Lowered
Westinghouse Electric & Manufacturing Company.

Figs. 1914-1915—Trolley Wheel with V-Groove, No. 10

Figs. 1916-1917—Trolley Wheel with U-Groove, No. 20

Eureka Tempered Copper Works

Fig. 1918—Standard Trolley Wheel with Oil Chamber
Standard Brass Foundry Company

Fig. 1919—Graphite Trolley Wheel Bushing
Graphite Lubricating Company

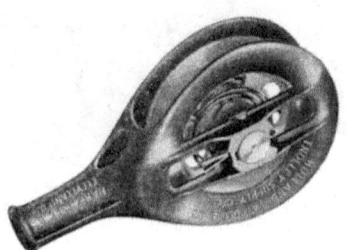

Fig. 1920—Holland Trolley Harp, Type D

Fig. 1921—Holland Trolley Harp, Type C

Fig. 1922—Holland Trolley Harp, Type B

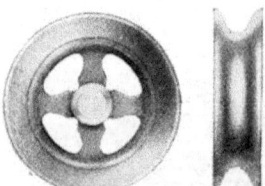
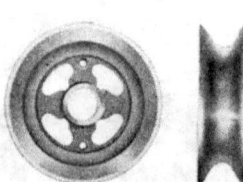

Figs. 1923-1924—Holland Trolley Wheel, V-Groove

Figs. 1925-1926—Holland Trolley Wheel, U-Groove

Holland Trolley Supply Company

Figs. 1927-1928—Holland Sleet Wheel

TROLLEYS

Figs. 1929-1932—Hensley Trolley Wheel and Axle

Fig. 1933—Hensley Trolley Harp, No. 3

Fig. 1934—Hensley Trolley Harp, No. 5

Hensley Trolley Company

Fig. 1935—Hensley Sleet Scraper

Figs. 1936-1938—Hensley Trolley Harp Contact Springs and Washers

Fig. 1939—Axle for Hensley Trolley Wheel

Hensley Trolley Company

Figs. 1940-1943—Kalamazoo Trolley Wheels and Harp
Star Brass Works

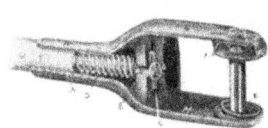
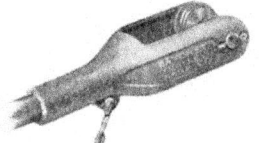

Figs. 1944-1945—Bayonet Trolley Harp
Bayonet Trolley Harp Company

Fig. 1946—B-V Sleet Cutter, Running Forward

Fig. 1947—B-V Sleet Cutter, Running Backward

Bonney-Vehslage Tool Company

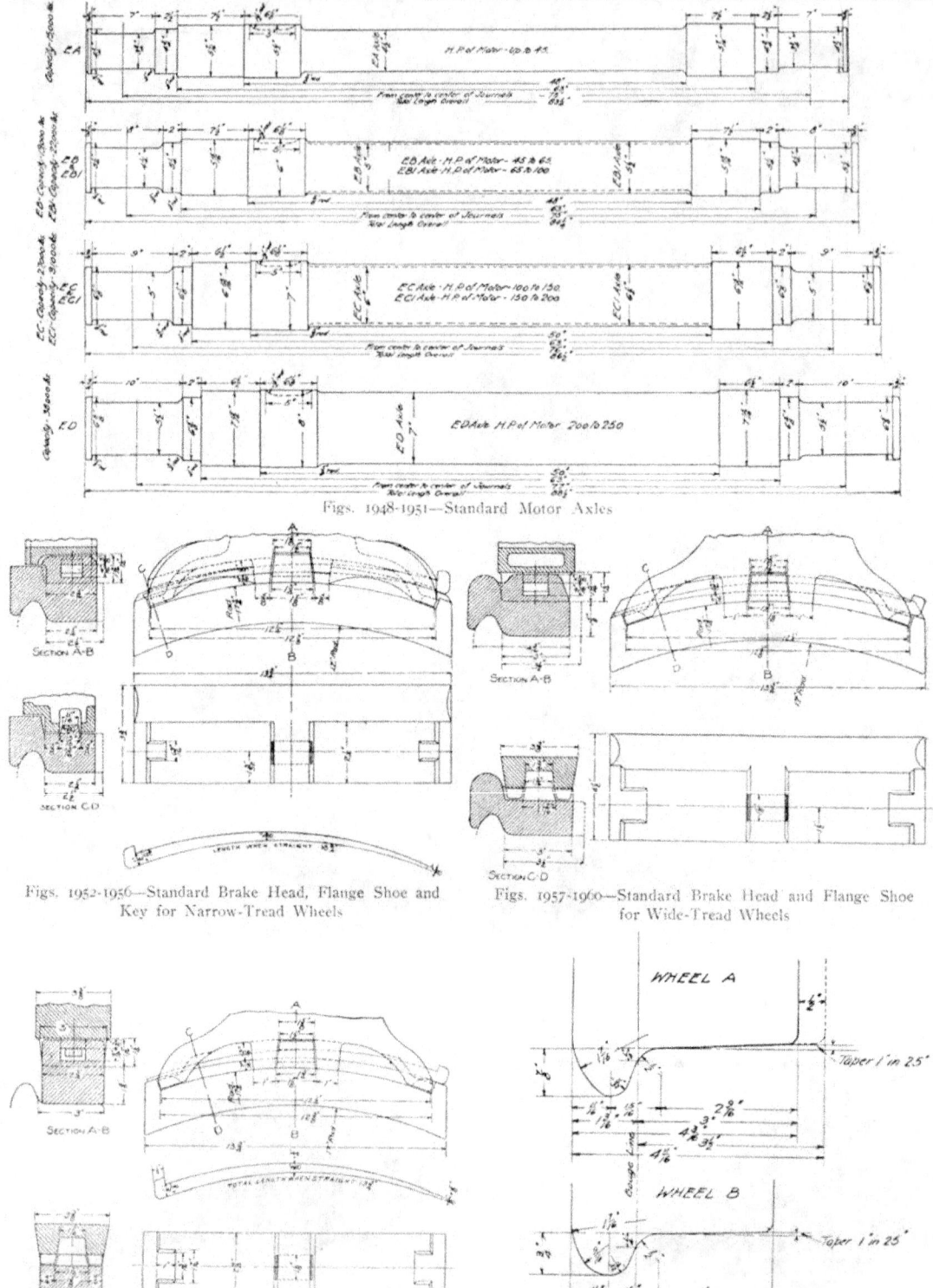

Figs. 1948-1951—Standard Motor Axles

Figs. 1952-1956—Standard Brake Head, Flange Shoe and Key for Narrow-Tread Wheels

Figs. 1957-1960—Standard Brake Head and Flange Shoe for Wide-Tread Wheels

Figs. 1961-1965—Standard Brake Head, Unflanged Shoe and Key for Wide-Tread Wheels

Figs. 1966-1967—Standard Treads and Flanges for Wide and Narrow-Tread Wheels

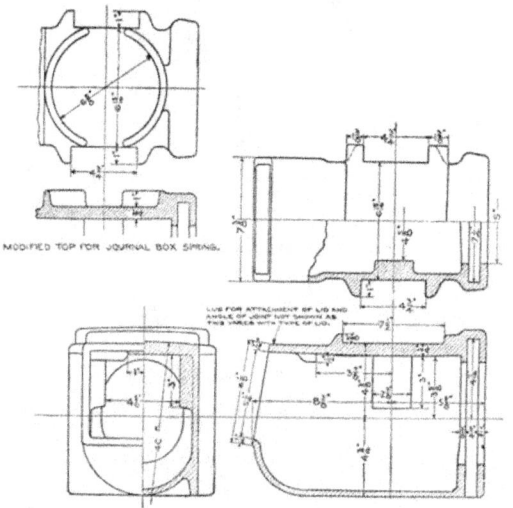

Figs. 1968-1972—Standard Journal Box for Journals
3¾ in. x 7 in.

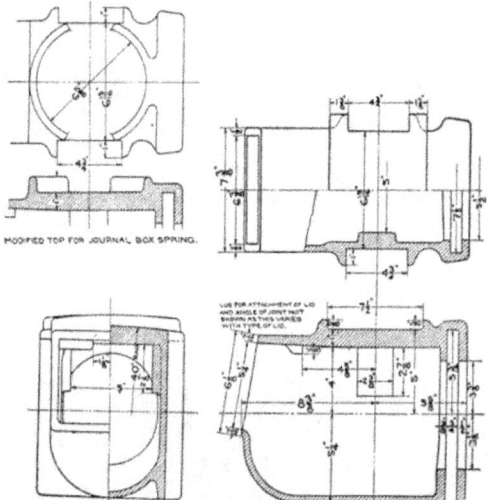

Figs. 1973-1977—Standard Journal Box for Journals
4½ in. x 8 in.

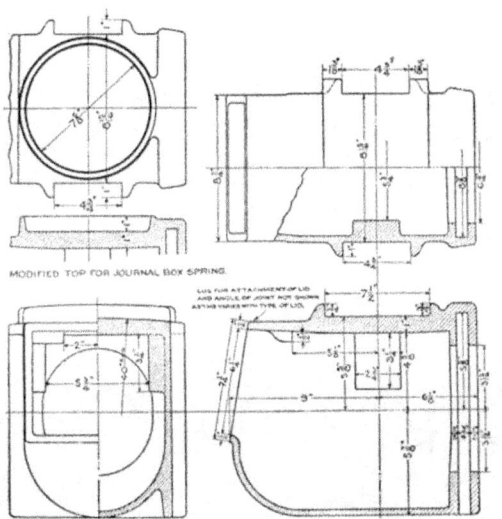

Figs. 1978-1982—Standard Journal Box for Journals
5 in. x 9 in.

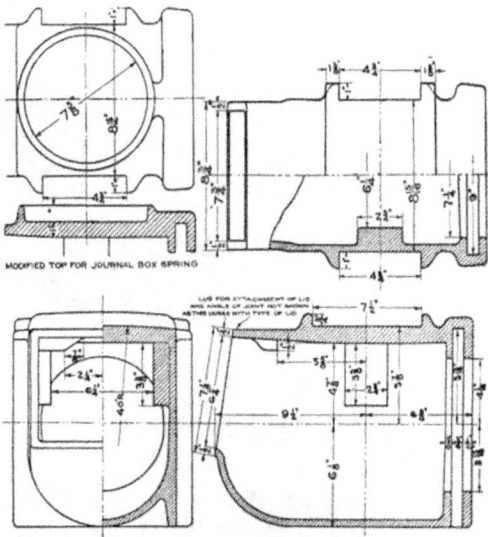

Figs. 1982-1987—Standard Journal Box for Journals
5½ in. x 10 in.

Railway Motors
For All Classes of Service

BOX FRAME

200 Horse Power

160 Horse Power

Railway operating officials are urged to investigate the great saving in maintenance cost which the modern Westinghouse Railway Motors afford.

125 Horse Power

100 Horse Power

Interpole
and
Non-Interpole

75 Horse Power

SPLIT FRAME

60 Horse Power

50 Horse Power

40 Horse Power

Westinghouse Electric & Manufacturing Co.

Atlanta	Buffalo	Denver	Los Angeles	Philadelphia	Salt Lake City
Baltimore	Chicago	Detroit	New Orleans	Pittsburg	San Francisco
Boston	Cincinnati		New York	St. Louis	Seattle

Westinghouse Electric & Mfg. Co., of Texas, Dallas and El Paso, Texas.
Canada: Canadian Westinghouse Co., Ltd., Hamilton, Ont.
Mexico: Compania Ingeniera, Importadora y Contratista, S. A., Successors to G. & O. Braniff & Company, City of Mexico.

Unit Switch Control System

Fairmount & Clarksburg Traction Co. Train
Equipped with Westinghouse Hand-Operated Unit Switch Control System

THE Westinghouse Unit Switch Control System is destined to become the standard of the country. It contains all the essentials of successful operation, viz.: light weight, simplicity, accessibility, reliability and low maintenance cost.

Ask nearest office for Circular 1089

Westinghouse Electric & Manufacturing Co.

Atlanta	Boston	Chicago	Denver	Kansas City	New Orleans	Philadelphia	St. Louis	San Francisco
Baltimore	Buffalo	Cincinnati	Detroit	Los Angeles	New York	Pittsburg	Salt Lake City	Seattle

Canada: Canadian Westinghouse Co., Ltd., Hamilton, Ont. Westinghouse Electric & Mfg. Co. of Texas, Dallas and El Paso, Texas.
Mexico: Campania Ingeniera, Importadora y Contratista, S. A., successors to G. & O. Braniff & Company, City of Mexico.

Railway Motor Lubrication

Cross section of waste-packed, Armature-Bearing Housing for Split Frame Motor.

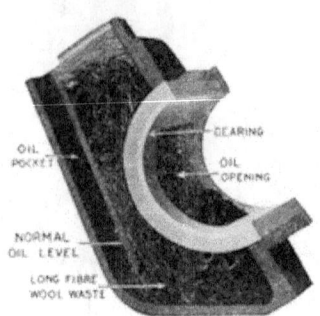

Cross section of waste-packed, Axle Cap and Bearing for Box Frame Motor.

The armature and axle-bearing housings are provided with separate oil channels, enabling the inspector, at inspection periods, to determine exactly the quantity of oil required,—no waste of oil. The large oil reservoirs make it necessary to replenish the oil, or inspect bearings only once a month.

The illustrations show how oil is fed to the bearings through capillary attraction only, being thoroughly filtered before reaching the bearings.

This method of lubrication saves thousands of dollars yearly, not only in reduced oil consumption and increased life of bearings, but also by reducing to a minimum the costly repairs due to armatures rubbing pole pieces.

Circular 1172 contains a detailed description of these bearings; ask for it.

Westinghouse Electric & Mfg. Co.

Atlanta Boston Chicago Denver Kansas City New Orleans Philadelphia St. Louis San Francisco
Baltimore Buffalo Cincinnati Detroit Los Angeles New York Pittsburg Salt Lake City
Westinghouse Electric & Mfg. Co. of Texas, Dallas and El Paso, Texas. Canada: Canadian Westinghouse Co., Ltd., Hamilton, Ont.
Mexico: Compania Ingeniera, Importadora y Contratista, S. A., Successors to G. & O. Braniff & Company, City of Mexico.

Railway Type Circuit Breaker

A positive protection against sudden overloads.

Superior blow-out action substantially reduces the burning of the arc tips and arc chutes.

Reliability in action disrupts the most severe short circuits, without undue noise, or expulsion of molten copper particles.

The solid moulded arc chutes have no cracks to vent gases and flare-backs.

Arcing tip is carried on brass casting, and pressure on machined surfaces provided by a steel spring which does not carry current.

The auxiliary tripping knob closes the magnetic circuit when tripped by hand, thus giving full blow-out on hand trip.

All working parts are accessible.

Fully described in Folder 4059; mailed upon request.

Westinghouse Electric & Manufacturing Co.

Atlanta   Boston   Chicago   Denver   Kansas City   New Orleans   Philadelphia   St. Louis   San Francisco
Baltimore   Buffalo   Cincinnati   Detroit   Los Angeles   New York   Pittsburg   Salt Lake City   Seattle
Westinghouse Electric & Mfg. Co. of Texas, Dallas and El Paso, Texas.
Canada: Canadian Westinghouse Co., Ltd., Hamilton, Ont.
Mexico: Compania Ingeniera, Importadora y Contratista, S. A., successors to G. & O. Braniff & Company, City of Mexico.

Brakes For Electric Railway Systems

Development in the Art of Braking has been as rapid, as varied, as full of interesting and vital problems, and as replete with accomplishment of far-reaching importance and value as the history of transportation itself.

Westinghouse Brakes for electric cars are made to meet every operating condition, safely and efficiently—from single car service to the longest trains on electrified steam roads. Typical equipments are:

SM-1 Equipment. A straight-air brake for ordinary single-car operation. Simple and easily handled.

SME Equipment. A straight-air brake with automatic emergency feature, for single-car, intermittent two-motor car, or motor car and trailer service. Combines the flexibility of straight-air operation in normal service, with many of the safety features of automatic operation in cases of emergency.

AMM Equipment. An automatic brake for one to five car train service; all motor cars or motor cars and trailers. Has graduated release, quick recharge, quick service and high-emergency-pressure, and may be provided with straight-air release.

AML Equipment. The most efficient form of the purely automatic brake for high-speed service on trains of any length. Has graduated-release, quick-service, quick-recharge, quick-action and high-emergency-pressure.

Electric-Pneumatic System. The highest development in the art of train braking. Insures absolute, instantaneous and uniform brake action on each car in a train of any length. While being operated electrically, all the pneumatic functions are in reserve, available for instant service with maximum braking power if required.

Westinghouse Traction Brake Co.
GENERAL OFFICES, PITTSBURG, PA.

ATLANTA, Candler Building
BOSTON, Exchange Building
CHICAGO, Railway Exchange Building
CLEVELAND, Schofield Building
COLUMBUS, Columbus Savings and Trust Bldg.
DENVER, Majestic Building
HOUSTON, TEX, 403 Hawthorne Ave.
MEXICO CITY, MEXICO, 4a Calle Pte. de Alvarado, No. 100
NEW YORK, City Investing Building
ST. LOUIS, 1932 North Broadway
ST. PAUL, Endicott Building
SAN FRANCISCO, Pacific Building
PORTLAND, ORE., Spalding Building

FOR CANADA: Canadian Westinghouse Co., Limited, Hamilton, Ontario

NUTTALL ∴ PITTSBURG

Makers of

Nuttall Case Hardened Gears and Pinions

Nuttall Trolley Wheels

Nuttall Trolley Harps

Nuttall Trolley Poles

Nuttall Trolley Bases

Nuttall Sleet Scrapers

Nuttall Sleet Wheels

Nuttall Flexible Cushion Couplings

The high physical properties of the material in Nuttall Gears and Pinions assure long life and minimum breakage.

AVERAGE PHYSICAL PROPERTIES.

Grade Material	Tensile Strength	Elastic Limit	Elongation % in 2 in.	Reduction in Area %
Standard Cast Steel Gear	65000–70000	30000–35000	20–22	25–30
Special Cast Steel Gear	75000–80000	40000–45000	20–22	30–35
XX Cast Steel Gear	85000–90000	50000–55000	20–22	30–35
SS Rolled Steel Gear	125000–130000	80000–85000	15–17	30–35
NS Steel Pinion	90000–95000	55000–60000	20–25	40–45
SS Steel Pinion	125000–130000	80000–85000	15–17	30–35

NUTTALL ∴ PITTSBURG

Agencies in

| Boston | Philadelphia | Pittsburg | Chicago | San Francisco | Spokane |
| New York | Atlanta | Cincinnati | St. Louis | Seattle | Portland |

INDEX TO ADVERTISEMENTS

	Page
Ackley Brake Co.	22
Adams & Westlake Co.	18
Allis-Chalmers Co.	36, 37
American Brake Co.	32
American Mason Safety Tread Co.	28
Baker Heating & Supply Co., William C.	16
Baldwin Locomotive Works	43
Benolite Co.	18
Brill Co., The J. G.	50, 51, 52, 53, 54, 55
Cincinnati Car Co.	49
Columbia Machine Works & Malleable Iron Co.	35
Commonwealth Steel Co.	30
Consolidated Car Fender Co.	27
Consolidated Car-Heating Co.	20
Crouse-Hinds Co.	14, 15
D & W Fuse Co.	22
Dayton Manufacturing Co.	16
Dorner Railway Equipment Co.	22
Duff Manufacturing Co.	34
Elastic Tip Co.	19
Electric Cable Co.	26
Electric Railway Journal	40
Emery Pneumatic Lubricator Co.	32
Galena Signal Oil Co.	33
General Electric Co.	10, 11
Graphite Lubricating Co.	12
Gould Storage Battery Co.	15
Hale & Kilburn Manufacturing Co.	19
Hanna Co., J. A.	48
Heywood Bros. & Wakefield Co.	19
Holland Trolley Supply Co., The	12
Homer Commutator Co.	34
Howard & Co., James L.	14
International Register Co., The	18
Jeandron, W. J.	15
Johns-Manville Co., H. W.	29
Kerite Insulated Wire & Cable Co.	9
Kerschner, W. R.	38
Laconia Car Co. Works	45
Langslow Co., The H. R.	17
Long Company, E. G.	38
Lord Manufacturing Co.	13
McConway & Torley Co.	41
McCord Manufacturing Co.	21
National Brake Co.	23
National Brake & Electric Co.	24, 25
National Metal Molding Co.	39
Niles Car & Manufacturing Co.	48
Nuttall, R. D.	6
Pay-as-You-Enter Car Corp.	46, 47
Pay-Within-Car Co.	46, 47
Perry Ventilator Co.	22
Prepayment Car Sales Co.	46, 47
Samson Cordage Works	13
Scarritt-Comstock Furniture Co.	19
Smith Heater Co., Peter	16
Standard Steel Works Co.	42
Taylor Electric Truck Co.	44
Trolley Supply Co.	12
Union Spring & Mfg. Co.	28
Universal Safety Tread Co.	28
Van Dorn Coupler Co.	39
Watson Insulated Wire Co.	9
Westinghouse Electric & Mfg. Co.	1, 2, 3, 4
Westinghouse Traction Brake Co.	5
Whipple Supply Co.	30
Whitmore Manufacturing Co.	31
Wilson Trolley Catcher Co.	13
Wonham, Sanger & Bates	26
Wood Co., Chas. N.	13

CLASSIFIED DIRECTORY OF ADVERTISERS

Alloy and Bearing Metals.
Westinghouse Electric & Mfg. Co.

Anti-Climbers.
Whipple Supply Co.

Axles.
Baldwin Locomotive Works
Brill Co., The J. G.
Cincinnati Car Co.
Standard Steel Works Co.

Basket Racks.
Adams & Westlake Co.
Brill Co., The J. G.
Dayton Manufacturing Co.
Howard & Co., James L.

Batteries, Dry.
Johns-Manville Co., H. W.

Batteries, Storage.
Gould Storage Battery Co.

Bearings for Trucks and Motors.
Brill Co., The J. G.
Columbia Machine Works & Malleable Iron Co.
General Electric Co.
Taylor Electric Truck Co.
Westinghouse Electric & Mfg. Co.

Bells and Gongs.
Adams & Westlake Co.
Brill Co., The J. G.
Dayton Manufacturing Co.
General Electric Co.
Howard & Co., James L.
Trolley Supply Co.

Bolsters, Car and Truck.
Baldwin Locomotive Works
Brill Co., The J. G.
Cincinnati Car Co.

Brake Hangers.
Brill Co., The J. G.

Brake Rods.
Columbia Machine Works & Malleable Iron Co.

Brake Shoes.
Brill Co., The J. G.
Columbia Machine Works & Malleable Iron Co.
Dorner Railway Equipment Co.
Taylor Electric Truck Co.

Brakes, Brake Systems and Brake Parts.
Ackley Brake Co.
Adams & Westlake Co.
Allis-Chalmers Co.
American Brake Co.
Brill Co., The J. G.
Columbia Machine Works & Malleable Iron Co.
Dayton Manufacturing Co.
Kerschner, W. R.
National Brake Co.
National Brake & Electric Co.
Taylor Electric Truck Co.
Westinghouse Traction Brake Co.

Brushes, Carbon.
General Electric Co.
Jeandron, W. J.
Westinghouse Electric & Mfg. Co.

Bumpers, Car Seat.
Brill Co., The J. G.
Cincinnati Car Co.
Elastic Tip Co.

Car Step Lifters.
Consolidated Car Fender Co.

Car Trimmings.
Adams & Westlake Co.
Brill Co., The J. G.
Cincinnati Car Co.

Columbia Machine Works & Malleable Iron Co.
Dayton Manufacturing Co.
Hale & Kilburn Mfg. Co.
Howard & Co., James L.

Cars, Passenger, Freight, and Express.
Brill Co., The J. G.
Cincinnati Car Co.
Dorner Railway Equipment Co.
Gould Storage Battery Co.
Hanna Co., J. A.
Laconia Car Co. Works
Niles Car & Mfg. Co.
Pay-as-You-Enter Car Corp.
Pay-Within-Car Co.
Prepayment Car Sales Co.

Castings, Grey, Iron, and Steel.
Columbia Machine Works & Malleable Iron Co.
McConway & Torley Co.
Standard Steel Works Co.
Union Spring & Mfg. Co.

Catchers and Retrievers, Trolley.
Lord Manufacturing Co.
Trolley Supply Co.
Wilson Trolley Catcher Co.

Circuit Breakers.
General Electric Co.
Westinghouse Electric & Mfg. Co.

Closets, Flush and Dry.
Dayton Manufacturing Co.
Howard & Co., James L.

Clusters and Sockets.
Adams & Westlake Co.
General Electric Co.
Westinghouse Elec. & Mfg. Co.

Compressors, Air.
Allis-Chalmers Co.
General Electric Co.
National Brake & Electric Co.
Westinghouse Traction Brake Co.

Contact Fingers.
Lord Manufacturing Co.

Controller Regulators.
Lord Manufacturing Co.

Controllers and Parts.
Allis-Chalmers Co.
Columbia Machine Works & Malleable Iron Co.
General Electric Co.
Johns-Manville Co., H. W.
Kerschner, W. R.
Lord Manufacturing Co.
Westinghouse Elec. & Mfg. Co.

Cord, Trolley, Bell, Register, and Sash.
Adams & Westlake Co.
Brill Co., The J. G.
International Register Co., The
Samson Cordage Works
Trolley Supply Co.

Cord Connectors.
Adams & Westlake Co.
Dayton Manufacturing Co.
Samson Cordage Works
Wood Co., Chas. N.

Couplers.
Brill Co., The J. G.
Cincinnati Car Co.
McConway & Torley Co.
Van Dorn Coupler Co.
Westinghouse Traction Brake Co.

Curtains, Curtain Fixtures, and Curtain Material.
Brill Co., The J. G.

(7)

CLASSIFIED DIRECTORY OF ADVERTISERS—Continued.

Door Operating Devices.
Consolidated Car-Heating Co.

Doors and Door Fixtures.
Adams & Westlake Co.
Brill Co., The J. G.
Dayton Manufacturing Co.
Hale & Kilburn Mfg. Co.
Howard & Co., James L.

Fare Boxes.
Brill Co., The J. G.
Langslow Co., The H. R.

Fenders and Wheel Guards.
Brill Co., The J. G.
Cincinnati Car Co.
Consolidated Car Fender Co.
Worham, Sanger & Bates.

Fire Extinguishers.
Johns-Manville Co., H. W.

Forgings, Drop and Car Truck.
Columbia Machine Works & Malleable Iron Co.

Fuses and Fuse Boxes.
Columbia Machine Works & Malleable Iron Co.
D & W Fuse Co.
General Electric Co.
Johns-Manville Co., H. W.
Westinghouse Elec. & Mfg. Co.

Gates, Car.
Adams & Westlake Co.
Brill Co., The J. G.
Cincinnati Car Co.
Dayton Manufacturing Co.

Gear Cases.
Columbia Machine Works & Malleable Iron Co.
General Electric Co.
Kerschner, W. R.
Westinghouse Elec. & Mfg. Co.

Gears and Pinions.
Columbia Machine Works & Malleable Iron Co.
Dorner Railway Equipment Co.
General Electric Co.
Kerschner, W. R.
Nuttall Co., R. D.
Whipple Supply Co.

Harps, Trolley.
General Electric Co.
Holland Trolley Supply Co.
Nuttall Co., R. D.

Headlights.
Adams & Westlake Co.
Brill Co., The J. G.
Crouse-Hinds Co.
General Electric Co.
Trolley Supply Co.
Westinghouse Elec. & Mfg. Co.

Heaters, Electric.
Consolidated Car-Heating Co.
Johns-Manville Co., H. W.

Heaters, Hot-Air.
Smith Heater Co., Peter.

Heaters, Hot-Water.
Baker Heating & Supply Co., Wm. C.
Smith Heater Co., Peter.

Insulating Compounds and Varnishes.
Benolite Co.
General Electric Co.
Johns-Manville Co., H. W.
Westinghouse Elec. & Mfg. Co.

Insulation.
Johns-Manville Co., H. W.

Jacks.
Brill Co., The J. G.
Duff Manufacturing Co.

Journal Boxes.
Brill Co., The J. G.
McCord Mfg. Co.

Lamps and Lanterns, Signal.
Adams & Westlake Co.
Dayton Manufacturing Co.

Lamps, Incandescent.
General Electric Co.
Westinghouse Elec. & Mfg. Co.

Lightning Arresters.
General Electric Co.
Lord Manufacturing Co.
Westinghouse Elec. & Mfg. Co.

Locks, Door.
Adams & Westlake Co.
Brill Co., The J. G.
Dayton Manufacturing Co.
Howard & Co., James L.

Locomotives, Electric.
Baldwin Locomotive Works.
Brill Co., The J. G.
General Electric Co.
Westinghouse Elec. & Mfg. Co.

Lubricants, Oil and Grease.
Galena Signal Oil Co.
Graphite Lubricating Co.
Holland Trolley Supply Co.
Whitmore Manufacturing Co.

Lubricators, Air Brake.
Emery Pneumatic Lubricator Co.

Meters, Car.
Worham, Sanger & Bates.

Motor Repair Parts.
Columbia Machine Works & Malleable Iron Co.
General Electric Co.
Homer Commutator Co.
Westinghouse Elec. & Mfg. Co.

Motors, Electric.
Allis-Chalmers Co.
General Electric Co.
National Brake & Electric Co.
Westinghouse Elec. & Mfg. Co.

Paints and Varnishes, Insulating.
Benolite Co.
General Electric Co.

Paints and Varnishes for Woodwork.
Whipple Supply Co.

Poles, Trolley.
Columbia Machine Works & Malleable Iron Co.
Dorner Railway Equipment Co.
Holland Trolley Supply Co.
Trolley Supply Co.

Rattan.
Brill Co., The J. G.
Hale & Kilburn Mfg. Co.

Registers and Register Fittings.
Adams & Westlake Co.
Brill Co., The J. G.
Cincinnati Car Co.
Dayton Mfg. Co.
International Register Co., The.

Repair Shop Machinery.
Columbia Machine Works & Malleable Iron Co.
Duff Manufacturing Co.

Resistance, Grid.
General Electric Co.
Kerschner, W. R.
Westinghouse Elec. & Mfg. Co.

Rheostats.
General Electric Co.
Westinghouse Elec. & Mfg. Co.

Roofing, Car.
Johns-Manville Co., H. W.

Saloon Fixtures.
Adams & Westlake Co.
Dayton Manufacturing Co.

Sanders.
Brill Co., The J. G.
Dayton Manufacturing Co.

Sash Fixtures.
Adams & Westlake Co.
Brill Co., The J. G.
Dayton Manufacturing Co.
Howard & Co., James L.
McCord Mfg. Co.

Scrapers, Track.
Brill Co., The J. G.
Cincinnati Car Co.

Seats.
Brill Co., The J. G.
Hale & Kilburn Mfg. Co.
Heywood Bros. & Wakefield Co.
Starrett-Comstock Furniture Co.

Shades, Vestibule.
Brill Co., The J. G.

Signals, Car and Train.
Consolidated Car-Heating Co.

Signs, Destination.
Brill Co., The J. G.
Columbia Machine Works & Malleable Iron Co.

Skids.
Lord Manufacturing Co.

Slack Adjusters.
American Brake Co.
Brill Co., The J. G.

Sleet Wheels and Cutters.
General Electric Co.
Holland Trolley Supply Co.
Nuttall Co., R. D.

Snow Plows.
Brill Co., The J. G.
Columbia Machine Works & Malleable Iron Co.
Consolidated Car Fender Co.

Springs, Car and Truck.
Brill Co., The J. G.
Hanna Co., J. A.
Niles Car & Mfg. Co.
Standard Steel Works Co.
Taylor Electric Truck Co.
Union Spring & Mfg. Co.

Sprinklers.
Brill Co., The J. G.

Steps.
Brill Co., The J. G.
American Mason Safety Tread Co.
Universal Safety Tread Co.
Whipple Supply Co.

Switches, Electric.
Consolidated Car-Heating Co.
General Electric Co.
Westinghouse Elec. & Mfg. Co.

Third-Rail Shoes.
General Electric Co.
Westinghouse Elec. & Mfg. Co.

Treads, Safety.
American Mason Safety Tread Co.
Brill Co., The J. G.
Universal Safety Tread Co.
Whipple Supply Co.

Trolley Bases.
General Electric Co.
Holland Trolley Supply Co.
Nuttall Co., R. D.

Trolley Wheels and Bushings.
General Electric Co.
Graphite Lubricating Co.
Holland Trolley Supply Co.
Johns-Manville Co., H. W.
Nuttall Co., R. D.
Trolley Supply Co.

Truck Parts.
Long Co., E. G.

Trucks.
Baldwin Locomotive Works.
Brill Co., The J. G.
Cincinnati Car Co.
Commonwealth Steel Co.
Dorner Railway Equipment Co.
Hanna Co., J. A.
Laconia Car Co. Works.
Niles Car & Mfg. Co.
Taylor Electric Truck Co.

Turnstiles.
Langslow Co., The H. R.

Ventilators, Car.
Perry Ventilator Co.

Vestibules, Portable.
Brill Co., The J. G.

Weather Strips.
McCord Mfg. Co.

Weed Burners.
Commonwealth Steel Co.

Wheels.
McConway & Torley Co.
Standard Steel Works Co.
Taylor Electric Truck Co.

Wires and Cables.
Electric Cable Co.
General Electric Co.
Kerite Insulated Wire & Cable Co.
Watson Insulated Wire Co.
Westinghouse Elec. & Mfg. Co.

Wiring Specialties.
Crouse-Hinds Co.
National Metal Molding Co.

Woodworking Machinery.
Allis-Chalmers Co.

Wrenches, Car Truck.
Columbia Machine Works & Malleable Iron Co.

Specify
KERITE

Insulated Wire and Cable

FOR

Car Wire—Car House Wire—Lighting—Power—Signalling—Feeder-Telegraph and Telephone

The actual test of time has proven Kerite to be the most efficient, safe and durable insulation known.

Kerite insulated wires and cables installed half a century ago are in service to-day.

The reliability and economy resulting from the use of Kerite insures the greatest service per dollar of expenditure.

Kerite Insulated Wire & Cable Company

INCORPORATED BY W. R. BRIXEY

Sole Manufacturer

Hudson Terminal, 30 Church St., NEW YORK

Western Representative:
WATSON INSULATED WIRE CO.
Railway Exchange, CHICAGO, ILL,

1200 Volt D. C. System

At this writing, the recognized standard for interurban railways

THE 1200 volt D. C. System has met with unqualified success because it is a rational development of standard equipment, now used on 600 volt roads. It makes use of standard generators, rotary converters, railway motors and control, insulated for the increased potential. The same degree of reliability has been secured as in ordinary city systems.

In both construction and operating cost, the 1200 volt system has shown a marked reduction over the 600 volt system. As far as comparative figures can be secured, no other system for the average interurban road has yet been perfected which can show as large returns on the investment.

General Electric Company

Largest Electrical Manufacturer in the World

Principal Office: Schenectady, N. Y.

Maintain Ⓖ Quality

It doesn't pay to sacrifice the efficiency of original equipment by using inferior renewal parts.

THE same reasons that influenced the selection of GE original equipment argue for the purchase of GE renewal parts.

The same materials are used; there is the same care in workmanship. And it stands to reason that parts made from the same patterns and jigs will fit better.

Parts for General Electric supply shipments are taken from the same stock as the original material. Prices furnished upon application.

2936

General Electric Company
Largest Electrical Manufacturer in the World

Sales Offices in all large cities

Holland Trolley Wheels and Harps

Current taken from side of wheel and harp instead of through hub and bearings. ¶ Large contacting surfaces. ¶ Wear on harp reduced to the minimum by renewable brass washers. ¶ Hollow axle lubrication. All harps reversible — fit on outside trolley pole — fouling of wire absolutely prevented.

Holland Sleet Wheels

and Cutters are interchangeable with wheels in Holland bases without the use of tools.

Holland Trolley Bases

Ball Bearing, Roller Bearing, Self Cleaning, Reversible.

Holland Anti-Friction Pin Plate

will convert your ordinary base into a ball-bearing base at less than half the cost of a new one.

¶ Order Holland Supplies on approval. We stand the carrying charges *both ways* if they do not make good.

THE HOLLAND TROLLEY SUPPLY CO.
Schofield Building, Cleveland, Ohio

Trolley Retrievers
Trolley Catchers
Bases
Headlights, Arc ᴬᴺᴰ Dash

Send for Complete Catalogue

The Trolley Supply Co.
Canton, O., U. S. A.

The First

bronze and graphite trolley wheel bushings on the market were

Bound Brook Bushings

—and they are still first in quality.

They are long-lived, self-lubricating, and add to the life of the wheel.

Standard sizes always in stock. Specials made promptly for the same satisfactory service.

Packed fifty in a box. Look for the trade mark and the green label—and write for booklet and prices.

GRAPHITE LUBRICATING CO.
2 CHURCH STREET   BOUND BROOK, N. J.

When Ordering New Cars Specify Lord Equipment

M.V.G. ARRESTERS. The body or element in these arresters is a highly hygroscopic mass. It holds moisture in suspense in fixed and definite form. This suspended moisture is maintained in a static conductor form. On account of the mechanical and chemical structure, this is permanently maintained in a practical manner, and is commercial. It is a perfect static conductor of absolute uniformity, acting as a barrier to the dynamic current. This body is sealed in a glazed porcelain housing. Each arrester is provided with a tell-tale, which records the passage of the discharge. They are made for car, station, or line, mounted in wool or iron weather-proof housing, as conditions require.

DUO CONTACT FINGERS have a renewable and reversible pure copper contact tip. By means of the reversible tip the life of a finger proper (which is the highest grade of extruded bronze) is prolonged indefinitely. The tip is 100% longer lived than any other. These fingers and tips are interchangeable, and made to fit standard controllers.

THE CONTROLATOR is a controller regulator. It insures uniform and regular acceleration. There is but one moving part, viz., the detent. The detent engages and locks the controller at each step in the forward movement, but does not interfere with return to the off position, from any point on the controller, making it impossible to feed the motors other than as predetermined. It is adaptable to all standard controllers, and for various handles. Made of malleable iron and steel.

EARLL RETRIEVERS prevent damage, accidents and delays, when the trolley wheel jumps the wire. They consist of two parts. The back is malleable iron. The front is made of pressed steel. A central shaft supported at both ends, carries a drum to which the rope is attached. A recess in the front end of the drum, carries a tension spring, which takes up the slack in the rope. A recess in the opposite end of the drum carries a heavy flat spring, called the retrieving spring, which is wound up and locked, and revolves with the drum. The sudden movement of the drum when the trolley jumps, causes the outer end of the retrieving spring, through the medium of the centrifugal pawl, to be released from the drum, and simultaneously locked to the back of the retriever. The drum then revolves under the action of the retrieving spring, winding up the rope with force sufficient to pull the trolley down. Pulling out the rope again rewinds or sets the retrieving spring. This is accomplished by short pulls or ratcheting, and not one long continuous pull. As much rope must be pulled out as was wound up in pulling the pole down. When this has been done the retrieving spring is again automatically locked, and the drum runs freely under the action of the light tension spring. The No. 5 retriever with the EMERGENCY RELEASE makes it possible to quickly disengage the retrieving mechanism, and replace the trolley on the wire.

THE BRADSHAW CAR SKID, a device by which crippled cars, by their own power, can be brought to the shop. It is a steel cradle, which accommodates motor and truck without danger of derailment or damage to car. Practically no limit to speed. Motor and truck are securely fastened to the cradle by the four chains with turnbuckles and hooks. Used successfully under the heaviest double truck interurban cars. Disabled cars have been mounted and under way in 15 minutes.

WRITE FOR BULLETINS C, I, F, L, & P.

LORD MANUFACTURING COMPANY
213 WEST 40th STREET.   NEW YORK

Wilson Trolley Catchers and Retrievers

Standard in
BOSTON
CHICAGO
PHILADELPHIA
WASHINGTON
ST. LOUIS
PITTSBURG
MILWAUKEE
SEATTLE
ALBANY
and many other cities all over the world.

50,000 IN DAILY USE

WILSON TROLLEY CATCHER CO.
BOSTON, MASS.

BAY STATE CORD CONNECTORS

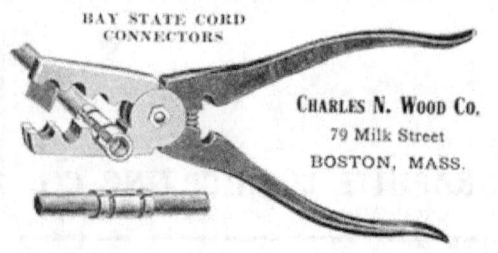

CHARLES N. WOOD CO.
79 Milk Street
BOSTON, MASS.

SAMSON SPOT  TROLLEY CORD

Made of extra quality fine cotton yarn, braided firmly and smoothly, and thoroughly waterproofed. Far more durable and economical than ordinary roughly braided cord. Can be distinguished at a glance by our trade mark, the Spots in the cord.

SAMSON
SOLID BRAIDED BELL and REGISTER CORD

Made of the same extra stock, and guaranteed free from the imperfections of braid and finish which destroy common cords so quickly. Costs less and wears much longer than leather or rawhide (send for tests). All colors and sizes, with or without wire centre.

Send for samples and full information

SAMSON CORDAGE WORKS
BOSTON, MASS.

HEADLIGHTS
FOR TRACTION SERVICE

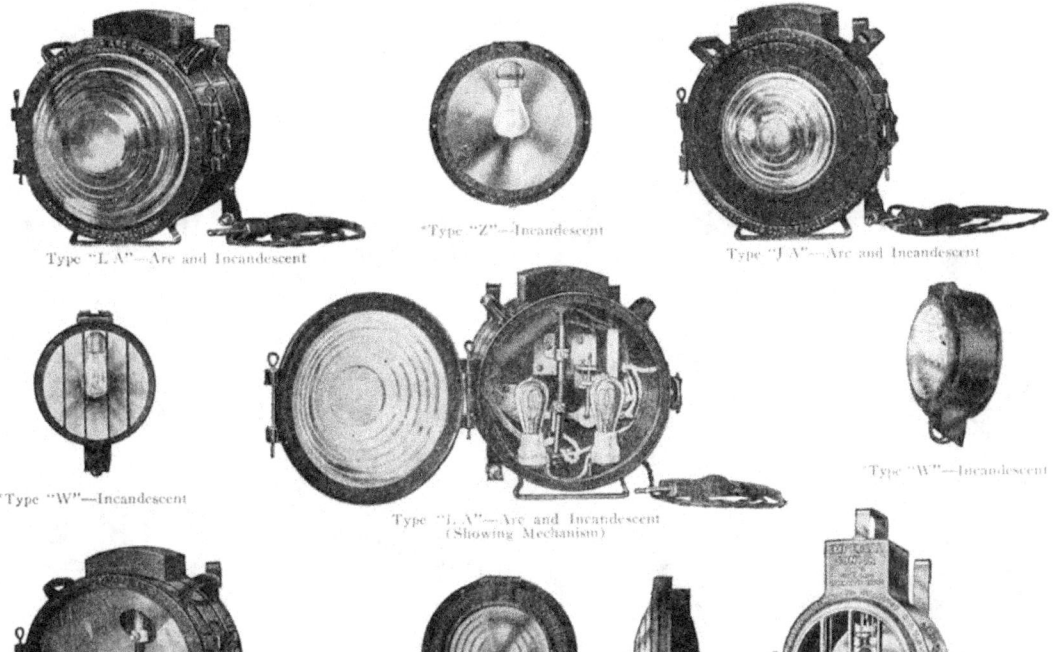

Type "LA"—Arc and Incandescent
"Type "Z"—Incandescent
Type "JA"—Arc and Incandescent
"Type "W"—Incandescent
Type "LA"—Arc and Incandescent (Showing Mechanism)
Type "W"—Incandescent
Type "LB"—Arc and Incandescent
"Type "Z"—Incandescent (Front View) (Side View)
Type "V"—Arc

*Types "W" and "Z" made with Plain, Grid and Semaphore Lens Doors.

Many Other Types of Electric Headlights Shown in our Headlight Catalogues.   Copies Free!

CROUSE-HINDS COMPANY
SYRACUSE, N. Y.

NEW YORK, 30 Church Street   CHICAGO, 303 Dearborn Street   CINCINNATI, 234 W. 4th Street

---

James L. Howard & Co. HARTFORD, CONN.

RAILWAY CAR SUPPLIES

Parlor, Sleeping and Day Car Trimmings
in Bronze, Brass, Silver, Nickel and Oxidized Metals

PATENT DOUBLE SLIDING DOOR FIXTURES	PATENT REMOVABLE BOTTOM BAGGAGE RACKS
" " " " LOCKS	" WATER CLOSETS AND DRY HOPPERS
Specially designed for Steel Cars	with automatic Seat Raising attachments

CONDULETS
FOR CAR WIRING

Complete Listings of Condulets and Covers in Bulletin No. 100.   Write for Copy, Now!

CROUSE-HINDS COMPANY
SYRACUSE, N. Y.

NEW YORK, 30 Church Street   CHICAGO, 303 Dearborn Street   CINCINNATI, 234 W. 4th Street

---

INTERBOROUGH RAPID TRANSIT CO.
BROOKLYN RAPID TRANSIT CO.

USE **LE CARBONE BRUSHES** EXCLUSIVELY

750,000 Le Carbone brushes are in daily service in the United States. The reasons why: Uniform quality; *No* commutator wear; Long life.

W. J. Jeandron,   172 Fulton St., New York

THE DAYTON MFG. CO. - Dayton, O., U.S.A.

Brass or Bronze Trimmings of Every Description, Basket Racks, Door Locks, Switch Locks, Electric Fixtures, Signal Lamps, Oil, Acetylene, Electric Arc and Incandescent Headlights, Gongs, Bells, Water and Dry Closets, Sanders

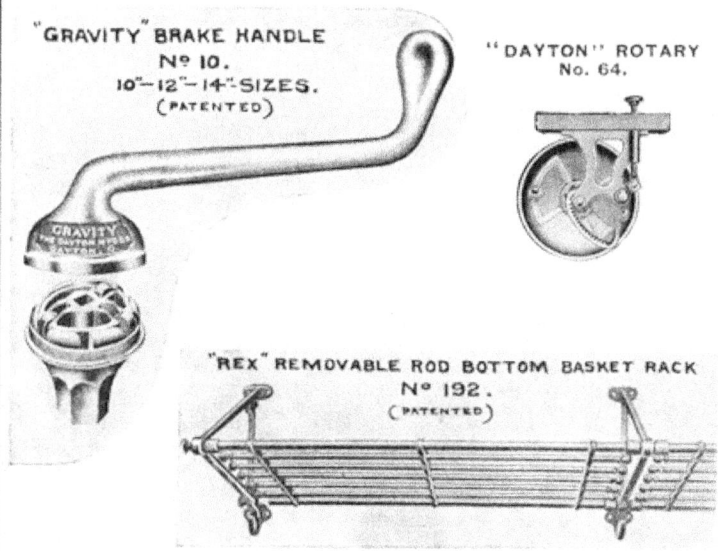

CAR HEATERS

Inventors and Manufacturers of

FORCED VENTILATION HOT AIR HEATERS

Pioneer Manufacturers of

HOT WATER SYSTEMS FOR ELECTRIC CARS

25 Years' Experience

The Peter Smith Heater Co.
Detroit, Michigan

The Mighty Midget Hot Water Car HEATER

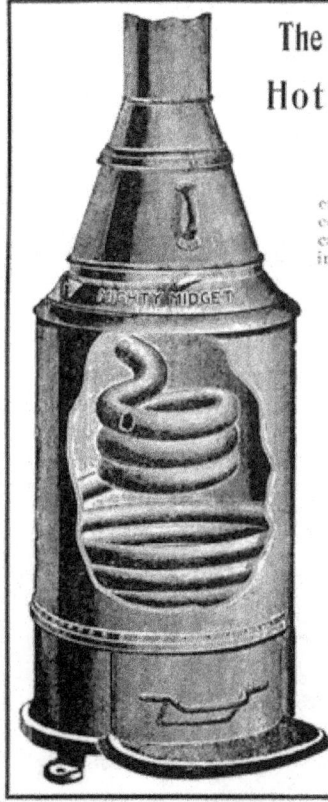

entirely eliminates gaseous atmosphere in your cars, and is economical in fuel consumption.

Requires little attention—forming the ideal efficient heater for interurban lines.

Water circulates from the coil surrounding fire box through pipe down one side of car and back the other.

Provision is made in an overhead expansion chamber for supplementary water supply and expansion of heated water.

Ask us for details.

THE WILLIAM C. BAKER HEATING & SUPPLY CO.
143 Liberty Street
NEW YORK

The Langslow Prepayment System
The First and Only Complete Solution of the Fare Collection Problem

The Langslow System forces every conductor to account for every passenger whether he pays his fare in cash, transfers, tickets, or fare checks.

The system makes use of a fare box and improved turnstile which has none of the objectionable features heretofore associated with such devices. The turnstile and fare box are electrically connected.

When a fare is deposited in the fare box it operates the release mechanism in the turnstile and admits one passenger.

Releases are built up automatically in the turnstile. If five nickels are dropped into the fare box simultaneously the turnstile will admit five passengers to the car and then lock—until another fare is deposited for the next passenger.

By means of a cam and arms which slide through the support, the turnstile is made to require only 7 or 8 inches of space and this is taken from where it can well be spared.

The shape of the arms is such that there is no danger of ramming an entering passenger and the turnstile can be made instantly reversible if desired. It is also equipped with a foot release, but every passenger passing the turnstile is recorded and this record shows exactly how many passengers have entered the car.

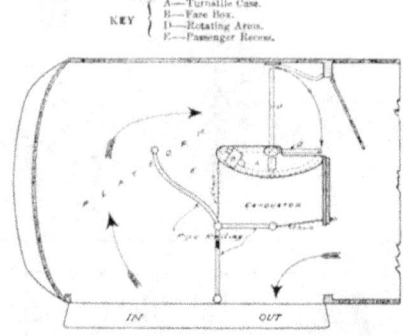

PLATFORM LAYOUT FOR LANGSLOW PREPAYMENT SYSTEM

KEY
A—Turnstile Case.
B—Fare Box.
D—Rotating Arms.
E—Passenger Recess.

In the fare box every cash fare is automatically registered and then drops into a box from which the conductor can remove the money at any time, thus making it available for change making.

A common way to use this system is to have the cash fares dropped into the box, where they are registered automatically. Transfers are handed to the conductor who passes the passenger into the car by means of the foot release on the turnstile. The difference between the registration on the box and the registration on the turnstile must then be balanced by the number of transfers and tickets collected by the conductor.

The system can also be used where all fares—cash, transfers or tickets—are dropped into the box.

Another use of this system is for park entrances or stations. In such installations it does away with the wasteful duplication of ticket seller and ticket taker. In fact, both fare boxes and electric releases for turnstile may be applied readily to any type of turnstile or revolving closure, thus making scrapping of existing equipment unnecessary. Both turnstile and fare box are unconditionally guaranteed for a full year.

To demonstrate the value of this system we are willing to install it on a car at our own expense and maintain it for a sufficiently long period to show what results can be accomplished.

Catalogs and other information will be sent upon request.

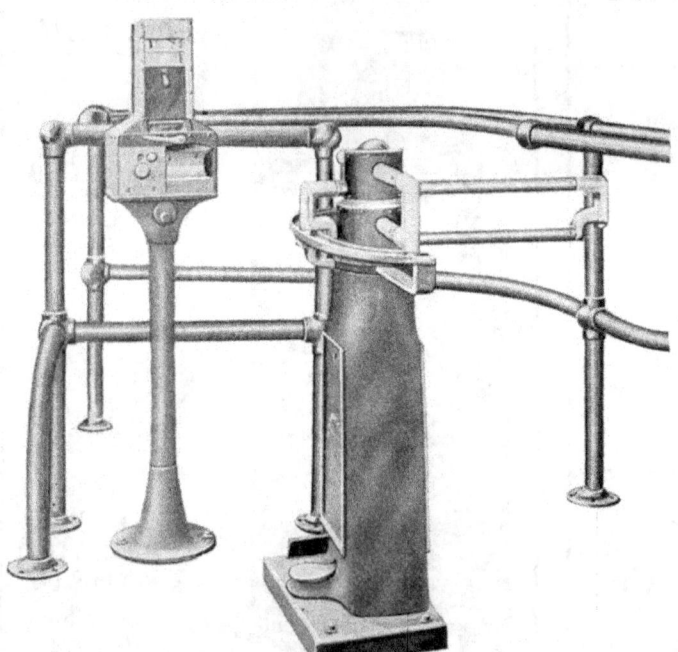

The H. R. Langslow Co.
Rochester, N. Y.

ADLAKE

Car Lighting Fixtures
Car Hardware
Signal Lamps and Lanterns
Headlights

LET us know your wants in particular and we will send you detailed information. We issue catalogs as follows:

No. 120—Adlake Signal Lamps, Tail Lamps, Bridge Lamps, etc. A complete line to which we are constantly adding articles of exceptional merit.

No. 121A—Adlake Railroad Lanterns for car and yard service. (Its information regarding Adlake Ventilation, Outside Wick Raiser and Incased Oil Pot may save you hundreds of dollars.)

No. 124—Adlake Car Lighting Fixtures (Oil, Gas, Electric); the most complete and up-to-date catalog of its kind published.

No. 127—Adlake Car and Ship Hardware, including everything in the trimming line. A storehouse of information.

No. 126—Adlake Headlights (Oil, Gas, Electric) for steam and electric railways.

Also, we issue special bulletins on new articles we manufacture.

The
ADAMS & WESTLAKE CO.
CHICAGO, U.S.A.

NEW YORK OFFICE: No. 30 Church Street
EASTERN WORKS AND OFFICE: 2042-2052 N. 10th Street, Philadelphia, Pa.

Cable Address: "Adlake, Chicago."

EFFICIENCY

is the keynote of success to-day.

Because
International Registers

are more efficient than others, they are now the standard equipment of more than 60% of the larger electric railways in cities of 100,000 and over.

The International Register Company
Registers, Fittings, Trolley and Bell Cord
Heeren Badges and Ticket Punches
625 West Jackson Boulevard, CHICAGO.

BENOLITE

Insulating Varnishes

Possess
GREATEST Dielectric Strength
UNEQUALLED Flexibility
EXTREME Durability

ESPECIALLY Suitable for Railway Apparatus

Benolite Company
PITTSBURG, PA.

HEYWOOD-WAKEFIELD UNIVERSAL SEATS

FOR ALL CLASSES OF SERVICE
Complete Catalog upon request

Heywood Brothers and Wakefield Company
NEW YORK   WAKEFIELD, MASS.   CHICAGO

TRADE WALKOVER MARK CAR SEAT

No. 199-A WALKOVER SEAT.

Neverbreak Pressed Steel parts, withstand the most severe service. Lightest and Strongest seat made, giving a distinct saving in power and maintenance.

Notice its superior construction and substantial appearance. Specify and insist on our seats for your new Electric Cars; they cost less, in the end, than the worthless imitations sometimes offered instead.

The Hale & Kilburn Mfg. Co.
PHILADELPHIA   -   NEW YORK   CHICAGO

Seats for Interurban and Street Railways

Full Steel Spring backs and seats

Imitation Leather or Plush

No. 35½. Rattan, Stationary Back. Malleable Iron and Steel Construction, Canvas Lined, Rattan Cover, Steel Springs.

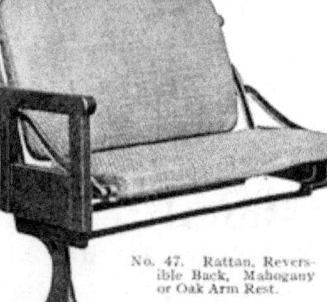

Ask us for full Details, Blueprints and Prices

Scarritt= Comstock Furniture Co.
ST. LOUIS, MO.

No. 47. Rattan, Reversible Back, Mahogany or Oak Arm Rest.

Save The Rack and Smash on CAR SEATS

and reduce one serious item in your maintenance expense by using these

Soft Rubber Car Seat Bumpers

Style No. 1783. $4.50 per 100

Style No. 513 light. $5.00 per 100

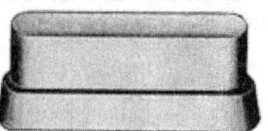

Style No. 1784. $4.00 per 100

These illustrations show various types of some of the numerous shapes and types in stock
Write for catalogue describing other styles.

THE ELASTIC TIP COMPANY
Patentees and Manufacturers
370 Atlantic Avenue, Boston, Mass.

Consolidated Car-Heating Co.

A FEW OF OUR ELECTRIC SPECIALTIES

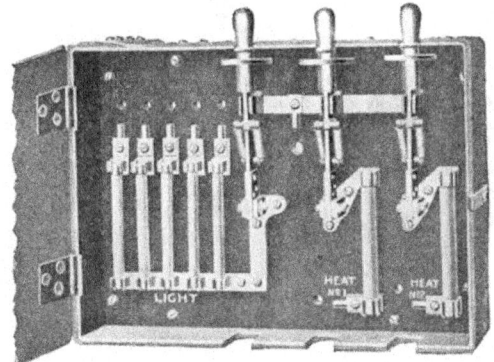
SPECIAL SWITCH PANELS

600-VOLT BUZZER

TRAIN DOOR SIGNAL

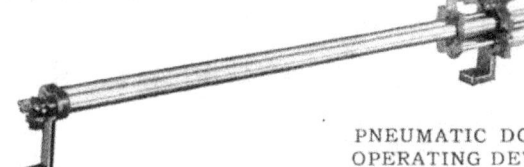
PNEUMATIC DOOR OPERATING DEVICE

ALL-STEEL CROSS SEAT ELECTRIC HEATER

SPECIAL RELAYS FOR BATTERY CHARGING, ETC.

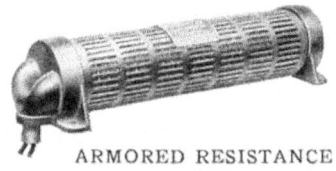
ARMORED RESISTANCE UNIT

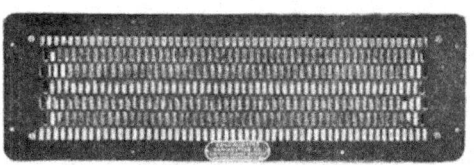
ALL-STEEL PANEL ELECTRIC HEATER

CATALOG SHOWING OUR FULL LINE WILL BE SENT ON REQUEST

RESISTANCE TUBES OF ALL TYPES

WE SHALL BE PLEASED TO FIGURE ON YOUR SPECIAL REQUIREMENTS

ALBANY   **NEW YORK**   **CHICAGO**

Top View

This shows side compression weather strip, dust deflector and gravity wedging sash-lock in operative position as applied complete to one side of window.

Weather Strips

Universal top and bottom weather strips and brass holding channels as applied to single and two-part sash.

Improved Ratchet

Note the improvements in the Universal Deck Sash Ratchet. Arrow "A" indicates a guard flange extending up behind the spring plunger. Arrow "B" points to a flanged bushing extending through the ratchet and bearing upon the spring case. These features positively prevent ratchet and case becoming accidently disarranged.

The Constantly Increasing Use of
Universal Window Fixtures
For Electric Car Equipment
Is Sufficient Evidence of Their Superior Service

Stop Rack and Lock

These illustrations show the Universal Continuous Stop Rack and the gravity wedging lock for single, double or compound sash. Made of stamped bronze or steel.

Universal Window Fixtures embrace notable improvements in car window designs. They provide automatically for all conditions arising from expansion or contraction of sash or casing, due to varying temperatures and weather conditions.

These fixtures contain gravity wedging locks which insure a light, non-rattling joint between the sash and outside stop and a cushion for the sash enclosing. A flexible weather stripping at the top, bottom and sides, allows loose-fitting, easily operated sash and insures dust-proof, air-tight joints around the window. Adaptable for wood or steel window construction.

Ask for our complete catalog
Blue prints and detailed information
cheerfully supplied on request.

McCord Manufacturing Co.
CHICAGO - DETROIT

Rebuilt Cars of Every Description

With or Without Electrical Equipment

These cars, for all practical purposes, are as good as new, look like new and will do the work of new cars—and **at a big saving in price.** In reconstructing, all defective timbers are replaced, giving the cars the same life as new cars.

We always have in our shops cars ready to operate and others in course of rebuilding.

We also handle motors, controllers, car trucks, steam engines and generators.

Let us send you photos and complete specifications.

THE DORNER RAILWAY EQUIPMENT CO.   332 S. Michigan Ave., Chicago

---

THE BRITISH ACKLEY BRAKE CO.	ACKLEY BRAKE COMPANY	DEUTSCHE ACKLEY BREMSEN CO.
Norfolk Street, Strand London, England.	50 Church Street New York City, U. S. A.	m. b. H. Krausenstrasse 42-43 Berlin, S. W. 19, Germany.

SOLE MANUFACTURERS AND LICENSORS FOR THE ENTIRE WORLD OUTSIDE OF UNITED STATES, CANADA, MEXICO AND HAWAIIAN ISLANDS, FOR THE

ACKLEY · ADJUSTABLE · BRAKE
THE STANDARD GEAR BRAKE OF THE WORLD

PATENTED EVERYWHERE.

——AGENCIES——

EUROPEAN
C. DUBBELMAN
11 Place de Louvain, Brussels.
SCHMASSMANN & CO.
110 Bahnhofstrasse, Zurich.
G. S. ALBANESE, INGENIEUR
62, Rue Saint-Lazare, Paris.
ING. S. BELOTTI & CO.
Corso P. Romana, No. 76-78, Milan, Italy.

SOUTH AMERICAN
FREDERICO H. BAGGE
Calle San Martin 201, Buenos Aires.
WALTER BROS. & CO.
Rua de Quitanda 141, Rio de Janeiro.

EASTERN
SALE & FRAZAR, LIMITED
Tokio, Yokohama, Kobe.
CHINA GENERAL ENG. CO.
15 Canton Road, Shanghai.
FRANK L. STRONG, M. E.
34-40, Calle Exchague, Manila, P. I.
R. W. CAMERON & CO.
Sydney, Melbourne and Wellington, N. Z.

Specify PERRY VENTILATORS
FOR YOUR NEW CARS

Designed for special requirements of frequent stop service. In use on far the greatest number and variety of City and Inter-City equipment.

Pure air a-plenty, at both speed and stops, with least depression of temperature. No draughts. No rain or snow—always in action. Low first cost, no maintenance. Round or flat roofs.

Make no mistakes—use only the demonstrated kind.

PERRY VENTILATOR CO.
BOSTON OFFICE: 178 Devonshire Street
F. C. STOWELL, Sales Mgr.

"DELTABESTON" MAGNET WIRE

 is insulated with pure asbestos which has been treated in such a manner that its insulating properties are exceptionally high. At the same time its wonderful resistance to heat renders it absolutely indestructible by any temperature to which it may be subjected in commercial service.

Manufactured in Round, Square and Rectangular Sections

WE ARE SPECIALISTS ON HEAT AND MOISTURE PROOF COILS

Our Fuses are Particularly Designed for Severe Railway Service

D & W FUSE COMPANY, Providence, R. I.

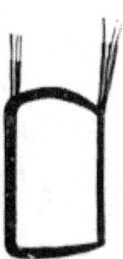

Peacock and Ackley Brakes

will stop your heaviest car on your worst grade, gently, but surely.

¶ The properly designed brake linkage gives the same braking power at the wheels that your air brake does.

¶ It is impossible to apply this power so suddenly as to lock the wheels, grind the track and cause great wear and tear on the trucks and rolling stock. With Peacock and Ackley Brakes the motorman "feels" the shoes contacting with the wheels and the power back of them. He can bring the car to as quick and as easy a stop as occasion requires. The advantages of this in braking cars on long grades, in cases of air brake failure, in emergencies of any kind is tremendous. Larger and heavier cars can be operated with these efficient brakes without any power brake equipment.

The Peacock Brake

The Ackley Adjustable Brake

¶ The eccentric drum directly below the gear takes up all the slack on the first turn. Power ratio is increased for the final tightening of shoes on wheels by the increased taper of chain drum.

¶ All movable parts turn on roller bearings, insuring ease of operation and long life service. The brake chain winds on a perfectly smooth drum with a resultant doubling of the life of the chain. No special chain is necessary. A straight or twist link chain can be obtained locally for replacement when the original chains wear out saving about half the cost of repairs on ordinary brakes. No stock of repair parts is required. The brakes will outlast your cars.

Our claims as to efficiency and durability are backed by the use of Peacock and Ackley Brakes on over 500 roads throughout the country.

SOME OF THE PROMINENT RAILWAYS USING PEACOCK AND ACKLEY BRAKES:

Chicago City Railway
Third Avenue Railway (New York City)
Metropolitan Street Railway (New York City)
United Railways and Electric Co. (Baltimore)
Pittsburg Railways
The Indiana Union Traction Co.
The Detroit United Railways
The United Railways of San Francisco
The Nashville Railway and Lt. Co.
New Orleans Railway and Lt. Co.

Chicago Railways Co.
Union Street Railway (New York City)
The Cincinnati Traction Co.
International Railway (Buffalo)
The Illinois Traction System
The Boston Elevated
The Metropolitan St. Railway (Kansas City)
The Toronto Railway Co.
The Montreal Street Railway Co.

Let us assist you in laying out a brake rigging that will give you the best results. Whether you are rehabilitating old cars or specifying new equipment our Engineering Department can be of assistance to you. We make no charge for this service—avail yourself of it. Write:

NATIONAL BRAKE COMPANY
888 Ellicott Square, BUFFALO, N. Y.

National Air Brakes

National Type ½" Piston Valve

Motorman's Valves

National type ½ inch piston valve is made without ground joints. A seat of durable, specially treated leather, prevents leakages. The use of this valve eliminates the necessity of grinding valve seats to an air tight fit, besides insuring ease of operation and low maintenance expense.

Write for Bulletin No. 388.

Emergency Valves

National type "C" emergency valve can be used in connection with any standard type of ½ inch motorman's valve. It combines the safety features of automatic air, without complicating the simplicity of the straight air brake equipment. Variable release and positive, reliable operation at all times are a few of its leading advantages.

Bulletin No. 389 on request.

National Type "C" Emergency Valve

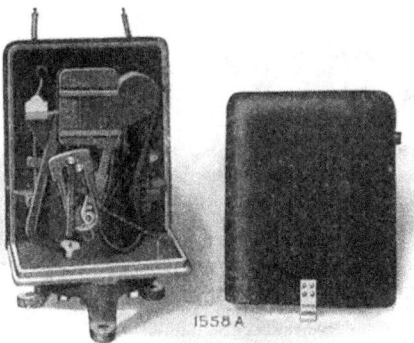

National Type "R" Governor with Cover Removed

Automatic Governors

National type "R" governor—with magnetic blow-out—is of the diaphragm type and has no valves to get out of order. It is compactly built with the few working parts so arranged that friction is reduced to a minimum. This insures positive, reliable operation under the most severe conditions of service.

Send for Bulletin No. 390.

National Brake & Milwaukee

NEW YORK: 111 Broadway
CHICAGO: 1344 First Nat. Bank Bldg.

National Air Compressors

Air Brake Compressors

National air compressors best meet the exacting requirements of modern electric traction systems. They are strongly designed, compact units, combining high efficiency, absolute safety and ease of maintenance with complications entirely eliminated. All working parts are readily accessible for inspection or repairs. Built in capacities ranging from 11 to 50 cu. ft. of free air per minute.

Write for Bulletin No. 376.

National Type "A-4" Compressor

Portable Outfit with CC-3 Compressor

Portable Outfits

National portable outfits can be easily hauled from place to place and the power applied just where it is needed. They eliminate extensive piping with consequent wasteful leaks and are especially adapted for service where floor space is limited. Capacities—11 to 75 cu. ft. of free air per minute. Equipped either with direct or alternating current motor.

Publication No. 391 on request.

Type "3VS" Compressor

A motor driven, direct connected, single stage air compressor with complete automatic controlling device. Strong, rugged construction a noticeable feature. Well adapted for service around car barns and shops. Built in capacities of from 50 to 300 cu. ft. of free air per minute. Furnished either with direct or alternating current motor.

Send for Publication No. 387.

150 cu. ft. Type "3VS" Compressor with Alternating Current Motor and Combined Automatic Control

Electric Company
Wis., U.S.A.

PITTSBURG: 9th and Penn. Ave.
ST. LOUIS: 405 Security Building
LONDON, ENG.: 14 Great Smith Street

C. H. ELEC. CAR METER

Is an Ampere Hour Meter with our Patent Cyclometer Dial, which is strong in construction and easy to read.

There are over 3,000 of these Car Meters in use at present.

Dead Accuracy Guaranteed

SOME MERITS OF THIS METER

1—Moderate first cost.
2—Low cost of *maintenance* due to
  (a) Sound mechanical construction.
  (b) Very light armature, practically floating in mercury.
  (c) The perfect natural cushion which mercury affords to the jarring of the car.
3—Negligible inertia, causing the meter to take up peaks of current immediately.
4—**Perfect comparison between drivers.**
5—**A check on actual current consumption.**
6—An approximate check on the station meters.
7—An indication of any defect causing increased consumption.

H. B. UNIVERSAL LIFE GUARD

THE cost of maintaining projecting fenders, no matter of what design, their inefficiency in all cases when persons are lying prone on the track and the difficulties experienced in operating cars with such dangerous extensions have created a demand for an efficient wheel-guard. A wheel-guard to be EFFICIENT, must act instantaneously; to be RELIABLE, should be entirely automatic; and to be ECONOMIC, simplicity of design and strength of construction are a necessity. The "H. B." Life Guard is shown to be the only wheel-guard to fulfill these requirements by the number in use, by the fatalities prevented and by the unanimous opinion of street railway experts.

WONHAM, SANGER & BATES
30 Church Street, New York
141 Milk Street, Boston
2 Laurence Pountney Hill, London, E. C.
San Jose, Costa Rica

Twelve Years Ago

we started business in a rented loft in Newark.

In 1905 we bought a section of land in Bridgeport, and put up two buildings. To-day we own our entire plant. We have completed our sixth building and have begun plans to double our floor space and output.

A coming concern is always better than one that "has been" or "is."

To sell our product we *must* make it better than the other man.

We *must* give more value for your money.

We *must* keep making our reputation.

The material we manufacture is the best of its kind. Our shipments cover the whole country and we are doing business direct abroad.

We have grown out of the cramped quarters in Newark, and into our big plant in Bridgeport, because we have worked hard; because we have served our customers as faithfully as we knew how; because we have never stopped looking for points where we might improve, and whenever we have found such a point we have gone at it hard.

It takes a product of high quality to cause such a rapid, steady growth as this. Why not find out about it?

The Electric Cable Co.
17 Battery Place, New York

Makers of
Magnet Wire, Weatherproof Wire and Cables, Rubber Covered Wires and Cables
National Electric Code Standard

| Boston | Philadelphia | Richmond | San Francisco |
| Chicago | Cleveland | Pittsburgh | St Louis |

5274

Providence Fenders and Wheel Guards

The Fender

is composed of two distinct parts, the Cradle and the Cushion. The Cradle, which is six feet wide and three feet long, is formed of curved steel ribs tempered to a point that will bend before breaking, and arranged parallel to the axis of the car. The back of this Cradle is hinged to the front of the platform by means of adjustable brackets, so that it may be turned up against the Dash, or down, so that its front edge will rest on the track, or set to occupy, and be carried, in any intermediate position. Two steel bars attached to the cradle, and projecting to the rear under the platform, hold the cradle at any desired height. By means of a latch or trigger, being pressed by the Motorman's foot, the cradle is released so that its front edge drops to the ground. The front edge of the cradle consists of a steel rod, passing through eyes formed on the ends of the curved ribs. On this rod, and between the curved ribs, are rubber rolls one and three-quarter inches in diameter. This Fender is made for use on Interurban and Suburban Cars. It is large enough and strong enough to pick up a horse and carry it, without injury, until the car can be stopped. In the use of this fender, if the motorman does his duty and drops it to the track, there is not the slightest danger of the car being derailed, from running over an animal. If the car is running at a high rate of speed, the animal will be thrown clear from the track, but if running at a moderate speed, the fender will pick up the animal and hold it, until the car is stopped.

The Wheel Guard

or Underneath Fender is made in two general types; one attached directly to the body of the car and the other attached directly to the truck platform.

Both are operated automatically by a swinging gate set a sufficient distance in front of the fender. The pressure on the gate rearwards, drops the fender. The action is positive and instantaneous no matter what the position of the trucks are, relative to the body of the car in rounding curves, or when the brakes are suddenly set.

In addition to the automatic gate, both types can be operated by foot from the platform of the car, or automatically by air simultaneously with the setting of the brakes.

Resetting device can be furnished if desired.

The materials used in construction are malleable iron and steel.

The special advantages of this Wheel Guard are: Its front edge is normally carried high and is free to rise.

Its front edge is elastic and will accommodate itself to any irregularities in the road bed; it is also formed so as to retain an object when once on the fender.

Its design and construction are such as to prevent the scooping and retaining of snow which is so destructive to the usual wheel guards. Its operating mechanism is simple and positive. The dropping of the wheel guard is accelerated by powerful springs which maintain it to the road bed when down.

Simple and quick adjustment is provided to accommodate the carrying height of both the fender and the gate to any condition of road bed.

Provision is made for turning the gate up temporarily, without the use of tools, in emergencies such as snow storms or road bed construction.

For further information and price lists, address

THE CONSOLIDATED CAR FENDER CO.

Manufacturers of the Providence Fender and Wheel Guard

Office and Factory:

PROVIDENCE R. I.

Branch Office: 110 East 23d Street, New York

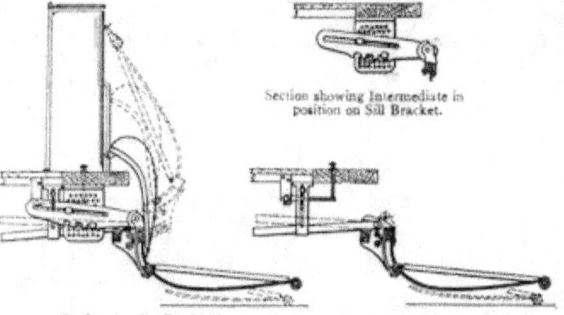

Section showing Intermediate in position on Sill Bracket.

Section showing Fender down and, in dotted lines dropped, also swung up.

Section showing Quadrant and Drop.

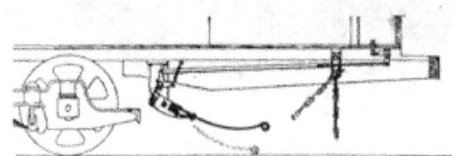

Section showing Wheel Guard attached to body of car and operated either by apron or motorman's foot.

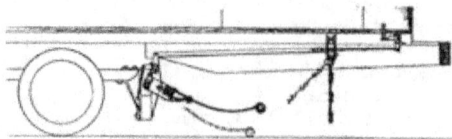

Section showing Wheel Guard attached to pilot board and operated either by apron or motorman's foot.

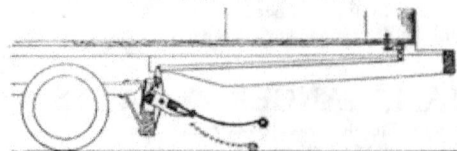

Section showing Wheel Guard attached to pilot board and operated by motorman's foot only.

The Universal Safety Tread

is made from a steel baseplate in which holes are punched forming corrugations of projecting steel teeth. Solid lead strands are rolled into these rows, the steel teeth are then clamped firmly into the lead holding it securely in position. The lead extends through to the bottom of the baseplate, riveting itself thereto. The teeth form a broken surface and this fact makes the UNIVERSAL an ideal safety tread as it is **non-slipping in all directions**. The two metals are so proportioned that the wear is uniform thus presenting a **non-slipping surface of lead** until the tread is entirely worn out. The UNIVERSAL is the **only tread on the market possessing this feature**. It offers a maximum service both as to prevention of accidents, where 90% of your claims arise, and as to economical maintenance due to long life service. Its efficiency and economy in maintenance are vouchsafed by its use on the leading railways of the country. We solicit your investigation into this matter.

Our catalogue gives full details.

Cut showing Single-Piece Car Step

Cut showing Three-Piece Car Step

UNIVERSAL SAFETY TREAD COMPANY
141 Milk Street, Boston, Mass.
New York, 50 Church St.   Philadelphia, 1103 Land Title Bldg.

Mason Safety Tread

for car steps, vestibules or station platforms of wood, metal or concrete.

The base is rolled sheet steel or hard brass with U shaped grooves. Soft metal lead or carborundum grains are filled into the dove-tailed rectangular grooves to form a gripping surface for firm foothold.

Karbolith Sanitary Flooring

is a chemical composition that makes an absolutely clean, solid and fireproof flooring. The cement bond employed to fill the interstices firmly unites Karbolith with the supporting base. Specify it on your new work or in rehabilitating old station platforms, waitingroom floors, etc. It is durable and slightly elastic. Installed on wood, cement, iron or stone.

Curved or Straight to Fit Street Railway Car Steps

American Mason Safety Tread Co.
702 Old South Building   —:—   Boston, Mass.

Union Spring & Mfg. Co.

Manufacturers of

SPRINGS

of Every Description

for Electric Traction and Interurban Cars

Steel Castings and Light Pressed Steel Shapes

GENERAL OFFICE:
OLIVER BLDG., PITTSBURGH, PENNA.

50 Church St., New York   700 Fisher Bldg., Chicago
Missouri Trust Bldg., St. Louis
American National Bank, Richmond, Va.

H. W. Johns-Manville Co.

J-M Ceilinite—A Fireproof Insulation for Steel Cars

This lining consists of a felt, made of pure Asbestos and reinforced on the back with pure Asbestos Cloth. Is absolutely fireproof and practically indestructible.

Makes an ideal lining for fireproofing, sound deadening and insulating ceilings, side walls, etc., of electric cars; also for fireproofing switch boxes and other electrical apparatus. It is strong, flexible and easy to apply.

"Noark" Fuses and Boxes

"Noark" Fuses are made in all capacities, styles and voltages, and to suit special conditions if required. "Noark" Boxes are made in gas, water and weather-proof styles for low and high tension service.

J-M Transite Asbestos Wood

Fire and heat have practically no effect on this material as it is made of pure Asbestos fibre and binding cements and contains nothing that can burn. Makes an excellent material for car floor linings, fireproof partitions, and as a protection against fire around electrical apparatus.

J-M Ebony Asbestos Wood for switchboards and electrical insulation has a higher electrical resistance than slate, marble or fibre. It takes a high polish, and can be grained and worked similar to ordinary wood.

J-M Electrobestos Arc Deflectors

These Arc Deflectors are made of Asbestos and other fireproof insulating materials moulded under enormous pressure, producing great density and mechanical strength. They have high electrical resistance and are absolutely fireproof and unaffected by extreme temperatures. Furnished to fit any make or type of controller.

J-M Transite Asbestos Controller Linings

These linings eliminate danger of fire, shock to motorman or passengers and are a positive prevention against short-circuiting or grounding to the metal casing. They are non-conductors of electric currents and are absolutely fireproof.

Made to fit inside the controller covers of all shapes and sizes of railway controllers.

J-M Friction Tapes and Splicing Compounds

The fabric used in J-M Friction Tapes is closely woven, uniform throughout and has exceptional strength. Both sides are heavily and evenly covered with insulating compound and every thread thoroughly impregnated. Have great adhesive properties.

J-M Splicing Compounds are made of pure Para Rubber. They form into a homogeneous mass of rubber after being applied, without artificial heat, making an absolutely water-tight joint which actually improves with age. Are of uniform thickness and superior strength.

J-M Asbestos Tape and J-M Niagrite for Cable Insulation

J-M Asbestos Tape is a thin, closely woven fabric about .015 of an inch thick furnished in widths of ½", ¾" and 1" with salvage edges. Used for insulating field coils in motors, etc., wrapping small wires or cables and wherever a thin asbestos insulation can be used. For heavier service such as feeder cables in subways, manholes, tunnels, etc., J-M Niagrite should be used, a heavy fireproof tape of pure asbestos in strips 3 inches wide and 3 feet long.

J-M Asbestos Tubing for Conductors

This Tubing is extensively used for covering motor leads, conductor wires of arc lamps and all electrical wires where a superior protection against heat or flame is required. It is very flexible, absolutely fireproof and will take any insulating compound.

Write our Nearest Branch for Catalog

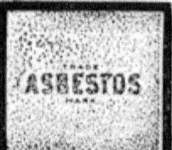

Baltimore	Cleveland	London	New Orleans	San Francisco
Boston	Dallas	Los Angeles	New York	Seattle
Buffalo	Detroit	Milwaukee	Philadelphia	St. Louis
Chicago	Kansas City	Minneapolis	Pittsburg	

For Canada:—THE CANADIAN H. W. JOHNS-MANVILLE CO., LIMITED
Toronto, Ont.   Montreal, Que.   Winnipeg, Man.   Vancouver, B. C.

For Great Britain and Continent of Europe:
TURNERS & MANVILLE, LTD., Hopetoun House, 5, Lloyds Ave. London, E. C. (1356)

The Hedley Anti-Telescoping and Anti-Climbing Device

Prevents Damage Suits and Saves Equipment

Combination Anti-Climber
Draw Head Steel Casting
Made to Any Size

"Light Weight" Anti-Climber
for City Cars
7" x 1" Rolled Steel

"Heavy Weight" Anti-Climber
for Interurban Cars
5½" x 2" Rolled Steel

"CORRUGATED CHANNEL SECTION"

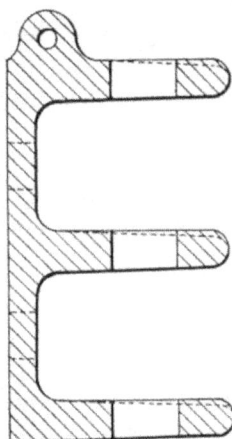

"Rolled Steel" Buffers with horizontal ribs.

Replaces ordinary buffer on new equipment.

Bolted to old buffer on existing cars.

Also made as a combination draw head.

In case of collision, the corrugations or ribs interlock, thus preventing car platforms from climbing and minimizing danger of telescoping.

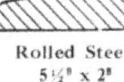

Steel Casting
Made to any size

Rolled Steel
7" x 1"

Rolled Steel
5½" x 2"

Whipple Supply Company

50 Church St., New York   First National Bank Bldg., Chicago

Announcement Card of the Commonwealth Steel Co.

THE COMMONWEALTH STEEL COMPANY of St. Louis, whose Cast Steel Pullman Trucks and Platforms and other car and locomotive devices are standard on leading railroads, announce the very satisfactory service of their CAST STEEL MOTOR TRUCKS that are in use on various electric interurban and city traction lines. They are most efficient and economical and quite up to the Commonwealth standards so long established in steam-road equipment. ¶ THE COMMONWEALTH GASOLINE WEED BURNER is now also being manufactured for use on traction lines.

::   Catalogs, designs and full particulars will be gladly furnished on request   ::

Whitmore's
Gear Protection Composition

will make gears and pinions last five times as long—it will give better results than any other lubricant on the market.

The above cut shows the condition of a gear and pinion, after one year, nine months and twenty-three days' service on an interurban car in Central New York

It was installed August 3d, 1908, and removed September 11th, 1909, for exhibit Denver Convention, out of service only 21 days. Total mileage, up to that date 53,232 miles. The same gear and pinion were returned, placed in service, making an additional mileage of 51,100 miles, again removed for exhibition October Convention, 1910, total mileage 104,332 miles. Weight of car, 62,100 pounds.

The lower cut shows a gear and pinion after 113,793.77 miles of service on a city car in Illinois. Put in service December 6th, 1908. 10 pounds **Whitmore's Gear Protective Composition** added July 23d, 1909, after a mileage of 39,924.45 miles. 3 pounds **Whitmore's Gear Protective Composition** (winter) added November 29th, 1909, and 2 pounds **Whitmore's Gear Protective Composition** (summer) added July 7th, 1910. The lubricant was still in excellent condition when removed from service September 23d, 1910.

Write for detailed information.

The Whitmore Mfg. Co.
Cleveland, Ohio U. S. A

Westinghouse American Automatic Slack Adjuster

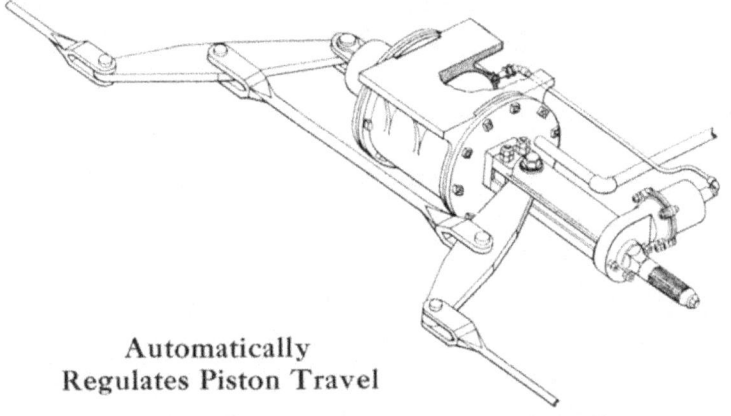

Automatically Regulates Piston Travel

Its use secures maximum brake efficiency by insuring uniform piston travel. Device does not operate until adjustment is required, resulting in minimum wear of adjuster parts.

FOR INFORMATION ADDRESS THE

AMERICAN BRAKE COMPANY, St. Louis, Mo.

Automatic Lubrication

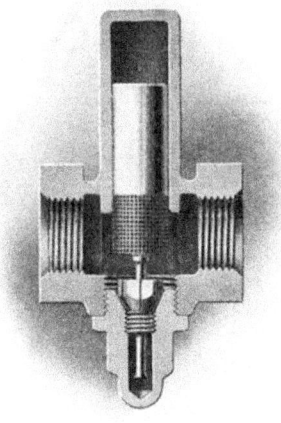

The EMERY PNEUMATIC LUBRICATOR **Automatically** lubricates Brake Valves, Feed Valves, Triple Valves and Brake Cylinders.

This Lubricator is inserted in the air supply pipe of the brake system close to main reservoir. All air passing into service pipes is thereby charged with lubricant which is carried to all surfaces in contact with the air current,

INSURING UNIFORM LUBRICATION

WRITE FOR PARTICULARS

The Emery Pneumatic Lubricator Company
1932 North Broadway, St. Louis, Mo.

Why Experiment?

Can you afford to jeopardize your equipment by trying cheap oils under inexperienced experts? It costs money to shut down your plant or lay out a car. You can lose the earning power of that equipment, as well as incurring a repair bill.

Galena Oils are used on a large majority of the railway equipment of the United States and Canada, and are recognized as the acme of lubrication perfection. They are compounded of the best lubricating ingredients, and will insure you against annoyance and failures, and in the long run will result in lower cost because of their greater lubricating qualities. Galena Oils are the only brands that will fill these requirements. We guarantee the cost per 1000 miles and 1000 kilowatt hours.

Galena-Signal Oil Company
FRANKLIN, PA.

Our Electric Railway Jacks Are Rapid and Durable

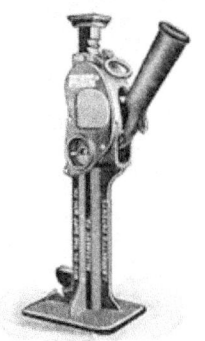

The many types and sizes of **Genuine Barrett Jacks**, of which we are the sole manufacturers, have won preference through their durability and efficiency. They handle electric railway equipment rapidly in car barn or repair shop, and our special-design **Barrett Emergency Jacks**, for individual car equipment, are unexcelled for quick and reliable service.

Every **Genuine Barrett Jack** is guaranteed to be made by skilled machinists, and to contain the finest materials obtainable. This "quality" policy maintained for nearly thirty years has made **Genuine Barrett Jacks** standard.

No. 22. "BARRETT" EMERGENCY JACK

No. 19. "BARRETT" AUTOMATIC LOWERING JACK, 15 Tons Capacity

"BARRETT" MOTOR ARMATURE LIFT

We make two types of Armature Lifts—the "Barrett" Lift which is equipped with a "Barrett" Automatic Lowering Jack; and the "Wheel and Screw" lift which lifts with a screw. Each is equipped with either flat or flanged wheels and is made for any depth of pit. The screw lift is adapted for use in close quarters.

We are the largest manufacturers of Lifting Jacks in the world. Our **Duff-Bethlehem Forged Steel Hydraulic Jacks** and our **Duff Ball-Bearing, Geared Ratchet Screw Jacks** have become famous for their economical operation.

Write for the largest Jack catalogue ever published.

THE DUFF MFG. CO.
ESTABLISHED 1883
50 CHURCH ST. NEW YORK.
PITTSBURGH, PA. U.S.A.

Homer Commutators are High Grade First, Last and All the Time

Only pure Hard Drawn Lake copper bars are used in our street railway commutators.

For Engine Generators we use Hard Drawn Lake copper bars, and for small special commutators, Roll Drop Lake copper bars. Only Amber Mica Segments and India Mica Rings are ever used for insulating a Commutator built in our factory.

Homer is the long life, high efficiency commutator.

Write for further details and prices.

**THE HOMER COMMUTATOR COMPANY
CLEVELAND, O.**

Columbia Babbitting Moulds

The only device which will babbitt axle bearing halves in center and make same strictly interchangeable.

Columbia Controller Handles

Fit all makes and types of controllers. Made of brass, or malleable iron.

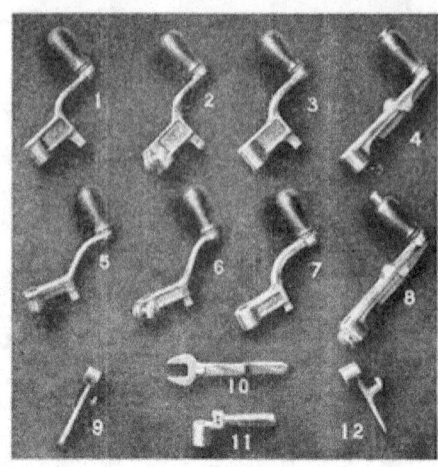

Armature Banding and Heading Machine

Self contained and instantly adjusted tension and feeling attachment. No straddling of wire by operator. Worm drive enclosed in air-tight, dust-proof case. All bearings bronze.

All Steel Gear Case

Absolutely oil, water and dust tight. Top and bottom are flanged over sides and ends with brackets bent over sides to remove all strain from rivets.

Pinion Puller

Quickly removes pinions, wiping rings or armatures. Adjustable swinging head. Small hand wheel for ordinary adjustment. Large wheel for quick application. Grippers and Yokes are of best crucible steel.

Winding Machine for Armature and Field Coils

Stopped or started instantly. Occupies only 4 feet floor space. Worm drives enclosed in oil and dust proof cases. Extension spindle for small coils, spools or magnets.

Columbia Ratchet Brake Handles

Automatically hold the chain taut at the point to which motorman has pulled it. No Pawl for motormen to kick loose for releasing. Made in brass or malleable iron.

Columbia Commutators

For motors and generators. Segments made from hard drawn copper bar with soft sheet mica insulation.

Other Columbia Specialties:—Malleable Iron Gear Cases—Trolley Wheels—Field and Armature Coils—Axle Straighteners—Armature and Axle Bearings—Armature Buggies—Steel Trolley Poles—Pit Jacks—Car Trimmings. Ask for details.

Columbia Machine Works & Malleable Iron Company
Atlantic Avenue & Chestnut Street, Brooklyn, N. Y.

Allis-Chalmers Railway Motors
BOTH INTERPOLE AND NON-INTERPOLE

40 to 90 H. P.
On Either
500 or 600 Volts
Direct Current
Circuits.

Many Improvements that Lengthen the Life of Railway Motors and Lower the Maintenance Costs are Found in ALLIS-CHALMERS Motors for Both City and Interurban Service.

LATEST DEVELOPMENTS IN RAILWAY MOTORS

Allis=Chalmers Type 301; with a nominal rating of 40 H. P. at 500 volts.

Allis=Chalmers Type 302; with a nominal rating of 55 H. P. at 500 volts.

Allis=Chalmers Type 303; with a nominal rating of 75 H. P. at 500 volts.

Allis=Chalmers Type 501; Interpole, with a nominal rating of 50 H. P. at 600 volts or 42 H. P. at 500 volts.

These motors give continuously satisfactory service under the ever-varying conditions of electric traction service.

Send for Bulletins
Describing Them

Allis-Chalmers Company
District Offices in all Large Cities   General Offices, MILWAUKEE, WIS.

Allis-Chalmers Air Brake Equipment

Allis-Chalmers
Engineer's Valve

A A 6 COMPRESSOR

Allis-Chalmers
Air Whistle

Greater reliability and lower maintenance costs account for the adoption of ALLIS-CHALMERS Air Brake Apparatus by all the leading Electric Railway Companies. Many of the largest companies use these equipments exclusively because they have proven to be the most satisfactory under all conditions of service.

ALLIS-CHALMERS Air Brake Equipments can be furnished for any combination of motor cars and trailers.

Car Equipped with Allis-Chalmers Motors, Controllers and Air Brakes

Allis-Chalmers Company
General Offices, Milwaukee, Wis.
OFFICES IN ALL PRINCIPAL CITIES

The Air Brake Valve is Automatically Locked

by the removal of the handle when

The Automatic Air Brake Lock

is used. The valve cannot be tampered with nor released unless the handle is replaced. Hand Set Screw insures close contact of handle and valve stem and compensates for wear of stem. Absolutely prevents mischievous passenger opening air valve on rear platform of car.

Catskill Gears and Pinions

Solid or Split. All Sizes and Types. Our Split Gears with 8-1" bolts and 4-¼" stud bolts will hold as firmly as a Solid Gear.

Write for further details and prices.

W. R. Kerschner
Sole Sales Agent.
Room 1882, 50 Church St., New York

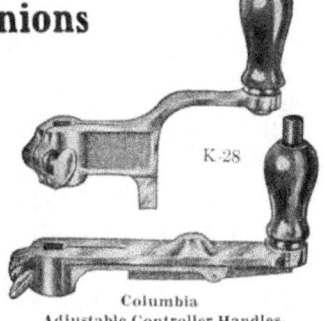

K-28

Columbia Adjustable Controller Handles.

E. G. Long Company
50 Church Street, New York.

Manufacturers   Merchants   Agents   Exporters

Appliances and Accessories for Cars and Trucks

Repair and Renewal Material of Every Kind

Springs, Castings, Forgings, Chain, Journal and Axle Bearings, Wheels and Axles, Armature and Field Coils, Gears and Pinions, Commutators, Gongs, Headlights, Fenders and Life Guards, Drawbars and Couplers, Trolley Harps and Wheels, Trolley Poles and Bases, Trolley Catchers and Retrievers, Brakes and Brake Parts, Etc., Etc.

E. G. Long Company
50 Church Street, New York.

"SHERARDUCT"

is Sherardized on Interior and Exterior

The **Only** Conduit manufactured in which the **Interior** is alloyed and covered with zinc the same as the **Exterior**, both the **Inside** and **Outside** being Sherardized and rendered **Rust-Proof and Non-Corrosive.**

Send for Sample.

"NATIONAL" METAL MOLDING

The Ideal Method of
Metal-Encased
Exposed Wiring

A Complete
Line of
Fittings

Consider the use of the "NATIONAL" in connection with car wiring on account of its ease of installation and the adaptability of its Fittings to the various conditions met with in exposed wiring construction work. Send for Sample and Catalog.

NATIONAL METAL MOLDING CO.,   PITTSBURGH, PA.

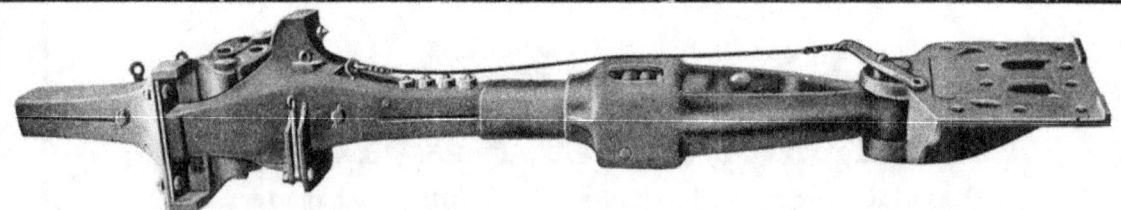

Exceptional Durability—Rapid, Positive and Easy Coupling and Uncoupling on Curve, Straightaway or Grade—
Reinforced Interchangeable Wearing Parts—Greater Gathering Range, Insuring
Absolute Connection—Greater Economy

ARE POSSESSED BY

VAN DORN DRAWBARS

Van Dorn drawbars have proven by their superior excellence and many points of advantage the best all around drawbars for electric railway service in the market. They are simple in design, occupy less space, are especially built to withstand strain with interchangeable, reinforced wearing plates where they are most needed. The M. C. B. type has greater gathering range and vertical play with protective stops to prevent knuckles oscillating out of position. They are easily installed and are coupled and uncoupled with ease and speed. We make more than 100 different styles of rigid, tight-lock drawbars. Write for full information.

Van Dorn Coupler Co., 2325 S. Paulina St., Chicago

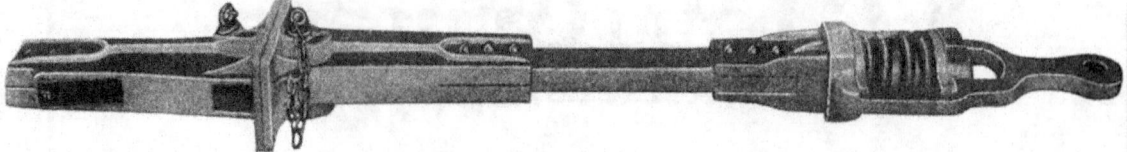

MANUFACTURING
AND
SELLING

In the manufacture of an article great care is exercised in the selection of raw material, the best machinery is employed, and every process and detail is carefully studied with a view to **production at minimum cost.**

And yet when the finished product is ready for sale, many manufacturers hesitate to use means which will positively help to place that product on the **market at minimum cost.**

For instance, if in the manufacture of a given article it is found that some new machine will materially cut down the cost of production, that machine is promptly purchased.

How is it in the selling? Comparatively few manufacturers make proper use of that greatest single selling force —**advertising**—real advertising—sales-helping of the most comprehensive and effective character.

No selling plan in the electric railway field is complete or economical unless it includes suitable advertising in the ELECTRIC RAILWAY JOURNAL.

From its inception—over 26 years ago—in the early horse-car days, the Journal has been the acknowledged leader in this great field. To-day, not only throughout North America, but all over the world—wherever there are electric railways, tramways, or electrified steam roads—the Journal circulates and is recognized as **the authority.**

Its subscribers include presidents and vice-presidents, general managers, purchasing agents, superintendents, chief engineers, electrical engineers, engineers of power stations, master mechanics, foremen and heads of departments generally, of the operating street and interurban electric railways and the chief officers and active incorporators of new lines, as well as bankers, promoters, capitalists, manufacturers, dealers, contractors, consulting engineers and others directly or indirectly engaged in this field.

Whatever you may have that electric railways use, or should use, can be effectively and profitably advertised in the Journal.

May we show you how?

Electric Railway Journal
239 West 39th Street, New York

Janney Radial Coupler

Exceptionally wide range of lateral movement.
Facilitates passing of cars over curves and tangents.
Eliminates lateral buckling.
Prevents car sills coming in contact on curves.

The Coupler for Electric and Interurban Railway Service

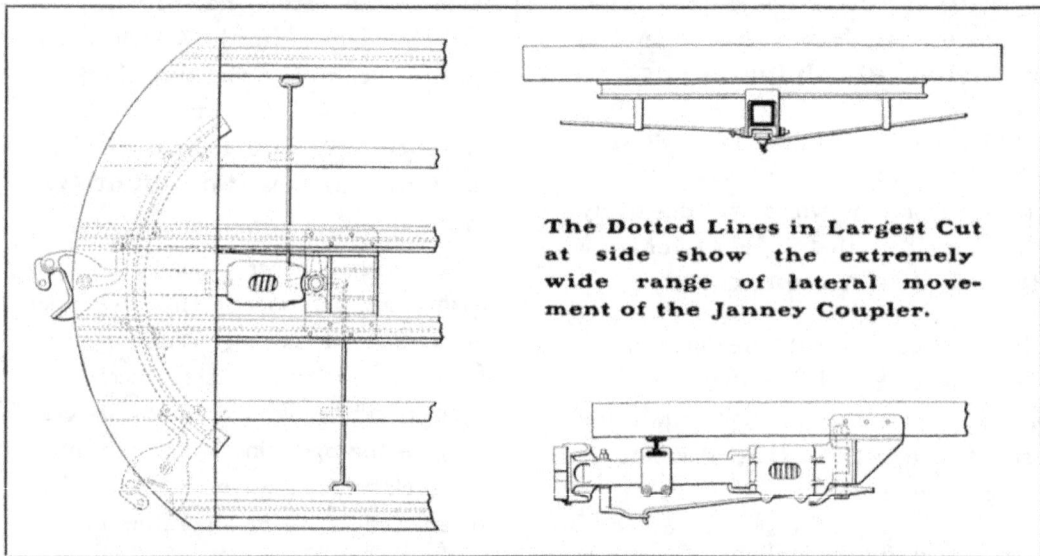

The Dotted Lines in Largest Cut at side show the extremely wide range of lateral movement of the Janney Coupler.

Couples automatically by impact on curves or straight track without requiring trainmen to go between ends of cars.

Interchangeable with couplers on steam cars.

Operates perfectly on curves of 35-foot radius.

Conforms to the requirements of Safety Appliance Laws and to the recommendations of Standardization Committee.

Blue prints gladly sent upon request.

Special designs made to suit requirements.

The McConway & Torley Co.
Pittsburgh, Pa.

STANDARD
STEEL WORKS COMPANY
Makers of High Efficiency Railway Car Equipment

Solid Rolled Steel Wheels
Steel Tired Wheels
Steel Tires for Re-Tiring
Special Steel Heat-Treated Axles
Correctly Designed Car Springs
Steel and Iron Castings
Steel and Iron Forgings

For forty years the "Standard" brand has been recognized as the mark of supreme quality. The long experience, constant upholding of quality of products, unequalled facilities of this company are full assurance of the highest possible degree of service to customers.

General Offices: Morris Bldg., Philadelphia

New York, N. Y.	Cleveland, O.	St. Louis, Mo.	Chicago, Ill.
St. Paul, Minn.	San Francisco, Cal.	Portland, Ore.
Richmond, Va.	Pittsburg, Pa.

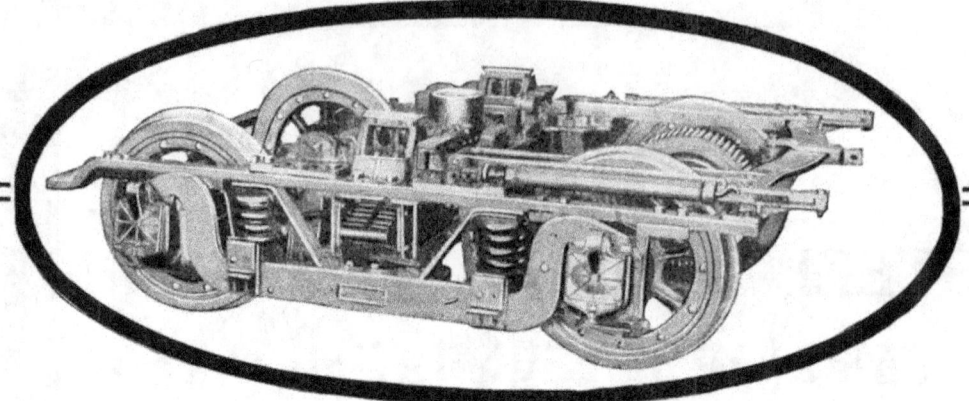

Motor Truck

The time to order your trucks is before the car is built

This obviates many difficulties in design and construction, and insures a well balanced and easy-riding car.

Baldwin Trucks

are largely used and give general satisfaction, for the reason that they are well made. This warrants the safety and long life of the truck with minimum cost of maintenance. The design in each case is worked out with a view to the easy-riding qualities of the car under which it is placed.

Baldwin Locomotive Works
Philadelphia, Pa.
Branch Offices

New York, Hudson Terminal
St. Louis, 1614 Wright Building

Chicago, Railway Exchange
Portland, Ore., Couch Building

Trailer Truck

TAYLOR IMPROVED S. B. TRUCK

TAYLOR M. C. B. TRUCK

TAYLOR ELECTRIC TRUCK CO.
TROY, N. Y., U. S. A.

BRANCH OFFICE, 1137 FIRST NATIONAL BANK BUILDING, CHICAGO, ILL.

Taylor Single and Double Trucks

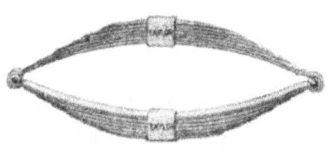

We manufacture
Elliptic and Coil Springs
for all makes of trucks.

Are constructed to meet all requirements of electric railways, reducing the cost of maintenance, and increasing dividends by saving power, road bed, motors, and car bodies.

In **Taylor Designs** there is maximum strength, with the weights reduced to a minimum.

Taylor Trucks are the easiest riding in service.

T M C
Taylor Malleable Center
Steel Tired Wheel

5 times stronger, yet about **100** lbs. lighter in weight than any other Steel Tired Wheel made. **Noiseless in service.**

The Storage Battery Car

A Proven Success

Thirty cars like illustration operating daily in New York City

A FULL DAY'S OPERATING SCHEDULE ON ONE CHARGE

LOW CURRENT CONSUMPTION

LOWEST INSTALLATION INVESTMENT OF ANY SYSTEM OF ELECTRIC TRACTION

Tell us about your conditions—length of road, grades, schedule—and we will be glad to advise just what can be accomplished.

Gould Storage Battery Co.

Batteries of High Efficiency, Low Maintenance and Long Life.

General Offices:—341-347 Fifth Avenue, New York.   Works:—Depew, N. Y.

Boston, 89 State Street.   Chicago, Rookery Bldg.   San Francisco, Atlas Bldg.

Laconia Light Weight Semi-Convertible Car for
City and Interurban Service.

The seating capacity of the car shown in the illustration is forty passengers and the total weight of the car body is under 14,000 lbs., being much lighter than any other satisfactory car body yet produced of equal carrying capacity. The lower section of windows drop into recesses extending slightly below floor level. The upper section is moved up past the weather board into the roof. The design of this car provides increased head room and improved ventilating facilities with liberal seating accommodations, in addition to being a perfect semi-convertible car, as the entire windows go out of sight when necessary.

Cars of this design in actual service have shown a saving of $87^{7}/_{10}\%$ per car per day in power consumed, or on a basis of ten cars they would save $3,186.36 per year in power consumed over ordinary cars. Practically everything is steel construction under the window stool. If interested, write us at

The Laconia Car Co. Works, Laconia, N. H.

BOSTON OFFICE: 141 MILK STREET.

Pay-As-You-Enter Car

Operating Advantages of the Prepayment Idea
as demonstrated by
Pay - As - You - Enter Car

Accidents from the front of cars are practically eliminated, as the door is not opened until the car has come to a full stop, and the car is not started until the door is closed.

Pay-As-You-Enter Car Platform

The use of folding or sliding doors on the rear platform, and the presence of the conductor at that point, prevent accidents at the rear end.

Of almost equal importance to the obvious increase of revenue due to the adoption of the Prepayment Idea, is the inevitable improvement in schedules.

In handling hundreds of passengers the saving of a second or two on each transaction runs into hours.

An hour saved means a saving all down the line in the operating department, wages, power consumption, etc.

During peak-load hours particularly, every second saved means money to the company—and satisfaction to the public.

Prepayment Car Sales Co.
Sole Licensor for
THE-PAY-AS-YOU-ENTER CAR CORPORATION
Principal Office:
50 Church Street
NEW YORK

PHILADELPHIA
1024 Filbert Street

CHICAGO
417 S. Dearborn Street

FACTORY, 515 LAFLIN STREET, CHICAGO
ELECTRIC SERVICE SUPPLIES CO., General Sales Agent

Pay-Within Car

The Adaptability of the Prepayment Idea
as exemplified by
and Pay-Within Cars

The application of the Prepayment Idea is not restricted to any one type or size of car. It has proven successful not only on standard city cars in centres of congested traffic, but also in long-haul interurban and suburban service.

Where the traffic is light, as in the smaller cities of the West and South, the conductor is dispensed with; the vestibules being so arranged that the motorman can do his own work as well as that of the conductor, without leaving his station at the front of the car.

In the matter of platform and door arrangement great flexibility obtains. Platforms may be long or short, and the means of controlling the entrance and exit of passengers may be folding doors, sliding doors or gates, operated manually or by compressed air.

You cannot get away from the fact that, no matter what type of car you operate, the Prepayment Idea applies to and improves your operating conditions.

All of the patents covering this field being now in the hands of a central organization, operating companies are assured absolute patent protection.

Pay-Within Car Platform, with Manually Operated Folding Doors

---

Prepayment Car Sales Co.
Sole Licensor for
THE PAY-WITHIN CAR COMPANY
Principal Office:

PHILADELPHIA   **50 Church Street**   CHICAGO
1024 Filbert Street   NEW YORK   417 S. Dearborn Street

FACTORY, 515 LAFLIN STREET, CHICAGO

ELECTRIC SERVICE SUPPLIES CO., General Sales Agent

48-Ft. Center Vestibule City and Suburban Steel Car.

48-Ft. Interurban Trailer Coach.

46-Ft. Single End, Light Interurban Car.

45-Ft. Single End, 3-Compartment, Interurban Car.

45-Ft. Express, Baggage and Freight Car.

50-Ft. Double End, 3-Compartment, Interurban Car.

41-Ft. Double End, Suburban Car.

51-Ft. Single End Passenger and Smoking Car.

42-Ft. Double Truck, Single End, P. A. Y. E. Car.

55-Ft. Single End Combination Observation Car.

39-Ft. Double Truck, Double End, City Car.

58-Ft. Smoking, Express and Baggage Car.

32-Ft. Single Truck, Double End, P. A. Y. E. Car.

62-Ft. Buffet, Parlor and Observation Car.

40-Ft. Construction, Freight and Locomotive Car.

56-Ft. Single End, Semi-Parlor, Interurban Car.

If you expect to buy Cars, write for our Catalog. It contains full details of these and many other types. It may assist you in preparing your specifications. It is of the loose leaf style and always up-to-date. We make all kinds of Cars for all kinds of service. Wood, Semi-Steel and Steel. City, Suburban, Interurban, Private, Parlor, Freight and Work Cars.

Niles Car & Mfg. Co., - Niles, O.

General Sales Office, 312 Electric Bldg., Cleveland, O.

Designers and Builders of Every Type of Electric and Steam Railway Equipment

Specifications and Designs Submitted Upon Request

The Cincinnati Car Co.
Winton Place
CINCINNATI, OHIO

CAR AND TRUCK PARTS AND SPECIALTIES

AXLES. The absolute accuracy and superior finish which characterize our axles are due to the improved machinery and methods employed. Axles are furnished to any specification and facilities and capacity insure prompt deliveries.

BEARINGS, TRUCK. Journal and side bearings of every description.

Brill "Half-Ball" Brake Hanger

BELLS, CONDUCTORS' SIGNAL. The Brill "Retriever" Bell (patented) is an improved type in which the cord does not pass under the clapper, thus avoiding the possibility of the cord catching or deadening the sound. The weight of the clapper combined with its leverage enables it to retrieve the cord through three long cars. The bell, bracket and parts are made of solid bronze. It is made with four- and six-inch bells.

BOLSTERS, CAR. Built-up steel bolsters and cast steel bolsters of Brill standard types. Bolsters built to specification.

BOLSTERS, TRUCK. Cast steel and built-up bolsters for Brill trucks and for special designs.

BRAKE CHAIN SLACK ADJUSTERS. The Brill Adjuster winds up slack chain rapidly and gives the greatest ratio of work to power. This adjuster can be used on any brake shaft of standard diameter—1¾ inches below the floor.

BRAKE HANDLES. The Brill Ratchet Brake Handle (patented) excells in strength, simplicity, rapidity and effectiveness. A spring and upper ratchet comprise all the movable parts aside from the handle. It is made of bronze or malleable in seven sizes. No. 3401 is the size generally used—height over all, 11¾ inches and distance between centers of brake shaft and knob, 12½ inches.

BRAKE HANGERS. The Brill "Half-Ball" Brake Hanger (patented) is the only device of the kind which has proved faultless in every particular. It is self-adjusting for wear and therefore noiseless. On January 1st, 1911, this hanger was in use on one hundred and fifty-two different railways. It consists of a pair of forged hangers with half-ball ends. The half-ball ends are held firmly in sockets by a spiral spring in tension on a bolt which bolt passes through the ends and socket castings with sufficient play for necessary lateral motion. The "Half-Ball" Hanger is used on all Brill trucks and is made for any type of truck with either inside- or outside-hung brakes.

BRAKE RIGGING, EQUALIZING, DOUBLE-TRUCK CAR BODY. The Brill standard equalizing body brake rigging for double-truck cars is capable of modification to suit every style of car and truck.

BRAKE SHAFTS. Forged steel brake shafts furnished in any size required.

BRAKE SHOES. A large variety of brake shoes are carried in stock including A. E. R. A. and M. C. B. types. For cast wheels the Brill shoe is almost invariably specified for Brill trucks. This shoe is made of soft iron with oblong sections of wrought iron set in the contact surface.

BRAKE SHOEHOLDERS. Brill, A. E. R. A., and M. C. B., types are furnished.

BUMPERS, CAR. Composed of a single solid forging, the Brill Angle-Iron Bumper (patented) possesses all the qualities essential to large effectiveness. It is made in shapes and sizes suitable to every style of car.

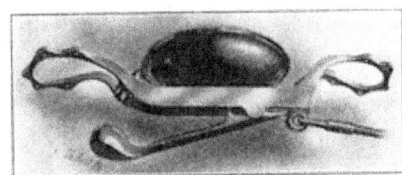

Brill "Retriever" Signal Bell

CAR TRIMMINGS. Every item of car hardware used in city and interurban rolling stock can be supplied in most cases from the large stocks kept on hand or if of special character can be promptly made from immense collections of patterns which cover every possible requirement.

CENTER PLATES. In the Brill Improved Center Plates the lower plate has an extra large space for oil and an anti-friction-metal ring which receives all of the wear. The upper plate is tapped for an oil pipe which extends up through the car floor.

THE J. G. BRILL COMPANY, PHILADELPHIA

Wason Manufacturing Co., *Springfield*; Danville Car Company, *Danville*;
John Stephenson Company, *Elizabeth*; American Car Company, *St. Louis*;
G. C. Kuhlman Car Co., *Cleveland*; Compagnie J. G. Brill, *Paris, France*; *London*,
110 Cannon St., E. C., Cable "Axles."

CORD, BELL AND TROLLEY. All of the standard cords are carried in stock.

COUPLERS. The Brill Radial Draw Bar (patented) has a draw-and-recoil spring on the bar which is the entire drawing and buffing apparatus. It is made of channels for cars of more than thirty-foot bodies. Standard size of bar is four feet between centers of draw bolt and drop pin holes; the channel bar, four feet three inches.

CURTAINS AND CURTAIN FIXTURES. Curtains and fixtures of every description for closed and open cars.

DOORS AND DOOR FIXTURES. Vestibule, body-end and partition doors of all hinged and sliding types. Fixtures and operating devices for every purpose.

FARE BOXES. There are five types of Brill (patented) fare boxes and several modifications of each of these types to suit unusual conditions. Three of these types are arranged to be attached to the platform floor and two to the conductor's railing. The No. 3 and No. 4 are most widely used. No. 3 is a four-compartment-till all-steel box 4 x 18½ inches, and 43½ inches high over all, made with and without totalizer. No. 4 is a single-compartment-till box with steel case 6 x 9¼ inches, and 20¼ inches high over all, made with and without totalizer. Each of the Brill fare boxes has the same mechanical principles and these have proved the safest, simplest and most efficient in operation and the most substantial and durable in construction.

FENDERS AND WHEEL GUARDS. Every type of fender and wheel guard furnished.

GATES, FOLDING. For compactness, strength and adaptability to all conditions, there is nothing on the market that equals the Brill Folding Gate (patented). It is made on

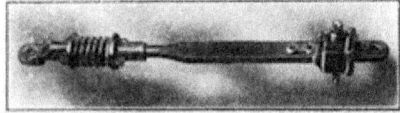

Brill Radial Draw Bar

the pantagraph principle of flat bars or channels, for any width of opening, any height, and may be attached to the car body, vestibule, dasher, or may be arranged to fold on the outside of the vestibule or dasher.

GONGS, PLATFORM. For many years the Brill "Dedenda" Gong (patented) has been in standard use on the principal railways at home and abroad. The gong is made in twelve- and fourteen-inch sizes. The castings are made for two and three-quarter and six-inch thicknesses of platform crown-piece.

GUARDS, WINDOW. Made of rods or wire screens to suit every requirement.

HEADLIGHTS. All standard makes furnished.

HEADLININGS. Three-ply veneer or composition, cut to size, varnished, or painted and striped, ready to install.

JACKS, CAR. The Brill "Hercules" Car Jack consists of two wooden uprights, well braced and reinforced with iron, and containing the raising mechanism, and a steel plated plank

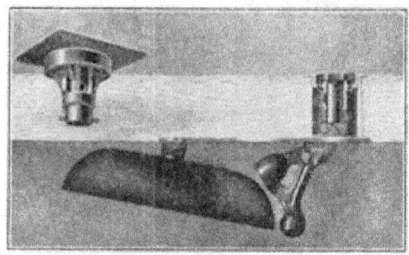

Brill "Dedenda" Gong

on which the end of a car can be easily raised by one man at each lever.

JOURNAL BOXES. For high-speed trucks, an improved box similar to the A. E. R. A. standard is used, the chief difference being that the Brill box has the front and rear ends of the oil well of equal height. The journal box for city trucks of Brill type has a patented dust-proof feature and has been in successful use for more than ten years.

MATS, CAR FLOOR. Rubber, coco-fiber and wooden slat mats of all dimensions; also rubber tiling.

MOTOR LIFTS. The Brill Motor Lift is a powerful machine for pit work and is suited to the heaviest work and the roughest usage. From floor to top of table on lowered position is thirty-four inches; the table is capable of eighteen inches adjustment.

MUTUALLY-OPERATING DOOR MECHANISM. The Brill mechanism (patented) is a reliable and efficient device for double-door operation. Four sheaves, two chain wheels, two chains, two rods and a latch plate comprise the apparatus. The sheaves and chain wheels are bushed with phosphor-bronze.

PLATFORM KNEES. The Brill Channel Steel Platform Knee (patented) is lighter than the ordinary plated timber knee and is capable of supporting three times the heaviest load it will be required to carry. It also markedly improves the appearance of the car. This knee is furnished for any length of platform and is now being used on the majority of prepayment cars.

PANELS, SEAT END. Brill round-corner seat-end panels (patented) for open cars give more entrance space. The double curvatures

THE J. G. BRILL COMPANY, PHILADELPHIA

Pierson, Roeding & Company, *San Francisco*; Giovanni Checchetti, *Milan*; Noyes Bros., *Melbourne, Sydney, Dunedin, Brisbane, Perth*; C. Dubbelman, *Brussels*; Shewan, Tomes & Co., *Hong Kong, Canton, Shanghai*; F. H. Bagge, *Buenos Aires*; International Machy. & Eng. Co., *Mexico, D. F.*; Thomas Barlow & Sons, *Durban*.

of the panel makes them very strong so that they aid materially in stiffening the posts and supporting the seats. Curtain grooves are cast in the panels, allowing the curtains to be drawn to the floor.

RATTAN, SNOW SWEEPER. An ample supply of rattan in all lengths is kept in stock ready for prompt shipment. Complete sets of segments for Brill and Kuhlman sweeper brooms or single segments, made or filled at short notice.

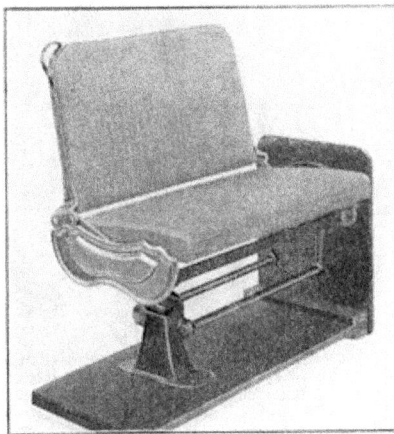

Brill "Winner" Seat

REGISTERS AND REGISTER FITTINGS. All standard makes furnished.

SAND BOXES. The unique feature of the Brill "Dumpit" Sand Box (patented) is a double hopper which successfully prevents moisture, that creeps up the hose, from getting into the sand. It is impossible to keep the sand-wick from forming in the hose, but it is possible to prevent the wick from having any connection with the sand in the box and that is the principle on which this box is designed.

SASHES AND SASH FIXTURES. Single and double sashes for side, end and vestibule windows; plain, wire glass and art glass deck sashes. Sash locks, lifts, metal stiles and other parts and fixtures.

SEATS. Every type of car seat is manufactured in our Seat Department. The Brill "Winner" Seat mechanism (patented) is comprised of few parts, operates smoothly and excels in durability. "Winner" seats are furnished with eighteen and twenty-four-inch plain and three-part backs. They are made with one-piece pressed-steel pedestals, pressed-steel aisle and wall plates and angle-iron crossings. Cricket legs are furnished, if desired. All seats are upholstered in any style of material; woven cane of Brill manufacture is made of hard, glossy cane smoothly and closely twill-woven by improved looms and processes Seats with eighteen-inch backs are also made spindle, slat and open cane backs. Self-adjusting foot-rests and wooden arm-rests are furnished, if desired. Longitudinal seat cushions and backs are made in all lengths and widths. Frames, springs, padding, covering and all parts are of superior material and workmanship.

SEATING MATERIAL. Canvas lined woven cane for seat cushions and unlined woven cane for seat backs, of Brill manufacture, are made in all widths, from eighteen to thirty-six inches, even inches. Plush, leather and imitation leather furnished in standard and special colors.

SEATS, MOTORMEN'S. These seats are made in circular type with screw adjustment for height, and in saddle type with pin adjustment for height. The saddle type seat folds against the dasher.

SIGNAL FLAGS. Single and double-stitched signal flags in all standard materials.

SIGNAL LAMPS. All standard makes furnished.

SIGNS. Destination signs for hood and side deck done in plain block letters promptly furnished in any quantity. Illuminated signs of standard makes supplied.

SPRINGS, CAR AND TRUCK. Brill springs comprehend every type used on electric and steam railways from the smallest spring used in cars to the heaviest locomotive driving spring. The grade of steel used is the Pennsylvania Railroad Analysis. Our enlarged spring manufacturing plant is equipped with

Brill "Dumpit" Sand Box

the most advanced types of machinery and oil-burning furnaces and operated with the best skilled labor obtainable. We have a distinct advantage, being car and truck builders, of having complete records which enable us to fill orders for springs with exact knowledge of requirements.

STEPS, PLATFORM. The Brill step for dropped platforms is powerfully constructed, neat appearing and is made for any width between car-body end-panel and platform crown-piece. Separate step hangers and toe guards furnished.

THE J. G. BRILL COMPANY, PHILADELPHIA

Wason Manufacturing Co., *Springfield*; Danville Car Company, *Danville*; John Stephenson Company, *Elizabeth*; American Car Company, *St. Louis*; G. C. Kuhlman Car Co., *Cleveland*; Compagnie J. G. Brill, *Paris, France*; *London*, 110 Cannon St., E. C., Cable "Axles."

STEPS, ROOF. Plain and folding roof steps are made in bronze and iron.

TRACK SCRAPERS. The three special features of the Brill Track Scraper are, elastic arms, diagonal cross-bracing and removable shoes. The blades may be drawn up to any desired height by the handle and dropped instantly on the track by kicking the trigger. Made for any gage of track. Extra blades and wear shoes are carried in stock and ready for prompt shipment.

TRAP DOORS AND TRAP DOOR FIXTURES All standard makes furnished.

TREADS, SAFETY. All standard makes furnished.

VESTIBULE CENTER SASH ADJUSTERS. The Brill Vestibule Sash Adjuster is a neat contrivance which exactly fills the requirements. Small catches on the sash engage the points of a metal rack screwed to the side of each post. Sash springs prevent rattling and hold the sash away from the points while being raised or lowered. This device is almost invariably used in vestibuled cars built by us.

VESTIBULE DOOR CONTROLLERS. The Brill Vestibule Door Controller consists of a roller mounted vertically on the upper corner of the outer leaf of the folding door and which moves between a guide rail attached to the lintel of the door and a parallel rail. Spring catches at top and bottom hold the door open and spring hinges open the door part way so that a light push with one hand is only necessary to fold it completely back.

VESTIBULES, PORTABLE. The Brill Portable Vestibule is substantially though lightly constructed. It bears directly on the dasher railing, is held upright by straps around

Electric Locomotive for Heavy Service

the hood supports and is connected to the hood by a narrow canvas bellows. The central sash is arranged to slide to one side and the side sashes are stationary.

WHEELS. All standard makes of cast iron, steel and steel-tired wheels furnished.

CITY AND INTERURBAN CARS

BAGGAGE CARS. Steel and wooden cars of every description.

COMBINATION OPEN AND CLOSED CARS. The Brill "California" type (patented) is a single truck car with closed compartment at the center. A pair of angle irons, with the upper flange under the side sills, is offset and prolonged to support the long dropped platforms without strain to the body. Ingress and egress are facilitated by the dropped platforms which have running boards only thirteen inches from the track, and twelve inches from board to platform.

CONSTRUCTION AND GENERAL UTILITY CARS. Cars suited to every requirement.

Brill Track Scraper

CONVERTIBLE CARS. The Brill Convertible Car (patented) with and without running boards, has gained an important place amongst city types and is now in operation on seventy-eight different railway systems. The window system is practically the same as in the Brill Semi-Convertible Car. Both panels and sashes slide into roof pockets. The sliding panels are made of two sheets of thin steel with air space between.

DOUBLE-DECK CARS. Every type of single and double-truck top-seat car, with and without canopies and enclosures, with longitudinal seats on the deck, facing outwardly, or transverse seats.

ELEVATED AND SUBWAY CARS. We delivered a large number of cars during 1910 to the New York and Chicago Elevated Lines; have furnished cars to the New York Subway System and for service in the Belmont Tunnel and East Boston Tunnel. Our facilities for building all-steel cars are unsurpassed.

EXCURSION CARS. Open center-aisle cars with low sides or with sides protected by screens. Platform cars enclosed with iron railing, covered with a canvas canopy.

INTERURBAN CARS. Steel, semi-steel and wooden cars for interurban service have established the reputation of their builders for superiority of design, material and workmanship. The Brill semi-convertible window system is frequently included in interurban car designs and is adaptable to the arched-top twin-window arrangement.

LOCOMOTIVES, ELECTRIC. Every type of electric locomotive for hauling freight and baggage cars and for industrial purposes, including mine locomotives.

THE J. G. BRILL COMPANY, PHILADELPHIA

Pierson, Roeding & Company, *San Francisco*; Giovanni Checchetti, *Milan*; Noyes Bros., *Melbourne, Sydney, Dunedin, Brisbane, Perth*; C. Dubbelman, *Brussels*; Shewan, Tomes & Co., *Hong Kong, Canton, Shanghai*; F. H. Bagge, *Buenos Aires*; International Machy. & Eng. Co., *Mexico, D. F.*; Thomas Barlow & Sons, *Durban*.

OPEN CARS. The only practical double-truck open car is the Brill "Narragansett" type (patented). A double-step is provided by having the upper step on the middle web of Z-iron sills. The width over all is no greater than a single-step double-truck open car, as the sill step is within the line of the posts.

PARLOR AND PRIVATE CARS. The compartments are finished in rich woods handsomely carved and inlaid, and the upholstering and appointments are all of the most luxurious character. A number of these cars

Kuhlman Long-Broom Sweeper

have included the Brill Semi-Convertible System, which adds to their comfort in summer.

PLAIN ARCH ROOF CARS. The Brill Plain Arch Roof is much stronger than the monitor type. It increases head room, has advantages in connection with ventilating systems, the windows can be considerably higher and it is specially suited to the Brill Semi-Convertible Window System. Another point in its favor is that it can be covered with canvas made in a single piece without seams and is therefore absolutely water proof.

POSTAL CARS. These cars are completely equipped with all modern appliances to facilitate the rapid handling of mail.

SEMI-CONVERTIBLE CARS. The Brill Semi-Convertible Car (patented) continues to hold the first place amongst city and interurban types. For the last five years thirty per cent. of all cars built in the United States have been of this type. The system is suited to both curved and straight sided construction and twin-window arrangements. The lower sash engages the upper, on being raised, and with one motion both sashes slide into the roof pocket. Eliminating wall window pockets adds six to seven and one-half inches to the interior width, does away with unsanitary and rubbish collecting recesses and reduced glass breakage. The window sills can be as low as desired, the standard height being twenty-four and five-eighths inches from the floor.

SNOW PLOWS. The Brill and Wason types of single and double-truck snow plows are used on many of the principal city and interurban railway systems in the northern States. No unnecessary weight has been incorporated in the double-truck cars as the plows are removable and the cars are used in baggage and express service during the greater part of the year. The plow lifts are arranged for operation by either air power or hand or both.

SNOW SWEEPERS. The two types of sweepers illustrated are used by large number of city railway systems in the northern States and represent our standard practice in design and construction. The brooms are operated by chain and sprocket gearing from a motor driven shaft. Aside from the length of the brooms, the short broom sweeper differs from the other only in details.

SPRINKLING CARS. The Brill Centrifugal Sprinkling Car (patented) has a centrifugal pump operated by a direct-connected 20 H. P. motor, both on platform at one end of the car, supplies pressure for distributing water uniformly for 35 feet on each side of the track. The same pump will fill the tank from a lake or stream fifteen feet below track or the tank may be filled in the usual manner. The shaft of the centrifugal pump is the only wearing surface. The amount and direction of the water is always under perfect control by patented sprinkling head

STEEL CARS. Our steel construction departments are equipped with the most modern appliances and our facilities for handling large orders insure early delivery.

STEEL UNDERFRAMES. The increasing demand for steel underframes has developed a variety of types applying to passenger and baggage cars for all forms of city and interurban service.

CITY AND INTERURBAN TRUCKS

No. 21-E SINGLE-TRUCK. (Patented) Cars mounted on this truck are carried two inches lower than on any other single-truck.

Brill Standard Sweeper

No rivets, no built-up work, no possibility of getting out of square, no sagging at the ends. The spring arrangement gives complete support and steady cushion—no bounding motion, solid forged side frames.

No. 22 SINGLE-MOTOR TRUCK (Patented). Seventy-five per cent. of the load is on the drivers, giving traction that enables it to start rapidly and climb heavy grades. When taking curves, a spring-post between the pony wheels is compressed by an inclined plate attached under the car transferring for the time more of the load to these wheels. The brake

THE J. G. BRILL COMPANY, PHILADELPHIA

Wason Manufacturing Co., *Springfield;* Danville Car Company, *Danville;*
John Stephenson Company, *Elizabeth;* American Car Company, *St. Louis;*
G. C. Kuhlman Car Co., *Cleveland;* Compagnie J. G. Brill, *Paris, France; London,*
110 Cannon St., E. C., Cable "Axles."

system includes differential levers which proportion the amount of pressure on each pair of wheels according to the load which they carry.

No. 22 SPECIAL SINGLE-MOTOR TRUCK (Patented). This truck is the same as the No. 22 except that the side frames are cast with a connection between the side bearing frame extension and the pony wheel yoke.

No. 27-F SHORT BASE PIVOTAL TRUCK (Patented). Three sets of springs give the truck its superior riding qualities and include a cushioned lateral motion to the car body. The car body receives the full benefit of the spring motion of the ellipties and of the coil springs in the links as the weight and torque of the motors only affect the journal springs. By bringing the load to bear on the frames at wide-apart points close to the yokes produces a leverage against the outside-hung motors and in favor of frame stability. The standard wheel base is four feet six inches.

No. 27-G SHORT BASE PIVOTAL TRUCK (Patented). This truck has a wider range of service and is more extensively used than any other type. Semi-elliptical springs take the place of equalizing bars. Spring links cushion the side swing, amplifying the action of the semi-elliptical springs, and cushion the load upon the frames. The elastic side swing prevents jarring of the car at the entrance of curves, and gives soft contact of wheel flanges with rail heads. The standard wheel base is four feet six inches.

No. 27 M. C. B. INTERURBAN TRUCK. The one-piece solid forged side frames which are a fundamental feature of this truck, provide greatest strength where it is most needed and make possible a transom, tie-bar and end-crossing construction which insures permanent squareness and rigidity to the entire frame.

Double-Truck Nose Plow

The accessibility of the brake parts is an important feature secured by this frame. The bolster is made of a single steel casting. Truck is made for four sizes of journals $3\frac{3}{4} \times 7$, $4\frac{1}{2} \times 8$, 5×9 and $5\frac{1}{2} \times 10$.

No. 34 SHORT BASE PIVOTAL TRUCK (Patented). This truck is suitable for either motor or trailer service. The frame is of the arch-bar type with each side frame composed of a single casting including yokes and extensions. Angle transoms and flat bar ends of crossings are substantially secured to the side frames. Journal springs and large diameter nested coils in rocking castings under the bolster ends furnish easy riding qualities. Standard wheel base four feet.

No. 39-E SINGLE MOTOR TRUCK (Patented). The two large surface railway systems of New York City have adopted the 39-E truck as their standard truck after investigation of first and operating cost and maintenance charges and the features on which they are dependent, such as weight, power consumption, accelleration, step-heights and wheel slippage. By having the pony-wheels toward the car ends

Brill Centrifugal Sprinkling Car

the overhang is reduced to a greater extent than with any other type of pivotal truck. With thirty-inch driving wheels the steps may be fourteen and three-eighths inches from the rail; from step to platform, twelve inches, and from platform to car floor, eight and one-quarter inches. A simply-devised differential brake system proportions the pressure of the shoes on both pairs of wheels and prevents skidding. The truck has a cast steel bolster and solid forged side frames.

No. 50-E MOTOR FREIGHT TRUCK. This truck has a diamond frame with powerfully gusseted transoms and end-crossings. The truck is in all essential features a high-class freight car type such as is used on steam railways with the necessary variations to provide for inside hung motors. The bolster is mounted on four coils at each end.

No. 57 TRAILER TRUCK. An arch bar type with journal springs and large diameter coil springs supporting the bolster. The truck is built for five sizes of journals, $2\frac{1}{2} \times 5$, 3×6, $3\frac{3}{4} \times 7$, $4\frac{1}{2} \times 8$ and 5×9.

SOLID FORGED SIDE FRAMES. Brill

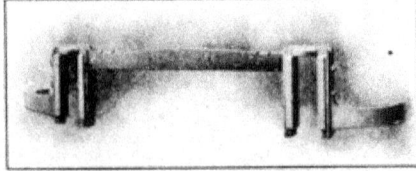

Brill Solid Forged Side Frame.

trucks are the only ones built with side frames —side bar, yokes and extensions—solid forged in a single piece.

THE J. G. BRILL COMPANY, PHILADELPHIA

Pierson, Roeding & Company, *San Francisco*; Giovanni Checchetti, *Milan*; Noyes Bros., *Melbourne, Sydney, Brisbane, Perth*; C. Dubbelman, *Brussels*; Shewan, Tomes & Co., *Hong Kong, Canton, Shanghai*; F. H. Bagge, *Buenos Aires*; International Machy. & Eng. Co., *Mexico, D. F.*; Thomas Barlow & Sons, *Durban*.

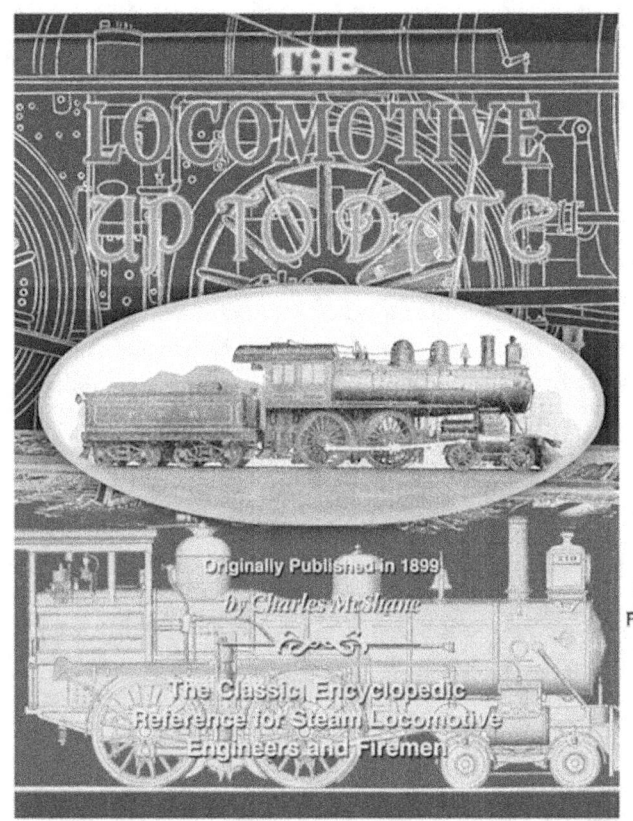

When it was originally published in 1899, **The Locomotive Up to Date** was hailed as "...the most definitive work ever published concerning the mechanism that has transformed the American nation: the steam locomotive." Filled with over 700 pages of text, diagrams and photos, this remains one of the most important railroading books ever written. From steam valves to sanders, trucks to side rods, it's a treasure trove of information, explaining in easy-to-understand language how the most sophisticated machines of the 19th century were operated and maintained. This new edition is an exact duplicate of the original. Reformatted as an easy-to-read 8.5x11 volume, it's delightful for railroad enthusiasts of all ages.

Originally printed in 1898 and then periodically revised, **The Motorman...and His Duties** served as the definitive training text for a generation of streetcar operators. A must-have for the trolley or train enthusiast, it is also an important source of information for museum staff and docents. Lavishly illustrated with numerous photos and black and white line drawings, this affordable reprint contains all of the original text. Includes chapters on trolley car types and equipment, troubleshooting, brakes, controllers, electricity and principles, electric traction, multi-car control and has a convenient glossary in the back. If you've ever operated a trolley car, or just had an electric train set, this is a terrific book for your shelf!

ALSO NOW AVAILABLE FROM PERISCOPEFILM.COM!

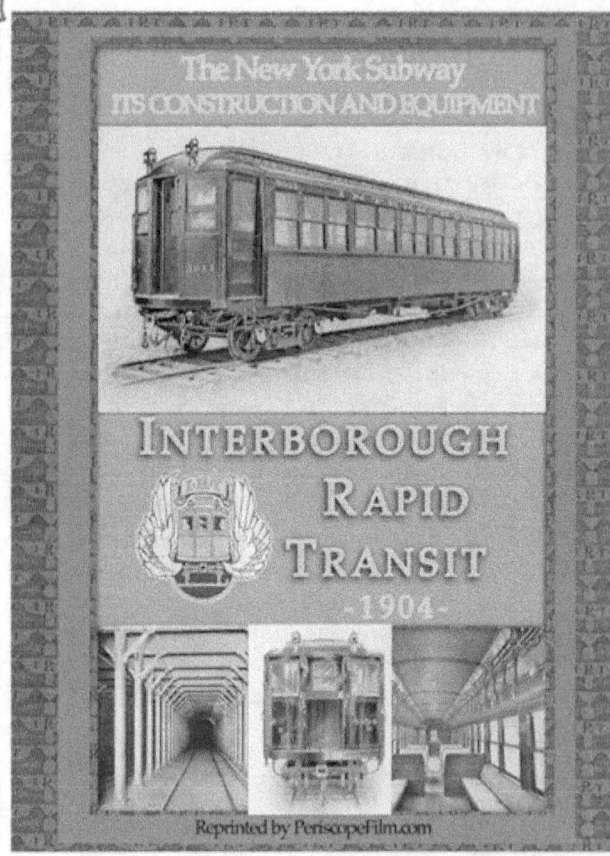

On October 27, 1904, the Interborough Rapid Transit Company opened the first subway in New York City. Running between City Hall and 145th Street at Broadway, the line was greeted with enthusiasm and, in some circles, trepidation. Created under the supervision of Chief Engineer S.L.F. Deyo, the arrival of the IRT foreshadowed the end of the "elevated" transit era on the island of Manhattan. The subway proved such a success that the IRT Co. soon achieved a monopoly on New York public transit. In 1940 the IRT and its rival the BMT were taken over by the City of New York. Today, the IRT subway lines still exist, primarily in Manhattan where they are operated as the "A Division" of the subway. Reprinted here is a special book created by the IRT, recounting the design and construction of the fledgling subway system. Originally created in 1904, it presents the IRT story with a flourish, and with numerous fascinating illustrations and rare photographs.

Originally written in the late 1900's and then periodically revised, A History of the Baldwin Locomotive Works chronicles the origins and growth of one of America's greatest industrial-era corporations. Founded in the early 1830's by Philadelphia jeweler Matthais Baldwin, the company built a huge number of steam locomotives before ceasing production in 1949. These included the 4-4-0 American type, 2-8-2 Mikado and 2-8-0 Consolidation. Hit hard by the loss of the steam engine market, Baldwin soldiered on for a brief while, producing electric and diesel engines. General Electric's dominance of the market proved too much, and Baldwin finally closed its doors in 1956. By that time over 70,500 Baldwin locomotives had been produced. This high quality reprint of the official company history dates from 1920. The book has been slightly reformatted, but care has been taken to preserve the integrity of the text.

NOW AVAILABLE AT
WWW.PERISCOPEFILM.COM

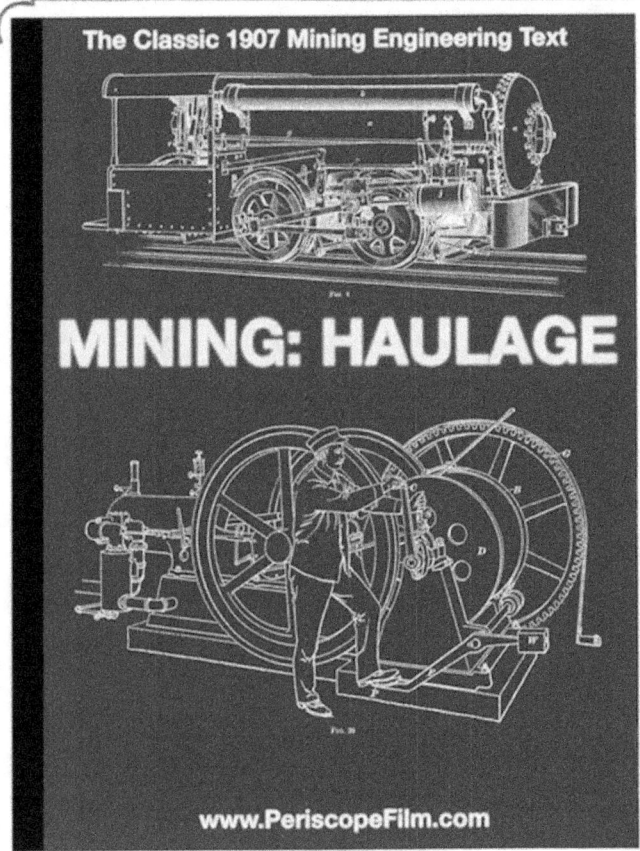

The technology of mining is the subject of this fascinating book, and two companion volumes, all of which were originally published in 1907. Mining: Haulage details the railways that operate in the underground world of the mine. The book contains over 300 pages of text, numerous illustrations, and a set of examination questions for the mining sciences student. It contains chapters about steam locomotives, electric locomotives and wiring, and cable railway systems and the principles behind them. It also examines compressed air, gravity and rope, and animal haulage. This historic book has been reprinted in its entirety. It's a treat for anyone who ever worked underground, or for anyone who ever wondered, "How does that work?"

331 Pages, 8.5x11, softbound

Mining: Hoisting details the elevators, hoists and component machinery used to lift miners, supplies and ore. It contains over 200 pages of text, numerous illustrations and a set of examination questions for the mining sciences student. The book examines electric, steam and hand-powered hoists and explains the principles behind them in detail. It also delves into the control and signaling systems used to ensure safe and reliable operation.

232 Pages, 8.5x11, softbound

ALSO NOW AVAILABLE FROM PERISCOPEFILM.COM!

©2008-2010 Periscope Film LLC
All Rights Reserved
ISBN #978-1-935700-25-8
www.PeriscopeFilm.com

www.ingramcontent.com/pod-product-compliance
Lightning Source LLC
Chambersburg PA
CBHW080933300426
44115CB00017B/2805